ISBN 978-0-282-97724-5
PIBN 10875343

1 MONTH OF FREE READING

at
www.ForgottenBooks.com

By purchasing this book you are eligible for one month membership to ForgottenBooks.com, giving you unlimited access to our entire collection of over 1,000,000 titles via our web site and mobile apps.

To claim your free month visit:
www.forgottenbooks.com/free875343

English
Français
Deutsche
Italiano
Español
Português

www.forgottenbooks.com

Mythology Photography **Fiction**
Fishing Christianity **Art** Cooking
Essays Buddhism Freemasonry
Medicine **Biology** Music **Ancient**
Egypt Evolution Carpentry Physics
Dance Geology **Mathematics** Fitness
Shakespeare **Folklore** Yoga Marketing
Confidence Immortality Biographies
Poetry **Psychology** Witchcraft
Electronics Chemistry History **Law**
Accounting **Philosophy** Anthropology
Alchemy Drama Quantum Mechanics
Atheism Sexual Health **Ancient History**
Entrepreneurship Languages Sport
Paleontology Needlework Islam
Metaphysics Investment Archaeology
Parenting Statistics Criminology
Motivational

No. 13545

United States
Court of Appeals
for the Ninth Circuit

R. W. MEYER, LIMITED,

Appellant,

vs.

TERRITORY OF HAWAII,

Appellee.

Transcript of Record

Appeal from the Supreme Court for the
Territory of Hawaii

FILED

APR 27 1953

PAUL P. O'BRIEN
CLERK

Phillips & Van Orden Co., 870 Brannan Street, San Francisco, Calif.

No. 13545

United States
Court of Appeals
for the Ninth Circuit

R. W. MEYER, LIMITED,

Appellant,

vs.

TERRITORY OF HAWAII,

Appellee.

Transcript of Record

Appeal from the Supreme Court for the
Territory of Hawaii

Phillips & Van Orden Co., 870 Brannan Street, San Francisco, Calif.

INDEX

[Clerk's Note: When deemed likely to be of an important nature, errors or doubtful matters appearing in the original certified record are printed literally in italic; and, likewise, cancelled matter appearing in the original certified record is printed and cancelled herein accordingly. When possible, an omission from the text is indicated by printing in italic the two words between which the omission seems to occur.]

Transcript of Proceedings—(Continued)

Witnesses—(Continued)

iv.

NAMES AND ADDRESSES OF ATTORNEYS

P. CASS, Esq.,
2168 City View,
Eugene, Oregon, and

S. SHAPIRO, Esq.,
506 Stangenwald Bldg.,
Honolulu, Hawaii,

> Attorneys for defendant in error-
> appellant.

RHODA V. LEWIS, Esq.,
Deputy Attorney General of Hawaii,
Iolani Palace, Honolulu, Hawaii, and

T. W. FLYNN, Esq.,
Special Deputy Attorney General,
Territory of Hawaii,
1071 Bishop Street,
Honolulu, Hawaii,

> Attorneys for Territory, plaintiff in error-
> appellee.   [1*]

In the Supreme Court of the Territory of Hawaii

No. 2829

In the Matter of the Application of R. W. MEYER, LIMITED, to Register and Confirm Its Title to Land Situate in Molokai, County of Maui, Territory of Hawaii.

NOTICE OF APPEAL TO THE UNITED STATES COURT OF APPEALS FOR THE NINTH CIRCUIT

Notice is hereby given that R. W. Meyer, Limited, defendants in error above named, hereby appeal to the United States Court of Appeals for the Ninth Circuit from the Decision, Decree and Judgment of the Supreme Court of the Territory of Hawaii made and entered in the above entitled cause on the 23rd day of June, 1952.

Dated at Honolulu, T. H., this 25th day of June, 1952.

R. W. MEYER, LIMITED,
Defendant in Error

PHIL CASS & SAMUEL SHAPIRO
Its Attorneys
/s/ By PHIL CASS

Clerk's Certification attached.

[Endorsed]: Filed June 25, 1952.   [4]

[Title of Supreme Court and Cause.]

STATEMENT OF JURISDICTION

Comes now R. W. Meyer, Limited, by Phil Cass & Samuel Shapiro, its attorneys, and make the following Statement of Jurisdiction:

This is an appeal taken from the Decision, Decree and Judgment of the Supreme Court of the Territory of Hawaii made and entered in the above entitled cause on the 23rd day of June, 1952;

The amount in controversy exceeds the sum of $5,000.00, exclusive of interest and costs;

This appeal is taken under authority of Title 28, USCA S 1293 permitting appeals to the United States Court of Appeals for the Ninth Circuit from all final decisions of the Supreme Court of the Territory of Hawaii, in all civil cases where the amount in controversy exceeds $5,000.00, exclusive of interest and costs.

Dated: Honolulu, T. H., June 25, 1952.

PHIL CASS & SAMUEL SHAPIRO
/s/ By PHIL CASS,
Attorneys for R. W. Meyer, Limited,
Defendant in Error.

Clerk's Certification attached.
[Endorsed]: Filed June 25, 1952.

[Title of Supreme Court and Cause.]

APPLICATION FOR WRIT OF ERROR

To the Clerk of the Supreme Court of the Territory of Hawaii:

Please issue a writ of error in the above entitled cause to the Registrar of the Land Court of the Territory of Hawaii, on behalf of the Territory of Hawaii, plaintiff - in - error, returnable to the Supreme Court of the Territory of Hawaii.

Dated: Honolulu, T. H., July 7, 1950.

TERRITORY OF HAWAII,
Plaintiff-in-Error
/s/ By THOMAS W. FLYNN,
Deputy Attorney General, Territory
of Hawaii [2]

[Title of Supreme Court and Cause.]

ASSIGNMENT OF ERRORS

Comes now the Territory of Hawaii, plaintiff-in-error above-named, respondent and contestant in a cause lately pending in the Land Court of the Territory of Hawaii, entitled "In the Matter of the Application of R. W. Meyer, Limited, to register and confirm its title to land situate in Molokai, county of Maui, Territory of Hawaii", and the said Territory of Hawaii states that in the proceedings in said cause in said Land Court, and in the decision made and entered on the 27th day of January 1950, and in the decree made and entered therein on the 10th day of April 1950, there was and is manifest and prejudicial error in the particulars hereinafter set forth, that is to say:

Assignment of Error No. 1

The court erred in decreeing that the boundaries of the lands sought to be registered were in accordance [4] with the survey and map filed by the applicant, the same not being supported by the evidence adduced before the Land Court.

Assignment of Error No. 2

The court erred in failing to sustain the claim of the Territory of Hawaii to a portion of the lands sought to be registered, the said claim being fully and conclusively supported by the evidence.

Assignment of Error No. 3

The court erred in finding that royal patent grant No. 3539 to R. W. Meyer was issued on a portion of grant 3437 to R. W. Meyer.

Assignment of Error No. 4

The court erred in refusing to dismiss the application on the ground of failure of the application to be supported by a correct map and description.

Assignment of Error No. 5

The court erred in finding that Waihanau Valley was in the lands of Kahanui, the same being contrary to the evidence.

Assignment of Error No. 6

The court erred in holding in its decision that the deceased surveyor, one Mr. Monsarrat, was expressing merely an opinion as to the boundaries of the lands in question, being the lands of Kahanui, whereas this surveyor had in fact determined and described, and made a map of, the lands in question and the Hawaiian government had issued its grant on the basis of such determination and description and map. [5]

Assignment of Error No. 7

The court erred in failing to accord to official government registered maps and surveys the weight to which they were and are entitled.

Assignment of Error No. 8

The court erred in considering the awards of lands of Kahanui "by name only" where the application for registration of title was and is based solely upon the grants, by map and description, by the Hawaiian government.

Assignment of Error No. 9

The court erred in finding that "an award by name only conveys all property within its boundaries as known and used from ancient times" where the application herein involved has as its claim of title only the grant by the Hawaiian government, said grant being accomplished by map and detailed description, and there being no award or conveyance "by name only."

Assignment of Error No. 10

The court erred in its ruling that a written description prevails over a map or plat in a deed or grant, in this case where the court has failed to ascertain preliminarily whether there is a real or factual variance between the description and the map or plat.

Assignment of Error No. 11

The court erred in applying the rule that natural monuments prevail over maps and plats, in this case where the natural monument was not called for or identified. [6]

Assignment of Error No. 12

The court erred in finding a natural monument called for in the words "head of the valley", the same being general descriptive language and not a definitely ascertainable monument.

Assignment of Error No. 13

The court erred in finding the northern boundaries of the lands sought to be registered to be described by a natural monument, such finding being contrary to the evidence.

Assignment of Error No. 14

The court erred in finding that the intention of the original parties to the grant was to convey "some of the Makanalua lands", there being no evidence in support thereof.

Assignment of Error No. 15

The court erred in finding that the original grantee "did in fact describe the lands which he requested", there being no evidence in support thereof.

Assignment of Error No. 16

The court erred in finding that "an amended description was attempted to be included in the re-issued grant No. 3437 but it did, in fact, not include and did exclude the parcel which the applicant now claims ownership in fee" and notwithstanding such finding failed to deny the application on the obvious ground that the original grantee failed to receive the excluded portion of lands. [7]

Assignment of Error No. 17

The court erred in failing to find that grant 3539 was a separate grant from grant 3437, while in its decision the court specifically states that certain correspondence "refers to ridge lands between the two valleys which later became grant 3539".

Assignment of Error No. 18

The court erred in permitting testimony based on conversations with alleged "kamaainas".

Assignment of Error No. 19

The court erred in receiving purported "kamaaina" testimony on the part of witnesses who were not and could not be qualified as kamaainas.

Assignment of Error No. 20

The court erred in receiving into evidence any and all hearsay and purported "kamaaina" testimony, where the claim of title was on the basis of grants issued by maps and detailed descriptions by the Hawaiian government.

Assignment of Error No. 21

The court erred in admitting into evidence, and

refusing to strike from the record, the testimony
of each of the following witnesses for the applicant:
Theodore Searle, Thomas Cummins, Christina Meyer
Tuitele, Bertha Meyer Aubrey, Ernest L. Meyer
and Penn Henry Meyer, and of William Meyer (the
latter testimony being admitted from the record of
a former trial). [8]

Assignment of Error No. 22

The court erred in receiving into evidence applicant's Exhibit R, the affidavit of one A. Mauritz,
the same not being admissible in evidence.

Assignment of Error No. 23

The court erred in receiving into evidence applicant's Exhibits S and T, being deeds of other
lands to applicant's predecessor in title, the same
not being admissible in evidence.

Assignment of Error No. 24

The court erred in receiving into evidence applicant's Exhibit W, copy of petition in eminent
domain proceedings filed in the Second Judicial
Circuit, Territory of Hawaii, entitled "Territory,
etc., vs. Otto S. Meyer, et al.", the same not being
admissible in evidence.

Assignment of Error No. 25

The court erred in finding that after a grantee
accepts a patent grant of land from the government, it was thereafter material to consider what
the grantee had applied to purchase.

Assignment of Error No. 26

The court erred in failing to find that the government map was controlling as to what constituted the remnant of Kahanui.

Assignment of Error No. 27

The court erred in finding that the grantee was to "receive all the valley lands necessary to be conveyed for the purpose of saving fencing", the same being contrary to the evidence. [9]

Assignment of Error No. 28

The court erred in concluding from prior correspondence between the government and original grantee that there was an ambiguity in the grant, there being neither patent nor latent ambiguity in the grant.

Assignment of Error No. 29

The court erred in finding that "Monsarrat's map and plat accompanying the grant shows a variance in fact in the northern and eastern boundary as compared to later maps", the same being contrary to the evidence.

Assignment of Error No. 30

The court erred in finding that the whole of the lele of Kahanui was "purchased by name" at the auction, the same being contrary to the evidence.

Assignment of Error No. 31

The court erred in applying as a rule of law, a proposition that in the interpretation of a grant the grant itself, together with "all the surrounding facts and circumstances" is the determining factor, the same being contrary to the true rule of law.

Assignment of Error No. 32

The court erred in finding the head of Waihanau Valley to be the big waterfall, the same being contrary to the only admissible evidence.

Assignment of Error No. 33

The court erred in failing to apply the rule of law that where there is no ambiguity in the descriptions and maps used in the conveyance, the same are to be taken as the conclusive evidence of the intention of the parties. [10]

Assignment of Error No. 34

The court erred in failing to apply the rule of law that where a conveyance is made by description and map, the map and description are binding upon the parties.

Assignment of Error No. 35

The court erred in failing to apply the rule of law that a government survey must be given preference over a private survey where there is a dispute.

Assignment of Error No. 36

The court erred in failing to apply the rule of law that the field notes and maps of the original surveyor are the primary evidence as to the true location of boundaries.

Assignment of Error No. 37

The court erred in failing to apply the rule of law that a surveyor's only duty is to relocate the courses and lines at the same place where originally located by the first surveyor on the ground.

Assignment of Error No. 38

The court erred in denying motion of the Territory for dismissal of the application at the conclusion of the evidence introduced on behalf of the applicant.

Wherefore, the said respondent, plaintiff-in-error, the Territory of Hawaii, prays that said decree [11] of April 10, 1950, be reversed, and that the cause be remanded to the Land Court of the Territory of Hawaii for dismissal of the application, and for such other relief as may be just and equitable under the circumstances.

Dated: Honolulu, T. H., July 7, 1950.

TERRITORY OF HAWAII,
Plaintiff-in-Error,

/s/ By THOMAS W. FLYNN,
Deputy Attorney General,
Territory of Hawaii.

[Endorsed]: Filed July 7, 1950. [12]

[Title of Supreme Court and Cause.]

WRIT OF ERROR

The Territory of Hawaii to: The Registrar of the Land Court of the Territory of Hawaii.

Application having been made on behalf of the Territory of Hawaii, a respondent in the above entitled cause, for a writ of error in said cause,

You are commanded forthwith to send to the Supreme Court of the Territory of Hawaii the record in said cause.

Witness the Honorable S. B. Kemp, Chief Justice of the Supreme Court of the Territory of Hawaii, this seventh day of July, 1950.

[Seal]   /s/ LEOTI V. KRONE,
    Clerk of the Supreme Court of the
    Territory of Hawaii.   [16]

To the Clerk of the Supreme Court of the Territory of Hawaii:

The execution of the within writ of error appears by the record hereto annexed, dated this twenty-sixth day of July, 1950.

[Seal]   /s/ [Illegible]
    Registrar of the Land Court of the
    Territory of Hawaii.   [17]

In the Land Court of the Territory of Hawaii
Application No. 1483

[Title of Cause.]

AMENDED APPLICATION

To the Honorable, the Judge of the Land Court:

The undersigned, R. W. Meyer, Limited, a corporation organized and existing under the laws of the Territory of Hawaii, hereby applies to have the land hereinafter described brought under the provisions of Chapter 307, Revised Laws of Hawaii, 1945, and to have its title therein registered and confirmed as an absolute title, and it declares:

(1) That it is a corporation, duly organized and

existing under and by virture of the laws of the Territory of Hawaii and that it is the owner in fee simple of forty-one fifty-fourths (41/54) undivided interest in and to those certain parcels of land situate on the Island of Molokai, County of Maui, Territory of Hawaii, described and bounded as follows:

Being all of Grant 3437 to R. W. Meyer, and Grant 3539 to R. W. Meyer on a portion of Grant 3437 to R. W. Meyer.

Beginning at the Government Survey Triangulation Station "Puu Kaeo" on the edge of Waikalu Valley and on the boundary between Kahanui 3 and Kamiloloa, and running by true azimuths measured clockwise from South:

1. 86° 03' 5118.70 feet along the land of Kamiloloa to a "+" cut in rock;
2. 138° 44' 15" 3370.70 feet along the land of Kaunakakai (Land Court Application 632) to a "+" cut in rock; [35]
3. 134° 36' 4785.00 feet along the land of Kalamaula to a "+" cut in rock;
4. 142° 14' 2854.00 feet along the land of Kalamaula to a "+" cut in rock;
   Thence along the top edge of pali along the Waihanau Valley in the land of Makanalua in all its turns and windings, the direct azimuth and distance between points being:
5. 289° 53' 1387.30 feet to a pipe;
6. 204° 42' 424.60 feet down spur at the head of Waihanau Valley in the land of Makanalua to a spike on edge of Waihanau Falls;

7. 246° 16′ 856.50 feet up spur at the head of Waihanau Valley in the land of Makanalua to a pipe;

   Thence along the top edge of pali along the Waihanau Valley in the land of Makanalua in all its turns and windings for the next six courses, the direct azimuths and distances between points being:

8. 127° 40′ 1400.00 feet;

9. 180° 47′ 2950 feet;

10. 238° 00′ 550.00 feet;

11. 159° 00′ 1600.00 feet;

12. 163° 00′ 850.00 feet;

13. 209° 00′ 400.00 feet to a place called "Hoalae";

   Thence along the top edge of pali along the Waialeia Valley in the land of Kalawao in all its turns and windings for the next 13 courses, the direct azimuths and distances between points being:

14. 272° 52′ 400.00 feet;

15. 338° 15′ 2100.00 feet;

16. 346° 45′ 2150.00 feet;   [36]

17. 42° 15′ 550.00 feet;

18. 345° 05′ 500.00 feet;

19. 5° 00′ 500.00 feet;

20. 353° 43′ 500.00 feet;

21. 357° 58′ 1082.60 feet to a pipe;

22. 331° 35′ 1400.00 feet;

23. 311° 12′ 400.00 feet;

24. 27° 52′ 319.80 feet to a pipe;

25. 294° 36′ 15″ 2030.40 feet;

26. 231° 36′ 3877.70 feet;

Thence along the top edge of pali along Wai-kolu Valley in all its turns and windings for the next 4 courses, the direct azimuths and distances between points being:

27. 349° 32′ 1421.70 feet to Government Survey Triangulation Station "Kaluahauoni";
28. 302° 23′ 30″ 1703.30 feet;
29. 329° 16′ 30″ 3329 feet;
30. 339° 58′ 2543.70 feet to the point of beginning and containing an area of 1195 Acres.

(2) That Applicant is the owner in fee simple of a forty-one fifty-fourths (41/54) undivided interest in said property, and at the last assessment the said land was assessed at one thousand two hundred sixty-eight dollars ($1,268.00).

(3) That Applicant does not know of any mortgage or incumbrance affecting said land, nor that any other person has any estate or interest therein, legal or equitable, in possession, remainder, reversion, or expectancy, save and except the following:

1. That the Territory of Hawaii is occupying said land as a watershed as tenants by sufferance.

2. That the following persons own undivided shares in the properties shown hereunder.

* * * * * [37]

That Applicant obtained title to said lands:

1. By deed of Theodore T. Meyer, et al., dated November 28, 1935, recorded in Book 1375 Pages 145-147 (Abstract Page 75).

2. By deed of Bertha Aubery (unrecorded).

3. By deed of Victoria Meyer Ackerman dated

December 31, 1933, Book 1375 Pages 148-149 (Abstract Page 79).

4. By deed of Miala Meyer dated February 15, 1935, Book 1375 Pages 150-151 (Abstract Page 80).

5. By Decree in Equity No. 3958, in the Circuit Court of the First Judicial Circuit at chambers entitled Christina Tuitele, et al., vs. Margaret Ann Meyer, et al., dated November 25, 1938 (Abstract Page 102).

That Applicant is occupying said lands through its tenant by sufferance, the Territory of Hawaii.
* * * * *   [39]

Dated: Honolulu, T. H., this eighth day of September, 1947.

                    R. W. MEYER, LTD.,
          By THEODORE SEARLE,
                    Its President,

          By NELSON TUITELE,
                    Its Secretary.   [43]
* * * * *

[Title of Land Court and Cause.]

ANSWER OF TERRITORY OF HAWAII
TO FIRST CAUSE OF ACTION
* * * * *

Comes now the Territory of Hawaii by Walter D. Ackerman, Jr., Attorney General, one of the respondents herein, and hereby answers the first cause of action of the amended application on file herein and demurs to the second cause of action thereof, as follows:

For answer to the first cause of action:

I.

Respondent alleges that, of the land claimed by the applicant and sought to be registered in this proceeding, applicant is not the owner of that certain piece of land shown colored in green on the map hereto annexed, marked Exhibit A, and made a part hereby by reference, said piece of land being hereinafter more particularly described, and that applicant does not own any interest in said piece of land. Respondent alleges that said piece [55] of land is part of the Ahupuaa of Makanalua, L. C. Aw. 11216, Apana 11, to Kekauonohi. That at the time of filing of this application and at all times involved in this proceeding and at the present time the Territory of Hawaii has been and is the owner of Makanalua, including said piece of land. That said piece of land, hereinafter called the "disputed area", is more particularly described as follows:

Portion of the land of Makanalua, L. C. Aw. 11216 Apana 11 to Kekauonohi, conveyed to the Minister of Interior by the Administrator of the Estate of L. Haalelea by deed dated May 9, 1866, recorded in Book 21 on page 207.

Beginning at the southeast corner of this parcel of land, the south corner of Grant 3539 to R. W. Meyer, at a point on the north boundary of Grant 3437 to R. W. Meyer, and on the top of the ridge between Waihanau and Waialeia Valleys, the coordinates of said point of beginning referred to Government Survey Triangulation Station "Puu Kaeo" being 6017.22 feet north and 9191.83 feet west, and the direct azimuth and distance to said point of beginning from Government Survey Triangulation Station "Kaohu" being 305° 50′ 6180 feet, as shown on Government Survey Registered Map 1890, and running by azimuths measured clockwise from True South:

Around the head of Waihanau Valley in the land of Makanalua along Grant 3437 to R. W. Meyer, for the first three courses, the direct azimuths and distances between points being:

1. 105° 11′ 1517.50 feet;
2. 152° 00′ 740.00 feet;
3. 145° 02′ 309.50 feet;
4. 204° 42′ 424.60 feet down pali to spike at edge of water fall;
5. 246° 16′ 856.50 feet up pali to pipe on top of edge of the pali bounding the easterly side of Waihanau Valley;   [56]

Thence along Grant 3539 to R. W. Meyer, along the top edge of the pali bounding the easterly side of Waihanau Valley, in all its turns and windings, for the next three courses, the direct azimuths and distances between points on the top edge of said pali being:

6. 318° 02′ 373.10 feet to a pipe;
7. 331° 35′ 1400.00 feet;
8. 347° 58′ 30″ 538.00 feet to the point of begining.

Approximate Area: 50 Acres.

II.

Respondent further alleges that applicant's map inaccurately depicts the boundaries of Grants 3437 and 3539, and inaccurately depicts the topography of said lands and the Waihanau Valley, and further, that neither said map nor the amended application shows the owners and occupants of all adjoining lands, as required by law, this information being wholly omitted as to the adjoining land of Makanalua.

III.

Further answering paragraph (1) of the amended application respondent denies that Grant 3539 to R. W. Meyer was issued on a portion of Grant 3437 to R. W. Meyer, and alleges that said Grant 3539 constitutes a separate grant for a piece of land not covered by said Grant 3437. That on the map hereto annexed as Exhibit A, said Grant 3437 is shown colored in red and said Grant 3539 is shown colored in yellow. That said Grants 3437 and 3539, omitting the disputed area colored in green on said map (Exhibit A), but not contesting applicant's description as to points of difference where the interests of the Territory of Hawaii are not materially prejudiced, cover two tracts of land [57] the metes and bound of which, separately described, are as follows:

Grant 3437 to R. W. Meyer

Beginning at Government Survey Triangulation Station "Puu Kaeo" on the top edge of the pali bounding the westerly side of Waikolu Valley, said triangulation station being at the southeast corner of this grant, and the northeast corner of the land of Kamiloloa, thence running by azimuths measured clockwise from True South:

1. 86° 03' 5118.70 feet along the land of Kamiloloa to a + cut in rock;

2. 138° 44' 15" 3368.50 feet along the land of Kaunakakai (Land Court Application 632) to a + cut in rock;

3. 134° 36' 4785.00 feet along the land of Kalamaula to a + cut in rock;

4. 142° 10' 2854.00 feet along the land of Kalamaula to a + cut in rock;
   Thence for the next seven courses, around the head of Waihanau and Waialeia Valleys, the direct azimuths and distances between points being:

5. 289° 53' 1387.30 feet along Waihanau Valley in the land of Makanalua;

6. 325° 02' 309.50 feet along same;

7. 332° 00' 740.00 feet along same;

8. 285° 11' 1517.50 feet along same;

9. 297° 06' 44.30 feet to a pipe;

10. 294° 34' 30" 2028.40 feet along Waialeia Valley in the land of Kalawao;

11. 231° 36' 3877.70 feet along same;
    Thence to the point of beginning along the top edge of the pali bounding the westerly side of Waikolu Valley in all its turns and windings for the next four courses, the direct azimuths and distances between points on the top edge of said pali being:

12. 349° 32′ 1421.70 feet to government survey triangulation station "Kaluahauoni";
13. 302° 23′ 30″ 1703.30 feet;
14. 329° 16′ 30″ 3329.10 feet;
15. 339° 58′ 2543.70 feet to the point of beginning.
    Approximate Area: 995 Acres.   [58]

Grant 3539 to R. W. Meyer

Beginning at the south corner of this parcel of land, at a point on the north boundary of Grant 3437 to R. W. Meyer, and on the top of the ridge between Waihanau and Waialeia Valleys, the coordinates of said point of beginning referred to Government Survey Triangulation Station "Puu Kaeo" being 6017.22 feet north and 9191.83 feet west, and the direct azimuth and distance to said point of beginning from Government Survey Triangulation Station "Kaohu" being 303° 50′ 6180 feet, as shown on Government Survey Registered Map 1890, and running by azimuths measured clockwise from True South:

Along the top edge of the pali bounding the easterly side of Waihanau Valley in the land of Makanalua, in all its turns and windings, for the next nine courses, the direct azimuths and distances between points on the top edge of said pali being:

1. 167° 58′ 30″ 538.00 feet;
2. 151° 35′ 1400.00 feet to a pipe;
3. 138° 02′ 373.10 feet to a pipe;
4. 127° 40′ 1400.00 feet;
5. 180° 47′ 2950.00 feet;
6. 238° 00′ 550.00 feet;

7. 159° 00′ 1600.00 feet;
8. 163° 00′ 850.00 feet;
9. 209° 00′ 400.00 feet to a place called "Hoalae"; Thence to the point of beginning along the top edge of the pali bounding the westerly side of Waialeia Valley, in the land of Kalawao, in all its turns and windings for the next twelve courses, the direct azimuths and distances between points on the top edge of said pali being:
10. 272° 50′ 400.00 feet;
11. 338° 15′ 2100.00 feet;
12. 346° 45′ 2150.00 feet;
13. 42° 15′ 550.00 feet;
14. 345° 05′ 500.00 feet;
15. 5° 00′ 500.00 feet;
16. 353° 43′ 500.00 feet;
17. 357° 58′ 1082.60 feet to a pipe;
18. 331° 35′ 1400.00 feet;
19. 311° 12′ 400.00 feet;
20. 27° 52′ 319.80 feet to a pipe;
21. 117° 06′ 44.30 feet along Grant 3437 to R. W. Meyer to the point of beginning.

Approximate Area: 150 Acres.   [59]

IV.

Further answering paragraphs (1), (2) and (3) of the first cause of action of the amended application:

(a) Respondent admits that applicant is a corporation duly organized and existing under the laws of the Territory of Hawaii.

(b) Respondent admits that applicant is the

owner in fee simple of an undivided interest in the land sought to be registered in this proceeding, excepting and excluding therefrom the disputed area which is owned by the Territory of Hawaii, but respondent is without knowledge or information sufficient to form a belief as to the extent of applicant's undivided interest, and therefore neither admits nor denies the allegations with respect thereto but leaves applicant to its proof thereof.

(c) Respondent admits that the land sought to be registered has been assessed for taxation at the value of one thousand two hundred sixty-eight dollars ($1268) but alleges that the land so assessed for taxation did not include the disputed area, the same being the property of the Territory of Hawaii.

(d) Respondent denies the allegations set forth in the sixth and seventh lines of paragraph (3) of the first cause of action, page 3 of the amended application, and the last two lines of paragraph (3) of the first cause of action, middle of page 5 of the amended application. Respondent alleges that it is occupying the disputed area above described by virtue of its own right as owner, that respondent is not occupying any [60] other portion of the lands sought to be registered in this proceeding, and that respondent is not a tenant by sufferance, or any other class of tenant, of the applicant.

(e) Respondent is without knowledge or information sufficient to form a belief as to the remaining allegations of paragraph (3) of the first cause of action (which begins on page 3 of the amended application) and therefore neither admits nor denies the same but leaves applicant to its proof thereof.

* * * * *   [61]

Wherefore, this respondent prays:

1. That the first cause of action be dismissed as to the disputed area, and that said area be ordered, adjudged and decreed to be not the property of the applicant. [63]

2. That applicant be ordered and directed to revise and correct its map and application, so as to properly depict and set forth the boundaries of Grants 3437 and 3539, and so as to show the owners and occupants of all adjoining lands, as required by law.

3. That the second cause of action be dismissed.

Dated at Honolulu, T. H., this twenty-eighth day of November, 1947.

TERRITORY OF HAWAII,

By WALTER D. ACKERMAN, JR.,
Attorney General of Hawaii,

By RHODA V. LEWIS,
Assistant Attorney General,
Attorney for Respondent.

* * * * *   [64]

[Title of Land Court and Cause.]

DECISION

There is one issue presently before the Court for determination at this time which may be designated as the issue created by the pleadings under the first cause of action or Count I of the application which heretofore by stipulation approved by the Court would be heard and determined through appeal by the parties prior to proceeding with the remaining ground of application. And in that connection, may I suggest to counsel now that perhaps it would be advisable for the record to file a written stipulation to that effect. The issue concerns the boundaries of Grant 3437, issued on October 29, 1899 and of Grant 3539, issued on May 5, 1891, both to R. W. Meyer as grantee, the present applicants being successors in title, as alleged in the application of the original grantee R. W. Meyer.

The area in dispute has been very clearly delineated in green coloring in Exhibit A annexed to the answer of the Territory and has been referred to in these proceedings as the disputed area. This area designated as the disputed area is more particularly described commencing on page 2 of the answer and pertains to lands in upper Kahanui, raising the overall question to to whether the applicant is the owner of these lands. In that connection, the Territory alleges ownership of the disputed parcel as a portion of the Ahupuaa of Makanalua, Land Court Award [69] 11216, Apana 11, to Kakauonohi, and further alleges the Territory as owner of the entire area of Makanalua.

As to the grants the question for determination is whether or not Grant 3539 to R. W. Meyer, as a grant, was issued on a portion of Grant 3437 to R. W. Meyer, the same grantee, and in that connection raises the question in dispute as to the boundary of Grant 3437, particularly the northern line thereof.

By way of answer the Territory admits that the applicant is the owner in fee of an undivided interest in the land sought to be registered, save and except the disputed area referred to; that is, the applicant has title to whatever is included in the two grants save and except, of course, the disputed area.

The applicant claims Grant 3437 and urges an metes and bounds description in the grant, the applicant likewise urging the same as to Grant 3539, and that as such, the original grantee R. W. Meyer, creating the collateral question of fact as put by the applicants, as to whether or not the original grantee did receive what he applied and paid for.

As to the natural topography, the question arises in that aspect of the evidence of a determination of what constitutes "the head of Waihanau and Waialea Valleys" or, more particularly, the interpretation of the written description of the use of the language "the head of the valley," or admittedly, "the head of Waihanau Valley."

In that connection, the applicant contends that Waihanau Valley is in Kahanui, the Territory conversely claiming that Waihanau Valley is in Makanalua. The ultimate fact, therefore, for determination is the interpretation of the language "the head of Waihanau Valley," and a resulting determination of the boundary line on the ground created thereby. [70]

Much testimony and documentary evidence has been offered and received which brings the question in this particular proceeding to the weight to be accorded to the testimony and documentary evidence, very little of which is, to say the least, in accord with that offered by each party, one against the other.

There is testimony of surveyors and engineers, living surveyors or deceased surveyors and one deceased engineer, as admitted from the transcript in Law 14859.

It is the Court's understanding of the rule that all testimony by surveyors and engineers in a matter of this nature is to be given such weight as it is entitled to by way of opinion and conclusions. One of the deceased surveyors, namely, Mr. Monsarrat, and his works, have been the constant source of reference to, and the offering of his works and alleged works in the proceedings. Reference has been made to his excellent reputation as a surveyor for many years. However, the fact does remain that Mr. Monsarrat nevertheless is or was a surveyor, and testimony of that nature, together with all other testimony of a corresponding nature, must still be entitled to and be weighed as other testimony of surveyors and engineers in any particular given case. The fact that Mr. Monsarrat or any other

engineer was at one time accorded the reputation of
being perhaps, and he may well have been the outstanding surveyor in the Territory of his time, let
us assume, does not in the Court's understanding of
the rule regarding the weighing of testimony entitle
that testimony to be considered ipso facto as conclusive. It is not the rule of evidence as I understand it. If it were, the effect of reception of that
nature of evidence would defeat the very foundation
of the basic value of evidence in a case of this nature, which is its probative value, in arriving at
the ultimate decision on the facts presented, and as
weighed in [71] the light of all the facts, circumstances, and evidence in any particular case.

In this case, where we are concerned with issues
under the evidence of facts, the testimony being
presented from numerous sources, there is testimony
of laymen, living laymen, one deceased, by way of
affidavit, living lay persons as members of the family of the original grantee. There is testimony of
surveyors, both living and deceased, there is testimony of an engineer now deceased, all covering a
period of over sixty years last past. Further, there
are documents in the form of official government
maps and official government surveys, official government correspondence and maps and surveys of
the non-governmental surveyors.

In that connection, all of the testimony has been
of assistance to the Court in arriving at the ultimate
fact to be determined here; all parties are, I am convinced, more than sincere and continue to be, in
their efforts to arrive at a determination of the
ultimate question of fact. But, nevertheless, the rule

must be borne in mind that the testimony of surveyors and engineers is, as I understand the rule, merely opinion and conclusions of professional men as such, and as such, as heretofore stated, are not for that reason accepted or to be accepted as conclusive in the face of other credible and reliable evidence.

The lands of Kahanui and Makanalua were both originally awarded by name only and not by survey description of boundaries. As the Court understands the rule in that connection, an award by name only conveys all property within its boundaries as known and used from ancient times. That is the law of this jurisdiction insofar as I am able to ascertain it. That is, the natural monuments prevail in any question in dispute.

There were numerous maps introduced as evidence herein, and [72] in the opinion of the Court, having reviewed over the past week end all the numerous maps and documents and all of the exhibits, the basis of all of them, that is almost all of them, is the parent map work and field notes of Mr. M. D. Monsarrat. Monsarrat's plat accompanies Grant 3437.

Further, it is the Court's opinion that Monsarrat's map and plat accompanying the grant shows a variance in fact in the northern and eastern boundaries as compared to later maps.

The law in that connection, as I understand it, is that where a description varies from the map or plat the written description prevails and controls over the plat.

Further, upon the survey aspect, there has been

much testimony of courses and calls and distances. Under the evidence there were mixed calls of every conceivable nature embracing courses and distances, natural boundaries and adjacent boundaries. As I understand the law in that connection, and applicable to the facts before the Court, the rule is that natural monuments as set forth in a written description, if ascertainable, prevail over the maps and plats where there is a conflict. This for the obvious reason that natural monuments are physical and factual, and, of course, resultingly speak for themselves.

As to the correspondence, all correspondence considered, the Court is of the opinion that the correspondence does in fact disclose what the grantor intended to convey and the grantee intended to receive, as to the general area to be conveyed. Further, that the correspondence shows that the grantee was to receive all the valley lands necessary to be conveyed for the purpose of saving fencing, and this even if it should incidentally include some of the Makanalua lands. At that time both the remnants of Makanalua and Kahanui were, of course, government lands. [73]

The Court further finds that R. W. Meyer, the original grantee, did in fact describe the lands which he requested, and the reasons described by Meyer, and designating them as "the remnant of Kahanui, which is part and parcel of my land and the whole thereof." Resultingly, the whole of the lele of Kahanui, in the Court's opinion, was purchased by Meyer at the auction, that is, purchased by name.

Further, that R. W. Meyer, the original grantee, complained that the description of the boundaries did not appear to be explicit, that is, with respect to the northern boundary. Resultingly, an amended description was attempted to be included in the reissued Grant 3437 but it did, in fact, not include and did exclude the parcel which the applicant now claims ownership in fee. Further, that the correspondence refers to ridge lands between the two valleys which later became Grant 3539, a portion thereof, and in that connection was referred to as being of so little value as not worth surveying.

Applying the rules, therefore, as the Court understands them in a proceeding wherein the grantee or the successors in interest of an original grantee are parties, or in this case an applicant, the rule, as I understand it, being that in the interpretation of a grant, as applied to this case, where the sovereign is the grantor and Meyer, the citizen, a grantee, the intention of the parties as drawn from the instrument, namely, the grant, viewed in connection with all the surrounding facts and circumstances, is the applicable rule of law to be applied.

Accordingly, the Court, upon the one issue now before it, will find and so holds that under all of the evidence and testimony and the law applicable thereto, and the record herein, viewed in connection with all the surrounding facts, that it was the intention of the grantor to convey to R. W. Meyer by Grant 3437 all [74] of the remnant of Kahanui not theretofore granted to him and to vest in the original grantee R. W. Meyer all of the land or lele of Kahanui; which would include the question of boundary now for determination, the big fall in Waihanau Valley and the head of the valley, which the Court finds, as a matter of fact, to be the big fall, and the resulting boundary, the line at the top of the big fall.

The Court further finds the applicant is the owner in fee simple of an undivided interest in the disputed area, to be determined, however—there is no testimony before the Court and in the light of the comments made in the examiner's report, Penrose C. Morris, filed August 22, 1947, that question will remain open for further determination solely upon the extent and quantum of the undivided interest of the applicant; that the applicant, subject to that, is the owner in fee simple of the disputed area described and delineated in green coloring on the map attached to the answer as Exhibit A herein; further, that the applicant is the owner in fee simple, vested with an undivided interest to be determined at a later date, for the reasons heretofore stated, in all of the lands described in Paragraph No. I of the amended application at Pages 1, 2 and 3 of the amended application. Further proceedings in this matter will await, of course, counsel's move in the premises.

However, upon the instant matter, pursuant to the Court's oral findings just made, a decree embracing the findings and incorporating therein the findings of the Court, will be signed on presentation.

Dated this twenty-seventh day of January, 1950, at Honolulu, T. H.

[Seal]   EDWARD A. TOWSE,
           Second Judge of the Land Court.

[Title of Land Court and Cause.]

DECREE

In accordance with the stipulation filed herein by which the applicant and the respondent, Territory of Hawaii, agreed that the issue of the boundaries of the land under application and the title to the part of said lands shown to be disputed, as between said parties, should be finally adjudicated before any issue of law or fact presented pursuant to Act 207, Session Laws of 1947, shall be heard, and in accordance with the decision fined herein,

It is hereby ordered and decreed that the boundaries of the land subject to the application herein run in accordance with and as shown in the survey and map filed herein by the applicant, and that the applicant has a fee simple title to a forty-one fifty-fourths (41/54) undivided interest in said lands.

That respondent Territory of Hawaii's claim to a portion of the said land, as shown in its answer and the map attached thereto, is not sustained. [77]

The true boundaries of said land are as follows:

Forty-one fifty-fourths (41/54) undivided interest in and to those certain parcels of land situate on the Island of Molokai, County of Maui, Territory of Hawaii, described and bounded as follows:

Being all of Grant 3437 to R. W. Meyer, and Grant 3539 to R. W. Meyer on a portion of Grant 3437 to R. W. Meyer.

Beginning at the Government Survey Triangulation Station "Puu Kaeo" on the edge of Waikalu Valley and on the boundary between Kahanui 3 and Kamiloloa, and running by true azimuths measured clockwise from South:

1. 86° 03′ 5118.70 feet along the land of Kamiloloa to a "+" cut in rock;
2. 138° 44′ 15″ 3370.70 feet along the land of Kaunakakai (Land Court Application 632) to a "+" cut in rock;
3. 134° 36′ 4785.00 feet along the land of Kalamaula to a "+" cut in rock;
4. 142° 10′ 2854.00 feet along the land of Kalamaula to a "+" cut in rock;
    Thence along the top edge of pali along the Waihanau Valley in the land of Makanalua in all its turns and windings, the direct azimuth and distance between points being:
5. 289° 53′ 1387.30 feet to a pipe;
6. 204° 42′ 424.60 feet down spur at the head of Waihanau Valley in the land of Makanalua to a spike on edge of Waihanau Falls;
7. 246° 16′ 856.50 feet up spur at the head of Waihanau Valley in the land of Makanalua to a pipe;
    Thence along the top edge of pali along the Waihanau Valley in the land of Makanalua in all its turns and windings for the next six

courses, the direct azimuths and distances between points being:

8. 127° 40′ 1400.00 feet;
9. 180° 47′ 2950 feet;
10. 238° 00′ 550.00 feet;
11. 159° 00′ 1600.00 feet;
12. 163° 00′ 850.00 feet;
13. 209° 00′ 400.00 feet to a place called "Hoalae"; Thence along the top edge of pali along the Waialeia Valley in the land of Kalawao in all its turns and windings for the next 13 courses, the direct azimuths and distances between points being:
14. 272° 52′ 400.00 feet;
15. 338° 15′ 2100.00 feet;
16. 346° 45′ 2150.00 feet;
17. 42° 15′ 550.00 feet;
18. 345° 05′ 500.00 feet.
19. 5° 00′ 500.00 feet;
20. 353° 43′ 500.00 feet;
21. 357° 58′ 1082.60 feet to a pipe;
22. 331° 35′ 1400.00 feet;
23. 311° 12′ 400.00 feet;
24. 27° 52′ 319.80 feet to a pipe;
25. 294° 36′ 15″ 2030.40 feet;
26. 231° 36′ 3877.70 feet; Thence along the top edge of pali along Waikolu Valley in all its turns and windings for the next 4 courses, the direct azimuths and distances between points being:
27. 349° 32′ 1421.70 feet to Government Survey Triangulation Station "Kaluahauoni";

28. 302° 23′ 30″ 1703.30 feet;
29. 329° 16′ 30″ 3329 feet;
30. 339° 58′ 2543.70 feet to the point of beginning and containing an area of 1195 Acres.

Subject, however, to that certain proceeding in Eminent Domain filed in the Circuit Court of the Second Judicial Circuit, Territory of Hawaii, Entitled, Territory of Hawaii, by Walter D. Ackerman, Jr., its Attorney General, Plaintiff, vs. R. W. Meyer, Limited, et al., defendants, being Law No. 1518 of said Court and Notice of Pendency of Action filed in said proceeding dated September 22, 1948, filed for record in the Bureau of Conveyances as Lis Pendens Document No. 580.

Dated at Honolulu, T. H., this tenth day of April, 1950.

[Seal]　/s/ EDWARD A. TOWSE,
Judge of the Land Court,
Territory of Hawaii.　[80]

In the Supreme Court of the Territory of Hawaii
October Term 1951
[Title of Cause.]

OPINION OF THE COURT

Argued April 17, 1952.　Decided May 19, 1952.

Le Baron, J., and Circuit Judges Corbett and Brown in Place of Towse, C. J., and Stainback, J., Disqualified.

Public Lands—survey and disposal of government lands of the Kingdom of the Hawaiian Islands—

statutory requirements of prior survey and of public record thereof—compliance—a prerequisite of sale—royal patents by necessary implication drawn in conformity with survey.

Compliance with statutory requirements that government lands be accurately surveyed before sale and that the surveys resulting therefrom be kept as public records not only constitutes a prerequisite of sale, but by necessary implication, indicates that the royal patents conveying those lands by surveyed description and map were drawn in conformity with those official surveys so made and kept.

Same—same—royal patents—surveyed description and map on face of patent as parts of the grant—construction—official survey and substantiating government surveys and maps—construed together with grant. [345]

In construing a royal patent all parts of the grant are to be considered in conjunction with prior official survey and substantiating government surveys and maps registered before the patent was drawn and since kept as public records.

Same—same—same—same—unambiguous grant—parol evidence at variance with or contradictory to terms of grant inadmissible.

If there be no ambiguity, parol evidence is inadmissible to vary or contradict the terms of the grant.

Same—same—same—same—parol evidence admissible on question of location.

Where the question is one of location as distinguished from one of construction, parol evidence is admissible to connect the land with the grant or to apply the grant to the land.

Boundaries—description—natural and permanent objects.

A natural and permanent object is of no probative value in establishing the boundary of land conveyed by surveyed description and map if the grant, official survey, the work of the government surveyor and substantiating government surveys and maps contain no description of that object or reference to it and there is no evidence directly connecting it with the land conveyed.   [346]

Opinion of the Court by LeBaron, J.

This is an action in the land court. The applicant is a Hawaiian corporation and claims a forty-one fifty-fourths (41/54) undivided interest in fee simple to certain lands on the island of Molokai as described in its application. The applicant's original source of title thereto is from Kalakaua, King of the Hawaiian Islands, who conveyed unawarded government lands, "situated at Kahanui in the island of Molokai," to R. W. Meyer by two separate and distinct grants. The first is Royal Patent Number 3437, dated October 13, 1888, but subsequently canceled and a new patent of the same number substituted for it on October 29, 1889, to correct misspellings in the names of the two main valleys adjoining the land conveyed on its northern boundary. The new patent, hereinafter referred to as Royal Patent Number 3437, however, made no difference in the location of that boundary or in that of any other boundary, the new, in the same language and with identical sketch map attached as the old, describing that land and stating that it contains an area of 1048 acres more or less. The second grant is Royal Patent Number 3539, dated May 5, 1891, which, with sketch map attached, describes the land conveyed as begininng at a certain point on the northern boundary of Royal Patent Number 3437, extending north along center of ridge and containing an area of 20 acres more or less. Thus were conveyed government lands totaling an area of 1068 acres "more or less."

Two causes of action are alleged by amended application. In the first cause the applicant seeks to have its undivided interest registered and confirmed as an absolute title. The lands subject to that interest are referred to in such application as "all of Grant 3437 to R. W. Meyer and Grant 3539 to R. W. Meyer on a portion of Grant 3437 to R. W. Meyer," and as "containing [347] an area of 1195 acres." The amended application alleges that the Territory is a tenant of the applicant on those lands by sufferance. In the second cause the applicant seeks to have its claim for rentals upon an implied contract adjudicated against the Territory. To the first cause of action, the Territory filed an answer which lays claim of title to an area in dispute of 50 acres within the area claimed by the applicant. It alleges that applicant's map inaccurately depicts the boundaries described by Royal Patents Numbers 3437 and 3539 and inaccurately depicts the topography of the lands conveyed and of Waihanau

Valley so as to include a portion of Waihanau Valley within the lands conveyed, which portion is a part of the adjoining land of the Makanalua and constitutes the area in dispute. It further admits that the "applicant is the owner in fee simple of an undivided interest in the land[s] sought to be registered in this proceeding, excepting and excluding therefrom the disputed area which is owned by the Territory of Hawaii," but denies that the Territory is a tenant by sufferance, alleging that it is only "occupying the disputed area above described by virtue of its own right as owner." To the second cause of action the Territory filed a demurrer. But that demurrer was not considered below, the issues raised by it to the second cause of action being reserved for future determination until a time after the issues raised by the answer to the first cause of action had been finally determined. Nothing concerning the second cause of action, therefore, is before this court for appellate review. The first cause of action alone was tried below.

The sole issue before the land court for determination by stipulation of the parties was the location of the middle western portion of the northern boundary of Royal Patent Number 3437, the locations of the extreme western and the eastern portions of that boundary, as well as those of the entire eastern, southern [348] and western boundaries not being in dispute but admittedly established by the description in the grant, consistent with prior existing government surveys and maps. That issue required the land court to interpret the language of the call for the western portion of the boundary between the agreed point certain on the extreme northwestern tip of Royal Patent Number 3437 and that designated as triangulation point "A," to the southeast on the northern boundary thereof, where the center ridge line of Royal Patent Number 3539 joins that boundary at the edge of Waileia Valley. Such language calls for a meander line commencing with "a stone marked with a cross at the edge of Waihanau Valley thence around the head of the Waihanau" Valley to "A" as the southeast point above set forth. Over the objection of the Territory, the land court on such issue admitted parol or extrinsic evidence of ancient boundaries on the theory that Royal Patent Number 3437, as well as the other patent, constituted a grant "by name only." On that evidence, it in effect interpreted the language of the call to mean a portion of boundary "as known and used from ancient times" and determined the intention of both patents to convey, not according to surveyed descriptions, but according to ancient boundaries. It therefore found that the language "at the edge of Waihanau Valley thence around the head of the Waihanau" Valley described an ancient boundary, as depicted in the amended application, so as to include the disputed area. Consistent therewith, the land court entered a decree sustaining the applicant's claim of title to the disputed area and denying that of the Territory.

The Territory relies upon eight specifications of error covering its thirty-eight assignments of error. No useful purpose would be served by setting them forth. Suffice it to say that they challenge, inter alia, the description in the amended application depicting the middle western portion of the northern [349] boundary of Royal Patent Number 3437 and the adoption of it by the land court; the admission of parol or extrinsic evidence to prove that such portion constitutes an ancient boundary; the underlying theory of the land court's finding that the intention thereof was to convey, not according to surveyed descriptions based upon existing government surveys and maps, but according to ancient boundaries in disregard of such descriptions; and its failure to properly apply the language of the call for such portion of the boundary to the ground, as well as to limit the inquiry of trial to a following of the steps of the government surveyor who made the actual survey and maps for the government before the unawarded government land was conveyed by Royal Patent Number 3437, as indicated by those surveys and maps and by the supporting field notes of the government surveyor. Those specifications, however, present before this court the same issue of location and require it to interpret the same language of the call for the middle western portion of the northern boundary of Royal Patent Number 3437 as presented and required below.

The applicant does not seriously argue before this court that either royal patent constitutes a grant "by name only," even though the theory that both of them did is the essential basis of the decree from which the Territory sued out the instant writ. Indeed, it could not do so with cogent reason. Admit-

tedly, both patents are of the same character of
grant. The call to be interpreted, however, is in
Royal Patent Number 3437 and only the character
of that patent need be considered. The land conveyed thereby, being government land of more
than three hundred dollars in value, was required
by statute not only "to be correctly surveyed" before it was sold but to be sold "at public auction,"
the survey likewise being required to "be kept in
the office of the Minister [of the Interior], open to
inspection of any one who may desire [350] to examine the same." (Haw. Comp. L. 1884 §§ 47, 42,
sub-par. 1.) Compliance with these statutory requirements constituted a prerequisite of sale. That
prerequisite was fully met. Thus, the land was actually surveyed in 1885 by the government surveyor,
one M. Douglas Monsarrat, now deceased, who made
extensive field notes. His survey and field notes, together with four official government surveys and
maps made in accordance with them, were filed and
registered with the office of the Minister of the Interior in 1886 and since that time have remained public records in the files of the government. As already
indicated, the patent issued in 1888 and reissued in
1889. It describes the land by metes and bounds and
by other calls consistently with those surveys and
maps. Fastened between its pages is a sketch map as
a part of the patent on its face. That map clearly
outlines the shape of the land conveyed and portrays the courses of its boundaries. It indicates not
only the commencing point of survey but other government survey stations on the boundary lines of

the land conveyed. It also shows the location of adjoining lands, inclusive of the upper ends of the valleys bordering from the north. Moreover, such map is on the same scale as a corresponding government survey and map of 1886, so that tracings of one would substantially coincide with those made from the other.

The patentee was fully aware of the character of Royal Patent Number 3437 as a grant by surveyed description and map in contradistinction to one "by name only." He himself was a surveyor. It was he who advised the government by letter that "M. Douglas Monsarrat surveyed this piece of land" and enclosed with his formal application for the patent Monsarrat's surveyed description of it. After purchasing that land at public auction and after issuance of the patent in 1888, the patentee claimed that an additional piece of land should have been included. But he was reminded by the Minister of the Interior that "the sale [351] was made by a map and detail description both made by Mr. M. D. Monsarrat, excluding the piece which you claim." In response to that reminder he conceded that "it would be illegal to add anything to a Royal Patent for a piece of land sold by survey" and he merely had misspellings corrected by a reissuance of the patent. Thereafter he applied for and purchased the piece claimed by him as the ridge land adjoining the northern boundary of the patent at point "A," which would have been unnecessary had the patent been a grant "by name only" so as to include within its ancient boundaries that piece. He thus acted consistently with the obvious character of the patent, which on its face manifested the grant's intention to convey land according to the surveyed description and map contained in the grant, there being no intention to convey land according to what had been "known and used from ancient times."

The determinative source of the surveyed description and map as parts of Royal Patent Number 3437 on its face was the reservoir of official surveys and maps, as well as supporting field notes, filed and registered in the office of the Minister of the Interior where the patent was prepared. Indeed, compliance with the statutory requirements of prior survey and of public record of that survey not only constituted a prerequisite of sale but by necessary implication indicates that the sale was made and the patent drawn in conformity with such survey. Resort, therefore, may be had to that public record, as well as to the other public records substantiating it, for the purpose of controlling the calls in the grant. Those public records are to be construed with the grant should it require construction. (See Newman v. Foster, 3 How. [U.S.] 383, 34 Am. Dec. 98; Steele v. Taylor, 3 A. K. Marsh [Ky.] 225, 13 Am. Dec. 151; Vaught v. McClymond, 155 P. [2d] 612 [Mont.]; Lyon v. Fairbanks, et al., 79 Wis. 455, 48 N. W. 492.) But no construction is required of the grant, [352] which admittedly is a valid conveyance without any patent ambiguity appearing on its face. Consistent with the excellent reputation of the government surveyor as the outstanding surveyor of his time in the Hawaiian Kingdom, the grant contains no errors or mistakes to be corrected and gives rise to no latent ambiguities when its language is applied to the ground.

The crux of the case concerns the location of a portion of boundary, rather than a construction of the grant, and involves the admissibility of parol or extrinsic evidence. Upon that crucial point this court has authoritatively declared the settled law to be, where, as here, there is no ambiguity, that "parol evidence is inadmissible to vary or contradict the terms of the grant." (Ookala S. Co. v. Wilson, 13 Haw. 127, 131.) It further likewise declared that "It is also settled that parol evidence is admissible when the question is one of location as distinguished from one of construction, that is, such evidence is admissible to connect the land with the grant or to apply the grant to the land." (Ookala S. Co., v. Wilson, supra.) These principles, simply stated, are decisive of the solution of the problem before this court, the objective being to give effect to nothing else but the grant's intention to convey land according to its surveyed description and map.

Within those principles, parol or extrinsic evidence was properly employed to locate all the boundaries of Royal Patent Number 3539. Illustrative thereof, the applicant applied to the ground not only the language of the grant for a surveyed line along the center of a ridge but a more definite survey of the land itself by the government surveyor on file with the government, presumably as a part of the grant, and readily located the boundaries of the land conveyed. The natural monument descriptive thereof was found by that process to be the continuous contour line of the entire eastern edge of Waihanau Valley and of the [353] entire western edge of Waileia Valley as parallel valleys between which the ridge extended to the north from point "A" on the northern boundary of Royal Patent Number 3437.

Within the same principles, parol or extrinsic evidence was properly employed to locate all the boundaries of Royal Patent Number 3437 except the middle western portion of its northern boundary, the location of that portion being in dispute. Illustrative thereof, the applicant applied to the ground the language of the grant for the extreme western portion and for the eastern portion of the northern boundary and readily located those portions. Likewise, the entire eastern boundary of Royal Patent Number 3437 was located. The language of the call for the eastern boundary is comparable to that for the northern. It calls for a meander line commencing with the eastern terminal point of the course for the northern boundary at the edge of Waikolu Valley "thence along the edge of Waikolu Valley to initial point," also on the edge thereof. The natural monument, descriptive of and common to the extreme western and eastern portions of the northern boundary and the entire eastern boundary, was found by that process of application to be the contour line of continuous mountains meandering along the edges of the respective three adjoining valleys similar to that surrounding the ridge land of Royal Patent Number 3539. In this connection, the Territory had no difficulty in applying the language of the call for the western portion of the northern boundary of Royal Patent Number 3437 to the ground. In doing so, the natural monument descriptive of the middle western portion of that boundary was found to be a continuation of the contour line connecting the extreme western portion with the eastern portion thereof and common to the boundary as a whole. Indeed, any competent surveyor, even without the aid of the government surveyor's field notes, would have had no difficulty in so locating such middle western portion of the northern boundary by the same process. This [354] is indicated by the topography of Waihanau Valley, to which the language of the call is directed with respect to the edge and head of that valley.

To appreciate that topography and to understand that call, the ordinary and usual meaning of the word "valley," the word "head" and the term "around the head" of a valley must be borne in mind so that the language of such call may be properly applied to the ground. The pertinent definition of a valley in Webster's dictionary is "an elongate depression * * * between bluffs, or between ranges of hills or mountains." That of a head is "the end of anything regarded as the upper end, through being higher, being associated with the head of a person, being opposite to the foot, or any like association of ideas; as the head of a * * * valley * * *." The term "around the head" of a valley denotes a line of curvature with its apex at the topmost part of the upper end of the valley. It has the same meaning as that of the term "along the edge" of a valley, when limited to the upper end, and has a comparable meaning to that of the term "around the shoulder" of a valley or other protruding parts thereof.

Waihanau Valley is "an elongate depression * * * between * * * mountains." Its foot is to the north toward the sea and its head to the south toward the center of the island, the head being "the upper end, through being higher." Its floor, down which runs a stream, progressively ascends in elevation but the mountains creating the definitive depression remain fairly constant at an elevation of 2600 feet on the western edge and 2700 feet on the eastern. When the parts of that valley are depicted by an association of ideas to corresponding parts of a person the wide depression between the mountains before they commence to converge may be termed "the body"; the adjoining narrowing depression as those mountains converge may be termed "the shoulders"; the adjoining long gorge where those mountains converge and run almost parallel to each other may be termed "the neck"; and the adjoining wider and shorter ravine where those mountains diverge at the southern end of the gorge and then reconverge at the southern edge of the valley may be termed "the head." By like association of ideas, the crown or topmost part of the head may be placed at the point where the mountains reconverge by an overlapping of ridges at an "S bend" of the stream bed so as to virtually terminate the definitive depression, except for the stream bed, the contour lines of those ridges

being at the elevation of 2400 feet at the center
point of overlap, which is the southern edge of the
valley at the crown of its head. Thus, the entire edge
of the valley forms a hairpin loop with an elevation of 2600 feet on the western side of the valley,
one of 2400 feet on its southern side and one of
2700 feet on its eastern.

The language of the call for the western portion
of the northern boundary of Royal Patent Number
3437 demands that it be interpreted objectively in
relation to the physical features of Waihanau Valley so that every word be given significance. When
this is done the meaning is plain and signifies a
meander line commencing with "a stone marked
with a cross at the [western] edge of Waihanau
Valley thence [curving along that edge in a southerly direction to the topmost part of the valley's
upper end] around the head of Waihanau" Valley
and thence east to point "A." That language, so
interpreted, calls for a single meander course which
is southeast, south and east and within which are
confined the necessary turns and windings of the
valley's edge.

Strongly corroborative of that meaning as the
true interpretation of the language of the call for
the western portion of the northern boundary is the
sketch map as a part of the grant itself. That map
portrays the same meander course for that portion
of boundary and, without dispute, does so correctly
for the [356] extreme western portion of the same
boundary, as well as for the eastern portion. In

further corroboration thereof, the official government surveys and maps all identify the same meander course of the same boundary and may be resorted to for the purpose of controlling the call for that boundary. On one of them the government surveyor, in his own handwriting, marked the letter "K" as a triangulation point upon that course. That point is admittedly located with certainty in his field notes by being twice coordinated with different government survey stations and other fixed points. It therefore further not only identifies the same meander course but controls the call for the boundary along that course. Nor it there anything to the contrary to be found in the grant or in those public records. Thus, the single meander course is identified with absolute certainty as one along which runs the western portion of the northern boundary. Such identification operates to amplify the meaning of the language of the call for that portion as interpreted by this court. No other meaning suffices to meet the grant's intendment. That meaning therefore governs the location of that portion as to course. Consistent therewith, the answer of the Territory correctly describes and locates such portion and in doing so properly excludes the disputed area from the land conveyed by Royal Patent Number 3437.

Needless to say, the amended application of the applicant contradicts the meaning of the language of the call for the middle western portion of the northern boundary of Royal Patent Number 3437 as interpreted by this court. In doing so, the amended application not only contradicts but varies the terms of the grant itself, so as to add the area in dispute to land conveyed, and thereby violates the grant's intention and encroaches upon the land of the Territory. This the applicant accomplished by ignoring the sketch map's portrayal of the single meander course for the entire [357] western portion of the northern boundary as a part of the grant, by refusing to be guided by official government surveys and maps or to follow in "the footsteps" of the government surveyor, and by improperly applying the language of the call to the ground. Illustrative thereof, the applicant in its amended application creates four courses out of the single meander course by departing due north from the western edge of Waihanau Valley at a point it arbitrarily fixed, which is short of point "K" further southeast along such edge, so as to go down its side for a depth of four hundred feet at the base of its head to the floor of the valley, where there are several spectacular big waterfalls, then up the opposite side of the valley to its eastern edge for a height of six hundred feet and then along that edge due south to point "A." Applicant's excuse for so cutting off the head of the valley is premised solely upon parol or extrinsic evidence. That evidence consists of the testimony of various witnesses, the correspondence between the patentee and the Minister of the Interior, letters of Monsarrat and other documents. It deals generally with ancient boundaries and specifically with the big waterfalls. It tends to prove, assuming without deciding such probative tendency, that the top of those falls has been considered "since ancient times" to be the head of the Waihanau Valley as a natural monument descriptive of an ancient boundary and was used and regarded by the patentee for the purpose of marking the middle western portion of the northern boundary of Royal Patent Number 3437.

Although the law is well-settled that parol or extrinsic evidence is admissible to locate and explain natural monuments descriptive of the land conveyed, no citation of authorities is necessary to say that such evidence is inadmissible to locate and explain any object not descriptive thereof. Moreover, the test of whether an object be such a natural monument so as to mark a [358] boundary of the land conveyed is that it must be connected with that land. The parol or extrinsic evidence relied upon by the applicant does not meet that test. It pertains to the object of the big waterfalls but does not connect that object with the land conveyed. Nor do the surveyed description and map as parts of the grant, the official government surveys and maps and the work of the government surveyor, none of which describes such object to mark a boundary of the land conveyed. The evidence so relied upon therefore has no probative value or force to prove anything descriptive of the middle western portion of the northern boundary of the land covered by Royal Patent Number 3437. (See Vireca Corporation v. Cole, et al., 129 S. W. [2d] 433 [Tex. Civ. App. 1939].) Nor does that evidence purport to locate and explain any monuments, natural or artificial, which are descriptive of such portion. On the contrary, it completely ignores them, as well as their locations. It does so by radically departing from the well-established and easily ascertainable single course of boundary and by substituting for the descriptive monuments along that course the big waterfalls located elsewhere. This attempt to supplant a course of boundary and to displace descriptive monuments upon it is beyond the permissible limits of parol or extrinsic evidence, otherwise boundaries delineated by surveyed description and map could always be disturbed. In short, the evidence relied upon by the applicant goes outside the land conveyed by grant on surveyed description and map, in contradiction of and at variance with the terms of the grant itself. It therefore is inadmissible and constitutes no valid excuse in law or in fact, either for the applicant to claim the area in dispute or for the patentee to have used and regarded, if he did, the big waterfalls for the purpose of marking any portion of boundary for the land conveyed by Royal Patent Number 3437. [359]

The decree of the land court is reversed and the cause remanded below with instructions to order the applicant to amend its amended application by striking out the disputed area, in lieu of an order dismissing such application, and for such further proceedings as may be consistent with this opinion.

T. W. Flynn, Special Deputy Attorney General (W. D. Ackerman, Jr., Attorney General, and T. W.

Flynn, Deputy Attorney General, on the briefs), for plaintiff in error.

P. Cass (S. Shapiro with him on the brief) for defendant in error.

/s/ SAM LeBARON,
/s/ R. CORBETT.

[Endorsed]. Filed May 10, 1952. [360]

In the Supreme Court of the Territory of Hawaii
October Term 1951

No. 2829

In the Matter of the Application of R. W. MEYER, LIMITED, to Register and Confirm its Title to Land Situate in Molokai, County of Maui, Territory of Hawaii.

JUDGMENT ON WRIT OF ERROR

In the above entitled cause, pursuant to the opinion of the Supreme Court rendered and filed on the nineteenth day of May, 1952, and pursuant to the order of the Supreme Court rendered and filed on the sixteenth day of June, 1952, denying the petition for rehearing, the decree appealed from is reversed and the cause remanded to the Land Court of the Territory of Hawaii with instructions to order the applicant to amend its amended application by striking out the disputed area, in lieu of an order dismissing such application, and for such further proceedings as may be consistent with said opinion.

Dated at Honolulu, Territory of Hawaii, this twenty-third day of June, 1952.

By the Court:

/s/ LEOTI V. KRONE,
Clerk.

Approved:

/s/ SAM LeBARON,
Associate Justice.

[Endorsed]: Filed June 12, 1952. [375]

[Title of Supreme Court and Cause.]

SUPREME COURT CLERK'S CERTIFICATE

I, Leoti V. Krone, clerk of the Supreme Court of the Territory of Hawaii, do hereby certify that all of the documents and items listed in the index to the certified record on appeal to the United States Court of Appeals for the Ninth Circuit in the above-entitled case are the originals on file in said matter and the above court pursuant to Order to Include Original Exhibits in Record, filed June 25, 1952, and in pursuance of the praecipe filed June 25, 1952. I further certify that the original record, comprised of two volumes, of the Supreme Court, numbered 2829, is transmitted herewith, together with all of the original exhibits and the transcript of evidence, No. 1483, two volumes, filed in the above court. I further certify that the said Supreme Court record No. 2829, two volumes, and all exhibits and transcript of evidence, in two volumes, are attached hereto. I further certify that all costs in connection with the transcript of the record to the United States Court of Appeals for the Ninth Circuit have been paid by the attorneys for the appellant.

In witness whereof, I have hereunto set my hand and affixed the seal of the above court this fifteenth day of September, 1952.

/s/ LEOTI V. KRONE,
Clerk. [417]

In the Land Court of the Territory of Hawaii

Application No. 1483.

In the Matter of the Application of R. W. MEYER, LIMITED.

TRANSCRIPT OF EVIDENCE

The above entitled and numbered cause came on for hearing on the 11th day of January, 1950, at 9:30 a.m.

Before: Honorable Edward A. Towse, Judge, presiding.

Appearances: Phil Cass, Esq., for the Applicant; Thomas W. Flynn, Deputy Attorney General, for the Territory of Hawaii. [1*]

(The clerk called the case.)

---

* Page numbering appearing at bottom of page of original Reporter's Transcript of Record.

The Court: Are the parties ready?

Mr. Cass: The applicant is ready, your Honor.

Mr. Flynn: Ready for the Territory, your Honor. [2]

* * * * *

Mr. Cass: As to the present hearing, the applicant and the Territory, the only persons who are contesting the title, have entered into a stipulation that the Court may hear and try and determine the title issues normally the function of the Land Court, and separate and apart from those special issues, jurisdiction for which is conferred by the Session Laws of 1947, and that no hearing will be had on any issue of law or fact under the Session Laws of 1947 until the question of title to the land has been judicially determined finally.

Is that your understanding, Mr. Flynn?

Mr. Flynn: That is about correct. I would endeavor to clarify only slightly, for convenience.

Mr. Cass: Please clarify.

Mr. Flynn: To the effect that the parties are now to proceed in the Land Court under only the first cause of action in the application, which is simply the standard type of Land Court application for the registration of land. The second cause of action, being that coming under the special legislation of 1947, to be entirely disregarded until a final judicial determination as to the merits of the first cause of action.

The Court: I understand final disposition contemplates an appeal.

Mr. Cass: It does.

Mr. Flynn: Possibly including an appeal.

The Court: Possibly. Let's make it definite.

Mr. Flynn: Definitely. In other words, appeal if the party takes one, yes.

The Court: The stipulation as offered will be approved. Let the stipulation appear of record. [3]

* * * * *

Mr. Cass: In discussion of this matter yesterday the parties agreed that the issue of title, which is an issue of boundaries, concerns only the interpretation of the language of the grants "Around the head of Waihanau and Waialeia Valleys" and does not concern the boundaries, which are assured by traverse, on the boundary of Kamiloloa, Kaunakakai, and Kalamaula or the boundaries of Waialeia Valley or Waikolu Valley, which have never been questioned, but simply the boundary of the area shown on the maps and in the answer of the Territory as being approximately 50 acres lying above Waihanau Falls.

The Court: That is that portion delineated in green in the exhibit attached to the answer?

Mr. Cass: Yes.

Mr. Flynn: Yes, your Honor.

Mr. Cass: Is that your understanding of the issues?

Mr. Flynn: Yes.

The Court: Very well. Let that stipulation and the offer be approved and entered of record.

* * * * *

Mr. Cass: This land comprises a lele of the Ahupuaa of Kahanui. The history of the land is that the land was awarded as a Mahele award in 1848, the Mahale award being Award No. 48. Later the [4] land by name was awarded under Land Commission Award 7755 and one-half of the land of the Ahupuaa of Kahanui. Rudolph W. Meyer, from whom title descends in this matter, bought a one-half interest in the Ahuputaa of Kahanui by name and occupied this land for many years.

In 1885 Mr. Monsarrat, a surveyor for the Government who then was engaged in surveying by traverse the lines now accepted as the southern and western boundaries of this land, to fix the boundaries of the lands which border this. He was not surveying Kahanui but was surveying the lands that border it to fix their boundaries.

Meyer was then in occupancy of the land and had been for many years. He was informed by Monsarrat and Mr. Alexander, Mr. Monsarrat's superior in the Land Office, that by some error or some reason this lele of Kahanui was not shown in the Government records as being part of the patent issued on Land Commission Award 7755. That apparently was the first information that he had that the land which he was occupying and which he had bought by name was not covered in the patent.

In 1886 Monsarrat prepared a description of this land, which Meyer attached to an application in a series of letters to the Government for a patent award or the privilege of purchasing all land which he occupied. He first made his application in 1888. And accordingly, in his letter he made an application to purchase the land "Which I now occupy

and which I believed was mine'' for $500. Where-
upon, the Government advertised the sale of this
lele by name only and sold it to Meyer for $500.
Thereafter a patent was drawn up in the language
of Monsarrat's survey, which proved to be inaccurate in names. Monsarrat's [5] survey did not
differentiate between the Valley of Waihanau and
the Makanalua boundaries. Meyer returned the
grant for correction and that first patent was thereupon cancelled and a new patent embodying the
names that Meyer had suggested was issued.

Sometime later, when Meyer received the new
patent, he found that a section of the land itself
was not shown in the sketch attached to the patent.
The language ''Around the head of the valleys''
would have been broad enough to have covered this
new parcel of land if it had not been that the
sketch attached clearly did not show this projection
out into the flat lands. Again he wrote to the Government. And the Government admitted that the
land in this projection out into the flat land should
have been included because it was intended to sell
the whole of the lele of Kahanui to Meyer, and said,
however, that the original grant could not now be
corrected to include this particular land because
they interpreted the law to be that it would not
allow the Minister of Interior to change a grant
which had been made under survey and map, but
offered to sell to Meyer the additional land for
$10. Meyer sent his $10 in and was issued a grant.
Before he was issued a grant again the boundaries
to the new grant came up.

Monsarrat was not available in the office of the Land Commissioner and J. D. Brown, known as Jake Brown, was in charge of the survey department and knew nothing at all about the boundaries, according to his letter. However, Monsarrat finished a survey line from some map of his, from which he said Meyer could get a rough estimate of the length of the spur and the description of the land. Jake Brown wrote a letter saying [6] that he would come to Molokai on a shooting trip and he would bring along a surveying instrument and get a better description. He did come to Molokai, but it was raining. There may have been other reasons why he did not do it, but he never set foot on the land of Kahanui or made any survey whatsoever. They simply took this straight line that Monsarrat had furnished for purposes of other distances, with the point projected into the land and issued a patent in which they patented the line only, not the area on top of the ridge but a straight line following that line out.

When the patent had been issued and came to the attention of Brown again, he wrote a letter acknowledging the mistake and setting forth the description which he had furnished the Land Office, which was a description "Around the edge of the pali," a piece of land of which this line was the center. He estimated the area at 20 acres. The actual area was 200 acres. This never was incorporated in a new grant but the letter of Brown correcting the patent has been used as delineating the boundary of that land, which now is not in dispute.

The land below this, the land of Makanalua, was also a Mahele award. It was an award to Haalelea. He was of the family of royalty. When the lepers were first to be placed on the land it was thought that leprosy would be stamped out in just a few years, and Haalelea offered this land of his, together with the lands of Kalaupapa and Waikolu for a leper settlement. It was agreed by the medical men that if they took the lepers over there and let them die off there would be no more leprosy in Hawaii. That happened in about 1860. I am not sure of that particular date. But in 1866 Haalelea's administrator [7] deeded the land of Makanalua to the Government by deed, and the Government's title to the land of Makanalua along which the disputed boundary line runs, as far as their title to the Makanalua land goes is based upon the deed of Haalelea's administrator to the King.

Meyer himself was a surveyor for the Board of Education for school lands. He was Land Commissioner for the island of Molokai, he was attorney in fact for Haalelea, he was attorney in fact for Princess Ruth, who was predecessor of the Bishop Estate; he was also business manager for the Leper Settlement.

In 1883 he got a deed for this half of the Ahupuaa of Kahanui from the secondary awardee by its ancient boundaries. The other half of the Ahupuaa of Kahanui belonged to the Princess Ruth and from the Princess Ruth came to her niece Pauahi Bishop. In 1884 he bought that other half of the

land from Bernice Pauahi Bishop, becoming the
sole owner of this land. [8]

* * * * *

Mr. Flynn: The principal point which the Government has taken ever since the very extensive
litigation in various phases was [12] begun has
been that the lands involved here were conveyed
or given to the applicant's predecessor by grant, by
map and description, the grant being by map and
description.

Our principal point of law is that where the
grant is made by map and description and where
the map and description may be reconciled with
each other and reconciled on the ground and reconciled from all other data available to assist the parties in determining their rights, those are controlling
and cannot be rejected except by clear, unequivocal
and incontrovertible evidence. And we expect little
or no difficulty in showing that the survey of the
lands described in the first grant are adequate to
bring the boundary line to where it always was as
far as the Government was concerned, and that
the survey of the second grant, an admittedly in-
adequate survey, still would not have bearing on
the 50 odd acre parcel of land which is in dispute
here. [13]

* * * * *

BERNARD H. McKEAGUE

a witness called by and on behalf of the applicant,
being first sworn, was examined and testified as
follows:

(Testimony of Bernard H. McKeague.)

Direct Examination

* * * * *

Q. (By Mr. Cass): What is your profession?

A. Registered professional surveyor.

Q. How long have you been a registered professional surveyor? A. Sixteen years.

Q. Do you speak Hawaiian?

A. No, but I understand it fairly well.

Q. What has been your experience in surveying boundary lines in Hawaii?

A. I started in 1925 with the Bishop Estate and had experience in other offices, later, about eleven years, with Mr. Mann, and then since 1941 in business for myself, during all this time doing surveying work of the old boundaries, including ahupuaas [16] and kuleanas.

Q. In connection with your surveys, Mr. McKeague, how do you determine the lines which you are to run on an old boundary?

A. If it is an ahupuaa, kamaaina evidence together with the old description, if any. These boundaries usually follow definite topographic features.

Q. Did you prepare the map accompanying the application in this matter? A. I did.

Q. What did you do in connection with locating on the ground the boundaries of this land?

A. That is, Kahanui 3?

Q. Yes. You may go over and point on the map, if you wish.

A. Yes. My principal work on the ground was

(Testimony of Bernard H. McKeague.)
in the vicinity of the disputed area, that is, from
this rock marked with a cross, which is Monsarrat's point X, over and around to this point Y,
across the gulch to where his point "Ridge A"
was and northerly to a portion of the area, the
flat area covered under Grant 3539 to R. W. Meyers,
and back across the Big Fall to Monsarrat's
point X.

Q. Did you actually go on the pali around to
take your shots, all the way around that northern
boundary?

A. No, I did not. On Monsarrat's "Ridge A"
I located the boundary for probably a thousand
feet and then on the point "Monsarrat's Dry Tree"
I located the edge of the pali for about another
thousand feet northward.

Mr. Flynn: Excuse me. I did not get that.

(The answer was read by the reporter.)

Mr. Flynn: May I ask you to point out again on
the map, [17] please?

A. That is where I plotted the point to identify
the position as it pertains to my map. For other
points I probably can use an X circled here near
the bearing 353 degrees 43 minutes as being the
northerly limits of my locating the top edge of the
pali on the Waialeia side and probably the same
at the end of cross 127 degrees 40 minutes.

Q. (By Mr. Cass): I note that the map you
are pointing to there has red lines and figures on it.
Do those appear on the map that is on file?

A. It does not.

(Testimony of Bernard H. McKeague.)

Q. What do those lines and figures represent?

A. They represent the shots that Monsarrat took from these established points on the Kalamaula boundary and some of the points along the Waikolu boundary.

Q. They are identified, as you have mentioned, as "Point A," "Dry Tree," and so forth, written onto your map?

A. That is right.

Mr. Cass: May we offer that map in evidence?

The Court: Any objection?

Mr. Flynn: No objection, your Honor.

The Court: It will become Applicant's Exhibit A in evidence.

(The map referred to was received in evidence as Applicant's Exhibit A.)

Q. (By Mr. Cass): Now, in determining the boundary of this land, did you refer to the patent?

A. I did not. Where it pertains to the northerly —the northerly boundary? [18]

Q. Did you read the patent?

A. I did.

Mr. Cass: The patent is already in the abstract, if the Court please. I offer a photostat copy of Patent 3437. That is the same one that was in evidence before, although the certificate may have been lost on it.

Mr. Flynn: The clerk's notes from the 1936

(Testimony of Bernard H. McKeague.)

trial are here. I have no objection, your Honor.

The Court: It will become Applicant's Exhibit B in evidence, Patent No. 3437, a photostatic copy thereof.

(The photostatic copy of Patent No. 3437 was received in evidence as Applicant's Exhibit B.) [19]

* * * * *

Q. (By Mr. Cass): Now, Mr. McKeague, reading from the exhibit which is in evidence, the grant reads, as Course No. 4, "North 37 degrees 56 minutes west 2854 feet along Kalamaula to a stone marked with a cross at the edge of the Waihanau Valley, thence around the head of the Waihanau and Waialeia Valleys to the Government Survey Station 'Kaluahauoni,' the direct bearing and distance being 79 degrees 07 minutes east (true) 8631 feet."

Did you identify the boundary described thusly before you put it on your map?

A. What was that question again?

Q. Did you take your boundary off of the grant here and identify it on the ground?

A. In determining the northerly boundary as it pertains to that fourth course, "thence around the head of the Waihanau [20] Valley and Waialeia Valley," I further explored the meaning of that and decided and determined that the boundary, that it meant that it went from this point, this cross on

(Testimony of Bernard H. McKeague.)

a rock, around the top edge of this gulch overlooking Waihanau Valley, across Big Fall, to the upper edge, and northeasterly from Big Fall, thence around the westerly edge of Waihanau Valley, around Hoalae Point, still following the top edge of the pali, along the westerly side of Waialeia Valley and around the head of Waialeia Valley to the point Kaluahauoni.

Q. How did you come to that conclusion? What evidence did you have or obtain as to the location of that line on the ground?

A. There were letters in correspondence between Meyer and Government officials, corrections in the original patents, to show the intent of what was intended to be conveyed in the original application by Meyer.

Mr. Flynn: If the Court please, I want to make a slight interruption. Although he is entitled to testify from conclusions, from the examination of correspondence and other documents, I believe properly the applicant must be required to have those in evidence as the best evidence themselves and then the witness will be allowed to draw his conclusions from them and point specifically to what he refers to as bases for his conclusions. Mr. Cass, are you now offering this? [21] * * * * *

Mr. Cass: This letter to Thurston, July 4, 1888, the response of Thurston, July 27, 1888, to Meyer, or rather a letter from J. F. Brown to Thurston, July 27, 1888, reporting on the application, the formal application of Meyer to purchase the land for

(Testimony of Bernard H. McKeague.)

$500, dated the 31st of August, 1888, accompanied by a description of survey. I offer those in evidence.

The Court: Any objection?

Mr. Flynn: No objection.

The Court: Very well. Let all be marked Exhibit C of the applicant. The letter from Meyer to Thurston, dated July 4, 1888, Exhibit C-1; the letter of Brown to Thurston, July 27, 1888, C-2; the application and accompanying description of survey, dated August 31, 1888, C-3. In evidence.

(Applicant's Exhibits C-1, C-2, and C-3 were received in evidence.)   [22]

* * * * *

Mr. Cass: It may help in reference. I am reading from the typed copy of the letter of Meyer, dated July 4, 1888.

(Reading.) * * * * * [23]

Then, following that, on July 27, 1888, J. F. Brown reported to Thurston: (Reading.) [25]

* * * * *

Then Meyers writes again to Thurston, on the 31st of August, 1888. (Reading.)

* * * * *

Those are the letters contained in the file. This blueprint, however, has in addition to the letters, the survey mentioned. [26]

* * * * *

Mr. Flynn: It is the three documents. I had thought it was only the one. So that you can let

(Testimony of Bernard H. McKeague.)
the record note that C-1-A is the typewritten copy
of all three letters referred to in Exhibit C.

The Court: Very well. Let the record so show.
Exhibit C-1-A.

Mr. Flynn: Thank you.

The Court: Will then become C-1-A, B, and C,
of the applicant. That is the typewritten copy.

(Applicant's Exhibits C-1-A, B, and C, were
received in evidence.) [27]

* * * * *

The Court: Let the photostat of the advertise
ment of October 4, 1888, in the Daily Pacific Commercial Advertiser become Exhibit D-1 of the applicant, in evidence; the news item, dated October 11,
1888, becomes D-2 in evidence.

(The documents referred to were received
in evidence as Applicant's Exhibits D-1 and
D-2.)

* * * * *

The Court: Letter dated July 31, 1888, from
the Department of Interior to R. W. Meyers, becomes Applicant's Exhibit E in evidence.

(The document referred to was marked Applicant's Exhibit E and was received in evidence.) [28]

* * * * *

The Court: Letter of August 6, 1888, Depart-

(Testimony of Bernard H. McKeague.)
ment of Interior to Meyer, will become Applicant's
Exhibit F in evidence.

> (The document referred to was marked Ap-
> plicant's Exhibit F and was received in evi-
> dence.)

* * * * *

The Court: It will become Applicant's Exhibit G
in evidence, letter from Thurston to Meyer, dated
August 30, 1889.

> (The document referred to was marked Ap-
> plicant's Exhibit G and was received in evi-
> dence.) [29]

* * * * *

The Court: The letter of the Department of Interior to Meyer, dated October 17, 1889, becomes
Applicant's Exhibit H in evidence.

> (The document referred to was marked Ap-
> plicant's Exhibit H and was received in evi-
> dence.)

* * * * *

The Court: Very well. Let the letter of Brown
to Thurston, dated November 12, 1889, become Applicant's Exhibit I-1.

Mr. Cass: And the letter of Meyer to Thurston,
dated October 23, 1889——

The Court: Will become Exhibit I-2 of the applicant's in evidence. [30]

Mr. Flynn: You have those two in reverse order,

(Testimony of Bernard H. McKeague.)
but that does not make any difference. That does not matter.

> (The documents referred to were marked Applicant's Exhibits I-1 and I-2 and were received in evidence.)

Mr. Cass: Now I offer in evidence a photostatic copy of the original grant, not for the purpose of establishing boundaries by the original grant but because the original grant has corrections made in the handwriting of Meyer, I believe. The original grant is corrected to change the names of the Waihanau Valley and the name of Waialeia Valley is substituted for that of Makanalua in that fourth course. Is there any objection to that?

Mr. Flynn: No objection. I might call the Court's attention to the fact that the handwriting referred to by Mr. Cass is extremely indistinct on this copy but we will probably be able to agree as to the exact wording of it.

Mr. Cass: Yes.

The Court: Is that offered for the purpose of the corrections noted on the photostat, limited to that solely?

Mr. Cass: That is for that purpose only.

The Court: It will become Applicant's Exhibit J in evidence.

> (The document referred to was marked Applicant's Exhibit J and was received in evidence. * * * * * [31]

(Testimony of Bernard H. McKeague.)

The Court: Photostatic copy of original Grant 3539 becomes Applicant's Exhibit K in evidence.

(The document referred to was marked Applicant's Exhibit K and was received in evidence.)

Mr. Cass: I offer in evidence the letter from J. F. Brown, Hawaiian Government Survey Office, dated May 22, 1891, with the inscription "Signed by Brown" attached.

* * * * *

(The document referred to above was marked Applicant's Exhibit L and was received in evidence.)

Q. (By Mr. Cass): Now, Mr. McKeague, you have heard the description of the letters that I have read and have sat here and seen the letters themselves as I passed them in for entry into evidence in this case, as exhibits. Are those the letters which you examined when you made up your mind where the boundary of the land was supposed to run?

A. That is right.

Q. Did you make any other effort to locate on the ground where the survey lines should run by way of gaining information from other sources? [32]

A. I made inquiries with the kamaainas and I was informed that they all knew the boundary to run along the Big Fall.

Mr. Flynn: If the Court please, I am going to

(Testimony of Bernard H. McKeague.)

make an objection to that answer as not being strictly responsive to the question but primarily because the conclusion is expressed by the witness that he made inquiry of kamaainas, whereas I believe the Court could take judicial notice that kamaainas have been particularly extinct since 1912, according to a number of Supreme Court decisions, and I move to strike that portion of the witness' answer wherein the witness states he found from kamaainas where the boundaries were. * * * * *

The Court: The objection is sustained. The portion of the answer objected to will be stricken. For the record also, let the record show that Mr. Flynn's original objection—now that these other exhibits are in evidence—is overruled.

Q. (By Mr. Cass): Having talked to kamaainas and examined letters and the grant, as you stated, where did you place the boundary of the disputed area between Makanalua and Kahanui?

Mr. Flynn: Objection, if the Court please, to that portion of the question calling for the witness' referral to his talk to kamaainas, when that has just been stricken [33] by the Court:

The Court: The objection is sustained.

Mr. Cass: If the Court please, what he told them is sustained—is objectionable, but the fact that he actually obtained knowledge from them is very similar to the proposition that a policeman cannot relate what was told him in a confession but he can tell what he found as a result of that confession.

(Testimony of Bernard H. McKeague.)

The Court: That is not the form of the question, Mr. Cass. Perhaps it can be rephrased.

* * * * *

Q. (By Mr. Cass): Well, whom did you talk to, Mr. McKeague, that you considered kamaainas?

A. Willie Meyer, who is about sixty-four years old, a member of the Meyer family, who in turn was a little boy, and the boundary was pointed out to him by his grandfather; two daughters of the original Rudolph Meyer, Aunty Pearl and another member of the family who is about eighty-seven years [34] old; and there was a kid there, Penny Meyer, who roamed those hills in the early days with the older folks, and he also said that the boundary——

Mr. Flynn: Wait a minute. May I interrupt, please?

A. (continuing): ——was at the Big Fall.

Mr. Flynn: May I interrupt the answer, if the Court please? I submit this is not admissible. If those individuals are capable of giving kamaaina testimony, they must be present in court for cross-examination and cannot be brought in this way. I submit further that the Supreme Court in the late 1890s and again about 1912 indicated that kamaaina testimony within the meaning of that term as used many years ago, even when land commission awards were involved, is not the type of testimony offered now. [35]

* * * * *

Mr. Flynn: If the Court please, at the time of the recess I had just made an objection to the na-

(Testimony of Bernard H. McKeague.)

ture of the questioning by counsel for the applicant, the purpose of which was to bring forth from the witness, who is a surveyor, that he contacted kamaainas for information, and I objected on the ground that kamaaina testimony has a specific and limited meaning in Hawaiian land law, and on the further ground that if there are any qualified kamaainas or were at the time of this witness' work that their own testimony would be the best evidence of this matter, and I objected further on the ground that the decisions of our own Supreme Court many years ago specifically refer to the nature of kamaaina testimony and in their references and discussions have diclosed that the type of limited testimony is that which was then available from original Hawaiians or those who were in existence on the lands and whose business it was to know the lands in the various divisions and subdivisions of the lands in the Territory, specifically ahupuaas and other subdivisions.

(The Court thereupon heard the argument of counsel upon the objection.)

The Court: The question that brought forth the objection was what people Mr. McKeague had contacted. He thereupon started to testify as to what certain individuals had told [36] him and thereupon Mr. Flynn objected.

Mr. Cass: I will withdraw that testimony and permit it to be stricken, and I will ask Mr. McKeague this.

Q. (By Mr. Cass): Now, Mr. McKeague, you

(Testimony of Bernard H. McKeague.)

testified that you had talked to kamaainas. Is this survey an expression of what those kamaainas told you where the boundaries run?

Mr. Flynn: My objection is a little bit more specific.

The Court: I would think, for the record, Mr. Flynn, that now is the time for the objection formerly made.

Mr. Flynn: Then I will renew the objection that I formerly made, together with the argument in support of the objection.

The Court: The objection is overruled.

Mr. Flynn: May I save an exception, please, your Honor?

The Court: An exception may be noted. [37]

* * * * *

The Court: Let the blueprint of the map attached to the application become Applicant's Exhibit M in evidence.

(The map referred to was marked Applicant's Exhibit M and was received in evidence.)

Q. (By Mr. Cass): Now, go ahead, Mr. McKeague, and from this map explain how you reached those boundaries.

A. In determining the boundary along the northerly side of this application, in running from this point, this cross in rock, following around the head of the Waihanau Valley, through Big Falls, which is known as Kaulahuki and up along the easterly

(Testimony of Bernard H. McKeague.)
side of Waihanau and back around Hoalae to Kalawao, on the westerly side of Waialeia Valley and
around the head of Waialeia Valley to the trig
station Kalauhauoni was determined by all the
evidence that I could get, including the kamaainas,
the commission's letters that were submitted in evidence, related maps, descriptions, and notations that
were made on the original application as to the
boundary running around the—the notation that
was made at the foot of the original patent, [38]
thence around the head of Waihanau Valley, following the pali to Kalawao and around Waihanau
Valley to the Government triangulation station,''
I took that to mean around the head or around
Kalawao Valley and around the Waialeia Valley
to the Government survey station.

Mr. Cass: I would like the record to show that
the witness in indicating the boundary line followed
the boundary shown upon the blueprint map up
there as presented by the applicant.

The Court: The record may so show. [39]
* * * * *

Q. (By Mr. Cass): Have you prepared an elevation chart showing the elevations of the land
coming up Waihanau Valley, up the Fall and up
to the disputed boundary of the Government?

A. Yes, I have prepared a profile.
* * * * *

(The map referred to was received in evidence as Applicant's Exhibit N.) [40]
* * * * *

(Testimony of Bernard H. McKeague.)

Q. Now, will you show us where the Big Fall is on your profile?

A. The Big Fall is indicated on this map as 5 plus 80, elevation 2200, top of Kaulahuki or Big Fall.

Q. That, I notice on your sketch map, is broken into apparently two falls. Is that what is known as the Big Fall in both sections or is there a separate name for each section?

A. I have labeled the one section by the two names, Kaulahuki and Big Fall.

Q. Where did you get those names?

A. The name "Kaulahuki" was shown on some registered maps and by the description in W. H. P. survey of the land of Makanalua.

Q. You place Kaulahuki at that point, from those two?   A. Yes, I did. [41]

* * * * *

Mr. Flynn: May I ask once again, if the Court please, to have the witness clarify that and refer again to the points? I have difficulty following this.

A. I will start from the bottom of the Waihanau Valley or floor, at 2,000 feet. The first rise is 2,117 feet—117 feet. And that is at a point 15 feet from the lower point. Then the next rise is 83 feet to 5 plus 80, the elevation being 2,200 feet up to the top of Kaulahuki or Big Fall.

Q. (By Mr. Cass): Now, did you measure the height of the fall at the point where the Government survey line crosses the stream? There is a waterfall there, is there not?

(Testimony of Bernard H. McKeague.)

A. Referring to the fall at Waiau?

Q. Yes.

A. That elevation was measured by the Territorial Survey Office and I applied those elevations to this profile.

Q. And what does the Territorial Survey Office plot that as? [42]

A. At 29 plus 0 the elevation is 2,385.

Q. How much is the Fall itself?

A. About 25 feet.

Q. About 25 feet. Have you ever gone up that Waiau Fall?

A. No. I stepped over the Fall, but I couldn't get down to it. I had to go around it to get under it.

* * * * *

Cross Examination

Q. (By Mr. Flynn): Mr. McKeague, you have stated in general terms that you referred to the old correspondence which is now in evidence here as giving you information as to where this northern boundary of Kahanui is located. May I say first the northern boundary of Grant 3437. Is that correct?

A. I believe my answer was "Government information as to the intent of where that boundary should be under the application made by Meyer for the land that was desired."

Q. Will you please refer specifically as to where in those documents you find evidence of the intent?

A. The first thing I tried to do as far as that description that refers "to the head of Waihanau and Waialeia Valleys" is to explore everything that

(Testimony of Bernard H. McKeague.)

is in connection with that course. In the original patent 3437, at the bottom it said—they had in pencil "thence around the head of Waihanau Valley, around the pali to Kalawao and around the Waialeia Valley" gave me the first clue as to the intent. Then the letters just supplemented my belief that Monsarrat did not survey the [43] land of Kahanui 3—rather than the land of Kamolo, Kaunakakai. Also, the description which he prepared was prepared before the grant was made and was not intended to convey the land that was applied for by Mr. Meyer. In one of the letters from Mr. Monsarrat to Mr. Meyer, when he was in Pukoo, he admitted that the lands on either side belonged to the Government, that it made no difference in his mind where that line went, but it did make a lot of difference as far as Mr. Meyer was concerned where the boundary of his application went. Following the ancient boundaries, which, interpreting his notation that he made on the original patent, went around the head of the valley, along the lines that I have accepted as the boundary as intended to be conveyed.

Q. (By Mr. Flynn): You say in one of the letters from Monsarrat to Mr. Meyer?

A. That is right.

Mr. Flynn: Is that letter in evidence? I don't believe it is, if the Court please. I am sorry to interrupt again. [44]

* * * * *

(Testimony of Bernard H. McKeague.)

Mr. Cass: It has not been offered. I don't believe it is marked in this case.

* * * * *

The Court: It will become Applicant's Exhibit O in evidence. Letter from M. D. Monsarrat to Mr. Meyer, dated June 25, 1890.

(The letter referred to was marked Applicant's Exhibit O and was received in evidence.)

* * * * * [45]

The Court: Letter from the Department of Interior to Mr. Meyer, dated November 22, 1889, becomes Applicant's Exhibit P in evidence.

Mr. Cass: That is the one in which he says he is going to take a surveying instrument along.

Mr. Flynn: I have no objection to this. Are you offering it, Mr. Cass?

Mr. Cass: Yes.

The Court: Letter dated July 15, 1890, from Brown to Meyer, becomes Applicant's Exhibit Q in evidence.

(The documents above referred to were marked Applicant's Exhibits P and Q and were received in evidence.)

Mr. Cass: Now, I have here a copy of an affidavit of A. Mauritz, which is found in the file of Law Number 14859. I have asked the clerk for a certified copy and will replace [46] it with a certi-

(Testimony of Bernard H. McKeague.)

fied copy as soon as the clerk can prepare such a copy. They could not find the file. And I offer in evidence this copy, subject to later check and verification of the contents and signature. We will withdraw it if it cannot be sustained, although I know it can. This is a carbon copy of the record of the Supreme Court.

Mr. Flynn: I will object to this offer, your Honor. [47]

* * * * *

Mr. Flynn: I will stipulate to the death but will ask the Court for a brief delay until I check that statute and I ask that I be permitted further argument on that.

The Court: Let it be marked "R" for identification".

    (The document referred to was marked Applicant's Exhibit R for identification.) [48]

* * * * *

Q. (By Mr. Flynn): Now, I will ask the witness to examine this letter of 1890, from Monsarrat to Meyer, and restate what conclusion, if such it was, that you drew from it?

A. The conclusion that I got from the letter was that the matter refers to the description of a survey made by Pease, wherein he quotes, "Following always a stonewall separating this land from the land called Pohakuloa, thence south 12 degrees 0 minutes east 15 chains and thence to the top of the mountain ridge called Hoalae, then following along the top of the pali bounding Makanalua Gulch or ravine on its

(Testimony of Bernard H. McKeague.)

easterly side to a certain mountain peak,'' which in Pease's description called it—he calls it Kaula-huki also.

Q. Mr. McKeague, you are reading now from your own notation, are you not, rather than from this letter of 1890?

The Court: Exhibit O.

A. That is right. I can read from the letter also. It is from my notes. I can read it from the letter also.

(Reading from Exhibit O.) [49]

* * * * *

Q. May we refer to your first map that you presented in evidence today?   A. This blueprint?

Q. No. I believe you called it your work sheet. ·

A. Yes.

Q. Exhibit A. On the basis of your knowledge derived from the several letters and pieces of correspondence between Mr. Meyer and the government officials and also this letter from Mr. Monsarrat to Mr. Meyer, which is Exhibit O, is it not correct to state that the land referred to in this letter of June 25, 1890, from Mr. Monsarrat to Mr. Meyer, was only that covered by this ridge shown on your map as Grant 3539 to R. W. Meyer?

A. My conclusion is the opposite one of all the letters and does not necessarily refer to the specific letter.

Q. May I call your attention to your own map, which shows this ridge as Grant 3539 to R. W. Meyer?   A. What is the question again?

(Testimony of Bernard H. McKeague.)

Q. I am just calling your attention to it.

A. Yes. [50]

Q. Now I want to ask you, wasn't this ridge the land constituting the Grant No. 3539?

A. It comes by the supposed description of this finger of land here. It starts from Monsarrat's point A, which I marked "Portion of 3539" to our mark and includes this piece here.

Q. This grant was issued in 1891, was it not?

A. That is my recollection.

Q. This grant did not purport to convey any land that was contained in Grant 3437, did it?

A. It was intended to convey the balance of the land that Mr. Meyer applied for and did not get.

*　*　*　*　*　[51]

Q. At no time in the correspondence did Grant 3539 become described as including any land which had previously been conveyed under Grant 3437, is that correct?　A. That is my understanding.

Q. And the description in Grant 3539, together with the more corrected description shown in the various government records in evidence, still do not show Grant 3539 as including any of the lands intended to be in Grant 3437, is that correct?

A. That is right.

Q. So Grant 3539 was a separate grant of a separate piece of land, was it not?

A. That is right.

Q. And Grant 3539 by both the description in the grant and by the more accurate or more comprehensive description that should have been made

(Testimony of Bernard H. McKeague.)
in the grant touched Grant 3437 at only one point.
Is that not correct?   A.   That is right.
* * * * *

Q.   (By Mr. Flynn): And continuing, Mr. Mc-
Keague, with where we were at the recess, I will
show you Applicant's Exhibit L, which is a letter
addressed to Mr. R. W. Meyer, May 22, 1891, signed
by J. F. Brown, Government Survey Office, and
included as an extra page a description of a portion
of Government land Kahanui, Molokai, and ask you
if you have seen this before?   A.   Yes, I have.

Q.   Did you consider this in doing your work
and this surveying problem along with the other
materials we have discussed?   A.   I have.

Q.   Calling your attention to the description of
"Portion of Government land Kahanui, Molokai,"
which reads as follows: "That tract of land lying
on the top of the ridge between the Waihanau and
Waialeia Valleys, and bounded by the upper edge
of the palis of these valleys, the center line of this
ridge being described as follows: Beginning at a
point on the northern boundary of Grand 3437 to
R. W. Meyer, this point bearing south 56 degrees
10 minutes east true, distant 5180 feet from station
on 'Kaohu,' thence by true bearings," and so forth.
"Beginning at a point on the northerly boundary
of Grant 3437" is where you have marked "M. D.
M's ridge A", is it not?   A.   That is it.

Q.   That is the beginning description of that
tract of land as shown in this description? [55]

A.   According to that description, that is right.

(Testimony of Bernard H. McKeague.)

Q.   And then it reads: "That tract of land lying on the top of the ridge between the Waihanau and Waialeia Valleys, and bounded by the upper edge of the palis of these valleys." According to this description, then, Mr. McKeague, beginning from ridge point A there is only the Waihanau Valley on the westerly side of that line, is there not?

A.   That is according to the description.

Q.   And you agree, then, do you not, that no part of Grant 3437 was mentioned in this description except that single beginning point?

A.   That is right.

Q.   Then do you not agree that Grant 3539, either by the actual description in the grant or by the more appropriate description in the records of the Government Survey and Land Offices was not intended to include any portion of the Land previously described as being in Grant 3437?

A.   That is my understanding.

Q.   Now, the matters we have already discussed show that Grant 3437 was issued in its final form in October 1889; Grant 3539, this ridge, was issued in 1891. Correct?   A.   That is right.

Q   Then, is there anything in the grants themselves or the descriptions to show that Grant 3539 was issued on a portion of Grant 3437? [56]
* * * * *

A.   There is not. [57]
* * * * *

Mr. Flynn: This may be slightly premature, your Honor, but I think it is appropriate to bring

(Testimony of Bernard H. McKeague.)

it into the record at this time. I will move the Court to make a ruling denying as admissible for registration the portion of the description which contains the words, following the words "Grant 3539 and R. W. Meyers," the words, "On a portion of Grant 3437 to R. W. Meyer," as being contrary to law and as being contrary to the legal evidence now before the Court.

The Court: The question is premature. It will be denied at this time.

Q. (By Mr. Flynn): Mr. McKeague, we might leave Grant 3539 for the time being and return to Grant 3437. I believe your earlier testimony showed, and as exemplified in this map, which is Exhibit A, that you examined the field notes of the surveyor M. Douglas Monsarrat. Is that correct?

A. That is right.

Q. And from those notes you made many of those plottings as shown in red on your map?

A. That is right.

Q. Will you state which field notes you examined, or do you recall?

A. I have photostat copies of the notes. From Government survey field book No. 359. [62]

Q. Can you give just the pages?

A. Pages 110, 111, 112, 113, 114, 125, 126, 129, 130, 131, 132, 133, 134, 141, 142.

Mr. Flynn: You haven't offered these in evidence, Mr. Cass?

Mr. Cass: No.

Mr. Flynn: I would like to offer in evidence as

(Testimony of Bernard H. McKeague.)

Territory's Exhibit 1 the field notes just referred to by the witness as being a basis for his compilations shown on Exhibit A.

Mr. Cass: We object, if the Court please. [63]

* * * * *

The Court: Why not put that question to the witness and ask him if he did use the notes for the computation of the boundary.

Q. (By Mr. Flynn): Did you use these notes in your work to ascertain the boundaries in dispute, Mr. McKeague?   A. I did not.

Q. You did not even examine them to see where they went to?

A. I examined the notes and plotted the notes to see where it lies on the ground, exactly on the ground.

Q. Haven't you testified that you also examined maps of Monsarrat?

A. Not in this area, that he prepared. [65]

* * * * *

Q. (By Mr. Flynn): I was asking you, Mr. McKeague, about these field notes, and you enumerated them and have handed them to me. You have enumerated the pages which you did examine to establish the various points shown on your map. Correct?   A. That is right.

Q. Now, I will refer you to M. D. M's ridge point A that is shown on the field notes.

A. By the——

Q. (interrupting): If it is shown on the field notes——

(Testimony of Bernard H. McKeague.)

The Court: Let the witness explain his answer, if any.

A. This M. D. M. ridge point A was completed from observations [66] made from M. D. M's point Y and M. D. M's Kauna Gulch, the location of which I wanted to know.

Q. Did you check this ridge point A on the ground? A. I did not.

Q. Did you check it from any work that you did? A. I did not.

Q. So you accepted M. D. M's ridge Point A as accurate? A. By plotting, I did.

Q. And M. D. M's ridge point A you have previously shown is the beginning point of the description of Grant 3539. Isn't that so?

A. I did not come to that conclusion.

Q. The beginning point of Grant 3539 calls for, in its description, this point A, does it not?

A. That is right.

Q. Now, M. D. M's X, which is Monsarrat's X, you have marked down at this extreme northwesterly corner of Grant 3437. Correct?

A. That is right.

Q. Did you note there——

Mr. Cass: That is southwesterly, isn't it?

A. Northwest.

Mr. Cass: All right.

Q. (By Mr. Flynn): Did you note there the field notes of Monsarrat occupy Point X?

A. That is right.

Q. And from there he took various shots to

(Testimony of Bernard H. McKeague.)

other points, did he not?   A.   That is right.

* * * * *

Q.   Monsarrat did take a sight from his Point X
to Kaluahauoni Triangulation Station, did he not?

A.   That observation indicated on the map is
280 degrees and 49 minutes.

Q.   It is the observation I ask you about, is it
not?   A.   Yes.

Q.   Now, that point is the one referred to—I am
sorry—that sight is the one referred to in the description of Apana 3 of Kahanui, Grant 3437?

A.   I don't recall because I wasn't interested in
the sights as pertains to the grant.

Q.   I am referring to Grant 3437. I call your attention to the first page of applicant's Exhibit B,
a photostat copy of Grant 3437, at the bottom of
which there is a course reading "North 37 degrees 56 minutes west 2854 feet along Kalamaula
to a stone marked with a cross at the edge of the
Waihanau Valley"; can you not identify that as
M. D. M's Point X?

A.   The end of the course you just read, that is
right.

Q.   The next course after the one I just read
reads: "Thence around the head of the Waihanau
and Waialeia Valleys to the Government Survey
Station 'Kaluahauoni,' the direct bearing [68] and
distance being south 79 degrees 07 minutes east
true 8631 feet."

Does that not refer to this bearing we were

(Testimony of Bernard H. McKeague.)

just talking about a minute ago, going from Point X to Kaluahauonia Triangulation Station?

A. That is possible but this does not jibe with the patent. The distance is not shown on this map.

Q. Did you endeavor to check this distance?

A. I did not.

Q. And you say it does not jibe with the patent?

A. This line as I show it on the map does not indicate the distance and that bearing and distance as shown on the description of the patent is not shown on the map here. I don't recall whether they are identical or not.

Q. You have examined this patent to determine, both from dates and other sources, the intended description of the boundaries, have you not?

A. Not in its entirety for my purposes in establishing a boundary in this application.

Q. Did you endeavor to establish the boundary without regard to the patents?

A. Where it shows the intention of the conveyance under the patent I did, but values of the bearing and distance I did not.

Q. So you disregard in your survey here this entire patent?   A. No.

Q. Are you disregarding portions of it?

A. No.

Q. If I understand your answer correctly, to what I asked you a minute ago, you said something to the effect that the [69] bearing and distance shown on the patent here does not correspond to the

(Testimony of Bernard H. McKeague.)
line you have drawn from Point X to the Kaluahauoni Triangulation Station.

A.   That is right. For the simple reason I did
not show the distance and the distance is shown on
the patent.

Q.   Can you show the distance now, if you have
instruments?

A.   It is quite possible if I have the computation.

Q.   Can you do that if you have time?

A.   I think we probably have it; I don't know.

Q.   Why did you disregard this language in this
patent: "The direct bearing and distance being
south 79 degrees 07 minutes east (true) 8631 feet"?

A.   Because that bearing and distance does not establish the boundary of the grant. The call distance
around and so forth is what we are concerned with.

Q.   Do you mean to say that as a surveyor in
examining a grant you can take one part of a call
and disregard the remainder of the same call?

A.   No.

Q.   But you did state you disregarded this language about "The direct bearing and distance being
south 79 degrees 07 minutes east (true) 8631 feet,"
is that correct?

A.   I disregarded the values but not the intent
of the thing. They are two different things altogether.

Q.   Did you regard this distance at all?

A.   Offhand, as I said, I don't recall whether I
did or not, because as far as I was concerned I was
more concerned with the call "Beginning around

(Testimony of Bernard H. McKeague.)

the head of Waihanau and Waialeia Valleys." A direct bearing and distance, like many other [70] courses, is a meandering line, a direct line, and does not establish the boundaries.

Q. But this is a direct bearing and distance at least from Point X to Kaluahauoni Triangulation Station, is it not?

A. That is right. That is called for in the patent. That is right.

Q. Do I understand you, then, to say that you disregarded this distance matter because as long as you followed around what you thought was the head of the valley or what you interpreted to be the head of the valley, you found the distance to be off?

A. Because the bearing and distance was a direct line and the bearing and distance does not state the boundary,—the boundary can be broken up when it is a meandering line into four or five different courses. It is a mathematical thing to give a direct bearing distance between two points wherein the inbetween boundary is a meandering line.

* * * * *

Q. Don't you have to check out each point of the patent if you find it appropriate to disregard some point to point?

A. I have answered that question. [71]

* * * * *

Mr. Flynn: There was a question there a moment ago that I would like to have answered or

(Testimony of Bernard H. McKeague.)
rather repeated by the reporter, if the Court please.

(The question was read by the reporter.)

A. If the points are recognized on the ground and it ties in with the patent, we will use it. In this case the M. D. M's X on the ground marker, that cross on rock, is well established, the Kaluahauoni Trig Station at the end of what is supposed to be the course given in the patent is well established, the values in between are the changes slightly from the patent, [72] but along that line it connects up the call distance "Around the head of Waihanau and Waialeia Valleys" the direct bearing being such.

* * * * *

Q. If I read your writing properly here, Mr. McKeague, from X to Kaluahauoni Triangulation Station is 280 degrees 49 minutes. Am I correct?

A. That is right.

Q. The patent I have before me reads, "The direct bearing and distance being south 79 degrees 07 minutes." Is that a discrepancy?

A. About 4 minutes. He changed it to azimuths. That bearing should read "280 degrees 53 minutes."

Q. Very close, in other words?   A. Yes.

* * * * * * [73]

Q. Are there two different methods of computing this bearing?

A. Shall I say two different methods of presenting the direction of a line.

Q. All right. Can you tell me which two they are?

(Testimony of Bernard H. McKeague.)

A. One is near the segment from the south, in this case 39 degrees. No. 79 degrees and 7 minutes. That is southeast 79 degrees and 7 minutes is deducted from 360 degrees to arrive at an azimuth.

Q. So that comes very close then?

A. That is right.

Q. Thank you. I notice you have a point marked K. You found this in Monsarrat's field notes?

A. That is right.

Q. And you checked it out in what way?

A. All I did was plot it on this map.

Q. What is plotting? Will you just explain what that is that you did in this case?

A. By parallel ruler and protractor and starting from the point M. D. M's Kauna Gulch point and ruling off this azimuth 143 degrees, to this point R, which would be intersected by another sight from Kaluahauoni Trig Station by the azimuth [74]   97 degrees 22 minutes and by intersection from the Point R located on the map.

Q. You call that Point R?

A. K. I am sorry.

Q. It is Point K?   A. K.

Q. Will you explain, and I hope this is not repetitious, how you examined Monsarrat's field notes and then examined his maps? I will withdraw that. Did you examine Monsarrat's map of 1886, on file in the survey office of the Government?

A. To the best of my knowledge there are no maps in connection with Kahanui as it pertains to this survey.

(Testimony of Bernard H. McKeague.)

Q. I mean Monsarrat's map of Molokai in 1886, on file in the Government Survey Office?

A. Yes, I have.

Q. You have examined it?   A. Yes.

Q. Do you recall whether you examined a one thousand foot or two thousand foot map?

A. Offhand, I don't.

Q. Was it sometime ago, some months or years ago that you examined it?

A. Two or three years ago. Almost four years ago.

Q. Do you remember examining only one map of Molokai by Monsarrat or two or more maps?

A. I don't recall any number at all.

Q. You do recall looking at some map or maps of Molokai by Monsarrat, is that correct?

A. Very vaguely, yes. [75]

Q. Did you ever look at any of those maps where Apana 3 of Kahanui is drawn in?

A. I don't recall.

Q. You don't recall?   A. No.

Q. You may have seen a map of Monsarrat's which included Apana 3 of Kahanui on Molokai?

A. That is possible; I don't recall.

Q. I rather thought that you did not use that at all in your surveying work for this Land Court registration, is that correct?

A. That is right.

Q. You used the grants themselves, is that right?

A. It helped me to determine certain phases of the land that was acquired by Meyer. [76]

* * * * *

(Testimony of Bernard H. McKeague.)

Q. What was your next step after examining the grants?

A. Going into all these letters, correspondence, maps, descriptions, in old maps.

Q. Will you please state what old maps there were that you went into?

A. They were in the survey office, certain registered maps. Some of the lands had been mapped by Surveyor Nahala and by Surveyor Pease.

Q. That was a map and description of what?

A. It was an old map.

Q. Of what?

A. The land of the lower part of Makanalua.

Q. I assumed you were going to proceed. You may, if you will. That is the first map or description you have discussed now aside from the grant.

A. The patent, the grants, the different letters in connection with the acquiring of the whole Kahanui 3, the boundary as surveyed by Monsarrat along Kalamaula, Kaunakakai, and Kamiloloa.

Q. I am going to interrupt the questioning, Mr. McKeague, because you refer to your examination of registered maps and other old maps. You have mentioned only one. I will ask you if you can tell me what others you have examined?

A. There was one by Monsarrat. I believe the registered [77] number is 1728.
* * * * *

Q. When you examined this first map you referred to as an old one of the lower section of

(Testimony of Bernard H. McKeague.)
Makanalua, did you make any notes about that for your own use?

A.   In one or two cases, where it refers to Waihanau Valley and the Point Iliilika.

Q.   Was that map or description of any use to you in arriving at your conclusions as to the boundaries of these lands?

A.   Not for the boundary but the call of the name Waihanau, as to the location of Waihanau.

* * * * *

Q.   You refer to Monsarrat's registered map No. 1728. Do you have any notes or data from your examination of that map?

A.   I prepared a map using part of that information. I have a composite map here of all the data that I had wherein Monsarrat's data was used in the lower section, and then I located, by M. A. Wall, the boundary near the boundary of Kaohu, Kalamaula, at Kaohu, to as nearly as possible determine the lower and upper ends of the land of Makanalua. So that [78] upon that map I can as nearly as possible plot the Pease description, so that I can get up to a point he calls Kaulahuki.

Q.   Do I understand you now to say from Monsarrat's registered map 1728 you compared data in Pease's map?

A.   No, I did not say that. I used part of Monsarrat's map in the lower end and compared that with the map that I prepared or that was prepared by Wall and in some instances by the survey office, or other recognized surveys, so that the location

(Testimony of Bernard H. McKeague.)

of the big Fall as it pertains to the whole of Makanalua could be determined.

* * * * *

Q. (By Mr. Flynn): Referring again, Mr. McKeague, to this map of Makanalua, which you have just mentioned. This was done by you just this past month, is that correct?

A. That is right. Labeled that. The finish date of the map is labeled just this past month. The worksheet was [79] started quite some time ago.

Q. And in connection with your work on that you used Pease's map?

A. No. Pease had no map, to the best of my knowledge.

Q. You used Monsarrat's map?

A. In the lower section. I was only concerned with trying to see if Pease's location of Kaulahuki —that is why I prepared this map, and only for that purpose. I was not trying to determine the boundaries of Makanalua.

Q. Then this was used solely to determine that Kaulahuki section in Pease's description?

A. That is right.

Q. Not shown in his map?

A. In his description.

Q. You have not seen any map of Pease's, is that correct, of Makanalua?

A. I don't recall seeing any.

Q. How did you arrive at the location of Kaulahuki?

A. In the description prepared by Pease, he de-

(Testimony of Bernard H. McKeague.)
scribes the easterly boundary and then the westerly
boundary, and there was no known survey on his
part. He starts from a shot and gives the bearing
and distance, and the calls, "And then to the mountain peak called Kaulahuki." Then he starts from
a shot again from the westerly boundary and continues on up and comes to the head of the peak he
calls Kaulahuki.

Q. You have placed that peak at the waterfalls,
is that correct?   A. Yes.

Q. But the language in Pease's description calls
for a peak [80] known as Kaulahuki or a peak
called Kaulahuki. I have a description by Pease, I
think, and I would be glad to offer it to you, if you
would like.

A. I have it here. The language he uses is, in
the case of an easterly boundary of Makanalua,
"After leaving the point of Hoalae, thence——"
* * * * *

Q. You may proceed.

A. "Thence along the top of the pali bounding
Makanalua gulch or ravine on its easterly side, to
a certain mountain peak at the head of said ravine
called 'Kaulahuki.'" That is the language he uses
in describing the easterly and westerly boundaries.

Q. Kaulahuki is referred to by him as a mountain peak?

A. "At the head of a ravine" also.

Q. Yes, but no mention whatever of a waterfall.
Is that correct?   A. No. [81]
* * * * *

(Testimony of Bernard H. McKeague.)

Q. Did you examine a survey by Harvey?

A. I used part of Mr. Harvey's work in making reference, as far as reference is concerned. [82]

Q. Did you examine a survey by Mr. Newton?

A. Yes, I have a copy of that map and I have used part of that data furnished by that map.

Q. From all of your work or rather your data did you not find in one or more of those maps a purported northern boundary of Grant 3437 which ran from Point X through Point K to Point A?

A. The maps shown, in that general direction, yes, but whether they went through Point K and reached A, I don't know.

Q. Do you recall any maps showing that?

A. There was one prepared by Wright, Harvey & Wright, I believe, that showed the boundary reaching in that general direction.

Q. Was that map of any use to you in your own computations and compilations?

A. Just for mathematical purposes, yes.

Q. You, I presume, did not agree with the boundary shown on that map?

A. That is naturally correct.

Q. Mr. Newton's map, did it not also show the boundary running from Point X through K to A?

A. I don't recall whether it went from X through Point K to Point A, but it was a map showing a line in that general direction.

Q Now, this registered map No. 1728 of Monsarrat, did you check that and endeavor to ascertain on it where Points A, K and X would be?

(Testimony of Bernard H. McKeague.)

A. The registered map 1728, to the best of my knowledge, [83] does not show Points X, K and Ridge A. It does not come out that high. He was interested in the survey of Kalaupapa Settlement.

Q. As far as registered map 1728 is concerned, it meant nothing to you or rather it was used by you for no other purpose except to check some of the lower portions of Makanalua?

A. No. The upper portions to determine Kaulahuki Falls near the Big Falls. I wanted to determine one point and only one point: If the point Kaulahuki is correct.

Q. Can you recall whether registered map No. 1728 by Monsarrat shows Apana 3 of Kahanui?

A. I have here a tracing from that map 1728. How accurate it is I do not know, but this should give you a good idea of what that map shows. [84]

* * * * *

Q. (By Mr. Flynn): Can you point out, Mr. McKeague, where on this map you located Kaulahuki?

A. Kaulahuki was never located on this map.

Q. Then will you describe in what way you used this to change the location of Kaulahuki?

A. I used the topography, which is shown on the lower part, which I considered fairly accurate. The upper part I considered very inaccurate. For that reason I located the topography, which was actually located on the ground by surveys made in the case of Kalamaula survey made by Monsarrat, the ridge point from Hoalae mauka was located by

(Testimony of Bernard H. McKeague.)

both Wall and myself to be accurate. The other points were also located by me.

Q. Excuse me. What ridge points were located to be accurate? [85]   A. The points located.

Q. What points?

A. At the Big Falls, for instance. At this point. The relative positions of these points with regard to this, as best as I can, was considered fairly accurate. It is a compilation of the physical features as they relate to one another. The lower end located—as I was once given a U. S. Geodetic survey, it fits in with Monsarrat's location of his stonewall reference and other references in here. I consider that the upper part of his map is not accurate according to the data available to me.

Q. Is this tracing to the same scale as your map of Makanalua?   A. That is right.

Q. I want you to lay this tracing over as close as it can be done. This tracing shows Waihanau Valley continuing up to a point well beyond where you have established Kaulahuki or your map. Is that not so?   A. That is right.

Q. And this tracing from a point Alae—I will withdraw that please, Mr. Reporter.

The point Alae on this tracing of the very old map is most likely identical with the point Hoalae that is shown on your map?   A. That is right.

Q. They are meant to be the same points, are they not?   A. That is right.

Q. The description of Pease that you have re-

(Testimony of Bernard H. McKeague.)

ferred to reached this point Alae or Hoalae, did it not?   A. That is right. [86]

Q. From there on it was by general language "Following the top ridge and ridge or peak known as Kaulahuki, at the head of a ravine," isn't that so? . A. That is right.

Q. On this tracing wouldn't the head of the ravine be at this extreme tip of the map?

A. That is according to Monsarrat's map, which I considered very inaccurate in the upper limits.

Q. But you are telling me that you have taken Pease's description and distinguished it from what is shown on Monsarrat's map or I mean on this map or this tracing?

A. No. I did not use this Pease description on Monsarrat's map. I used Pease's description on the composite map, and I compiled the map.

Q. You did use Monsarrat's map for the extreme upper ends of what he placed in here as Waihanau Valley, is that correct?

A. I just used the accurate location of the topography about two-thirds of the way up because it is almost evident that he was only interested in the lower section of Makanalua to round off his map in the upper limits. He just evidently fudged on that portion, but I was not interested in using that portion of the map for my purposes. [87]

* * * * *

Q. Can you examine these exhibits and advise me just which ones or which parts of letters or

(Testimony of Bernard H. McKeague.)
correspondence gave you the information you regarded as satisfactory?

The Court: Hand to the witness the applicant's exhibits for examination.

A. I probably can answer that question without examining these, that in reading the whole thing, between the Government officials and Meyer, that the intention of the parties concerned was to convey all of the land that he bought and paid for and had occupied all those years.

Q. I want to ask you specifically the material in these documents or exhibits which gave you that indication. I therefore ask you to examine the exhibits and answer the question that way. [89]
* * * * *

A. For a specific answer, I would say no, but it is a collective information I got as to the intent of what was desired under the correspondence as to what they wanted to convey. It was not as if I say from this correspondence, regular, definite bearing and distance and very specific evidence by language, that the boundary followed along the lines that I chose.

The Court: Mr. McKeague, let me suggest this. I think we will move along a lot faster. The question now on cross-examination, in the light of your testimony, is that you have used certain documents, and that you have enumerated. The question now is whether or not included in those documents are the exhibits which have been admitted in this proceeding thus far. Those exhibits are before you. Now,

(Testimony of Bernard H. McKeague.)
please just look through them and just answer yes
or no, if you recall or if you don't recall, say so,
which of those exhibits in evidence you used perhaps in addition to others to arrive at your intention.

A. I refer more specifically to the notation at
the bottom of the first patent to Grant 3437, at the
bottom of which is the correction made or intended
to be made of the course, "Thence around the head
of Waihanau Valley," and so forth. [90]
* * * * *

Q. Now, can you refer to any other items among
this correspondence [92] or these exhibits to support your conclusions as to what the parties intended?

A. The fact that in Pease's description, for one
thing, he called the Big Fall "Kaulahuki." And
yesterday I did not recall seeing Pease's map, but
I found a tracing, which is registered number 505,
—and although Pease is known on record as being
a careless surveyor,—I found in this particular
case, scaling the map from Hoalae up to the Big
Fall, he comes within a couple of hundred feet of
the Big Falls on the easterly boundary of Waihanau Gulch or valley.

Q. But Pease called for a peak by the name of
Kaulahuki, didn't he?

A. And the head of the——

Q Please answer that yes or no. Will you? Did
he call for a peak known as Kaulahuki?

A. That is right.

(Testimony of Bernard H. McKeague.)

Q. The Big Falls could not be called a peak, could it?

A. He chose to call it a peak, although he says a ravine, "At the head of a ravine" also.

Q. Can a surveyor finding an area of land headed by a falls refer to that as a peak?

A. As I said, the word "peak" is what he chose to use together with the wording "At the head of said ravine," and I believe the word "ravine" applies more than the words "mountain peak" in this particular case.

Q. What is a mountain peak?

. A. It is the top of a mountain, like Punchbowl or I mean Leahi or any other prominent projection of land.

Q. Is there any possibility of a surveyor, even a poor [93] surveyor, confusing a mountain peak with a waterfall?

A. No. A mountain peak is very definite. As I said, Pease just chose to call this particular point a mountain peak or the head of said ravine. It is a conflicting statement in his own language.

Q. You are saying, then, that he chose to call a waterfall a mountain peak?

A. Yes, and he qualified it with "The head of said ravine."

* * * * *

Q. Now, will you take a look at the cancelled grant with the notation at the bottom? Have you any idea whose writing that is, Mr. McKeague?

A. No.

(Testimony of Bernard H. McKeague.)

Q. You don't know.   A. I don't know.

Q. Do you think it might be Mr. Meyer's?

A. Quite possible.

Q. Do you think it might be Monsarrat's?

A. It could be possible also.

Q. You have stated that you relied on this writing to show the intentions of the parties as to what was to be included?   A. That is right.

Q. Does your exhibit there have the reverse side, including the plat, the map?   A. Yes.

Q. This contains additional writing, does it not, "At an [94] area above the north line of this map"?

A. That is right. It indicates Waihanau Valley.

Q. And it also indicates Waialeia Valley?

A. Over the old Makanalua Valley. He scratched out the word "Makanalua" and in pencil wrote "Waialeia."

Q. Down below here is written "Makanalua," is it not?   A. That is right. In pencil.

Q. Would it appear to you that the handwriting above the plat saying "Waihanau Valley and Waialeia Valley" over the crossed out "Makanalua Valley" is similar or identical to the handwriting at the foot of the grant?

A. I did not try to compare that at that time.

Q. Would you just take a look now?

The Court: This witness is not a handwriting expert.

Mr. Flynn: I don't mean to qualify him as such, your Honor, or hold him to any ability of that sort, but to the naked eye I believe there is a definite

(Testimony of Bernard H. McKeague.)
similarity in the writing, and I would like to ask
him if he agrees with it.

A. I don't think so.

Mr. Cass: I object to it as immaterial and not
proper cross-examination.

The Court: Objection sustained. [95]

* * * * *

Mr. Flynn: I will now question him on the final
grant, Grant 3437, Exhibit B.

* * * * *

The Clerk: It is Applicant's Exhibit B.

* * * * *

Mr. Flynn: It is the grant from which title
stems to the applicant.

Mr. Cass: That is a conclusion of counsel.

Mr. Flynn: It is in the abstract, your Honor,
and it is in the pleading as well.

The Court: Proceed.

Q. (By Mr. Flynn): The grant, Mr. McKeague,
Exhibit B, contains both a description and a map,
does it not?   A. That is right.

Q. As a general principle of surveying, where a
grant contains a description and a map, both are
to be considered in determining the lands conveyed
to the grantee, are they not? [96]

* * * * *

A. Not necessarily, is my answer. If the map
was prepared at the same time as the description
and prepared under the supervision of the author
of the description, it is correct.

Q. (By Mr. Flynn): I am asking about princi-

(Testimony of Bernard H. McKeague.)
ples of surveying. Where you find a grant containing a description and a map, do you not begin in
determining the lands conveyed by the grant to
check as to whether the map and description were
prepared by the same party? [97]
* * * * *

A. I did.

Q. And what did you find?

A. That there is no evidence, as far as I can
find, that Mr. Monsarrat plotted those shots as
shown in his field book and that the sketch was
prepared at the same time that the patent was issued or when he wrote his description, in 1886, as
I recall.

Q. Did you confine your search for material to
the field books of Mr. Monsarrat?

A. And I inquired for all maps available that
he had in the Survey Office. It was my understanding that a lot of his field books and records were
supposed to be in the office of Wright, Harvey &
Wright. I went to Wright, Harvey & Wright's
office and tried to get all information, if they had
any, of Monsarrat in connection with this work,
and I [98] could not get anything there.

Q. Did you examine any of the registered maps
of Monsarrat at or about this time in the Government Survey Office to determine whether the field
notes had ever been placed by him on any of his
maps?

A. That I did, and I could not find anything
like that.

(Testimony of Bernard H. McKeague.)

Q. You could not find anything like that?

A. That is right.

Q. Do you recall looking at a 1,000-foot to the inch map and a 1,000-foot to the inch worksheet on file and registered in the office of the survey department of the Territory, made and prepared by M. D. Monsarrat, covering Central Molokai and dated in 1886?

Mr. Cass: We object. More than one question being asked at once.

Mr. Flynn: I will be glad to ask the first part, if he checked the 1,000-foot map.

A. I have a section of that map, 1,000-foot, made by Monsarrat, a blueprint.

Q. The 1886 map?

A. I don't recall the date of the map because I just took a sectional point of the map.

Q. Do you have that among your papers now?

A. No. It is in my office.

Q. Do you recall a worksheet on the scale of 1,000-foot to the inch?   A. No.

Q. Do you recall examining a map of Central Molokai by M. D. Monsarrat, dated in 1886, made on a scale of 2,000 feet [99] to the inch?

A. Yes.

Q. You do?   A. Yes.

Q. Do you also recall a working sheet from which that map was made or did you examine only the map?

A: I only examined the blueprint.

Q. The blueprint?

(Testimony of Bernard H. McKeague.)

A. Of the 2,000-foot map.

Q. Where did you find that blueprint?

A. It was furnished to me by the Survey Office, to the best of my knowledge.

Q. It is in the Territorial Survey Office, as far as you can recall now?   A. That is right.

Q. Did you find Kahanui, Apana 3, on that map?   A. As I recall, yes.

Q. Did you check that area on that map against this map or sketch in the grant?

A. I did not.

Q. Was there any reason why you refrained from doing so?

A. Because I did not think it was an accurate location of the topography in that vicinity.

Q. Did you determine that by simply looking at the map?

A. In mapping my location of the conditions on the ground, yes.

Q. Was this the time that you rejected any further consideration of the map or sketch attached to the grant?

A. I don't recall when I made that rejection because this [100] work was continued over a period of time and I worked at this thing for perhaps weeks or months.

Q. Do I understand now that you did examine this map or sketch attached to the grant?

A. I did.

Q Did you ascertain whether any of the lines were reasonably accurate?

(Testimony of Bernard H. McKeague.)

A. There was nothing to ascertain as far as values are concerned except to probably superimpose that line over an accurate topographic map.

Q. Was there any specific time, Mr. McKeague, that you definitely rejected this map or sketch attached to the grant?

* * * * *

A. As I said earlier, I worked on this thing for a period of weeks or months, and I don't know when my conclusion was reached in rejecting this sketch.

Q. I am only asking you now if you concluded to reject entirely this map or sketch as of any value in the grant?   A. That is right.

Q. You did conclude that?

A. That is right.

Q. Did you thereafter confine yourself to the material in the description in ascertaining the lands which were conveyed to the grantee?

A. The course "Thence around the head of Waihanau Valley," [101] and so forth, has been my principal point of exploration.

Q. If you will take a look at the map or sketch attached to the grant——

A. You mean Exhibit B?

Q. Exhibit B. Can you state from looking at it whether it is drawn to scale?

A. I did not check that. It is possible.

Q. You stated, Mr. McKeague, that Mr. Pease's reputation as a surveyor was not so good.

A. That is right.

(Testimony of Bernard H. McKeague.)

Q. Will you state your understanding of Monsarrat's reputation as a surveyor?

A. Excellent.

Q. Among the best, was he not?

A. That is right.

Q. Was his reputation not also quite widespread for his excellent memory?

A. That I don't know. My knowledge of the man is brief. That he was an excellent surveyor.

Q. And he did extensive surveying work on these islands and particularly on Molokai, in 1885 and 1886, did he not?

A. That is my understanding.

Q. These field notes that you have looked at and which you stated you looked at in the course of your work indicate to you that he did extensive surveying in that general region, in Central Molokai. Is that not right?   A. That is right.

Q. Is it not true that a very large part of his surveying work is still accepted as entirely correct?

A. That is right.

Q. And a very large part of that surveying work is still the foundation for present-day surveyors in rechecking old land boundaries or associated matters?

A. To the best of my knowledge, that is right.

* * * * *

Q. Now, referring once again to the descriptive language of Surveyor Pease as to the boundaries of Makanalua. If you will excuse me a moment, I will have to refer to it myself. Do you find yours?

(Testimony of Bernard H. McKeague.)

A. Yes.

Q. If you will read the part from where the first metes and bounds descriptions ends at "Alae" or "Hoalae."

A. Yes. "Thence to the top of the mountain ridge called Hoalae."

Q. I am sorry. Oh yes. Yes. Further on now. That is correct.

A. "Thence following along the top of this pali bounding Makanalua gulch or ravine or its easterly side, to a certain mountain peak at the head of said ravine called 'Kaulahuki' ".

Q. Yes. "Following the top of the pali," does it say? [104]   A. That is right.

Q. Look at your map, which is your Exhibit A. Will you follow me from Hoalae on? This is the top of the pali?   A. That is right.

Q. Does the pali end here?   A. No.

Q. The pali keeps going, does it not?

A. Just for about three or four hundred feet.

Q. Three or four hundred feet?   A. Yes.

Q. Is there no pali along here?

A. There is.

Q. Then why do you say three or four hundred feet?

A. The nature of the pali or the precipice changes. You can call this a pali and it would not necessarily be as steep as the pali here. This pali, between this point and this point, can be traversed much easier than the pali on this side.

Q. Yes, but if I understood you a minute ago,

(Testimony of Bernard H. McKeague.)

you said the pali does not continue beyond this three or four hundred foot space?

A. That is right. But it changes as to its steepness.

Q. But it does continue as a pali?

A. That is right.

Q. It continues all the way down here, does it not?   A. That is right.

Q. To this area you have referred in your map, Exhibit A, as a portion of Grant 3539 to R. W. Meyer?   A. That is right. [105]

Q. Wouldn't this general area, being this portion at the extreme southerly tip of Grant 3539, be a peak or a mountain peak?   A. No.

Q. It could not be?   A. No.

Q. Will you state what it is?

A. It is sort of a grassy plateau that slopes gradually down towards Waialeia Valley.

Q. Where, then, in this description does the pali follow? I am sorry. Not in this description. I want to get the record straight, your Honor. Where, as shown on your map, Exhibit A, does this pali follow?

A. It follows the conventional boundary line as shown by the long dash and dot to two dotted lines indicated here, and in this particular area by the course No. 23, 311 degrees 12 minutes, 400 feet; Course 24, 27 degrees 52 minutes, 319.80 feet, and on through by the next course, 294 degrees 36 minutes 15 seconds, a distance of 2030.40 feet.

Q. You reached this point, referred to as M. D.

(Testimony of Bernard H. McKeague.)

M's Ridge A, as shown on your map. Is that not where this pali ends and a new pali begins?

A. No. It is a continuous pali from Hoalae all along the head of Waialeia Valley, up around to the survey station.

Q But the direction changes sharply, does it not? A. That is right.

Q. This pali, and I am referring again to the line towards the extreme northerly end—no—southerly end of Grant 3539, bounds this valley area in here, does it not, and separates [106] it from this valley area in here. A. That is right.

Q. Is this plateau-like area not raised above the ridge formations you have shown going down into each valley?

A. You are speaking of the new boundary line as I indicate it here by Course 311 degrees 12 minutes?

Q. I am speaking of this entire little area on this map, approximately three acres.

A. It slopes down from the Waialeia Valley.

Q. So that there should properly be two palis here, should there not? One along this extreme tip of this disputed valley, we will call it, and the other at the edge of the approximately three-acre area, where it slopes down to Waialeia Valley. Is that not so? A. That is right.

Q. And the area surrounded by these two palis, we will refer to for convenience, that three-acre area, does it not constitute a mound or peak, as you view it from, say, the middle of Grant 3539?

(Testimony of Bernard H. McKeague.)

A. No, because you cannot see the area that slopes away from the southwesterly side of that little three-acre piece.

Q. Do you see this pali, the one on the lower valley?

A. That is right. And you cannot see the other area from Monsarrat's Point X, Y and so forth.

Q. You cannot see that?

A. You cannot see that until you are there.

Q. Is there not in the general area of this ridge A or in this Grant 3539 a rise or mound or peak?

A. The terrain starting from Monsarrat's Dry Tree, through [107] Ridge A, on up in the easterly direction, was more or less the same, viewing that from across the disputed area.

Q. No. I am asking about viewing it from the approximate center of Grant 3539.

A. When I was on this grant the plateau as shown here by the word "Meyer" on Grant 3539, I didn't think it was necessary or I didn't notice anything that would indicate a peak.

Q. Or mound?   A. Or mound.

Q. Or any hill?

A. The terrain was just about the same, viewing it in a general location.

Q. May we take a look at your contour map? I beg your pardon. I thought this had been introduced in evidence. Is that incorrect?

Mr. Cass: It is marked up above there.

The Clerk: No, not that one.

(Testimony of Bernard H. McKeague.)

Mr. Flynn: This one does not seem to be marked.

Q. (By Mr. Flynn): Looking at your contour map of this same—excuse me. This is a three-acre area? A. Yes.

Q. This is supposed to be three acres?

A. Yes.

Q. Very well. That is what I am talking about then. A. That is right.

Q. Look at your contour map. Does that not appear to be raised up above the immediately adjacent land?

A. Not necessarily. It shows that the contour slopes both ways from that area and the intervals are set at 100-foot [108] angles.

Q. Is this a contour line?

A. That is right. That is the 2,600-foot contour line.

Q. And there is a contour line from here?

A. That is right. That is the 2,700-foot.

Q. Is this a contour line here?

A. That is right. That is the 2,700-foot contour line sloping down the other way.

Q. And you say this includes the approximately three-acre parcel, is that not so?

A. That is right.

Q. And then a short distance away is the 2600-foot contour line, isn't that so?

A. That is right.

Q. And a slightly longer distance, in the westerly direction or towards the disputed valley area,

(Testimony of Bernard H. McKeague.)

the disputed gulch area, is likewise a boundary and the 2600-foot level, is that not right?

A. That is right.

Q. Does that not show that this three-acre parcel is raised above the lands immediately around it?

A. Not necessarily. It shows there is a high contour break between the Kahanui side and the Waialeia Valley.

Q. It is a raised area, then?   A. Yes.

Q. Is not that raised portion visible from, say, approximately the middle of Grant 3539?

A. As I recall, I did not try to make a particular observation, but I believe it is the same as this plateau area, [109] generally speaking. There is nothing prominent.

Q. This plateau area as shown on your contour map is 2500 feet?   A. That is right.

Q. And the three-acre area we have been talking about is 2700 feet?   A. That is right.

Q. Does it not appear to you from examining your own contour map that that would be visible as a raised area from the plateau area of 3539?

A. The rise is gradual from 2500 to 2700, so it does not have to be very pronounced as a peak, one that you would see, something like Punchbowl or Leahi.

Q. But it could be visible as a peak, not pronounced, is that not so?   A. No.

Q. Could it be visible as a mound or raised area?   A. Not in that direction.

Q. Nothing in your contour map shows it would

(Testimony of Bernard H. McKeague.)

be interfered with, does it? Now, referring to the same map and to the 2500-foot contour, the plateau area, and placing with my finger the direction to and including the three-acre parcel——

A. (interrupting): The rise is still gradual and there is nothing abrupt, although there is a 200-foot difference in elevation, so that one would indicate above the 2700-foot contour or the three-acre piece there would be a peak, observing it from the 2500-foot contour line.

Q. Is it observable at all from here or have you stated you don't recall? [110]

A. From here, at the course marked 318 degrees 2 minutes, 373.10 feet, it seems to me I saw that point more or less on the same gradual rise.

Q. Beyond this point you did not see anything, in a southerly direction, that would be very close to it, is that correct? A. I don't understand.

Q. What I have in mind is that examining your own contour map, beyond this point, it drops down to 2600 feet, this being the 2700-foot area, in the immediate vicinity, isn't that right?

A. The land drops off, down, for perhaps 50 feet in about maybe 500 feet, and it is a gradual rise towards the trig station or in a northeasterly direction.

Q. The visible portions in the gradual rise beyond the three-acre parcel are noticeable as such are they not? By that I mean they are obviously visible points well away from the three-acre parcel, isn't that so?

(Testimony of Bernard H. McKeague.)

A. That is right. That is observed from the point I stated before, 318 degrees 2 minutes, 373.10 feet.

Q. Then do we not get back to the proposition that this three-acre area is equivalent to a mound or peak and rises, possibly generally, from Grant 3539?

A. No. That was not my observation.

Q. You don't recall seeing it that way?

A. No.

Q. It does look that way on your contour map, doesn't it?

A. On the contour map the contours which were superimposed on the geological survey indicate that it does. [111]

Q. Did you do any of this contouring yourself?

A. No. There was a compilation of the geological survey and the observations made by Mr. Newton in his survey of the floor of the valley, and I just corrected it. I assumed that the elevations given of the floor of the valley and the geological survey on the top, the one I used, and this map was prepared for a different purpose.

Q. Then you did not do any taking of elevations yourself?   A. No.

Q. Did you take elevations at this place you were talking about on direct examination?

A. Where there are differences in elevations, yes, but running the true level to see whether it jibes with the elevations or the data by Mr. Newton, no.

(Testimony of Bernard H. McKeague.)

Q. You did not take these level elevations then, you simply took the differences between elevations at these points?   A. That is correct. [112]

* * * * *

The Court: Has the contour map been offered?

Mr. Cass: It has not.

The Court: Do you desire to offer it?

Mr. Cass: I have no desire to offer it. [113]

The Court: It has been used and referred to in much of the testimony here.

Mr. Cass: If you wish the record clear, I will offer it for the record, but I have no—I am not interested or I am not endorsing the contour map at all. The contours there are contours from the Government map, not from this surveyor's own knowledge.

The Court: Does counsel have any objection to it becoming a Court's exhibit?

Mr. Cass: Not a bit.

The Court: Very well. Let the contour map become Court's Exhibit 1.

(The contour map referred to was marked Court's Exhibit 1 and was received in evidence.) [114]

* * * * *

Mr. Flynn: I would like the record to show, your Honor, that this is a controlled topographic mosaic, showing portions of the land of Kahanui and Waihanau Valley, Molokai, T.H.; topography by photogrammetric methods; date of photo, De-

(Testimony of Bernard H. McKeague.)

cember 23, 1949; containing the printed identity of R. M. Towill, Civil Engineer and Surveyor.

The Court: The record may so show.

Q. (By Mr. Flynn): I will ask you to examine Territory's Exhibit 1 for Identification, Mr. McKeague, and I ask you if you can recognize this topographic photo?

A. In general, I think so. [115]

* * * * *

Q. (By Mr. Flynn): I now will ask the witness if upon examining this mosaic he can find or point out the matter we referred to before as the locality where he has placed the head of Waihanau Falls or the boundary of the disputed area as he supposes it to be.

A. Since there are no identifying marks on this photograph to indicate the point I have used it will be difficult for me to point, other than to make a guess, as to the first point that you have here, about nine inches from the lower left-hand corner, which seems to show a pool at the top of which is where I believe I have located the Big Fall.

Q. All right. Will you mark this place you have referred to in this last answer of yours; mark it with—it should be identified in some way.

The Court: Put any symbol that you want.

Mr. Flynn: "Peak" and the letter A there follows below, so it may be seen. Very well. [117]

* * * * *

Mr. Cass: I will insist that this map with the lines drawn thereon, which are not topographic

(Testimony of Bernard H. McKeague.)
or relative topographic originally, be identified and proven before this witness has to point to any location or any other point on this in which he may be assisted by the lines so drawn.

Mr. Flynn: That is not much of an objection, your Honor, but I would be very happy to postpone the further cross-examination [119] on this exhibit until after it is properly put in evidence.

The Court: Very well.

* * * * *

Q. (By Mr. Flynn): Now, Mr. McKeague, we can return to your map which is Applicant's Exhibit A. You have testified, if my recollection is accurate, that the pali or the top of the pali begins from the point Hoalae and follows around the entire broad area of Grant 3539, to which I am pointing, continues beyond the point marked "M. D. M's Dry Tree," and approximately three or four hundred feet thereafter. Is that correct?

A. As it pertains to that plateau, that is right.

Q. Didn't you also testify that the pali still continues beyond that point all the way along to approximately this area marked "M. D. M's Ridge A"?

A. That is right. Where you previously followed. It went along the Waialeia Valley side of the break, which is around the three-acre piece.

Q. This is all the same pali, from M. D. M's Ridge A, around the Waialeia Valley side of the three-acre piece, and continuing all the way to the end of Grant 3539, shown as the Point "Hoalae"?

(Testimony of Bernard H. McKeague.)

A. On the easterly side of this Grant 3539 and on the Waialeia Valley side, your answer is "correct", it follows all the way from Ridge A to Hoalae. [120]

Q. And on the westerly side, we just agreed, it likewise follows all the way from Hoalae to and including the beginning or northerly point of this small three-acre piece? A. That is right.

Q. Now, to arrive at the point you have referred to as Kaulahuki, as set forth in Pease's description, you have departed from this pali, have you not, and come down to this waterfall?

A. That is right.

Q. The description does not call for any departure from the pali, does it?

A. Following the head of the ravine, the break in the pali from that point on where I make that departure changes drastically from a very steep pali here to one which could be traversed on foot or by animals, and that is not the case in the part of Waihanau Valley that is shown as the boundary.

Q. The break you are speaking of is three or four hundred feet beyond the point at which you have departed from this pali in the boundary, is that not so? A. No, that is not so.

Q. Didn't I understand you to say a while ago just words to the very effect, Mr. McKeague, now, that this pali continues on beyond some three or four hundred feet beyond the point "Dry Tree"?

A. In its general shape, and then takes a sharper break as it pertains to the word "pali" in reference

(Testimony of Bernard H. McKeague.)

to boundary, the answer is not right. As it pertains to the word "pali" as to abrupt change in the land, yes.

Q. Consider for a minute that you are at this point— [121] Hoalae—looking in an almost direct southerly line, as shown, compared with this early showing—true north. Is that correct? Can there be any point at this spot marked "M. D. M's Dry Tree" where the pali breaks off, discontinues?

A. I never made that observation.

Q. How far back on Grant 3539 have you looked, or rather from what point, looking at this map, have you on Grant 3539 looked in a southerly direction?

A. I looked from the vicinity of "Dry Tree," Monsarrat's "Dry Tree," I looked both ways.

Q. Were you never north, on Grant 3539, of Monsarrat's point "Dry Tree"?

A. I was. I walked down there but my observation was only in the northerly direction. I walked down quite a ways to observe the nature of the pali and lay of the land.

Q. Will you state approximately how far down you walked?   A. Approximately half way down.

Q. Approximately near M. D. M's Ridge C?

A. That is possible or it may be where the letter "A" in the word "Kahanui," the first letter "A" in the word "Kahanui 3."

Q. Another six or eight hundred feet beyond Ridge C, maybe?   A. About a half mile.

Q. Half a mile. Beyond Ridge C, I asked?

(Testimony of Bernard H. McKeague.)

A.   Oh, I am sorry. Probably about four or five hundred feet.

Q.   But you made no observations looking southerly from there, is that correct?   A.   No.

Q.   Now, with regard to the survey of Grant 3437, how far [122] down in the valley below the intake did you go?

A.   I did not go beyond the first fall.

Q.   The first fall. In which direction?

A.   That is right at the intake, but I sent a rodman down to the Big Fall and located the intervening falls. [123]

* * * * *

Q.   Above the intake or going southerly did you do any actual surveying? [124]   A.   No.

Q.   Will you relate to us just what you did do above the intake in the course of your work on this survey?

A.   I walked to the floor of the valley and came up to about the fourth fall that was shown on Mr. Newton's map, and was not able to scale it, so I went back.

Q.   You were not able to scale the fall?

A.   It is about eight or ten feet.

Q.   But it is impassable, is that right?

A.   No. It is passable; with some help you can scale it.

Q.   But you did not try it?

A.   I did not try it because I was alone.

Q.   Was there a pool there?

(Testimony of Bernard H. McKeague.)

A. Yes, there was a pool there, about sixty feet across.

Q. In your direct examination did you not identify that as Waiau?

A. No. I did not go that far.

Q. Did you go to Waiau at any time?

A. Yes. What I thought was Waiau. But my approach was from the southerly side.

Q. Will you take this pencil and mark on this map where Waiau is?

A. Right here (indicating).

Q. Will you write it in below? You have it as "Waiau Falls." Isn't there also a pool there?

A. That is right.

Q. Did you go along this stream to any points above Waiau?

A. Yes. I approached the floor of the valley by coming down from a point above Ridge A and scaling down the sides [125] to the bottom of the valley or into the stream bed and all the way down to Waiau Falls.

Q. You have referred to a general area where the distance 143.00 appears, about one inch below the word "grant" on this map, Exhibit A. Correct?

A. That is right. And my entering the floor of the valley should be a little higher up, at the letter "t" in the word "grant" just referred to. [126]
* * * * *

Q. In locating the head of the valley you undoubtedly follow around the ridge beginning with M. D. M's X, as shown on your map, is that not so?

(Testimony of Bernard H. McKeague.)

A.   That is right.

Q.   The language here is "Boundary follows along top edge of pali." Do you know that?

A.   That is right.

Q.   If you will follow my pencil, beginning from the point M. D. M's X, I am following along the top edge of the pali, am I not?

A.   That is right.

Q.   And I reach this point, where you take a line down to [128] the Big Falls, is that not right?

A.   That is right.

Q.   To follow along the top edge of pali I simply continue along there, do I not?   A.   Yes.

Q.   Through Point K?

A.   That is right.

Q.   Here, to the head of the valley, then drop off from the top edge of the pali at that point?

A.   Up there (indicating). For this reason, this edge of the pali is much steeper than the portion shown in hachures, from there on up (indicating).

Q.   But this is still distinctly the top edge of the pali, is it not?   A.   That is right.

Q.   What I am pointing to is the area beyond Point K.   A.   That is right.

Q.   And if a surveyor in locating a head of a valley does so only while following the top edge of a pali, there is no reason to leave that top edge of the pali and go down to the Big Falls, is there?

A.   Very definite reasons in this particular case.

Q.   Aside from any particular case, if a surveyor is marking out a valley by following the top edge

(Testimony of Bernard H. McKeague.)

of a pali, does he arbitrarily leave the pali, where there is no natural marker to take him away from it?

A. If he has to locate the top of the pali throughout its whole length he has got to go along the same ridge regardless of whether it has any reference to boundaries or not, if you [129] are just locating the pali.

Q. Yes. If you are locating a valley entirely surrounded by palis there would be no reason to leave at this point that you have marked, is there?

A. There are probably good reasons to leave it.

Q. If a valley is bounded solely by the language "top edge of the pali," and referring that language to this map, there is no reason to leave the top edge of the pali at this point and descend to the Big Falls, is there?

A. Your question is hard to answer because if you are to locate the top of the pali as it pertains to a valley, you continue on up indefinitely until it peters out at the very end.

* * * * *

Q. (By Mr. Flynn): Looking at the ground that you looked at and starting from M. D. M's X as shown on your map and then following along the top edge of the pali and looking for a head of a valley which is bounded only by the top edge of a pali would loosely give you "continuing beyond this point," wouldn't it? [130]

* * * * *

(The question was read by the reporter.)

(Testimony of Bernard H. McKeague.)

Q. (By Mr. Flynn): To take you well beyond the point at which you have shown and descend to the falls through Point K, continuing on as shown on your map, and even clear out of the Kahanui area and beyond, would it not?

The Court: Now.

Mr. Cass: Now, the words of the grant are "Around the head of Waihanau Valley." Waihanau is a place name. How would he determine the edge of a valley by following the pali all the way around to the head of the gulch? That is not material to this case and does not prove where Waihanau Valley goes. The question of surveying does not enter into this deal at all and it is not proper cross-examination. How he would determine the head of a valley as described in a [131] grant, when the valley is described by place name, is determined by where the place name ends, not where the physical contours of the land continue up several miles, several miles on up. Both the Government and the applicant concede that the valley goes a long ways beyond both boundary lines. The Government claims that we cross the valley at one point and we say we cross it at another. So that following the edge of the palis a way up, as is indicated they are several miles above the top of the falls, has nothing to do with the case or with fixing the boundaries of Waihanau.

Mr. Flynn: This is a great statement about what the Government concedes, your Honor. It is not in the case at all that the Government concedes that

(Testimony of Bernard H. McKeague.)

the valley goes around the—it is not in the evidence here, it is not in any testimony. And I would like to ask the Court to note my request to strike all this part of the so-called objection which is pure testimony on the part of counsel.

The Court: The motion to strike is denied. What is the relevancy of the question?

Mr. Flynn: I am questioning him on his own map and the markers shown on it, Exhibit A.

The Court: As a matter of cross-examination, what is the relevancy of the question asked? The objection is on the relevancy of the question.

Mr. Flynn: As a check on the accuracy of the survey. As a check, rather, on the accuracy of the map and where the map shows the boundary follows along the top edge of the pali. And I can certainly ask him if the top edge of the pali does not continue beyond the point where he has shown a boundary [132] marker.

The Court: The objection is overruled. Proceed.

Q. (By Mr. Flynn): Do you remember the question, Mr. McKeague?

A. Will you repeat the question, to be sure?

(The question was read by the reporter.)

The Witness: Will you repeat it again, please? I am not prepared at this time to answer that question.

Q. (By Mr. Flynn): Is it not so shown on your map?

A. As it pertains to the words "and surrounds" —no, but as a location of the top edge of the pali

(Testimony of Bernard H. McKeague.)
continues indefinitely, shall I say, until it peters
out to the very extreme southeast end of the gully.

Q. (By Mr. Flynn): For clarification, Mr. Mc-
Keague, your own surveying work does not go beyond this point, approximately in the "T" of the
word "grant"? Grant 3437. Isn't that right?

A. That is right.

* * * * *

Q. (By Mr. Flynn): May I see the Exhibit B,
please? Calling your attention, Mr. McKeague, to
Exhibit B, which is the Grant 3437, the final grant,
issued October 20, 1889, and [133] specifically calling your attention to the map or sketch, do I recall
correctly that you stated this map or sketch could
have been drawn to scale but you didn't know
from examining it?   A. That is right.

Q. And you never found any material in the
Survey Office to indicate to you whether that was
drawn from a map on record?

A. In the south and southwesterly sides the lines
seem to indicate that they follow properly surveyed
lines, but there is no way on the record I could
find that shows that the line on the northerly side,
which is abutting what is indicated on the sketch
here as Waihanau Valley and Waialeia Valley, as
being plotted to scale; and none of the records that
I could find of any of Monsarrat's notes to show
that he located the line as shown on the sketch
except in its extremities.

Q. Specifically, though, am I correct in saying
that you do not recall seeing any map or any record

(Testimony of Bernard H. McKeague.)
in the Survey Office which would show even the south and west lines of this to have been the basis for the map or sketch on the grant. Is that correct?

A. That is right.

Mr. Flynn: I have here, if the Court please, Registered Map No. 1288, containing the identification of "Molokai, middle and west section, 1:24,000, and containing in the center of the map the following identification: "Hawaiian Government Survey, W. D. Alexander, Superintendent. Molokai. Middle and west section. Map and survey by M. D. Monsarrat. Scale 1:24,000 or 2,000 feet equals 1 inch. 1886." I will ask leave to introduce this exhibit as Territory's Exhibit [134] for Identification No. 2, and rather than have it marked at this time will ask leave later to submit photostat copies of the portion of this exhibit which will be concerned with the testimony.

The Court: Any objections? It will become Territory's Exhibit 2 for Identification.

(The map referred to was marked Territory's Exhibit 2 for Identification.)

Q. (By Mr. Flynn): Calling your attention, Mr. McKeague, to this map, do you not see at the extreme right-hand side an area of land marked "Kahanui" and down below, well down below marked "Apana 3"?   A. Yes.

Q. That is in black printing or rather—I will withdraw that. The words "Kahanui" below that "1048 acres" below that "Apana 3" are in black print, are they not?   A. That is right.

(Testimony of Bernard H. McKeague.)

Q. Between the words "Kahanui" and the words "1048 acres" there is inked in the following: "Gr. 3437, R. W. Meyer," is that correct?

A. That is right.

Q. I will ask you to examine that piece of this map we have referred to and then examine the sketch or map attached to Grant 3437, and I will ask you if they appear to be substantially similar? Will you answer that question?

A. That is right.

Q. They do?   A. They do.

Q. Do they not even appear to be identical?

A. No.

Q. On the boundaries do they not appear to be identical, as to "Kahanui 1048 acres"?

A. In the southern and southwesterly boundary they seem to be identical, but where it has a meandering line following from Puu Kaeo, along Waikolu and along Waialeia and Waihanau Valleys, it is not necessarily identical.

Q. They appear very similar, though, do they not?   A. In a very general way, yes.

Mr. Cass: Is this supposed to be a tracing off of that?

Mr. Flynn: I think it is a tracing off the grant. However, I will mark it for identification.

Mr. Cass: Let's lay it over the map and find out.

Mr. Flynn: That is what the testimony is going to be. I will show to the Court here a tracing and

(Testimony of Bernard H. McKeague.)
ask that it be marked Territory's Exhibit 3 for Identification.

The Court: The tracing will be marked Territory's Exhibit 3 for Identification.

(The tracing referred to was marked Territory's Exhibit 3 for Identification.)

Q. (By Mr. Flynn): Mr. McKeague, I show you Territory's Exhibit 3 for Identification and ask you whether it does not appear to be a tracing of the map or sketch shown on Grant 3437.

A. It does.

Q. I will now lay this tracing over the map or sketch accompanying Grant 3437, and ask you whether the lines showing the boundary of Kahanui 1048 acres are not virtually or substantially identical with those in the grant? [136]

A. Substantially, it is.

Q. I will now return your attention to Territory's Exhibit 2 for Identification, and ask you whether this tracing, which is now laid over the 1886 map of Kahanui or rather the 1886 Government map by M. D. Monsarrat, with reference specifically to that portion marked "Kahanui 1048 acres,"——

Mr. Cass: If the Court please——

The Court: Let counsel finish his question.

Mr. Cass: I thought he had finished.

Q. (continuing): ——isn't very similar to the tracing which was found to be substantially identical with the grant?

Mr. Cass: If the Court please, this is way be-

(Testimony of Bernard H. McKeague.)

yond direct examination and cross-examination. The witness testified that he had not seen it. Now if it is the intention of the Government to prove that this map was in existence, and it was a tracing, it is not a part of the cross-examination of this witness. The witness has testified that he had not ever seen such a map and had no reason to believe it is a tracing. The fact that it is a tracing is not part of his testimony. [137]

* * * * *

The Court: I don't have any notes on this witness's testimony that he referred to this particular map.

Mr. Flynn: No. You are correct, your Honor. He says he did not. I now want to show it to him for the purpose of proving, even on the cross-examination of this witness, that the map contained in Grant 3437 was that on record in the Government Survey Office at the time this grant was issued. [139]

The Court: I understand that. The objection goes to your doing it on cross-examination. That is the objection.

Mr. Flynn: I submit it is absolutely proper cross-examination when everything this surveyor did and has testified to as doing in establishing the boundaries is now to be considered.

Mr. Cass: But what he didn't do cannot be brought into the record for the first time on cross-examination.

The Court: The objection is sustained at this time.

(Testimony of Bernard H. McKeague.)

Mr. Flynn: Note an exception.

The Court: It is improper cross-examination.

Mr. Flynn: Note an exception, if the Court please.

The Court: An exception may be noted. I do not mean you are precluded from any showing you want to make during the course of this hearing, Mr. Flynn, on any proper sequence of testimony, but on the grounds of the objection made, as being improper cross, as I understand the rule the objection must be sustained.

Mr. Flynn: This concerns my recollection only slightly, but I want it clarified.

Q. (By Mr. Flynn): Did you not state a few moments ago, Mr. McKeague, that the map or sketch attached to Grant 3437 showing Kahanui 1048 acres appears to be substantially the same as that shown on this registered map dated 1886?

A. The boundary along the southerly and south-westerly sides seems to show and the boundary along Waikolu Valley, Waialeia Valley and Waihanau Valley in a general way, yes.

Q. Now, having seen the map of 1886 and having examined the sketch plan or map attached to Grant 3437, are you not prepared [140] to state that the map on Grant 3437 was and did depict just what the Government conveyed to R. W. Meyer in 1889?   A. No.

Mr. Cass: We object, if the Court please. The grant and the tracing are not part of this witness's testimony in chief, nor are they any part of a proper

(Testimony of Bernard H. McKeague.)
cross-examination nor are the maps themselves admissible on direct examination. So the opinion solicited from this witness as to the amount of land conveyed, and so forth, goes way wide of his direct examination.

Mr. Flynn: On the basis of what counsel is saying, your Honor, I am virtually authorized to make a motion to deny the application for registration now, because there is not a sufficient survey to back up the application. That is an alternative to a ruling of the Court that the entire survey and all matters pertaining to it are before the Court on direct examination and therefore open to cross-examination.

Mr. Cass: But counsel is trying to put in something here that the surveyor said he never considered in making the survey.

The Court: That is the point.

Mr. Flynn: Then it is very proper to show that he should have considered it and on cross-examination it is proper to do that.

The Court: It is definitely premature. The objection is sustained.

Mr. Flynn: Note an exception.

The Court: An exception may be noted. [141]

* * * * *

Q. (By Mr. Flynn): Will you return to the map, please, Mr. McKeague? Calling your attention to the top edge of the pali as shown on your map, from Monsarrat's Point X, following around to the point where you depict the extreme northerly boundary of Grant 3437, can you estimate the drop from the

(Testimony of Bernard H. McKeague.)
top of the pali to the stream on the westerly side of the stream? You may refer to your contour map if it will be of any assistance to you.

A. That means down to the floor of the valley from this point here, which is at the end of the course marked 1387.3, down to the floor of the valley?

Q. To the point where you put the boundary there, I believe that is at the head of the first falls as you come up from Makanalua. Is that correct? Or the third falls as you go down from the intake?

A. Oh, yes. The third falls. That is right. Six hundred feet.

Q. Six hundred feet?

A. Oh, no. That is to the very bottom. It is four hundred [142] feet.

Q. Four hundred feet from the top edge of the pali?　　A. That is right.

Q. To the point at the head of the Big Falls?

A. As shown on my map, yes.

Q. Four hundred feet?　　A. That is right.

Q. Now, the drop from the pali at approximately Point K, M. D. M's Point K, to the stream.

A. About two hundred feet to two hundred fifty feet.

Q. About two hundred fifty feet?

A. Two hundred to two hundred fifty feet.

Q. Is this the stream as shown on your contour map, which I am pointing to, just above the word or figures here, "2300," which is about an inch below

(Testimony of Bernard H. McKeague.)

the word "Waiau," where it reads "Area 49 acres"? Am I pointing to this properly?

A. Yes, that is the stream bed.

Q. Yes?   A. Yes.

Q. You say from the top of the pali to the stream bed at Point K is around 250 feet?

A. Yes.

Q. These are 100-foot contour lines, are they not, on your map?   A. That is right.

Q. I follow this 2600-foot contour line, which is slightly below the top of the pali. Is that correct, at Point K, approximately?

A. Yes, that is right. [143]

Q. And then following along the 2500-foot line?

A. That is right.

Q. 2400-foot line?   A. Yes.

Q. 2300-foot line?   A. Yes.

Q. And then the stream bed?   A. Yes.

Q. Isn't that 350 feet, then?

A. From this point. That is right.

Q. From the top of the pali?

A. In that particular spot.

Q. Instead of 250 feet?

A. That is compiled from the U. S. Geological Survey map, and I did not make any observation as to the relative difference in elevation from the top of the pali down to the stream bed.

Q. I only asked if it was shown on your map. I wanted to correct the 250 to 350 feet. Three hundred and fifty feet is now more accurate, is it not?

A. My answer is the same. The difference in

(Testimony of Bernard H. McKeague.)

elevation is from the records of the U. S. Geological Survey, and I did not make any observation on it from the top edge of the pali to the bottom of the stream bed.

Q. Is it not shown on this map as more like 350 feet rather than 250 feet?   A. That is right.

Q. Look at your blueprint, marked Exhibit M. You show an extensive ridge coming down to the floor of the stream at a [144] point——

Mr. Cass: Approximately Waiau Falls, isn't it?

Q. (By Mr. Flynn): ——very well. At a point approximately Waiau Falls. Is that correct?

A. That is right.

Mr. Flynn: I might note that there isn't any Waiau Falls noted here or anything of the sort, so I will say just above, on this map, the letter R, which letter R is followed by the letter W. Is that correct?   A. That is right.

Q. Did you from your own work arrive at those hachure line divisions or did you take that from other material available to you?

A. They do not follow any recorded notes. That is just a draftsman's indication that there is a difference in elevation in the direction downward from the part that is a little to the right of the distance marked 424.60 feet down towards the stream bed.

Q. Where did you get it to put it on your map that is submitted with this application?

A. My observation on the ground that there is a drop from that point down to the stream bed, and

(Testimony of Bernard H. McKeague.)

as I said, there is nothing recorded as to that difference in elevation.

* * * * * [145]

Q. From observations on the ground, your map shows a lack of any ridge coming down near the stream at this point we have agreed is approximately Waiau. Is that correct?

A. That is right. And also, it could have been followed all the way up because the different spurs coming down to the stream bed. They are throughout the whole floor of this gulch. And hachures do not pretend to show the exact spurs or gullies or ridges.

Q. Without pretending to show them exactly, they are supposed to be fairly consistent, are they not, so that if there is a spur on this side comparable to one on this side, and I am referring to both sides of the stream at approximately Waiau, should it not be shown? [146]

A. If it is very significant and if it is needed for mapping purposes, I show it. Any more than I disregard showing some gullies up here. I was only showing the general terrain, if it is possible to do so.

Q. Do you recall, from observation, whether or not there is a spur coming well down beyond the point shown on your map and nearly to the stream bed at approximately Waiau, a spur coming from the east to the west?

A. For about an inch, starting from part of the stream bed immediately above the letter "R", which is before the letter "W", there is a spur that starts

(Testimony of Bernard H. McKeague.)
from there and goes on up for about an inch on the map and it dissipates, as far as I can remember.

Q. But you did not put any part of that spur on your map? A. I did not.

* * * * * [147]

Q. (By Mr. Flynn): Mr. McKeague, referring back to your map, which is Exhibit A, we have previously referred to the language "Boundary follows along the top edge of pali," which is contained on your map and set forth just southeasterly of the cross on rock or M. D. M's X. Am I correct so far?

A. The southerly side, yes.

Q. Yes, the southerly side.

A. The southerly side of the line indicated by the line 289 degrees 53 minutes, 1587.3 feet.

Q. You stated that the top edge of the pali does continue beyond the spur ridge which goes down to the Big Falls and does continue beyond and approximately through Point K and continues on around until it hits the point marked M. D. M's Y? Correct? A. That is right.

Q. Did you walk along the top edge of the pali in the course of your work and continue beyond the spur ridge going down to the Big Falls and beyond Point K?

A. I did. Not in its entirety, but inspecting a point here and there.

Q. But you did walk beyond Point K?

A. That is right.

Q. Did you walk as far as Point marked M. D. M's Y? A. No. [148]

(Testimony of Bernard H. McKeague.)

Q. Did you walk as far as a point which would be just west of the spot we have now marked as Waiau Falls?   A. I did.

Q. Would you, to the best of your recollection, state that you did walk along the top edge of this pali?

A. I went about two or three hundred feet beyond the point marked by the dot and indicated by the letter B, in a southerly direction.

Q. The letter B you have just inserted in pencil, have you not?   A. That is right.

Q. On your map, Exhibit A?

A. That is right.

Q. As you walked along this top edge of the pali and as you reached the spur ridge or the area where the spur ridge descends down to the Big Falls, what is the visibility to the point down to the spot you have referred to as the Big Falls?

A. I would estimate that I could see perhaps 300 to 350 feet from the top of the spur, in that general direction.

Q. Can you see the bottom of the valley at the Big Falls from up there?   A. No.

Q. You cannot see it?   A. Cannot see it.

Q. Let's assume a surveyor is following along the top edge of this pali, and continuing beyond the spur ridge that leads down to the Big Falls, and continues to the point marked K, which you have previously stated is M. D. M's survey point K. I gather from what you have stated a minute ago the there would not be any ascertaining from this top

(Testimony of Bernard H. McKeague.)

of the pali as to [149] whether or not the valley is impassable at that point referred to as the Big Falls? Correct?

A. Will you start your question all over again? It is too long and I cannot follow your continuity at all.

Q. I will try to put it this way. A surveyor is confining this present trip to a walk along the top edge of the pali, and he goes beyond this spur ridge and to Point K. Correct?

A. You mean in that neighborhood? You are assuming that?

Q. I am assuming this, yes.

A. That is an assumption?

Q. That is right. That the surveyor looks down into the valley as he takes that walk; is he able to see whether that spot at the Big Falls is passable or impassable?

A. No, he cannot determine that.

Q. Now, referring to the marks in red dotted lines or dash lines on your map, you have stated that these were points and plottings in M. D. M's survey field book. Is that correct?

A. That is right.

Q. From your examination of his field notes I believe you stated that Mr. Monsarrat never went down into this valley. Correct? By this valley I am referring to the area where the Big Falls is located.

A. I could not find anything in his records or field notes to indicate that he went down to the bottom of that valley.

(Testimony of Bernard H. McKeague.)

Q. Did you find anything in his field notes or any of his records to indicate that he ever went below the top edge of the pali, following the line we have previously talked about, that is to say, from M. D. M's survey Point X through K and again following back down to M. D. M's Y? [150]

A. There is nothing I can find in the records to show that M. D. Monsarrat left this plateau and entered the floor of the valley at any one point.

Q. Or at any point at all. Isn't that correct?

A. To the best of my knowledge, that is right.

* * * * *

Q. You did state, did you not, that from this point where the spur ridge goes down to the Big Fall, the Big Fall itself—The head of the Big Falls is not visible, isn't that so? What was your purpose in checking out and plotting——

A. (interrupting) From that point, that is right.

Q. (continuing) ——all the lines in red which you found [151] to be in Monsarrat's field book?

A. I wanted to know just where the points were that are shown in his field notes actually on the ground by plotting so that I could more graphically see what he had done.

Q. Why did you want to see what Monsarrat had done?

A. Just naturally, to see how good his work was as it pertains to the boundaries of Kahanui, and if it has merit in that respect.

Q. You understood then that Monsarrat did

(Testimony of Bernard H. McKeague.)

draw the description for Kahanui or did write the description for Kahanui?   A. Yes.

Q. Did you also understand that he had drawn a map of Kahanui?

A. No. Not at the time he wrote the description. I have no way of knowing when that map was made or whether that map was made by Monsarrat himself or whether it was plotted by a draftsman, and it was marked on the map, the blueprint which I saw indicated it was a map by Monsarrat.

Q. Will you indicate that blueprint, please?

A. It is a sectional print of a place as I recall I got from the Survey Office and just made a sectional print, and on that sectional print it did not have all of the information as to date and all that, but I did know that map was a result of Mr. Monsarrat's work.

Q. And it may have been Mr. Monsarrat's map?

A. He may have been the maker of the map and he may not have been the maker of the map.

Mr. Flynn: I would like to have this document marked Territory's Exhibit for Identification.

The Clerk: Exhibit No. 4. [152]

The Court: Territory's Exhibit 4 for Identification.

(The document referred to was marked Territory's Exhibit 4 for Identification.)

Mr. Flynn: For the benefit of counsel and the witness, I will explain what that is.

(Testimony of Bernard H. McKeague.)

Mr. Cass: This is a tax map.

Mr. Flynn: No. That is a reduction made from the map of Mr. McKeague's which is filed with this application for registration, a reduction in scale from the original map on file with this case, to a scale of 2,000 feet to the inch.

Mr. Cass: A photostatic reduction, isn't it?

Mr. Flynn: Correct, yes.

Q. (By Mr. Flynn): Mr. McKeague, I show you Territory's Exhibit 4 for Identification, which I have claimed is a reduction, a photostatic reduction of your map filed with this application No. 1483.

The Court: Exhibit M.

Mr. Flynn: Exhibit M is the blueprint of it. The reduction to which I am referring is from the original map or the original tracing filed with the application.

Q. (By Mr. Flynn): As I was saying, this purports to be or is represented by me to be a reduction of 2,000 feet to the inch of your map. I will ask you whether from an examination of this exhibit you are satisfied that my claim is correct?

A. That is right.

Q. We have previously discussed Territory's Exhibit 3 for Identification, which is a tracing, and you stated, upon seeing this tracing laid over the map or sketch accompanying the grant, that it is substantially identical with the map [153] or sketch accompanying the grant. Correct?

A. With the qualification that it is correct as to the boundary on the southerly and southwesterly

(Testimony of Bernard H. McKeague.)

sides and very nearly the same as it follows Wai-kolu Valley and Waihanau Valley.

Q. Did you not also say that it was substantially identical with the entire northern boundary as shown on the map or sketch accompanying the grant? A. Substantially, yes.

Q. Now, I will lay this tracing over Territory's Exhibit 4 for Identification, which is a 2,000-foot to the inch reduction of your map filed with this application, and ask you how the boundaries as shown on the tracing compare with the reduction of your map?

A. Except along the southwesterly and southerly boundary it is not identical.

Q. There is a very wide differentiation along the northern boundary, is there not?

A. That is right.

Q. Mr. McKeague, I would ask you to trace on this tracing in a dotted line your boundary in the Waihanau Valley area.

Mr. Cass: Do you have a red or blue pencil or a colored pencil? If any tracings are made over that——

The Witness: This is a blue one.

Q. (By Mr. Flynn): You use your own judgment in fitting the lines that do fit together and try to be accurate.

A. Will you repeat your question, please?

Q. I ask you to trace the boundary as shown on the reduction of your map on this tracing. I am confining it to the [154] extreme northern point,

(Testimony of Bernard H. McKeague.)

northwesterly point of the boundary of Apana 3 of Kahanui.   A.   Meaning here? (indicating)

Q.   Yes.

Mr. Cass.   All of it.

Q.   (By Mr. Flynn):   Maybe you had better examine that a little bit.

A.   Do you want me to continue through on around?

Q.   As far as you can, yes. I am referring specifically to Grant 3437.

A.   Then I will have to pick it up here, where it touches the tracing. From here on up to here.

Q.   No. Just a minute. Your map does not distinguish between 3437 and Grant 3539, does it?

Mr. Cass: I don't know.

A.   That is right.

Mr. Cass: No line is drawn on the original map between the two grants on that boundary.

Q.   (By Mr. Flynn):   Then I will ask you to demonstrate the boundary between Point X and approximately the middle of the ridge known as Grant 3539, as shown on your map. Do you follow me now?

A.   No. I didn't quite get the question.

Q.   I am asking you to trace or rather to mark on this map——   A.   On the tracing?

Q.   On the tracing, the boundary of Kahanui between Monsarrat's Point X and Monsarrat's ridge Point C, as shown on your map Exhibit A.

(Witness marks on exhibit.) [155]

Q.   That is far enough as far as I am con-

(Testimony of Bernard H. McKeague.)

cerned. Now, if you will draw on this tracing, while holding the tracing over the Territory's Exhibit 4 for Identification a dotted line along the top of the ridge, which is Grant 3539, to its extreme southerly end or the equivalent of Monsarrat's ridge Point A as shown on your map Exhibit A, a dotted line, however it shows on your own map.

A. I just wanted to get the direction.

Q Now, will you please draw a dotted line between the boundary as shown by you on the westerly side of Grant 3539 to the line you have just drawn, which is the pali along the easterly side. A dotted line. Thank you.

Now, as we have seen, this tracing is on a scale of 2,000 feet to the inch. Correct?

A. That is right.

Q. The boundary shown on the tracing, which is also that on the map or sketch attached to Grant 3437—examine it from the beginning point on the north boundary, which is Point X. It goes southerly beyond your boundary point approximately 2,000 feet, does it not?   A. That is right.

Q. And the boundary you make beginning at that point of differentiation we have just referred to turns easterly and goes over to the offset ridge in a distance of approximately 1100 or 1200 feet?

A. That is right.

Q. Now, looking at this tracing, will you identify approximately on the tracing Point K as it appears on your map Exhibit A. Hold this however you find it convenient to do so. [156]

(Testimony of Bernard H. McKeague.)

A.   About here or in here (indicating).

Q.   That is approximately Point K?

A.   Yes.

Q.   Very well. Will you place on this tracing as approximate as you can, from examining your map Exhibit A, M. D. Monsarrat's Point A?

A.   It would be difficult for me to get the relative position of this ridge here with respect to the intersecting lines and the grant lines.

Q.   Can you approximate it? You will not be held to any precise location. Or if you like, you may place it on Territory's Exhibit 4 for Identification and locate it that way. Mark it "A" please.

Point "A" then on this sketch comes out directly at the line where you show the termination of the —correction—the southerly direction of the ridge which is Grant 3539. Correct?

A.   That is right.

Q.   And Point "A" likewise comes out directly at a point on the line, the northern boundary line of the tracing of Grant 3437. Correct?

A.   That is right.

* * * * *   [157]

Q.   We have previously discussed your map with reference to the hachuring showing the spur ridge which descends to Waiau Fall from the top of the ridge which is a portion of Grant 3539, and I believe you stated that the spur ridge does descend farther than is shown by hachuring on your map. Is that correct?   A.   That is right.

(Testimony of Bernard H. McKeague.)

Q. Doesn't that spur ridge extend just about to the stream itself?   A. That is right.

Q. Will you take a blue pencil and hachure in the balance of that spur ridge?

Now, from the point you have previously re-ferred to as the fartherest southerly point in the stream to which you walked, to this spur ridge descending from the 3539 pali would be approxi-mately a distance of a thousand feet, would it not? * * * * *   [158]

A. As an approximation, since I indicated that perhaps this point, 191 degrees shown on the map, was the spot I stopped, I would say that is about 600 feet.

Q. About 600 feet?   A. Yes.

Q. Would it be reasonable to say that this other spur descending from the point we have marked as "B" was less than 500 feet in a direct line from the point where you stopped?

A. Yes.
* * * * *

Q. Scale first from this numeral number 9 in red pencil to [159] the end of the spur which de-scends from the westerly pali of Point "B", which I shall mark with a "C", in black pencil. After that scale in a virtually direct line to the upper portion of the spur which descends from the east-erly ridge or the ridge which is a portion of Grant 3539 to the stream in the center of the valley at a point which I shall mark "D" in black pencil.

A. The distance from red No. 9 to the point

(Testimony of Bernard H. McKeague.)

marked in pencil "C", which is easterly and below Point "B" is 500 feet by scaling; this distance "D" which is the beginning of the spur towards Waiau Falls, is about 750 feet.

Q. Very well. Now, from this point marked in red pencil with the numeral 9, looking southerly along the continuation of the stream and the ridges, the spur ridges on both sides of the stream, are you able to view the two overlapping ridges shown here, being the ridge descending from the point "B" on the westerly pali to the floor of the stream and the ridge descending from the easterly pali of this valley, which is Grant 3539?

A. Simplifying your question, do I understand you correctly, you just want to know the view where I stopped, from red figure 9 to Point "C" to "D"?

Q. Yes.

A. I do not recall at this time whether I was able to see that spur at the end of Point "C" and the beginning of the spur that goes to the Waiau Falls, starting at Point "B". I did, however, go to a point which I marked on my notes here as Fall No. 4, starting from the intake and counting the falls as I went up, and it is quite possible I could see [160] this Point "C" and to the top or what I considered the top of—at the Point "D".

Q. Is it not also possible that you as you were standing near or even in the stream at Point 9 and looking southerly you saw these two overlapping ridges in a formation which would appear to be

(Testimony of Bernard H. McKeague.)
the end of this valley where the stream is running?

A. No, because the other parts of the stream bed are comparable to that; that winds back and forth with spurs supposedly bending the stream bed.

Q. Would it not be possible from several points along that stream, looking southerly, to see overlapping ridges which would appear to close out the valley as you are standing in it there?

A. There are several points that would appear as such.

Q. And from down there at various points along the stream there are several points that would appear to be a head of the valley that you are down in; is that correct?

A. No. I would consider it as head of the valley.

Q. I am only asking you, if as you stand down in the stream, and looking up towards the overlapping ridges that appear to close out the valley that you are standing in, such could have been a head of the valley to a person that was making that view? Correct?

A. No, I would not get that impression.

Q. But you did state there are points, both this one shown by "C" and "D" and other points, where the stream turns which, as you look at them appear to close out the valley that you are in? [161]

A. If I understand your question, I lose sight

(Testimony of Bernard H. McKeague.)
of the stream bed. That is right, because of the
abrupt change in the direction of the stream bed.
* * * * *

Q. I am asking you if the hachuring in the blue
pencil marks fits the condition on the ground better
than the lack of it previously contained in your
map?

A. As it pertains, the spurs that starts at Point
"D" and goes to Waiau Falls, yes; but to say there
is a ridge that comes down from the top, where M.
D. Monsarrat's Ridge Point A is, and continues
on down through "D", no.

Q. You don't recall any such ridge?

A. No. There is no such ridge.

Q. Any such spur ridge?

A. No spur that starts from the very top. The
beginning of the spur that starts from Waiau Ridge
starts from "D". It sort of flattens out and dissipates itself. If you start from Waiau Falls and
work your way up to "D".

Mr. Flynn: I want these series of photographs,
all pasted upon heavy transparent paper, to be
marked as Territory's Exhibit 5 for Identification.

The Court: Territory's Exhibit 5-A, B, C. [162]

Mr. Flynn: Territory's Exhibits 5-A, B, C.

The Court: Territory's Exhibit 5 for Identification, 5-A, 5-B, 5-C, from left to right.

  (The photographs referred to were marked
  for identification as Territory's Exhibits 5-A,
  5-B, and 5-C.)

(Testimony of Bernard H. McKeague.)

Q. (By Mr. Flynn): I will ask you to examine each of these three pictures contained in Territory's Exhibit 5 for Identification, Mr. McKeague, and ask you whether you can identify any of the areas as including those which we have discussed as being shown on your maps and as to which you have been on the ground?

(Witness examines Territory's Exhibit 5 for Identification.)

Mr. Flynn: If I may be allowed to help you.

The Court: That is necessary for such a greatly reduced photo.

Mr. Flynn: I would be very glad to do it.

Q. (By Mr. Flynn): I will refer you to the ridge we have previously shown to be Grant 3539. I will point to this area just above the center line of the entire photo, on the first picture, which is Territory's Exhibit for Identification 5-A, and advise you that that is the ridge area contained in Grant 3539 except for the extreme southerly portion of that ridge or the very narrow ridge area to the south of the broader area. I will then point out to you that the second picture, Territory's Exhibit 5-B for Identification, is a continuation of the same area, the overlapping being approximately one-half of the first picture; and similarly, the third picture is a continuation of the second, the overlapping again roughly [163] being one-half of the second picture. And I will call your attention to the stream or stream bed noticeable at the extreme left-hand side of the first picture, Territory's Exhibit 5-A,

(Testimony of Bernard H. McKeague.)

tracing it along as I see it, and indicate to you that this point at the extreme right-hand side of the picture 5-A is where you have placed your boundary or the area we have previously referred to as the Big Falls, and show you the same point in the second picture, which is very near the center of this picture, and point out to you that in the third picture that area is already off the picture.

* * * * *   [164]

Q. (By Mr. Flynn): Mr. McKeague, you have shown on the picture 5-B, which we are now looking at, a point which you are satisfied is the location of the high waterfall. Correct?

A. That is right.

Q. From which you can follow the course of the stream upward, can you not?

A. That is right. [172]

Q. Will you follow slowly along the course of the stream and demonstrate to the Court, counsel, and myself?

(Witness indicates on exhibit.)

Q. (By Mr. Flynn): Will you stop at Waiau, if you can identify it to your satisfaction, Mr. Mc-Keague?   A. Right here (indicating).

Q. Now, referring to your map Exhibit A, the point on this picture at which you have stopped is identical with the pencil mark on your map Exhibit A as Waiau Falls?   A. That is right.

Q. I will call your attention to the picture and ask you whether the ridge or spur ridge from that

(Testimony of Bernard H. McKeague.)
point upwards to the ridge which is Grant 3539 is not plainly visible?

A. For a short ways up, maybe two or three hundred feet, perhaps four hundred feet.

Q. Now, I ask you whether at that same point there is not a very marked overlapping between that ridge and the ridge which descends to Waiau Falls or just north of Waiau Falls from the top of the ridge on the westerly side of that valley?

A. There is.

Q. A very marked overlapping. Correct?

A. That is right.

Q. Then, from that picture are you satisfied that the spur ridge shown beginning from the spot Waiau Fall on your map Exhibit A and going upward in an easterly direction to the ridge of Grant 3539 is now a much more accurate picturization on your map of the true condition on the ground?

A. That is right.

* * * * * [173]

Redirect Examination

Q. (By Mr. Cass): Beginning at the cross on a rock, from and whence the description runs "Thence around the head of Waihanau Valley and Waialeia Valley," is there any difference between the steepness of the pali on the side that you have included in the map as distinguished from the side that you have excluded from the map?

A. There is a definite difference, in this respect, that one would not venture in this particular case just above the cross on rock and above M. D.

(Testimony of Bernard H. McKeague.)

M's X and venture down towards the bottom from this point, whereas above this point it seems like a good many places you can descend into the bottom of the valley from the top.

* * * * *   [175]

Q. Now, you examined Pease's notes and particularly that part of Pease's notes you were cross-examined on from the point Hoalae to the head of the gulch. Is there anything in Pease's notes or from the observations taken by Pease, if any, that would ever indicate that Pease ever went up on top of the plateau?

A. No, there is nothing that I can tell from his description from the map that he did go up to the top of the plateau.

* * * * *   [176]

Q. Is it possible to see this three-acre piece referred to here from any point on the bottom of the canyon?

A. I have no way of knowing; I wasn't anywhere near the bottom of the canyon.

Q. Now, this tracing and the 2,000 feet to the inch reduction of the map that we offered for identification here, I will ask you to complete in blue pencil on your overlay the boundary—you have already traced in the boundary from here to here. Now, I will ask you to trace in the boundary to **Kaluahauoni** as it appears on the overlay the same way, with the blue pencil or with the red pencil.

* * * * *   [177]

Q. (By Mr. Cass): Now, this red line that ap-

(Testimony of Bernard H. McKeague.)
pears upon this tracing, Territory's Exhibit 3 for
Identification, is an overlay of your map reduced to
2,000 feet to the inch scale over the map, the tracing,
as it existed?   A. That is right.

Q. This area in here has been referred to as a
pali, pointing to the tip of the larger portion of
Grant 3539, coming back to the three-acre piece.
What is the character of the pali towards Waialeia?   A. Very steep.

Q. Very steep. What is the character of the
pali on the side towards Kahanui?

A. Accessible on foot.

Q. It is accessible on foot clear up to the top?

A. Yes. * * * * * [178]

Recross Examination

Q. (By Mr. Flynn): Mr. McKeague, in your
redirect examination you referred to the description by Pease. I will ask you to look at that description now. You read a portion of that description which has to do with the easterly boundaries of
the lands of Makanalua, the ahupuaa of Makanalua, one of the portions of the description reading
as follows:

"Thence S. 12 degrees E. 15 chains and thence to
the top of the mountain ridge called Hoalae, thence
following along the top of the Pali bounding Makanalua gulch or ravine on its easterly side, to a
certain mountain peak, at the head of said ravine,
called Kaulahuki."

Will you now read the description for the west-

(Testimony of Bernard H. McKeague.)

erly [180] boundary of the lands of Makanalua?

A. (Reading from document): "The westerly boundary of this land commences on the sea, at the corner of land called Kalaupapa, at a certain large flat stone, laying a short distance above the sandy beach, running from thence S. 81 degrees 30 minutes E. 14.81 chains to a certain Hala tree, thence S. 86 degrees E. 1.42 chains, S. 25 degrees 30 minutes E. 14.85 chains, S. 40 degrees S. 8 chains, S 27 degrees E. 23.10 chains. S. 18 degrees E. 36 chains, S. 19 degrees E. 30.30 chains, always following an old path, (overgrown) to a certain Hala tree, thence S. 47 degrees 30 minutes E. 5.60 chains and S. 7 degrees 30 minutes E. 24.54 chains to the river at a certain bend, from thence following along southerly bank of the river, S. 45 degrees E. 29 chains, to the foot of the mountain ridge called Ililika, thence to the top of Ililika and from thence following along the top of the Pali bounding Makanalua gulch or ravine, on the west, to a certain mountain peak at the head of said gulch called Kaulahuki, comprising an area of twelve thousand five hundred acres, more or less. W. H. Pease".

Q. Yes, now Mr. McKeague, examining this description by Pease, you find that on both the easterly and westerly boundaries of the lands of Makanalua the course requires the going along the top of the pali to a mountain peak called Kaulahuki, correct?

A. That is a portion of it, yes.

Mr. Flynn: No further questions, your Honor.

The Court: Next witness. * * * * [181]

THOMAS P. CUMMINS

called as a witness on behalf of the plaintiff, being first duly sworn, was examined and testified as follows:

Direct Examination

* * * * *

Q. (By Mr. Cass): Are you related to the Meyer family? A. By marriage.

Q. How long have you been married to a member of the Meyer family?

A. Thirty-four years.

Q. Are you familiar with the lands of upper Kahanui, that is what is known as mauka Kahanui? A. I am.

Q. How long have you been familiar with that land? A. Since 1916. * * * * *

Q. Now [196] in your early acquaintance with the land, did you ever note the fencing of this area, where the fences were?

Mr. Flynn: If the Court please, I want to make an objection as to this all being incompetent, irrelevant and immaterial to this boundary question.

The Court: The purpose, Mr. Cass?

Mr. Cass: Why in the letter of Meyer requesting the allotment of additional land appears the statement that the awarding of that additional land would save fencing. Now the question of what is fenced and what was considered necessary to fence as to do with Meyer's mental conception of the area of land which he was going to get. I wish to prove by this witness the nature and extent of the fencing of this particular area.

(Testimony of Thomas P. Cummins.)

The Court: From 1916 forward?

Mr. Cass: And what he knows of old fences that might have been in existence at that time.

The Court: Objection overruled.

Mr. Flynn: Note an exception, if the Court please.

The Court: Exception may be noted.

Mr. Flynn: May I make a further objection that any data as to fencing or other outside material, that is to say, outside the description and map accompanying the grant, is inadmissible until such time as the description and map are found to be in error.

The Court: All right, the objection on that ground is also overruled. [197]

Mr. Flynn: Exception, if your Honor please.

The Court: Exception may be noted.

* * * * * [198]

Q. (By Mr. Cass): Was there any fence anywhere else on the boundaries of this land?

A. No, I didn't see any other fences. There were no fences in this section here (indicating) at all. There were none on this ridge nor none on this edge here (indicating). In this section here there were, and there were some ironwood trees in this section (indicating), I don't know whether built for windbreak or reforestation or what. There was kind of a dense growth of big trees in that section.

Q. Were there cattle on the land when you knew it?   A. There were.

(Testimony of Thomas P. Cummins.)

Q. As to the pali boundaries, were there any fences on the pali boundaries?

A. You mean in this?

Q. Yes, there and across where the pali is.

A. No, there were no fences at all. After you left the property on this side (indicating) and went down that gully, you come up into this section here (indicating), there were no fences until you get around in this area here (indicating).

Mr. Cass: That's all.

Cross Examination

* * * * * [199]

Q. (By Mr. Flynn): From where the cattle left Grant 3437, was that not somewhere in the neighborhood of the part of the Kalamaula road and from north to south? I ask that because I believe that is where you pointed.

A. That's right. They came in from this direction to the lower lands of Meyer.

Q. And that roadway did not connect at all with this point?

A. Not that road, not the way they brought the cattle in. It came in this direction (indicating), towards the Meyer lands at Kalae. That is the beginning of the Meyer lands.

Q. Yes. Now did I understand you to say you have seen cattle taken from this very point, Kaohu, to this area shown as around point X in rock?

A. No, I have seen them brought out from this area (indicating) to this area (indicating).

(Testimony of Thomas P. Cummins.)

Q. By 'out of this area' you have referred to the small area of Kahanui immediately above the central part of [202] Kalamaula and immediately to the right of the mark plus or X in rock?

A. That's right.

Q. Now there is a mere trail, is there not, between Kaohu and the plus in rock?

A. About four feet wide in places.

* * * * * [203]

CHRISTINA M. TUITELE

called as a witness on behalf of the plaintiff, being first duly sworn, was examined and testified as follows:

Direct Examination

Q. (By Mr. Cass): Are you a member of the Meyer family of Molokai?   A. Yes, I am.

Q. What relation are you to Rudolph W. Meyer, Sr.? [205]   A. He is my grandfather.

Q. Do you know when he first came to this country?

A. Well, when he first came to this country I wasn't born then, you see.

Q. In your family history, your knowledge of the family, can you tell us when Mr. Meyer approximately came to this country?

A. Oh, many, many many years, but I don't really know what date or what year.

Q. How old are you, please?

A. I am sixty-two years old.

Q. Born in 1887?

(Testimony of Christina M. Tuitele.)

A. Yes, December 27th.

Q. Where were you born?

A. I was born in Honolulu here and raised on Molokai.

Q. Where in Molokai?   A. Up at Kalae.

Q. Where is Kalae in relation to the Meyer lands?   A. Well, just Kalae, Molokai.

Q. Do you know where Kahauni 3 is?

A. Yes, I do. We used to roam in there too and up at Kahanui.

Q. When did you first become acquainted with upper Kahanui?

A. Well, when grandfather Meyer was alive, well, I was old enough to understand and to know when he asked us grandchildren to go up to the mountains with him, with our uncles and aunts and cousins.   [206]

Q. How did you go?

A. Well, we went on a bullock cart as far as the bullock cart could go. Then we would leave the bullock cart way up on top of a big mountain, and we would walk down this great big valley into this other side. That is the whole of Kahanui.

Q. Now do you know where the Big Fall is? The big waterfall?   A. Yes, I do.

Q. Where was that in connection with those trips with your grandfather?

Mr. Flynn: Excuse me. I want to make an objection to the competency, relevancy and materiality, your Honor, similar to my objections before that the testimony of this nature is inadmissible

(Testimony of Christina M. Tuitele.)

for purposes of establishing boundaries where the description and map in the grant has not yet been disproved or shown to be inadmissible.

The Court: Objection overruled.

Mr. Flynn: Exception please.

The Court: Exception may be noted. Proceed.

Mr. Cass: Will you read the question?

(The question was read by the reporter.)

A. Kahanui, yes. My grandfather always told us up at Kahanui there.

Q. Now did you ever go to the neighborhood of these big waterfalls?

A. Yes, we did. We used to go on picnics. Yes, and [207] grandfather used to just tell us and show us what we owned and what we didn't own.

Q. Now were there any marks there at that time in existence that he pointed out?

A. Well, yes, he did. He had landmarks up, and he had put kapu signs up. I remember that so well.

Q. Where were those kapu signs in relation to the Big Falls?

A. Well, those signs were put up right on top of the falls to keep the lepers from going up to our land where the water was. Grandfather didn't want the lepers to go up in there.

Q. How near to the top of the Big Falls were these kapu signs?

A. Oh, I should say, oh, about two feet.

Q. About two feet from the top of the falls?

A. Yes.

Q. And were the lepers allowed to go up on top

(Testimony of Christina M. Tuitele.)

of the falls?   A. No, they were not allowed.

Q. How long did you continue to be familiar with this area? By the way, you were married before you married Mr. Tuitele, were you?

A. Yes, I was married to Dr. Goodhue.

Q. Did Dr. Goodhue come to Molokai to court you and marry you?   A. Yes, he did.

Q. Where did you conduct your courtship?

A. Up at Kalae. [208]

Q. Up at Kalae?

A. Yes, at Kahanui, I guess.

Q. Did you go on picnics with Dr. Goodhue?

A. Yes, many times, and we used to go out shooting all around those hills and mountains, and he shot many a deer and goats.

Q. Did you go up to the Big Falls?

A. Yes, I did.

Q. How old were you then?

A. At that time I was going onto 18.

Q. Going onto 18 years old?   A. Yes.

Q. Now Dr. Goodhue, did he take you right back to Honolulu when he married you?

A. No, he used to be the physician for the leper settlement, and I lived there with him for about 30 years.

Q. In the leper settlement?

A. In the leper settlement. And every Saturday or Friday afternoon he and I would go up and spend the week end with my mother and father. That is, up at Kalae.

(Testimony of Christina M. Tuitele.)

Q. Did you ever go up the bottom of Waihanau Valley?

A. Well, no, I couldn't get up in there.

Q. You couldn't get up in there?

A. No, but we used to ride, when we used to go hiking up there, we used to walk along the edges, oh yes, from on top, not down below.

Q. Not down below?   A. No.   [209]

Q. Were there any fences on the edge of the pali?

A. There were no fences up there, but grandfather put these kapu signs along the line because if grandfather was to put a fence up, it would run for miles and miles down big gulches, up and down. He said he couldn't do it.

Q. Did they keep cattle on this land up there?

A. Yes, they did. I remember so well, we used to go up and drive cattle, wild cattle, wild horses and wild turkeys. We raised turkeys up in there.

Q. Where did you go in to get your cattle?

A. Well, we had two ways of getting in there. We used to go through the Molokai ranch, now it is Molokai ranch. The other was was right through down that big valley down through part of Waihanau, up into Kahanui.

Q. You went down to Waihanau Falls and up the other side?   A. Yes.

Q. That was the shortcut you drove cattle?

A. Yes, because if we didn't take that shortcut it would take us days to bring the cattle and ourselves down. The trail used to be so narrow. There

(Testimony of Christina M. Tuitele.)

is one place—I can't remember the location—I went by there one day while my uncles were shooting, and I was riding my horse and it got frightened and it jumped to one side; that road was only that wide (indicating) from where it would drop into that big valley.

Q. You brought the cattle up that trail?

A. Oh, yes. [210]

Q. Weren't the cattle pretty wild?

A. Yes, they were very very wild.

Q. What did you do when they were too wild to drive?

A. Well, grandfather and my uncles, they used to get a tame bullock, oxen, and chain the wild bullocks with the tame ones and the tame one would lead.

Q. That would take them up over the trail?

A. Yes.

Q. Did you know Dr. Moritz?

A. Yes, I knew Dr. Moritz when my grandfather used—Dr. Moritz used to be very friendly.

Mr. Flynn: If the Court please, the objection I made before, I would like the record to note runs to all this testimony, and the ruling applies and the exception noted.

The Court: That is correct.

Mr. Flynn: Very well, your Honor.

* * * * * [211]

Q. Now going back to your grandfather, Rudolph W. Meyer, who was your grandmother?

(Testimony of Christina M. Tuitcle.)

A.   My grandmother, I don't know her Hawaiian name. Her name was Kalama Dorcus Meyer.

Q.   Do you know what Hawaiian family she came from?

A.   From Pukoo, Molokai, Auntie Bertha knows.

Q.   And then your father and your Auntie Bertha are half Hawaiian?   A.   Yes.

Q.   Do you speak Hawaiian?

A.   I can speak very little of it, but I understand every word of it.

Q.   Now when you were a child at Kalae, were there old Hawaiians around the place?

A.   Yes, we had Hawaiians do all the work. There were cowboys. They used to go with Grandfather Meyer. Grandfather used to survey all that property up there. Grandfather was a surveyor himself.

Q.   These cowboys, Hawaiian cowboys, that you knew when you were a child, drove cattle into this land?   A.   Yes, they did.

Q.   And brought them back over this path? [212]

A.   Yes.

Q.   Did you ever learn from them any of the traditions of the boundaries of the Kahanui?

Mr. Flynn: I want to object, if the Court please. The question calls for a conclusion of the witness as to what she was told may have been traditions. It is inadmissible as hearsay.

Mr. Cass: That is allowed in land boundaries.

The Court: The form of the question, Mr. Cass, I think is objectionable. Perhaps you could reframe it.

(Testimony of Christina M. Tuitele.)

Mr. Cass: I was just asking whether she had ever been told anything about the boundaries.

The Court: The objection is to the use of the word traditions.

Q. (By Mr. Cass): Did they ever tell you anything of their knowledge of the boundaries of Kahanui?

Mr. Flynn: I will object again as hearsay, as an effort to bring in kamaaina testimony, which is inadmissible, second-hand.

(Argument on objection.)

Mr. Flynn: My further objection, for clarification is that all such evidence is inadmissible where there is a map and description accompanying a grant on which claim of title is based.

The Court: Objection overruled.

Mr. Flynn: Exception, please, your Honor.

The Court: Exception may be noted. Proceed.

Q. Did they tell you their knowledge of the boundaries of Kahanui?   A. Oh, yes.

Q. What did they tell you about the boundaries of the land around the Big Falls in that area?

A. Grandfather and my uncles told his grandchildren that belonged to us.

Q. Well, how about the cowboys? Did they ever tell you anything about it?

A. Yes, the cowboys knew about it too. Grandfather told them what we owned.

Q. Well, the old Hawaiians, did they ever differ with your grandfather on that boundary?

A. No, they never did.

(Testimony of Christina M. Tuitele.)

Q. Now you stated that you went on picnics in Bullock cart?   A. Yes.

Q. In your family how early did the children start to ride horses?

A. Well, when I first rode a horse, I was about four years old. We were taught to ride when we were very young, to ride horses.

Q. Did you keep on going in the bullock cart after you learned to ride the horse?

A. No; the older people like my aunties, mother and Grandmother Meyer, they were the ones that rode in the bullock cart then. We rode on horses.

Q. Down to this same place on horses? [214]

A. Yes, exactly.

Q. You started to ride down there just as soon as you were able to ride a horse?   A. Yes.

Q. And certainly you were not more than ten years old when you started to ride that way.

A. I was younger than that.

Q. Much younger than that?   A. Yes.

Q. So that your recollection of going on picnics down there first in bullock carts starts when you were approximately five years old or younger?

A. Yes.

* * * * * [215]

Q. Is Waihanau in the leper settlement or in the Kahanui land?   A. It is in Kahanui lands.

Q. Waihanau, you are sure it is in your own lands?   A. Grandfother always told us that.

Q. Were there any fences at all in this valley to keep the cattle down away from the waterfall?

(Testimony of Christina M. Tuitele.)

A. Well, Mr. Cass, we had boundary marks put up, but no fences, because grandfather couldn't get into this valley and up again, because it was so thick with lehua trees and ferns. It was impossible. * * * * * [216]

Cross Examination

Q. (By Mr. Flynn): Mrs. Tuitele, do you remember a location in those lands known as Waihanau?   A. Waihanau?

Q. Yes.   A. I think I do.

Q. Can you say approximately where Waihanau was from the Big Falls?

A. Well, all grandfather told us was that the whole place was Kahanui.

* * * * * [218]

Q. Now going from the seacoast toward Waihanau into the valley, about how far would you ever go, do you recall?

A. Way up to the waterfall there; but there were waterfalls like one would be here (indicating) and one would be again up here (indicating) but we couldn't get up to the other ones. We went down to the first one.

Q. The first waterfall was a long way from the Big Falls point where you went picnicking?

A. Yes.

Q. That's right?   A. Yes.

Q. And it was absolutely impassible beyond that first waterfall, wasn't it?   A. Very much, yes.

Q. So that was as far as the lepers come?

(Testimony of Christina M. Tuitele.)

A.   There used to be an old trail which was there at Makanalua, and the lepers used to go up that trail into the Meyer estate. That's why grandfather put all these kapu signs up.

Q.   That first waterfall was several miles toward the sea, or several miles makai of the Big Waterfall that [224] you are talking about, correct?

A.   Well, I'll tell you where the waterfalls are. I am taking from Kalaupapa, you see.

Q.   Yes.

A.   It would be about ten miles, I should think, from where the ocean is. That goes right into that valley. That is Waihanau Valley.

Q.   Yes; and about approximately how far from the seacoast to this first waterfall you are talking about?   A.   I don't know.

Q.   Would it be maybe half-way toward the other big waterfall where you used to picnic?

A.   Yes, I think it would be more than half-way.

* * * * *   [225]

Q.   Can you give me any approximation, any estimate of how far that first waterfall is from the seacoast? It doesn't matter if it is accurate.

A.   I know, but I cannot say.

Q.   You think it was more than five miles?

A.   Yes, I think so, because you see that Waihanau Valley, it runs in several miles from up in that fall there way down to the ocean. I wouldn't know how many miles it would be.

Q.   All right. Now Mrs. Tuitele, you referred to

(Testimony of Christina M. Tuitele.)
the two ways to get into Kahanui, one through
Molokai.   A. Yes.

Q. And the other was by a trail?   A. Yes.

Q. It was from other Kahanui lands, was it not?
A. Yes.

Q. From Kananui apanas one or two?
A. Yes.

Q. And I believe you said that that trail took
you [226] *Waihanau* Falls.

A. Yes. Kanhanui. That was the fall. Waihanau
Falls are down, you see. The whole mountain there,
the whole place, grandfather always told us it was
called Kahanui. * * * * *

Q. Mrs. Tuitele, at this place where you went
picnicking, you saw it was a short distance from
a Big Falls, is that correct?   [227]

A. I don't know.

Q. In that space, that particular location where
you went picnicking, were there three falls in a
row, one after another?   A. I don't recall.
* * * * *   [228]

BERTHA MEYER AUBREY
a witness called by and on behalf of the applicant,
being first sworn, was examined and testified as
follows:

Direct Examination

Q. (By Mr. Cass): What relation are you to
Mr. Rudolph W. Meyer, Sr.?

A. He is my father.

Q. Who is your mother, Mrs. Aubrey?

(Testimony of Bertha Meyer Aubrey.)

A. My mother is Mrs. Kalima Apanu Meyer.

Q. What was her Hawaiian family name?

A. Kalima Apanu.

Q. Her family?   A. Her family is Apanu.

Q. Where did you mother's family come from?

A. Makolelau, Molokai.

Q. Where were you born? [232]

A. Born at Kalae, Kahanui.

Q. That is on the land of Kahanui?

A. Yes. We were all raised on that land. Kalae, Kahanui.

Q. When you were a child did you have Hawaiian servants in your home?

A. Yes, we did. That is all we could have, Hawaiian help. There was nobody around there but Hawaiians.

Q. How long did you live at Kalae?

A. I lived there until I got married.

Q. When were you married?

A. I have forgotten now. In 1907.

Q. In 1907?   A. Yes.

Q. How old are you, Mrs. Aubrey?

A. I am now 81 years old.

Q. That would mean that you were born in 1868?

A. Yes.

Q. Now, do you know the land of Kahanui, Apana 3, the land that is on the edge of the Waihanau and Waikolu Valleys?   A. Waiakapua.

Q. What does that mean in Hawaiian?

A. The water for the pigs.

(Testimony of Bertha Meyer Aubrey.)

Q. When did you first come to know the land known as the water for the pigs?

A. Well, my father had a lot of cattle in there, a lot of cattle run there, he had hogs, turkeys, and deer, had all those things running on that flat land.

Q. Do you know when he first put cattle and deer on that land?

A. Well, I kind of forget. I know it was a very long time [233] ago.

Q. Was it before you knew of the land?

A. Oh, no. My father had got the land then and put the cattle up there.

Q He got the land then?

A. Yes. But I cannot tell you the date because father does not always tell us about his business. We were all very small at that time.

Q. Did you go onto this land of Kahanui, mauka, when you were a girl?

A. Yes. We all roamed around there. We gathered shells and we made leis. Very often we went up there. And when my father was living we often went up on a picnic right near the—what you call it now—Waihanau Gulch, at the edge of Waihanau Gulch. That would be often on Sundays that we would go there on picnics and stay there all day, roaming around, even going down into the valley to make leis, gather shells, land shells, and shrimps and all those little things down in the big water hole there.

Q. Did you ever go down to the big water hole?

(Testimony of Bertha Meyer Aubrey.)

A.   Yes. Went down on the ieie. That is the only way we could go down.

Q.   That is the name of a vine?

A.   That is the name of a vine—ieie. Of course, all Hawaiians know that.

Q.   It is like a rope, isn't it?

A.   Yes, it is like a rope.

Q.   You climbed down from the top of the Big Falls?

A.   Yes. When we got down there—we had no idea there [234] was such a great big waterfall. That is the only one. We didn't know there was any more higher than that. Only that one we knew. I went down with my brother and mother and sister. I was quite grown up then, about in my twenties. I was over twenty at that time.

* * * * *

Q.   Were there any signs or indications along the line of the Big Falls at that time?

A.   Do you mean boundary?

Q.   Yes.

A.   Well, my father always had these redwood posts on the top and there was a stone there too and that is the boundary of the Waihanau—of the Kahanui—of the Waihanau, yes.

Q.   Where was this stone located?

A.   Right near the redwood pole.

Q.   Were they near the edge of the fall or farther back?   A.   No, up on the top.

Q.   Right on the top of the falls?

A.   Yes. Right up on the top because we used to

(Testimony of Bertha Meyer Aubrey.)

go up that way to Waiakapua, flat land, up above the Waihanau. That is where we had the cattle running. There was an old trail where we would go up and come back and they used to drive the [235] cattle that way too, up and down that way. I would go with them too because I was just like a tomboy at that time. I would go with my brothers. I had six brothers.

Q. Did you ever go on picnics at this place on the ox cart?

A. You mean where, the flat land?

Q. Yes, or down to the waterfall?

A. We had picnics below the waterfall. That is where we used to go. Father used to go too. And then we would get up on the horse. We had an ox cart to take us up there. There was no wagon of any kind. Only horses. My brothers used to ride and father used to go over to the flat land, where they raised the cattle.

Q. The falls you talk about are those Big Falls that you climbed down on the ieie?

A. Yes. That is the falls I know.

Q. Where is that in relation to Waihanau Valley?   A. That is Holae, Makanalua.

Q. What is Holae in Makanalua?

A. That is the name of the—that is the boundary.

Q. That is the boundary?

A. That is the boundary of Kahanui.

Q. Did you ever talk to any of the old Hawai-

(Testimony of Bertha Meyer Aubrey.)
ians who worked for you about the boundary lines,
where your land ran?

A. Well, the old people that I used to know as
a child, they used to tell us stories about these
lands up there, old lands up there. The people used
to stay around those places and tell us about the
high hills and big gullies, streams, and waterfalls.
That is what they used to tell us when we were
small. [236]

Q. These old Hawaiians, were they Molokai
folk?

A. Yes, they are Molokai folks; they worked for
my father.

Q. From that same area?

A. Yes, near Kalae. They lived about two miles
from our place. They had a little hut up near where
we got our water from, and they lived there. Quite
a few native Hawaiians used to live up there.

Q. That is just above Meyer Lake?

A. Yes.

Q. How many brother did you have?

A. I had six brothers.

Q. Did they all live there on Molokai?

A. Yes, they all lived up there.

Q. Did they all work on the place or did they
have jobs somewhere else?

A. No. They all worked on the place until after
my father passed away and older brother went
over to Kamaleia and he started his own business.
He is the only one that left home. You know, he
lived on the same place and he came home all the

(Testimony of Bertha Meyer Aubrey.)

time, but he had his own ranch there at Kamaleia, and afterwards he bought a piece of land at Puukoolau.

Q. Were any of those brothers older than you?

A. Younger brother. He died in New York.

Q. One younger brother?

A. Yes. And then I came first and then he is the youngest in the family.

Q. All of them were older than you?

A. Yes, except this younger brother.

Q. Except this younger brother? [237]

A. Yes.

Q. They worked on the place. Did they work on this upper Kahanui, mauka?

A. Yes. Where they put the cattle in there. They built the fence up there for the cattle when my father was living then. The brothers all worked on the land until after my father passed away. They never left home. Only the girls, when they got married. Four sisters or three with myself makes four.

Q. They drove their cattle along the path that passed by the high falls?   A. Yes.

Q. That path was there when you first knew the land?   A. Oh, yes. When I could remember.

Q. An ancient path?

A. Yes. An ancient path. Very narrow in some places. Very narrow. I couldn't say now but it is quite narrow in some places.

Q. But it is a path that was ancient when you were a girl?

(Testimony of Bertha Meyer Aubrey.)

A. Yes. It went from our home up to Waia-kapua.

Mr. Flynn: Excuse me, please. May I get that path again, where it went?

A. We go up by the lake.

Q. (By Mr. Flynn): By Meyer lake?

A. Yes. And then we go up to Puakoolau and then that little valley and you go down and up on the other side.

* * * * * [238]

Mr. Cass: Your witness, Mr. Flynn. You may cross examine.

Mr. Flynn: If the Court please, I will move to strike all of this testimony insofar as it purports to contain any evidence as to location of the boundary now in question before this Court on the ground that such evidence is inadmissible where the claim of title is by grant including description and map, where the said grant and its map and description have not been shown to be faulty or erroneous.

The Court: The motion to strike on that ground is denied.

Mr. Flynn: Exception, please.

The Court: An exception may be noted.

Mr. Flynn: I will now move to strike on the ground of vagueness and indefiniteness and lack of certainty any testimony sufficient to constitute any evidence of boundary.

The Court: Motion to strike on the grounds mentioned [239] just now will also be denied.

(Testimony of Bertha Meyer Aubrey.)

Mr. Flynn: Note an exception, if the Court please.

The Court: An exception may be noted.

Mr. Flynn: If the Court will excuse me just one moment.

Cross Examination

* * * * *

Q. (By Mr. Flynn): I see. What is included in the lands you have mentioned as Waiakapua; is that of Kahanui?

A. Yes, that is all Kahanui. [240]

Q. It is Waiakapua and the term "Kahanui" refers to exactly the same place?   A. Yes.

Q. Plateau?

A. Yes. That is all in Waihanau and Waiakapua is on the up side.

Q. The upper side?

A. Waihanau is along side of the ridge as you go up.

Q. Waihanau is along side of the ridge as you go up?   A. Yes.

Q. Do you say Waihanau is included in Kahanui?

A. Yes, that is in Kahanui. Kanalua or Makanalua. That is all in there.

Q. Is any part of Makanalua in Kanalua?

A. All in there. That is wholly Makanalua.

Q. Looking at it the other way, is Kahanui in any part of Makanalua?

A. Kahanui is the name of all the land around Molokai.

(Testimony of Bertha Meyer Aubrey.)

Q. Your Kahanui includes many lands below the mountain lands too, does it not?

A. Not my father's property. All in where the gulch is, that is all Kahanui. The whole of Waihanau is in my father's property. That is my father's property. He always told us that was his land, our land, and nobody else's. That is what he said.

Q. Do you remember whether your father owned any part of Makanalua?

A. Makanalua is the—Kahanui is in Makanalua—I mean Waihanau. The whole of Waihanau is in Makanalua.

* * * * *   [241]

Q. Now, you used to go to the picnic grounds in bull carts, is that right?

A. Yes, when we were all small.

Q. All the way?

A. No. Only go as far as Puukawao because there is a gully that goes down and up and we couldn't go up. But that is all Waihanau. Puukawao is the name of the valley. The cart would only go as far as Puukawao. That is where we would picnic. And all the children wanted to go down in the valley and gather shells.

Q. Did you picnic right at the point Puukawao?

A. Yes, right at the point. That place used to be nothing but ieie.

Q. There are no falls right there, are there?

A. Not where Puukawao go down in the valley. Water running there all the time.

(Testimony of Bertha Meyer Aubrey.)

Q. Down in the valley?

A. Yes, down in the valley.

* * * * *

Redirect Examination

* * * * * [242]

Q. (By Mr. Cass): You said at one time that Waihanau was in Kahanui and at another time you said that Waihanau was wholly in Makanalua.

A. Yes.

Q. Which is right?

A. Well, I think it is in Makanalua.

Q. It is in—— A. It is Makanalua.

Q. It is wholly in Makanalua?

A. Yes, in Makanalua.

Q. Where is the head of that Waihanau Valley that is in Makanalua?

A. I don't remember that.

Q. Where did you father say his title run to in connection with Kahanui?

A. I don't remember.

* * * * * [243]

Mr. Cass: Now I wish to renew my offer as to Mauritz's affidavit; first, on the ground that the statute allows the introduction of affidavits which are on file in any Circuit Court action, and second, on the ground that it is a statement of a disinterested witness who is now dead.

The Court: Any opposition to the offer, Mr. Flynn?

Mr. Flynn: Yes, your Honor. I oppose it on both [244] grounds on which it is offered. As to the first ground, that the statute authorizes such admissibility, which is the statute or rather Section 9884, Revised Laws of Hawaii 1945, I will submit to the Court that the entire Section 9884 is confined exclusively to the proof or admissibility of documents only insofar as examined copies or authenticated copies may be offered. The statute gives no authority or no determination that any particular document, affidavit or other paper is admissible as evidence in a case. As to the second ground, I will say, and this would somewhat apply as to the first ground too, that the offer in evidence of this affidavit must be rejected because the maker of the affidavit was never subjected to cross-examination, and the admissibility of anything in the nature of statements or testimony is determined by the presence or lack of presence or opportunity for cross examination. The affidavit, as the record in the prior case will show, was refused when an offer was made to put it into evidence in the former case.

* * * * *   [245]

The Court: Objection overruled. Exhibit R of the applicant, heretofore offered for identification as R, will be received in evidence as Applicant's Exhibit R.

(The document referred to was received in evidence as Applicant's Exhibit R.)

Mr. Flynn: And my exception may be noted, if the Court please?

The Court: You may have an exception.

Mr. Flynn: And I make an objection on the additional [246] ground that the declarations in the affidavit are those constituting declarations outside of and contradicting the description and map contained in the grant on which claim of title is based, and that the description and map within the grant have not been disapproved or rejected, and that such evidence is therefore inadmissible on that ground.

The Court: The objection also on the grounds just stated is overruled.

Mr. Flynn: May my exception be noted?

The Court: An exception may be noted to that ruling.

Mr. Cass: Now I offer in evidence as an addition to the abstract in this case the deed of Lono Wahine to R. W. Meyer, covering one-half of the Ahupuaa, and a deed by B. P. Bishop to Meyer, covering the other half. They have identical legal positions so I assume that there is an objection to their admission and it can relate to both exhibits.

* * * * *

Mr. Flynn: Both deeds are dated 1883. The correspondence and exhibits now in evidence shows that Mr. R. W. Meyer, the grantee of Kahanui in these deeds, who was also the grantee of the two grants on which claim of title is now based, the claim of title now being based exclusively on the two grants, I submit that these deeds are wholly inadmissible. [247]

Mr. Cass: The law says we must produce all documents which may have a bearing upon this title. These particular deeds should have been included by the abstract, at the head of the patent, I believe. The patent is merely a quit-claim. If there are two patents, the oldest patent rules and if the person produces an abstract for the latter patent, then the second patent may be introduced. The same way with this deed. The letter of Meyer, if you will recall, says that "Here is the land which I now occupy, had purchased and thought that I owned." The letter of the minister of the interior says that the records which he examined shows that Meyer does own an equity but that he cannot have a patent. And the basis of giving him the right to buy for $500 was partly on the basis that he already owned in equity 500 acres of this land and the other 500 acres he wanted to buy. These two deeds are in substantiation of Meyer's first letter that he had bought this land and was in occupancy for some years before the application for the patent. And his claim is that he had a right to believe that he had purchased all this land was more than just simply something out of thin air. It has to do with the title to this land, and as such he always brought in the Land Court abstract, just as we put in the lease agreements and so forth of the Land Commission ahead of the patents.

Mr. Flynn: May I respectfully refer the Court to the amended application now before the Court?

The Court: What portion, Mr. Flynn?

Mr. Flynn: The first page of the amended application, [248] where it says the applicant is the owner, and so forth, of those certain parcels of land described and bounded as follows, and then says,

"Being all of Grant 3437 and Grant 3539, and so forth." Page 5 shows that this applicant obtained title to said lands from the following, and then recites four deeds, and, No. 5, a decree in equity. There is no claim anywhere in the application that any of the title to the lands now claimed dates back to any transactions prior to the time of the two grants 3437 ad 3539.

Mr. Cass: There is no requirement that in the application the party is limited tq the original grant. It says that the land is the same as described in the grant, and it is. Our description of the grant is "Apana 3 of Kahanui." And this is the deed which covers all of Kahanui, regardless of whether more land might have been conveyed than in the patent. At least it covers all that is in the patent because the patent and the papers connected with the patent show it was the grant of an apana of Kahanui. The advertisement of the sale to Meyer describes the land purely as a lele of Kahanui.
* * * * * [249]

The Court: The objection is overruled. The deed dated June 28, 1883, will become Applicant's Exhibit S in evidence, and the deed dated October 25, 1883, will become Applicant's Exhibit T in evidence.

Mr. Flynn: May my exception be noted?

The Court: Exceptions may be noted.

(The documents referred to were received in evidence as Applicant's Exhibits S and T.)
* * * * * [250]

ERNEST DONALD MEYER

a witness called by and on behalf of the applicant, being first sworn, was examined and testified as follows:

Direct Examination

* * * * *

Q. (By Mr. Cass): What is your relationship to Rudolph W. Meyer, Senior?

A. He was my grandfather.

Q. Where·were you born?

A. I was born at Kalae, Molokai, on the land of Kahanui.

Q. How old are you?

A. I am 58 years old.

Q. How long did you live on the land of Kahanui?　　A. All my life.

Q. Are you familiar with the land known as Mauka-Kona, Kahanui?　　A. That is Apana 3.

Q. Of Kahanui?　　A. Yes.

Q. How long have you been familiar with that land?

A. Oh, since I was about 10 years old, when I used to ride a horse to go with my father and my uncles.

Q. Do you know the boundaries of Kahanui?

A. Yes, I know the boundaries of Kahanui.

Q. How did the boundaries of Kahanui become known to you?

A. From my father and my uncles, they used to tell me "This is our land; our boundaries run——"

(Testimony of Ernest Donald Meyer.)

The Court: Mr. Meyer, you will have to speak a little [252] louder, please.

Q. (By Mr. Cass): Your father's name was what? A. Henry R. Meyer.

Q. When was Henry R. Meyer born?

A. That I do not know. I never kept a record of it.

Q. What was his number in the sons of Rudolph W. Meyer; was he No. 1, No. 2, in age, or how? A. He was No. 3 in age.

Q. No. 3 in age. How old was he as compared to your uncle Otto? A. That I don't know.

Q. Now, referring specially to the boundary of Kahanui 3 that runs across the upper end of Makanalua Leper Settlement. Do you know where that boundary runs?

Mr. Flynn: If the Court please, may I interrupt and make my objection to the giving of any of this testimony. It is parol evidence, evidence by reputation. My objection is that such is not admissible unless and until the expressed description in the grant or grants, including the map or maps, has been refuted or found to be in error.

The Court: The objection on that ground is overruled.

Mr. Flynn: May I object further that the witness cannot give testimony in the nature of kamaaina testimony on land boundaries, not being qualified.

The Court: That objection is also overruled.

Mr. Flynn: An exception noted to each ruling?

(Testimony of Ernest Donald Meyer.)

The Court: An exception may be noted as to each ruling.

Mr. Cass: Will you read the question, please, Mr. Reporter? [253]

(The question was read by the reporter.)

A. Above the high waterfall; above the waterfall.

Mr. Flynn: What was the last part of the answer?   A. Above the waterfall.

Q. (By Mr. Cass): When you say "Above the waterfall," where do you mean above the waterfall, some distance back or otherwise?

A. No. The highest waterfall.

Q. Is it at the highest waterfall?   A. Yes.

Q. Do you know the name that we have been applying to this high waterfall?

A. Some of the old people used to tell me it was Kaulahuki, was the name of the high waterfall. [254]

* * * * *

Q. (By Mr. Cass): Now, as to the far side of the land, that is the land beyond the stream as you enter this land, is that straight up and down or is it a gradual slope?

A. Straight up and down.

Q. I mean the place where the path goes?

A. Oh, it is a gradual slope.

Q. It is a gradual slope?   A. Yes. [255]

* * * * *

The Court: Cross examine.

Mr. Flynn: If the Court please, I will move

(Testimony of Ernest Donald Meyer.)

first to strike all of the testimony for vagueness and uncertainty, insufficiency in itself, to have any bearing on location of the boundaries between Kahanui and Makanalua.

The Court: The objection is overruled. An exception may be noted.

Mr. Flynn: Thank you.

* * * * *

Q. (By Mr. Cass): Do you know where the lands of Waihanau lie?

A. Below the waterfall.

* * * * *

Cross Examination

Q. (By Mr. Flynn): Mr. Meyer, you have referred to a high waterfall?   A. Yes.

Q. At the point you were talking about, is there just one fall there?

A. Just two; one smaller than the high one. [257]

Q. There are just two falls, is that correct?

A. Yes.

Q. About how close are they to each other?

A. Oh, I think about, a rough guess, about 200 feet.

Q. About 200 feet apart, approximately?

A. Yes.

Q. Now, as you approached those falls from the upper lands of Kahanui and going towards Kalaupapa, which is the larger of those two falls?

A. The second one is the largest.

Q. The second one?   A. Yes.

(Testimony of Ernest Donald Meyer.)

Q.   Were you ever down below the first fall and the head of the second fall?

A.   Yes, I was down there.

* * * * *

Q.   You say these waterfalls were known as Kaulahuki?   A.   Yes.

Q.   Was the first or the second fall called Kaulahuki? [258]   A.   The second fall.

Q.   The second fall as you go down the valley?

A.   Yes.

Q.   Have you ever heard of the term "Kaulahuki" as referring to a mountain peak?

A.   No, I haven't heard.

Q.   So you say that Kaulahuki as told to you by the oldtimers was the second fall?   A.   Yes.

Q.   It is the larger of the two falls?

A.   Yes.

Q.   Was there a third fall near either of the other two falls?

A.   No, not that I know of. [259]

* * * * *

Q.   What is the boundary or boundaries on the north?

A.   The edge of the valley is the boundary on the north.

Q.   Which valley?   A.   Waihanau Valley.

Q.   Waihanau Valley?   A.   Yes.

Q.   Is there any other valley bounding any other part of Kahanui?   A.   No.

Q.   Did you ever hear of Waikolu Valley?

A.   Yes, I heard about it, yes.

(Testimony of Ernest Donald Meyer.)

Q. Do you know where it is?

A. On the north, I guess. I am not sure.

Q. Do you know whether any of the mauka Kahanui lands went as far as Waikolu Valley?

A. Along the edge of Waikolu Valley.

Q. Along the edge of Waikolu Valley?

A. Yes.

Q. That is one of the boundaries then, isn't it?

A. Yes.

* * * * *

Q. You have said that the large falls has the name Kaulahuki?

A. Yes. That is the name of the falls. That is only the [262] fall.

* * * * *

Q. As you come up along that journey I am speaking of mauka from the Big Falls, towards the other land upstream, what is the general formation of the lands?

A. Well, they have a stream and pools and small gulches.

Q. Small gulches? A. Yes.

Q. As you walk mauka, what is there on your right? A. Just the side of the gulch.

Q. The side of the gulch? A. Yes.

Q. Does the side of the gulch go up very high?

A. Oh, it is passable; you can go in and out.

Q. I beg your pardon?

A. It is passable. You can go in and out of those gulches. Not so high.

(Testimony of Ernest Donald Meyer.)

Q.   On your left as you walk mauka, what is the general formation of the land?

A.   The side of the gulch too?

Q.   The side of the gulch.   A.   Yes.

Q.   Can you climb it?

A.   Yes, you can.   [263]

* * * * *

PENN HENRY MEYER

a witness called by and on behalf of the applicant, being first sworn, was examined and testified as follows:

Direct Examination

* * * * *

Q.   (By Mr. Cass):   Where were you born?

A.   At Kalae, Molokai.

Q.   What relation are you to Rudolph W. Meyer, Senior?   A.   Grandson.

Q.   Who was your father?   A.   Otto Meyer.

Q.   In the sequence of sons, where does Otto Meyer come in? Is he the oldest or the youngest or in between, of the sons of Rudolph W. Meyer?

A.   He is the second oldest, I think.

Q.   The second oldest. Do you know about when he was born?   [268]

* * * * *

Mr. Flynn: Born about 1858.

* * * * *

Q.   Were there any cowboys or other employees of Rudolph W. Meyer that went with you in the operation of this land?

A.   They did, but they are all dead now.

(Testimony of Penn Henry Meyer.)

Q. They are all dead now. Did you ever learn from them or from your father the location of the boundaries of the Meyer land?

A. My father and my uncles always told me about the boundaries of the Kahanui land.

Q. Are any of your uncles still alive?

A. None of them.

Mr. Flynn: If the Court please, may I interpose my objection to this testimony? General reputation or information received from the father and uncles, first, as hearsay, and secondly, as being inadmissible where the title to the land is claimed by grant containing descriptions and maps, and parol evidence of any nature is inadmissible unless and until the description and the maps and grant or deeds are refuted [269] or found to be ambiguous.

The Court: Objection overruled. **An exception may be noted.** * * * * *

Q. (By Mr. Cass): Now, do you know where the land of Waihanau lies?

A. The land of Waihanau lies, according to my father, he said it was below the Big Falls.

Q. Do you know if any name was given to the Big Falls by your father or these older Hawaiians?

A. I used to hear some of the Hawaiians say it used to be Kaulahuki.

* * * * *

Cross Examination

Q. (By Mr. Flynn): Mr. Meyer, what is your own age?   A. I am 47. [270]

* * * * *

(Testimony of Penn Henry Meyer.)

Q. Now, you have heard of the name of the Big Falls as Kaulahuki; have you heard of any name of the stream above the Big Falls as you go mauka?

A. Above the Big Falls, my father used to call it all Kahanui, the whole valley right up to the mountain.

Q. That is the name of the whole area? [271]

A. That is right.

Q. All the lands above. Have you heard of any name for the stream alone?   A. No.

* * * * *

Q. Have you ever traveled from the Big Falls and along the stream mauka to the upper lands?

A. You mean up the valley?

Q. Yes.   A. Yes, I did.

Q. From the Big Falls, all the way up?

A. Above the Big Falls?

Q. Above the Big Falls, going mauka?

A. That is right.

Q. And you have traveled along the stream as you have gone up?

A. Once in a while up the stream; most of the time we crossed over to the other side of the ridge there, they call it Waialeia, the lower end of Kahanui. [272]

* * * * *

Q. Were cattle, if you know, ever on this upper ridge along Waialeia?

A. They used to come down the valley there from upper Kahanui to a place they used to call

(Testimony of Penn Henry Meyer.)

Waiakapua, they used to come right down the valley along the ridge.

Q. Were they ever on that upper ridge there?

A. Yes, they were sometimes.

Q. They were? [273]   A. Yes.

Q. You say cattle would come along the valley?

A. There is a ridge there and they came right down that ridge into the valley. There used to be a trail there. Always a good trail to travel.

Q. You say that was from Waiakapua?

A. That is right.

Q. And Waiakapua included how much of the Kahanui lands?

A. That is the biggest area up there. I don't know. About a thousand acres or more.

Q. Will you say Waiakapua included about all of the mauka Kahanui lands?

A. That is the top end of Kahanui.

Q. Do you know the boundaries of mauka Kahanui by the term Apana 3, or does that mean anything to you?   A. No, I don't.

Q. That doesn't mean anything to you. All right. Now, you refer to a boundary on the north, on the Leper Settlement side, as Kaulahuki or the Big Falls?   A. That is right.

Q. Does that boundary join any other lands owned by Meyer or owned by the Meyer Corporation, if you know?

A. No. Just Kahanui. They call the whole place Kahanui. That is all.

(Testimony of Penn Henry Meyer.)

Q. Kahanui is the name also of a large area of lower lands, isn't it? [274]

* * * * *

A. It is divided. There is a forest boundary running between lower Kahanui and upper Kahanui.

Q. There is a forest there?

A. And there is a trail going through.

* * * * *

Q. Do you know the name of the locality at that point where the trail begins?

A. The name, they used to call that name Kaohu. There is a trig station there. [275]

* * * * *

Q. Did I understand you to say that you take the trail from approximately Kaohu to the upper or mauka Kahanui lands and through the forest reserve area?   A. That is right.

Q. Can you estimate the distance from the beginning of that trail to the point where you reach the upper Kahanui lands, just an estimate?

A. I think it runs about three quarters of a mile or one mile. Somewhere around there.

Q. About three quarters of a mile or one mile?

A. Yes.

Q. That is to the beginning of Kahanui?

A. Yes.

Q. Now, when you arrive at the beginning of the mauka Kahanui lands, is there any marker or point or land marker to tell you where the beginning is?

(Testimony of Penn Henry Meyer.)

A. Yes, there is a cross on a stone there.

* * * * *

Q. Have you ever been over the lands with any survey groups? A. Yes, I did.

Q. When did you do that, and at what times, if more than [276] once?

A. Just once I have and that was 1947.

Q. In 1947? A. Yes.

Q. Whom were you with at that time?

A. Mr. McKeague. [277]

* * * * *

Q. Now, getting back to the survey parties again, do you recall ever hearing whether a Mr. Fred Harvey made a survey of the lands in the general area of that makai boundary of Kahanui?

A. Yes, I heard about it. [280]

* * * * *

Q. Can you state just approximately how long ago it was?

A. I think within 15 years or more, I think.

Q. Fifteen years or more ago? A. Yes.

Q. But you had nothing to do with his survey party? A. No, I did not go out.

* * * * *

Q. Do you recall when the Hawaiian Homes Commission put a tunnel in that general area?

A. You mean what year it was?

Q. Or approximately what year, yes.

A. I think they started in 1924 and completed it in 1925, if I am not mistaken. [281]

* * * * *

(Testimony of Penn Henry Meyer.)

Q. Were you ever on the lands in the vicinity of that tunnel during the time it was being constructed?   A. I did.

Q. You were there?

A. Well, I used to go hunting all the time. We used to pass above the tunnel work.

Q. You used to go hunting and would pass above where they were putting the tunnel in?

A. Yes. The old trail going down the ridge and up the other side.

Q. What about that old trail going down the ridge and up the other side?

A. That is going up to Waialeia Valley, going down that valley, Waialeia Valley.

Q. You would go through there on a hunting trip?   A. Yes.

Q. Down that trail and up to the ridge on the Waialeia side, is that correct?   A. Yes.

Q. And this was above or beyond or mauka of where they were putting in the tunnel?

A. Right above.

Q. Right above?   A. Right above.

Q. By "right above," will you estimate how far?

A. Going down the valley it is about, I would say, about [282] 100 feet away, but going up the other side it is right opposite the tunnel.

* * * * *

Q. As best you can remember, what was the nearest waterfall to the point where you crossed the stream on the old trail?

(Testimony of Penn Henry Meyer.)

A.   There is no waterfall right by the old stream, I mean by the old trail.

Q.   No waterfall by there?   A.   No. [283]

Q.   Was there any waterfall mauka or above the old trail?

A.   They don't call it a fall. There is a pool there.

Q.   There was a pool mauka of the old trail?

A.   Yes.

Q.   About how far mauka, can you recall?

A.   Well, I should say about a thousand feet maybe, more or less. I am not sure. [284]

* * * * *

Q.   Did you go up as far as that pool that you have referred to, which was approximately a thousand feet mauka of the old trail?

A.   We crossed on top there. [285]

* * * * *

Q.   As you walked along the stream, Mr. Meyer, in this same mauka direction from the Big Falls on upward to the larger area of the flat lands, do not the ridges coming from the sides, that is, coming from the top of the level lands up above, down to the stream, do any of those ridges come right to the stream bed or are they set back for quite a distance?

A.   I think there is one a way up that comes right down to the bed. The valley is split, see?

Q.   The valley is split there?

A.   Yes. * * * * * [286]

Q.   I am speaking of the ridge you have referred

(Testimony of Penn Henry Meyer.)

to as one that comes right down to the stream bed. Can you recall where that ridge comes from, whether the Waialeia side or the——

A. (Interrupting) It comes from Waiakapua, a way above Waialeia.

Q. Above Waialeia?

A. Up the valley, the Kahanui Valley, runs way up; it is about two or three thousand feet above the pool there.

Q. Two or three thousand feet above the pool?

A. Or maybe more, I don't know.

Q. You have referred to the pool approximately a thousand feet mauka of the point where the old trail crosses the stream.   A. That is right.

Q. Does that pool or did that pool ever have a name?   A. Yes. Waiau pool.

Q. That was Waiau pool?   A. Yes.

Q. I believe you said there was no waterfall around that pool?

A. Just a little drop; I cannot say it is a water-fall.

Q. Just a little drop?   A. Yes.

Q. Is the little drop right into the pool or is it above or below?

A. It falls into the pool. * * * * * [287]

Q. Do you recall, Mr. Meyer, aside from Harvey's surveying party, whether any other surveying parties were in or around these lands, specifically the makai boundary, in the twenties or early thirties?

(Testimony of Penn Henry Meyer.)

A. Just Jorgenson and Wright, Harvey and Wright. * * * * * [291]

Q. You have referred to the area along the stream above or [292] mauka of the point you call Kaulahuki as the valley, haven't you?

A. Yes.

Q. Do you know whether that valley or any part of that valley has a name?

A. Yes. They used to call it Kahanui Valley.

Q. They used to call it Kahanui Valley. Can you give us an estimate or approximation as to how far up that Kahanui Valley runs or to what point on the land can you refer as the end or ends of that Kahanui Valley?

A. It runs almost clean up to the top.

Q. Almost clear up to the top?   A. Yes.

Q. Almost as far up as where the old mountain home used to be?

A. Passed the mountain home.

Q. Even past that?   A. Yes.

Q. Now, as you are on the top land or flat land above the old trail, on the Kalamaula side, and you look down into the stream there, can you see the stream from the top of the pali?

A. All along the ridge you can, yes.

Q. Along the ridge you can. I am speaking of the ridge on the Kalamaula side, on the right-hand side as you go mauka?   A. That is right.

Q. Okay. Can you estimate the distance or elevation from the top of that ridge to the stream bed?

(Testimony of Penn Henry Meyer.)

A. I will say it is 500 feet or more.

Q. Five hundred feet or more. And to the ridge across the valley there, where the trail goes up to what we will call [293] the Waialeia Ridge of Kahanui, can you estimate the elevation there from the bed of the stream to the top of the pali?

A. Not less than 500 feet.

Q. It is approximately the same on both sides?

A. Almost the same. [294]

* * * * *

Q. This cross on the stone is on the top of the pali, isn't it?   A. That is right.

Q. As you follow along on the top of the pali, as you walk along there, going mauka, is there any flat land to your right?

A. On the Kalamaula side?

Q. Yes.

A. Yes, there is flat land there, right to the cliff.

Q. I beg your pardon?

A. Right to the cliff. Right to the pali there.

Q. Right to the pali?   A. Yes.

Q. Do you know whether any of that flat land belongs to Kahanui or is it all Kalamaula? [295]

A. I don't know about the boundaries there.

Q. Do you know whether any part of that flat land is in Kahanui?

A. There might be a narrow strip, but I don't know.

Q. As far as you recall, there were no cattle up along that strip, is that correct?

(Testimony of Penn Henry Meyer.)

A. No. They used to drive them back and forth sometime. That is, from the upper part they used to drive the cattle. That is the passage through there.

Q. That is the pass through there. You would drive them between the upper part and Kaohu, do you mean? A. Yes.

* * * * *

Q. Was there any stretch of lands on which cattle could be grazed between those points or did you at all times follow this narrow strip all the way down to Kaohu?

A. No, they never used to leave any cattle there.

* * * * * [296]

Q. (By Mr. Flynn): Mr. Meyer, I was just asking you about cattle that you would take, going mauka from approximately the cross on the stone towards the flat lands up mauka. Those were only stray cattle?

A. Whatever broke loose, we would bring them down that way before. * * * * * [297]

Q. Yes. I am trying to get placed in my own recollection of these lands where the cattle would be from that strayed onto this little area around the cross on the stone.

A. That is from upper Kahanui.

Q. From upper Kahanui? A. Yes.

Q. I see.

A. They never used to graze around there though. When we used to drive cattle some of them used to break away from up above and hide in the

(Testimony of Penn Henry Meyer.)

forest and we would generally go back the next day and hunt them out and bring them down to where the cross is and pass through that path there.

Q. Are you referring there to the point or rather to upper Kahanui as the Waialeia side or as to the large flat lands in [298] Waiakapua?

A. The whole area that the cattle used to roam. Waialeia and Waiakapua.

Q. So they might be from either place?

A. Every time when we drove cattle we used to drive them all up and come around the other way, along the road there.

Q. Where did the road run?

A. The road is on the right of where the old forest mountain house used to be.

* * * * *

Q. Was there another roadway makai of that?

A. Just a trail.

Q. Just a trail?   A. Yes.

Q. Was that the trail that came from Kaohu over to the point known as cross on stone?

A. There are two trails, one on the upper and one on the—they split there, two trails, one goes to Kaohu and one comes down to the Kalamaula side. [299]

Q. Kalamaula side, there is a trail too?

A. That is the trail they generally drove the cattle on.

Q. Was there ever any occasion to take cattle from the trail beginning at Kaohu and go over to the cross on stone and then go to the upper lands?

(Testimony of Penn Henry Meyer.)

A. Often take them back to the upper lands.

Q. Either way, either up or down on that trail?

A. Not that I know of; only the stray ones.

* * * * *

Q. Beginning from the cross on the stone, did you follow along the top of the pali?

A. That is right.

Q. And did that trail go beyond the top of the pali? I mean go along the top of the pali beyond the old trail that led down to the stream bed?

A. It follows the edge of the valley all the way up to the mountain house.

Q. And you went beyond the point that was the old trail going down to the stream bed? [300]

A. Yes.

Q. You went beyond that point?

A. Just keep on going straight up, yes.

Q. Did it go past the point we referred to as Waiau?   A. Yes, way past that.

Q. Was there any point where you could go down any of the ridges to Waiau as you followed along the top of the pali?

A. Do you mean to take cattle down or something?

Q. First, to take cattle down, yes.

A. Not during my time; not that I know of.

Q. Was there any point where you could go down to Waiau yourself, just persons?

A. Oh, yes, you could go up and down.

Q. You could go up and down?

A. Three or four or five places.

(Testimony of Penn Henry Meyer.)

Q.   Were there three or four or five places you could go down from the top of the pali and across the stream and up to the other side of the Waialeia side?   A.   That is right.

Q.   Three or four or five places?

A.   When we would go hunting we would cross any where we wanted. [301]

* * * * *

Mr. Cass: I have nothing further, if the Court please. I have to present one more exhibit, which is in the course of preparation, and that consists of the notation of the contents of a file in the Archives concerning the construction of a water pipe at Kalaupapa, the dates when it was started and the dates when it was finished, and the course of the pipe line. I will present that as soon as it is finished, subject to any objection the defendants may have.

The Court: Otherwise, you are through?

Mr. Cass: Otherwise, I am through.

The Court: You will be permitted to reopen for that limited purpose. Are all your exhibits properly in, all those marked for identification, either in or rejected? Did you check your list? [305]

Mr. Cass: I don't believe I have any in for identification.

The Clerk: Nothing; just the affidavit that was received. That was the only one for identification.

The Court: Very well. Is the Government ready to proceed?

Mr. Flynn: First, if the Court please, I wish to make a motion to the Court to enter an order denying the application for registration on the ground, first, that it is supported by inaccurate and insufficient description and map, for the reason that it erroneously shows the lands to consist of Grant 3437 and Grant 3539 on a portion of Grant 3437, this being shown both in the map and in the descriptions in the application, and the same are patently defective by the unambiguous language of the grants themselves and by the unambiguous restatements contained in the correspondence between the minister of the interior Thurston and the original grantee R. W. Meyer.

The Court: Do you have more than one ground?

Mr. Flynn: Yes, your Honor.

The Court: Perhaps you can recite all the grounds you have for the record and then we can take them up for argument one by one.

Mr. Flynn: Yes.

The second ground is that the claim of title is based upon two grants, both containing descriptions and maps, and the descriptions and maps to have been shown to be either defective or ambiguous; that evidence or testimony showing other or additional lands to have been within the intentions [306] of the parties is therefore inadmissible, and that the said maps and descriptions filed with the application are contrary to and contradictory with maps and descriptions in the two grants upon which claim of title is made for the application.

Those will be my only two grounds, your Honor.
* * * * *

The Court: The motion, upon both grounds, as stated, is denied.

Mr. Flynn: I note an exception, please.

The Court: An exception may be noted for the record. [307]
* * * * *

Mr. Flynn: I have discussed with counsel for the applicant numerous exhibits we expect to offer and we have arrived at an agreement as to a portion of them, which I will start with now and the others will be brought in as the testimony proceds.

The first is a letter from M. D. Monsarrat to Professor W. D. Alexander, Honolulu, dated May 27, 1885, at Kaunakakai.

Mr. Cass: I have seen it.

The Court: Any objection? [308]
* * * * *

Mr. Cass: I have no objection to it. Your Honor, the only comment I have on it is that it refers to the boundary of Kahanui, and it is agreed between the parties that the portion of Kahanui referred to in that letter is not the portion under application at the present time.

Mr. Flynn: I so stipulate, your Honor. I might state that this particular exhibit is introductory in nature at the most to the work of M. D. Monsarrat, but I would ask leave of Court to read it into the record.

The Court: Received in evidence as Territory's Exhibit 6.

(The document referred to was received in evidence as Territory's Exhibit No. 6.)

* * * * *

Mr. Flynn: The next offer is a packet of three letters, all from M. D. Monsarrat to Professor W. D. Alexander, the first dated at Kaunakakai, July 17, 1885, the second dated at Kaunakakai July 31, 1885, the third dated at Pukoo February 7, 1889.

Mr. Cass: If the Court please, these are the same photostats that have been heretofore used in litigation between the parties. There is perhaps some underlining in [309] the photostats to which we do not object.

The Court: Let the record so show. It will become Territory's Exhibit 7-A, letter of July 17, 1885, Territory's Exhibit 7-B, the letter of July 31, 1885, and Territory's Exhibit 7-C, the letter of February 7, 1889.

(The documents referred to were received in evidence as Territory's Exhibits 7-A, 7-B, and 7-C.)

* * * * *

Mr. Flynn: I next offer a certified photostatic copy of description of Grant 3539 to R. W. Meyer, made from the original papers of Grant 3539 on file in the office of the commissioner of public lands, Territorial Office Building, Honolulu.

Mr. Cass: I think that is the same as the one I offered. I have no objection to it going in.

The Court: It will become Territory's Exhibit 8 in evidence.

(The document referred to was received in evidence as Territory's Exhibit 8.)

Mr. Flynn: As the last non-controversial exhibit, I will offer a certified photostatic reproduction of the description of the boundaries of the ahupuaa of land called Makanalua. [310] That is certified before L. M. Whitehouse, Surveyor, Territory of Hawaii, on the 28th day of September, 1936.

Mr. Cass: No objection.

The Court: It will become Territory's Exhibit 9 in evidence.

(The document referred to was received in evidence as Territory's Exhibit No. 9.)

Mr. Cass: May I ask what the date of the survey note was, that it shows?

The Clerk: April 8, 1945.

Mr. Flynn: If counsel has no objection, I will state that the correct date is 1865. It would appear as 1845. It actually isn't even 1845 either. It is that the writing is indistinct and the correct date is 1865. If counsel wishes to challenge it, we will verify it.

Mr. Cass: I don't challenge it. I believe it was 1865.

* * * * *

H. E. NEWTON

a witness called by and on behalf of the Territory, being first sworn, was examined and testified as follows:

Direct Examination

Q. (By Mr. Flynn): Will you state your full name? A. H. E. Newton.

Q. Your occupation, Mr. Newton?

A. Senior cadastral engineer, Territorial Survey Department.

Q. Are you a registered surveyor, Mr. Newton? [311] A. I am.

Mr. Cass: I will stipulate that he is qualified as a surveyor.

Mr. Flynn: Stipulate that he was qualified as a surveyor and has been so——

Mr. Cass: For a long time, yes.

Mr. Flynn: Approximately 30 years.

Mr. Cass: I will so stipulate if he will so state.

Mr. Flynn: And qualified to act and appear as a surveyor for the Land Court of Hawaii for approximately 25 years.

Mr. Cass: Yes.

Q. (By Mr. Flynn): How long have you been with the Territorial Survey Department?

A. I started in 1900.

Q. And have you been with that department continuously since 1900? A. Yes.

Q. Did you know M. D. Monsarrat in his lifetime? A. Very well.

Q. Did you know J. F. Brown or Mr. Jake Brown in his lifetime?

(Testimony of H. E. Newton.)

A. Yes, I knew Mr. Brown also.

Q. In the course of your work as a surveyor for the Territorial Survey Department, have you had occasion to make surveys of land boundaries within the Hawaiian Islands?   A. Yes.

Q. Have you also had occasion to examine older existing surveys of land boundaries within the Hawaiian Islands?   A. I have. [312]

Q. Have you had occasion to check any records within the Territorial Survey Department of surveys performed by M. D. Monsarrat?

A. Yes, many times.

Q. Many times. Have you had occasion to check or examine maps in the Territorial Survey Department made by M. D. Monsarrat?   A. Yes, sir.

Q. Have you used the information or data on such maps for any boundary surveying work that you have done yourself?   A. Yes.

Q. You stated that you were familiar with the work of M. D. Monsarrat. From your familiarity, can you state whether he obtained the assistance or help of kamaainas in his surveying?

A. Yes. He did the original surveying for these ahupuaas to open up the government lands and adjoining private lands and he had kamaainas to guide him through.

Q. He used them frequently or consistently, could you state?

A. Oh, yes, consistently. He surveyed practically the whole island of Molokai. [313]

* * * * *

(Testimony of H. E. Newton.)

Q. (By Mr. Flynn): Mr. Newton, do you recall the time or approximately the time of the death of Mr. Monsarrat?

A. I don't remember the date.

* * * * *

Q. Now, Mr. Newton, are you familiar with the lands known as Kahanui, Apana 3, on the island of Molokai? A. Yes.

Q. Have you ever surveyed those lands or any portion of those lands?

A. I surveyed portions of the lands.

Q. Roughly or approximately what portions did you survey?

A. I surveyed the makai section, the lower section adjoining the Leper Settlement and the boundary between Kalamaula and Kahanui boundary—I mean the boundary between the two lands, Makanalua and Kahanui. Not all the way through but about three or four courses mauka.

Q. Did you examine any older or existing surveys of those lands in the course of your own surveying work around those [315] boundaries?

A. I did.

Q. What existing or older surveys did you examine?

A. The Kalamaula survey. In fact, that is all that adjoins this particular piece of land. And Kaunakakai on one side. That is right. Kaunakakai and Kalamaula.

Q. Did you find and examine any surveys of Kahanui, Apana 3, itself?

(Testimony of H. E. Newton.)

A. There was a survey made by Monsarrat of that piece of land.

Mr. Cass: Objected to; that is not responsive.

Mr. Flynn: I asked him if he found or examined any survey of Kahanui, Apana 3, itself.

The Court: Objection overruled.

A. What I examined was a survey made by Monsarrat of Apana 3.

Q. Of Kahanui? A. Of Kahanui.

Q. Did you find any record of a description by Monsarrat of his survey of Apana 3 of Kahanui?

A. Yes. [316]

* * * * *

Q. (By Mr. Flynn): Mr. Newton, where did you find a survey or record of a survey by Monsarrat of Kahanui, Apana 3?

A. We have a copy of the survey right in the survey office.

Q. Right in the Territorial Survey Office?

A. Yes.

Q. Did you check that particular survey, examine it or use it in any way, when making your own survey that you have spoken of as a portion or the northern boundary portion of Kahanui, Apana 3?

A. Yes, I used Monsarrat's survey.

Q. Did you arrive at a conclusion of your own as to the northern or any portion of the northern boundaries of Kahanui, Apana 3? [317]

* * * * *

(The question was read by the reporter.)

(Testimony of H. E. Newton.)

Q. (By Mr. Flynn): My question, Mr. Newton, was this: Did you arrive at a conclusion of your own?

A. My conclusion is based on interpreting the survey made by Monsarrat.

Q. You did arrive at a conclusion based on interpreting Monsarrat's survey? A. Yes.

Q. Did you prepare a map?

A. I did, of a portion, not of the whole Kahanui itself, just the lower portion and along the boundary of Makanalua.

Q. Is this map you prepared based on the surveying work that you did and confined generally to the area in which you did do surveying work?

A. Yes.

Q. Was your principal activity in conducting this survey retracing of the survey by M. D. Monsarrat? A. Yes. [320]

Q. Did you use any maps made by M. D. Monsarrat?

A. I used several maps that are filed in the survey office.

Q. Made by M. D. Monsarrat?

A. Made by M. D. Monsarrat.

* * * * *

Q. Mr. Newton, have you seen either the original grant or a photostat copy of the original Grant No. 3437 to R. W. Meyer? A. Yes, I have.

Q. Bearing date October 29, 1889, covering lands at Kahanui? Showing you Exhibit B of the applicant, I will ask you if you have seen that before?

(Testimony of H. E. Newton.)

A. Yes, I have seen this before.

Q. Do you recall referring to that grant and its language?   A. Yes.

Q. At or about the time you did your own surveying work?

A. Yes, I used this as a guide or aid in my surveyng work, Mr. Flynn. [321]

* * * * *

Q. (By Mr. Flynn): Mr. Newton, I show you a large map entitled "Map showing portions of boundaries of lands of Kahanui, Makanalua, and Kalamaula, Island of Molokai; scale: 1 inch equals 200 feet. Survey and map by H. E. Newton, September 1936," and ask you if you are the author and creator of this map?

A. I am.

Q. You have previously stated you did surveying work on the question of the northern boundaries of Kahanui and you referred to Makanalua and Kalamaula. Does this map reflect the survey work you have previously referred to?

A. Yes, it reflects my opinion of the boundary, the northern boundary of Grant 3437. [322]

* * * * *

(The document referred to was received in evidence as Territory's Exhibit No. 10.)

* * * * *

Q. (By Mr. Flynn): Mr. Newton, I will show you a large map bearing the following identification: "Hawaiian Government Survey, W. D. Alexander, Supt. Molokai. Middle and west section. Map

(Testimony of H. E. Newton.)

and survey by M. D. Monsarrat. Scale: 1/12000 or 1,000 feet equals 1 inch. 1886 worksheet,'' and bearing below in blue stamp "M. D. Monsarrat, Surveyor, dated Honolulu, September 1886, H Islands,'' and ask you whether you have seen this map before?

A. I have.

Q. Did you examine or check or use this map in any way in doing the survey work you have spoken of on the northern boundary of Kahanui?

A. Yes, I have.

Q. Is this a registered map of the survey department of the Territory of Hawaii?

A. It is.

Q. Bearing register No. 1259?

A. Yes. [324]

* * * * *

(The document referred to was received in evidence as Territory's Exhibit No. 11.)

* * * * *

Q. (By Mr. Flynn): Mr. Newton, I show you this large map entitled "Hawaiian Government Survey, W. D. Alexander, Supt., Molokai, middle section, map and survey by M. D. Monsarrat, scale: 1/12000 or 1,000 feet equals 1 inch, 1886, registered map 1260,'' and ask you if you have seen this map before? A. I have.

Q. Did you examine or use this map in any way in your own survey work as to the northern boundary of Kahanui, Apana 3?

A. Yes. I used this map as a guide in determining the north boundary of Grant 3437.

(Testimony of H. E. Newton.)

Q. Is this an official map, an official registered map in the records of the survey department of the Hawaiian Government?   A. It is.

Mr. Flynn: I similarly offer this map, being registered [326] map 1260, in evidence.

Mr. Cass: We object. The face of the map itself shows it was not in existence at the time the grant was issued; that the map contains data of the grant of 1889 that couldn't possibly have been on this map in 1886 or 1888, when this grant was issued, and there is no way that he can tell or that anyone else can tell what data was on that map in 1888, when the grant was issued, except that we know that the map itself was not completed at the time of the grant, and it has no evidentiary value on the boundary as established by the grant itself.

Mr. Flynn: All of which, if the Court please, goes to the weight and reliability of the map and has nothing to do with its admissibility in evidence at this point.

Mr. Cass: We are trying to establish the boundaries of this land as it existed in 1888. That is the point of the grant that is before the Court. Maps which are in existence in the survey office and on their face show that they are not of the date that they purport to be, of 1886, but are compiled at some later date—I haven't examined the map carefully, but I think if you will look at it you will find there are notations up there up to 1900, and there is no way in the world anyone can tell about

(Testimony of H. E. Newton.)

that map, when it was compiled. Certainly it was never compiled in 1886.

The Court: As to those matters the applicant may examine the witness on cross examination. But as to its admissibility, the objection is overruled. Registered Map 1260 will be Territory's Exhibit 12 in evidence. [327]

* * * * *

(The document referred to was received in evidence as Territory's Exhibit No. 12.)

Q. (By Mr. Flynn): Mr. Newton, I show you this large map, bearing identification "Hawaiian Government Survey, Molokai, middle and west sections, M. D. Monsarrat, Surveyor; scale: 2,000 feet equals 1 inch;" and a worksheet likewise bearing stamp "M. D. Monsarrat, Surveyor, Honolulu, September 20, 1886, H. I." I will ask you whether you have seen this map before?

A. Yes, I have seen this map before.

Q. Did you examine or check or use this map in any way in performing the survey work as to the northern boundaries of Kahánui, Apana 3, to which you previously testified?

A. Yes, I consulted this map also.

Q. And is this a registered map, is this an official registered map in the records of the survey department of the Territory of Hawaii?

A. It is.

Mr. Flynn: I will offer this map in evidence.

Mr. Cass: What is the register number?

(Testimony of H. E. Newton.)

The Court: 1289.

Mr. Flynn: Yes, register number 1289; it is shown at the extreme left-hand end of the map. I offer this map under the same conditions as the other official maps, namely, that the photostat which we offer as the exhibit covers that portion of the map which has to do with the present controversy.

Mr. Cass: We object, if the Court please. The same objection as entered as to the other maps, and in addition [328] thereto, there is nothing on it to show that the map itself was ever prepared by Monsarrat.

The Court: The same ruling. Received in evidence as Territory's Exhibit 13, in evidence.

(The map referred to was received in evidence as Territory's Exhibit No. 13.)

Q. (By Mr. Flynn): Mr. Newton, I show you a large map bearing the following identification, "Hawaiian Government Survey, W. D. Alexander, Supt. Molokai. Middle and west sections. Map and survey by M. D. Monsarrat. Scale: 1/24,000 or 2,000 feet equals 1 inch. 1886. Being registered map No. 1288." I will ask you whether you have seen this map before?

A. Yes. I have consulted this map also.

Q. Did you consult or check this map in performing the survey work we have mentioned with regard to the northern boundaries of Kahanui, Apana 3?   A. Yes, sir.

(Testimony of H. E. Newton.)

Q. Is this an official registered map in the records of the survey department of the Territorial Government? A. Yes, sir, it is.

Mr. Flynn: I offer this map in the same manner as the other maps, that is to say, the photostatic copy.

Mr. Cass: Same objection.

Mr. Flynn: (Continuing with offer) ——of the exhibit will be substituted for the original.

The Court: Same ruling. It will be received in evidence as Territory's Exhibit 14.

(The document referred to was received in evidence as Territory's Exhibit 14.) [329]

Q. (By Mr. Flynn): Mr. Newton, I show you a large map bearing identification as follows: "Working sheet. Hawaiian Government Survey, W. D. Alexander, Supt. Molokai. Survey and map by M. D. Monsarrat, Surveyor. Scale: 1,000 feet equals 1 inch. Dated 1895 and bearing registered number 1890." I will ask you whether you have ever seen this map before?

A. Yes, I have also consulted this map.

Q. In the course of the work on the survey of the northern boundaries of Kahanui?

A. Yes, sir.

Q. Is this an official registered map in the office of the Territorial Survey Department?

A. It is.

Mr. Flynn: I offer this map in evidence in the

(Testimony of H. E. Newton.)

same way, that is to say, a photostat copy of the portions covering the area in litigation here will be furnished.

The Court: Any objection?

Mr. Cass: Same objection.

The Court: Same ruling. It will become Territory's Exhibit 15 in evidence.

(The document referred to was received in evidence as Territory's Exhibit No. 15.)

Q. (By Mr. Flynn): Mr. Newton, I show you a book bearing the title "Molokai Surveys, M. D. Monsarrat, Surveyor. 1885. Field Book 2, register number 359," and ask you whether you have ever seen this field book before?

A. Yes, I have consulted this field book.

Q. Did you consult this field book or any portions of it [330] in the course of your work in boundary surveying as to the northern boundary of Kahanui, Apana 3, on Molokai? A. Yes.

Mr. Flynn: I will offer as Territory's Exhibit for Identification these photostats, the first page or title page of which shows "Molokai Surveys, M. D. Monsarrat, Surveyor. Field Book 2. 1885. Register No. 359." [331]

✳ ✳ ✳ ✳ ✳

The Court: It is being offered solely for identification at this time. Let the field book be marked for identification only as Territory's Exhibit 16.

(Testimony of H. E. Newton.)

(The document referred to was received and marked Territory's Exhibit No. 16 for Identification.)

* * * * *

Q. (By Mr. Flynn): Mr. Newton, from your knowledge of the records of the Territorial Survey Department, can you state whether M. D. Monsarrat was a surveyor in the employ of the Hawaiian Government in 1885? A. He was.

Q. He was? A. Yes, sir.

Q. Can you state whether this field book No. 2 bearing register number 359 is an official record of the survey department of the Hawaiian Government and the Territory of Hawaii?

A. It is. [332]

Q. I will show you, Mr. Newton, a group of photostats, the first page bearing the title "Molokai Surveys, M. D. Monsarrat, Surveyor, Field Book 85, Register No. 359," and ask you whether these pages, which are excerpts from the original book, are ones which you consulted in the course of your survey work as to the northern boundaries of Apana 3, Kahanui, Island of Molokai?

A. Yes, they are.

Q. I will call your attention to various markings or underlinings in red pencil.

Mr. Cass: We have no objection to the underlining and markings.

Mr. Flynn: This is for identification. Thank you.

Q. (By Mr. Flynn): There being some of which

(Testimony of H. E. Newton.)

on each of the pages of these photostats, and ask you whether you know who made those markings and underlinings?

A. They were underlined by myself.

Q. They were underlined by yourself?

A. Yes.

Q. Were the marks on the sketches in red crayon or pencil also made by yourself?

A. Yes, sir, they were made by myself. [333]

* * * * *

Q. (By Mr. Flynn): For what purpose or purposes, Mr. Newton, did you make these underlinings and various markings in red pencil or crayon?

A. I was retracing Mr. Monsarrat's actual field work on this map. I found notes which he took at different stations and at different boundary points and at sights to monuments on the ground in several cases and to triangulation stations.

* * * * *

Mr. Flynn: I will now offer in evidence as an exhibit for the Territory the original Molokai surveys Field Book [334] No. 2, Register No. 359, now in the custody of the survey department as an official record of the Territorial Government, and ask leave at the same time to withdraw the original field book and substitute the photostated pages which the witness has identified. [335]

* * * * *

The Court: Where specifically, in the pages offered, is there reference to the disputed area?

Mr. Cass: Reference to Waihanau is to the upper

(Testimony of H. E. Newton.)

boundary of the other Kahanui and of the northern boundary of Kalamaula.

Mr. Flynn: Pages 109 and 110 bear date August 21, 1885, and show the occupation of station Kaohu by the surveyor Monsarrat, with shots to Kaluahauoni, to waterfall, to Kahanui, to Kalamauli, to Point X, to Kahanui and Kalamaula Y, to Ridge B, to Ridge C, to Dry Tree W. all identified or nearly all—I think all identified in previous testimony in this case as points within Kahanui, Apana 3, the identifications specifically including that of the applicant's surveyor's map and exhibit, on which he points out these locations.

The next pages are 111 and 112, which show Monsarrat occupied Point Y at the boundaries of Kahanui and Kalamaula [336] and took sights to Kauna Gulch, to Point X, at the boundary between Kahanui and Kalamaula, to Dry Tree W and to Point Ridge A. This pair of pages has for its second a number of penciled sketchings on which is shown Kahanui, readily identifiable as some of the lands herein involved, being identified by the Point Y shown on the applicant's map and also the Point Kaluahauoni, which is the triangulation station.

The next pages, 113 and 114, show the surveyor occupied Point Z at the boundary between Kalamaula and Kahanui and took shots to Ridge B and Ridge C, again both of which have been identified as being in the Kahanui, Apana 3 lands, and as to which the surveyor for the applicant made reference.

(Testimony of H. E. Newton.)

The next pages, 129 and 130, again show the Point Kauna Gulch at the boundaries, a three cornered boundary between Kalamaula, Kaunakakai and Kahanui, all sufficiently identified. This also shows Waikolu Gulch on the extreme easterly ends of land identified as Kahanui; it also shows Puu Kaeo, which is the beginning point of the description of Kahanui, Apana 3.

The next pages withdrawn from the field book and photostated are 131 and 132, showing that the surveyor occupied the triangulation station Puu Kaeo and took sights to boundary Point Y, at the boundaries of Kahanui and Kalamaula, boundary Point X and boundary Point Kauna Gulch.

Page 132 being pencil sketches showing Point Puu Kaeo and various boundary delineations.

Pages 133 and 134 showing occupation by the surveyor of station Kaluahauoni and the taking of shots to boundary Point X [337] between Kalamaula and Kahanui, boundary Point Y between Kalamaula and Kahanui, and Kauna Gulch, also to Ridge B, also to Ridge point or rather to boundary Point Z, also to point Ridge A, also to Point K. The second part of that, which is Page 134, likewise contains a pencil delineation of portions of Waihanau Valley, Waialeia Valley, with the identification of boundary Point Y, boundary Point Kauna Gulch, triangulation station Kaluahauoni, also Point K.

The last is pages 141 and 142, showing that the surveyor Monsarrat occupied station Kauna Gulch

(Testimony of H. E. Newton.)

and took sights to Point Ridge A, to Point Y on the boundary between Kalamaula and Kahanui and to Point K. This page 142 contains a sketch showing portions of the boundary, showing Point K, showing boundary Point Y between Kalamaula and Kahanui. [338]

* * * * *

Q. (By Mr. Flynn): Mr. Newton, you have previously testified that you examined a survey of Kahanui, Apana 3, by Mr. Monsarrat. Is that right?

A. Yes.

Q. Did you examine the field notes contained in registered field book No. 359 with relation to the survey of Apana 3, Kahanui, by Mr. Monsarrat?

A. I did.

Q. Did you find in the field notes contained in registered field book No. 359 notes which were identifiable as covering the survey of Apana 3, Kahanui, by M. D. Monsarrat? A. Yes.

Mr. Flynn: I now offer the photostats in evidence.

Mr. Cass: I ask the privilege of cross examining the witness on the points in question.

The Court: The request is granted.

Q. (By Mr. Cass): Mr. Newton, you have said that you have found evidence in this field book bearing upon the survey of Apana 3. Now, excluding the data of the south and westerly boundary, which is surveyed by traverse, will you tell what point you found in this book that was identified by Monsarrat as being points on the northerly and easterly

(Testimony of H. E. Newton.)

boundary which is in dispute, in his notes? [343]

* * * * *

A.   Now on page——

Q.   The pages are the same?

A.   Yes, they are the same. On page 109, from Kaohu station he sights to Kahanui, Kalamaula.

* * * * *   [344]

Q.   (By Mr. Cass): Will you point out where Monsarrat himself on those notes has stated that this point is a point in the boundary line of Kahanui 3, in the disputed boundary?

A.   Well, to go back a little further, he started with letters back and forth, in which they discovered this piece of Kahanui, which was shown to him by some kamaainas, and he was going to——

Q.   Just answer the question. The field book is the thing we are talking about.

A.   And he actually made the survey and he has marked it "Kahanui." "K. H." would stand for Kahanui, which was this piece of land he was surveying, Apana 3.

Q.   He wasn't surveying Kahanui. Where does it say he was?

A.   It says it right in here. He took sights to the waterfall and then he took sights to this Point X, which is on the boundary of Kahanui and Kalamaula. Those are the surveyor's field notes.

Q.   What boundary of Kalamaula?

A.   Kahanui and Kalamaula to an X.

Q.   That is the one? [345]   A.   Yes.

(Testimony of H. E. Newton.)

Q. That is not disputed. It is the undisputed boundary line.

A. I am fixing the boundary. Then he went to Y. Kahanui to Kalamaula Y.

Q. Yes. That is not the question. Show us where he has any points in there marked on the disputed boundary of Kahanui 3. I am not talking about this undisputed boundary down here, this X and Y here, but the boundary that you have run up here or the boundary that is laid down in the application. Where does he say that that survey pertains to that boundary?

A. After he got through making his survey——

Q. Where does he say it?

A. The description was written by Monsarrat.

Q. Where does he say it in his notes, that this is the boundary?

A. You cannot write a description when you are taking sights.

Q. He was not surveying the boundary there. Continue and find out where Monsarrat has said that that is the boundary.

A. Common sense. If he was running between two known lines, it is running the boundary.

Q. Show it. Where does it say so.

A. He took shots to this Y, which is on the boundary.

Q. It is not on the boundary. It is down here in Kalamaula.

A. That is what he says.

Q. Yes.

(Testimony of H. E. Newton.)

A.   That he is on that particular boundary. [346]

* * * * *

The Court: Now, Mr. Newton was under direct examination at the termination of the last session or was being examined relative to the mention or the offer of the field book by Mr. Cass, I believe, at the termination of the last session. Do you want to proceed with that phase now, Mr. Cass? [351]

Mr. Cass: The last question asked the witness was a request to him to indicate on the field book notes where any entry appears thereon that specifically refers to any point as being the boundary of Kahanui along the line now in dispute, and he was given overnight to look into the book.

H. E. NEWTON

a witness called by and on behalf of the Territory, having been previously sworn, resumed the stand and further testified as follows:

The Court: Now do you understand the tenor of the question?

The Witness: Yes.

Q.   (By Mr. Cass): Do you want to answer it?

A.   Mr. Monsarrat plotted these notes in the exhibit here on his work sheet and he showed the north boundary as running through—— [352]

* * * * *

Q.   (By the Court): Mr. Newton, the question is very direct and concise. Reading from the excerpt

(Testimony of H. E. Newton.)

which you now have in your hand, consisting of several pages of the field book, just read from that excerpt, without any explanation at this time.

A. It doesn't say definitely that it shows the boundaries of Kahanui outside of just the heading; the heading itself refers to the survey of the land of Kalamaula and Kahanui.

Q. The only definite statement is contained in the heading? A. Kahanui boundary mauka.

Q. Now, you may explain that statement just made in any respect you desire. [353]

* * * * *

A. I will start over again. This survey was made by Monsarrat in 1885 and it is in field book No. 359, recorded in the survey department. On page 111 of the field book. Monsarrat occupied Station Y on the boundary of Kalamaula and Kahanui and took shots to Puu Kaeo and azimuth 297 degrees 17 minutes, and took slope angles, 32 degrees 35 minutes, and then he took a sight to Kaulahuki, 310 degree 32 minutes 30 seconds [354] at an angle of 45 degrees 51 minutes 30 seconds, and he also took a sight to Puu Kaeo. I have already read that.

Mr. Cass: If the Court please, he is merely reading into the record that which has not been admitted. I object to reading into the record this document before it is admitted, and the word for word reading of these notes. Before these notes are admissible it must be proved that these are from the survey attached to the letter for the sale of the property, the survey by Monsarrat in 1886.

(Testimony of H. E. Newton.)

The Court: The objection is overruled at this time. The answer is merely by way of explanation to your preliminary examination on the admissibility of the field book. Proceed.

A. (Continuing): He took a sight to Kauna Gulch Point, 314 degrees 35 minutes 30 seconds and at an agle of 48 degrees 53 minutes 30 seconds. Took a sight to Kahanui and Kalamaula, 142 degrees 7 minutes, angle 237 degrees 25 minutes, to Dry Wood Tree W, 291 degrees 29 minutes, angle 286 degrees 47 minutes. To Point Ridge A, 253 degrees 32 minutes, angle 348 degrees 50 minutes. Then he went to a new station on the Kalamaula boundary, marked X.

Q. (By the Court): Mr. Newton, for the further clarification of all concerned, can you use this map here, or any other map that is now an exhibit here, and explain those as you go along? I do not think the mere reading of those surveys will be of much assistance to any of us.

A. The beginning point is Kaohu station, marked here.

The Court: Let the record show the witness is now making his designation on Territory's Exhibit 10.   A. Shall I start all over again? [355]

The Court: Without reading, if you want to refer to what you have in your hand, just point them out and designate them on Exhibit 10.

A. Most of the points are off this map. But I see a sight to Kaluahauoni, that point there, triangulation station, sighted a waterfall, 297 degrees

(Testimony of H. E. Newton.)

28 minutes. From Kaohu he sighted to a waterfall. He sighted to a point, Kahanui and Kalamaula boundary, Point X, which is this point here. Then he sighted again at boundary Point Y, at that point. Then he sighted on Ridge B. That is this point on the map. And to Ridge C, which is that point. Dry Tree W, this point. I do not see any point or sight to Ridge A. Now he moves his instrument to boundary Point Y, here, and sights to Kaluahauoni station and to Puu Kaeo, to Kaulahuki, and thence he takes a sight to Kauna Gulch, which is this point here, and to Kahanui-Kalamaula boundary X, which is this point, and to Dry Tree W on the ridge, which is this point, then to Point Ridge A, which is here. And now he moves to Kahanui-Kalamaula Point X, which is here, and sights to Kaohu, which is here, a back sight, to various stations. Thence Kahanui-Kalamaula boundary Point Y and then a sight to Z, which is down here. Then the same sights up to Dry Wood Tree W and to Ridge B, at the end of the ridge, and to Ridge C, in between. Thence to Kaluahauoni. And then he moves now to station Z and takes a sight to X, this point, and thence a sight to Puu Kaeo, also a triangulation station, also to triangulation station Kaluahauoni, and then a sight to a waterfall, and thence sights to Ridge B, then Ridge C, this ridge, and then he moved to Puu Kaeo, which is off the [356] board here, and sighted Point Y and X and Kauna Gulch, these three points on the boundary between Kahanui and Kalamaula. And he

(Testimony of H. E. Newton.)

went over to Kaluahauoni station and sighted to Point X on the boundary of Kalamaula and Kahanui; also a sight to Y, on the same boundary, and to Kauna Gulch on the same boundary, and sighted to Ridge B and to Point Z on the Kalamaula-Kahanui boundary, and then a sight to Point K on the Kalamaula-Kahanui boundary. Point K here. And then he goes to Kauna Gulch and thence sets up here and sights to Kaluahauoni, this azimuth, and then he sights on Point Ridge A and then Point Y on the Kalamaula-Kahanui boundary and then Point K, sights to Point K. And that is the end of it. * * * * * [357]

The Court: Mr. Flynn, do you want to proceed with your foundation on the field book?

Q. (By Mr. Flynn): Mr. Newton, you have stated that your surveying work was largely a retracing of the survey by M. D. Monsarrat, as to which you referred, both to his maps and to his field notes. Correct?   A. Yes, sir.

Q. You have marked on your maps Points X, K and A. I will withdraw that.

You have marked on your maps Points X, K and A. Have you found these same points on any existing maps by M. D. Monsarrat?

A. Yes. * * * * * [358]

Mr. Flynn: May we see Registered Map 1289?

The Court: Is that Exhibit 13?

Mr. Flynn: I am sorry. 1259, which is Exhibit 11.

The Court: Exhibit 11.

Mr. Flynn: I believe it would be preferable

(Testimony of H. E. Newton.)

to look at the original, even though it is on this exhibit.

Q. (By Mr. Flynn): Mr. Newton, I show you Registered Map No. 1259 and call your attention to the area marked "Kahanui, area 1048 acres," and ask you whether you find on there any of the symbols or letters you have previously pointed out on your map and referred to in the field notes?

A. Point X at the northwest corner of the land of Kahanui under Grant 3437 to Meyer and Point Y, which is on the boundary between Kalamaula and Kahanui, and Kauna Point which is the boundary of Kalamaula and Kahanui and also at the corner of Kaunakakai. Those are the three points I referred to. And also to Point K, which was sighted by Monsarrat on the upper edge of the pali of the Waihanau Gulch, above the top edge of the pali. Thence Point A on the top of the ridge, which is also on the north boundary of Kahanui and a point of beginning of the second grant to Mr. Meyer. That is as far as I went.

Q. (By the Court): What boundaries of Kahanui have you just referred to now, with reference to northeast, south or west?

A. Point A, which is on the north boundary.

Q. North?   A. North, yes, Kahanui.

Mr. Flynn: And Point K is on what boundary, Mr. Newton?

A. Point K on Monsarrat's map is on the north boundary [359] of Kahanui.

The Court: Proceed.

(Testimony of H. E. Newton.)

Q. (By Mr. Flynn): Mr. Newton, you have examined the map accompanying the grant, have you not, namely, Grant 3437?   A. Yes, sir.

Q. You have also examined the map accompanying Grant 3539?   A. I have.

Q. Can you state whether you have checked the map of Grant 3437 against the portion of the map marked "Kahanui" now before you?

A. I have.

Q. Do you find Grant 3437 map to correspond to the map or rather to Kahanui Grant 3437 as shown on this 1886 map of Monsarrat?

A. It does. I have compared them.

Q. You have stated, Mr. Newton, that you have examined much of the work of M. D. Monsarrat?

A. Yes.

Q. You have examined much of his writing?

A. Yes. I know his handwriting.

Q. Can you state whether these points he referred to as Y, X, K and A are in the handwriting of M. D. Monsarrat?

A. Yes, they are all Monsarrat's. [360]
* * * * *

Q. (By Mr. Flynn): Mr. Newton, I will ask you to look at Registered Map 1289.

The Court: That is Exhibit 13 of the Territory.

Q. (Continuing): Which is M. D. Monsarrat's map, work sheet of 1886, on a scale of 2,000 feet to the inch, and I will ask you to look at the portion of it shown within the boundaries of Kahanui, Apana 3, 1048 acres. From an examination of this map and from an examination of the map accom-

(Testimony of H. E. Newton.)

panying the grant incorporated into Grant 3437, can you state whether the map on the grant corresponds to Kahanui as shown on this map?

Mr. Cass: If the Court please, we object to the question. We object to the use of the two maps until it is shown whether or not the sketch on the map was taken from the grant or the sketch from the grant was taken from the map. If they do compare it is just possible that the sketch on the map is taken from the grant sketch, without survey.

Mr. Flynn: That is up to proof by him.

The Court: Let counsel finish his objection.

Mr. Cass: There is no evidence in here as to when these marks were made on the map. The witness testified it was a progressive map. [361]

* * * * *

Mr. Flynn: If the Court please, I wish to challenge that statement by counsel as to what the witness testified to as a progressive map. I believe if the record were to be examined it would be found to be only a statement by counsel. He has not been asked that question.

* * * * *

The Court: Do you want that testimony to be read?

Mr. Flynn: I would be willing to defer checking that testimony until counsel finishes his objection. We may be able to proceed without it. If not, we will then ask the testimony be rechecked. [362]

* * * * *

(The question was read by the reporter.)

(Testimony of H. E. Newton.)

Mr. Cass: My objection is that there is no probative value unless it is shown that the sketch on the grant was taken from the map, and not the map sketch was entered from the grant or from some other sketch.

The Court: For the record, Mr. Flynn, what is the relevancy?

Mr. Flynn: The only logical and sound inference is that this map of 1886 shows Kahanui to be substantially identical in proportion and scale to the map accompanying the grant. That is the minutely explicit evidence, that the map in the grant was based on this map.

The Court: The objection is overruled. Proceed.

Q. (By Mr. Flynn): I will ask you, Mr. Newton, whether upon examination you can state whether Kahanui, Apana 3, 1048 acres, as shown on this work sheet of M. D. Monsarrat, of 1886, corresponds to the map accompanying Grant 3437?

A. Offhand, I would say it does, without having the grant itself.

Q. Just a minute. Let me offer you the grant to examine, which is Exhibit B, I believe.

A. They are practically the same.

Q. All right. Now, I will ask you to examine Registered Map 1288.

The Court: Exhibit 14.

Q. (By Mr. Flynn): Being a map of 1886 by M. D. Monsarrat, on a scale of 2,000 feet to the inch, and ask you once again to examine the map accompanying the grant, and the showing on this

(Testimony of H. E. Newton.)

map being "Kahanui 1048 acres in Apana 3," and ask [363] you if they correspond?

A. The boundaries correspond.

Q. The boundaries do correspond?

A. Yes.

Q. I will ask you specifically about the correspondence, if any, of the boundaries at the western end of the northern boundary, and ask you whether they do correspond, and by "western end" I am referring specifically to points shown on your map as Points X to A?   A. Yes, they do.

Q. I will ask you, from your work on this survey problem, including all of the work you did, all of the maps and documents you have examined and upon which you have based your conclusions, I will ask you whether you can express an opinion, I will ask you if you can express an opinion as to whether the map accompanying Grant 3437 and incorporated into that grant was based upon or taken directly from the two maps of 1886 of M. D. Monsarrat that you have just examined?

A. Yes, they were taken from Mr. Monsarrat's map, his survey and map both.

Q. In your own survey work on this boundary problem, you stated you were retracing the footsteps of the original surveyor Mr. Monsarrat. Isn't that right?   A. Yes.

Q. In doing so, did you refer to the various points in his field book 359 you read off a while ago?   A. I did.

Q. Did you find from your own examination

(Testimony of H. E. Newton.)

that those points checked with the maps of Monsarrat you have examined? [364]

A. Yes. I found his marker points there; I checked on those and also located the edge of the pali, the top edge of the pali along the top edge of Waihanau Valley.

Mr. Flynn: I offer the field notes in evidence, your Honor.

The Court: The field notes have been offered, Mr. Cass. Any objection?

Mr. Cass: I have stated by objection to the field notes. And the further objection that this grant was made upon a survey of Monsarrat attached to the grant and that there has been no evidence that this is a field book or field notes of that survey. In fact, the letters accompanying or about the same date, of Monsarrat to Alexander, show that he was then engaged in an official survey of different lands and that the survey in question had nothing to do with the boundary now in dispute.

The Court: Objection overruled. Field Book No. 2 of Mr. Monsarrat will become Territory's Exhibit 16 in evidence.

(The document referred to was received in evidence as Territory's Exhibit No. 16.)

The Court: Are you going to arrange those for the purpose of an exhibit, Mr. Flynn, the photos?

Mr. Flynn: Yes. If the Court please, I will ask leave to withdraw the field book itself and substi-

(Testimony of H. E. Newton.)

tute the pages as the Territory's exhibit inasmuch as the pages include the only material on which the field book will be referred to.

The Court: Any objection, Mr. Cass?

Mr. Cass: No objection.

The Court: Let the substitution be made. [365]

* * * * *

Q. (By Mr. Flynn): Mr. Newton, referring to your map, which is Territory's Exhibit 10, I will call your attention to the red markings "waterfall," and you have up above the Roman numeral (I), further on and just directly above, mauka, of that point you have a mark for "waterfall" and II, a third waterfall slightly farther above, marked III. Did you take sights to this first waterfall from any position?   A. Yes, I did.

Q. From where?

A. From Kaohu triangulation station and from Point Z and [366] Point X.

Q. Were any of those same sights taken by Monsarrat; and you may refer to the field notes if you wish.

A. Yes. He took a sight to a waterfall to boundary Point X.

Q. Just to the waterfall. Did you find such?

A. Yes.

Q. From what point?

A. From Kaohu triangulation station to waterfall, bearing azimuth of 297 degrees 28 minutes.

Q. Did you find whether that bearing checked with your own bearing on the ground?

(Testimony of H. E. Newton.)

A. Yes.

Q. Does it check?

A. It checks on the ground.

Q. I note numbers here at the first waterfall, just makai of the red, marked 2005, just makai of the first marker 2117. Are those your bearings?

A. Yes. That is the elevation that I observed.

Q. Those were the elevations you observed?

A. Yes.

Q. You made the elevation measurements?

A. Yes.

Q. Is that likewise the case as to the third waterfall, where you have a number 2210?   A. Yes.

Q. I am sorry. That is the second waterfall, No. 2210?   A. Yes. .

Q. The third waterfall, No. 2272?

A. Yes, sir. Those are my elevations. [367]

Q. All the way up there?   A. Yes.

Q. You show a fourth waterfall several hundred feet above the third and the identifying marker IV, the elevation 2309, and similarly a fifth one still going makai?

A. Yes. Those are all mine.

Q. With the V. Continuing on up to IX above —I will withdraw that—IX and far on up to X. Did you go up the entire area from Waterfall No. 1 to Waterfall No. 10 along the course of the stream?

A. I did.

Q. Will you describe the general topography on your way from Waterfall No. 1 to Waterfall No. 9? I refer to that number because I think it is shown

(Testimony of H. E. Newton.)

to be slightly mauka of the boundary as drawn or as shown by this map, and therefore into the undisputed or upper portions of Kahanui, Apana 3, if the Court please.

A. I did not quite get the question.

Q. I ask you to describe the general topography are you traveled from Waterfall No. 1 to Waterfall No. 9.

A. These three waterfalls, 1, 2, 3, are very high and impassable. The falls up above there are not so high. There are some good swimming pools there. Between Pool 5 and Pool 8 the stream takes an "S" bend and there is a ridge coming down from the westerly side down to the pool, which I believe is Waiau Pool, and another ridge which comes down from the peak on this spur ridge between Kalawao and Makanalua there, comes down the ridge, runs right down to the stream so that the two ridges cross each other on either side of the [368] stream. This is all enclosed in. You cannot see beyond this point. You don't get a clear view because it is shut off by those two ridges coming down together, crossing each other. And above that the stream begins to branch out and it is not one stream from there on, after you pass that boundary.

Q. Approximately below Waiau is there a single stream?

A. Yes. This is a single stream below the Waiau Falls.

Q. Now, Mr. Newton, did you also go along the

(Testimony of H. E. Newton.)

top of the pali from points or through points beginning at X and through K? Did you personally go along there?

A. Yes. I located the edge of the top of the pali all the way through. I took in all the little angles and from my line there I passed through Point K, which Monsarrat showed in his field notes, and over to a spur ridge running down towards the stream and crossing the stream about the top of the Waiau Pool there and thence up the ridge on the easterly side of the stream, up to Monsarrat's Point A on the top of the peak, on the top of the ridge there, and this point is on the mauka boundary of Grant 3437, and it is also the initial point or point of beginning of Grant 3539. Then it continues all along the top of the ridge to Waihanau and to Kaluahauoni triangulation station.

Q. You stated, Mr. Newton, as you come up the stream and as you approach the area you have referred to as where the two ridges appear to overlap or where the two ridges do overlap, one from the west and one from the east, the appearance is one of closing off of the valley.

A. Yes, you get that impression. [369]

* * * * *

Q. (By Mr. Flynn): Mr. Newton, I was referring to your testimony of a few minutes ago, that as you walked up the stream and reached the point you have shown to be the vicinity of Waiau Falls you found a closing off appearance in topography. I am asking you what you find as you are on the top

(Testimony of H. E. Newton.)

of the ridge, walking along from Point K to the point marked "pipe"?

Mr. Cass: We object. The witness was asked whether it appeared to be closed off. Counsel is assuming that the witness answered. That question was not allowed. There is no such evidence here that the witness said that it appeared to be closed off. We will admit that there is a different appearance in the valley there that you can see at that place. If that is the answer to it. But I cannot see how that is material unless it is proven that Monsarrat saw it.

The Court: Objection overruled on that ground.

* * * * * [371]

A. I think I answered that. I followed the top of the pali and thence down a spur ridge running in an easterly direction and crossing the stream at Waiau Falls, thence up another spur ridge on the east side, which takes you right up to the point, to a peak at the Point A of Monsarrat, on top of the ridge. And that I know, from where I have seen the ground, that gives you the idea that this portion is one valley, it gives you the impression that this is the head of a valley.

Mr. Cass: If the Court please, we object to the impressions and move that the witness' statement of his impressions be stricken.

The Court: The last part of the answer, as to his impression, will be stricken.

Mr. Flynn: If the Court please, I do not to belabor this, but that description is sufficient to show

(Testimony of H. E. Newton.)

what the witness found on the ground. It is not a matter that is determined by his use of the word "impression." It is all a portion of the descriptive language of what his findings were.

The Court: The last part of the answer was unqualifiedly the use of the words "give the impression." That is the [372] matter at issue here on this witness' testimony. The ruling will stand.

Proceed.

Mr. Flynn: I will note an exception, if the Court please.

The Court: An exception may be noted.

Q. (By Mr. Flynn): Now, I will ask you, Mr. Newton, whether any of the other falls along this stream and above or mauka of the falls 3 are impassable?

A. Some would be passable if you went right through the fall but most of them you can cut a trail or something around, clear to the top.

Q. I believe you stated that the falls in the vicinity of Waiau are the biggest along the stream after the first three falls. Is that correct?

A. Yes.

Q. And what is the elevation of that falls?

A. That falls is 22 feet.

Q. 22 feet high?   A. Yes.

* * * * * [373]

Q. (By Mr. Flynn): I call your attention, Mr. Newton, to Applicant's Exhibit A, which is a map previously identified as having been made by Mr. McKeague. I now call your attention to the red

(Testimony of H. E. Newton.)

printing on this map showing "M. D. M's Point X." Does that correspond to where you placed Point X on your map?   A.   It does.

Q.   I will show you where, in red printing, there is the mark "K". Does that correspond to where you placed Monsarrat's Point K on your map?

A.   Just about the same place.

Q.   Similarly, as to M. D. M's Y?   A.   Yes.

Q.   And M. D. M's Ridge A?   A.   Yes.

Q.   Now, I will ask you to take a blue pencil, Mr. Newton, and draw on this map, Applicant's Exhibit A, the line or [374] approximate line of the northern boundary of Grant 3437 to R. W. Meyer as shown by your survey.

Mr. Cass: If the Court please, we object to his marking the map with anything as shown by his survey. If he wants to show on the map where the ancient government monuments are there, all right, but he has not so far identified in his own survey any boundary line at all. He has identified an overlay of government maps but his boundary line is not—he cannot fix a boundary line. All he can do is trace the steps of the other surveyor. And if he wants to mark up there where his ground line follows the government survey, as such a line we have no objection, but not as testimony that they are lines of boundary.

The Court: The question of boundary is your ultimate determination. These matters are not of very much probative value. I don't think there is any objection to the relevancy or materiality of it.

(Testimony of H. E. Newton.)

Are there any marks or symbols on there in green or rather blue?

Mr. Flynn: There is one area in blue.

The Court: Use a green pencil then. The objection is overruled.

The Witness: Do what now? Mark out the Monsarrat line? Please read the question.

(The question was read by the reporter.)

The Court: Hand the witness a rule if he needs it.

The Witness: No, I don't need it.

(The witness did as requested in the question.)

Q. (By Mr. Flynn): That is enough. I was only asking for the area that was in between Ridge Point A and Point X. [375]

Mr. Flynn: Now, let me see some of these Territory's exhibits, from 11 to 15, beginning with 11.

Q. (By Mr. Flynn): I will show you, Mr. Newton, Territory's Exhibit 11, being working sheet of M. D. Monsarrat map, 1886, on which is shown Grant 3437 to Meyer, Kahanui, area 1048 acres. I will correct that latter statement. On which is shown Kahanui, area 1048 acres, and in the writing below "Apana 3," and ask you whether the northern boundary of Kahanui, Apana 3, as shown on this map corresponds in any way to the boundary between Points X and A as you have now drawn them on this map, which is Applicant's Exhibit A?

* * * * *

(Testimony of H. E. Newton.)

A. They do. Very close.

Q. Now, I will show you Territory's Exhibit 12, which is a map and survey by M. D. Monsarrat, 1886, and ask you to make the same comparison between Kahanui, Apana 3, as shown on this map, insofar as it concerns the western end of the [376] northern boundary of Kahanui, Apana 3, and in comparing it with that boundary line you have drawn in green pencil on Applicant's Exhibit A, ask you whether the boundaries correspond?

A. Yes, they compare very closely with Monsarrat's work sheet.

Q. Very well. I will similarly show you Territory's Exhibit 13, which is Hawaiian Government Survey, Molokai, middle section, by M. D. Monsarrat, Surveyor, Scale: 2,000 feet to 1 inch, working sheet, again showing you on this 1886 map Kahanui, Apana 3, 1048 acres, and call your attention to the western section of the northern boundary of Kahanui, Apana 3, and ask you to compare the same with the green line you have drawn on Applicant's Exhibit A, and ask you whether those boundary lines correspond?

A. Yes, they do; they correspond very closely.

Q. I will similarly show you Territory's Exhibit 14, map and survey by M. D. Monsarrat, Scale: 2,000 feet to the inch, 1886, showing Kahanui, Apana 3, 1048 acres, and ask you whether as shown on this map the western end of the northern boundary of Kahanui, Apana 3, corresponds to the

(Testimony of H. E. Newton.)

green line you have drawn on Applicant's Exhibit A?

A. It does; it corresponds to the line I have drawn on my map.

Q. To the line you have drawn in green pencil?

A. In green pencil on Exhibit A of the applicant.

Q. I will show you Territory's Exhibit 15, working sheet, Hawaiian Government Survey, survey map by M. D. Monsarrat, Surveyor, Scale: 1,000 feet equals 1 inch, 1895, and ask [377] you to examine on this map the area shown as Kahanui, Grant 3437, Meyer, and ask you to compare this map with Applicant's Exhibit A and specifically comparing the boundary line at the north boundary, the western end of the north boundary, as you have shown it in green pencil, and ask you whether that corresponds to this map which is Territory's Exhibit 15?

* * * * *

Q. (By Mr. Flynn): In retracing Mr. Monsarrat's work, where did you find his northern boundary of Kahanui, Apana 3, as compared with where you have placed the northern boundary of Kahanui, Apana 3?   A. Practically the same.

Q. Practically the same?   A. Yes.

Q. What point or points did you find in Mr. Monsarrat's work to correspond to points that you have checked yourself along [378] the northern boundary of Kahanui, Apana 3?

A. Beginning at the northwest corner there, at

(Testimony of H. E. Newton.)

Point X, and following along the top edge of the gulch and passing through K and thence continuing on the top of the pali, in a southerly direction, and thence running down a spur ridge to the east and crossing the stream at about the south bend there, and up a spur ridge on the east side of the stream, right up to Monsarrat's Point A, the peak at the top of the ridge overlooking Kalawao, thence continuing along the top edge of the ridge and around the head of Waialeia Valley to Kaluahauoni station. That is just the northerly boundary.

Q. In that last answer, Mr. Newton, you have referred to your map, which is Territory's Exhibit 10, have you not?   A. Yes.

* * * * * [379]

Q. (By Mr. Flynn): Mr. Newton, you have stated that you have located the northern boundaries of Kahanui, Apana 3?   A. Yes.

Q. What lands adjoin the northern boundary of Kahanui, Apana 3, between points as shown on your map, Exhibit 10, Points X and A?

A. Starting from the Point X on the Kalamaula-Kahanui boundary, the northern boundary of Grant 3437 runs along the top edge of the pali along Waihanau Valley.

Q. And Waihanau Valley is in what lands, if you know?

A. Waihanau Valley is in the land of Makanalua.. * * * * * [380]

Q. (By Mr. Flynn): Is any part of the Waihanau Valley in the land of Kahanui?   A. No.

(Testimony of H. E. Newton.)

Q. I show you, Mr. Newton, Territory's Exhibit 11, the 1,000 foot to the inch working sheet of Monsarrat, dated 1886, and call your attention to Kahanui, Apana 3, and ask [381] you whether the words "Waihanau Valley" appear on this map?

A. It does.

Q. I will ask you to examine this map and state if you can tell where the boundaries of Waihanu Valley are with relation to the southern or mauka end of that valley?

Mr. Cass: We object to the witness stating where the boundary of the valley is unless it is so delineated on the map.

Mr. Flynn: I am referring to the delineation, if any, on the map.

The Court: Objection overruled.

A. Makanalua?

Q. (By Mr. Flynn): Waihanau Valley.

A. Waihanau Valley. Waihanau Valley starts quite a ways down below Kaohu triangulation station and the boundary runs up along the top edge of the pali and over or to this X, Monsarrat's Point X, at the northwest corner of Kahanui and Makanalua, thence follows along the top edge of the pali, passing through Point K, according to this map, and through the word "Waiau" and up to Point A, thence following along around the head of Waialeia——

Q. No. My question was only as to Waihanau Valley.

A. Oh. Waihanau Valley. Just up to Point A at

(Testimony of H. E. Newton.)

the top of the ridge, the north boundary of Kahanui.

* * * * * [382]

Q. (By Mr. Flynn): I will show you Territory's Exhibit 13, Mr. Newton, which is the work sheet of M. D. Monsarrat, surveyor, scale of 2,000 feet to the inch, and call your attention to where the words "Waihanau Valley" appear and ask you whether any portion of the southern boundary of Waihanau Valley, where it joins what appears to be the northern boundary of Kahanui, Apana 3, is shown on this map?

A. The valley seems to stop at the northern boundary of the land af Kahanui.

Q. As shown on this map?

A. As shown on this map.

Q. I will show you, Mr. Newton, Territory's Exhibit 12, which is a map and survey of M. D. Monsarrat, 1886, and point out to you that this map contains the words "Waihanau Valley" and also "Kahanui, area 1048 acres, Apana 3", and ask you whether Waihanau Valley as shown thereon, or rather ask you if you can state where the southern boundaries of Waihanau Valley are shown on this map?

A. The photostat shows the boundary running along the northern boundary, it stops at the northern boundary of the land of Kahanui.

Q. Examining this map, Mr. Newton, can you locate approximately the point of the waterfall

(Testimony of H. E. Newton.)

shown on your own map as Waterfall I, your own map being Territory's Exhibit 10?

A. Yes, I can. [383]

Q. Can you mark it in red pencil, please?

(Witness does as requested.)

The Court: For the record, what symbol or writing is inserted?

Mr. Cass: Red?

Mr. Flynn: It is just a blot at this point. May I insert the figure 1, No. 1? It is difficult to tell with this pencil.

* * * * * [384]

Mr. Flynn: I had just asked the witness to locate and mark the approximate point of the Waterfall I, as shown on his own map, which is Territory's Exhibit 10. We had just made some markings in red pencil. I will ask leave, which I am sure won't be disputed, if I will make the marking in blue ink where the witness had been.

The Court: Indicating the waterfall.

Mr. Flynn: Indicating Waterfall No. I.

The Court: Very well.

Q. Calling your attention, Mr. Newton, to the scale of this map, which is 1,000 feet to the inch, ask you to estimate the distance from the waterfall, as you have marked it there, from Waterfall No. I to the extreme southerly or mauka end of Waihanau Valley?   A. About 3,000 feet.

Q. To what point did you show that marking, as relating to your own map, Territory's Exhibit 10?

A. From the Waterfall No. I up to Point A;

(Testimony of H. E. Newton.)

the peak on the top of the ridge overlooking Waialeia Valley.

Q. Can you locate the approximate point, Waiau, on this map, Territory's Exhibit 12, from close to the point that you have just marked?

A. The point Waiau—No, no, I take it back. Are you referring now to the approximate location of Waiau?

Q. Yes. I have marked this with a circle in blue ink. I will write the words "Waiau,"—I will ask you to give the approximate distance from the waterfall to the circle marked on this map, Territory's Exhibit 12, calling your attention to the waterfall marked with a cross, the other being marked I, to indicate the—— [385]

A. Nearly 2,000 feet.

Q. Now, Mr. Newton, I will show you Territory's Exhibit 15, photostat of the working sheet, survey map of M. D. Monsarrat, scaled 1,000 feet equals one inch, dated 1895, and again call your attention to the lands we have already discussed, one show Kahanui, 3437 Meyer, the other showing Waihanau Valley itself, also showing the point previously referred to as Waiau, ask if you can locate on this map the approximate location of the same Falls, No. I, as shown on your map, Territory's Exhibit 10?

A. Approximately through the second letter "a," —approximately through the second letter "a" in the word "Waihanau."

(Testimony of H. E. Newton.)

Q. The second letter "a" being the "a" following the letter "h" in the word "Waihanau?"

A. Yes.

* * * * *

Q. I ask you, Mr. Newton, whether any portion of the words "Waihanau Valley" are written or printed in this map at a [386] point or points above the location of Falls No. I, as you have placed it on there?

A. The word "Valley" is entirely above the Waterfall No. I.

Q. Are not the letters "nau," the last letters of "Waihanau" also entirely above Waterfall No. I?

A. Yes. That is my recollection. It takes in the letters "nau" and "Valley."

Q. And by "above" you mean mauka, or southerly, of the Falls, do you not?

A. Mauka or southerly, they are both the same.

Q. Now, Mr. Newton, we have previously referred to a survey, rather the description of Makanalua, which is Territory's Exhibit 9, in which you stated you referred to, in the course of your surveying work on this boundary question, and I call your attention to the following portion of the description by Pease, reading as follows: "following always a stone wall separating this land from the land called Pohakuloa, thence South 12° East 15 chains, and thence to the top of the mountain ridge called Hoolae, thence following along the top of this Pali bounding Makanalua gulch or ravine on its easterly side, to a certain mountain peak at

(Testimony of H. E. Newton.)

the head of said ravine called Kaulahuki." I will call your attention to the latter portion of this description, on the second page thereof, reading as follows: "To the foot of the mountain ridge called Ililika, thence to the top of Ililika, and from thence following along the top of the Pali bounding Makanalua gulch or ravine on the West, to a certain mountain peak at the head of said gulch called Kaulahuki," did you draw any,—did you form any opinion from your examination of all of these materials that have been placed in evidence and which you [387] discussed as being the basis for your own work as to the location of the mountain peak called Kaulahuki?

Mr. Cass: We object to the opinion of the witness.

The Court: Objection overruled.

A. I have.

Q. Can you show on your own map, which is Territory's Exhibit 10, where, on your own map, Kaulahuki, as set forth in Pease's description, Territory's Exhibit 9, is located?

A. It is marked Ridge Point "A," which is on the North boundary of Grant 3437 Meyer, and the initial point of Grant 3539 to Meyer. It is the peak on the top of the ridge overlooking Waialeia Valley.

Q. Now, I will ask you the same question, Mr. Newton, with reference to the map which is Applicant's Exhibit "A," and ask if you can state

(Testimony of H. E. Newton.)

where on that map Kaulahuki, as shown in the description of Pease, is located?

A. This hill (witness indicating). There was some evidence that it was 3.40 acres. Otherwise I will have to identify it by these arrows here pointing to the space on the top of the ridge and marked "Portion of Grant 3539 to R. W. Meyer."

Q. Looking at this map, Exhibit "A", is that area, or any portion marked in the M. D. Monsarrat's survey as Ridge "A"?

A. Yes, it is marked on the map here "M. D. Monsarrat Ridge A."

Q. Now, what did you do to ascertain the location of Kaulahuki, Mr. Newton, what did you refer to, what material did you refer to, what did you find on the ground?

A. I referred to Pease's survey of the Land of Makanalua, and also took a photograph,—had one done by my assistant, who was working with me. Took a picture of that Valley [388] looking up Waihanau Valley from a point near Kaohu Station. There is a picture which shows a peak on the ridge overlooking the Waialeia Valley.

Q. I show you this photograph, Mr. Newton, and ask you if you can identify it?

A. Yes, this is the picture that we took——

Q. Just a minute. You say this is a picture that you took, or that was taken?

A. Of the waterfalls in the Waihanau Valley. That was the idea of taking the picture, to take a

(Testimony of H. E. Newton.)

picture of the waterfall, but we got the background also.

Mr. Flynn: I will show this to Mr. Cass, if the Court please.

Mr. Cass. This is offered for identification?

Mr. Flynn: I offer it in evidence.

Mr. Cass: No objection.

The Court: It becomes Territory's Exhibit 17 in evidence.

(The photograph above referred to was received in evidence and marked Territory's Exhibit 17.)

Q. Now, Mr. Newton, I will ask you to examine this photograph, and ask you whether you can locate on it the waterfall you have referred to as Waterfall Roman numeral I on your own map, Territory's Exhibit 10?   A. Yes, I can.

Q. Can you point to it please?

A. (Witness indicates.)

Q. Can you mark it in a small circle with ink?

A. (Witness does so.)

Q. Can you look at this photograph, Mr. Newton, and locate [389] on it the point you have referred to as Pease's Kaulahuki?   A. I can.

Q. Will you point it out, please?

A. Yes. (Witness indicating.)

Q. Will you encircle that point with pen?

A. (Witness does so.)

Q. Now, Mr. Newton, you have stated that this

(Testimony of H. E. Newton.)

view as shown in this photograph is familiar to you?   A. Yes.

Q. You have referred to this peak shown in the photograph as Kaulahuki, can you state whether or not there are other peaks from this view, at the point where this picture was taken?

A. No peaks, no prominent peaks.

Mr. Flynn: If the Court please, if counsel has no objection I will write in "waterfall" at one point and "Kaulahuki" at the other.

Mr. Cass: No objection.

Q. Mr. Newton, you have also stated that you also examined Pease's Map of Makanalua?

A. I have.

Q. From an examination of that map, and examination of the description by Pease, can you state whether Kaulahuki, shown on that map, corresponds to the point Kaulahuki as you have marked it on this photograph?

A. I didn't show any Kaulahuki there, but the site I can identify as Kaulahuki——

Q. I am referring to Pease's map?

A. On Pease's map, oh, yes.

Q. Mr. Newton, I will ask you to refer to your own map [390] again, Territory's Exhibit 10, and ask you if you can state what the points are on that map, shown to be marked in green pencil?

A. Those were black points which Mr. Monsarrat put on the top edge of the ridge, and he took observations for his survey down in the Leper Settlement.

(Testimony of H. E. Newton.)

Q. Do you know when, or approximately when, he was making the survey down in the Leper Settlement?

A. I have really forgotten the exact date, around 1890 somewhere,—probably 1895.

* * * * *

Q. How were they plotted on there, if you know?

* * * * *

A. These points were observed by Monsarrat, which we studied from his survey in the lower section, and on different sections he would intersect these at the edge, at the Pali of the ridge.

Q. How, or from what source do you know that those points were made by Mr. Monsarrat, Mr. Newton? [391]

A. I will follow it through in his field books,—field notes.

* * * * *

The Court: They become Territory's Exhibit 18 for Identification.

(The documents referred to were received and marked Territory's Exhibit 18 for Identification.)

* * * * *   [392]

Mr. Flynn: I now offer as Territory's Exhibit 18-A for Identification, a pack of photostats, the title, "Molokai Survey, M. D. Monsarrat, Surveyor, Field Book 8, Register No. 365," bearing date 1894, and ask that they be marked for identification.

(Testimony of H. E. Newton.)

The Court: They may be marked Territory's Exhibit 18-A for Identification.

(Documents referred to were marked Territory's Exhibit 18-A for Identification.)

* * * * *

Q. Can you state, Mr. Newton, whether the points marked in green pencil on your map, Territory's Exhibit 10, are based upon data contained in Territory's Exhibits 18 and 18-A for Identification?   A. Yes.

Q. Are they?   A. Yes.

* * * * *   [393]

Q. (By Mr. Flynn): Mr. Newton, I show you a cardboard type envelope, bound with a pink string or ribbon, entitled, "Document No. 1369, Grant 3437, description by R. W. Meyer, Kahanui, Molokai. Letter from J. F. Brown, re above 11/28/05. Tracing enclosed," and I will ask you to examine them and say whether you recognize them?

A. Yes, I have seen these before.

Q. I will ask you, Mr. Newton, whether these are from the files and records of the survey department of the Territory?

A. Yes, they are filed with the records of the survey department.

Q. The identification at this time of the envelope, Document 1369, is that an identifying number of the survey department [397] records?

A. It is. * * * * *

Q. (By Mr. Flynn): I believe you stated, Mr.

(Testimony of H. E. Newton.)

Newton, that you were acquainted with J. F. Brown during his lifetime?   A. Yes, I was.

* * * * *

Q. Do you happen to know whether prior to the time Mr. Brown was in the land department he had been with the survey office? [398]

A. Yes; he was a surveyor.

Q. Have you had occasion in the past to refer to Mr. Brown's work or any portions of his work?

A. Yes, I have.

Q. Have you examined any of his writings or specifically his signature?

A. Yes, I know his signature.

Q. I will ask you if on the first page of the papers accompanying this envelope marked "Document 1369" you can identify the signature at the bottom of that page?

A. Yes. That is signed by J. F. Brown himself.

Q. I will ask you if on the third page of those pages included in this envelope you can recognize the signature at the bottom of the page?

A. Yes, I do; that is Brown's signature.

Q. This is the same J. F. Brown who, according to the records now exhibits in this case, drew the map and description for Grant 3539, is it not?

A. Yes, that is right. The spur ridge.

* * * * *

Q. And Mr. J. F. Brown is dead now, is he not?

A. Yes, he is dead.

* * * * *

(Testimony of H. E. Newton.)

Mr. Flynn: I offer the photostats in evidence as [399] Territory's Exhibit 19.

* * * * *

(The documents referred to were received in evidence as Territory's Exhibit 19.)

* * * * *

Q. Mr. Newton, do you speak or understand the Hawaiian [402] language?   A. I do.

Q. Do you speak it and understand it both?

A. Well, I can speak it fairly well; I can understand it a little better.

Q. You can understand it a little better. Do you know the meaning of the term "Kaulahuki"?

A. Yes, I do.

Q. Will you state to the Court what the meaning of that term is?

A. "Kaulahuki" means to pull with a string or rope, like in a tug-of-war perhaps.

Q. Like in a tug-of-war?

A. Something like that. It could be in a tug-of-war game, for instance. It could be two sides pulling. That would be Kaulahuki. But generally it means to pull with a string or rope.

Q. From your knowledge of Hawaiian, has it been used as referring to the type of situation where there is a pulling of the rope from the two ends, as against a middle area of it, such as a tug-of-war?

A. After seeing the applicant's map here, I think that just about fits the case.

Q. Will you point that out, please?

(Testimony of H. E. Newton.)

A. Generally they have a small mound in between the two teams, on either side, and this would be that mound, that is in the middle. And we have two very narrow ridges and one can barely walk here and across there.

Q. Pointing to Applicant's Exhibit A, Mr. Newton, will you [403] identify those points more specifically?

A. The peak itself would be identified on Applicant's map as a portion of Grant 3539 to R. W. Meyer. The highest point naturally would be the peak. Some narrow ridges would be the space between the middle point and the two teams that are on either side; one team would be this R. W. Meyer piece, being a portion of 3437, and the other team would represent Grant 3539 to R. W. Meyer. You have to have in a tug-of-war game a team on either side with a mound in the middle, and the space in between the two teams, and you pull one way or the other to win. I believe that is where they got the name "Kaulahuki" itself.

Q. From one of the points in Field Book No. 359, which is Territory's Exhibit 16, I believe, you made reference to a point referred to by Monsarrat as "Kaulahuki." I will ask you to find that in this field book, or rather these photostats, and I will also ask you to examine the original map No. 1259. The photostat will be good enough. Have you located that, the mention of that point in the field notes, Mr. Newton? A. Yes, in several places.

Q. Now, I will ask you to examine Territory's

(Testimony of H. E. Newton.)
Exhibit 11 and ascertain whether you can locate
the point "Kaulahuki" as shown on this map and
ascertain whether it is correlated to the one shown
in the field notes?

A. Kaulahuki as referred to in Monsarrat's
field book is the name of a triangulation station
which Monsarrat used in his survey.

Q. And this triangulation station named Kaulahuki is where with relation to Kahanui, Apana
3? [404]

A. It is pretty nearly on the south boundary of
Kahanui, Apana 3, and it is south of Grant 3437
to R. W. Meyer.

Q. And this map being 1,000 feet to the inch,
will you estimate how far south it is of the nearest
boundary of Kahanui, Apana 3?

A. About 4,000 feet.

Q. About 4,000 feet?

A. Yes. South of the south boundary.

Q. From your study of all these various maps
and these field notes, Mr. Newton, does that Kaulahuki triangulation station point have any relation to the Kaulahuki you have previously referred
to as used by Pease?   A. None whatever.

Q. None whatever. Now, while I have before us
Territory's Exhibit 11, the 1,000-foot to the inch
working sheet of M. D. Monsarrat, 1886, I will call
your attention to the area at the north boundary of
Kahanui, Apana 3, and ask you, Mr. Newton, what
the line markings are, for example, beginning at
the point you have previously identified as Point

(Testimony of H. E. Newton.)

X? Just a minute. I am sorry. The original map is still better. The lines I am referring to are pencil lines. I will ask you what they are intended to describe or represent?

A. They are what you call hachure lines which are drawn on a curve along the edge of the steep incline to show the difference between the level land and the beginning of a slope, such as going down into the stream. The hachuring was put on the side where the slope is.

Q. I will ask you whether on this map, which is Registered Map No. 1259, those hachure lines show a pali beginning at [405] Point X, following through Point K, following through Waiau and up to Point A?

A. The hachuring begins at X and runs to Point K; there is a ridge that runs down to Waiau. It is colored in on the boundary of Kahanui.

Q. Kahanui, Apana 3?

A. Apana 3. That is going through Point A. Then some more hachuring lines, which shows the top edge of the Waialeia Valley.

Q. That is as far as I have asked you about at this point, Mr. Newton.

May I look at Registered Map 1890?

Now, if you will look at Registered Map 1890. I am showing you Registered Map 1890, which is Territory's Exhibit No. 15, Mr. Newton. I will ask you whether this contains hachuring marks similar to those on Territory's Exhibit 11, which is Registered Map 1259, at the points on the northern

(Testimony of H. E. Newton.)

boundary of Kahanui shown as X and K?

A.   It does.

Q.   Does this map also contain hachuring marks in the neighborhood or coming from Ridge 3539, Grant 3539, Kahanui?

A.   Yes, the hachuring lines are on the westerly side of Grant 3539 all the way and also around into Waialeia Valley; it shows hachuring lines and the top is flat. The land itself seems to be flat land.

Q.   Are those hachure marks also referred to by surveyors as smudge lines, Mr. Newton?

A.   Smudge lines, yes, in a way, but they run differently; instead of lines or a group of lines they have kind of circles, [406] circles showing the different slopes.

Q.   Look at your own map, which is Territory's Exhibit 10. I call your attention to the lines immediately adjacent to Points X and K and I will ask you whether those are properly referred to as smudge lines?

A.   Yes, sir, those are smudge lines.

Q.   And those are to indicate what?

A.   To indicate the slope from the higher elevation down towards the stream.

Q.   Is the purpose of those smudge lines similar to the hachure marks we have just referred to on the two old maps by Monsarrat?

A.   Yes, the same thing.

* * * * *

Q.   Did you examine Pease's map of the Ahupuaa of Makanalua and consider it in relationship

(Testimony of H. E. Newton.)

with existing maps of M. D. Monsarrat, which maps are now in evidence in this case? A. Yes.

Q. And ascertain the relationship of the point "Kaulahuki" on Pease's map, if it has any relationship, to the waterfall [407] point marked on your map, Territory's Exhibit 10, as "Waterfall I"?

A. Well, the description made by Pease——

Q. I am referring to the map only at this point.

A. Oh, the map. The upper section of the land——

Q. Of Pease's map?

A. ——of Pease's map was just sketched in up to a peak at the head of Waihanau Valley, and it came back on the other side.

Q. Which is the other side?

A. On the other side of the—on the westerly boundary of Makanalua, by metes and bounds up to Ililika, I believe the point is, on the upper slope of Makanalua Valley, and then it was a general description, "Thence around the edge of the pali to this high peak called Kaulahuki."

Q. Did Pease, both from the easterly and westerly sides of Makanalua, refer to this peak as Kaulahuki? A. Yes. [408]

* * * * *

Q. What I have in mind, once more, Mr. Newton, as far as the map is concerned, realizing that it is only sketched in mauka or south of points Hoalae and Ililika, can you state from your examination of that sketching in whether the point on

(Testimony of H. E. Newton.)

that map at the top called Kaulahuki on the map is below or above the Waterfall I as shown on your map, Territory's Exhibit 10?

A. It is above that, from my map.

Q. It is above that?

A. It is above that, yes.

Q. I show you, Mr. Newton, Territory's Exhibit 8, which is a certified copy of the description of Grant 3539 to R. W. Meyer from the original papers of that grant in the files in the office of the commissioner of public lands of Hawaii, and ask you whether you have examined this photostat or the original of it in the course of your survey work on this boundary problem?

A. This is a description made by J. F. Brown.

Q. I have asked you if you have examined it before?   A. Yes, I have examined it.

Q. I call your attention to the following wording: "That [409] tract of land lying on the top of the ridge between Waihanau and Waialeia Valleys and bounded by the upper edge of the palis of these valleys, the center line of this ridge point described as follows."

I will ask you to go to the blackboard and upon Applicant's Exhibit A, the map, point out the beginning point as shown on this description, if you can do so.

A. The initial point of Grant 3539 is on the north boundary of Grant 3437 to R. W. Meyer, so that we have a point and a boundary line, and that point is also tied up to Kaohu triangulation sta-

(Testimony of H. E. Newton.)

tion given on the map to the initial point, which is a fixed point. It is tied into the triangulation system.

Q. What is the name or designation of that fixed point as shown on Applicant's Exhibit A?

A. The courses are not numbered.

Q. Examine the blueprint.

A. Yes. Except the end of course 24 which is described in the applicant's description, or the beginning of course No. 25. It is the end of course 24 and the beginning of course 25.

Q. Will you state whether that point is identified now on Applicant's Exhibit A?

A. That particular point?

Q. Yes.

A. It is written in there on the map, M. D. M's Ridge A.

Q. And is that or can you state whether that coincides or is identical with the beginning point in the courses given in this description of Grant 3539, Territory's Exhibit 8?

A. Yes, it would be identical. [410]

Q. Yes. Now, reading that description from its beginning point, the beginning of the first course, to the conclusion of it, is any portion of Waihanau Valley included in the lands conveyed by that Grant 3539?

A. Not in the grant. Of course, it may be a narrow strip on the top there. They may be entitled to a strip of land along the top ridge itself to where the pali starts.

(Testimony of H. E. Newton.)

Q. Examine this map, Applicant's Exhibit A. Would that strip of land at the top, which you have referred to as the top ridge, include any portion of Waihanau Valley?

A. Well, it would not include any up to the pali itself, the top of the pali.

* * * * *

Q. (By Mr. Flynn): I will call your attention, Mr. Newton, to the map accompanying and forming a part of the description by J. F. Brown, entitled, "Description of portion of the Government land, Kahanui, Molokai," being Territory's Exhibit 8, and ask you whether you find any definition of the edge of pali on that land—in that map? [411]

A. Yes. It is written right on the face of the map, on both sides, on the easterly side and on the westerly side of the ridge, the spur itself.

Q. I will ask you to trace now the definition of "edge of the pali" from the north to the south, that is, from makai to mauka, and ask you to state where or to what point the line designating the edge of the pali terminates?

A. The edge of the pali on the westerly side terminates at the edge of the Waihanau Valley and on the easterly side of the grant it terminates at the westerly edge of Waialeia Valley and extends up as far as the north boundary of Grant 3437.

Q. Now, from an examination of the map accompanying or a part of Territory's Exhibit 8, can you state whether the point you have just shown as the mauka or southerly termination of that ridge

(Testimony of H. E. Newton.)

of land is identical with the point shown on Applicant's Exhibit A as "M. D. M's Ridge A"?

A. Yes, it is the same point.

Q., That is what I am asking you.

A. Yes, that is the same point. M. D. M's Ridge Point A.

Q. Mr. Newton, examining further this map accompanying and forming a part of Territory's Exhibit 8, is the southerly or mauka boundary of Waihanau Valley clearly defined? A. Yes.

Q. Will you state where that southerly or mauka boundary of Waihanau Valley is with relation to the line you have previously drawn in green pencil on Applicant's Exhibit A?

A. That line is on the northerly boundary of Grant 3437. It is determined by M. D. Monsarrat practically on the line [412] I have determined by my survey.

Q. I will ask you this, then. Is there a substantial correspondence or identity between the southern or mauka boundary of Waihanau Valley, as shown on the map in Territory's Exhibit 8, with the line you have drawn in green on Applicant's map, Exhibit A?

A. It would be one and the same line.

* * * * *

Q. (By Mr. Flynn): Now, Mr. Newton, please, we had prior to the recess been examining Territory's Exhibit 8, being the description and the map of Grant 3539 of J. F. Brown, description and map by J. F. Brown, and I was just calling your at-

(Testimony of H. E. Newton.)

tention to the Applicant's Exhibit B, which is a photostat of the original grant issued to R. W. Meyer. I will ask you now whether the southern or mauka boundary of Waihanau Valley as shown on Territory's Exhibit 8 compares or corresponds with the southern or mauka boundary of Waihanau Valley as shown on Applicant's Exhibit B?

A.   The section above Waihanau Valley corresponds with the sketched plan and Grant 3437.

Q.   From examining them in this manner can you tell whether they correspond closely or roughly or how?

A.   They seem to be drawn to the same scale, 2,000 feet to the inch.

Q.   Would you like to hold the one map much more closely to the next one? Now will you answer that question as to [413] whether they correspond closely or roughly, or how?

A.   I would say closely. They correspond closely.

Q.   Now I will show you Territory's Exhibit 11, where it shows Kahanui Apana 3 and also where it shows Waihanau Valley, and I will ask you to examine that and then examine the map accompanying the grant, which is Exhibit B, and state whether the southern or mauka boundary of Waihanau Valley as shown on the map, which is Territory's Exhibit 11, compares with that southern boundary of Waihanau Valley as shown on Applicant's Exhibit B, compares or corresponds?

A.   They seem to be alike, only they are drawn

(Testimony of H. E. Newton.)

on a different scale, one is slightly larger than the other.

Q. Now, I will show you Territory's Exhibit 12, which is the map and survey by M. D. Monsarrat of 1886, and call your attention to the southern boundary of Waihanau Valley on that map and ask you how it compares or corresponds with the southern boundary of Waihanau Valley as shown on the map which is part of Grant 3437, Exhibit B of the applicant?

A. They seem to correspond with each other; as I say, only one is a little larger scale than the other.

Q. Yes. Now, I will show you Territory's Exhibit 13, which is the working sheet of M. D. Monsarrat, surveyor, at a scale of 2,000 feet to the inch, showing the stamped date with Monsarrat's stamp, September 20, 1886, and call your attention to the southern boundary of Waihanau Valley as shown on this map, Exhibit 13 for the Territory, and ask you whether that southern boundary corresponds to the southern boundary of Waihanau Valley as shown on Applicant's Exhibit B, Grant 3437, the map connected therewith? [414]

A. They seem to correspond with each other.

Q. Can you state whether the seeming correspondence is close or approximate or rough?

A. As close as you can scale it. Very close, I would say.

Q. Now, I will show you Territory's Exhibit 14, which is the map and survey by M. D. Monsarrat bearing date 1886, on a scale of 2,000 feet to the

(Testimony of H. E. Newton.)

inch, and call your attention to the southern boundary of Waihanau Valley. And we will have to get the original map once again to examine this properly. And I will ask you whether the southern boundary of Waihanau Valley shown on the map, which is Territory's Exhibit 14, compares with the southern boundary of Waihanau Valley as shown on the map incorporated in Grant 3437, which is Applicant's Exhibit B?

A. They seem to correspond with each other.

Q. Is the seeming correspondence approximate or rough or close?

A. Close. They are both on the same scale and they seem to be identical.

* * * * *   [415]

Q. (By Mr. Flynn): Mr. Newton, will you step up to this board, please? I show you Applicant's Exhibit M, which is a blueprint of the Land Court map and description filed with the application, and call your attention to Grant 3437 to R. W. Meyer, Kahanui 3. Now, you have stated that you have examined this grant before and that you have also examined Grant 3539 and that you have examined many of the letters between the parties at the time when the issuance of the grants and many of the documents on record in your own survey department of the Territory concerning these grants. I will ask you to draw in red pencil on this blueprint the northern boundary of Kahanui 3 where it joins the southern boundary of Waihanau Valley, if you can do so from your examination of this blueprint?

(Testimony of H. E. Newton.)

A. Kahanui is in two parts here.

Q. Yes, but first I am asking you to draw the——

A. Described in Grant 3437?

Q. Yes.   A. It begins at——

Q. I ask you only for the northern boundary, which is the southern boundary of Waihanau Valley.

> (Witness draws boundary between Waihanau Valley and Kahanui 3.) [423]

Q. (By Mr. Flynn): Now, from the way you have indicated the boundary between Waihanau Valley and Kahanui 3, Mr. Newton, it appears that Grant 3539 joins Kahanui 3 at only one point, which we have previously referred to as Point 1 and which is referred to or demonstrated on this blueprint map, Exhibit M, by the word "pipe" just under the circled number 24. Is that correct?

A. Yes, that is correct.

Q. From your examination of this grant——

Mr. Cass: If the Court please, may I interrupt? If the Court please, I am not objecting to the marking of these maps. It has been done before in the other maps, and of course this is all opinion testimony of this witness, it is not factual in any way, but I am not objecting to the marking of the maps, according to his opinion, and agree to have the opinion before the Court for what it is worth.

The Court: Proceed.

Q. (By Mr. Flynn): I was referring, Mr. Newton, to your knowledge of these grants from an

(Testimony of H. E. Newton.)

examination of them and various letters and documents pertaining to them and including your own survey work to determine the boundary between Kahanui 3 and Waihanau Valley. I will now ask you whether Grant 3539 to R. W. Meyer is on a portion or any portion of Grant 3437?

A. No. Not at all. No.

Q. I will call your attention to the wording in the area shown on this map, Applicant's Exhibit M, within the ridge boundaries of Grant 3539 to R. W. Meyer, the words to which I will call your attention are "Grant 3437." Is it correct [424] to place those words "Grant 3437" within the same area shown to be Grant 3539?

A. No. The Grant 3539 is only on the spur ridge and does not include any portion of Grant 3437.

Q. Grant 3539 was a wholly separate grant, Mr. Newton?   A. Yes, sir.

* * * * *

Q. (By Mr. Flynn): Calling your attention, Mr. Newton, to your own map, which is Territory's Exhibit 10, I will ask you what was your purpose in plotting the points marked with a green pencil on the spur ridge Grant 3539?

A. Those were points on the edge of the ridge which Monsarrat had located from his survey of Kalaupapa there and he had flags at these different points along the edge of the ridge, which he sighted on from stations below. [425]

Q. And from field books 7 and 8 of Monsarrat you have made those plottings, have you not?

(Testimony of H. E. Newton.)

A. Yes.

* * * * *

Q. (By Mr. Flynn): Yes. Mr. Newton, if you will step over here now, I will show you Territory's Exhibit 15, which is the working sheet of M. D. Monsarrat, surveyor, scale 1,000 feet to the inch, 1895, and calling your attention to the area marked "Waihanau Valley" immediately to the north of the word "Waiau" shown here to be on the northern boundary of Waihanau, Grant 3437 to Meyer, this being dated 1895, can you state whether the field note work of Monsarrat shown by books 7 and 8 bearing dates 1894 and 1895 appear to have been incorporated into this map? A. Yes.

Q. And will you state whether the extreme mauka or southern boundary of Waihanau Valley, where it joins Kahanui, Grant 3437, was in 1895 placed by Monsarrat substantially where it was shown in the other maps done in 1886? [426]

A. Yes.

Q. Mr. Newton, I will show you Territory's Exhibit 3 for Identification, which contains a tracing marked "Kahanui 1048 acres" all in pencil, on which some lines have been superimposed in blue and in red pencil, and ask you whether the tracing itself was made by you or under your direction in the survey department?

A. Yes; I remember that.

Q. May I see Exhibit B, please? I will lay the tracing over the map incorporated in Grant 3437,

(Testimony of H. E. Newton.)

and ask you if this tracing appears to be one of this map in the grant?

A. The pencil line agrees with the map itself, with the sketch plan.

Mr. Flynn: May I see Territory's Exhibit 11 and 12, please? And 13 and 14, Mr. Clerk, please.

Q. (By Mr. Flynn): I will show you Territory's Exhibit 13, Mr. Newton, which is a working sheet map by M. D. Monsarrat, surveyor, on a scale of 2,000 feet to the inch, bearing stamp date 1886, and holding the tracing over that portion of this map, which is Territory's Exhibit 13, and I will ask you if the boundaries shown on the tracing correspond to those on the map?

A. They do.

Q. Between points known to you as X and A, is the correspondence close or precise?

A. It is very close.

Q. Is it substantially identical?

A. Yes, sir.

Q. Very well. Now, I will follow the same step with [427] regard to Territory's Exhibit 14, which is the map and survey by M. D. Monsarrat, scale of 2,000 feet to the inch, bearing date 1886, and ask you whether the boundaries shown in the tracing correspond to those of Kahanui Apana 3 as shown on the map?

A. The map does not show the entire grant itself, but what is shown on the photostat is fairly consistent.

Q. Between points we have previously referred

(Testimony of H. E. Newton.)

to as X and A, is the correspondence very close or precise? A. Practically precise.

Mr. Flynn: Thank you; I will offer Exhibit 3 for Identification in evidence.

* * * * *

The Court: Let the tracing become Territory's Exhibit 3 in evidence.

(The tracing referred to was received in evidence as Territory's Exhibit 3.)

Mr. Flynn: I offer Territory's Exhibit No. 4, the photostat reduction of the map of Mr. Mc-Keague, which is Applicant's Exhibit M, and which map Applicant's Exhibit M is a blueprint.

* * * * * [428]

The Court: It will become Territory's Exhibit 4 in evidence.

(The photostat reduction of map, referred to above, was received in evidence as Territory's Exhibit 4.)

* * * * *

Q. (By Mr. Flynn): Mr. Newton, I will show you Territory's Exhibits 5-A, B, and C, for Identification, and ask you whether you have previously examined these photographs? A. Yes, I have.

Q. I will ask you whether you can identify them or state what lands they cover? This is A, this is B, this is C.

A. These photographs of the spur ridge, which

(Testimony of H. E. Newton.)

are parts of Kahanui lands, the lands of Kahanui which are covered by Grant 3437 and 3539.

Q. Does Waihanau Valley area show in any of these pictures? A. Yes. [429]

Q. You can identify it in the second picture, which is Territory's Exhibit 5-B for Identification?

A. Yes, I can see the ridge and stream. I know it is about where that is on the map.

Q. Can you see any ridges we have referred to as transverse or overlapping ridges? A. Yes.

Mr. Flynn: I will offer these as Territory's Exhibits 5-A, B, and C.

Mr. Cass: No objection.

The Court: They will become Territory's Exhibits 5-A, 5-B, and 5-C, the three photostats mounted on plastic, reading left to right, A, B, and C, respectively, in evidence.

(The three photographs mounted on plastic were received in evidence as Territory's Exhibits 5-A, 5-B, and 5-C.)

* * * * *   [430]

Mr. Flynn: I have here a photostat reduction of the map of which Applicant's Exhibit M is a blueprint, this reduction being to a scale of 2,000 feet to the inch, the previous one—or rather to a scale of 1,000 feet to the inch, the previous one having been 2,000 feet to the inch. I will show it to counsel.

Mr. Cass: We have no objection to its admission.

(Testimony of H. E. Newton.)

The Court: It will become Territory's Exhibit 20 in evidence.

(The document referred to was received in evidence as Territory's Exhibit 20.)

Q. (By Mr. Flynn): Mr. Newton, examining the Applicant's Exhibit B, which is Grant 3437, I call your attention to the map incorporated in this grant and will ask you if you can locate in the area of the map the approximate location of the Big Fall which has previously been referred to as Waihanau Falls and also as Kaulahuki?

A. It is just below the north boundary of this grant. It would be about where the letter "e" in the word "Valley", I believe.

Q. The letter "y" of the word "valley" then would be mauka or southerly of the Waihanau Falls, is that correct?

A. Very close to the "e" in the "valley"; right in that vicinity there.

* * * * *   [432]

Cross-Examination

Q. (By Mr. Cass): Mr. Newton, the Applicant's Exhibit A, now on the board up there, contains a number of lines and other symbols which appear on other maps. Are these lines and symbols lines on which part of the technical description of boundaries and so forth—I refer to this line here of a dash and two dots—is that the technical way of denoting a surveyed boundary?

(Testimony of H. E. Newton.)

A.   Yes, that is.

Q.   Then I take it wherever that line appears on this map there is some evidence somewhere of an actual survey on the ground, or it is supposed to be so indicated?

A.   Well, if they are running out of a boundary that would indicate what it meant.

* * * * *   [433]

Q.   Now, these dotted lines here, apparently between stations, are for showing directions?

A.   You mean the dash-dotted line?

Q.   No. Just the little dots.

A.   The dotted line shows a direct line between two points.

Q.   It is not intended as a boundary line?

A.   No, not the boundary line. The dash and two dots represent the boundary line.

* * * * *

Q.   In taking Monsarrat's survey of 1885, this boundary here then, I take it, you have checked to determine whether or not these monuments, distances and directions are the same as appear in that survey notebook? I am speaking now of this southerly boundary and the—southerly and the westerly boundary, the bottom lines.

A.   I don't know whether that is absolutely correct, but these are the courses that are given in the grant itself.

Q.   And those courses are taken from what?

A.   By Monsarrat, the description of Kahanui.

Q.   Have you got any survey book of Monsar-

(Testimony of H. E. Newton.)

rat's at or about the time of this grant that shows a different survey or a separate survey made by him of this southerly line—these bottom lines?

* * * * * [434]

A. Not necessarily. It may be on the boundary, on hills or other vantage points.

Q. At a station it is customary to put some sort of monument, either a flag or some other object, to relocate the station, is it not? [435]

A. Yes.

Q. Now, the next column is "Object," and the object is what you sight. Do the objects you sight at necessarily imply that they are on a boundary?

A. No.

Q. Are those objects marked with a flag station always or might they be any natural object that could be picked up from an instrument?

A. It all depends on what you are actually doing. It may be just some object the station, or for some work they would probably flag the points that they want to locate.

Q. This is my impression. Correct me if I am wrong. That when the surveyor sets up his instrument at a station he takes a sight to various objects, first for the purpose of relocating that station in the event that is necessary, and second for the purpose of triangulating objects which may be used later in the survey to locate the entire line over which he is going, or for some other purpose. Is that right?

(Testimony of H. E. Newton.)

A. Well, while he is doing that, that is what he would do.

Q. Every time he would set up he would shoot permanent objects, monuments if possible, from which some surveyor if going back to those objects or monuments could shoot back and locate reasonably accurately the position of that station on the ground?

A. Yes. That is why they have these triangulation stations. Somewhere to start from.

Q. The next column is headed—I cannot make out exactly what that is; apparently it is an A——

A. "Az". for azimuth. [436]

Q. Azimuth. That is the reading taken from the instrument at the station of each object named, is it not?   A. Yes.

Q. "Dist." in the next column means distance?

A. Distance.

Q. That is not necessarily filled in?

A. Of course, if you are sighting at flags, they may be distant points, but the close points are generally taped by a rod that is used.

Q. The next is "Angle." What is the angle?

A. The actual angle that you obtain by sighting at one point and then to the second point. You can get that angle in between the two points.

* * * * *   [437]

Mr. Cass: Admittedly, this has nothing at all to do with the maps in issue up here, and I am using these pages purposely so that the general explanation may not be warped or biased either by. myself

(Testimony of H. E. Newton.)

or anyone else in regards to that opinion testimony.

* * * * *

Q. And that page is cross-lined and contains a sketch. Where would that sketch be from?

A. Well, it is just a flat sketch; he sketches as he goes along with his work. [439]

Q. Whatever he thought, made at the time, to identify his work, he would sketch in at that time?

A. That would be a guide when he made his map, to kind of picture the area.

Q. And it would be the guide when he made his map?   A. Yes.

Q. These triangles with dotted lines are what?

A. Triangulation stations.

Q. Here is an entry "Rock S"; that would be a description on a map?

A. No, no; it is just a point, a sub-station.

* * * * *

Q. Some of these points are triangles with a dot in. What does that mean?

A. Triangulation station.

Q. And the circle with a dot means what?

A. Generally a sub-station.

Q. Each one of these points, or with very few exceptions, is followed by either a triangle or a dot or a circle with a dot, some of them followed by a circle and a dot. Would that be something marked on the ground by him or something simply picked up and sighted to?

A. Both. If he puts in no station there he can occupy, he puts in his own station, probably a

(Testimony of H. E. Newton.)

spike or a wooden peg or something, or a cross on rock or something.

* * * * *   [440]

Q. Now, on page 16 of this book is a sketch showing pencil lines drawn in. What does the solid pencil line mean; is it a boundary line?

A. The lines drawn in between these two stations, and when they do that they are getting a base line; this sketch shows he was trying to get a point across a gulch, using these two bases to figure out his distance to the point on the other side of the gulch.

Q. The dotted lines mean merely sights?

A. Sights to the station on the opposite side of the gulch.

Q But the solid lines mean the accurately measured distance?   A. Yes, for a base.

Q. For a base between two stations?

A. Yes.

Q. On page 14 is a straight line between stations, with apparently five stations indicated. Taking the survey itself and the data on this side, would you say that those straight [441] lines indicate a boundary?

A. Oh, it doesn't say. If he was running a boundary line he would probably have the name of the land. Generally he used simply the dash and two dots for a boundary line.

Q. Did he in his book ever put the dash and two dots on the boundary lines?

A. I don't know.

(Testimony of H. E. Newton.)

Q. On page 48 are straight lines. Apparently from stations. This is the seacoast, as I understand it? A. Yes.

Q. Marked "sea"? A. Yes.

Q. Stations on the seacoast or near the seacoast have straight lines running up with Kamiloloa, Government, or konahiki? A. Konahiki, yes.

Q. Kamiloloa Government and Paakea. Do those lines represent the division or boundary lines between those parcels?

A. Yes. It shows that he showed the adjoining lands and these lines in between are the boundary lines.

* * * * *

Q. (By Mr. Cass): Now, referring again to Exhibit A.

* * * * * [442]

Mr. Flynn: May I ask that the record show that the map, the source of all this discussion, is Applicant's Exhibit A?

The Court: Proceed.

Q. (By Mr. Cass): That is my understanding of these marks on this map and any surveyor would interpret them that way.

A. Well, that was the idea.

* * * * * [443]

Q. In determining the edge of a pali in surveying, will it be likely that two surveyors, one working from the top of the pali and traversing what he conceived to be the edge, would make the same boundary of the land as one working from the bot-

(Testimony of H. E. Newton.)

tom of, say, a thousand foot pali and looking up?

A. Generally in a country like that, where land is fifty cents an acre, they generally take just a few shots along the top edge of the pali or flag and cut in.

Q. But if the pali drops off sharply and slopes less sharply back several hundred feet, the man on top might take the edge of the pali where it was less sharp and the man working below would take where there was an abrupt drop, isn't that right, according to what he could see?

A. It is up to the surveyor doing the work.

* * * * *   [445]

Q. (By Mr. Cass): Now, this map, referring to Registered Map No. 1259, Exhibit 11, which is labeled "Working sheet, W. D. Alexander, superintendent; M. D. Monsarrat, dated September 17, 1886" on the face of the map, this map contains the lands of Kalawao, Palaau, Naiwa, Kahanui, Kalamaula, Kaunakakai, Pupukeo, and Kamiloloa, together with other lands. Can you say whether or not all these lands on this map were surveyed in 1886 or 1885?

A. The map is dated 1886 and the field book may be a little earlier.

Q. The field book may be earlier?   A. Yes.

Q. This is only part of Molokai, the center section, apparently, and it contains—do you know whether or not this is the first map or sketch that portrays Kahanui 3, later granted as Grant 3437?

A. I am not sure whether that is the first map

(Testimony of H. E. Newton.)

or not. It cannot be very far off. It may be No. 2,
I don't know.

Q. Now, inviting your attention to the southerly
and westerly boundaries of Kahanui 3, as it appears
on this map, that boundary is marked with a dash
and two dots. What does that indicate?

A. That is simply for the boundary line.

Q. All right. Now, is that simply for a surveyor's boundary line?

A. Well, the boundary line. Sometimes they are
not even surveyed, the boundary lines.

Q. Do you know who actually did the draftsman's work on this map? [446]

A. The working sheet is generally, on a job like
this it takes months and sometimes years, a couple
of years, and the drafting work is done right where
you are doing your work. It is a progressive map.
You do your field work and then you come back and
probably take a week or so off and fill in your field
notes and go out again when it is good days for the
field work, and on the rainy days you stay in and
do your office work.

Q. That is the general custom?   A. Yes.

Q. But as to this particular map, do you know
whether Monsarrat came back from Molokai and
entered the surveys of these various lands himself
by drafting them on the land?

A. Yes. Those are Monsarrat's printing.

Q. That is his printing. Is the "land of Kahanui" his printing?   A. It could be.

(Testimony of H. E. Newton.)

Q. Is the word "Grant 3437 Meyer" his printing?

A. No. That came later, after the grant was issued.

Q. But that is not Monsarrat's printing, no matter when it was put on there?   A. No.

Q. The word "Waialeia" out here apparently covers an old erasure on the map. Is that printing Monsarrat's printing? It is different letters than the rest of it?   A. I believe it is.

Q. The word "Waikolu Valley" up here, is that Monsarrat's?   A. I believe so.

Q. Can you tell me any other lands that are on this map [447] where the name of the land is in lower case letters and set in by Monsarrat?

A. I don't get that question.

Q. These are all capital letters, "Kamiloloa Government, Kaunakakai, Kalamaula, Kahanui." Those are all in capitals. Can you tell me why the words "Waialeia Valley, Waihanau Valley, Waikolu Valley" appear in small letters, that is, lower case letters?

A. These are the names of the lands, the ahupuaa or ili, while these are merely the gulches.

Q. Now, I invite your attention to the northern boundary of Kahanui 3, as it appears on this map. There is no dash and two dot lines of that boundary. What does that indicate?

A. This colored line here indicates the limits of Grant 3437 to Meyer in Kahanui, Apana 3.

Q. And what does the lack of the dash and two

(Testimony of H. E. Newton.)

dots on that boundary indicate; that it was not yet surveyed finally?

A. Probably he hadn't written the description; the grant was made later, after the map had been completed.

Q. Was made after the map was completed?

A. I believe the grant was later.

* * * * * [448]

Q. But this was put in without a dot and dash line sometime after this particular map was made?

A. Yes. He had to have something to base the boundary line on and that was his determination of the boundary of Kahanui Apana 3.

Q. And you say you have no knowledge of any survey that Mr. Monsarrat may have then made except the survey he made when he was determining this boundary marked with dots and dashes on the south and west line of this?

A. The correspondence shows that there was a lele in there that was not surveyed and they wanted him to make the survey.

Q. Do you know whether that has any indication that he was ever on the ground to make the survey?

A. He actually—his field notes show where he took actual sights to all points.

Q. That is his field notes of the survey of this lower line here. I am speaking about this undotted smudge line that runs on the northern and westerly boundary of this land. Is there anything in the field

(Testimony of H. E. Newton.)

notes that shows he ever was on the land in connection with that?

A. He had a habit of putting flags——

Q. I am speaking about——

A. That is what he said; he was setting flags with his kamaainas on a different part of that land, and he had found and discovered there was a piece up in here, and he was taking some Hawaiian kamaainas up to show them the piece.

* * * * *   [449]

Q. That is the first letter to Alexander. His having discovered a piece of land lying on the edge of the valley, part of the Ahupuaa of Kahanui. May 27, 1885. This has nothing to do with it. The next letter, I believe.

Mr. Flynn: July 31.

Mr. Cass: That has to do with the survey of lower Kahanui. Now, here is the letter of July 17, 1885.

Q. (By Mr. Cass): I invite your attention to the underlined portion of this. "Yesterday I was mauka of Meyer's with kamaainas on the boundary of Ilole." Where is Ilole? Indicate on the map the area of Ilole, Kahanui, and Kalamaula. Kalamula is over here.

"I had to go to Pukoo to get a kamaaina."

Pukoo is a way off and practically across the country straight across from Kahanui, is it not?

A. About half way over to Halawa. That would be about the east end of the island, about in the middle of the island.

(Testimony of H. E. Newton.)

Q. "And yesterday the kamaainas showed me a piece of Kahanui a way mauka, on the edge of the palis." Now, in the letter of July 31, 1885 to Alexander, and, by the way, these letters are all in the Archives or from the records of the Government, are they not? A. Yes.

Q. Reading. "I enclose a rough sketch of the lands that I am now working on so as to give you a little idea of the way they are mixed up."

Have you got that sketch?

A. I don't remember. What sketch do you mean?

Q. The one mentioned there. A rough sketch of the land he was working on. Probably it is down here.

And further in the letter: "I show on the sketch the piece of Kahanui that I spoke to you about. It is part of the land belonging to government and konohiki, but the konohiki portion has been awarded by survey and this piece is left out."

Have you got that sketch?

A. I don't know what sketch you are referring to.

Q. I am referring to the one mentioned in that letter. The letter has an enclosure. Have you got the enclosure?

A. No. In fact, he wouldn't know because he had no survey of it.

Q. He wouldn't have to have a survey of it if he sketched what the kamaainas told him what the boundaries were.

A. But he would have to make a survey before

(Testimony of H. E. Newton.)

he could get proper boundaries for the ili itself.

Q. Let me understand that, Mr. Newton. That he had to have a survey on the ground to determine, to lay off the boundaries of this land, before he could determine the boundaries?

A. He had kamaainas. From his letter he had kamaainas who said that there was a lele of Kahanui up in this vicinity there, and he was going to get some kamaainas. He had to go somewhere to get some kamaainas to show him where this particular land was.

* * * * *   [451]

Q. A few days later he said, "I show you a sketch of the land I spoke to you about." That is the land of Kahanui that had been shown him by those kamaainas. That sketch would contain, would it not, the information that he had received from the kamaainas as to the boundary, the land markers, roughly where those land markers lay?

A. They just say, "This is a piece of Kahanui and this was down to the gulch," in the general description. They would not go around if they were passing by. They would have to go and get instruments.

Q. That is the only record we have of kamaainas ever telling Monsarrat, as far as you know, anything about this land. Do you mean the whole boundary of this land was based upon just a casual conversation while he was engaged in another survey?

A. These boundaries of Kahanui would really

(Testimony of H. E. Newton.)

depend on the determination of the boundaries of the adjacent lands.

Q. The lower boundary, yes.

A. Where they have already been awarded.

Q. Yes.

A. Then the only remaining part would be gulch, which would be the natural boundary, and the edge of the pali.

* * * * *   [452]

Mr. Cass: I am cross-examining on an exhibit of the Government which was studied by this witness, and that sketch was mentioned. I want to know about that sketch, what facilities he had at the time to make such a sketch.

The Court: The subject of the sketch is referred to in one of the exhibits, which opens it up to cross-examination. The nature of this question, in fact, the exact words were, "How would he do it if he did it?" If this witness knows, [453] he is a qualified surveyor, and if he knows, he may answer the question. If you don't know and have no idea, say so, Mr. Newton.

A. I think I have some idea. That they had kamaainas for the boundaries of the land of Kamiloloa, which would establish the southerly side, the southerly boundary of this land of Kahanui. Thence along the southwest boundary, we already have the fixed boundaries of the land of Kaunakakai and Kalamaula down to Points X and Y near Kaohu station. Now, the land that is in question is easterly of that, on the top of the pali. The Wai-

(Testimony of H. E. Newton.)

kolu Valley and the Waialeia Valley. The southwesterly boundary has already been determined and
all he had to do was to make a survey of the location of the edge of the pali.

Q. (By Mr. Cass): I note on this map in pencil the word "Waiau." Does that word "Waiau"
appear in any part of the survey of this land or
the field books of Monsarrat concerning this land?

A. Monsarrat showed it in his field book, yes.
There is a waterfall or swimming pool.

Q. Will you show me?

A. It shows "Waiau" there (indicating).

Q. Will you show me?

A. It has the word "Waiau" on it.

Q. From which point did he give you that; can
you give me the word?

A. On his sketch plan he has it.

Q. On the sketch plan?

A. In his field notes somewhere. I don't know
just [454] where.

* * * * *

Q. (By Mr. Cass): Run through the description here and see if you can find the word "Waiau"
any place in the blueprint.

Mr. Flynn: Let me see this, please. It is not in
evidence.

Mr. Cass: Let me have the other one, please.

Q. (By Mr. Cass): Here is the photostat which
picks out the pages. Find where "Waiau" is mentioned in those pages, please, and if it is mentioned,
where it is located.

(Testimony of H. E. Newton.)

A. It is on page 112 of Field Book 359. Monsarrat has a sketch of the land of Kahanui and just below Point A he has, at the bottom of the valley, of the stream there, he has the word "Fall" indicated in red in the sketch. It does not say "Waiau Fall", but he says, shows a fall there. Just where it crosses the boundary, sketched as crossing the stream. That is, there was a waterfall there at least. It proves to me that the result of Monsarrat's work, he put it in as Waiau Falls, where it crosses the stream. His map shows that.

Q. It does not show in his field book at any location?   A. I do not find it here.

Q. And if you cannot find it, it is not there. As I understand it, this map starts below and this survey includes these particular lines and these lands. When the next surveying job was done these were all resurveyed in here, or was the next section just put on to the end of this map?

A. I believe a new map was made altogether of the other [455] section.

Q. But the new map was simply a copy of the section already in?

A. Yes. The adjacent boundary of the land would be shown on the second map.

Q. The adjacent boundaries are shown, but the work is unchanged. For instance, the boundaries of Kamiloloa, if they are shown on a compiled map of the whole island of Molokai, would be taken right off of this map and scaled to the scale of the new map?   A. Generally, yes.

(Testimony of H. E. Newton.)

Q. There would be no resurvey of the lands of Kamiloloa for the purpose of making a completed map of another job?

A. No, unless it was necessary to get a little more additional information.

Q. But that is the general practice, is it not, you make a survey of one section, complete the map, make a survey of the next section, complete the map, and continue on until you have the complete map of Molokai, or of some other island, and then the whole is one complete map, which is then based actually on copies of the previous maps. Isn't that correct?

A. Yes. The island map would just show the large lands, not the small areas.

Q. But whatever would be shown on the large maps would be taken off of the other maps?

A. Yes.

Q. So that in this series of maps that the Government has offered, the land of Kahanui, as shown here, has been recopied from the same sketches that appear in the previous maps, [456] simply to complete the map, isn't that true?

A. It is based on previous maps.

Q. Yes. So that if a tracing follows the lines of this work sheet here, the same tracing will follow the lines on these other Government maps as long as there is no resurvey of Kahanui?

A. That is the idea.

Q. Yes. In other words, as far as Kahanui is concerned, there is one map here, it has been copied

(Testimony of H. E. Newton.)

into other maps from the authority of this sketch or this map?   A. Based on Monsarrat's map.

Q. All of them?

A. They are all Monsarrat's.

Q. So that actually as the survey and the map of Kahanui, there has been one map copied into a number of different maps of various areas, including Kahanui, but just the one survey and one map of Kahanui has been used in the copying?

A. That is my belief. I am not positive but that is my belief.

Q. The authority then for each map for the boundaries is the authority for the first map that was made?

A. The boundaries are defined on two sides and the easterly and the northerly boundaries are also indicated as running along the pali lands.

Q. It is definite in that the boundary follows the natural monument or pali?   A. Yes.

Q. But as to the location of those palis on the ground, it is indefinite, isn't that true? [457]

A. It did not take every angle on the edge of the pali. You have them scattered so that you do not have every peak in there. Land at fifty cents an acre.

Q. This is an overlay of the Government's map on a reduction to the same scale of the surveyed maps?

Mr. Flynn: May I interrupt, please? The overlay is taken from the grant and the map on the grant and the evidence so shows. Counsel has re-

(Testimony of H. E. Newton.)

ferred to the Government map. That is not accurate.

Q. (By Mr. Cass): You compared this overlay with the Government map of the same scale and found it practically identical, did you not?

A. Yes, according to Monsarrat's map there, it was practically identical.

Q. You also overlaid it on the sketch attached to the grant and found it identical or practically so?

A. As I said, along the gulch, along Waikolu and Waialeia Valleys the surveyor did not locate all the little angles along the top of the pali. It was more of a sketch but it took in all the land from the fixed boundaries over to Waialeia Valley and Waikolu Valley. Modern surveying has taken in all the little angles which gives it a different shape altogether.

Q. Do I understand, Mr. Newton, then, that this northern and westerly boundary is a sketched boundary and not a surveyed boundary of that sketch?

A. Monsarrat did locate certain points along the top edge of the pali but he did not have enough.

Q. When? [458]

A. When he was down in the valley.

Q. He had not located them in 1888, had he?

A. I don't know.

* * * * *

Q. On that overlay, upon the first approximately 2,000 feet of this overlay the Government line there is approximately 500 feet out, isn't it?

(Testimony of H. E. Newton.)

A. It is possible.

Q. From the line that you yourself determined to be the edge of the pali?

A. As I say, I did not locate anything in Kahanui.

Q. No. But here is your lower sketch or your map, Exhibit 10. It shows a line of the edge of the pali, the lower edge, where it is lettered in "Kahanui Grant 3437 to R. W. Meyer." It [459] varies from the overlay by at least 500 feet?

A. That portion from above the word "Kahanui" there, "Grant 3437 to R. W. Meyer", that was just taken off of Monsarrat's map. The one we are on, to Waikolu Valley, I had nothing really, no location of my own there.

Q. But the first line of Monsarrat's map, for the first 2,000 feet starting from cross on rock, Point X, on your map is there an overlap anywhere from 500 to a thousand feet? In error, is it not?

A. Which one? Point X here?

Q. Yes.

A. No, no. It starts right at the same point. No.

* * * * *   [460]

Q. Here is a red pencil. You can make a dotted line for that so that it will show up. If you will refer back to the tracing so that you can say, without reference to the topographical features, where the line is supposed to run, superimposed on this map. That is what I want. I don't want the topographic description of the line but where that line itself would run.

(Testimony of H. E. Newton.)

A.   You mean Monsarrat's line?

Q.   The line that is on this Government map.

A.   Yes.

Q.   Yes.

A.   I will say at this time, first, that I located nearly every angle in the top of pali where Monsarrat just took a few sights, so mine is an irregular line and Monsarrat has a curved line to the edge of the pali, so his line would be a curved line.

Q.   Just line it in, please.

A.   It begins at Point X, at the northwest corner of the land of Kahanui, Grant 3437 to R. W. Meyer.

Q.   I invite your attention to the shape of the Government's map there, that is, this line here, and ask you whether the line that you have drawn follows the shape of that—of the [461] Government's line here?

A.   It is the same. I mean fairly close.

Q.   In your opinion, then, what you have drawn on that map is fairly close to the Government's original line here?

A.   Yes. Monsarrat's survey.

Q.   I am not talking about Monsarrat; I am talking about the one that is on the map.

A.   Yes. Well, Monsarrat made the Government survey map.

Q.   And that, to the best of your ability, is a representation of the Government's map?

A.   Yes, up as far as the ridge point.

Q.   As far as the ridge point?   A.   Yes.

(Testimony of H. E. Newton.)

Q. That is enough. Now, may I have the next map in point of age?

Mr. Flynn: Exhibit 12, No. 1260.

Q. (By Mr. Cass): Now, on the outside this is marked "No. 2, Molokai, central, reg. 1260."

A. Yes, sir.

Q. "1 to 12,000." Now, Mr. Newton, in relation to the last map we had up here, which was the work sheet, what does this map represent?

A. This map represents the middle section of Molokai, map and survey by M. D. Monsarrat in 1886, 1 inch equals 1,000 feet.

Q. Then, as I understand it, this is a completed map?

A. And it is registered map No. 1260.

Q. Yes. And, as I understand it, this map, then, is the completed map of which the other was a work sheet? [462]

A. Yes. This is on the same scale.

Q. Can you tell me from what survey or surveys this map was compiled; would it be the same survey as the work sheet?

A. Yes, probably with a few additions.

Q. Yes. This map is dated 1886. How come Grant 3539 to Meyer appears on the summit of the ridge when that grant was not granted until two or three or four years later?

A. Our maps are kind of progressive maps. After these lands are granted and the Government has no more interest in that particular piece, they insert the title.

(Testimony of H. E. Newton.)

Q. They insert the title. Do they insert anything else?

A. The area, the grant, and the grantee.

Q. Do they insert additional topographic features?

A. Yes. Anything new like a pipe line, for instance. That has been added on. The pipe line which is shown in blue is added on to the map.

Q. When was that pipe line added on to the map? A. I don't see the date there.

* * * * *
[463]

Q. Do you remember about when that was put in? A. I don't know.

Q. You don't know?

A. I haven't made many trips to Molokai. If I were to look up the records I could find out.

Q. That appears on the documents?

A. But I haven't looked at the records.

The Clerk: Exhibit 5-A, B, and C.

Mr. Cass: That appears on Exhibit 5-C.

A. I wouldn't know.

Q. (By Mr. Cass): It appears in the lower right-hand corner of Exhibit 5-C?

A. I would not know anything about it because I am not too familiar with that section.

Q. Now, in connection with this map, have you any record of an additional survey made by any person by which this dash and two dot line was put on the northern and westerly boundaries of the land sketched in. There is no such mark on the work sheet.

(Testimony of H. E. Newton.)

A. I don't think there has been any other surveying outside of Monsarrat's, which map shows on some of the other Government maps, but it seems to me that this Land Court survey is about the first complete survey of that area.

Q. That is, actually following the line on the ground?

A. That is a more accurate survey of the edge of the pali.

Q. You don't know that this boundary here does accurately follow the line on the ground?

A. No, I don't. In fact, the top of the pali, the edge of the pali is the boundary. [464]

Q. Somewhere along in there the boundary runs?

A. Yes.

Q. It follows the natural monument, the edge of the pali?   A. Yes.

Q. And the monument controls?   A. Yes.

Q. That is, as I understand it, the monument controls. There has been no substantial change in the shape of Kahanui on this map from that in the work sheet?

A. No. They have been practically done within a year or two of each other.

Q. One is practically a copy of the other or it should be a copy of the other?

A. An exact copy with additions probably.

Q. If there is any addition there would be some surveyor's note to show the reason for the addition, would there?

A. They generally put that in blue or something

(Testimony of H. E. Newton.)

like that to indicate something has been added.

Q. You don't see anything of that sort on Kahanui 3?

A. No, but this map came later.

* * * * *

Q. Yes, but no change in the survey appears?

A. No. The boundary remains the same.

Mr. Cass: Now, may I have the next map in point of time?

Q. (By the Court): Mr. Newton, according to the note on the map and the color legend there, the Kahanui area there is one of three pink shades, which the legend designation has either award by survey, award by name or title questionable. Which one would obtain here as to the color? They are faded and shaded, I believe.

A. I believe it is more like Kamiloloa and probably Kahanui Apana 3.

Q. And that, according to the legend, would be on the questionable?

A. Yes, title questionable.

* * * * *

Q. (By Mr. Cass): The coloring would be put on before the lettering. You don't mean that Kahanui section up here, which from your judgment of colors, is in the title questionable class?

A. The date is 1886.

Q. Yes, but it also appears as a grant to Meyer. Then the grant to Meyer was noted after the map was colored.   A. Yes.

Q. Then the shape of this and the coloration of

(Testimony of H. E. Newton.)

that area in there, in your opinion, was noted in the map before any grant was made to Meyer?

A. What?

Q. It was noted before the grant was made to Meyer?

A. You mean the boundaries of the land?

Q. Yes.

A. It was unawarded land so Mr. Meyer—I mean Mr. Monsarrat was making this survey for the first time to determine the boundary.

Q. Then the coloration and the boundaries were on there before the grant was issued to Meyer?

A. What is the date of the grant? [466]

Q. The grant is 1888.

A. It was after the map was made.

Q. The date 1886, does that refer to the survey date or the map date?   A. The map date.

Q. Then everything that appears at a date later than 1886 must have been added after the grant or after the map was made?   A. Yes.

Q. And in 1886 there had been no survey by traverse of this boundary in here?

A. No. Mr. Monsarrat made that survey.

Q. He made a survey but a survey by traverse had never been made at the time this map——

A. (interrupting): No. Only points were located at certain points along the edge of the pali and a boundary between Kalamaula and Kaunakakai and Kamiloloa.

Q. Yes. But the boundary we are disputing had

(Testimony of H. E. Newton.)

never been surveyed by traverse at the time this map was made?

A. Well, Monsarrat was making the survey then, at the time he was on Molokai, and from his letters to Alexander of the survey department he said that the kamaainas or someone had showed him a piece of unawarded land, being a portion of the land of Kahanui.

Q. That is true. He made a survey of the land. But I am speaking of the survey by traverse, actually the surveyor going out and putting flags and running his instrument and having his chain and cutting brush along this line of the north and westerly boundaries. That had never been done at [467] that time?

A. No. Only the westerly and southerly and the easterly and northerly boundaries were run along the monument of the top of the pali.

Q. They simply were described by monument?

A. Yes, by monument.

Q. There is no pretense at all that this boundary line follows the monument?

A. That was the line that was established by kamaaina evidence and Monsarrat reproduced it on his map.

Q. You mean kamaaina evidence established the line of the palis or told Monsarrat that the line of the palis was the boundary?

A. Yes. The kamaaina evidence told him that the boundary was along about in there. That is why he put it in there.

(Testimony of H. E. Newton.)

Q. In accordance with the description "along the edge of the pali"?   A. Yes.

Q. Wherever the edge of the pali run, the kamaainas told him the line run?

A. According to his letters to the office.

Mr. Cass: May I have the next map, please?
* * * * *

The Clerk: Exhibit 14. [468]

Q. (By Mr. Cass): This is apparently the same map we had before, only on a reduced scale, is it not?

A. I just wanted to take in a little more.

Q. This runs clear down to the end of Molokai, on a reduced scale?

A. Yes, on a scale of 1 inch to 2,000 feet.

Q. And as you testified, as these sections are put together the sections are fitted in at the boundaries of the various sections as they appear and the interior is not changed?   A. No.

Q. So that this, although it is on a scale of 2,000 feet to the inch, is plotted or traced from the other map or photostat, I presume it is traced from the other map because the other map is one section?

A. And there may be additions.

Q. There may be additions?   A. Yes.

Q. But they would show on this map?

A. Yes.

Q. From your inspection up there, has there been any material alteration of the shape of the plat on this map?

(Testimony of H. E. Newton.)

A. No. It is drawn on a smaller scale, that is all, a different scale.

Q. And this is the map from which apparently the sketch that appears attached to the grant was taken?   A. That is possible.

Q. Yes. On all those boundaries up there with the exception of the Government survey points and the statement in the grant that it follows the pali, are any land markers [469] or monuments set out?

A. Not in the grant itself.

* * * * *

Q. I asked you if there appears on this map, for the record, any indication along the disputed boundary lines or on the Waikolu boundary line, anything other than the straight line, showing a natural monument described by name or otherwise on the map itself?

A. It is a reproduction of the larger scaled map and it would be absolutely the same as the other.

* * * * *

Q. That last boundary, starting from the point "cross on rock" there, is there any land marker other than the survey station mentioned?

A. It runs along the top edge of the pali, around the Waihanau Valley, and across the stream, up to the top of the spur ridge.

Q. I am speaking of the language of the grant. There is no stream mentioned in the grant, is there?

A. No. The map is a part of the description also. [471]

(Testimony of H. E. Newton.)

Q. Would you look at the grant there and find out where the word is that makes the map a part of the description?

A. That is according to law, when you issue a patent.

* * * * *

Q. But is there any natural monument or other monument from the point "cross on rock," around Puu Kaeo, is any natural boundary fixed or described other than the general line of the pali?

A. The general line of the pali is on the top edge of the Waihanau Valley, according to Monsarrat's map, thence he crosses a gulch or stream in Waihanau, thence in a meandering line along the top edge of Waialeia Valley to Kaluahauoni station.

Q. Yes. Now, going back to Mr. Monsarrat's field notes. Have you your copy there? This is mine. Now, I invite your attention to the bottom of page 112, which is from the station [472] marked "cross on a rock" apparently, the word "waterfall," has a bearing of 297 degrees 20 minutes 30 seconds. I am through with this map. I am not going back.

A. Are we going to read some more on it?

Q. No. This is pau. Now, from this point "cross on a rock" here, using roughly these various lines, shots, topography markers, can you tell which waterfall was meant by this entry? Taking it from point "cross on a rock," referring to Applicant's Exhibit A.

(Testimony of H. E. Newton.)

A.   Well, he referred to a Waiau Falls.

Q.   Now I am talking about taking it from the bearing of 297 degrees 20 minutes. Here is 280. From that same point. Ten degrees farther to the left. [473]

* * * * *

A.   297 degrees 20 minutes 30 seconds is from a point on the boundary of Kahanui—not Kahanui but Makanalua and Kalamaula, the point down near Kaohu station, Point Z.

Q.   From a line 297 degrees 20 minutes plotted in, from Kaohu station, in this Exhibit A, what waterfall is he referring to there?

A.   Naturally he was sighting to this large waterfall.

Q.   To the big waterfall, wasn't he?

A.   Yes, sir. That is the very point, Point Z.

Q.   Yes. Now, Mr. Newton, if Mr. Monsarrat has made a sketch purporting to be the boundaries of a line and on the line he has placed a natural monument, would you say that the boundary indicated runs through that natural monument?

A.   Well, if it is indicated somehow or mentioned in the description, that would have to be definite. You cannot guess at it.

Q.   Suppose he has on the same page that he has sketched the boundary line and suppose he has in his shots indicated not only one place a natural monument of that sort but he has put in the sketch showing the boundaries of the line of the particular monument or the word describing that monu-

(Testimony of H. E. Newton.)

ment. Would you say that that monument then was on the boundary line intended by Monsarrat? [474]

* * * * *

A. It seems to me that if he intended to go through the waterfall he would have said "along to the waterfall and through the waterfall." The boundary says it runs along the top edge of the pali, around the head of Waihanau Valley. If that went to the waterfall, he would surely say "to the waterfall."

Q. Mr. Newton, I am speaking now of the sketch in his field book. He sketched the boundaries of this land in his field book and noted a monument on the sketch that he had in the field book, showing the boundaries by that monument. Would you say that that monument then was on the boundary?

A. No. He located that point. Yes, he located the waterfall to show it on his map but when he actually wrote his description he said it ran along the top edge of the pali.

Q. Please answer the question I asked. If he has located and noted the monument and has made a sketch in his field book showing the boundaries of the line in question running through that monument, would you say that that natural monument was on the boundary?

Mr. Flynn: I will object to the question as without foundation unless counsel makes a showing to the witness that such a sketch exists in the field book.

Mr. Cass: All right, we will do that.

(Testimony of H. E. Newton.)

Q. (By Mr. Cass): Mr. Newton, I invite your attention to [475] page 112 of Exhibit 16, Monsarrat's notes. That is the same page upon which the word "waterfall" appears?

A. Yes. I see it. Yes, I have it.

Q. The only place where "waterfall" appears on that page, on the right-hand side of the page, is a sketch with the words "Kahanui" on one side of a straight boundary line and "Waihanau Valley" on the other side of that boundary line.

Mr. Flynn: I object already, your Honor. It is not identified as a straight boundary line.

The Court: Let counsel finish his question.

Q. (By Mr. Cass): At about the center point of that straight line that appears on that sketch is "waterfall." Do you recognize what I have been saying in connection with this sketch?

A. Yes, I see it.

Q. That word "waterfall" appears directly on the boundary line indicated by Monsarrat. Would you say that that waterfall indicated by Monsarrat there is the same waterfall indicated in his survey notes?

Mr. Flynn: I will object to the question. The statement in the question that the word "waterfall" appears in the boundary line is insufficient until that is established as a boundary line. Counsel must first ask what that line is.

Mr. Cass: I do not have to. I have already asked him. I asked him before in my examination what these symbols meant in this book and he said

(Testimony of H. E. Newton.)

that where a straight line runs between two points and the names appear on either side of the line, it was a boundary line.

Mr. Flynn: That wasn't all of what he said. He also [476] referred to straight lines between fixed points for the convenience of the surveyor. This one has not been identified as a boundary line and I will object until it is.

* * * * *

The Court: We are concerned here with the sketch, of course, and according to this witness's designation a solid line does indicate a boundary in these field books. I think the designation is proper.

The objection is overruled.

Mr. Flynn: I will note an exception.

The Court: An exception may be noted. [477]

The Witness: Shall I answer the question?

The Court: Yes.

A. The line running from the point X? Is that the idea?

Q. (By Mr. Cass): The line running straight up the page from point X?

A. From Point X.

Q. Through "waterfall" to the Government survey station at Kaluahauoni?

A. If you will read the description there, the boundary itself is "around the head of the Waihanau Valley and the Waialeia Valley to Kaluahauoni station," and then he gives a direct bearing between two fixed points, the cross on rock and

(Testimony of H. E. Newton.)

Kaulahuki, which is a straight line, but the boundary is following the head of the valley, the head of the valleys.

Q. That is not what I asked you before. I asked you whether or not the waterfall that appears on there is not on the boundary line?

A. It happens to be on the line as you draw the line from X to Kaluahauoni, but it does not say a word about the waterfall.

Q. I am not talking about anything but what this sketch bears, Mr. Newton. If you will confine yourself to the sketch, we will get along better.

A. Yes; it happens to go through the waterfall.

Q. I am asking you particularly if this sketch, which shows the station on the boundary line between Kalamaula, Kaunakakai and the other portions which he surveyed, with lines indicating those boundaries, the lines leading from those stations, indicating the boundares of the various tracts which he [478] surveyed, and continuing around here to a tract labeled "Kahanui," which is a waterfall on the boundary, if that is not a boundary line?

A. It is not, to my knowledge of surveying, what this sketch actually shows. This is merely a direct bearing and distance between the two points.

* * * * *

Q. This is Applicant's Exhibit J, being the grant that was issued at first. I invite your attention to the sketch attached to the grant and particularly to the wording above the sketch there "Waihanau Valley" and the wording "Makanalua

(Testimony of H. E. Newton.)

Valley" printed in and scratched out and the words "Waialeia Valley" inserted. Is that handwriting in the handwriting of Monsarrat?

A. Yes, it is Monsarrat's handwriting.

Q. Now, in the exhibit we have just had before us, the [479] survey book, Territory's Exhibit 16, turning again to the sketch on page 112, I invite your attention to the words "Waialeia Head" and the scratched out words "Makanalua Gulch."

A. Yes.

* * * * *

Q. (By Mr. Cass): Does not that indicate to you that the sketch in Monsarrat's field book was used to prepare the description by Monsarrat that is used in the grant?

A. Partly. The original grant, which was cancelled—shall I say anything more?

The Court: Yes.

A. The original grant was cancelled because there were mispelled words and they thought it was better to write a new description of the land of Kahanui Apana 3. So they [480] made some corrections. That is why these corrections were added to the bottom of the original grant written by Monsarrat himself. "Thence around the head of the Waihanau Valley, following the pali to Kalawao and around the Waialeia Valley to the Government survey station." I believe it was the Government survey station at Kaluahauoni. And then the sketch plan is also added too. In the original sketch plan they only have the Makanalua Valley, and

(Testimony of H. E. Newton.)

then it was corrected in pencil by Monsarrat to read "Waihanau Valley and a spur ridge in be_ tween," and then Waialeia Valley.

Q. The same corrections appear in his survey notes, do they note?   A. I believe so.

Q. Well, look at them.

A. I have the survey notes.

Q. You have the survey notes right in front of you, the sketch?

A. No. You gave me the one that was cancelled.

Q. No. I am speaking of the sketch now. The same corrections that were made on this grant appear in the sketch that we have in the field note-book?

A. Yes. The field notebook shows this to be Waihanau Valley. It was written over the word "gulch," which was scratched out. Then where Waialeia Valley is should be——

Q. Makanalua?

A. "Makanalua Gulch", which was scratched out and the word "Waialeia" inserted.

Q. And those are the same corrections that were made on [481] the reissued grant, were they not?

A. Yes. The name of the valley "Waialeia" was incorrect in the original.

Q. Does that or does that not indicate to you that this sketch was used by Monsarrat in the preparation of his description of this land?

A. These corrections were made by Monsarrat.

Q. I ask you, does it indicate to you that he

(Testimony of H. E. Newton.)
used this sketch in making his description of this land?

A. Well, this survey was made by Monsarrat from his own map, yes.

Q. And from his field notes and sketches?

A. He had reproduced his field notes on a map and then he made a description from his map.

Q. Mr. Newton, I wish you would answer the questions. A. I am answering them.

Q. And not evade them.

A. He could not write the description before making his map. [482]

* * * * *

Mr. Cass: Go back to the question I asked before.

Q. (By Mr. Cass): Does the change in the field book, which is apparent on its face, and the change upon the cancelled grant, which appear as changes in the permanent grant, indicate to you that Mr. Monsarrat used this sketch in his field notebook?

The Court: Mr. Newton, do you understand the question?

Q. (continuing): In preparing the description of the land to be conveyed by the grant?

The Court: Do you understand the question, Mr. Newton?

A. The sketch is not drawn to scale so that you have to reproduce——

Mr. Cass: Another argument. [483]

(Testimony of H. E. Newton.)

A. (continuing): ——it before you can even write your description.

The Court: Do you understand this question?

A. The sketch in the field book, you cannot draw a description from the sketch in the field book.

The Court: Let me repeat. Do you understand the question that was just put? Do you understand that question?

A. I don't quite grasp the question. I don't quite grasp what he is trying to get at.

The Court: All right, Mr. Cass, repeat your question then.

Mr. Cass: Will you please repeat the question?

(The question was read by the reporter.)

A. Naturally he did.

Q. (By Mr. Cass): He did. Then it is apparent from the field book and from the lack of any other field book in your records that Mr. Monsarrat did not run a separate survey to determine that description but took it from the notes of this particular survey. Isn't that true?

A. He was making a general survey and this was part of the survey.

Q. Oh, please answer the question, Mr. Newton.

A. In his survey of the line there he actually surveyed this piece of land. * * * * * [484]

Q. (By Mr. Cass): Now, Mr. Newton, I have asked several times during the course of this trial if there is any proof in your own personal knowledge or in the records of the survey office as to

(Testimony of H. E. Newton.)

who [486] actually put the sketch of Kahanui on the various Government maps that have been in existence. Is there such proof?

A. I cannot say absolutely.

Q. Each time I have asked that you have answered with a statement as to the customs of the survey office. Do you know or do you not know whether Mr. Monsarrat actually put those things on his map, speaking of the sketch of Kahanui?

A. Well, I would like to see the sketch. I know Mr. Monsarrat's handwriting.

Q. I am not speaking of the handwriting; I am speaking of the Government's maps now.

The Court: Mr. Newton, you have undoubtedly been a witness in many many cases, but the requirement in law is that you answer the questions directly to facts within your own knowledge.

A. Yes.

The Court: Do you feel that because you do not have any facts within your own knowledge or you do not know something, do not feel that you are not entitled to say so. If you don't know, say so. If you do have those facts within your own knowledge which will answer the question, please answer the question accordingly.   A. Yes.

The Court: But you are definitely entitled on facts that you don't know—for instance, the instant question, you either know or you don't know. If you don't know, immediately state that you don't know. I think if you will bear that in mind it may help you.

(Testimony of H. E. Newton.)

The Witness: Will you repeat the question?

Mr. Cass: Please, Mr. Reporter, read the question.

(The question was read by the reporter.)

A. I don't know definitely.

Q. (By Mr. Cass): Now, speaking of the sketch which is attached to the patent 3437, do you or do you not know who placed that sketch upon the map? A. I don't know definitely.

Q. Do you or do you not know whether the sketch attached to the patent was made before the boundary marked on Monsarrat's work sheet, that is the first map we had here, was traced in with that red line? A. I don't know definitely.

Q. You don't know whether or not that tracing was actually on a Government map prior to 1888?

A. I don't know unless I am just told by the date of the map itself.

Q. But the map, you testified, had additions from time to time; that is right?

A. Any additions were very few. [488]

* * * * *

Mr. Cass: Now, may I have again Monsarrat's work sheet, the original, the first one.

Q. (By Mr. Cass): Now, the work sheet here has on its smudge line a point marked K, apparently used with the dividers to mark things off. That is the point you adopted for your boundary point? [494]

A. Yes. K was one of the points.

Q. What other points located on this work

(Testimony of H. E. Newton.)

sheet?   A. Point A, on top of the ridge.

Q. K and A are the two points that appear to be marked upon that boundary at all. Now on the ridge over here appears——   A. "Tree W."

Q. "Tree W."?   A. Yes.

Q. Point "C"?   A. Yes.

Q. And to Point B?   A. "B."

Q. And on the upper Waikolu edge of the valley is what?   A. "B".

Q. And there appears in this work sheet a number of pin pricks along the outside edge of this, throughout that entire boundary?

A. Yes.

Q. Now, what were those pin pricks put there for?

A. Well, I believe they were the little pin pricks that went through onto the finished, onto another sheet, onto the final map.

Q. The final map?

A. I have my opinion of the production of the second map. There was the work sheet and then there was the finished sheet.

Q. And that is the method used by surveyors to transfer from one map to another, to put pin pricks through from one to the other and then to connect them on the other side? [495]

A. Yes, sir.

Q. You testified the other day that there is nothing in the field books that were introduced in evidence to indicate that any of these lines are on

(Testimony of H. E. Newton.)

the boundary of anything. I am speaking now of this I have just referred to.

A. No, they are not mentioned in the description itself, but they are shown on this working sheet as colored in to establish the limits of the land of Kahanui.

Q. But you don't know who colored that in, except by guess?

A. Monsarrat is responsible for the map.

Q. Again, you don't know who colored that in, do you?   A. Well, Monsarrat——

Q. Do you know?

A. Well, I did not see him do it.

Q. Do you have any records to show that he did do it other than your guess from the fact it is his map?

The Court: Mr. Newton, do you know of your own knowledge whether Mr. Monsarrat——

A. I do not know positively.

The Court: ——whether Mr. Monsarrat inserted the red that Mr. Cass is asking about? You either know or you don't know. Do you know of your own knowledge as a fact that he did?

A. No. That was before my time so I would not know.

The Court: You don't know?

A. I don't know, at the time he did the job, no.

* * * * * [496]

Q. Let's see if I understand your testimony. You testified that there is in existence this map in the survey office, that it is as far as you know the

(Testimony of H. E. Newton.)

only map or the first map from which the boundaries of Kahanui are traced on other maps. Is that true? A. Yes.

Q. You don't know whether the tracing of this map was made by Mr. Monsarrat or some other person? A. I cannot say definitely.

Q. Do you even know when, by a reasonable number of years, when that was traced on there?

A. This map is dated 1886. It was around that time.

Q. Do you know that all your map data was as it appears now or was this data later? I am asking you if you know. A. I don't know positively.

Q. It might be that this was not added until after this was granted. Isn't that true?

A. Maybe. In fact, I don't know and I cannot say.

Q. And the boundary on the straight line or near straight line [497] boundaries is the boundary established by Monsarrat's survey of these lower kuleanas or lower ahupuaas and adopted as the boundary of Kahanui. That is what appears in the field book, isn't it? A. Yes.

Q. The upper boundary here is a boundary sketched in without any location or record of the actual point where this boundary lays on the ground?

A. I cannot say that definitely or positively, outside of looking on this map there seems to be other points going through.

Q. But have you any record or any monument

(Testimony of H. E. Newton.)

set up, that a surveyor would set normally if he made a traverse of that boundary and set it up as a traversed boundary?   A. He had flags.

Q. At the time that this survey was made?

A. Yes, he had flags on the boundaries. Yes. That is how he got his points. He sighted from the triangulation station over to these flags.

Q. Which point?

A. Flag Point X on the boundary of Kalamaula and Kahanui. He had a flag at Y on the same boundary.

Q. Those are monuments on that **boundary**?

A. Yes. He had to have flags to sight to. He had one at Kekeakula, at the southwest corner of Kahanui, and Puu Kaeo, which was a triangulation station, and Kaohu, which was a triangulation station, and Point A on the ridge.

Q. Does his book——

Mr. Flynn: Let the witness finish his answer, please. [498]

The Court: I don't think the witness finished his answer, Mr. Cass.

Mr. Cass: Go ahead.

A. And Point K on the northerly boundary of Kahanui, at the edge of the gulch. That completes the circuit. And thence back to X.

Q. (By Mr. Cass): Does his book show that either at K or A, you can look in the book if you wish to, that flags were set there, in the surveying of this land?   A. He just——

(Testimony of H. E. Newton.)

Q. Look in the book and tell me whether the book shows that.

A. I know what is in the book. He sights to this Point K, marked in the field book, where he actually took sights to K, to X and to Y.

Q. These down here at this boundary we acknowledge were sighted, but these to Points K and A, does his field book show that he put flags there?

A. It doesn't show definitely, but he had to sight on something.

Q. It could have been a wood tree or a rock as well as a flag, could it not, or a dead tree?

A. It says "dead tree."

Q. What do the field notes say about those points; what did he sight on?

A. Page 112 of Field Book 2. That is station Y or I mean boundary Point Y in Kalamaula and Kahanui. He sighted to Point A, Ridge Point A.

Q. Does it show whether it was a flag station or what it was? [499]

A. I don't know just how it was marked but he had a point which he sighted at as Ridge Point A.

Q. But there is nothing in the book to indicate that he, in all his sighting, went across Ridge Point A to establish a flag station, is there?

A. I can't say definitely but he was sighting on something which he designated as Point Ridge A, and he shows Point A on the sketch plan as being on the ridge.

Q. Undoubtedly he sighted at something up there, but what I want to know, did he ever cross

(Testimony of H. E. Newton.)
the valley to establish the point over there, and not
stand on the ridge and look at it.

A.   He sighted at some definite point because he
sighted several times at the same point.

Q.   Now, as to the other point——

Mr. Flynn: May this question be more definite,
instead of "to the other point," because there have
been many points mentioned, your Honor.

The Court: Do you understand the question?

Mr. Cass: I am referring to the point K.

* * * * *

The Witness: I will have to look all over for
this. [500]

* * * * *

Q.   No. I just want you to find Point K, where
he shot Point K.

A.   I think you can find it sighted from cross on
rock.

Q.   And from Point X to Point Y.

A.   From trig station Kalauhauoni he sighted to
Ridge Point A.

Q.   Yes, but I am asking about, I am speaking
of Ridge Point K now.

A.   Ridge point A was 59 degrees no minutes
and to Point K 69 degrees no minutes, and then
from Kauna Gulch——

Q.   Which is the next station up?

A.   At this point. He sighted to Point Ridge A,
154 degrees no minutes, and he has a sight along
Kalamaula and Kahanui boundary Y, 134 degrees

(Testimony of H. E. Newton.)

35 minutes 30 seconds and Point K, 143 degrees no minutes.

Q. My question was, is there any indication whether or not any monument or flag was established at Point K?

A. I cannot answer that definitely. He had to have something to sight on.

Q. I am just asking from the record. I am not asking from your own knowledge. But from the record, is there anything to indicate? [501]

A. He sighted to that point several times so there was something there; something was certainly there at the time of his survey.

Q. Now, Mr. Newton, there was something there that he had sighted on. We admit that.

Now, just go over to your other map over there, Territory's Exhibit 10. Starting at Point X, you traversed as near as you could the line of the pali shown around where your boundary is indicated, did you not?

A. Yes, I ran a traverse around and located the edge of the gulch, new gulch, yes.

Q. Now, at Point K, at Point K did you find any monument?

A. No; I didn't even look for it.

Q. You did not look for Monsarrat's monuments?

A. In fact, I was making a general location myself.

Q. You did not look for any of Monsarrat's monuments?

(Testimony of H. E. Newton.)

A. It did not call for a monument. [502]

* * * * *

Q. Now, from your map and your sights, Mr. Newton, is there any place on this boundary, referring to the lower boundary here, the X, Y, Z boundary, where you take a shot on a waterfall at Waiau? I am speaking of this boundary (indicating).

A. Yes, I know. From Waiau waterfall, about at this point on the map, in the bend of the stream, where Monsarrat seemed to have used the word "Waiau."

Q. I am speaking of your survey. Could you make a shot at that place called Waiau?	A. No.

Q. Can you see it?

A. No, you cannot see it.

Q. So, assuming that Monsarrat did all his work from the ridge, he never saw Waiau Falls, isn't that true?

A. Not the Waiau Falls that shows on his map.

Q. And there is nothing in his field books or notes to show that he ever knew of the existence of Waiau Falls, in the field survey of this land, is there?

A. I believe he has notes in his field book.

Q. Point them out, please?

A. It will take me some time. I believe he has; I am not positive. If you will give me an opportunity to look for them.

Q. Point them out in the survey.

* * * * *

(Testimony of H. E. Newton.)

A. In fact, I don't know where Waiau Falls is. The large [503] falls are not Waiau Falls.

Q. Of course not. But you testified you thought Waiau Falls was at the place where the line crossed the stream?

A. Yes. In fact, I located that waterfall or I mean a waterfall at that point, which I believe to be Waiau Falls referred to by Monsarrat.

Q. Mr. Monsarrat referred to some falls on the boundary, did he?

A. It shows on his map. That boundary crosses at about Waiau Falls.

Q. Crosses some falls. Which map are you referring to now, the sketch in his field book?

A. No, the map itself. The developed survey map shows that.

Q. The word "Waiau" appears?

A. Yes, Waiau there and the falls are right there. Right on this map it has "Falls Waiau," and that is at the, where the boundary crosses the stream to Ridge Point A.

Q. Couldn't that have been put there by Jake Brown when he identified the point for the sugar company?

A. No. It was on Monsarrat's map.

Q. I know it was on Monsarrat's map, but because the figures appear there does not mean that Monsarrat put them there?   A. It is his map.

Q. You have just said that it does not, that you have no way of knowing.

A. Positively, definitely.

(Testimony of H. E. Newton.)

Q. Now, apparently "Waiau Falls" appears on the map. Now there are two places that I can see in this field book, there may be more, on page 110. Refer to your own copy, please. [504]

A. Just a minute.

Q. That is the first sheet. At a point about two-thirds of the way down. Shooting from Kaohu.

A. Yes.

Q. What waterfall is that?

A. That is the Big Waterfall.

Q. All right.

A. He sights 297 degrees 28 minutes to waterfall.

Q. Now, from Point X—wait a minute now. Is that Point Z? No—here. Is this taken from Point Z?   A. That is on the boundary.

Q. That is on the boundary?

A. Boundary Z, yes. That is the point near Kaohu triangulation station. That is right near Kaohu station.

Q. That, then, is near the same station?

A. Yes.

Q. And shooting practically the same way, is that the same waterfall or is that Waiau?

A. No, that is the same waterfall.

Q. Now, at page 130.   A. I have it.

Q. At the top, it has "Makakupaia."

A. Makakupaia.

Q. Where is that? It is clear over here?

A. Yes.

Q. The next name is Kamiloloa. So that that is

(Testimony of H. E. Newton.)

the survey of this boundary in here, is it not?

A. Yes.

Q. The word "waterfall" appears in that exhibit at about [505] the sixth word down in the column, and that has nothing to do with either the Big Waterfall or Waiau, does it?

A. I don't believe so.

Q. Now, I don't find anywhere else in the pages which have been photostated as being material any reference to a waterfall anywhere. Have you found any other reference to a waterfall?

A. No. There are other waterfalls but not this particular waterfall. [506]

* * * * *

Q. All right. Now let's move to Grant 3539 to R. W. Meyer. I invite your attention to the sketch accompanying this grant.   A. Yes, sir. [507]

* * * * *

Q. As I understand it, Monsarrat shot this ridge we have all taken from a distance along stations that he personally went over there to establish, is that right?

A. We have a lot of stations in the lower portions of Kalaupapa Settlement and he had set flags all along the top edge of the ridge, on both sides, and those were shot in later when he was doing his work. He took sights to all of these flags which he had set on both sides of that ridge.

Q. Mr. Newton, you used the words "which he had set." You don't mean that Mr. Monsarrat per-

(Testimony of H. E. Newton.)

sonally went up to the top edge of the ridge there and staked flag poles up there?

A. No; he had kamaainas working for him.

Q. Those kamaainas were his workmen, and whoever set the flags went up there to where they could see the instrument and they took a shot at it?

A. Yes; he had several flags set around the entire ridge.

Q. Mr. Monsarrat did not actually climb over the land to each one of those flags; he had his men do that?

A. The men set the flags on the edge of the pali and Monsarrat took the field notes.

Q. The question is, was Monsarrat up on the edge of the pali with those men when those flags were set?

A. No, he did not go up to the top at all on that particular job.

Q. You spoke also of the height of Waiau Falls and you [509] said that you could cut a path around the side of the road, if I remember correctly, or that you could cut a trail around Waiau Falls and go around it. You could not climb the falls themselves. Do you remember saying that?

A. The falls are 22 feet high.

Q. But you said you could get around them by going around the side?   A. Yes.

Q. And you said you cut a trail there. You don't mean you actually cut into the wall on the side; you mean the brush on the trial?

(Testimony of H. E. Newton.)

A. Just brush and jungles in there, where they have the ieie vines. [510]

* * * * *

Q. Mr. Newton, has there been produced in this action all the documents relating to the title, claim of title of the Government to the area in dispute here, that are in existence so far as you know in the files of the survey office or the land commissioner? A. I believe so. [512]

Redirect Examination

Mr. Flynn: Now, if I may see our exhibits 11, 12, 13, and 14.

Q. (By Mr. Flynn): A while ago when Mr. Cass was questioning you, Mr. Newton, you looked at the original of Registered Map 1259 and pointed out that the line made up of a dash and two dots and then again a dash and two dots was a boundary line delineated on this map for the southern boundary of Kahanui and also the western boundary of Kahanui. Is that right? A. Yes.

Q. And no such line did exist for either the northern boundary or the western or the eastern boundary of Kahanui, Apana 3, is that correct?

A. It is a curved line, according to the plan.

Q. That does not appear on this map the dash and two-dotted boundary line? A. No.

Q. To determine as to those boundaries?

A. No.

Q. I will now show you Territory's Exhibit 12, which is the finished map of 1886, map and survey

(Testimony of H. E. Newton.)

of M. D. Monsarrat, bearing Registered No. 1260, and I will call your attention to the boundaries of Kahanui Apana 3 and ask you to state whether all of the boundaries, that is the north, east, south and west, are delineated in this finished map in the established manner by delineating the boundaries, namely, a line composed of a dash and two dots?

A. Yes, that is correct.

Q. Now, let's examine Territory's Exhibit 13, which is Registered Map No. 1289, being the 2,000-foot to the inch scale working sheet of Monsarrat of 1886, according to the stamp on it at least, and I call your attention again to the boundaries of Kahanui Apana 3 1048 acres, and ask you to point out whether all of these boundaries are marked out in the same boundary line of a dash and two dots?

A. Yes, that is correct.

Q. Now, calling your attention more carefully, is there not a solid line instead of a dash and two-dotted line between points equivalent to X and A, as shown on the many exhibits in this case?

A. Yes. On this particular map, yes.

Q. Now, if you know, was there a solid line, as distinguished from a dash and dot line, used for any particular purpose? Once again, if we may look at the original map, which is Registered Map No. 1289, it may be easier for you to answer it. This is the original of the map which has the solid line there.   A. Yes.

Q. And if you will note has solid lines in other places as well?

(Testimony of H. E. Newton.)

A. I really could not say just why I made a distinction between the two lines. This is one and the same boundary and half of it is a full line and the rest is a dash and two [518] dot line.

Q. Are there any other portions in the near vicinity of Kahanui Apana 3 where boundaries appear to be marked with a solid line instead of a dash and two-dot line?

A. Yes. Down near the coast line, the edge of the slope shown as a solid line or full line.

Q. I call your attention to Kalaupapa and Kalawao, being north of those areas and included within this map.

A. I take that back. That was in the ocean. Along the pali, sloping down into Kalaupapa and Kalawao.

Q. Then a solid line was used to indicate a boundary along the palis?

A. Yes. It seems to be that way.

Q. Now, Mr. Newton, I will show you Territory's Exhibit 15, which is Registered Map No. 1890, working sheet of Monsarrat, scale 1,000 feet to the inch, dated 1895, and call your attention once again to the boundaries of Kahanui, Grant 3437, Meyer, as shown on this map, and ask you whether all of the boundaries of Kahanui, Grant 3437, are again outlined in established boundary markings, namely, a dash and two-dot line?

A. Yes, that is correct.

Q. Now I will finally show you Territory's Exhibit 14, which is the 1886 finished map by M. D.

(Testimony of H. E. Newton.)

Monsarrat, scale 2,000 feet to the inch, and call your attention to Kahanui Apana 3, Grant 3437 to R. W. Meyer, apparently having been superimposed later, and ask you whether all of the boundaries of Kahanui Apana 3 on this map are delineated in the customary manner by a line composed of a dash and two dots? [519]

A.   Yes, that is correct.

Q.   I believe you have stated, Mr. Newton, that in your survey you find Monsarrat's northern boundary of Kahanui Apana 3 to correspond closely to your own northern boundary of Kahanui Apana 3 where that apana joins or is bounded by Waihanau Valley. Is that correct?   A.   Yes.

Q.   Does your boundary go through from Point X through fixed points K and A?   A.   Yes.

Q.   Does Monsarrat's boundary go through the same fixed points K and A from X?   A.   Yes.

Q.   And as far as the lines of the northern boundary are concerned through those fixed points, yours and Monsarrat's coincide, is that correct?

A.   Yes. Very closely. [520]

* * * * *

Mr. Flynn: I have before me the original transcript of the testimony from the records of the clerk of the First Circuit Court, bearing Transcript No. 884, in Law No. 14859. I offer into the record and if the offer is accepted I will read into the record the testimony of two persons now deceased, namely, Jorgen Jorgensen and Hugh Howell.

I do not believe counsel will dispute that the two persons are deceased.

Mr. Cass: I concede that they are deceased.

Mr. Flynn: To support this offer, I will state that the issue on which these two witnesses testified was identical with the issue in the present case, namely, the boundary between Kahanui 3 and Waihanau Valley. We are therefore offering this as testimony from a former trial of witnesses now decceased. [523]

* * * * *

The Court: Isn't that something that can wait until some other stage of the proceeding? Do you have any witnesses here waiting?

Mr. Flynn: Yes, I do.

The Court: Let's take them first.

MAX H. CARSON

a witness called by and on behalf of the Territory of Hawaii, being first sworn, was examined and testified as follows:

Direct Examination

Q. (By Mr. Flynn): Will you state your full name please? A. Max H. Carson.

Q. Your occupation or profession, Mr. Carson, please?

A. I have a dual position; I am chief hydrographer of the Territory and I am also district engineer of the geological survey, water resources division. [530]

* * * * *

(Testimony of Max H. Carson.)

Q. Now Mr. Carson, have you ever been on the lands of Kahanui Apana 3 and/or the lands of Waihanau Valley on the island of Molokai?

A. I have been on Kahanui; I am not sure whether it is Apana 3 or not, but the land that was involved in a condemnation suit back in 1929 or 1930.

* * * * *

Q. Can you state when you went into the lands of Waihanau Valley, approximately?

A. Yes. My first trip over there was in connection with that condemnation suit that I just mentioned. Mr. Hewitt had told me that there was a question likely to arise as to the value of the water rights there, and on the last day of March 1929 I went over there with Sam King and Francis Evans for the express purpose of finding out what I could on the ground in regard to the value of the water rights. [531]

* * * * *

A. Bill Meyer and Henry Waiwaiole were with me on both of these days pointing out the boundaries.

* * * * *

The Witness: Bill Meyer, yes.

* * * * *

A. April 1929, April 1 and 2. [533]

* * * * *

Q. (By Mr. Flynn): What, if you know, Mr. Carson, was the capacity of Henry Waiwaiole to the Meyer family interests, Meyer land interests?

(Testimony of Max H. Carson.)

A. He was one of the Meyer clan; I don't know the exact relationship. [535]

* * * * *

The Court: Mr. Carson, a minute ago you indicated you would like to amplify your statement relative to this information. [536] You may do so now, if you so desire.

A. I wanted to amplify it to the extent that, as I said in the first place, I had these men go around with me and point out these boundaries, and the reason that was done was because I wanted to measure the water at the boundaries. That was the purpose of my asking them where the boundaries were. I needed guides. I did not know the country. And they acted as my guides. I think that is sufficient.

Q. (By Mr. Flynn): If you will confine your answers for the time being at least, Mr. Carson, to what William Meyer did with you.

* * * * *

A. He took me up there along the ridge to a point just above where the boundary crossed the stream and told me the boundary was there.

Q. (By Mr. Flynn): Can you describe more definitely where that point was, Mr. Carson? [537]

A. It was a place called Waiau.

Q. It was a place called Waiau?

A. Yes. I measured just below the pool. It was one job to get down there too from the ridge.

Q. I show you, Mr. Carson, a map bearing the identification "Department of the Interior, U. S.

(Testimony of Max H. Carson.)
Geological Survey, topographic map of the island
of Molokai, Hawaii.''
* * * * *

The Court: It will become Territory's Exhibit
21 in evidence.

(The document referred to was received in
evidence as Territory's Exhibit 21.)

Q. (By Mr. Flynn): Now, showing you Territory's Exhibit 21, [538] Mr. Carson, and calling
your attention to the lands marked ''Makanalua,''
lands marked ''Kahanui Apana 3,'' I will ask you
if you can locate on this map the point you have
just stated was referred to you by William Meyer
as Waiau or the boundary between Waihanau Valley and Kahanui?

A. I would say it was about in here.
* * * * *

Q. I will ask you to mark a large X at that
point.   A. I will circle it.

Q. Or circle it. Will you write the word
''Waiau'' there? That is the location of Waiau as
shown to you by William Meyer?

A. That is as close as I can spot it on that map.
* * * * * [539]

Cross Examination

Q. (By Mr. Cass): Did you testify that Mr.
William Meyer was a representative of the Meyer
family?   A. Yes, I did.

Q. Where did you get any idea that Mr. Meyer

(Testimony of Max H. Carson.)
was a representative of the Meyer family?

A. When we got over there that night we were taken up to Otto Meyer's place at Kalae and we started out in the morning and Sam King introduced him to me as one of the Meyers that will show me around.

* * * * *

Q. Did you explain to anybody but William Meyer where you wanted to put your measurements?

A. Yes. Sam King knew.

Q. You explained to Sam King? [541]

A. Yes. They knew what I was there for and they took me around to show me their sources of water. We went not only there but to Waialeia and they have a number of springs in there and we went down and measured the springs.

Q. Sam King arranged, then, for William Meyer to show you around?

A. That is right.

* * * * *

Redirect Examination

Q. (By Mr. Flynn): Mr. Carson, what, if you know, was Sam King's capacity or connection with the Meyer interests at that time?

A. He prepared an appraisal of the whole property, which he submitted to Judge Robertson. He sent me a letter a few days after we got back, saying he was giving me a copy of his appraisal and statement that he had followed my figures on water pretty closely. Actually he followed them exactly.

(Testimony of Max H. Carson.)

Q. To your knowledge, was Judge Robertson counsel for the [542] Meyers at that time?

A. He was later. Whether he had already been retained, I don't know, but he represented them later in the case, I know. [543]

* * * * *

R. M. TOWILL

a witness called by and on behalf of the Territory of Hawaii, being first sworn, was examined and testified as follows:

Direct Examination

Q. (By Mr. Flynn): Will you state your name, please?   A. R. M. Towill.

Q. And your profession or occupation, Mr. Towill?

A. I am a civil engineer and land surveyor.

Q. Civil engineer and land surveyor?

A. Yes.

Q. Mr. Towill, I will show you Territory's Exhibit 5-A for Identification, Territory's Exhibit 5-B and Territory's Exhibit 5-C, which constitute a group of three photographs placed on a plastic paper, and ask you if you recognize these photographs?   A. I do. [544]

Q. Did you take these pictures, Mr. Towill, or were they taken under your supervision and direction?   A. I personally took them.

Q. These are photographs of the mauka lands of Kahanui, of Makanalua, of Waihanau Valley,

(Testimony of R. M. Towill.)

and in part the upper or mauka Kahanui, are they not, on the island of Molokai?

A. That is correct.

Q. These, of course, are airplane photographs, are they not, Mr. Towill?

A. They are aerial photographs taken from an aeroplane.

Q. Now, were those photographs taken in accordance with a procedure known as photogrammetry?   A. That is right.

Q. Will you state just what that process is, photogrammetry?

A. The nomenclature of photogrammetry, meaning measurement taken from pictures, the simple definition. [545]

* * * * *

Q. Now, the final map you are talking about, is that used in the same sense as the word you previously used—mosaic?

A. There are several types of finished maps that are made from aerial photography. First there is a planimetric map that is made from stereoscopic measuring instruments; that gives us polimetry and contours, and it is made on tracing paper and can be reproduced by either the blue or white print method. And then there are your mosaics, which are made in instruments to reproduce to scale the aerial photographs. It is also possible to superimpose on this mosaic the verticle elevations by means of contours.

Q. With regard to the vertical elevations by

(Testimony of R. M. Towill.)

means of contours, can you state from your own experience, Mr. Towill, whether you have found the vertical elevations by means of contours, that are placed upon shown in such products, accurate or reliable?   A. Very reliable, yes. [547]

* * * * *

Q. Mr. Towill, from examining the three pictures, Territory's Exhibits 5-A for Identification and 5-B and 5-C, it would appear that the same were taken in a series. Is that correct?

A. That is correct. In order to get the third dimension from pictures, using a stereoscope, it is necessary to have at least 50 percent overlap to insure proper stereoscope vision. However, the general practice is to take at least 60 percent for mapping purposes. In other words, about 60 percent of the picture is covered by another photograph in order to insure proper vision.

* * * * *

Q. As to these pictures, which are Territory's Exhibits 5-A, B, and C, for Identification, can you give the scale or the approximate scale?

A. These pictures are approximately 800 feet to the inch. [548]

* * * * *

Q. Now I will show you, Mr. Towill, Territory's Exhibit 1 for Identification, bearing the identification "Attorney General's Office, Territory of Hawaii. Control topographic mosaic showing portions of Kahanui and Waihanau Valley." Was this mosaic made by you or under your supervision?

(Testimony of R. M. Towill.)

A. It was made by me and under my supervision.

Q. Was this made from the photographs or additional photographs similar to Territory's Exhibits 5-A for Identification, 5-B and 5-C?

A. It was.

Q. What are the numerous black lines in this mosaic, Mr. Towill?

A. They represent the contour lines or different elevations of the area.
* * * * *

Q. The contour lines are how frequent?

A. These contour line control intervals are 40 feet.

Q. 40-foot intervals?   A. 40-foot intervals.
* * * * * [549]

Q. Can you state whether the mosaic here together with all of the contour lines thereon are an accurate reproduction of what you have seen both on the ground and from the air?
* * * * *

The Court: It will become Territory's Exhibit 1 unconditionally, in evidence.

(The document referred to was received in evidence as Territory's Exhibit 1.) [550]
* * * * *

The Court: For the record, let the witness state what the machine consists of, this stereoscopic machine now about to be used or offered for use.

(Testimony of R. M. Towill.)

Mr. Towill, will you describe the machine for the record?

A. The instrument is a type of stereoscopic instrument consisting of a mirror, a prism, which the mirrors reflect onto the prisms, which are set at the pupillary distance of the average person to show the photographs in the third dimension.

Q. (By Mr. Flynn): May I ask you, Mr. Towill, whether any average, ordinary, layman can use or see through this stereoscopic machine and get a good clear view of the single three dimensional photographs shown by the combination of the two photographs?

Mr. Cass: We object to the opinion of the witness on that matter. [552]

The Court: The objection is overruled.

A. Yes. It is very easy for the average person to view photographs through this stereoscope. I might add that for viewing photographs through a stereoscope it is necessary to adjust the two photographs to the pupillary distance of the individual. In other words, if I were to adjust two photographs for my pupillary distance, it might be a little out of focus for someone else not having the same vision. However, by manipulating or moving them into position under the stereoscope anyone should be able to see under the stereoscope, except people who have a vision only in one eye. Unless you have vision in both eyes it is impossible to use the stereoscope.

(Testimony of R. M. Towill.)

Q. (By the Court): That is the only physical limitation? A. Yes. [553]

* * * * *

Mr. Cass: I will withdraw my objections to the use of the machine in identifying objects in the way that it is suggested. The center picture can be loosen and used as an adjustable picture on the two outside pictures, and I believe then that anyone can see through the machine.

The Court: Very well.

* * * * *

Q. (By Mr. Flynn): Now, I will ask you to adjust the machine and examine the first two pictures, Exhibits 5-A and 5-B, through the stereoscope, Mr. Towill. A. Yes.

Q. Now, from your familiarity with these lands and also of the pictures which you have taken,—and may I call your attention to Applicant's Exhibit A, a map, and call your attention [557] to areas indicated by the word "intake" and just makai or northerly of that point, and ask you whether you know the name of the falls which it has been agreed was located just below that intake?

A. I don't know the name of the falls.

* * * * *

Q. You do, however, know where those falls are located, a short distance makai or below that intake. Is that correct?

A. I have been at this place.

* * * * *

Q. First I would ask you to trace up the course

(Testimony of R. M. Towill.)

of the stream on each picture from that falls point that you know.

A. Well, starting from the falls, on Photograph 5-A, on 5-B, the stream follows a southerly direction up for probably 400 feet and then it turns easterly, I guess that is. It turns westerly. And then it follows along a gradual curve for another 700 or 800 feet, in practically a southerly direction, and then it has a series of winds probably 300 or 400 feet in either direction, still following a southerly direction, and then we have almost an S bend in the stream, two ridges. As you go along from there the stream separates [558] into three forks, one running in a southerly or maybe a southeasterly direction, one in a southerly direction, and one in a southwesterly direction.

Q. Where is the separation of the stream into three forks with relation to the S bend and overlapping ridges point you have just referred to?

A. The first stream starts approximately 1200 feet up above, the one that continues of course, and then there is the one that goes to the southeasterly, it is probably 1600 feet. I will have to clarify that. The one that goes in the southeasterly direction is approximately 1200 feet. The one that runs in the southwesterly direction is probably 800 feet, and the main stream that continues on in a southerly direction, kind of a three-fingered fork. [559]

* * * * *

Q. (By Mr. Flynn): I will ask you now to examine Territory's Exhibit 1 for Identification. I

(Testimony of R. M. Towill.)

am sorry. It is Territory's Exhibit 1 in evidence.
* * * * * [561]

Mr. Flynn: All I am interested in is to get points marked on the mosaic and arrive at a condition where they can be checked with the stereoscopic view of the two photographs.

Mr. Cass: That is all right. The thought occured to me that the superimposition of the contour lines on there did not check up with the testimony or with the necessity of having two pictures to see the depth. [562]

A. The contours were made through the stereoscope plotting device by using two pictures and then they were traced and superimposed on a mosaic in their proper position.
* * * * *

Q. (By Mr. Flynn): Now, Mr. Towill, I will ask you to examine Territory's Exhibit 1 and state whether you can locate the S-bend in the stream and the two overlapping ridges area you have previously referred to. Now, I will ask you, Mr. Towill, if you can on this mosaic locate the S-bend in the stream and the two overlapping ridges we have previously referred to?

A. May I start at this falls and go up?

Q. Certainly.

A. Tracing along the center of the stream, in sort of a southeasterly direction, until we get to a point approximately 1600 feet above the falls; then the stream makes an almost right-angle bend in a westerly direction and then a sharp bend back to

(Testimony of R. M. Towill.)

an easterly or southerly direction, forming an S.

Q. Will you place some mark or line coming down the ridge from the easterly side and going back up across the ridge from the westerly side.

A. How is that now?

Q. I ask you to draw a line coming down from the ridge on the easterly side and going back up the ridge on the westerly side, the two overlapping ridges that you have already referred to or two lines if you find that necessary. [563]

(The witness does as requested.)

Q. Now, will you take your red crayon and follow the course of the stream, marking it out, from the S-bend to the Big Falls?

(Witness does so.)

Q. That is the center line of the stream?

A. That is the center line of the stream.

Q. I don't believe we need to mark it that way, once you have stated it for the record.

Now, I will ask you to examine the mosaic. Can you state the elevation from the center of the stream at the falls or directly above the falls to the top of the pali on the west?

A. About 400 feet.

Q. 400 feet. Approximately 400 feet?

A. That is an elevation.

Q. Yes. Can you give the difference in elevation from the center of the stream to the top of the pali, again on the west, from the point where you show the beginning of the S-bend in the stream as you go south. I am referring to this point here.

(Testimony of R. M. Towill.)

A. Approximately 280 feet.

Q. 280 feet?   A. Approximately 280 feet.

Q. Now, I will ask you to examine the stereoscopic view of Pictures 5-A and 5-B and I will ask you if you can trace the top of the pali between the two points at which you have just given the elevation measurements from the center of the stream. That would be from the point just above the [564] stream at the higher falls to the point just above the stream at approximately the S-Bend. I would rather have you trace it on the map.

A. All right, sir.

Q. You have done that?   A. Yes.

Q. You have marked an X and a Y there, is that correct?

A. Yes. The X is just above the large falls on the pali and the Y as it comes out of the valley onto the edge of the pali.

Q. Now, I will ask you to locate that on, first, the mosaic, the edge of the pali on the opposite or easterly side of the stream, first at the area directly above the falls.   A. Up to here?

Q. Up to the edge of the pali. First at the area above the falls. Well, then, first, will you estimate the vertical elevation from the center of the stream to the top of the pali on the opposite or easterly side? You have previously estimated it on the westerly side at the falls.

Q. At the falls on the easterly side of the valley, at the falls the land is not nearly as precipitous as it is on the westerly side of the falls, and

(Testimony of R. M. Towill.)

the pali—there are several series of palis between the falls and the actual pali along the top of the flat lands of the ridge. Is that what you want?

Q. Yes.

A. At the falls the elevation is approximately 2200 feet and up to the first ledge it is approximately 200 feet and then there is another pali area that goes up to another [565] 200 feet, making 400 feet, nearly, but on the top of the ridge it is rather flat and you have a gradual slope down for about 200 feet in elevation and then a little pali or drop and then a gradual slope again back to the stream. There are two palis along that side. The actual top of the pali is on top, I presume.

Q. Will you mark that actual top of the pali directly above the falls, on the east?

A. I have marked the lower.

Q. The lower of the palis?

A. The lower of the palis.

Q. Will you mark the higher of the two palis?
(Witness does so.)

Q. Now, will you trace along the higher of the two palis to a point where you are directly above or east of the S-bend in the stream?
(Witness does so.)

Q. Now, directly above the extreme mauka end or southerly end of the red line you have just drawn there is a small area, showing a higher elevation, and I am pointing to this circle about one and a half inches above the end of the last red line. Is that correct?

(Testimony of R. M. Towill.)

A. Yes. That contour is approximately 2700 feet. It is rather flat topped hill in that vicinity.

Q. Approximately 2700?

A. In elevation, yes.

Q. I will call your attention to this line as the 2600-foot line and ask you whether this is still approximate?   A. 2760 feet. [566]

Q. 2760 feet?

A. At the 2700 elevation, represented by the top contour.

Q. You say that is a small flat hill?

A. Rather a flat topped hill.

Q. I will show you Applicant's Exhibit A and ask you whether that small flat topped hill can be identified by you on this map, Applicant's Exhibit A?

A. Yes. That area is right in here. It shows the pali going around and the flat area on the top. I was pointing on the mosaic. It is just about at the end of the area of the portion of land 3539 to R. W. Meyer.

Q. That is a point in the neighborhood of the writing near "M. D. M's Ridge A"?

A. M. D. M's Ridge A is marked at the approximate location, yes.

Q. Now, returning to the stereoscopic view, Mr. Towill, I will ask you to trace the top of the palis on the first two pictures, Exhibits 5-A and 5-B, between the point you have referred to as the falls and the point referred to as the S-bend in the stream, asking you to place the top of the pali on

(Testimony of R. M. Towill.)

both sides?   A.   From the falls?

Q.   From the falls to the approximate area of the S-bend.

A.   I traced it on the westerly side. Now you would like it on the easterly side from the falls. These two lines I have drawn here.

Q.   You have not traced it on the westerly side here. This is the center line of the stream. You have traced it on the easterly side. [567]

A.   I have traced it on the westerly side in one of the photographs.

Q.   Yes, you have. That is right. If you will now add the easterly side.

A.   Which pali do you want?

Q.   I want the pali as it looks to you.

A.   The greater of the two? All right.

* * * * *

Q.   (By Mr. Flynn): Mr. Towill, returning to the stereoscopic view of the combined photographs 5-A and 5-B, I will ask you to trace on the photograph 5-B the outline of the top of the pali on the easterly side of the area we have referred to as Waihanau Valley or specifically between the points referred to [568] as Waihanau Falls and the S-bend above those falls in the stream?

A.   That has been done.

Q.   Yes.

Now, the lines as shown on the photograph, Exhibit 5-B, for the Territory, will you place also on the mosaic, Territory's Exhibit 1?

A.   The same lines?

(Testimony of R. M. Towill.)

Q. Yes.

A. Opposite the "s" in the "stream" there is a hill; this entire area on the easterly side of the hill, the flat area, breaks off into the large valley to the east and on the west side of the pali there is a flat that comes out for quite a ways before it breaks into the stream. Which of the two palis do you wish, or both?

Q. If you can do so I would ask you to place the lines exactly as you have them on the photograph. What you have now drawn is approximately identical with the——

A. It is the same.

Q. On that photograph. It is the same. Very well. The line on the photograph reaching makai or northerly of where you have now drawn it goes a considerable distance beyond the present makai end of the red line you have just drawn in. Is that correct? A. Yes.

Q. Then I will ask you, if you can do so, to trace the line on the mosaic so that it goes as far makai or northerly as that shown on the photograph. Now, if I may look at the photograph for adjustments. [569]

From an examination of the photograph I note a very considerable distance where your line on the easterly ridge or that area approximately above the stream, between points Waihanau Falls and S-bend in the stream is a single line at each end of which you show in an encircled line, apparently to cover broader points of the ridge formation. Am

(Testimony of R. M. Towill.)

I right?   A.   That is right.

Q.   Where you have the single line on the photograph?   A.   Yes.

Q.   On the photograph. Is the ridge formation
such where that single line is that the flat line between the edge or edges of the palis so narrow
that an encircling or larger line could not be drawn
and still stay along the flat land?

A.   That is correct. Where the single line appears
it is a hogback ridge; there is no flat on top at all.

Q.   You have previously referred, Mr. Towill,
on your mosaic to the small mound or hill or
raised piece of flat land at the elevation of 2760
feet and you have identified that on Applicant's
Exhibit A as coinciding with the small parcel of
flat land as shown as a portion of Grant 3539 to
R. W. Meyer, also containing the identification
"M. D. M's Ridge A", is that correct?

A.   That is correct.

Q.   I would ask you to mark "A" on the mosaic
at the point where it appears on the map, Applicant's Exhibit A, if you can do so.

A.   M. D. M's A?

Q.   M. D. M's "A".

A.   Yes, they do coincide. [570]

Q.   The two do coincide?   A.   Yes.

Q.   Very well. Now, on the photograph Exhibit
5-B you have drawn a line on the westerly top of
the pali above the stream from a point slightly
below or makai of the Big Falls to the point approximately next to the S-bend in the stream. I

(Testimony of R. M. Towill.)
will ask you if you will reproduce the same line
on the mosaic.

(Witness draws line on the mosaic.)

A. As to the westerly side of the stream from
the S-bend, the ridge coming up from the S-bend
along the edge of the rim of the pali to a point
approximately opposite the falls.

Q. Have you not traced that point somewhat
below or makai of the falls. A. Yes, I have.

Mr. Flynn: Now, for identification purposes, if
counsel has no objection, I will write for this line
the words "top edge of pali on westerly side of
stream" and along this red line the words "top edge
of pali along easterly side of stream."

Mr. Cass: I don't know that that is true. I know
that it is the opinion of this witness.

Mr. Flynn: I will ask this witness to write it
in then. It is what he testified to.

Mr. Cass: He has testified that in his opinion
that is the top of the pali, yes; but I won't stipulate that is a fact.

Mr. Flynn: I do not mean for you to; I mean
only for identification. [571]

Mr. Cass: For identification, yes. No reason why
I should object to the identification.

Mr. Flynn: And, Mr. Cass, I will identify in
here "center line of stream," all as testified to by
the witness.

Mr. Cass: I have no objection to you lettering
just what he has said that to be, for identification.

Mr. Flynn: That is what I mean.

(Testimony of R. M. Towill.)

Mr. Cass: Go ahead and write it in, Mr. Flynn. Anything he is doing in the way of identification merely lines the way his testimony is.

Q. (By Mr. Flynn): Mr. Towill, this is your Point A as coinciding with the Point A, M. D. M's Ridge Point A on the map, Applicant's Exhibit A?

A. That is right.

Q. May I ask you to identify Point A also on the photograph which is Exhibit 5-B for the Territory?

(Witness does so.)

Mr. Flynn: You may cross-examine.

Cross-Examination

Q. (By Mr. Cass): Mr. Towill, what is your understanding of the word "pali" in Hawaiian?

A. A precipice.

Q. A precipice. Then in your designation of the edges of the pali on this mosaic up here, you have tried to follow the edge of the precipice all the way around?　　A. That is correct.

Q. And where the slope is gradual, you would not call it a pali? [572]　　A. No.

Q. Now, just how steep in relation to your contour lines there does the land have to be before it is classified as a pali rather than a valley side or a gentle slope or other slope?

A. Will you repeat that question, please?

Q. I want to know, a drop off straight up and down is a pali?　　A. That is right.

Q. You come off at an angle of 30 degrees from

(Testimony of R. M. Towill.)

the vertical. No man can walk down. That is a pali. You come down at an angle of 45 degrees; a man can walk down it if he is careful. Is that a pali?

A. I would like to say that on the westerly side of this valley, Mr. Cass, where I have drawn a red crayon line, it is very precipitous down into the stream at all places with the exception of the little finger ridges going down, which are very precipitous from the top and go down at a very steep angle on the westerly side.

Q. Yes.

A. On the easterly side of this valley, from the top of the ridge, which in this instance the ridge is fairly flat on top, the ground or the country slopes gradually for an area or for a distance from the top of the flat to where it breaks off maybe to, oh say a 40 or 50-degree angle and goes at that angle for quite a distance, and then you have another little pali that breaks off. In other words, along this side there is a series of——

Q. (interrupting) A series of hard rock benches on the [573] edge of the valley wall here, where there are straight up and down places?

A. That is right, varying maybe from 10 to 30 or 40 feet.

Q. Yes. This is, according to the contour, 40 feet?   A. 40 feet, yes.

Q. And the lines that you have drawn here are in your opinion where the land becomes so steep that it becomes a pali?

A. No. These contours are drawn at the eleva-

(Testimony of R. M. Towill.)
tion of which they are numbered on the map, without regard to the pali.

Q. The red lines——

A. The red lines indicate the average of the top of the pali along there. Some places it runs along a precipice in order to join two precipices, and they can cross sloping land.

Q. This is 1 inch equals 300 feet, according to your scale?   A. That is right.

Q. Exhibit A is 1 to 400 feet, slightly smaller than this?   A. That is right.

* * * * *

Q. Is that a trail or does it show on the picture?

* * * * *   [574]

A. There is evidence of an open area zig-zagging down this ridge.

Q. And indicating on your map the first ridge on the westerly side that comes down into the Valley above the Big Falls, the second ridge that comes down into the valley above the Big Falls, counting the ridge that actually goes across Big Falls as one?   A. That is correct.

Mr. Cass: Nothing further.

The Court: Redirect.

Redirect Examination

* * * * *   [575]

Q. (By Mr. Flynn): I will ask you if you have been down to the Big Falls, Mr. Towill?

A. I have. * * * * *

(Testimony of R. M. Towill.)

Q. Have you when you have been down at approximately the Big Falls looked mauka up the stream?

A. Yes, I have traversed that stream for probably a half mile.

Q. Have you as you traversed the stream going mauka from the Big Falls observed the ridges which make the stream go into an S-bend?

A. Walking along the bottom or in the stream the overgrowth was such when I was there that it was difficult to see anything coming out at all. It was staghorn fern and occasionally a tree and unless you get up on the side someplace you cannot see hardly what the sides look like, you can only see from the top.

Q. I am asking you if, as you went along mauka from the falls towards the area, this S-bend in the stream, could you at any point see the two transverse ridges or overlapping ridges [576] you have referred to?

A. Yes. In getting out of there there is probably a 50-foot drop or a gradual drop from the stream down to the face of those precipitous falls, and to get down to there you come over on the side ridge and from the side ridge you can see up the valley and see those ridges. It is on the side of the stream, not in the stream.

Q. Did you see the two overlapping or transverse ridges at the point of the S-bend in the stream?   A. Yes.

Q. As you looked at those two overlapping

(Testimony of R. M. Towill.)

ridges, do those two overlapping ridges attain a position where they close off or block off the valley area?

A. There is that feature. The two ridges come across like this and you cannot see through them, no.

Q. Now, two more questions. Examining the stereoscopic view once again, you have stated that the valley at the point of the Big Falls is impassable as you go mauka. Assuming you are below the Big Falls, I will ask you whether from this view you can state if there are any other falls below the Big Falls which are an impassable point?

Mr. Cass: Now, you are asking him from traversing it himself or from the photographs?

Mr. Flynn: From the photographs.

A. There are two falls that appear in these two pictures—three falls that appear in these pictures. The one that I sighted on. You come down approximately, I will say, about 1200 feet, it looks like, or about 1400 feet, and there is a fall that is probably 160 feet high; and right down, [577] about 2500 feet possibly, there is another large fall which appears much larger than the upper one of the three.

Q. Of the three falls, the first being the Big Falls, we have consistently referred to as the one where you have been, and then one of the other two, are the other two as impassable or more or less so than the Big Falls which we will Call No. 1 for the purposes of this question?

(Testimony of R. M. Towill.)

A. The middle fall does not appear to be as precipitous as either of the other two. The lower of the three seems much higher and more precipitous than the other two.

Q. Than the other two? A. Yes.

Q. That lower one being approximately 2500 feet from the falls we have previously been referring to? A. That is correct.

* * * * * [578]

The Court: Call your next witness.

Mr. Flynn: If the Court please, by stipulation I can offer within a couple of minutes some testimony that would be given if the witness were here. Counsel is agreeable to my making this statement as to what his testimony would be if called and to have that read into the record as testimony given in the cause. The witness being Samuel Wilder King, Honolulu real estate broker and appraiser, whose testimony is that in 1929 he was employed by the Meyer family through their attorney, Judge Robertson, to make an appraisal of the Meyer lands on Molokai, that he did go on the lands with Mr. Max Carson, who has testified here, and a few other persons, and was shown the lands by Mr. William Meyer of the Meyer family.

Is that correct, Mr. Cass?

Mr. Cass: So stated by Mr. King and accepted.

Mr. Flynn: If the Court please, that concludes all the testimony to be offered by the Territory with the exception of the testimony of the two deceased witnesses, which is [579] to be read now in the record.

* * * * *

The Court: Proceed. Read it very slowly then.

Mr. Flynn: Yes. I will read from the transcript of testimony in Law 14859 of the Circuit Court of the First Judicial Circuit, Territory of Hawaii, beginning at page 213 of said transcript of testimony.

Mr. Cass: What is the title of the case, please?

Mr. Flynn: The case being entitled, William C. Meyer, et al., plaintiffs, versus the Territory of Hawaii, defendant.

The Court: Let the record show that the Court is now confirming its former ruling upon this offer, which is that it is open to objection upon the ground of relevancy, competency and materiality, without regard to the ruling or any ruling or any effect of any ruling of the presiding judge at the former hearing.

Mr. Flynn: Beginning on page 213.

The Court: What are you reading, the direct examination?

Mr. Flynn: Yes. I will read it all. (Reading.)

JORGEN JORGENSEN

was called as a witness on behalf of the defendant, being first duly sworn, testified as follows:

Direct Examination

* * * * *

Q. (By Mr. Kimball): Are you a registered professional surveyor?

(Testimony of Jorgen Jorgensen.)

A. I am a——

Q. Engineer?   A. Engineer.

Mr. Cass: We might shorten this. I will stipulate that Mr. Jorgensen was a qualified engineer and that he was employed by the Hawaiian Homes Commission to survey and construct a tunnel slightly above the Big Falls from the lands of Kahanui or from wherever the present intake of the tunnel is located to the lower land of Molokai. Maybe we can cut out two or three pages.

The Court: Do you accept the stipulation?

Mr. Flynn: Yes, your Honor, except that it saves us very little time.

* * * * *

Q. When was construction commenced?

Mr. Flynn: I will say in parenthesis that this refers to the tunnel construction.

A. I think it was in February 1924.

Q. And when was it completed? [581]

A. In October 1924.

Q. Before the construction was commenced I assume you ran a line for the tunnel, did you not?

A. I did.

Q. Before you ran the line for the tunnel, did you do any survey work?

A. I did, and I located, I tried to locate all the boundary between Kalamaula and Kahanui and I found every one of those corners.

Q. Everyone of Mr. Monsarrat's corners, you

(Testimony of Jorgen Jorgensen.)

Q.   Cornerstones. Did you consult any documents before you did your work?

A.   I did. I went to the Bureau of Conveyances and got a description and the boundary of Kahanui, that particular part of Kahanui.

Q.   What was the document that you consulted in the Bureau of Conveyances?

A.   I got a copy of the description of the boundary.

* * * * *   [582]

Q.   In addition to what you have testified already that you did, did you ask any person on Molokai whom you thought might know the boundaries of Kahanui?

* * * * *

A.   I did, I first consulted George P. Cooke. At that time he was executive secretary of the commission. He and I went up there together. Later when I started the survey for this business I employed Albert Meyer and he was with me there three or four years on a survey party or on pipe work and all kinds of things like I used him for and in this particular case I asked him as being an old-time person on Molokai, if he knew where this boundary was. After showing him the boundary stone, and he said he didn't exactly know, but he [583] pointed out a place to me up above a waterfall (indicating on paper) and he thought that was the direction the boundary went to.

* * * * *

Q.   Now, where was that place that **Mr. Meyer**

(Testimony of Jorgen Jorgensen.)

pointed out to you in relation to the intake of Waihanau Tunnel?

A. I should judge it was about 1,000 or 1,500 feet above where the intake is.

* * * * * [584]

Q. Is this Mr. Meyer living now?

A. I understand he is dead a couple of years ago.

* * * * *

Q. (By Mr. Kimball): Do you know what relation that Mr. Albert Meyer was to Mr. R. W. Meyer? A. So far as I know, he was a son.

* * * * * [585]

Q. Mr. Jorgensen, after you did the work you have told us about, prior to the time the construction of the tunnel was commenced, to what conclusion did you come with regard to the boundary between the government land and the Meyer land in the vicinity of the tunnel?

A. As near as I could figure out from the description given me from this description you showed me, I could not say that I would transgress on anybody's property, and to be sure of that I run my tunnel line, after I figured the tunnel line, I ran it over the top of the mountain, over the top of the spur from Kahapakai, to be sure I was outside the boundary of Kahanui.

The Court: Did you flag your line?

A. I did.

Q. (By Mr. Kimball): During the time the tunnel was being constructed, did anyone of the

(Testimony of Jorgen Jorgensen.)
members of the Meyer family make any protest
about it?

A. No, I was never approached on the subject.

Q. After the tunnel was constructed and during the time you were employed by Hawaiian
Homes Commission on Molokai, were any protests
made about the tunnel by any members of the
Meyer family? [589]

A. Not that I know of. None to me personally.
* * * * *

(Reading from transcript:)

Cross-Examination
* * * * *   [590]

Q. You located Point X?

A. I located this point (indicating) and as near
as I could see from the description of the boundary,
I seen that the boundary did go through the head
of Waihanau.
* * * * *   [591]

Q. The document to which you have referred,
that is, one like the one you used, had a sketch on
it, did it not?   A. No, I never saw it.

Q. You never saw a sketch?

A. I never saw a sketch.

Q. Before running your line, you did not see a
picture like that (indicating)?

A. Yes, I had that. I had a map showing——
* * * * *   [593]

Q. Is there any place in the line that you determined in your mind was the line of the land of

(Testimony of Jorgen Jorgensen.)

Kahanui which was the head of Waiahanau Valley?

A. There was no direct point, naturally I would say that the boundary line would go up toward the head of the valleys.

Q. What marks the head of a valley?

A. Well, you see it would be where the angle— the angle where there is no more valley.

Q. The angle where there is no more valley. Then why did you not go clear around instead of cutting across Waihanau Valley at this point here, marked "pipe" on Exhibit 6, instead of crossing the stream there, if that is where you crossed; is that where you crossed? [595]

A. No, I never go over there.

Q. You never did go over there?

A. No. I was satisfied with the boundary as we surveyed down here.

The Court: The witness points to the boundary Y-X and then brings his hand up towards the ridge line, up to K and around, but I do not know what he means thereby.

Q. (By Mr. Kemp): Were you not influenced more by the picture you saw than you were by any written contents?

Mr. Kimball: What picture?

Mr. Kemp: On the map he says he had before him.

Q. Is that not what influenced you?

A. No. Naturally I would look at the sketch and the—what influenced me was this: That it said "towards the head of the valleys."

(Testimony of Jorgen Jorgensen.)

Q. I beg your pardon, Mr. Jorgensen. Will you look at it again?

A. Yes. (Examining paper), "Thence toward"—

Q. No. "Around."   A. "Around."

Q. That is around the head?   A. Oh.

Q. Not "toward"?

A. Well, this, of course, that does not mention the Waihanau Valleys, it only says Waihanau and Waialeia Valleys.

Q. Yes. This one you are looking at, the other one you said you had did have the words in it. That is the only difference. Now if you are hunting for the head of a valley, if you don't go to the very end of the stream or water shed [596] that the valley forms, what natural object would stop you in finding the head of a valley?

A. That would be only waterfalls and places you could not get over.

Q. If I tell you the water, Waterfall No. 1, there is a waterfall that neither man nor beast, so it has been testified in this case, can go up or down, and that there is no other such place from that waterfall clear onto the head of this stream, what then would you say is the head of Waihanau Valley?   A. Well——

Q. The place where neither man nor beast could go up or down or——

A. Well, this stream; that is a big body in itself, you know.

Q. Yes.   A. All the way up.

Q. I am asking you now the specific question,

(Testimony of Jorgen Jorgensen.)

Mr. Jorgensen. You said if you are not going to take in the whole stream it would have to be some natural object, such as a waterfall, that you could not go up or down. Those were your own words, were they not?

A. Yes, but I want to modify that. That would not necessarily end the valley.

Q. I understand.

A. Because you could not get over it; you might be able to make headway on top.

Q. Yes. But you have answered me, if you are not going to take in the whole valley you would look for some natural [597] object that would be an obstruction that you could not pass; that is true, is it not?   A. Yes.

Q. Such as a waterfall?   A. Yes.

* * * * *

Q. At the place where you fixed as this line coming along here, you knew it would cross Waihanau Stream, as you said, some one thousand or some 1500 feet above the portal of the tunnel?

A. That was my——

Q. Estimate of——

A. My estimate and from all information I could get from persons who know, who thought they knew; they did not tell me they knew exactly, but they told me.

Q. But you could not find anything which you could define as a natural head of the valley at the point where it would cross?

A. No, but I also took this in consideration; di-

(Testimony of Jorgen Jorgensen.)
rect line from here to the trig station.

Mr. Kimball: What do you mean by here?

Mr. Kemp: X. [598]

The Witness: X. That line would still be above my intake.

Q. (By Mr. Kemp): Yes, but you know that a direct line given in that way does not mean that the direct line is the boundary, do you, Mr. Jorgensen?

A. Oh, I know that is simply the direction.

Q. Yes. That is a very common thing going along the seashore, is it not, you have got two points on the seashore and they connect the direct azimuth and distance between the two points, but that does not mean that the seashore, just that line, does it?

A. No.

Q. Nor that when you are going around the head of these two valleys that you are going to follow that direct line, would it, Mr. Jorgensen?

A. No.

Q. Did that direct line influence you in fixing your line where you did?

A. It gives me some way of directing where the intention was.

Q. Approximate that line.   A. Yes.

Q. You wanted to approximate that line?

A. Yes; it gives the direction.

Mr. Kemp: Yes. That is all.

Q. (By the Court): Mr. Jorgensen, a few moments ago, when the shorthand reporter could not hear you and all the lawyers gathered around the

(Testimony of Jorgen Jorgensen.)

board, and you were using your left hand to [599] indicate, you were indicating out from X up around that bend to K, and said something about Albert Meyer. Do you recollect what was on your mind at that time?

A. Well, what was on my mind was this. That I wanted to find out as near as I could if he knew anything where this boundary line was, because it is not described exactly, and he showed me the waterfall and a big pool way up above. He said he thought that was where that boundary line came.

Q. Did you go down to that waterfall?

A. I went up to it.

Q. You went up to it? A. Yes.

Q. What sort of waterfall was it?

A. It was not a very high waterfall, a waterfall say about 20 or 25 feet, and a big pool at the bottom of it.

Q. Did anybody give you any name for that pool? A. No, none whatever.

Q. When you were pointing to this bend up around from X to K. A. Yes.

Q. Around the ridge there, did you actually survey that ridge at the time you were laying out your tunnel there?

A. You mean over here (indicating)?

Q. No. You see where it is marked K?

A. Yes.

Q. Along from X to K is a broken ridge line. Do you see what I am indicating? A. Yes.

Q. My question is, did you actually walk along

(Testimony of Jorgen Jorgensen.)
that ridge [600] top there with your gang?

A.   I walked all the way around here and I made a. trail here, somewhere. Of course, it is hard to get down to the water, and furthermore made a trail all the way along my survey line to this tunnel.

Q.   You confined yourself from the upper part, from X to K?   A.   Yes.

Q.   Did you walk along that region with this Mr. Meyer you were referring to?

A.   I did.

Q.   Did you go up beyond with him?

A.   I think we went up there farther.

Q.   Was he in your gang when you made the location of the intake?   A.   He was.

Q.   Any other of the Meyer family come up around there at any time?

A.   I don't remember; I don't remember any of them.

Q.   At any time was the region of the lower falls marked on that map No. 6 as Falls 1 and 2, at any time were those ever pointed out to you as being within the or boundary of private land?

A.   No.

The Court: That is all I wanted.

* * * * *   [601]

The Court: Now you propose to read Mr. Howell's testimony, Mr. Flynn?

Mr. Flynn: Yes, your Honor.

The Court: Proceed under the same conditions and rulings relative to objections as to the prior testimony of Mr. Jorgensen.

Mr. Flynn: Reading, beginning at the top of page 281 of the transcript of testimony in Law 14859.

(Reading.) [618]

HUGH HOWELL

was called as a witness on behalf of the defendant, being first duly sworn, testified as follows:

Direct Examination

* * * * *

Q. (By Mr. Kimball): What is your profession, Mr. Howell?

A. Civil engineer and surveyor.

* * * * *   [619]

Q. Did you know Mr. M. D. Monsarrat in his lifetime?   A. Very well.

Q. Did you ever work with him?

A. Yes, in 1894.

* * * * *

Q. Are you familiar with his method of surveying?   A. Yes.

Q. What is your opinion of it?

A. I think there is no better surveyor, especially in those times. I never knew of any better surveyor than M. D. Monsarrat; very, very particular, very careful, and very meticulous in making his descriptions so that they will be followed by a later surveyor.

Q. Have you had occasion to consult maps prepared by Mr. Monsarrat? [620]

A. Very many times, yes.

(Testimony of Hugh Howell.)

Q. How do you find his maps?

A. Very clear and correct.

Q. Do you know whether or not Mr. Monsarrat made use of kamaainas in his field work?

A. Yes, always. I have had many conversations with him along those lines and that is the first thing he did was to get information from kamaainas who were living then. There are none of them living now of course.

Q. By kamaainas you mean whom?

A. Literally, children of the soil. It means the oldtimers that are acquainted with the vicinity. They gave him the information regarding boundaries of lands and corners and who made the surveys, and so forth.

* * * * *

Q. (By Mr. Kimball): Mr. Howell, have you had occasion to familiarize yourself with lands belonging to the Meyer family on the island [621] of Molokai in the vicinity of Waihanua Valley?

A. Yes.

Q. What was that occasion?

A. I was employed by Hawaiian Homes Commission to make extensive improvements to its water system, particularly to build new pipe lines from the outlet of Waihanau Tunnel down to their homestead area.

Q. When was that?

A. 1933. I made an early report, a preliminary report, I think in February, and began actual surveys for location and plans for the building begin-

(Testimony of Hugh Howell.)

ning in June, June 30, and it was necessary before expending a large sum of money—we planned to spend a quarter of a million dollars, it was necessary to find out whether the water source and tunnel system was on privately owned or government land.

Q. Now, what did you do in order to find that out?

A. I inquired first of Colonel Jorgensen, who had designed and built the tunnel. He assured me that he had made surveys, and he showed me his map showing that the tunnel lines were on government lands. I analyzed it and got hold of description of the Meyer property. Also then went to the government survey office and studied and analyzed the boundaries from Monsarrat's original working sheets and satisfied myself from both of those maps and surveys and base points on the ground, which I had identified by kamaainas to me, the most northerly corner, the end of the measured courses, there were several courses that Monsarrat measured, actually ran them out on the ground, and there is a course there that is very well known, and it agreed with the location of the [622] topography as shown on the map and as I observed on the ground. I went further than that, knowing that Mr. Harvey had made surveys up in that vicinity, I went to him and asked him if he had made a survey of that particular land. He said he had. I asked him, "How is that tunnel; is that tunnel on government land or Meyer property?" He said, "It is on

(Testimony of Hugh Howell.)

government land. You can go ahead fearlessly and protect your improvements.''

I also examined the land. I did not take any marks. I found that courses had been done, the courses of that land is not so much in the instrumentality as the interpretation of the description as given in the deed of that portion of Waihanau to the Meyers, I think it is 3400 and something, I have forgotten the exact number. But it is——

Q. Grant 3437?

A. 3437. I satisfied myself from those three different sources that we were indeed on government land, and went ahead fearlessly and put through the improvement, which cost approximately a quarter of a million dollars. I had not heard of anybody's report of private owners at that time or any claim at that time that the lands where our water system was to be were privately owned.

Q. In connection with the interpretation of the boundary line in this grant, did you make any observations or study of the topographical features of the land?

A. Yes. Inasmuch as the last two courses in that description are not by actual surveys but by statement that "Thence around the head of Waihanau and Waialeia Valleys,'' I assured myself by visual observation that the head of Waihanau Valley [623] at least, which was the only one I was interested in, was a considerable distance above the intake of our tunnel. An inspection of Monsarrat's map, which is very easily interpreted, shows clearly enough that

(Testimony of Hugh Howell.)

the boundary from the end of the last measured course runs along the top of the valley right at the top of the hachure marks, showing the slope of the palis, and then a quarter of a mile or so above that particular point I mentioned, it runs across Waihanau Valley. As a matter of fact, the end of Waihanau Valley, according to Monsarrat's map, is right at that point. Waihanau Valley is a local name. Above that is the land of Kahanui and below it is the land of Makanalua, according to Monsarrat's map. As I understand it, the grant sold to Mr. Meyer is in the land of Kahanui and apparently on his map the boundary of Kahanui and Makanalua is at the upper end of that portion of the valley that is called Waihanau.

Q. I hand you Exhibit 11 and ask you if that is a photostat of Monsarrat's working sheet?

A. Yes, this is undoubtedly a copy of the working sheet that I studied. Waihanau Valley, as you will see, apparently ends at the line designated by Monsarrat as the boundary of this grant from the point up here in Kamiloloa, along the Mahanui Road, I am very familiar with that road, I have gone up there a hundred times. That point is well known. The Meyers have a cabin right inside there. This course, this course, this course, the first three courses on the west side, were measured, the only ones measured.

Q. (By the Court): You are referring to the course where the letter Y and [624] X appear?

A. Yes. X is the end of those three courses. The

(Testimony of Hugh Howell.)

first course is not marked. The third, the head of
Waihanau Valley, is very definitely shown here, and
Waialeia Valley, which I am not particularly interested in, around to another point, which is very
definitely surveyed, Kaluahauoni, which is a government triangulation station, and then around
there. I could not conceive that there was any other
interpretation of the location of this land except
as shown on this map.

Q. (By Mr. Kimball): Now, Mr. Howell, can
you describe for us the topographical features which
you found or felt established the head of the valley?

A. From various points down here, Kaohu and
various other points, I walked down this pali, down
this place. In fact, I walked all along the valley
from station Kaohu you see over to the intake. It
was a terrible walk and I will never do it again.

Q. (By the Court): You say that is a terrible
walk?

A. A steep pali and sliding material, rather dan-
gerous. When I got started I wished I had not.
After I got started I did not stop; I had not time,
I had to go through.

Q. You mean it is terrible on the top of the
palis?   A. The tops of the palis all right.

* * * * *   [625]

A. All I wanted to bring out was I could see
the upper end of this where it looks as though the
valley was broken off by the fact the ridges are
running down in there and that looks like a logical

(Testimony of Hugh Howell.)

place to be called the end of Waihanau. That is just a local name.

Q. (By Mr. Kimball): What point now are you referring to?

A. Crossing the valley. Approximately northeast and southwest, approximately along the line of this boundary that is nearly northeast and southwest.

Q. Do you recall what direction the stream takes at that point?

A. You mean the point at the head of the valley?

Q. The point you have just been talking about?

A. Yes. Oh. It winds in there, winding around sort of a letter S in there, as a matter of fact, the valley, the valley goes up a way farther up, but the valley that is called Waihanau, according to this map, must end right there from the location of the words on Monsarrat's map made by his own hand. Waihanau is unquestionably a local name. It is not the name of a ahupuaa. The ahupuaa is Makanalua, and above that is Mahananini.

Q. Now, Exhibit 6, have you had occasion to study this map?

A. No. Very slightly; but I can see it is the map of this same region.

* * * * *.   [626]

Q. Can you tell us by proper indication on the map where the head of the valley is, as you considered it and have discussed it yourself?

A. Up above in here. "Waihanau Valley," printed in Monsarrat's own, by his own hand. I

(Testimony of Hugh Howell.)

know his writing. Right in here. It ends about here.

Q. (By the Court): Right here?

A. It ends about where his boundary crosses.

* * * * *

Q. (By Mr. Kimball): Is that the place where you noticed these two ridges?

A. Yes. Apparently going past each other, blocking off the valley. That is a very common occurrence in many places. I know what it is. It is a crook in the stream. I have seen that crook in the stream from up here somewhere. I did not identify it.

Q. Near where?

A. Up near where this boundary leaves this ridge, you have a letter in there; I can't see it.

Q. The word "pipe" in red?

A. Yes; that is the place. [627]

Q. You have looked across from that point?

A. Yes.

Q. Have you looked up to that point, rather, have you looked up the valley from the bottom or from a point near the bottom of the valley?

A. Yes. You could see it from down here somewhere. I don't remember just the point.

Q. Down where from where?

A. Down near the big waterfall you can see something blocking off the valley up at this point. I did not go down into this letter S in the stream, where our boundary was okay. It was not necessary. I was interested in determining whether this tunnel was on government lands or on privately

(Testimony of Hugh Howell.)

owned lands. I satisfied myself by consulting Monsarrat's map and working up in here and assured myself that the place he was shown is the logical—could be called logically the head of Waihanau Valley.

Q. Yes.

A. It is not the head of the whole valley, however. The whole valley goes way up farther, but that portion called Waihanau, that would be the logical place to call that little locality Waihanau.

* * * * *   [628]

Q. When you can see the condition you described farther up, were you right at the head of the big waterfall or down in the valley, somewhere near it?

A. I won't be certain about it but I know that I have noticed this sort of breaking off of the valleys from points below. It is so long a time.

Q. Can you see that condition from the trail going down?   A. Which trail?

Q. The trail going down to the intake?

A. Oh, I think so, yes. I would not be positive though. It has been two years since I was there and I would not be sure but I know I have seen that formation apparently blocking off the valley from some points below. Just where, I am not positive.

Q. And you also have seen that condition from points along the ridge, I take it?

A. Yes, from above.

* * * * *   [629]

(Testimony of Hugh Howell.)

Cross-Examination

Q. When you read the description in Grant 3437 where you had gone through all of the surveyed legs of the description wrote, "And thence around the head of Waihanau and Waialeia Valleys to government survey triangulation station"—

A. Kaluahauoni.

Q. ——"Kaluahauoni, the true azimuth and distance being so and so," you began to hunt for something to indicate where the head of those valleys was, did you not?

A. I took Monsarrat's line on the map.

Q. You were influenced by his map, rather than by any natural features?

A. Yes, but I did notice at that particular place that it seemed to be broken off. As this comes down farther above I could see what that breaking off was. It was two ridges, one from each side passing each other.

* * * * *   [631]

Q. Is there any such obstacle in the valley as that big waterfall at the point where you now say is the head of Waihanau Valley?

A. I went up above there, I suppose it is a quarter of a mile, that is pretty close to where Monsarrat's line shows, and I could not get up without actually cutting a trail up around the waterfalls considerably less higher than the big one we have been talking about. You could not get up there without cutting a trail. In fact, I had a rope

(Testimony of Hugh Howell.)

to go up there too. My men were more like monkeys than I and they gave me a rope and gave me a chance to pull myself up 25 or 30 feet, something like that.

Q. Mr. Newton has given us the benefit of the height of these various falls above the tunnel, and they range anywhere from seven feet to twenty feet in height.

A. I should not question that. I never had any occasion to measure them.

* * * * *   [632]

Q. I believe you stated on direct examination that after you reached the point we call X on Monsarrat's map, from there on the description of this survey depends upon interpretation?

A. Absolutely yes; the whole line from this point X way up [634] to the initial point.

Q. Yes.

A. Excepting the one point Kaluahauoni.

Q. Yes.

A. Fixed by interpretation; all the rest is interpretation.

Q. You have a distinct interpretation from that point Kaluahauoni to Point X?   A. Yes.

Q. There are many other interpretations from there on?

A. There are many interpretations from there on, not only interpretations on the ground but interpretations on Monsarrat's map. That is all I went by, as much as the interpretation on the ground, Monsarrat's map is the only information

(Testimony of Hugh Howell.)

that I know of that gives anything like the limits of Waihanau Valley. And I should call the limit of Waihanau Valley, which is only a local name of a small area, I should call the limit of Waihanau Valley is the boundary line of this grant as shown in the description on the map.

* * * * *   [635]

The Court: Any rebuttal, Mr. Cass?

Mr. Cass: Yes. I wish to introduce from this record the testimony of William A. Meyer, who is dead. Is that stipulated?

Mr. Flynn: That is stipulated.

* * * * *   [645]

Mr. Cass: Reading from page 139 of the record, transcript No. 884, in Law 14859, Circuit Court, First Judicial Circuit, William C. Meyer, et al., plaintiffs, versus The Territory of Hawaii, defendant.

(Reading.)

WILLIAM A. MEYER

called as a witness on behalf of the plaintiffs, being first duly sworn, testified as follows:

Direct Examination

* * * * *

Q. (By Mr. Kemp): You are a resident of Molokai?   A. Yes, sir.

Q. Born and raised there?   A. Yes, sir.

Q. Lived there all your life?

A. Lived there most part of my life.

(Testimony of William A. Meyer.)

Q. What relation were you to R. W. Meyer?

A. Grandfather.

Q. One of his sons your father?

A. Yes, sir.

* * * * * [646]

Q. You have lived on the lands of the Meyer estate all of your life? A. Yes, sir.

* * * * * [647]

Q. Have the older members of the Meyer family ever pointed out to you or told you where any of the boundaries of the lands of Kahanui, covered by Grant 3437, was? A. Yes, sir.

* * * * *

Q. What was the occasion for their giving you that information?

A. We were up hunting one day during the American Sugar Company's time and they had two men from the Coast, which they hired for shutting off deer from the lands, and one day after killing four or five deer we packed to Waihanau on top of the ridge, and these men stopped us and wanted to take us and have us arrested, and one of my uncles, Ben Meyer, told him he could explain the boundaries of his lands, and he did, and after he told him, he was satisfied and left us alone and we went home.

* * * * * [648]

Q. Can you locate on Exhibit B about where you were when accosted by these men?

* * * * *

A. It has always been customary when we went

(Testimony of William A. Meyer.)

out shooting on these lands of Kahanui, start from Kaohu to Kahanui, along the boundary and over to the edge of the valley looking into Waihanau.

Q. Where on that particular occasion did these hunters accost you?

A. After shooting a deer down in the stream of Waihanau we packed it on top of this ridge. While we were there the hunters came along the boundary and stopped us and asked us why we were shooting on their lands, and one of my uncles spoke up and said, "They are our lands," and he said, "I can satisfy you by showing you the boundaries." Which he did. He walked over here and showed him this boundary (indicating [649] on exhibit).

Mr. Kemp: It is already marked Y.

Q. You know where the mouth of the tunnel is now?   A. I do.

Q. Where was it with reference to the mouth of the tunnel?

A. Just about 10 feet above the mouth of the tunnel.

Q. Just about 10 feet above the mouth of the tunnel. You had started up?

A. Yes. We walked over and showed him this boundary and back again, and my uncle Ben told him our boundary was at the edge of the valley down to the highest waterfall, and after he showed them that, they were satisfied, so they went along their own way and left us alone.

* * * * *   [650]

Q. A narrow, rough ridge. You may now be

(Testimony of William A. Meyer.)

seated. In your younger days were you acquainted with any old-timers in that vicinity who are now dead and who made statements to you as to these lands?   A. Yes, sir.

Q. First, before asking you what they said, I shall ask you who the people were that made such statements to you?

A. An old Hawaiian by the name of Ku.

Q. Ku?

A. Another one by the name of Alalalona.

Q. Are they both dead?

A. They are both dead.

Q. Tell us what, if anything, you know that gave them special knowledge of the location of lands in that community?

A. They practically lived up in the same location where we are today, and they were cowboys on the ranch, and every time we would go out driving cr when we were driving they would always tell us where our boundaries were; they always kept us [653] posted. In fact, Ku was practically raised by my grandfather.

Q. Did they ever tell you what was the head of Waihanau Valley?   A. Yes, sir.

Q. What did they say was the head of Waihanau Valley?

A. The head of Waihanau Valley——

Mr. Kimball: Just a moment, Mr. Meyer. Object, if the Court please, on the ground the answer calls for hearsay, based on conclusions of persons now dead and could not be brought in. * * * * *

(Testimony of William A. Meyer.)

The Court: I overrule your objection at this time and allow the testimony to come in, Mr. Kimball. If you can satisfy the court by any authorities this idea of yours is more than an idea under the law, why, of course, you may attempt to bring it in. Objection will be allowed for the purpose of the record.

Q. (By Mr. Kemp): For the purpose of a little more specific information [654] as to who these men were, you say this man Ku was practically a member of your grandfather's family?

A. Yes, sir.

Q. Reared by him, with him as long as he lived?

A. Yes.

The Court: How old a man was he?

Q. (By Mr. Kemp): How old a man was he when you were talking with him?

A. Oh, I would say he was all of fifty years, anyway.

Q. How many years was that from now, back, when he was telling you this?

A. You mean how old?

Q. No. Give us an idea as to when it was.

A. He was about fifty when he was telling me this.

Q. About when was it he was talking to you about these lands; was it all at one time or over a period of years?

A. Oh, off and on, every time we went driving.

Q. How long has Ku been dead?

(Testimony of William A. Meyer.)

A. Ku has been dead about 30 years, I think; 30 or 35 years.

Q. Did he talk to you about it shortly before his death, or was it a long time before his death?

A. No; quite a while before he died.

Q. About how old were you when he was talking to you? A. About 20, between 19 and 20.

Q. Did he tell you where the head of Waihanau Valley was? A. Yes.

Q. Did he tell you anything about where the boundaries of the Meyer lands was in Waihanau Valley?

A. Yes. He always told us where the boundaries of the [655] Meyer lands in Waihanau Valley were.

Q. Where did he say the boundary was of Waihanau Stream? Did he point out to you or did he tell you something?

A. He told us we had right up to this point, and along down and he would always say that is the boundary of Waihanau.

The Court: I can't see where he is pointing.

Mr. Kemp: He is following the ridge he says exists there down to the waterfall, if I may interpret his testimony, through the waterfall and up the ridge on the other side to the top. That would be from D to E and from E to W.

Be seated again.

Q. What was the name of this other old man that talked to you about these boundaries?

A. Alalalona.

Q. Who was Alalaona?

(Testimony of William A. Meyer.)

A. He was another Hawaiian cowboy on the ranch.

Q. He had been with your family for a long time?   A. Yes, sir.

Q. Worked on the ranch under your grandfather?   A. Under my grandfather.

Q. Did he tell you where the head of Waihanau Valley was too?   A. Yes.

Q. And where the boundaries of your lands were?   A. Yes, sir.

Q. Did it coincide with what Ku had told you?
A. Yes.

Q. These two uncles, Otto and—— [656]
A. Ben.

Q. Otto and Ben, are they the only ones of your uncles that ever told you about boundaries up there?

A. All my uncles, in fact, told me about the boundaries.

Q. But the occasion that stands out in your mind right now is the one with the hunters?

A. I traveled with those two, Otto and Ben, most of the time.

Q. Did they ever in their talk state what was the head of Waihanau Valley?   A. Yes.

Q. What did they say was the head of Waihanau Valley?

A. The high falls is the head of Waihanau Valley.

Q. By that you mean the big waterfall, the E on this map?   A. Yes, sir.

Q. Where you pointed out the line coming down

(Testimony of William A. Meyer.)
off the ridge?   A.   Yes, sir.

Q.   Along a steep ridge.

Cross-Examination

Q.   (By Mr. Kimball):   The hunters or men who spoke to you back in about 1900, wasn't it?

A.   Between 1899 and 1901.

Q.   They were employees of the American Sugar Company, weren't they?   A.   They were.

Q.   Do you know whether or not the land of Makanalua was leased by the government to the American Sugar Company at that time? [657]

A.   It was.

Mr. Flynn: Just a minute, Mr. Cass. I have a correction on my copy. Where that question reads, "Do you know whether or not the land of Kalamaula was leased by the government to the American Sugar Company at that time?" I am quite confident that is correct. I wonder if you have any objection to that.

Mr. Cass: I have no objection to that because I am quite sure no part of the Leper Settlement was ever leased by the government and I know that Kalamaula was leased to the American Sugar Company.

Mr. Flynn: Yes. There are many other records that could back that up. If you will stipulate with me——

Mr. Cass: I will stipulate that word "Makanalua" is incorrect and should be "Kalamaula."

(Testimony of William A. Meyer.)

Mr. Flynn: The same way in the next question you read too.

Mr. Cass: I will repeat that question.

"They thought you were on Kalamaula and you showed them you were on Kahanui, when they stopped you, didn't you?

A. Yes.

Q. They didn't claim you were on lands called Makanalua, did they?   A. No.

* * * * *   [658]

Redirect Examination

Mr. Flynn: I make objection, if the Court please, to that portion of the testimony beginning on page 145 having to do with the examination of this witness William Meyer as to what he was told by the two cowboys Ku and Alalalona, my objection being is that it was hearsay, as raised by the question, raised by counsel at the time of the earlier trial, that it was not qualified as kamaaina testimony.

The Court: Objection overruled. The record contains ample foundation for its admission as kamaaina testimony.

Mr. Flynn: May my exception be noted, please.

The Court: Your exception may be noted.

Mr. Cass: Now, if the Court please, we offer in evidence a copy of the eminent domain proceedings in Circuit Court of the Second Judicial Circuit, Territory of Hawaii, entitled Territory of Hawaii by Lyman Bigelow, its Superintendent of Public Works, versus Otto Meyer, et al. I do not see any

(Testimony of William A. Meyer.)
number on it. It is stamped "Filed, January 6, 1929, Manuel Asui, clerk, and duly certified by the clerk. For some reason the number does not appear in the abstract.

Mr. Flynn: The entire offer of [663] the exhibit I regard as on a matter that is incompetent, irrelevant and immaterial to the present application for registration of the lands, and I will object on that ground.

* * * * *

The Court: The objection is overruled.

Mr. Flynn: Note an exception, please.

The Court: An exception may be noted. It will become Applicant's Exhibit W in evidence.

(The document referred to was received in evidence as Applicant's Exhibit W.)

Mr. Cass: Now, the description of the lands pertaining [664] to Grant 3437, R. W. Meyer, on page 6 of this exhibit, is apparently taken from the grant and does not vary except at the end of the paragraph this further description is included: "That said parcels of land hereinabove referred to and described are more fully set out and shown upon two maps attached hereto as Exhibit A and Exhibit B, which exhibits are hereby made a part hereof and incorporated herein." The difference between this description and the grant description is that the grant description has no words incorporating the maps attached into the description. The map referred to, which refers to these particular lands, is shown here by our application, the overlay interposed on the sketch attached to the grant; it appears that the sketch attached to the grant and the land under application is limited by a very similar sketch.

Mr. Flynn: Well, the sketch in this exhibit you have offered is substantially identical with the one of the grant shown by this tracing.

Mr. Cass: Yes. That is the point I was making.

Mr. Flynn: No question.

Mr. Cass: Now, in connection with the testimony of Mr. King and the testimony of Mr. Carson as to an appraisal that they were making, I offer in evidence and ask to be permitted to read it in evidence the report of Samuel W. King on that appraisal. It is contained in a letter dated April 11, 1929, and the pertinent parts are: "April 11, 1929. Directed to Judge A. G. M. Robertson, Castle & Cooke Building, Honolulu, T. H.

"Dear Sir: [665]

"Herewith is a summary of my appraisal of the Meyer lands on Molokai, included in the forest reserve that the government is desirous to condemn."

It contains the appraisal signed "Samuel W. King."

Is there anything further in that that you wish to go in?

Mr. Flynn: Do you want to introduce the whole letter in evidence?

Mr. Cass: It does not make any difference to me.

Mr. Flynn: Have you read enough of it that you want to go in?

Mr. Cass: It reads enough for me.

Mr. Flynn: I have no objection to that.

Mr. Cass: I offer that to show the Court the purpose of the survey and the limitations placed upon the lands that were then being surveyed and appraised, as being a different survey and appraisal than the actual boundaries claimed by the Meyers but limited to the boundaries as set out in the sketch attached to the condemnation action.

Mr. Flynn: Wait a minute. May I hear what that offer is again?

Mr. Cass: I offer this transcript of the case itself, showing the description of the lands which were being condemned, and now I offer the report of Mr. Samuel W. King of an appraisal made specifically limited to the lands under condemnation.

Mr. Flynn: I will make no objection to all of that.

* * * * *   [666]

The Court: Further rebuttal?

Mr. Cass: Mr. McKeague.

BERNARD H. McKEAGUE

a witness called by and on behalf of the applicant, having been previously sworn, was further examined and testified as follows:

The Court: The record shows that Mr. McKeague has been sworn.

Direct Examination

Q. (By Mr. Cass): Mr. McKeague, have you prepared an outline of the sketch appearing upon Grant 3437 blown up to 400 feet to an inch?

A. I have.

Q. Can you place upon the map on the board there the blown up or overlay of it and trace it on the map, Applicant's Exhibit A?   A. I can.

Q. Where that line would run if the map were laid on the ground. Now, can you by any means transcribe that mark onto the map below?

A. I can.

* * * * *   [667]

A. And I will trace from the trig station Kaluahauoni along that line to the cross X.

* * * * *

Mr. Cass: I have marked it "McKeague's tracing," the line that he just marked in there.

* * * * *

Q. Now, as I note on the map here, the line goes through or close to the point marked "pipe" at the end of the first dotted line course shown on the map there?   A. Yes.

Q. Now, from that point to the point where the green line and the line you have traced across the

(Testimony of Bernard H. McKeague.)

stream, do the lines [668] approximate each other?

A. Yes. At a point about 100 or 150 feet below, what is shown here as "Waiau Falls."

Q. That is where they coincide?   A. Yes.

* * * * *   [669]

Cross-Examination

Q. (By Mr. Flynn): Didn't you testify when you began all this business, at the very beginning, that Points A and K were well located as you checked them against Monsarrat's notes?

A. By plotting only as you see it on that map, Exhibit A.

* * * * *

Q. On those old maps you saw that the lines go through K to A, didn't you?

A. No, never. [670]

Q. Calling your attention, Mr. McKeague, to Exhibit 11, and your attention specifically to Point X at the extreme north tip of Kahanui 3.

A. Yes.

Q. Doesn't that line go through Point K?

A. On this map it does.

Q. Doesn't that line go through Point A?

A. On this map it does.

* * * * *

The Clerk: We have Exhibit V for Identification, copy of letter, Department of Interior, in the Archives.

Mr. Cass: I don't care about that. It is not important at all; except as to certain irrelevant conclusions that judges made before.

The Court: Do you want to withdraw it?

Mr. Cass: I will withdraw it.

The Court: Let Exhibit V of the applicant, the offer of it be withdrawn.

* * * * *   [671]

The Court: Are counsel still in agreement that the one issue of fact presently for determination is the determination of the language "the head of Waihanau Valley," how the resulting ground boundary line resulted from that finding? That is, as I understand it, the original stipulation.

Mr. Flynn: Yes, that is it.

Mr. Cass: Yes.

Mr. Flynn: In other words, the first cause of action is just to settle that boundary line.

* * * * * [674]

[Endorsed]: Filed July 26, 1950.

————

[Endorsed]: No. 13545. United States Court of Appeals for the Ninth Circuit. R. W. Meyer, Limited, Appellant, vs. Territory of Hawaii, Appellee. Transcript of Record. Appeal from the Supreme Court for the Territory of Hawaii.

Filed: September 17, 1952.

/s/ PAUL P. O'BRIEN,

Clerk of the United States Court of Appeals for the Ninth Circuit.

In the United States Court of Appeals
for the Ninth Circuit

No. 13545

R. W. MEYER, LIMITED   Appellant,

vs.

TERRITORY OF HAWAII,   Appellee.

APPELLANT'S STATEMENT OF POINTS
RELIED UPON

Comes now R. W. Meyer, Limited, Appellant, in
the above entitled cause, by its attorneys, Phil Cass
and Samuel Shapiro, and sets forth below the points
relied upon by it in its appeal to the above entitled
Court;

1. The decision of the trial court was fully supported by competent evidence and it was error by
the Supreme Court of Hawaii to reverse the decision of the trial court.

2. The issues before the trial court were restricted by a stipulation entered into by the parties,
that the sole issue to be tried was a question of the
location of boundaries on the ground, described in
the original grant as a course "around the head
of Waihanau and Waialeia valleys". The evidence
for the Applicant was factual oral testimony, supported by evidence of the intent of the parties and
the record of the surveyor who wrote the description
of the course at issue, fixing the boundary in accordance with Applicant's claim, while the Respondent Territory of Hawaii offered no proof or

evidence of the location on the ground of said line but relied on the opinions of government employees, without knowledge of the actual line, based upon a "meander line" of the said boundary, traced upon government maps at unknown times by unknown persons and reproduced without regard to known monuments by independent government surveys. It was error in the Supreme Court of Hawaii to accept and adopt the testimony so offered in fixing the boundary different from that adopted by the trial court.

3. The Supreme Court of Hawaii held in its opinion that a sketch attached to the original grant, which contained a "meander line", admittedly unsurveyed by traverse, and which contained no indication of monuments fixing said "meander line" on the ground, other than the starting and ending points, controlled the description of the land conveyed, and was superior in evidence to the language of the grant describing the course by natural monument. This was error by that court.

4. The Supreme Court of Hawaii held in its opinion that the boundary line adopted by the trial court required that the course adopted by the trial court to contain courses in addition to those of the "meander line" and thus altered a written instrument. This is contrary to the evidence, in that the course adopted passes over a ridge without width where the two valleys join. This ruling was error by the Supreme Court of Hawaii in that unsurveyed "meander lines" almost invariably require many courses when laid out by a traversed survey identifying the line on the ground, the adoption of the

line approved by the trial court does not require any course other than those located on the natural monuments described in the grant, and which the "meander line" purported to follow; the factual evidence shows that the boundary of the land known as "Waihanau valley" follows the trial court's line.

5. The Supreme Court of Hawaii held that there was a "vast reservoir" of maps in governmental files which showed and controlled the boundary. This is contrary to the evidence in that the government witnesses testified that all of the maps were copies of the original in varying scales, without additional surveys, so that there was but one map, if any, of evidenciary value, that this map was a "progressive map" with a sketch of the land under litigation added after the grant and without any survey or factual location of the line along the disputed boundary; that there never had been a survey of that boundary until the Applicant had it surveyed for this action; that there was no record as to the identity of the person who drafted the sketch on the original map and that many additions had been made by various parties unknown since the map was first made and no way existed to determine what was on any government map at the time of the grant. It was error in the Supreme Court of Hawaii to adopt or consider these map copies as having additional weight, if any, by virtue of the duplication.

6. The advertisement by which this land was sold by the government of Hawaii to the predecessor in interest of the Applicant, described the land as being the whole of the lele of Kahanui, in accord-

ance with a description on file, which is in evidence, and which does not refer to any map or other limitation on the description. The government has admitted the intent to convey the whole of the lele according to its ancient boundaries in the correspondence in evidence. If the actual location on the ground of the limits of the Waihanau valley had not been established by uncontradicted testimony in accordance with the finding of the trial court, the evidence of the intent of the parties, as shown by this government evidence, would have been binding on the court as fixing the line on the ancient boundaries, as shown by testimony of the witnesses and the survey of adjoining land by Pease, offered by the Respondent. As it stands, the evidence of ancient boundaries substantiates the testimony of the location of that monument. It was error for the Supreme Court of Hawaii to hold such evidence inadmissible in the face of the uncontradicted factual testimony it confirmed.

7. It was error for the Supreme Court of Hawaii to disregard the field notes of the surveyor who wrote the description for the grant, which, by sketch shown on page 112 of his field book, locates the line of the boundary as passing through the big water fall, and locates the Waihanau gulch below those falls.

8. It was error for the Supreme Court of Hawaii to direct the trial court to amend the decree by substituting the line of boundary claimed by the government for that in the decree when there was absolutely no evidence offered by the government by

persons familiar with the monument named locating that line or monument on the ground.

9. It was error for the Supreme Court of Hawaii to reverse a decree of the trial court founded on substantial evidence by a reconsideration of the weight, if any, of the evidence offered by the government and to try, de novo, the issue decided by the court below.

10. The issue tried in the Land Court was limited and stipulated by the parties to be the determination of the location on the ground of the location on the ground of the course described in the grant as "around the head of Waihanau and Waialeia valleys". The only evidence offered in the trial court and before the Supreme Court of Hawaii on appeal was that of the Applicant as to the location of that parcel of land known as "Waihanau valley", which was fixed as the name of the box canyon below the big falls, with the boundary being the line adopted by the trial court. It was error for the Supreme Court to attempt, by speculation, and without any evidence, to fix a boundary at any point not identified by evidence as the boundary of the valley, or to assume that the name "Waihanau valley" applied to any place not so identified.

Respectfully submitted,

/s/ PHIL CASS,
               Attorney for Appellant

[Endorsed]: Filed Oct. 27, 1952. Paul P. O'Brien, Clerk.

[Title of U. S. Court of Appeals and Cause.]

STIPULATION AND ORDER
Stipulation

It is hereby stipulated by and between the Appellant and Appellee by their respective counsel that for all purposes of the entitled appeal resort may be had to the original exhibits, in lieu of printing thereof.

Dated: November 5, 1952.

> R. W. MEYER, LTD.,
>> Appellant,

/s/ By PHIL CASS,
>> Attorney

> TERRITORY OF HAWAII,
>> Appellee,

/s/ By RHODA V. LEWIS,
>> Deputy Attorney General

Order

Pursuant to the Stipulation of the parties it is hereby Ordered that for all purposes of the above entitled appeal resort may be had to the original exhibits, in lieu of printing thereof.

Dated: November 10, 1952.

Approved:

> /s/ WILLIAM DENMAN,
> /s/ WILLIAM HEALY,
> /s/ WALTER L. POPE,
>> Judges, U. S. Court of Appeals for the Ninth Circuit

[Endorsed]: Filed Nov. 12, 1952. Paul P. O'Brien, Clerk.

No. 13,545

IN THE

United States Court of Appeals
For the Ninth Circuit

R. W. MEYER, LIMITED,

                           Appellant,

    VS.

TERRITORY OF HAWAII,

                           Appellee.

Appeal from the Supreme Court of the
Territory of Hawaii.

APPELLANT'S OPENING BRIEF.

PHIL CASS,
2186 City View, Eugene, Oregon,
SAMUEL SHAPIRO,
506 Stangenwald Building, Honolulu, T. H.,
Attorneys for Appellant.

FILED

APR 16 1953

PAUL P. O'BRIEN

Subject Index

Table of Authorities Cited

No. 13,545

United States Court of Appeals
For the Ninth Circuit

R. W. MEYER, LIMITED,

Appellant,

vs.

TERRITORY OF HAWAII,

Appellee.

Appeal from the Supreme Court of the Territory of Hawaii.

APPELLANT'S OPENING BRIEF.

Comes now R. W. Meyer, Limited, appellant in the above entitled case, and submits its opening brief in support of its appeal, as follows:

STATEMENT OF THE JURISDICTION OF THE COURTS.

This case originated in the Land Court of the Territory of Hawaii, by a petition to register and confirm the title of R. W. Meyer, Limited, an Hawaiian corporation, to lands situate in Molokai, Territory of Hawaii, which have a claimed reasonable value of $750,000.00, as set out in petition. The Land Court has jurisdiction of such cases, Section 12600, Revised Laws of Hawaii, 1945, and by special act of the

Legislature of Hawaii, contained in Act 207 of the Session Laws of Hawaii, 1947, additional jurisdiction to hear and determine the claim of applicant for rents and damages for occupancy of the land by the Territory, Copy of Act 207, Session Laws of Hawaii, 1947, annexed to amended application, certified record pages 34-39, which rental and damage claim is in the sum of $565,000.00. All of which value and claims depend upon the determination of the issue now before this Court of Appeal. The Supreme Court of Hawaii had jurisdiction of the case through a writ of error, issued on petition of appellee, R. 5, writ at R. 13, by virtue of Section 12635, Revised Laws of Hawaii, 1945. The jurisdiction of this Court lies on appeal from judgment on writ of error of the Supreme Court of Hawaii, under authority of Title 28, U.S.C.A., Section 1293, permitting appeals to the United States Court of Appeals for the Ninth Circuit from all final decisions of the Supreme Court of Hawaii, where the amount in controversy exceeds $5,000.00, exclusive of interest and costs. The value in excess of $5,000.00 is shown above.

STATEMENT OF THE CASE.

This is a case for registration of title under the Torrens System adopted by Hawaii. No issue is made of the basic title, but there is a dispute as to the boundary of the abutting lands where the appellee owns the Leper Settlement adjoining. (R. 61.) The issues were defined and limited by the parties to the issue of the location of this common boundary on the ground, stipulation being made and approved that this issue should be heard and determined, including appeal, before the supplementary action, second cause, for the damages, should be tried. (R. 43, 60, 61, and restated by the Court and agreed, R. 416.)

The controversy arises from the description in the original patent 3437 (Applicant's Ex. B), of the course "thence around the head of Waihanau (valleys) and Waialeia Valley". The applicant, appellant, claiming that the location of the line described was in accordance with a well-known, ancient land boundary of the original parcel, identified by parol evidence, the field book of the surveyor writing the description (Terr. Ex. 16), the acceptance of the boundary line claimed through many years of occupancy and exclusion of the lepers from this land by the predecessor in title of appellant and the government officials in charge of the leper settlement, the intent of the parties, as shown by the correspondence in evidence, and the topography showing a natural, impassable boundary at this point. The appellee claims that a sketch attached to the Patent 3437, by means of a meander line locates the boundary on the ground at a point some 2,000 feet above the line claimed by the appellant. The issues are raised by the amended application (R. 14) (erroneously indexed in the record as "Amended Application for Writ of Error"), with maps attached, the answer of the Territory of Hawaii (R. 18), with map attached, the assignment of errors by appellee in the Supreme Court (R. 5), and the opinion of the Supreme Court of Hawaii (R. 38).

The Land Court, after a hearing on the facts, adopted the testimony of the witnesses and other evidence of the location of the line as claimed by the appellant, and located the line as claimed. On writ of error to the Supreme Court of Hawaii, the decision was reversed. The Supreme Court of Hawaii held that the sketch controlled the boundary line over the location of that line on the ground as shown by parol and extrinsic evidence, and adopted the line given in opinion testimony of government surveyors, without any direct evidence as to the ground location, other than the laying out of the meander line of the sketch attached to the grant by means of office triangulation translated into a newly surveyed reproduction of the meander line on the ground.

The issues raised on appeal to this Court are as follows:

Is the sketch attached to the Patent 3437 controlling as a boundary line over the description "around the head of Waihanau Valley" as identified by the testimony of witnesses knowing that line, and extrinsic evidence as shown above? Raised by statement of points.

Can the testimony of surveyors be admitted to determine the location on the ground of a meander line on a sketch in the absence of any factual knowledge by the witnesses of the location on the ground of the monument described, which the meander line is supposed to indicate? Raised by statement of points.

Does the Supreme Court of Hawaii have jurisdiction on hearing a writ of error from the Land Court of Hawaii to reconsider the evidence and retry the facts? Raised by Section 12633, Revised Laws of Hawaii, 1945.

In view of the evidence and the finding of facts by the Land Court, was the reversal of its decree erroneous? Raised by statement of points, and by the decision in the Supreme Court of Hawaii. (R. 38.)

Does the factual location on the ground of a line of boundary described as a natural monument constitute "varying or contradicting a written instrument"? Raised by the opinion of the Supreme Court. (R. 39.)

Are "progressive maps," admittedly added to and changed since the date of the grant, without record or information as to the nature and extent of the changes, admissible to fix a boundary not identified on the map by monument? Raised by opinion of Supreme Court (R. 38) and statement of points.

Where a sketch is attached to, but not incorporated in by reference, a grant, having on its face no indication of topography, authorship, scale, directions or source of data, can such a plat control the boundary as against a description of a natural monument identified by witnesses and extrinsic evidence? Raised by assignment of errors (R. 5), opinion of Supreme Court (R. 38), and statement of points.

The argument follows the appellant's points (R. 417) in order, each point being copied at the head of the argument concerning it.

ARGUMENT.
POINT 1.
THE DECISION OF THE TRIAL COURT WAS FULLY SUPPORTED BY COMPETENT EVIDENCE AND IT WAS ERROR BY THE SUPREME COURT OF HAWAII TO REVERSE THE DECISION OF THE TRIAL COURT.

The parties limited the issue to be tried to the question of the location on the ground of a call in the patent (Ap. Ex. B) which reads "thence around the head of Waihanau Valley" (R. 42, 61, 412). This appears as an unsurveyed "meander line" (R. 43, 49, 54) between the property of the parties (R. 61) on a sketch attached to the patent (Ap. Ex. B). The Supreme Court of Hawaii held that the description of the call was unambiguous. (R. 47.) This leaves the sole issue to be determined a matter of fact, the location of the call upon the ground. Title, other than the location of the boundary, is undisputed.

What is a boundary is a matter of law. Where it is located on the ground is a matter of fact.

McCandless v. DuRoi, 23 Haw. 51;

Kelekolio v. Onomea, 29 Haw. 130;

Sale v. Pulaski, 117 S.W. 404;

Montana Mining Co. v. St. Louis, 183 Fed. 51;

Cole v. Mueller, 187 Mo. 638;

Boundaries of Pulehunui, 4 Haw. 239-243.

The true location of boundaries may be shown by parol evidence.

Hooten v. Comerford, 23 Am. St. 861 (Ann.).

Under the well established rule of law that such evidence is always admissible to apply a writing to its subject, and, therefore, to identify monuments called for in descriptions of tracts of land contained in patents and deeds.

Brown v. Huger, 21 U.S. 305, 16 L. ed. 125.

Where there is a dispute concerning the true location of natural objects called for in a grant or deed, and the evidence is conflicting, or where the evidence tends to show two or more natural objects that may answer the description, the boundary must be determined by the jury under the court's instruction.

Parran v. Wilson, 154 Atl. 449.

Natural objects called for in a grant may be proved by testimony not found in the grant but consistent with it.

Blake v. Dougherty, 5 Wheat. 359, 5 L. ed. 109.

The evidence which the Hawaiian Supreme Court rejected is as follows:

The land is a part of the Ahupuaa (land tract assigned to an overlord) of Kahanui. It is a lele (outlying tract separated from the main ahupuaa). The whole ahupuaa was originally awarded to the konohiki (overlord), including, by name, and unsurveyed, the lele. In order to perfect his title, the overlord was required to have the land surveyed and the survey filed, whereupon a patent granting the land in fee simple would issue. This overlord, by some mistake of the surveyor, failed to file the survey of the lele now in dispute, but transferred his title to the ahupuaa by deed, by ancient boundaries, to R. W. Meyer. (Ap.´ Ex. T-U.) Meyer was then in occupancy and had been since about 1850. (R. 188.) (Mrs. Aubery, born in 1868, was the youngest of nine children born at Kahanui of R. W. Meyer and his wife, a local Hawaiian girl.) He and his successors continued in occupancy until 1924 without any question being raised as to the boundary.

In 1885, M. D. Monsarrat, a government surveyor, was engaged in making a survey of lower Molokai along the southern boundary of the land in dispute (Terr. Ex. 16), verifying old surveys of lands, including the main Meyer ranch of Kahanui (Terr. Exs. 6 and 16), when he was advised of the existence of this lele (Terr. Exs. 6-7) by Kamaainas (persons raised on the land familiar with boundaries). He informed Meyer of the discrepancy in his title and Meyer had him write a description (Terr. Ex. 19) of the lele, which was later, by Meyer, furnished the government for the purpose of sale of the land to Meyer under the law (Sections 42, 43, 44, 45, Compiled Laws of Hawaii, 1884, Appendix page i. Monsarrat drew a sketch in his field book (Terr. Ex. 16, page 112) of the boundaries of the lele, placing that boundary on the big waterfall now claimed by appellant to be the "head of Waihanau Valley".

Meyer was a surveyor. (R. 178.) He was the agent for the leper colony and for the owner of Makanalua, from whom appellee takes title. (Ex. R, Ap. Ex. C-1.) In return for his services he had been promised a tract of land at a nominal sum. (Ap. Ex. C-1.) He had selected the Waihanau Valley, which was then a "part and parcel of the leper colony", as his tract, but, becoming convinced that lepers were a permanent feature, wanted no part of the "Waihanau Valley". (Ap. Ex. C-1.) He had for many years occupied the land above Waihanau Valley and had put up "kapu" (forbidden) signs on the top of the big falls, where there was an ancient boundary stone. (R. 174, 186, Ap. Ex. R.) This was expressly to keep the lepers off the lele which he occupied. (R. 174-186.) The officials in charge of the leper settlement cooperated in keeping the lepers off and recognized that boundary. (Ap. Ex. R, R. 174.)

When Meyer was advised of the defect in his title, he wrote Thurston, Secretary of the Interior, reciting the above facts, and asking that he be given a patent for his land. (Ap. Ex. C-1.) Thurston wrote back that a patent could not then be granted and that Meyer could either go to the legislature for relief or purchase the land title at public auction. (Ap. Ex. E.) Meyer then wrote Thurston offering to purchase the whole of the land occupied by him and constituting the ancient lele that he had bought by ancient boundaries, enclosing Monsarrat's description of the land. (Ap. Ex. C-3.) The land was then advertised as the "whole of the remnant or lele of Kahanui" (Ap. Ex.

D-2), under the law that required a description to be filed but did not require a map (see Section 42, Compiled Laws of Hawaii, 1884, Appendix page i). Maps and surveys are differentiated in Section 45. The land was accordingly knocked down to Meyer (Ap. Ex. D-2), and a patent issued (Ap. Ex. J). Meyer was dissatisfied with the description on the patent, and returned it to Thurston with a penciled notation of the true description on it in Monsarrat's handwriting. (Ap. Ex. J.) There had been attached to the patent by the "young man who fills out the patents" (Ap. Ex. L) a plat or sketch, with nothing on the sketch to indicate that it was to scale or that it was a surveyed map (Ap. Exs. J, B), the disputed boundary being run in as a "meandering line" (R. 43, 52, 53, 54), without monument, station or other location except the point of beginning and terminus (Ap. Ex. B). This is the first and only indication that Meyer ever had that the parcel had been sketched. He knew it had not been traversed. (Terr. Ex. 16.) Thurston, speaking from "an examination of the records", said that he would correct the clerical errors, but could not legally add to the area of the description. He offered to sell for a nominal sum at a private sale the excluded portion, which he admitted should have been in the original description of the lele. The original patent was corrected as to spelling of place names and returned to Meyer.

Meyer and his successors continued in possession of the land down to the big falls until 1924, when negotiations were commenced for its purchase by the

Territory, and, these failing, a condemnation suit was started, in 1929. (Ap. Ex. W.) The condemnation suit (Ap. Ex. W) was the first dispute as to this boundary which has persisted to now.

From the above, it will be seen that Meyer knew the boundary of Waihanau Valley to be below the big falls "wholly within the leper colony"; Monsarrat knew that the boundary was below the falls (Terr. Ex. 16), he ran the boundary through the falls in his field book and noted "Waihanau Valley" below the falls (R. 332, Terr. Ex. 16, page 112). He prepared the description from this sketch. (R. 334.) This is factual evidence of the location of this boundary known to the parties.

The following witnesses were all reared on the land from infancy. All but Tuitele were born on the land. All had contact with R. W. Meyer in his lifetime. All knew intimately the old Hawaiians of the neighborhood. They all testified positively that "Waihanau Valley" is the name of the box canyon below the falls and the falls constituted the boundary (as set out below).

Aubery, 82 years old (R. 184), daughter of R. W. Meyer (R. 183), picnicked with her father at the edge of the falls many years before the date of the patent (R. 185). Her father then occupied the land (R. 185), claimed it as his own, and had redwood posts and kapu signs at the head of the falls to keep off the lepers .(R. 186, 174, Ap. Ex. R). She was nursed and raised by the old Hawaiians who knew the boundaries. (R. 188.) The edge of Waihanau

Valley is the edge of the big falls. (R. 185.) There was an ancient boundary stone at the head of the falls. (R. 186.) There was a path across the head of the falls that was ancient when she was a girl. (R. 189.) Waihanau is wholly Makanalua, the leper settlement. (R. 192-193.)

Tuitele, 62 years old (R. 172), born in Honolulu (R. 173), but raised in Molokai on these lands from before she was four years old. Picnicked at the head of the big falls with her grandfather before she was four. (R. 173-180.) Married the doctor in the leper settlement and lived there thirty years. (R. 175.) There were redwood posts at the head of the falls from her earliest recollection. (R. 174.) She knows the location of the Waihanau Valley from her grandfather, the cowboys, the old Hawaiians, and her uncles, and her contact with the members and officials of the leper settlement. (R. 174, 178, 179.) Waihanau Valley runs from the sea to the big falls. (R. 182.) Waihanau Falls are below the land of her grandfather. (R. 182-183.)

Ernest Meyer, 58 years old (R. 198), grandson of R. W. Meyer, born on the land, spent all his life there. Knew his grandfather, his uncles, and the old Hawaiians in the vicinity. Learned the location of Waihanau from them. (R. 198.) Waihanau Valley lies below the big falls. (R. 199, 201.) The name of the high falls is Kaulahuki. (R. 200.)

Penn Meyer, 42 years old, born on the land, knew all the old folks (R. 205); quoting his father, he said the boundary was below the big falls which are named Kaulahuki (R. 205).

William Meyer, now dead, would be about 75 years old. Born on the land, lived there all his life. (R. 403.) Names old Hawaiians he knew who told him of the location of Waihanau over fifty years ago (R. 404-405); showed on the map "he is following the ridge he says exists there down to the waterfall, through the waterfall, and up the ridge to the top" (R. 407). The high falls at the head of Waihanau Valley, where he pointed out the line crossing the falls, there is a ridge, a steep ridge running down from one side, and up the other from the falls. (R. 409.)

The Territory introduced in evidence the description of the survey of Makanalua (the leper settlement) deeded to the government in 1866, description by Pease, 1865 (Terr. Ex. 9), by which the common boundary is described as "following the top of the pali bounding Makanalua gulch or ravine, on the west to a certain mountain peak at the head of said gulch called 'Kaulahuki'." It was agreed by Mc-Keague and Newton, the surveyors, that Pease never traversed this course, but "fudged it in". (R. 108, 281.) The name "Kaulahuki" given to the place at the head of the valley by Pease, described by him as a mountain peak, is shown to be the name of the big falls. (R. 200, 205, 80.) McKeague, a surveyor, made inquiry among kamaainas to locate the boundary. (R. 78.) He was informed that the name of the big falls was "Kualahuki" and drew his map as translation of the kamaaina testimony he had received. (R. 80.)

> "Monsarratt, surveyor, gave testimony that the survey and map before the commissioner was made along the lines which the above witnesses and other kamaainas had pointed out to him. We do not transcribe; it is not original testimony. What is admissible is that he has translated the description of the kamaainas into the definite expression of the survey. Boundaries of Pulehunui, 4 Haw, 239, 245."

Ernest Meyer: "The second fall of the big falls is called Kaulahuki. I have never heard the name Kaulahuki referred to a mountain peak." (R. 202.) Penn Meyer: "I used to hear some of the old Hawaiians say it (the big falls) used to be Kaulahuki." (R. 205, 206.) There is a mountain called Kaulahuki on Molokai, a government triangulation station, but it is about 4,000 yards south of the boundaries of this land and could not possibly be boundary monument, according to Newton, government surveyor. (Terr. Ex. 16, p. 111.)

Howell, government witness, says that the description under dispute is a matter of interpretation (R. 401) and that the name "Waihanau" is not the name of the whole watershed, but is the local name of a small area. (R. 402.)

The Supreme Court of Hawaii quotes with approval (R. 48) the case of *Ookala v. Wilson,* 13 Haw. 127, as follows:

> It is settled that parol evidence is admissible when the question is one of location as distin-

guished from one of construction, that is, such evidence is admissible to connect the land with the grant or to apply the grant to the land.

The issue before the court was exactly that. The Supreme Court so holds "The sole issue before the Land Court for determination by stipulation of the parties was the location of the middle western portion." (R. 42.) "The crux of the case concerns the location of a portion of boundary, rather than a construction of the grant" (R. 48), and quotes with approval *Ookala S. Co. v. Wilson,* 13 Haw. 127-131: "It is settled that parol evidence is admissible when the question is one of location, as distinguished from one of construction." (R. 48.) By stipulation and approval of the court, the court was limited; "determination of the language 'the head of Waihanau valley' how the resulting ground boundary line resulted from the finding? That is, as I understand it, the original stipulation." Mr. Flynn: "Yes, that is it." (R. 416.) The resulting *ground* boundary line is a question of location. Without proof of the location of the line on the ground the grant cannot be connected with the land, or the land with the grant. The erroneous assumption, by the Supreme Court, that "Waihanau Valley" is a generic term for the watershed, the line to be placed anywhere within that area, is responsible for the false authority placed with the opinion evidence adopting the "meander line", so called by all the surveyors and the Supreme Court (R. 43, 49, 53), of an unsurveyed (R. 314), untraversed (R. 322),

unidentified sketch and the maps copied therefrom
(R. 339), as superior to the definite, unambiguous
language (R. 47) of the call. Under any theory of
procedure, where there is a meander line unmarked
on the map by any landmark or monument, factual
parol testimony is required to tie the boundary in
and define its course on the ground, otherwise the
grant is defective and the description meaningless.
Even the erroneous adoption of sketches and maps
divorced from the field books of the surveyor, as
appears in the Supreme Court's opinion as being
superior to and overruling the written description,
requires some tie-in with the earth for identification,
which was not supplied by the appellee or from the
record.

Not one witness was produced by appellee familiar
with the ground. No one testified for the appellee
from the knowledge of the boundary, the location of
Waihanau Valley, or the identity of any monument
along the disputed line, except the monument "cross
on rock" where the line starts. Newton, the government's surveyor, laid out on the ground, from office
triangulation, the course of the meander line, but
looked for no monuments before making his own independent map. (R. 343.) His opinion and the opinion
of the other surveyors called by the government, all
admittedly based upon the acceptance of the meander
line as a rigid, permanent, controlling boundary, and
testifying directly that their opinions were taken from
the map. Newton: "I haven't made many trips to
Molokai, I am not too familiar with that section." (R.

318.) Howell: "The description of this survey depends upon interpretation." (R. 407.) Jorgenson: "I had a map" (R. 384, 381), can have no validity in fixing the ground line in the absence of either physical monuments or points, named in the description, by mathematical process.

———

POINT 2.

THE ISSUES BEFORE THE TRIAL COURT WERE RESTRICTED BY A STIPULATION ENTERED INTO BY THE PARTIES (R. 42, 61, 416) THAT THE SOLE ISSUE TO BE TRIED WAS THE QUESTION OF THE LOCATION OF BOUNDARIES ON THE GROUND DESCRIBED IN THE ORIGINAL GRANT AS A COURSE "AROUND THE HEAD OF WAIHANAU AND WAIALEIA VALLEYS". THE EVIDENCE FOR THE APPELLANT WAS FACTUAL, ORAL TESTIMONY, SUPPORTED BY DOCUMENTARY EVIDENCE OF THE INTENT OF THE PARTIES AND THE RECORD OF THE SURVEYOR WHO WROTE THE DESCRIPTION OF THE COURSE AT ISSUE, FIXING THE BOUNDARY IN ACCORDANCE WITH APPLICANT'S CLAIM. THE RESPONDENT TERRITORY OF HAWAII OFFERED NO PROOF OR EVIDENCE OF THE LOCATION ON THE GROUND OF SAID LINE BUT RELIED ON THE OPINIONS OF GOVERNMENT EMPLOYEES, WITHOUT KNOWLEDGE, BASED UPON A "MEANDER LINE" OF THE SAID BOUNDARY, TRACED UPON THE GOVERNMENT MAPS AT UNKNOWN TIMES BY UNKNOWN PERSONS AND REPRODUCED WITHOUT REGARD TO KNOWN MONUMENTS BY INDEPENDENT GOVERNMENT SURVEYS. IT WAS ERROR IN THE SUPREME COURT OF HAWAII TO ACCEPT AND ADOPT THE TESTIMONY SO OFFERED IN FIXING THE BOUNDARY DIFFERENT FROM THAT ADOPTED BY THE TRIAL COURT.

Monsarrat, surveyor, gave testimony that the survey and map before the commissioner was made along the lines which the above witnesses and other kamaainas had pointed out to him * * *

We do not transcribe this because it is not original testimony. What is admissible is that he has translated the description of the kamaainas into the definite expression of the survey. (R. 250-251.)

Survey and plat which might be in existence in any office of the government would not in itself be evidence of a boundary if it had not been incorporated in an award or patent.

Boundaries of Pulehunui, 4 Haw. 239-245.

It is also settled that parol evidence is admissible when the question is one of location as distinguished from one of construction, that is, such evidence is admissible to connect the land with the grant or the grant with the land.

Ookala v. Wilson, 13 Haw. 127-131.

There is a diagram on the face of the patent which shows that this course was along the coast but at present we are considering only the description contained in the patent.

Ookala v. Wilson, 13 Haw. 127-130.

It then went further and found on all the evidence that CE was the correct line and added that this was also the practical construction put upon the description for many years by the parties hereto and their predecessors, including the government, which is the owner, and the lessees, of the adjoining land * * * We cannot say that the trial court erred. (diagram attached.)

Ookala v. Wilson, 13 Haw. 127-136.

The natural monument along the entire front is given as the edge or shore of the sea. This, of course, would control courses, distance and area, in the absence of a clearly indicated intention to the contrary. (diagram attached.)

Brown v. Spreckels, 14 Haw. 399-405.

* * * The true location of boundaries may be shown by parol evidence (Hooten v. Comerford, 23 Am. St. 861, Ann. 6 LRA (NS) 938) under the well established rule of law that such evidence is always admissible to apply a writing to its subject, and therefore to identify monuments called for in descriptions of tracts of land contained in patents and deeds.

> *Brown v. Huger,* 21 U.S. 305, 16 L. ed. 125, 13 L.R.A. N.S. 958.

Natural objects called for in grant may be proved by testimony not found in grant but consistent with it.

Blake v. Dougherty, 5 Wheat. 359, 5 L. ed. 109.

The rule now generally established in the United States, however, is that evidence of common repute is admissible as to the location of a private as well as a public boundary line.

Ann. 47 Am. St. 602.

What are boundaries is a question of law and where they are is a question of fact.

Kelekolio v. Onomea, 29 Haw. 130.

The identity of a monument found on the ground with one referred to in a deed is a question for the jury.

McCausland v. York, 174 A. 383.

Where there is a dispute concerning true location of natural objects called for in grant or deed, and the evidence is conflicting, or where the evidence tends to show two or more natural objects that may answer the description the boundaries must be determined by the jury under the court's instructions.

Parran v. Wilson, 154 A. 449.

* * * The declarations of a former owner are admissible in evidence, but in order that they may be received, they must establish some fact, as a corner stone or particular marked line.

Boardman v. Reed, 6 Pet. (U.S.) 328, 8 L. ed. 415.

The boundary line of a public grant may not be changed by a survey or resurvey made several years after the original survey under which the land was granted (190 U.S. 452) nor are the decisions of the Land Department assuming to fix the boundary in accordance with the surveys admissible in evidence.

U. S. v. State Investment, 264 U.S. 206, 68 L. ed. 639.

What is the boundary between certain lands is a matter of law, but the location of that boundary is a matter of fact.

Kelekolio v. Onomea, 29 Haw. 130-134;

Smith v. Smith, 110 Mass. 302-304;

Whitehead v. Regan, 106 Mo. 231-236;

Taylor v. Femby, 22 So. 910-12;

Mitchell v. Williams, 76 S.E. 949;

McCandless v. DuRoi, 23 Haw. 51-53.

In that event the rule would apply that "course and distance will yield to known visible and definite objects whether natural or artificial". 5 Cyc. 913-921. This is unavoidable where, as here, the bank of the auwai, (water ditch) is the boundary. *McCandless v. DuRoi,* 23 Haw. 51-54.

The south bank of the auwai being irregular, the located points given in the former decree are to be taken as meander points merely, and are not to be regarded as points on the exact boundary * * * In other words, the straight lines from point to point, as shown on the plan attached to the description in the former case, were not intended to be, and are not, claimed to be boundary lines. They are mere meander lines * * * These are called meander lines and they are not the boundary of the tract, but they merely define the sinuosities of the stream which constitutes the boundary, and as a general rule, the mentioning in a deed or grant, of a meander line on the bank of a river as a boundary, will convey title as far as the shore, unless a contrary intention is clearly apparent, 4 RCL p. 97, See also 5 Cyc. 899, Whitaker v. McBride, 197 US 510-512, Freeman v. Bellegarde, 108 Cal 179-185, Stemstreet v. Jacobs, 118 Ky. 745-749, Tucker v. Mortenson, 126 Minn. 214. In Mitchell v. Small, 140 US 406-414, the Supreme Court said "It has been decided again and again that the meander line is not a boundary but that the body of water whose margin is meandered is the true boundary."
McCandless v. DuRoi, 23 Haw. 51-56.

The meander lines run along or near the margin of waters are run by the government for the pur-

pose of ascertaining the exact quantity of the
upland to be charged for, and not for the purpose of limiting the title of the grantee to such
meander lines.

> *McDade v. Bossier Levee Board,* 33 So. 628-
> 630, 109 La. 625, quoting and adopting defi-
> nition in *Hardin v. Jordan,* 11 S. Ct. 811,
> 140 U.S. 380, 35 L. ed. 428;
>
> *St. Paul & P. R. Co. v. Schurmeier,* 74 U.S.
> 272-286.

A meander line generally contains a call for a
natural object or monument which will usually
control over calls for course and distance.

> *State v. Armin,* Tex. Civ. App., 173 S.W. 2d
> 503-509.

A meander line is not a boundary.

> *City of Cedar Rapids v. Marshal,* 203 N.W.
> 932, 199 Iowa 1262.

"Meander line", whether state or national, is
not considered a boundary line.

> *McLeod v. Reyes,* 40 P. 2d 839-844, 4 Cal. App.
> 2d 143.

"Meander lines" are run in surveying fractional portions of the public lands bordering
upon navigable rivers, not as boundaries of the
tract, but for the purpose of defining the sinuosities of the banks of the stream.

> *Seabrook v. Coos Bay Ice Co.,* 89 P. 417-418,
> 49 Or. 237.

A "meander line" in an official survey is not
a line of boundary, but as said in Horne v. Smith,

15 S. Ct. 988, 159 U.S. 40, 40 L. ed. 68, is used
as a means of ascertaining the quantity of land
in the fraction which is to be paid for by the
purchaser.

Tolleston Club of Chicago v. Lindgren, 77 N.E.
818-820, 39 Ind. App. 448;

State v. Tuesburg Land Co., 109 N.E. 530-538,
61 Ind. App. 553;

Jones v. Pettibone, 2 Wis. 308-320.

A meander line is not a line of boundary, but
one designed to point out the sinuosity of the
bank or shore and a means of ascertaining the
quantity of land in the fraction which is to be
paid for by the purchaser.

Sherwin v. Bitzer, 106 N.W. 1046-1047, adopting definition in Whitaker v. McBride, 25 S.
Ct. 531, 197 U.S. 510, 49 L. ed. 857.

Meander lines are run in surveying public
lands to ascertain the quantity of lands subject
to sale, not to bound the tract.

Producer's Oil Co. v. Hanzen, 238 U.S. 325, 59
L. ed. 1330, 35 S. Ct. 755;

Security Land & Ex. Co. v. Weckley, 193 U.S.
188, 48 L. ed. 674, 24 S. Ct. 431;

French-Glenn Livestock Co. v. Springer, 185
U.S. 47, 46 L. ed. 800, 22 S. Ct. 563;

Niles v. Cedar Point Club, 175 U.S. 300, 44 L.
ed. 171, 20 S. Ct. 124;

Annotation 42 L.R.A. 510, 94 Am. St. 541.

A map means not only a delineation giving a
general idea of the land taken, but also such full

and accurate notes and data as are necessary to furnish complete means for identifying and ascertaining the precise position of every part, with courses and distances, so that every part can be found.

Hollister v. State, 77 Pac. 339, 9 Idaho 651.

So that the making of a map of an addition implies that the addition had been surveyed, and that such survey was marked on the ground so that the streets, blocks and lots can be identified.

Burke v. McCowen, 47 Pac. 367-368, 115 Cal. 481.

As to the official maps in the general Land Office, they represent nothing more than the draftsman's and commissioner's opinions and conclusions from the records and available information as to the location of the various surveys with reference the one to the other.

Weatherly v. Jackson, 71 S.W. 2d 259-263.

In an action involving boundary, fact that there were no marks on ground indicating location of lines as claimed by plaintiff was strong evidence that such lines never were surveyed or could not be ascertained.

Neill v. Ward, 153 A. 219, 103 Vt. 117.

A map or plot is not conclusive * * * or although it is annexed to an original grant and made a part thereof to indicate the shape and location of the boundaries.

Gunter v. Whiting Mfg. Co., 81 S.E. 1070.

The location of monuments is a question of fact for the jury.

Emvil v. Smith, 242 N.W. 407;

Wilson v. McCoy, 103 S.E. 42.

It was argued that the original maps and the reports should have been admitted as memoranda to refresh the memory of Mr. Barker the surveyor. Such memoranda may be used by a witness to refresh his memory, but may not be admitted as independent evidence.

Brown v. Reay, 96 Cal. 462-65;

Estate of Flint, 100 Cal. 391-99;

Estate of Benton, 131 Cal. 472-480;

Marcone v. Dowell, 178 Cal. 393-406.

The original survey and accompanying plat may always be considered to correct a mistake in the calls of a patent.

Combs v. Virginia Iron, 106 S.W. 815.

Registered Map 939 of the survey department of the Territory includes the outlines of the land of Kahua as a whole as well as many lands to the north and others to the south and has the words "Kahua 2nd" written substantially across the portion in dispute. This map was presumably based on patents and leases and perhaps upon kamaaina testimony, although this was not made to appear by the evidence. It is simply the conclusion that the government surveyor reached on practically the same evidence we are now considering. (See in re Pulehuni, 3 Haw. 239-251.)

Kahua, 20 Haw. 278-286.

THE SUPREME COURT HELD IN ITS OPINION THAT A SKETCH
ATTACHED TO THE ORIGINAL GRANT WHICH CONTAINED
A "MEANDER LINE" (R. 43, 49, 53) (ALONG THE DISPUTED
BOUNDARY), ADMITTEDLY UNSURVEYED BY TRAVERSE
(R. 321), AND WHICH CONTAINED NO INDICATION OF
MONUMENTS FIXING SAID "MEANDER LINE" ON THE
GROUND, OTHER THAN THE STARTING AND ENDING
POINTS (AP. EX. B), CONTROLLED THE DESCRIPTION OF
THE LAND CONVEYED, AND WAS SUPERIOR IN EVIDENCE
TO THE LANGUAGE OF THE GRANT DESCRIBING THE
COURSE BY NATURAL MONUMENT. THIS WAS ERROR BY
THE COURT.

The Supreme Court describes the line as a "meander line". (R. 43-49-53.) Newton, government surveyor and witness, testified that there were no monuments on this line (R. 324, 322), that there was no
survey by traverse (R. 322). He did not look for any
monument. (R. 343-344.) Monsarrat never did go to
the top of the pali on that job. (Pali, a precipice; R.
348.) The field book of the survey shows that Monsarrat never left the lower, surveyed boundary not
in dispute and never was anywhere on the meandering line. (Terr. Ex. 16.)

The sketch itself was not incorporated into any
map then in existence or taken from such a map, but
was added to the map by some person unknown after
the land had been granted to Meyer. (R. 321, 305-336-
339-338.) Brown, in his letter (Ap. Ex. L) refers
to "the young man who fills out the patents" in passing the buck for the hashed up description in Grant
3539, and the sketch attached to the grant is by some
unknown draftsman. (Newton, R. 336.) The map was
a "progressive map", had additions all through the

years (R. 336) without record as to the authority or the draftsman (R. 317, 321, 323, 336, 338). There is no record, and Newton did not know, if the data now appearing on the government map was on the map at the time of the sale or when it was put on. (R. 336, 339.)

A sketch physically attached to a grant, not referred to in the description, cannot control a boundary in defiance of the wording of the description. Natural monuments take precedence over sketches, courses, and distances.

> The natural monument along the entire front is the edge or shore of the sea. This, of course, would control courses, distance and area in the absence of a clearly indicated intention to the contrary (diagram attached to be disregarded).
>
> *Brown v. Spreckels,* 14 Haw. 399-405.

> Where lines are run by a surveyor his real location will always be followed; but where he does not run a line there is no location to be followed.
>
> *Kentucky Union Co. v. Hevner,* 275 S.W. 513.

> Natural monuments will control maps, plats and field notes in the absence of a contrary intention.
>
> 11 *C. J. S.* 605.

> A call for a natural monument, fixed, certain and enduring will generally control a description by reference to maps, plats or field notes.
>
> *Bergeron v. Babin,* 120 So. 384.

A "meander line" is not a boundary.

City of Cedar Rapids v. Marshal, 203 N.W. 932.

"Meander line", whether state or national, is not considered a boundary line.

McLeod v. Reyes, 40 Pac. 2d 839-844.

"Meander lines" are run in surveying fractional portions of the public lands bordering upon navigable waters, not as boundaries of the tract, but for the purpose of defining the sinuosities of the stream.

Seabrook v. Coos Bay Ice Co., 89 P. 417.

A "Meander line" in an official survey is not a line of boundary but, as said in Horne v. Smith, 15 S. Ct. 988, 159 U. S. 40, 40 L. ed. 68, is used as a means of ascertaining the quantity of land in the fraction which is to be paid for by the purchaser.

Tolleston Club of Chicago v. Lindgren, 77 N.E. 818-820.

A "Meander Line" is not a line of boundary, but one designed to point out the sinuosity of the bank or shore, and a means of ascertaining the quantity of land in the fraction which is to be paid for by the purchaser.

Whitaker v. McBride, 25 S. Ct. 531, 197 U.S. 510, 49 L. ed. 857;

Hardin v. Jordan, 11 S. Ct. 811, 140 U.S. 380.

A "Meander line" generally contains a call for a natural monument which will usually control over calls for courses and distances.

State v. Armin, Tex. Civ. App., 173 S.W. 2d 503-509.

The principal witness for the government was
Newton, the head cadastral engineer of the land office. (R. 223.) He testified solely to identify documents, to matters contained in the records and his
opinion of what those matters proved. (R. 318.) He
says: "The government map boundary on the disputed
line is a sketched line, a meandering line. (R. 325.)
It does not define the boundary, for the boundary
is the physical location of the pali. (R. 322-323.)
Sometimes boundary lines on government maps are
not even surveyed." (R. 303.) He believes that Monsarrat made the sketch of Kahanui that was added
to the government map after the map was completed
because the lettering on the other lands is definitely
Monsarrat's printing (R. 303), but the words "land
of Kahanui" "could be" his printing and the "Grant
to R. W. Meyer" on the sketch is not Monsarrat's
(R. 304), and was added after the map was finished.
(R. 321.) Lines indicated by dash and two dots
indicate surveyed lines. (R. 300, 305, 303.) This disputed line was put in without the dot and dash line
some time after the map was completed. (R. 305.)
Monsarrat enclosed a "rough sketch" in his letter
to Alexander July 31, 1885, Terr. Ex. 7-B (R. 307)
which may be the original of the sketch attached to
the grant, but at that time Monsarrat "had no survey
of it." (R. 307.)

"Q. A few days later he said 'I show you a
sketch of the land I spoke to you about.' That
is the land of Kahanui that had been shown him
by the kamaainas. That sketch would contain,
would it not, the information that he had received

from the kamaainas as to the boundary, the land
markers, roughly where those land marks lay?

A. They just say, 'this is a piece of Kahanui
and this was down to the gulch,' in the general
description. They would not go around if they
were passing by. They would have to go and
get instruments.

Q. That is the only record we have of kamaainas ever telling Monsarrat, as far as you
know, anything about this land. Do you mean
the whole boundary of this land was based upon
just a casual conversation while he was engaged
in another survey?

A. These boundaries of Kahanui would really
depend on the determination of the boundaries
of the adjacent lands.

Q. The lower boundaries, yes.

A. Where they have already been awarded.

Q. Yes.

A. Then the only remaining part would be
the gulch, which would be a natural boundary,
and the edge of the pali."

Can there be any doubt from the above, that the
disputed line was a meandering line, expressing the
information received by the surveyor from kamaainas
(old time residents familiar with the land, its place
names, and boundaries) with locations recorded in
his field book, (Terr. Ex. 16), placing the boundary
line through the falls, which he recorded by triangulation, and Waihanau gulch or valley below the falls?
Can there be any doubt that the line shown on the
sketch, if the sketch was indeed Monsarrat's and not
that of some draftsman, is a "Meandering line" without any intent that it should be a restriction on the

description or limit the title? Can there be any excuse in law for adopting the sketch as controlling the description or the "meandering line" of this anonymous sketch as limiting the title?

Where did the Supreme Court of Hawaii get authority for the statement that "His (Monsarrat's) survey and field notes, together with four official government surveys and maps made in accordance with them were filed and registered with the office of the Minister of the Interior in 1886 and since that time have remained public records in the files of the government." The maps in the exhibits on their face show that only one survey, that contained in the Field Book (Terr. Ex. 16), was ever made of any part of the land, and at the time of the grant the disputed land had not been surveyed. (R. 322.) The "four maps" (Terr. Exs. 11, 12, 13, and 14), are all from the same survey and are mere copies of the same one. (R. 313.) In fact, all of the maps purporting to be registered maps of this section are copies of the original.

"Q. Yes. In other words, as far as Kahanui is concerned, there is one map here, it has been copied into other maps from the authority of this sketch or this map?

A. Based on Monsarrat's map.

Q. All of them?

A. They are all Monsarrat's.

Q. So that actually as the survey and the map of Kahanui, there has been one map copied into a number of maps of various areas, including

Kahanui, but just the one survey and the one map of Kahanui has been used in the copying?
A. That is my belief.

*   *   *   *   *   *   *

Q. The authority, then, for each map for the boundaries is the authority for the first map that was made?" (R. 312-313.)

"Q. Do I understand, Mr. Newton, then, that this Northern and Western boundary is a sketched boundary and not a surveyed boundary of that sketch?
A. Monsarrat did locate certain points along the top edge of the pali, but he did not have enough.
Q. When?
A. When he was down in the valley. (Referring to surveys 7 and 8, dated 1890 and 1895, of the leper settlement, Terr. Exs. 18 and 18-a, which do not show any shots to the disputed boundary.)
Q. He had not located them in 1888, had he?
A. I do not know."

As shown supra, the part of the map that purports to be Kahanui, and which shows the meandering line of the boundary in dispute, is not identified as Monsarrat's work, and is positively declared by Newton to be lettered in handwriting other than Monsarrat's (R. 304) was added to the original map by some unknown person after the map was completed and after the patent was issued. (R. 321.) The Supreme Court of Hawaii never obtained any information that there were official government maps *showing the land of Kahanui* on file in 1888, at the time of the description, time of the sale, or time of the issuance of the patent, from the record of this case. Certainly not the maps on exhibition, all copied from one original, the original altered since the patent date. (R. 313.) The specific portion of the original showing Kahanui was added by unknown persons after the completion of the map and after the patent date. (R. 317, 321, 338, 336, 339.) Newton, custodian of the records testifies that all records pertaining to this patent have been entered as exhibits in this case. (R. 349.)

The finding, by the Supreme Court of Hawaii, that the sketch on the back of the patent was copied from a map is wholly contrary to the uncontradicted testimony of the government witness that the sketch was entered on the map after the grant was made. (R. 317, 321, 336, 338, 339.) Certainly, there is no evidence, and the Supreme Court did not find, that the parties to the sale of this lele to Meyer ever intended that the meandering line should control the title.

In practically every boundary case decided by the Supreme Corut of Hawaii where a patent was involved there was a sketch attached to the patent. In each of the cases considered, the testimony of witnesses determined the final decision.

Boundaries of Kahua, 20 Haw. 278;
Boundaries of Pulehunui, 4 Haw. 239;
Ookala v. Wilson, 12 Haw. 127;
McCandless v. DuRoi, 23 Haw. 51;
Bishop v. Mahiko, 35 Haw. 608.

The patent contains a diagram of the land granted. That diagram, with its markings that can be understood as the designation of a gully or holua tends to support the defendants contention that the third course is not erroneously stated in the patent as running NW; but maps or diagrams in patents or deeds, like other elements of description, are to be weighed in comparison with other elements of the description and other facts in the case. Whether such a diagram is to prevail over one or more inconsistent elements, or is to be overcome by such other elements is a question to be determined by the jury under proper instructions from the court.

Kelekolio v. Onomea, 29 Haw. 130.

It is to be noted in the above case that the diagram considered there actually marked the location of the gully, as does the sketch in the field book (Terr. Ex. 16) from which the description was taken in the present case, while there is no monument located on the sketch on the patent.

A map survey and plat which might be in exsitence in any office of the government would not in itself be evidence of a boundary if it had not been incorporated in an award or patent.

In re Pulehunui, 4 Haw. 239-251.

A registered map is not primary evidence.

Boundary of Kahua, 20 Haw. 278-286.

Although Mr. Burke had no connection with and personally knew nothing about the making by Mr. Cooley of the alleged 1911 survey, he was permitted to testify as to his interpretation of the lines and points shown in Exhibit B. Such testimony is valueless as evidence. "A surveyor's testimony is inadmissible except as to data from which he surveys, and testimony as to his location of a boundary line is incompetent where he has no means of verifying his survey" 11 CJS Boundaries, ¶ 107, p. 702.

Vaught v. McClymond, 155 P. 612-618.

The best evidence is the corners actually fixed upon the ground by the government surveyor. In default of which, the field notes and plats come next, unless satisfactory evidence is produced that the course was actually located upon the ground at a point different from that stated in the field notes.

Vaught v. McClymond, 155 P. 620.

As to the official maps in the general land office, they represent nothing more than the draftsman's and commissioner's opinions and conclusions from the records and other available information as to the location of the various surveys with reference one to the other. As additional information is obtained as, for example, from new field notes or reports of surveys or judgments, the maps are corrected and changed, and from time to time it becomes necessary to compile new maps.

Weatherly v. Jackson, 71 S.W. 2d 259-262.

But it is not absolute, as this court has also frequently decided. It will not be applied where, as here, the facts conclusively show that no body of water existed or exists at or near the place indicated on the plat, *or where, as here, there never was an attempt to survey the land in controversy.* (Italics added.)

> *Jeems Bayou etc. v. U. S.,* 260 U.S. 561, 67 L. ed. 402-406.

Citing:

> *Security Land v. Burns,* 193 U.S. 167;
> *Lee Wilson & Co. v. U. S.,* 245 U.S. 24;
> *Producers Oil v. Hanzen,* 238 U.S. 325, 338;
> *Horne v. Smith,* 159 U.S. 40;
> *French Glenn v. Springer,* 185 U.S. 47;
> *Chapman v. St. Francis,* 232 U.S. 186.

POINT 4.

THE SUPREME COURT OF HAWAII HELD IN ITS OPINION THAT THE BOUNDARY LINE ADOPTED BY THE TRIAL COURT REQUIRED THAT THE COURSE ADOPTED BY THE TRIAL COURT CONTAIN COURSES IN ADDITION TO THOSE OF THE "MEANDER LINE" AND THUS ALTERED A WRITTEN INSTRUMENT. THIS IS CONTRARY TO THE EVIDENCE, IN THAT THE COURSE ADOPTED PASSES OVER A RIDGE WITHOUT WIDTH WHERE THE TWO VALLEYS JOIN. (AP. EX. A, R. 372.) THIS RULING WAS ERROR BY THE SUPREME COURT OF HAWAII IN THAT UNSURVEYED "MEANDER LINES" ALMOST INVARIABLY REQUIRE MANY COURSES WHEN LAID OUT BY A TRAVERSED SURVEY IDENTIFYING THE LINE ON THE GROUND. (R. 97.) THE ADOPTION OF THE LINE APPROVED BY THE TRIAL COURT DOES NOT REQUIRE ANY COURSE OTHER THAN THOSE LOCATED ON THE NATURAL MONUMENTS DESCRIBED IN THE GRANT, AND WHICH THE "MEANDER LINE" PURPORTED TO FOLLOW; THE FACTUAL EVIDENCE SHOWS THAT THE BOUNDARY OF THE LAND KNOWN AS "WAIHANAU VALLEY" FOLLOWS THE TRIAL COURT'S LINE.

The fact that the two valleys are separated by a hogback ridge without width is shown by the maps admitted. Ap. Ex. M, Court's Exhibit 1, and Territory's Ex. 1, the mosaic photographs, Terr. Ex. 5-A, all show this feature. Surveyor Towill, who prepared the mosaic map for the appellee, testified:

"Q. (By Mr. Flynn.) From the examination of the photograph (Exhibits 5 A,B,C,) I note a very considerable distance where your line on the easterly ridge, or that area approximately above the stream, between points Waihanau Falls, S bend in the stream is a single line at each end of which you show an encircled line, apparently to cover broader points of the ridge formation. Am (372) I right?

A. That is right.

Q. Where you have the single line on the photographs?

A. Yes.

Q. On the photographs. Is the ridge formation such where that single line is that the flat line between the edge or edges of the pails so narrow that an encircling or larger line could not be drawn and still lay along the flat land?

A. That is correct. Where the single line appears it is a hogback ridge; there is no flat on top at all."

Mr. Towill, who prepared the photographic mosaic for the government, says that the meaning of the word "pali" is a "precipice". (R. 374.) The "top of the pali" is not a part of the description of the land contained in the description contained in the patent 3437. The words are taken from the description of the Pease survey of Makanalua (Terr. Ex. 9), where the description is qualified as follows: "Thence along the top of the pali *bounding Makanalua gulch or*

ravine.'' At the point of the big falls there is a precipice or pali extending across the entire depression.
(R. 130, 407.) The valley at the point of the big falls
is impassable. (R. 130, 165, 378.) The eastern side of
the valley above the big falls is a gentle slope, easily
traversible, with a series of hard rock benches interrupting the gentle slope in places, a slope of the
benches of "from 40 to 50 degrees" (R. 375), all
passable to men and animals and crossed by a trail.
"Following a pali" is impossible where there is no
pali.

> "Pali; (pa'li) n. A precipice; the side of a
> steep ravine; a steep hill; whatever stands up
> like a precipice; a cliff." (Andrews Hawaiian
> Dictionary, p. 524.)

The words "bounding Makanalua gulch or ravine"
are just as much a matter of description as the word
"pali". (R. 111.) A "gulch" or ravine" is not a
gently sloping valley. It is defined by Webster as:
"A deep or precipitous cleft, especially the sharply
hollowed bed of a torrent; a ravine" and "ravine" is
defined as "a depression worn out by running water,
larger than a gully, and smaller than a valley, esp.
a deep gorge." This definition applies to the portion
of Waihanau so identified below the falls. The line
of the description adopted by the trial court follows
this precipice across the box canyon up the steep
and untraversable walls of the two ridges on either
side of the falls (R. 165, 407) to the point where the
two valleys join at the ridge without width and constitute an unbroken traverse of the "pali that bounds

Makanalua gulch or ravine'' and the meander line that shows the "head of Waihanau and Waialeia valleys" thus joined.

The "high peak" which is a part of the Makanalua description, does not exist. (R. 120.) "A small mound or hill". (R. 372.) There is no "high Mountain peak" anywhere in the vicinity, as shown by the mosaic map (Terr. Ex. 1), McKeague's map (Ap. Ex. 1, Court's Ex. 1), the stereoscopic photographs (Terr. Ex. 5-A-B-C), and the photograph of the big falls (Terr. Ex. 17). McKeague testified that the point claimed by the government to be the "mountain peak called Kaulahuki is a flat, grassy mound, not appreciably higher than the rest of the valley walls. (R. 130.) Several witnesses testified (supra) that the name "Kaulahuki" is the name of the big falls. (McKeague, Ernest Meyer, Tuitele, Penn Meyer, William Meyer.) Pease's description is a government exhibit. The absence of any high mountain peak in the vicinity and the fact that Pease never went there strengthens the presumption that the description of Kaulahuki as a "mountain peak" is erroneous.

The line adopted by the Supreme Court, from the map and without any factual evidence of the ground locations of the monument the meander line purports to follow, does not follow a precipice above the big falls. The precipice ends at the big falls and the valley above is not so bounded. There is a path leading down the westerly valley slope, the slope may be traversed at almost any place. (R. 215.) "When we used to drive cattle some of them used to break away from up above and hide in the woods * * * When we would go hunting, we would cross anywhere we wanted." (R. 218.) Where the line crosses the valley there is no pali or precipice, no "Pali bounding Makanalua gulch or ravine." No gulch, no ravine, no authority in the description to leave the "head of the valley" and cross the stream. This actually requires a new course in the description, "thence down the ridge to the stream, across the stream, and up the slope on the far side", which is not required where the line adopted by the trial court follows a line of precipice all the way to where the boundries of the valleys join. See mosaic map Terr. Ex. 1, Photograph s Terr. Ex. 5 A-B-C.

The easterly slope, likewise has no pali. It is a gentle slope with rock outcroppings ten to forty feet high, forming steep places which are traversable, 40 to 50 degrees in slope. (R. 375.) This gentle slope follows back to the place where the pali bounding the ridge on the west side of the falls joins the steep precipice of Waialeia Valley. (Mosaic map, Terr. Ex. 1.) The line described by Meyer in his letter to Thurston of October 23, 1889 (Ap. Ex. I-2), as that which would "save some fencing." No fencing can be saved by adopting the government line. Meyer fenced off the boundaries of his land where the cattle could stray ((R. 171), but placed no fences along the government line, although he drove his cattle through there and there was nothing to keep them from straying. (R. 171, 176, 200, 213, 217.)

POINT 5.

THE SUPREME COURT OF HAWAII HELD THAT THERE WAS A "VAST RESERVOIR" OF MAPS IN GOVERNMENTAL FILES WHICH SHOWED AND CONTROLLED THE BOUNDARY. (R. 47.) THIS IS CONTRARY TO THE EVIDENCE IN THAT THE GOVERNMENT WITNESSES TESTIFIED THAT ALL THE MAPS WERE COPIES OF THE FIRST IN VARYING SCALES (1) (R. 311, 312, 323, 324), WITHOUT ADDITIONAL SURVEYS; (2) (R. 312, 313, 319, 324), SO THAT THERE WAS BUT ONE MAP, IF ANY, OF EVIDENTIARY VALUE; (3) (R. 312, 313, 319, 338, 339). THIS MAP WAS A "PROGRESSIVE MAP"; (4) (R. 317, 318, 303) WITH THE SKETCH OF THE LAND UNDER LITIGATION ADDED AFTER THE GRANT; (5) (R. 317, 318, 303, 304, 323, 334, 336, 339) WITHOUT ANY SURVEY OR FACTUAL LOCATION OF THE LINE ALONG THE DISPUTED BOUNDARY; (6) (R. 303, 305, 307, 311, 312, 319, 321, 322, 334), THAT THERE NEVER HAD BEEN A SURVEY OF THAT BOUNDARY UNTIL THE APPLICANT HAD IT SURVEYED FOR THIS ACTION; (7) (R. 319, 394), THAT THERE WAS NO RECORD AS TO THE IDENTITY OF THE PERSON WHO DRAFTED THE SKETCH ON THE ORIGINAL MAP; (8) (R. 334, 335, 336, 337, 338, 339) AND THAT MANY ADDITIONS HAD BEEN MADE BY VARIOUS PARTIES UNKNOWN SINCE THE MAP WAS FIRST MADE AND NO WAY EXISTED TO DETERMINE WHAT WAS ON ANY GOVERNMENT MAP AT THE TIME OF THE GRANT; (9) (R. 304, 310, 317, 318, 319, 320, 323, 336, 338, 394). IT WAS ERROR IN THE SUPREME COURT OF HAWAII TO ADOPT OR CONSIDER THESE MAP COPIES AS HAVING ADDITIONAL WEIGHT, IF ANY, BY VIRTUE OF THE DUPLICATION. (I HAVE COPIED INTO THE APPENDIX AT PAGE iii THE TESTIMONY REFERRED TO ABOVE. THE FIGURES IN PARENTHESIS REFERS TO NOTES IN THE APPENDIX.)

The maps were introduced "for what they were worth" under the procedure of the Land Court which calls for all documents purporting to show matters of title to be admitted. It is the contention of the appellee, adopted by the Supreme Court of Hawaii, that these maps, embodying the "meander line" sketch appearing on the modern versions introduced, control absolutely the boundary line. (R. 47.) This control is exercised by scaling off the meander line by office triangulation and reproducing it on maps of the government witness Newton, adopting such points of Monsarrat's "flag stations" as may, on the office copy, appear near the line as run, whether those points appear on the sketch of the boundary in the field book or not. Point "k", adopted by the government was unknown to Monsarrat at the time of making the field book sketch and was located as a triangulation point later in the book, but never visited and ignored as a monument by Newton in making his map. (R. 343.) Point "a" was never visited by Monsarrat, and "Waiau Falls," written in by some person unknown, can neither be seen from the surveyed line or anywhere Monsarrat is known to have been, but was actually unknown to Newton, although he claims it as a monument.

There is in the office of the department a map and survey notes on a separate paper taken to refer to it. We have no information whether he was the surveyor or copied what was in his handwriting. Nor have we any knowledge on which the survey was made (249). A survey and plot which might be in existence in any office of the government would not itself be evidence of a boundary if it had not been incorporated in an award or patent.

Boundaries of Pulehunui, 4 Haw. 239, 250, 251.

The rule that a government plat rules is not followed where there never was any attempt to survey the lands in question.

Jeems Bayou etc. v. U. S., 260 U.S. 561, 67 L. ed. 402.

But it is not absolute, as this court has frequently decided. It will not be applied where, as here, the facts conclusively show that no body of water existed or exists at or near the place indicated on the plat or *where as here, there never was an attempt to survey the land in question.* (Italics ours.)

Jeems Bayou (supra).

A map means not only a delineation of the land giving a general idea of the land taken, but also such full and accurate notes and data as are necessary to furnish complete means of identifying and ascertaining the precise position of every part, with courses and distances, so that every part can be found.

Hollister v. State, 77 P. 339, 9 Idaho, 657.

So that the making of a map of an addition implies that the addition had been surveyed, and that such survey was marked on the ground so that the streets, blocks and lots can be identified.

Burke v. McCowen, 47 P. 367-368, 115 Cal. 481.

Registered map 939 of the survey department of the Territory includes the outlines of the land Kahua * * * It is simply the conclusions of the government surveyor reached on practically the same evidence that we are now considering. See Re Boundaries of Pulehunui, 4 Haw. 239-251. Even though admissible, we deem it insufficient to counteract the showing of the Pelham plat and grant.

Boundaries of Kahua, 20 Haw. 278-286.

A call for a natural monument, fixed, certain and enduring will generally control a description by reference to maps, plats or field notes.

Bergeron v. Babin, 120 So. 384, 167 La. 833.

POINT 6.

THE ADVERTISEMENT BY WHICH THIS LAND WAS SOLD BY THE GOVERNMENT OF HAWAII TO THE PREDECESSOR IN INTEREST OF THE APPLICANT, DESCRIBED THE LAND AS BEING THE WHOLE OF THE LELE OF KAHANUI (AP. EX. D1), IN ACCORDANCE WITH A DESCRIPTION ON FILE (TERR. EX. 19), WHICH IS IN EVIDENCE, AND WHICH DOES NOT REFER TO ANY MAP OR OTHER LIMITATION ON THE DESCRIPTION. THE GOVERNMENT OFFICIALS ADMIT THE INTENT TO CONVEY THE WHOLE OF THE LELE ACCORDING TO ITS ANCIENT BOUNDARIES IN THE CORRESPONDENCE IN EVIDENCE. IF THE ACTUAL LOCATION ON THE GROUND OF THE LIMITS OF THE WAIHANAU VALLEY HAD NOT BEEN ESTABLISHED BY UNCONTRADICTED TESTIMONY IN ACCORDANCE WITH THE FINDING OF THE TRIAL COURT, THE EVIDENCE OF THE INTENT OF THE PARTIES, AS SHOWN BY THIS GOVERNMENT EVIDENCE, WOULD HAVE BEEN BINDING ON THE COURT AS FIXING THE LINE ON THE ANCIENT BOUNDARIES, AS SHOWN BY TESTIMONY OF THE WITNESSES AND THE SURVEY OF ADJOINING LAND BY PEASE, OFFERED BY THE RESPONDENT. AS IT STANDS, THE EVIDENCE OF ANCIENT BOUNDARIES SUBSTANTIATES THE TESTIMONY OF THE LOCATION OF THAT MONUMENT. IT WAS ERROR FOR THE SUPREME COURT OF HAWAII TO HOLD SUCH EVIDENCE INADMISSIBLE IN THE FACE OF THE UNCONTRADICTED FACTUAL TESTIMONY IT CONFIRMED.

Sections 42, 43, 44, 45 of the laws of Hawaii, 1884, which were in effect at the time of the grant, provide for a "survey" of all lands to be sold by the Minister of the Interior. But Section 45 makes it optional to

map lands. (Appendix, page iii.) In accordance
with this provision, Meyer adopted the "survey" of
Monsarrat, which was made up of a surveyed by
traverse lower boundary, and a description by monument of the northern and easterly boundaries. The
boundary adopted was the line of high, impassable
cliffs that wall off the lepers from the outside world
beginning at the sea and continuing around the whole
district of segregation. (See maps.) The whole of
this boundary constitutes the survey of the leper
colony itself as described by Pease (Terr. Ex. 9),
which was incorporated into the deed by which the
government obtained title to the adjoining land of
Makanalua in the leper settlement.

The "survey" was the description furnished by
Meyer in his application to purchase the land. (Terr.
Ex. 19.) Meyer was responsible for the accuracy of
that survey description. He also had a right to rely
upon the description as defining the land he bought
at public auction. This description (Terr. Ex. 19)
has no mention of a map or sketch. It adopts no map.
It is the sole requirement of legality of the sale, limiting the powers of the Minister of the Interior, and,
as such, fulfilled that requirement. No map is called
for in the law (Section 42, Comp. Laws of Hawaii,
1884; Appendix, page i.) The practice of the survey
and land departments in issuing patents was the
same as the United States Land Office practice, that
is, that there was attached to the patent a plat showing the approximate size and shape of the land for
the purpose of showing the acreage. These plats ap-

pear in almost every boundary case in the Hawaiian reports. They have been universally disregarded in favor of oral testimony fixing the lines on the ground.

The correspondence between the original parties, Meyer and the government officials unqualifiedly shows the intent of both parties that the whole of the lele should be sold at the auction and transferred to the purchaser (Applicant's Ex. C-1A, C-1B, C-1C, E, F. G. H. I-i, I-2, and P.) This intent controls the interpretation of all calls. (*Levy v. Lowell,* 24 Haw. 716-719.) If there is a doubt as to the location of any monument, the intent of the parties prevails. This intent was to convey according to a well known and existing boundary which happened to be also the ancient boundary of the lele, the "head of Waihanau valley". The evidence of ancient boundaries which the Supreme Court of Hawaii rejected corroborates the known location of this line on the ground. It is part of the impassable cliff above which the lepers could not climb. It was outside of the land of Waihanau which Meyer rejected as his choice because the land of Waihanau had been overrun by lepers, which was not the case of the land above the falls; it was at the place called Kaulahuki, where the surveyed boundary of the land of Makanàlua ended; and it was on the land occupied by Meyer under claim by ancient boundaries which he thought was his and which he applied to buy.

We are impressed that this line is a natural and probable one and that it is such adds weight to the testimony given for it.

In re Pulehunui, 4 Haw. 239, 254.

POINT 7.

IT WAS ERROR FOR THE SUPREME COURT OF HAWAII TO
DISREGARD THE FIELD NOTES OF THE SURVEYOR WHO
WROTE THE DESCRIPTION FOR THE GRANT, WHICH, BY
SKETCH SHOWN ON PAGE 112 OF THE FIELD BOOK (TERR.
EX. 16), LOCATES THE LINE OF THE BOUNDARY PASSING
THROUGH THE BIG WATERFALL, AND LOCATES THE
WAIHANAU GULCH BELOW THE FALLS.

The field notes of a survey, recorded in the official
field book, and filed with the Survey Department according to law, constitute the primary, basic evidence
of what was done by the surveyor in making his survey and, equally, what the surveyor did not do.

When reference is made in the decisions to the
intention of the surveyor, the purpose deduced
from what he did in making the survey and description is meant, and not one which has not
found expression in his acts.

Insofar as the field notes govern an area conveyed, that inquiry is not what the surveyor intended to do but, if it can be determined, what
he actually did.

Blake v. Pure Oil, 100 S.W. 2d 1009.

When a patent is based on a survey, the actual
footsteps of the surveyor are binding and must
be followed.

Outlaw v. Gulf, 137 S.W. 2d 787-94.

There is no authority for the assumption that the
surveyor did anything not recorded in the field book,
for it is his duty to so record his every act from
which the authority for his later maps may be drawn.
Monuments which appear as controlling lines of
boundary are the monuments which he has located

and noted in his field book. If he has located a waterfall, noted it in his field book, sketched it in his locating sketch as being the boundary, the waterfall so used is the waterfall identified in his field book and no other. Monsarrat located the big falls as a waterfall, the only one located in his field book or shown on the sketch therein. (R. 347-348.) This cannot now be shown to be a different waterfall, "Waiau Falls", entered in pencil on later maps in an unknown handwriting, and invisible to any point known to have been visited by Monsarrat. (R. 344.)

The justices of the Supreme Court of Hawaii were offered the sketch in the original field book, not the photostat, and examined that sketch while listening to argument on the writ of error. It is not mentioned in the decision. During the trial Newton, government surveyor, and principal witness, testified that the waterfall in the sketch was a landmark located on the boundary of Kahanui. "It is on page 112 of Field Book 359. Monsarrat has a sketch of the land of Kahanui and just below Point A he has, at the bottom of the valley, or the stream there, he has the word 'fall' indicated in red on the sketch. It does not say 'Waiau Falls', but, he says, shows a fall there. Just where it crosses the boundary, sketched as crossing the stream. That is, there was a waterfall there at least. It proves to me that the result of Monsarrat's work, he put it in a 'Waiau Falls', where it crosses the stream. His map shows that." (R. 311.)

This testimony of Newton, recanted later, was a deliberate falsehood. His later testimony on cross-examination, denies that this sketch is a sketch showing the boundary line of Kahanui, when he said that the line went through the waterfall. "It happens to go through the waterfall" (R. 330) and "It is not, to my knowledge of surveying, what this sketch actually shows. This is merely a direct bearing and distance between two points" (R. 330). There he lied again, clumsily, for an examination of the sketch, disregarding his sworn testimony ante that this was a sketch of Kahanui and that the line through the waterfall was the boundary, shows that the line goes through three points, Kaohu, Point X, and thence to Kaluahauoni. (Terr. Ex. 16, p. 112.) Definite bearings were taken from both of the first points, showing them to be situated widely apart. (Terr. Ex. 16, pp. 109-111.) A single line could not be a direct line from both points. Newton later says, in answer to a question if Monsarrat ever saw "Waiau Falls", that Monsarrat did not, and that he himself did not know where Waiau Falls was. (R. 345.) He did not look for any monuments on the disputed line because it did not call for monuments and he was just making a general location himself. (R. 313, 343.) The penciled "Waiau Falls" appearing on the map is not Monsarrat's handwriting.

Certainly, if Newton had gotten by with his first testimony that the sketch in the field book showed the line going over a waterfall, and that waterfall was named by Monsarrat in his field book as "Waiau Falls", the testimony would have been overwhelming for the appellee. As it is, the book speaks for itself and for Monsarrat. It is his record of what he did. He shot the big falls. He examined kamaainas who told him the landmarks, and the names of the landmarks controlling the boundary. He recorded the information in his field book, probably showed the data to his fellow surveyor Meyer, and had the description made from his recorded data. In it there in black and white for all the world to see. Page 109, a waterfall bearing 297 degrees, 28 minutes from Kaohu, page 111, a waterfall, the same fall, bearing 297 degrees, 20 minutes, 30 seconds from point Y. Kaluahauoni from Kaohu, 287 degrees, 44 minutes, from point X. "Cross on rock." 280 degrees, 49 minutes. The valley or gulch closed in at the waterfall by hashure marks and widening again above, and the location of "Waihanau gulch" written in below the fall. It is also there to see that at no time did Monsarrat ever traverse the disputed line. (R. 305, 307, 308, 313.)

POINT 8.

IT WAS ERROR FOR THE SUPREME COURT OF HAWAII TO DIRECT THE TRIAL COURT TO AMEND THE DECREE BY SUBSTITUTING THE LINE OF BOUNDARY CLAIMED BY THE GOVERNMENT FOR THAT IN THE DECREE WHEN THERE WAS ABSOLUTELY NO EVIDENCE OFFERED BY THE GOVERNMENT BY PERSONS FAMILIAR WITH THE MONUMENT NAMED LOCATING THAT LINE OR MONUMENT ON THE GROUND.

The location of a boundary line on the ground, which was the only issue before any court in this case, is a question of fact, not law, to be determined on oral and extrinsic evidence of fact, from which is excluded opinion testimony of surveyors and others concerning the location of monuments described in the description.

What are boundaries is a question of law and where they are is a question of fact.

Kelekolio v. Onomea, 29 Haw. 130;

McCandless v. DuRoi, 23 Haw. 51.

The identity of a monument found on the ground with one referred to in a deed is a question for a jury.

McCausland v. York, 174 A. 383.

Where there is a dispute concerning the location of natural objects called for in a grant or deed, and the evidence is conflicting or where the evidence tends to show two or more natural objects that may answer the description, the boundaries must be determined by the jury under the court's instructions.

Parran v. Wilson, 154 A. 449.

Natural objects called for in grant may be proved by testimony not found in grant but consistent with it.

Blake v. Dougherty, 5 Wheat. (U.S.) 359.

Opinion testimony of Surveyors is inadmissible to prove ground location of a boundary.

11 *C. J. S.* 701, Par. 107;

8 *Am. Jur.* 811.

Generally, reputation or tradition is admissible to prove ancient boundaries.

11 *C. J. S.* 698, Par. 106.

There is a distinction between *hearsay and evidence by reputation,* the latter being competent as to ancient boundaries, the former in case of declaration of deceased persons as to boundaries of more recent origin.

Corbett v. Hawes, 122 S.E. 478, 187 N.C. 653.

Family traditions are admissible as to a boundary, but are not to prove or disprove a title.

Boyd v. Ducktown Chem. (Tenn. App.), 89 S.W. 2d 360.

The rule now generally established in the United States, however, is that evidence of comman repute is admissible as the location of private as well as public boundary line.

Ellicott v. Pearl, 10 Pet. (U.S.) 412, 9 L. ed. 475.

If a public boundary, such as a county line, is the dividing line between two lots, any evidence tending to prove the proper location of the public boundary is relevant as to where the private division line should be located. Accordingly, it has been held that facts as to use and occupancy of other tracts by neighboring owners of land as to their erecting a fence and treating it as the county line for many years may be admitted in evidence in such dispute between owners of adjacent lands.

8 *Am. Jur.* 813, par. 95.

We use the word "kamaaina" above without translation in our investigation of ancient boundaries, water rights, etc. A good definition of it would be to say that it indicates such a person

as the above witness describes himself to be, a
person familiar from childhood with any locality.

Pulehunui, 4 Haw. 239, 245.

A map survey and plat which might be in existence in any office of the government would not
in itself be evidence of a boundary if it had not
been incorporated in an award or patent.

Pulehunui, 4 Haw. 239, 251.

Declarations of deceased persons, disinterested
at the time, in respect to boundary lines and corners, are admissible.

Boardman v. Reed, 6 Pet. (U.S.) 328, 8 L. ed.
    415;

Annotation, 94 *Am. St. Rep.* 678;

134 *Am. St. Rep.* 619.

The declarations of a deceased former owner
are admissible in evidence, but in order to be
admitted, they must establish some fact as a
corner stone or particular marked line.

Cadwalader v. Price, 111 Md. 310;

Annotation, 94 *Am. St. Rep.* 681.

Thus, the true locations of boundaries may be
shown by parol evidence, under the well established rule of law that such evidence is always
admissible to apply a writing to its subject, and,
therefore, to identify monuments called for in
descriptions of tracts of lands contained in patents and deeds.

Hooten v. Comerford, 152 Mass. 591;

Annotation, 6 *L.R.A.* (N.S.) 958;

Brown v. Huger, 21 U.S. 305, 16 L. ed. 125;

Blake v. Dougherty, 5 Wheat. (U.S.) 359, 5 L. ed. 109;

Holmes v. Trout, 7 Pet. (U.S.) 171, 8 L. ed. 644.

Where a description of premises is to be interpreted, the distinction seems sound and simple that if a witness (usually a surveyor) is attempting merely to construe the untechnical terms of a deed, map, or the like, his testimony is unnecessary and improper: * * *

Wigmore, 3rd Ed., par. 1956.

Where lines are run by a surveyor his real location will always be followed; but where he does not run a line there is no location to be followed.

Kentucky Union Co. v. Hevner, 275 S.W. 513; 11 *C.J.S.* 605.

A call for a natural monument, fixed, certain and enduring, will generally control a description by reference to maps, plats, or field notes.

Bergeron v. Babin, 120 So. 384, 167 La. 833.

The Land Court of Hawaii is a statutory court created to determine land titles according to the Torrens system. There are two appeals from its rulings; to the Circuit Court sitting with a jury for the retrial of the facts as certified by the Land Court (Section 12633), which is the only retrial of the facts permitted, unless a new trial shall be granted according to law. "After the trial in the circuit court there shall be no further trial of any issue of fact unless a new trial shall be granted according to law." (Last paragraph of Section 12633.) An appeal on writ of error lies to the Supreme Court of Hawaii on questions of law only. (Section 12635.)

The only question of issue was a question of fact. The Supreme Court, acting on writ of error, could pass upon questions of law raised by the specifications of error, but had no power to review the weight of evidence, or to order a verdict or decree on the facts.

The Supreme Court of Hawaii went on to elaborate its conclusions as to the boundary without benefit of evidence in a discussion of the topography involved. The basic error involved is, of course, the assumption that "Waihanau Valley" is the name of an entire watershed and that the "head" of the valley can be designated anywhere along its length. The valley involved runs as a watershed several miles above either line. (R. 399.) The maps show that above the line claimed by the government, the stream branches out and is shown indefinitely beyond the boundaries of Kahanui. R. 397.) The definition adopted by the Supreme Court of the "head" of a valley is "a line of curvature with its apex at the topmost part of the upper end of the valley". (R. 50.) This would be miles above, at the head of the stream. Certainly it cannot apply to a line crossing the depression at any other point. But "Waihanau" is shown by the evidence to be a local name, not of the whole valley, but of a part arbitrarily so called. (R. 397.) Jorgensen says, for the government, that the head of a valley is where it is closed off, as by a waterfall, or other impassable object, if it does not go to the limits of the watershed. (R. 386.) In this connection, Monsarrat was surveying land below the big falls at Ilole when the boundaries were pointed out to him. (Letters May, 1885, to Alexander, and July 17, 1885, to Alexander, Terr. Exs. 6 and 7-A.) From there the visible part of Waihanau valley extends only to the big falls with some background not containing any part of the government line. (Photo, Terr. Ex. 17.) He was there when the kamaainas said that the boundary was the head of Waihanau Valley. From that aspect, the head can only be the impassable falls which he shot first on August 21, 1885. (Field book, Terr. Ex. 16, and verified August 24, 1885.) He never left the ridge along the surveyed boundary as shown by the field book. (R. 344, 305.) He could not have known of Waiau Falls for they are invisible from the ridge. (R. 344. He erected no monuments on the disputed boundary and Newton did not even look for monuments on that line, knowing that Monsarrat never had been there. (R. 343.) Monsarrat put on his sketch every bearing he used to fix the boundary. The Supreme Court says that he marked the letter "k" on the boundary to mark the line, but his field book shows that the flag station K was not shot until August 30, 1885, from Kauna Gulch station, page 142 of the field book, and was not recorded as a monument in the field book or located on the sketch on page 112. Newton looked for none there, knowing none was called for. (R. 343.) The court overlooks the fact that the sketch attached to the patent was added to the map after the map was completed (R. 336) by some unknown draftsman (R. 321, 338), and that this draftsman copied exactly the sketch on the patent, not so marked, is not shown to have controlled that sketch by points which may have existed on the map for drafting purposes. Especially by point K. There was no monument at K. (R. 343.) Nothing but some object undescribed that made a flag point to be shot and triangled in from Kauna Gulch and Kaluahauoni for the future identification of these points. The sketch accompanying the day's work on August 30, 1885, from Kauna Gulch, page 142, shows a clear view down the valley, past the "S" curve claimed by the government as blocking the valley, lining in K and Kauna Gulch.

None of the points described appear in the sketch attached to the grant. If that sketch is a true copy of a government map no data appears on it to that effect, and the government "map" cannot be presumed to have contained any more data than the sketch. No map is referred to by the sketch, certainly not the map into which the sketch was afterwards copied. This data is the identification of the triangulation stations at Kaluahauoni and Kaeo without another indicated, measured, or described point on the entire boundary. Certainly there is nothing that would permit the owner to determine any point on the boundary by reference to the topography. To say that by this indefinite sketch the title was limited to the meander lines of its boundaries in spite of the description is beyond any stretch of legal decisions. This is plainly one of those sketches described in the decisions where the meander line was drawn to show the acreage to be paid for and not to limit the title. In view of the fact that Meyer furnished the description, made his upset bid by mail, and never was informed that there was a map in existence, if there was, how can the sketch, without scale, monuments, topographic features, directions or survey data limit his purchase?

POINT 9.

IT WAS ERROR FOR THE SUPREME COURT OF HAWAII TO REVERSE A DECREE OF THE TRIAL COURT FOUNDED ON SUBSTANTIAL EVIDENCE BY A RECONSIDERATION OF THE WEIGHT, IF ANY, OF THE EVIDENCE OFFERED BY THE GOVERNMENT AND TO TRY, DE NOVO, THE ISSUE DECIDED BY THE COURT BELOW.

The trial court was limited by the stipulation to determining a question of fact, not of law. The location of the line on the ground is always a question of fact for determination by jury or by the court sitting without a jury. (*Fentress v. Pokahontas,* 60 S.E. 633.)

After the trial of a question of fact in the Land Court there is an appeal on factual issues to a jury in the Circuit Court upon certified issues forwarded by the Land Court, and excluding all other issues. (R. Laws of Hawaii, 1945, Section 12633.) "After the trial in the circuit court there shall be no further trial of any issue of fact unless a new trial shall be granted according to law." (Section 12633, R. L. Hawaii, 1945, supra.) This section accents a difference in procedure between hearings by the Supreme Court on writs of error from the Land Court and writs of error in other courts. The limitation on retrials of issues of fact determined by Land Court procedure restricts the Supreme Court regardless of its jurisdiction over writs of error from other courts. The Supreme Court of Hawaii is given no jurisdiction by the statute to act in the determination of factual issues by trial *de novo,* or by considering the weight of evidence. The consideration of the evidence includes such matters as the examination of the exhibits other than for the purpose of adjudging the legality of their admission, weighing the opinion testimony of surveyors on the paper location of lines marked by monument unknown to the surveyors, or by mathematical process, or ruling on the intent of the parties as disclosed by lawful evidence.

In pursuing its study of the evidence to reach its own conclusion as to the facts, the Supreme Court disregarded all of the evidence of persons knowing the exact location of "Waihanau Valley", and disregarded the location of that boundary because the witnesses located it by natural physical features, on the ground that the natural features were not part of the description (R. 55), dismissing it as being associated with an imagined theory of the trial court that the grant was a grant by ancient boundaries. (R. 44.) "The underlying theory of the land courts finding that the intent was to convey, not according to surveyed descriptions, based upon existing government surveys and maps, but according to ancient boundaries in disregard of those descriptions.'' This statement is evolved from thin air. No such theory or fact is contained in the trial court's decision. The issue before the court was the determination of the location *on the ground* of a line described as ''the head of the Waihanau valley''. The surveyor who wrote the description took his language from kamaainas for a location well known from ancient times. (Terr. Exs. 6 and 7-B.) The advertisement for the sale of the land described it as the lele or remnant of Kahanui, as known by ancient boundaries. (Ap. Ex. D-1.) The deeds by which Meyer first came into claim of title to the land described the land by ancient boundaries. (Ap. Ex. S-T.) The letters of Monsarrat and Thurston to Meyer acknowledge that the whole of the lele was intended to be conveyed according to the description of the land filed by Meyer. The description of the land required to be filed and on exhibition in the office of the Minister of the Interior was that furnished by Meyer, containing no map. (Terr. Ex. 19.) It is the location on the ground of this ancient, well-known monument that was before the court. The only reference to the award of this land by ancient boundaries by the trial court was in connection with the first award of the ahupuaas of Kahanui and Makanalua by name only, and the establishing then of the ancient boundaries as the limits of the ahupuaas, and the persuasive effect on the present issue of the location of the named natural monument according to the description anciently known, of the course at the time. (R. 31.) Nowhere in the whole decision and decree of the trial court was ever any decision or theory that Grant 3437 was an award by name, as asserted by the Supreme Court. There can be no dispute that a purchaser at an auction which describes the lands as being the whole of a parcel, is entitled to an interpretation of courses named which will effectuate the intent and comply with the auction offer.

The ancient kamaainas who furnished that description to Monsarrat were so definite in the location of the line that Mansarrat triangulated the big falls, definitely located them and entered them in his field book as being the boundary. (Terr. Ex. 16, page 112.) He then located and sketched in the Waihanau Valley *below the falls.* This is the description and action of the surveyor contended for by the government in its evidence, that the "water fall" indicated was "Waiau falls" on the boundary until forced to acknowledge that "Waiau falls" is invisible from any place Monsarrat is known to have been, does not appear in any field notes, was unknown even to Newton, and is a mere 20 feet high, of such a slope that men can climb directly over and around it. (R. 400.) When Newton testified that a solid line with names shown on both sides is a boundary line, he knew that the solid line in the field book sketch indicated a boundary line, and so testified (R. 301, 311):

"A. It is on page 112 of Field Book 359. Monsarrat has a *sketch of the land of Kahanui* and just below Point A he has, at the bottom of the valley, of the stream there, he has the word 'fall' indicated in red in the sketch. It does not say 'Waiau Falls', but, he says, shows a fall there. Just where it crossed the *boundary,* sketched as crossing the stream. That is, there was a waterfall there at least. It proves to me that the result of Monsarrat's work, he put it in as 'Waiau Falls' where it crosses the stream. His map shows that."

(R. 327):

"A. He located that point. Yes, he located the waterfall *to show it on his map,* but when he actually wrote his description he said it ran along the pali."

But Monsarrat said no such thing, actually, the description in the patent is "from a stone marked with a cross at the edge of Waihanau Valley, thence around the head of the Waihanau (valleys) and Waialeia valley." Never a word of following the pali once the "stone marked with a cross" is reached, but "thence around the head of Waihanau valley" wherever that "head" was known to be. (Ap. Ex. B.) Newton then attempts to retract his former statement that the sketch is a sketch of Kahanui, and that the line is the boundary, but says "this is merely a direct bearing between two points". (R. 330.) There again he trips. The line referred to has located on it in a straight line the stations "Kaohu" and "x" the cross on rock, two points offset from the direct line to either by a considerable distance, as shown by the completed survey of this line by traverse. It could not possibly be a direction line to either and contain both. Further, Newton testified that direction lines were dotted lines. (R. 296.)

The original of that field book, opened at page 112, was examined by the justices of the Supreme Court at the argument of this case and no mention of the original work of Monsarrat as shown by his field notes is commented upon in the decision, no mention of the location of the waterfall by triangulation on the boundary, no mention of the sketch showing the location of Waihanau Valley below the falls, and no comment, but a complete acceptance by the court of Newton as an authority in locating a monument in a neighborhood strange to him, that he never knew, made no search for, and was incompetent to describe.

The court says that the trial court found that the intent was to convey "not according to surveyed descriptions". What surveyed descriptions? The line is admitted to be a "meander line" (R. 43, 49, 53, 52), a "sketched boundary" (R. 314). Monsarrat's field book is a record of what he did, and also a record of what he did not do, and definitely, he never traversed the disputed boundary, never surveyed the monument described, made no locations on the line of the pali, even, on the disputed boundary, but shot some flag stations several years later on the undisputed boundary "Waialeia Valley". (Terr. Exs. 18 and 18-A.) Monsarrat's survey was the only survey purporting to describe this land and all the records of the survey office pertaining to this boundary are on file as exhibits in this case. (R. 349.)

The Supreme Court says that these "surveyed" descriptions were based on "existing government surveys and maps" always referring to the disputed area. There were no traversed surveys. (R. 314, 319, 322.) What about maps:

The decisions of the Land Department assuming to fit the boundary in accordance with such surveys are not admissible as evidence.

U. S. v. State Investment, 264 U.S. 206, 68 L. ed. 639.

While the plat and survey may not be impeached in an action at law, facts and circumstances may be examined to determine the real intent of the grant as a whole, and if it affirmatively appears that the monuments shown on the plat or by field notes were erroneous or mistaken or that there was an intent that a certain boundary should be actually fixed the description of which would ordinarily have been construed otherwise, the boundaries actually intended by the grant shall prevail.

Horne v. Smith, 159 U.S. 40, 40 L. ed. 68.

Testimony of a surveyor is incompetent when he locates the line wholly from an ancient map which is not proved to be correct and which does not agree with another map of the same date.

Carpenter v. Fisher, 43 N.Y.S. 418, 12 App. Div. 622.

A surveyor is confined to questions of fact and cannot give as testimony conclusions of fact or of law which are for the determination of the jury or the court.

> Benten v. Montgomery Lumber Co., 142 S.E.
> 229.

Bounds and starting points are questions of fact to be determined by testimony, and surveyors have no more authority than other men to determine them upon their own motives.

> Radford v. Johnson, 8 N.D. 182, 184.

Surveyors should be confined to statements of facts, and not to express conclusions or presumptions.

> Clarke v. Case, 144 Mich. 148, 150.

Whether a survey was actually located on the ground or was an office survey is a matter on which the surveyor should not be allowed to express an opinion, but should be determined by the jury, from all the facts in evidence.

> Reast v. Donald, 84 Tex. 648.

It is not his business to decide questions of law or to pass upon facts which belong to the tribunal dealing with the facts.

> Jones v. Lee, 77 Mich. 35, 43;
> Northumberland Coal v. Clement, 95 Penn. 126;
> Virginia Coal Co. v. Ison, 114 Va. 144, 150.

We are to remember, then, that a document purporting to be a map, picture or diagram, is, for evidential purposes simply nothing, except so far as it has a human being's credit to support it. It is a mere waste paper, testimonial nonentity. It speaks to us no more than a stick or stone. It can of itself tell us no more as to the existence of the thing portrayed upon it than can a tree or an ox. We must somehow put a testimonial human being behind it (as it were) before it can be treated as having any testimonial standing in court. It is somebody's testimony or it is nothing. * * * But whenever such a document is offered as proving a thing to be as therein represented, then it is offered testimonially, and it must be associated with a testifier.

Two consequences plainly follow. On the one hand, the mere picture or map itself cannot be received except as a non-verbal expression of the testimony of some witness competent to speak of the facts represented.

Wigmore, 3rd ed., par. 791, p. 174.

The map or diagram, as testimony, must come in on the credit of some witness: yet this witness need not always be in court and testifying; for, by exceptions to the hearsay rule, a map * * * may be received on certain conditions, the document must be authenticated as genuinely the work of the person purporting to make it.

Wigmore, 3rd ed., par. 791, pp. 176-77.

Registered map 939 of the survey department of the Territory includes the outlines of the land of Kahua * * * it is simply the conclusions of the government surveyor reached on practically the same evidence that we are now considering. See In re Boundaries of Pulehunui, 4 Haw. 239-251. Even though admissible, we deem it insufficient to counteract the showing of the Pelham grant and plat B of Kahua. 20 Haw. 278, 286.

Boundaries of Kahua.

But the bounds are to be determined judicially, on evidence, and with notice to all parties concerned. The surveyor is not such an officer, and the tribunal constituted for the purpose cannot take the findings of the surveyor in lieu of or in contravention to proper testimony.

Pulehunui, 4 Haw. 239, 251.

Looking at the testimony of Hamar Kalama Imikia and Kekoa, we find that they are all of the class of men called kamaaina, born and having spent all their lives on Pulehunui or the next lands, who, therefore, have a reason to profess a knowledge of the ancient, traditional lines of boundary.

Pulehunui, 4 Haw. 239, 252.

Where natural monuments are designated on a plat referred to in a conveyance, but no survey is made upon the ground, the same rule is followed (precedence of calls for natural monuments) and the tract must be considered to be run by the monuments without regard for other elements of description, even though neither the certificate of survey nor the conveyance refers specifically to the monuments.

McIver v. Walker, 9 Cranch. (U.S.) 173, 3 L. ed. 694.

A survey is part of a map. The record of the survey is the field book, which is also part of the map. There have been placed on exhibit in this case a number of copies of one original map "with additions". In 1888 there was on file some map based on the 1885 survey of Monsarrat. This was an authorized survey of the lower section of Molokai which ended at the surveyed, undisputed lower boundary of the land in dispute. (Terr. Ex. 16.) It has been testified by Newton that his maps are "progressive maps". (R. 317.) That is, the original is not preserved and a new map made to include new surveys, but new matter is added from time to time in the office of the department, and there is no record kept as to the condition of the map at any time, nor as to who adds matter to the maps. (R. 338-339.) He says that he does not know and there is no record as to the matter shown on the 1886 map in 1888 when the patent was issued. (R. 336, 338, 339, 321, 317.) He says that the sketch which was added to the top of this map, extending the map to include Kahanui, was added after the grant (R. 338, 339, 321), and that there is no record to show what was on the exhibit at the time of the grant (R. 339), or whether the sketch on the grant, which was not part of the description furnished by Meyer as part of his description under the law (Terr. Ex. 19), was later copied into the government map and repeated by copy ever after (R. 313). Where did the Supreme Court get its facts from which it stated that there were "government surveys and maps on file"? Certainly no such evidence appears in this case.

The Supreme Court of Hawaii says of the witnesses who testified definitely as to the location of the monument Waihanau Valley and the location of the valley at its head. "The parol or extrinsic evidence relied on by applicant does not meet that test. It pertains to the object of the big water falls, but does not connect the object with the land conveyed." How can an object be more closely connected with the grant and the land than to swear that the big falls is the boundary known as the "head of Waihanau valley", that this line was marked by posts and an ancient boundary stone. They testified to many things showing their familiarity with the area, that they had lived there all their lives, that they had been told by (a) R. W. Meyer, the patentee, that Waihanau Valley lay below the falls, by (b) native Hawaiians who were the companions of their youth, even before the patent, that the ancient boundary known as Waihanau Valley was below the falls, (c) that the land claimed by Meyer as being the "land I bought by ancient boundaries the lele of Kahanui" was occupied by him for years before the grant and continued to be occupied as of right until 1924, and was not in dispute until the condemnation suit of 1929. They identify the landmark "Kaulahuki" as the big falls, and that is the monument marking the boundary of the adjoining land which the Territory acquired by deed. Meyer occupied the land above the big falls as clean lands, free from the taint of leprosy. He said that Waihanau Valley was overrun by lepers. (Ap. Ex. C-1.) How can a line be described on the ground other than by monuments, landmarks natural or artificial known and located by witnesses?

Although the Supreme Court states that parol evidence is proper to prove "a location" (R. 48), it dismisses all of the factual evidence on the strength of the meander line on the unidentified sketch, attached to the patent but not mentioned in the description, whose author is unknown, and the location of which on the ground is not supported by one word of factual testimony. All the government testimony amounts to is the several surveyors, Newton, Jorgensen, and Howell, having examined a map presented to them from the survey office, are of the opinion, that if the line were scaled off in the office, and from the triangulation thus obtained shots were taken from the monuments on the undisputed line, the line would run as claimed by the government, and that line would follow, roughly, a line of hills or valley crests found on the ground. Very roughly. Newton says the scaled line is more than 500 feet away from his line at the critical crossing of the stream (R. 314), and 1,500 feet out from the line of Waialeia Valley. (See Newtons map, Terr. Ex. 10.)

The Supreme Court calls this a "contour line of continuous mountains meandering along the edges of the respective three adjoining valleys similar to that surrounding the ridge land of Royal Patent Number 3539". This is not true. The contour line is not continuous, it breaks at the crossing of the stream where there is no pali or barrier, the line on the east side is the top of a gentle slope, not a mountain line, and there is no similarity between the precipice that surrounds Grant 3539 and the valley enclosed above the falls, which valley can be crossed at any point, and over which cattle can be driven and wander off from the path into the woods, there to remain hidden. (R. 215-216.)

The opinions of surveyors are not admissible to locate a boundary on the ground except where the boundary is delineated by mathematical points capable of technical location. Without the opinion testimony of the above surveyors, there is not one scintilla of proof of the government line.

Surveyors cannot give opinion evidence on boundaries.

9 *C.J.* 287, par. 345.

THE ISSUED TRIED IN THE LAND COURT WAS LIMITED AND
STIPULATED BY THE PARTIES TO BE THE DETERMINATION
OF THE LOCATION ON THE GROUND OF THE COURSE
DESCRIBED IN THE GRANT AS "AROUND THE HEAD OF
WAIHANAU AND WAIALEIA VALLEYS". THE ONLY EVI-
DENCE OFFERED IN THE TRIAL COURT AND BEFORE THE
SUPREME COURT OF HAWAII ON APPEAL WAS THAT OF
THE APPLICANT AS TO THE LOCATION OF THAT PARCEL
OF LAND KNOWN AS "WAIHANAU VALLEY", WHICH WAS
FIXED AS THE NAME OF THE BOX CANYON BELOW THE
BIG FALLS, WITH THE BOUNDARY BEING THE LINE
ADOPTED BY THE TRIAL COURT. IT WAS ERROR FOR THE
SUPREME COURT TO ATTEMPT, BY SPECULATION, AND
WITHOUT ANY EVIDENCE, TO FIX A BOUNDARY AT ANY
POINT NOT IDENTIFIED BY EVIDENCE AS THE BOUNDARY
OF THE VALLEY, OR TO ASSUME, WITHOUT PROOF, THAT
THE NAME "WAIHANAU VALLEY" APPLIED TO ANY
PLACE NOT SO IDENTIFIED.

The Supreme Court of Hawaii had no jurisdiction to rehear the case *de novo*, weigh the evidence and then order a decree in accordance with the new hearing, considering that the record of this case largely consists of demonstrations on maps and other exhibits which are, to say the least, blurred in identification, and the Supreme Court could not in any way have completely identified the lines indicated by the witnesses. The testimony of witnesses Howell (R. 391, 380) and Jorgensen was read into the record from a former proceeding without any identification of the lines purported to be identified from unidentified exhibits. (R. 397, 382.) This testimony is wholly unintelligible without such exhibits excepting where comment is made without the exhibits, such as Howell stating that the name "Waihanau valley" (R. 402, 397, 395) is a place name of a very small portion of the whole, and that the line shown on the sketch is a matter of interpretation (R. 401), and Jorgensen's statement that a ''head'' of a valley is a place, like a waterfall, over which you cannot pass (R. 386-387), including the admission of both witnesses that they took their conclusion from the map without any personal knowledge of the ground line or any competent kamaaina investigation (R. 381, 397, 400, 395, 393).

The Supreme Court was, in its retrial, if such was permitted, bound by the same rules of evidence as the trial court, and limited to the evidence contained in the record. It could not, for instance, turn to the ''reservoir of surveys and maps'' (R. 47), if such existed, outside the record. Newton testified that the whole of all records pertaining to the issue had been produced at the trial. (R. 349.) He said that at the time of the patent there was in existence only the survey of Monsarrat shown in Terr. Ex. 16, the field book containing the sketch of Kahanui from which the description had been taken, and identifying this waterfall on this sketched boundary as the big falls (R. 344-346, 311), locating Waihanau Valley below the falls (R. 332). He testified that at the time of the patent the sketch attached to the Grant 3437 had not been copied on to any government map (R. 321, 336, 338), but had been entered after the grant date (R. 339). If this is so, and the appellee relies upon Newton's testimony as to the location of the line claimed by it, the reservoir of maps resolves itself into nothingness, and it is conceded by Newton that at the time of the grant there was on file no map that contained a description of the land of Kahanui. (R. 304, 305, 321, 313.) If there was no map, no "reservoir", no survey of the disputed line by traverse (R. 314, 322, 321, 319), then or afterwards, no "footsteps of the original surveyor" (R. 305) on the line, no monuments (R. 324, 325) to identify it, either erected by the surveyor or placed there by nature and shown on the sketch, how could the opinion testimony of these surveyors overrule the factual testimony of witnesses who knew, as a fact, that Waihanau Valley lay below the big falls, and that the upper boundary of Waihanau was at the big falls (R. 332), the "head" of the valley according to every definition?

The location of the line by the Supreme Court was based upon no evidence contained in the record. There was not one word in the record that Waihanau Valley existed as a location other than below the falls. The name of the little valley above the falls is "Puukawao". (R. 192.) The name of the whole watershed is "Makanalua Valley" as shown by Pease's description introduced by the appellee. The name of the waterfall is "Kaulahuki", meaning to pull (up) with a rope. This is a logical name of a place where the only way to go up or down is to climb the ieie (R. 186), a ropelike vine, or to be assisted by a rope. The topography complies with the definition by Jorgensen of the head of a valley where the head sought is not the head of the watershed, a place where you can go no farther, like a cliff or a waterfall. (R. 387, 386.) The leper colony was selected by the government as a place of segregation where lepers might roam and by the cliffs be confined. The big falls does this. The Waihanau Valley, first selected by Meyer as his land, was overrun by lepers, so he wanted no part of it. (Ap. Ex. C-1A.) The proof of the location of Waihanau Valley, both as an ancient and well-known boundary and as the place intended by the parties to be the limit of the land conveyed, was indisputably proved by uncontradicted evidence. (McKeague, Aubery, Tuitele, Ernest Meyer, Mauritz, Penn Meyer, William Meyer, and Monsarrat's field book.)

The line of the appellee, adopted by the Supreme Court of Newton, his own line (R. 315, 343), office surveyed and located by Newton on his map without regard for monuments (R. 343) or the "footsteps of Monsarrat" purporting to be a translation of the line on the sketch attached to the grant, designated by all parties, Newton, McKeague, Howell, and the Supreme Court as a "meander line," a sketched boundary. (R. 314.) It appears on a sketch attached to the grant in accordance with the practice of United States surveyors and the land department of Hawaii of roughly sketching the land for the purpose of showing the amount of land conveyed, and indicating that there was a natural monument to be followed. The cases cited supra show that such a line is not a boundary. It is not identified by the appellee with any existing map or survey along the disputed line nor is the author or draftsman of the sketch shown. (R. 336, 338, 339.) The several maps introduced are all copies of the first with additions. (R. 313, 312, 339, 336, 323.) One of those additions was the sketch (R. 321, 336), placed on the first map after the grant and copied therefrom into all the succeeding maps without correction or further survey. (R. 313.) It misses the real line of the cliffs which is the accepted boundary, by 500 to 1000 feet (R. 314, 315), at the point claimed by the appellee, and by 1500 feet beyond where the line purports to cross into Waialeia valley. (Terr. Ex. 10.) If the error of location, ignored by the appellee and witness Newton, who was running his own line without regard for monuments (R. 315-343), was considered to be an error of deviation from the appellant's line (see maps) the error would be no greater in distance, possibly less.

The sketch shows no data as to distance, direction, or monument along the disputed line. (Ap. Ex. B.) The government appellee insists that the sketch may possibly (R. 338, 339) be the work of Monsarrat taken from the field book. That field book, the original record of survey (Terr. Ex. 16, p. 112) shows the line following the line of the impassable cliff formed by the big fall and its supporting ridges. The sketch does not refer to any map as controlling. No map of that area was in existence at the time of the grant. (R. 317; 321.) The intent of the parties (R. 331, Ap. Ex. C-1A, C-1B, C-1C, E, D-1, P, was to give Meyer all the land that he had occupied and claimed as his. (Ap. Ex. C-1-2-3.) The only knowledge of the boundary described by the grant in the possession of government officials was the information obtained by Monsarrat from old timers (kamaainas) describing the land by its ancient boundaries (R. 308, 322), which was repeated by him in his description "around the head of Waihanau valley". (R. 323.) The description was taken from the field notes. (R. 333, 384.) The field book was meticulously kept to show exactly what line was meant. (Terr. Ex. 16.) The line in the sketch explaining the locations passes through the big falls (R. 311, 330) and the location of Waihanau valley is entered purposely to show that Waihanau valley lies below the big falls. (R. 332.)

The Supreme Court of Hawaii, arbitrarily and without any citation of authority, or reason given except the fallacious assumption that the trial court had held that Grant 3437 had been awarded by ancient boundaries (R. 43, see R. 31), threw out all factual evidence of the location of Waihanau valley, disregarded the sketch from which the description was taken, ignored the letters of Monsarrat which he stated that he had obtained the description from kamaainas (Terr. Ex. 6, 7A, 7B), of an ancient boundary and described the land by what he had been told, waved aside the intent of the parties that the grant should contain all of the lele claimed by Meyer (Ap. Ex. B, C-1A, C-1B, C-1C, D, E, F, G, H, O, P), and created a new boundary from an unlocated, unsurveyed meander line not referred to in the description and located on the ground by a surveyor unfamiliar with the location of any monuments (R.

227), a stranger to the land (R. 318), who applied an office survey to the terrain in disregard of both the meander line and the known boundary, and created an opinion line 500 to 1000 feet from the office survey of the meander line as described by him as "following the pali" where the topography shows there is no precipice, across the valley where there is no barrier.

Dated, Eugene, Oregon,
    April 10, 1953.

Respectfully submitted,
    R. W. MEYER, LIMITED,
        Appellant,
    By PHIL CASS,
        SAMUEL SHAPIRO,
            Attorneys for Appellant.

(Appendix Follows.)

Appendix.

Appendix

42. The said Minister, by and with the authority of the King in Cabinet Council, shall have power to lease, sell, or otherwise dispose of the public lands, and other property, in such manner as he may deem best for the protection of agriculture, and the general welfare of the Kingdom, subject however, to such restrictions as may, from time to time, be expressly provided by law. And provided that no sale of one land or lot exceeding five thousand dollars in value shall be made without the consent of the King and a majority of the Privy Council.

TO REQUIRE THE SALE AND LEASES OF GOVERNMENT LANDS TO BE MADE AT PUBLIC AUCTION

Section 1. All sales or leases of government lands shall be made at public auction, after not less than thirty days' notice by advertisement in two or more newspapers published in Honolulu, in both the Hawaiian and English languages, excepting lands and portions of lands of less than three hundred dollars in value. All such sales shall be made at the door of the Government House, at Honolulu, and shall be cried by the Minister of Interior, or by one of his clerks, under his direction, who shall perform this service without extra compensation.

Notice of sale herein above required to be made, shall contain a full description of the land to be sold, as to locality, area, and quality, with a reference to the survey, which shall in all cases be kept in the office of the Minister open to inspection of any one who may desire to examine the case.

In case application has been made for purchase of a Government land, and a price has been offered for same, the price offered shall be published in the notice of sale as the upset price for which the land should be offered at public auction.

Section 2. The provisions of this Act shall not extend or apply to cases where the Government shall by quit-claim, or otherwise, dispose of its rights in any land by way of compromise or equitable settlements of the rights of claimants, nor to cases of exchange, or sales of Government lands in return for parcels of land required for roads, sites of Government buildings, or other Government purposes.

---

43. A Royal Patent, signed by the King, and countersigned by (the Kuhina Nui) and the Minister of the Interior, shall issue under the great Seal of the kingdom to the purchaser in fee simple of any government land or other real estate; and also to any holder of an award from the Board of Commissioners to quiet land titles for any land in which he may have commuted the Government rights.

44. All Royal Patents, leases, grants or other conveyances of any Government land or real estate, shall be prepared by and issued from, the Department of the Interior; and it shall be the duty of the Minister

of the Interior to keep a full and faithful record of all such patents, leases, grants, and other conveyances. Said record shall be open to public inspection, and he shall furnish a certified copy, under his official seal, of any instrument therein recorded, to any person applying therefor, upon being paid at the rate of fifty cents for every one hundred words. Every such certified copy shall be received as evidence in any judicial court of the kingdom, the same as the original instrument itself.

45. It shall be the duty of the Minister of the Interior to cause such surveys, maps, and plans of the Government lands, harbors, and internal improvements to be made as the public interests may require; which surveys, maps and plans shall be kept in his office for public inspection and reference.

TESTIMONY OF NEWTON, CHIEF CADASTRAL ENGINEER, SURVEY DEPARTMENT, GOVERNMENT WITNESS.

(1) 311 Q. When the next surveying job was done, these were all resurveyed in here, or was the next section just put on to the end of this map? A. I believe a new map was made altogether of the other section.

Q. But the new map was simply a copy of the section already in? A. Yes. The adjacent boundary of the land would be shown on the second map.

Q. The adjacent boundaries are shown, but the work is unchanged. For instance, the boundaries of

Kamiloloa, if they are shown on a compiled map of the whole island of Molokai, would be taken right off this map and scaled to the scale of the new map? A. Generally yes.

312 Q. There would be no resurvey of the lands of Kamiloloa for the purpose of making a completed map of the other job. A. No. Unless it were necessary to get a little more information.

*   *   *   *   *   *

Q. So that in this series of maps that the government has offered, the land of Kahanui, as shown here, has been recopied from the same sketches that appear on the previous maps, simply to complete the map. Isn't that true? A. It is based on previous maps.

Q. Yes. So that is a tracing follows the lines of the work sheet here, the same tracing will follow the lines on these other government maps as there is no resurvey of Kahanui? A. That is the idea.

313 Q. So that actually as the survey and map of Kahanui, there has been one map, copied into a number of different maps of various areas but just the one survey and the one map of Kahanui has been used in the copying? A. That is my belief.

323 Q. So that this, although it is on a scale of 2000 feet to the inch, is plotted or traced from the other map or photostat * * * A. And there may be additions.

324 Q. And this is a map from which, apparently the sketch that appears attached to the patent was taken? A. That is possible.

(2) 312 Q. But that is the general practice, is it not, you make a survey of one section, complete the map, make a survey of the next section, complete the map, and continue on until you have the complete map of Molokai, or of some other island, then the whole is one complete map, which is then based actually on copies of the previous maps, isn't that correct? A. Yes * * *

313 Q. The authority for each map for the boundaries is the authority for the first map that was made? A. The boundaries are defined on two sides and the easterly and northerly boundaries are also indicated as running along the pali lands.

Q. It is definite in that the boundary follows the natural monument or pali? A. Yes.

319 Q. (218) Now, in connection with this map, have you any record of an additional survey made by any person by which this dash and two dot line was placed on the northern and western boundaries of the land sketched in? There is no such mark on the work sheet. A. I don't think there has been any other surveying outside of Monsarrat's, which map shows on some of the other government maps, but it seems to me that the Land Court survey is the first complete survey of that area.

324 Q. I asked you if there appears on this map, for the record, an indication along the disputed boundary line or on the Waikolu boundary anything other than the straight line, showing a natural monument described by name or otherwise on the map

itself? A. It is a reproduction of the larger scaled map and would be absolutely the same as the other.

(3) 312 A. Yes, they would just show the large lands, not the small areas.

Q. But, whatever would be shown on the large maps would be taken off the other maps? A. Yes. 313 Q. (312) Yes, in other words, as far as Kahanui is concerned, there is one map here, it has been copied into other maps from the authority of this sketch or this map? A. Based on Monsarrat's map.

319 Q. You don't know that this boundary here does accurately follow the line on the ground? A. No, I don't. In fact the top of the pali, the edge of the pali is the boundary.

338 Q. Let's see if I understand your testimony, You testified that there is in existence this map in the survey office, that it, as far as you know, is the only map, or the first map from which the boundaries are traced on other maps. Is that so? A. Yes.

(4) 317 Q. This map is dated 1886. How come Grant 3539 to Meyer appears on the summit of the ridge when that grant was not granted until two or three or four years later? A. Our maps are progressive maps. * * *
318 Q. They insert the title. Do they insert anything else? A. The area, the grant and the grantee.

Q. Do they insert additional topographic information? A. Yes.

303 Q. Do you know who actually did the draftsman's work on this map? A. The working sheet is

generally on a job like this it takes months and sometimes years, and the drafting work is done right
where you are doing the work. It is a progressive
map. * * *

304 Q. Is the word "Grant 3437, Meyer" his printing? A. No. That came later, after the grant was
issued.

323 Q. * * * I presume it is traced from the other
map because the other map is in one section? A. And
there may be additions.

Q. There may be additions? A. Yes.

334 Q. Now, Mr. Newton, I have asked several
times during the course of this trial, if there is any
proof in your own personal knowledge or on the records of the survey office as to who (335) actually put
the sketch of Kahanui on the various Government
maps that have been in existence. Is there such
proof? A. I cannot say absolutely.

336 Q. Now, speaking of the sketch which is attached to the patent 3437, Do you, or do you not
know who placed that sketch upon the map? A. I
don't know definitely.

Q. You don't know whether or not that tracing
was actually on a government map prior to 1888?
A. I don't know unless I am told by the date of the
map itself.

Q. But the map, you testified, had additions from
time to time; that is right? A. Any additions were
very few.

339 Q. You don't know whether the tracing of this map was made by Mr. Monsarratt, or some other person? A. I cannot say definitely.

Q. Do you know that all your map data was as appears now or was this data later? I am asking you if you know? A. I don't know positively.

(5) Q. It does not show in his field book at any location? A. I do not find it here.

Q. And if you cannot find it, it is not there. As I understand it, this map starts below and this survey covers these particular lines and these lands. When the next surveying job was done these were all resurveyed here, or was the next section just put to the end of this map? A. I believe a new map was made altogether of the other section.

Q. But the new map was simply a copy of the section already in? A. Yes. The adjacent boundary of the land would be shown in the new map.

303 A. Well the boundary line. Sometimes they are not even surveyed, the boundary lines.

304 Q. And what does this lack of the dash and two dots on that boundary indicate; that it was not yet surveyed finally? A. Probably he hadn't written the description; the grant was made later, after the map had been completed.

305 Q. But this was put in without a dot and dash line sometime after this particular map was made? A. Yes. He had to have something to base the boundary line on and that was his determination of the boundary of Kahanui, Apana 2 (section 2).

Q. Do you know that has any indication that he was ever on the ground to make the survey? A. He actually—his field notes show where he took actual shots to all points.

307 A. No. In fact he wouldn't know because he had no survey of it.

Q. He wouldn't have to have a survey of it if he sketched what the kamaainas told him the boundaries were. A. But he would have to make a survey before (308) he could get proper boundaries for the ili itself.

Q. Let me understand that, Mr. Newton. That he had to have a survey on the ground to determine, to lay off the boundaries of this land, before he could determine the boundaries? * * * A. These boundaries of Kahanui would really depend on the boundaries of the adjacent land. Q. The lower boundaries, yes. A. Where they had already been awarded. Q. Yes. A. Then the only remaining part would be the gulch, which would be the natural boundary, and the edge of the pali.

314 Q. Do I understand Mr. Newton, then, that this northern and westerly boundary is a sketched boundary and not a surveyed boundary of that sketch? A. Monsarrat did locate points along the top edge of the pali but he did not have enough. Q. When? A. When he was down in the valley (referring to the survey Terr. Ex. 17 and 18, dated 1890 and 1894). Q. He had not located them in 1888, had he? A. I don't know.

319 I don't think there has been any actual surveying, outside of Monsarrat's, which map shows on some of the other government maps, but it seems to me that this Land Court survey is about the first complete survey of that area. Q. That is, actually following the line on the ground. A. That is a more accurate survey of the edge of the pali.

322 Q. That is true. He made a survey of the land. But I am speaking of the survey by traverse, actually the surveyor going out and putting flags and running his instrument and having his chain and cutting brush along this line of the north and westerly boundaries. That had never been done at the time, had it? A. No. Only the southerly and easterly and northerly boundaries were run along the monument the top of the pali. Q. They were simply described by monument? A. Yes, by monument. Q. There is no pretense at all that this boundary line follows the monument? A. That was the line that was established by kamaaina evidence and Monsarrat reproduced it on his map.

(6) A I don't think there has been any other surveying outside of Monsarrat's, which map shows on some of the other government maps, but it seems to me that this Land Court survey is about the first complete survey of the area.

(7) 334 Q. Now, Mr. Newton, I have asked several times during the course of this trial if there is any proof in your own personal knowledge or in the records of the survey office as to who actually put

the sketch of Kahanui on the various government maps that have been in existence. Is there such proof? A. I cannot say absolutely.

336 Q. Now, speaking of the sketch which is attached to Grant 3437, do you, or do you not know who placed that sketch upon the map? A. I don't know definitely.

337 Q. You testified the other day that there is nothing in the field books that were introduced in evidence to indicate that any of these lines are on (338) the boundary of anything. * * * A. No, they are not mentioned in the description itself, but they are shown on this working sheet as colored in to establish the limits of Kahanui. Q. But you don't know who colored that in except by guess? A. Monsarrat is responsible for the map. Q. Again, you don't know who colored that in, do you? A. Well Monsarrat * * * Q. Do you know? A. Well I did not see him do it. Q. Do you have any records to show that he did do it other than your guess from the fact that it is his map? The Court. Mr. Newton, do you of your own knowledge know whether Mr. Monsarrat—— A. I do not know positively. The Court. ——whether Mr. Monsarrat inserted the red line Mr. Cass is asking about? You either know or you don't know. Do you know of your own knowledge as a fact that he did? A. No. That was before my time so I would not know. The Court. You don't know? A. I don't know. At the time he did the job, no.

339 You don't know whether this tracing of his map was made by Mr. Monsarrat or some other person? A. I cannot say definitely.

(8) 304 Q. Is the word "Grant 3437 to Meyer" his printing (Monsarrat's)? A. No, that came later, after the grant was issued.

305 Q. But this was put in without a dot and dash line sometime after this particular map was made? A. Yes. * * *

310 Q. I note on this map in pencil the word "Waiau". Does the word "Waiau" appear in any part of the survey of this land, or the field books concerning this land * * *? (339) It does not in his field book at any location? A. I do not find it here.

317—Q. Can you tell me from what survey or surveys this map was compiled; would it be the same survey as the work sheet? A. Yes, probably with few additions. Q. Yes. This map is dated 1886. How come Grant 3539 to Meyer appears on the summit of the ridge when that grant was not granted until two or three or four years later? A. Our maps are kind of progressive maps. After these lands are granted and the government has no more interest in that particular piece, they insert the title. Q. (318) They insert the title. Do they insert anything else? A. The area, the grant, and the grantee. Q. Do they insert additional topographical features? A. Yes. Anything new like that pipe line, for instance. That has been added on. The pipe line which is shown in blue is added to the map. Q. When was that pipe line added to the map? A. I don't see the date there. * * * A. I would not know anything about it because I am not too familiar with that section.

319 Q. One is practically a copy of the other or it should be a copy of the other? A An exact copy with additions, probably.

323 A. And there may be additions. Q. There may be additions? A. Yes.

336 Q. You don't know whether that tracing was actually on a government map prior to 1888? A. I don't know unless I am just told by the date of the map itself. Q. But the map, you testified, had additions from time to time; that is right? A. Any additions were very few.

338 Q. Do you have any records to show that he did do it, other than your guess from the fact that it is on his map? A. I do not know.

394 Q. In connection with the interpretation of the boundary line in this grant, did you make any observations or study of the topographical features of the land? A. (Howell) Yes. Inasmuch as the last two courses in that description are not by actual surveys but by statement that "Thence around the head of Waihanau and Waialiea valleys".

* * * * * *

IN THE

United States Court of Appeals

FOR THE NINTH CIRCUIT

R. W. MEYER, LIMITED,

  Appellant,

vs.

TERRITORY OF HAWAII,

  Appellee.

Appeal from the Supreme Court of the
Territory of Hawaii.

BRIEF FOR APPELLEE

EDWARD N. SYLVA,
  Attorney General
  Territory of Hawaii

RHODA V. LEWIS,
  Deputy Attorney General
  Territory of Hawaii

  Attorneys for Appellee.

Subject Index

Table of Authorities

Cases

ii

TABLE OF AUTHORITIES

Statutes and Rules

No. 13,545

IN THE

United States Court of Appeals

FOR THE NINTH CIRCUIT

R. W. MEYER, LIMITED,

Appellant,

vs.

TERRITORY OF HAWAII,

Appellee.

Appeal from the Supreme Court of the
Territory of Hawaii.

BRIEF FOR APPELLEE

JURISDICTIONAL STATEMENT

This is an appeal pursuant to section 1293 of the Judicial
Code, noticed on June 25, 1952 (R. 4), appealing from a
judgment of the Supreme Court of Hawaii entered June 23,
1952 (R. 57). The case is one of boundary dispute, involving only local law. Therefore jurisdiction is dependent upon
the amount in controversy.[1]

---

[1] 28 U.S.C. 1293; *Sociedad Espanola v. Buscaglia,* 164 F. 2d 745
(C.A. 1st 1947), cert. den. 333 U.S. 867, 68 S.Ct. 790, 92 L.Ed. 1145;
De la Torre v. National City Bank, 110 F. 2d 381 (C.A. 1st 1939);
Robert Hind Ltd. v. Silva, 75 F. 2d 74 (C.A. 9th 1935).

Appellant's "Statement of Jurisdiction" (R. 4) is not an affidavit and may not be considered.[2] Pleaded amounts of value and damages, cited by appellant (Br. 1-2), are from the appellant's second cause of action which by stipulation (R. 60, 30) was not tried, has not been before the Supreme Court, and is not before this court. Alleged in the first cause of action was the value assessed for taxation (R. 17), but appellee denied that the assessment included the area here in dispute, the same being government property (R. 25), and in any event the alleged assessed value was only $1,268.

What does appear in the record is that the Territory, the appellee, has made extensive improvements in the area now claimed by appellant and here in dispute, commencing in 1924 with a value not shown (R. 381), and continuing in 1933 with a $250,000 project (R. 392-394). These improvements comprise a water system; the location of the intake of the water tunnel on the area in dispute appears upon comparison of the maps appended to the respective pleadings.

That the value in controversy in fact exceeds $5,000 is not contested by appellee, but since jurisdiction cannot be conferred by consent the question is whether the record is sufficient. The record is unaided by the order of the Supreme Court allowing the appeal[3] (not printed), since such an order now is surplusage.[4] Appellant has the burden of sustaining this Court's jurisdiction.[5]

As to the jurisdiction below, the same appears as follows: The case is one which arose on an application of the appellant in the Land Court of the Territory filed pursuant to

---

[2] 28 U.S.C. 2108 and cases cited supra, note 1.
[3] Cf. *Ihihi v. Kahaulelio*, 263 Fed. 817 (C.A. 9th 1920).
[4] *Fong v. James W. Glover, Ltd.*, 197 F. 2d 710 (C.A. 9th 1952).
[5] *De la Torre v. National City Bank*, supra.

sections 12600 and 12625 of chapter 307, Revised Laws of Hawaii 1945, relating to registration of title under the Torrens System, and amended pursuant to Act 207 of the Session Laws of Hawaii 1947, printed in the note.[6] To the amended application (R. 14-18), the Territory pleaded (R. 18-26). After decision by the Land Court a decree of that court was entered on April 10, 1950 (R. 35-38) and the case was taken to the Supreme Court of Hawaii by the Territory, appellee here, by a writ of error (R. 13-14) issued on July 7, 1950, hence within the required ninety days, pursuant to sections 9551 and 12635, Revised Laws of Hawaii 1945. From the judgment of the Supreme Court in favor of the Territory the case comes here. The opinion below is reported.[7]

---

[6] "ACT 207

"An Act to Authorize Litigation for the Determination of the Boundaries of Royal Patents Nos. 3437 and 3539, Kahanui 2 in the Island of Molokai and Claims for Rentals for the same.

"BE IT ENACTED BY THE LEGISLATURE OF THE TERRITORY OF HAWAII:

"Section 1. The land court of the Territory of Hawaii shall, subject to review by the supreme court as provided by law, have jurisdiction to hear and determine an application for land registration brought by any person claiming title or an interest in Land Patent Grant Nos. 3437 and 3539, against the Territory of Hawaii and others, and to determine therein the true boundaries of said land patents.

"Section 2. If such proceeding has been or shall be brought in the land court not later than two years after this Act becomes effective, there may be included therein claims for rental for occupancy of any portion of the said lands by the Territory or its agencies, and the court may award judgment for such rentals, and determine the person or persons entitled thereto, if it be found that the Territory or its agencies has been occupying such portion without right, without regard to any limitation of time for commencing action against the Territory otherwise imposed by statute, but no interest shall be allowed on such claim up to the time of rendition of judgment.

"Section 3. This Act shall take effect upon its approval."

[7] 39 Haw. 403.

STATEMENT OF THE CASE

Appellant filed its amended application in the Land Court for land designated as "all of Grant 3437 to R. W. Meyer, and Grant 3539 to R. W. Meyer on a portion of Grant 3437 to R. W. Meyer." (R. 15). Actually, and as held by the Supreme Court of Hawaii (R. 40, 46-47), these were two separate grants to appellant's predecessor in title, the first of which did not include the second. The relation of the two grants to each other is clear upon their face (Exs. B and K). Grant 3539, the second of the two grants, is for a ridge jutting out from the northern boundary of the first grant and touching it only at the base of the ridge. The descriptions and maps contained in the two patents (Exs. B and K) are reproduced at page I of the appendix, with a red line superimposed on each to show appellant's claim. (This part of the appendix hereinafter is referred to as Map I.)

The Territory's answer denied that Grant 3437 included the piece conveyed by Grant 3539, and described the two pieces separately (R. 21-24). This answer set the northern boundary of Grant 3437, between the western end of it and the base of the ridge, on a line southerly of appellant's claim and in accordance with the patent map. Thus there was placed in dispute a fifty acre area which the Territory says, and the Supreme Court held, never was granted by the government and still belongs to it. The fifty-acre area, called the "disputed area," is colored in green on the map appended to the Territory's answer which is reproduced at page II of the appendix, hereinafter referred to as Map II. On Map I the disputed area appears as the three-sided area between the superimposed red line, the ridge, and the northern boundary shown by the patent. (As to the ridge, reference is made to that portion of the cited map which reproduces Grant 3539, the later patent which granted the ridge. Grant 3437 did not grant and did not depict the ridge.)

As will appear, there is no middle ground between the appellant's line and the Territory's. Appellant does not say that there is, but seeks to sustain a right to cross over to the ridge, from west to east, along the red line (again referring to Map I).

The basis of appellant's claim is, as it was in the trial court, that this line should be fixed by parol testimony as to the ancient boundary. The basis of appellee's case is that the line should be fixed according to the survey description and map of the government surveyor Monsarrat incorporated in the patent. The trial court's primary error was in holding that the government survey, even though incorporated in the patent, constituted only an inconclusive opinion as to where the line should be (R. 29-31). From this primary error other errors followed, and the trial court decided that the appellant was the owner of the disputed area except as to a certain undivided interest not here involved (R. 34).

The Supreme Court reversed, holding the patent (Grant 3437 under which the disputed area is claimed) clear, certain and unambiguous, requiring a location which excludes the disputed area (R. 45-50, 52, 55-56). Accordingly, the Supreme Court ordered the disputed area excluded from the land court registration (R. 57). The evidence on which the trial court based its decision was extraneous and inadmissible, the Supreme Court held (R. 43-44, 48, 54-56).

The line of Grant 3437, now in dispute, consistently and

continuously has been placed by the government where it is placed by it today. This is stated because appellant seeks to inject an aura of uncertainty of the government's line by insinuating that it was not claimed until 1929 (Br. 10-11). The insinuation is entirely without basis. To the contrary, all maps, records, and official dealings between the government and the Meyer family, were on the basis of a boundary line placed where the government places it today, and it was not until after the government had constructed its water tunnel and intake in 1924 (R. 381-384) and made its further $250,000 of improvements in 1933 (R. 392-394) that the Meyer family claimed the intake site by the suit tried in 1936. (This was the trial at which was taken the testimony of witnesses now deceased, read from the record of that trial into the present record, R. 379-410.) The earlier suit resulted in a judgment sustaining the government's boundary line and the Meyer family took the case to the Supreme Court of Hawaii which held, precisely because the government always had claimed the disputed land, that the trial court lacked jurisdiction.[8]

Hence ensued the present suit, which was brought by the Meyer family, now occupying corporate status (see Abstract), in the Land Court of the Territory and with specific consent of the Territory to be sued (Act 207, Session Laws of Hawaii 1947, note 6).

---

[8] *Meyer v. Territory,* 36 Haw. 75, 77, 1942.

QUESTION INVOLVED

The question involved is:

Did the Supreme Court of Hawaii commit reversible error by holding that the grant is clear, certain and unambiguous, requiring
a location which excludes the disputed area?

This question is to be judged in the light of two well-
settled principles:

First: The case involves solely issues of local law. It is a
boundary dispute, in which the Supreme Court of Hawaii
has held that the line of a public land patent issued under
Hawaiian laws, is to be fixed according to the survey description and map of government surveyor Monsarrat incorporated in the patent, and not according to parol testimony as
to the ancient boundary of the land. The Supreme Court
has reviewed the record, has found in it no factual issue
that is not concluded by the Court's rulings of law, and has
ordered the Land Court to dispose of the case accordingly.
The case is a typical one for the application of the well-
settled principle that in matters of local concern,[9] including
land matters,[10] and the meaning and effect of local statutes
and local procedure,[11] there is to be no reversal of the

---

[9] *Waialua Agricultural Co. v. Christian*, 305 U.S. 91, 108-109, 59
S.Ct. 21, 83 L.Ed. 60; *De Mello v. Fong*, 164 F. 2d 232 (C.A. 9th
1947).

[10] *Kapiolani Estate v. Atcherley*, 238 U.S. 119, 35 S.Ct. 832, 59
L.Ed. 1229; *Lewers and Cooke v. Atcherley*, 222 U.S. 285, 32 S.Ct.
94, 56 L.Ed. 202; *Territory v. Hutchison Sugar Co.*, 272 Fed. 856,
859 (C.A. 9th 1921); *Pioneer Mill Co. v. Victoria Ward Ltd.*, 158 F.
2d 122 (C.A. 9th 1946).

[11] *De Castro v. Board of Commissioners*, 322 U.S. 451, 459, 64
S.Ct. 1121, 88 L.Ed. 1384; *Lord v. Territory*, 79 F. 2d 761 (C.A. 9th
1935); *Carey v. Hilo Finance and Thrift Co.*, 170 F. 2d 236 (C.A.
9th 1948); *Meyer v. Territory*, 164 F. 2d 845 (C.A. 9th 1947), cert.
den. 333 U.S. 860, 68 S.Ct. 738, 739, 92 L.Ed. 1139, 1140.

Supreme Court of Hawaii except for "manifest" error, that is, "clear departure from ordinary legal principles."

Second: Appellant's brief contains no specification of errors, as required by Rule 20, paragraph 2 (d). Instead appellant relies on ten point headings, copied from its "statement of points" filed pursuant to Rule 19, paragraph 6. These points really are summaries of argument. Further, appellant's statement of the questions involved does not show, as required by Rule 20, paragraph 2 (c), wherein the questions stated by it are raised on the record but instead states wherein they have been raised by itself in its "statement of points." There are hiatuses between the two, leaving much that is not tied to record citations that show appellant's right to raise the points. For example, appellant here is trying to impeach as of unknown origin (Br. Point 5, p. 41) the map which appears on the face of Grant 3437, despite the fact and without revealing, that the trial court found (R. 31) that the plat in the patent was Monsarrat's and that the parent map work and field notes were Monsarrat's, with which the Supreme Court simply agreed (R. 45). Specifications and arguments merit no consideration when not based on the record.[12] Appellant's brief is replete with this fault. In view of the first principle above stated, which requires appellant to show manifest error and clear departure from legal principles by the Supreme Court, this Court would be justified in dismissing the appeal or summarily affirming the Supreme Court.

---

[12] *Utley v. United States,* 115 F. 2d 117 (C.A. 9th 1940); *Simons v. Davidson Brick Co.,* 106 F. 2d 518, 521 (C.A. 9th 1939); *Buell v. Simon Newman Co.,* 154 F. 2d 35 (C.A. 9th 1946); *White v. Quittner,* 194 F. 2d 703 (C.A. 9th 1952).

ARGUMENT

THE SUPREME COURT WAS CORRECT IN ITS HOLDING THAT THE GRANT IS CLEAR, CERTAIN AND UN-AMBIGUOUS, REQUIRING A LOCATION WHICH EX-CLUDES THE DISPUTED AREA.

1. Historical background.

The history of Hawaiian land titles commences with the Land Commission, which was created by the Laws of 1846, p. 107, and dissolved as of March 1, 1855 by the Laws of 1854, p. 21. By the "Great Mahele" of 1848[13] a division of lands was made between Kamehameha and his chiefs, without survey.[14] An award of the Land Commission neverthe-less was required to be secured in order to obtain the title for which the Mahele paved the way,[15] and it further was required that a royal patent be obtained on the land com-mission award. Lands that were unawarded by the Land Commission remained in the government,[16] subject to cer-tain special acts not here involved. It was by virtue of such failure to secure an award that the government came into ownership of the "lele"[17] of Kahanui on the island of Molo-kai. Besides the lele, involved in this case, there is another Kahanui north and west of it. (Ex. A; Map II.)

The foregoing is merely background. This case involves Grant 3437, issued by the government after a sale at public auction, as will appear. The prior history of the land appears only by certain references thereto in correspondence.

---

[13] Explained in *Harris v. Carter*, 6 Haw. 195, 1877.

[14] *In the Matter of the Boundaries of Pulehunui*, 4 Haw. 239, 1879.

[15] *Kanaina v. Long*, 3 Haw. 332, 335, 1872.

[16] *Kenoa v. Meek*, 6 Haw. 63, 67, 1871; *Kahoomana v. Moehonua*, 3 Haw. 635, 1875; *Thurston v. Bishop*, 7 Haw. 421, 1888.

[17] "Lele" meaning literally "to jump" (Andrews Hawaiian Dic-tionary). Hence a non-contiguous piece of land held with a larger tract. See *In re Kakaako*, 30 Haw. 666, 668, 1928.

2. Land laws; requirement of survey; sale of this land by survey; trial court's error in this regard.

Two distinct methods of obtaining title are to be borne in mind, the first, by land commission award and patent issued in confirmation of the award, and the second, by a sale by the government in conformity with the land laws.

As to the first, it originally was possible to obtain a patent on a land commission award, without survey, according to the ancient boundaries. These boundaries were determined from the testimony of "kamaainas," who according to the Hawaiian custom from prehistoric times had knowledge of the boundaries, which was taught from father to son.[18] Concern was felt over the preservation of the kamaaina testimony;[19] indeed in the case cited in note 18, decided in 1879, some of the witnesses testified that "we are the only surviving kamaainas."[20] To put a stop to the practice of relying on the ancient boundaries there had been enacted in 1868 a law forbidding the issuance of "any patent, * * * in confirmation of an award by name * * *, without the boundaries being defined in such patent * * *."[21]

As to lands sold by the Minister of the Interior, the Laws of 1851[22] required them "to be correctly surveyed." This provision became section 47 of the Civil Code of 1859, so set forth in the Compiled Laws of 1884. The previous section, section 46, provided for the appointment by the Minister of the Interior of "suitable agents throughout the kingdom,

---

[18] *In the Matter of the Boundaries of Pulehunui,* supra, 4 Haw. 239 at pp. 240-241.

[19] *Akeni v. Wong Ka Mau,* 5 Haw. 91, 93, 1883.

[20] *In the Matter of the Boundaries of Pulehunui,* supra, 4 Haw. 239 at p. 245.

[21] Laws of 1868, p. 30, sec. 10.

[22] Laws of 1851, p. 52, sec. 4.

for the management and sale of government lands" and section 47 continued:

"SECTION 47. Every such agent shall procure the lands sold by him to be correctly surveyed; * * *."

By section 45 it further was provided:

"SECTION 45. It shall be the duty of the Minister of the Interior to cause such surveys, maps, and plans of the government lands, harbors, and internal improvements to be made as the public interests may require; which surveys, maps and plans shall be kept in his office for public inspection and reference."

The other pertinent laws are set forth in the appendix of appellant's brief and here are summarized. They provided[23] that:

The Minister of the Interior "shall have power to lease, sell, or otherwise dispose of the public lands, and other property, * * * subject, however, to such restrictions as may, from time to time, be expressly provided by law."

"All sales or leases of government lands shall be made at public auction, after not less than thirty days' notice by advertisement * * *, excepting lands and portions of lands of less than three hundred dollars in value."

"Notice of sale hereinabove required to be made, shall contain a full description of the land to be sold, as to locality, area, and quality, with a reference to the survey, which shall in all cases be kept in the office of the Minister open to inspection of anyone who may desire to examine the case."

"A Royal Patent, signed by the King, and countersigned by the Kuhina Nui and the Minister of the Interior, shall issue under the great Seal of the kingdom

---

[23] Civil Code 1859, sections 42-47, as amended by the Laws of 1876, Chapter XLIV, and the Laws of 1878, Chapter V, set forth in the Compiled Laws of 1884, pp. 11-13.

to the purchaser in fee simple of any government land or other real estate; * * *."

"All Royal Patents, leases, grants or other conveyances of any Government land or real estate, shall be prepared by and issued from, the Department of the Interior; and it shall be the duty of the Minister of the Interior to keep a full and faithful record of all such patents, leases, grants, and other conveyances."

It thus appears that, as correctly held by the Supreme Court (R. 44-45), the sale here involved was, and was required to be, by survey. The sale was open to the public, and all members of the public were entitled to an equal opportunity "to examine the case" on the basis of the public records. Testimony as to where the line anciently was can play no part in such a sale, the only question being where the survey has placed it.[24] Accordingly, the Supreme Court correctly held (R. 43-44, 48, 54-56) that the trial court erred in admitting "parol or extrinsic evidence of ancient boundaries on the theory that Royal Patent Number 3437, as well as the other patent, constituted a grant 'by name only' " (R. 43), and erred when "on that evidence, it in effect interpreted the language of the call to mean a portion of boundary 'as known and used from ancient times.' " (R. 43).

That the Supreme Court correctly typified the trial court's decision sufficiently appears from the following portions of it:

That the work of Monsarrat, the government surveyor who made the survey, "must still be entitled to and be weighed as other testimony of surveyors and engineers in any particular given case" (R. 29).

That "an award by name only conveys all property within its boundaries as known and used from ancient times" (R. 31).

---

[24] Infra, pp. 37-41.

That at the auction "the whole of the lele of Kahanui" was "purchased by name" (R. 32).

That it was the intention of the grant "to vest in the original grantee R. W. Meyer all of the land or lele of Kahanui; which would include the question of boundary * * *" (R. 33-34).

Appellant in its brief denies that the basis of the trial court's decision was a finding of intent to convey according to ancient boundaries (Br. 60), but nevertheless in its effort to uphold the trial court's decision gravitates to this theory again and again (Br. 11-14, 46, 55-56, 60-61, 69, 74-77).

3. Monsarrat's survey; sale of the land; issuance of the patents.

It being the duty of the Minister of Interior to have the government lands surveyed and mapped, M. D. Monsarrat, government surveyor, in 1885 was on the island of Molokai making such surveys. (Exs. 6 and 7). Monsarrat's reputation as a surveyor was excellent (R. 391).

On July 17, 1885 Monsarrat wrote Alexander[25] that "yesterday the Kamaainas showed me a piece of Kahanui away mauka on the edge of the palis * * *." (Ex. 7-A). Monsarrat went on to say in a subsequent letter that the piece had been left out of the Land Commission award (Ex. 7-B).

Monsarrat made field notes of his surveys and there are in evidence pages from his Field Book 2 of this period (Ex. 16). Thereafter Monsarrat mapped this land, making four maps dated 1886 (Exs. 11-14, R. 228-233), and wrote a description dated September 7, 1886 (see Grant 3437 file, Exs.

---

[25] Alexander was the Surveyor General.

C-1 to C-3).[26] This description appears in the patent, but with minor corrections, mostly in spelling (infra pp. 17-18). From Monsarrat's map was made the sketch map appearing as a part of the patent on its face. The Supreme Court so stated (R. 45-46). The trial court had so found (R. 31), as follows:

> "There were numerous maps introduced as evidence herein, and in the opinion of the Court, having reviewed over the past week end all the numerous maps and documents and all of the exhibits, the basis of all of them, that is almost all of them, is the parent map work and field notes of Mr. M. D. Monsarrat. Monsarrat's plat accompanies Grant 3437." (R. 31)

Appellant's brief largely is devoted to an attack on this map (Br. 26-27, 29, 31-33, 41, 68, 73, 75-76), although the trial court's finding is supported by substantial evidence (R. 248-51, 291-293, 302-305, 312-313, 333). Appellant's attack on the map, and on the findings concerning it, is embroidered upon cross examination (R. 335-339, 345) in which appellant's counsel differentiated between testimony of the witness Newton based on his knowledge of Monsarrat's handwriting and of survey office practice, and personal knowledge based on observation. The witness did not see Monsarrat do his map work and said so (R. 338). At no time did the witness say that the piece of land was mapped after the grant or that the original map was changed in any material respect. The attack on the map and findings concerning it also is embroidered upon testimony that the grant numbers and the name of the owner were printed

---

[26] There is no evidence whatsoever that Meyer had Monsarrat write the description, as stated by appellant (Br. 8). It is regular survey practice to map a survey, then write a description from the map. (R. 333)

in after the grants were issued (R. 303-304, 317-318, 320),
and that on some maps additions such as pipelines were indicated by special coloring (R. 318, 319-320), the boundary,
however, remaining the same (R. 320). The brief contains
many incorrect statements which will not be explored further in this regard, in view of the complete agreement of the
trial court and Supreme Court on the authenticity and origin of the patent map.

Monsarrat's worksheet is Exhibit 11, a map 1000 feet to
the inch. On it were marked in Monsarrat's own handwriting (R. 248) certain points appearing in his field notes as
X, K, A, and Y. While it is not necessary to go back of the
map appearing on the face of the patent or to go into the
field notes, as the Supreme Court held (R. 47), these points
were much referred to in the testimony and will prove convenient references. They were plotted by applicant's own
surveyor McKeague (Ex. A, R. 68-69, 93, 99) and by the
government surveyor Newton (Ex. 10, R. 246). Both
agreed as to the location of these points (R. 258-259) and
they correspond with Monsarrat's work (R. 262-263, Ex.
11). For convenience, we have marked these points in red
on Map II. We also have marked in red on Map II the line
of the direct bearing between X and Kaluahauoni Government Triangulation Station; this direct bearing is given in
the grant.

Turning now from the survey and map material to the
sale itself, the exhibits show that on July 4, 1888 R. W.
Meyer wrote the Minister of the Interior stating his discovery of the fact that there was no award of the "lele" of
Kahanui (Ex. C-1). The same letter spoke of Monsarrat's
survey, referred the Minister of the Interior to Monsarrat,

and made an application for purchase, offering $500. The offer was repeated by a letter of August 31, 1888 (Ex. C-3).

On October 4, 1888 the land was advertised for sale on October 10, 1888, at public auction. In response to the law's requirement that the notice of sale contain "a full description of the land to be sold, as to locality * * *," the notice described it as "the remnant or lele of the Ahupuaa of Kahanui on the Island of Molokai." (Ex. D-1).[27] In response to the law's requirement for a statement of the area the notice stated "an area of say 1000 acres". In response to the law's requirement for a statement of the land's quality the notice stated "mountain forest land". But the required "reference to the survey" was not supplied in the notice and the sale might well have been held invalid for that reason.[28] However the Supreme Court held that this requisite was met, due to the fact that the land actually had been surveyed, and the maps, survey and field notes were a matter of public record (R. 45, 47).[29]

---

[27] The land was *not* advertised as the "whole of the remnant or lele of Kahanui" as incorrectly stated by appellant (Br. 9, 44).

[28] *Hawaiian Government v. Cornwell*, 8 Haw. 12, 1890.

[29] Appellant cannot limit the record of the survey to the description sent in by Meyer (Br. 45, 58, 60). The sale was at public auction and governed by the entire public record of the survey, as held by the Supreme Court (R. 45, 47). This is evident from the law's requirement that the survey be kept "open to inspection of anyone who may desire to examine the case." Maps are specifically mentioned in the law as being open for public inspection and reference. Appellant itself regards the field notes as part of the survey (Br. 3, 8, 11, 30, 42, 47-50, 56-57, 61-63, 73, 76-77), and thereby accepts the principle that the record of the survey consists in more than the description.

In any event the whole matter of the survey and the effect of it was fully reviewed by the parties at the time, as shown in the next paragraphs of this brief.

It should be noted that appellant's citation of Exhibit 19 has no bearing, for this simply was an excerpt from Grant 3437 copied some years later. Of course the patent itself (Ex. B) is the best evidence.

A few days after the sale there was issued the patent afterward cancelled (Ex. J). This patent contained the same sketch map appearing in the final patent (Ex. B). The wording of the description was the same as that written by Monsarrat on September 7, 1886 (See Grant 3437 file, Exs. C-1 to C-3).

The next occurrence appears from Monsarrat's letter of February 7, 1889 to Alexander at Honolulu (Ex. 7-C). It there appears that in November, 1888, at Kaunakakai on Molokai, Meyer spoke to Monsarrat and Alexander about a "change in the notes of Kahanui piece that was sold to Mr. Meyer." Of this Monsarrat says in his letter: "That is around the Waihanau and Waialeia gulches." A proposed amendment of the description appears (R. 75) in three lines marked with an asterisk at the bottom of the first page of the October 13, 1888 patent (Ex. J), in the roughing in of the ridge on the map on the second page, and also a correction in names on the second page.

The proposed amendment of the description would have substituted for the language "Thence around the head of the Waihanau and Makanalua Valleys to the Government Survey Station 'Kaluahauoni' ", the language "Thence around the head of the Waihanau Valley following the Pali to Kalawao[30] and around the Waialeia valley to the Gov't. Survey Station Kaluahauoni." This change was not made. However, the valley east of the ridge, appearing in the description and patent when first written as "Makanalua", was corrected to read "Waialeia". (It is agreed that Waialeia

---

[30] Kalawao lies north and east of the tip of the ridge (See Ex. U). Hence to follow the pali all the way to Kalawao would have included the ridge in Grant 3437. The ridge was conveyed by Grant 3539 (infra).

is the correct name of the valley east of the ridge) .

It is significant that the trial court held (R. 33) that the "amended description [which] was attempted to be included * * * did, in fact, not include and did exclude the parcel [of] which the applicant now claims ownership in fee."

As to why the proposed amended description was not adopted we find that on October 17, 1889 (Ex. H) the Minister of the Interior wrote Meyer acknowledging receipt of a letter from him (Ex. G) , and saying that "the inaccuracy in spelling of names in said Patent will be corrected in a clean copy issued to you; it now awaits signature of King." The letter continues:

> "With regard to the addition which you claim ought belong to the land, and desire to be included in said Patent, I would say that upon examination of the records, I find the sale was made by a map and detail description both made by Mr. M. D. Monsarrat, excluding the piece which you claim; under these circumstances I cannot lawfully add anything to the area of the land included in this Patent.
>
> Mr. Monsarrat states however that the piece you desire is undoubtedly a part of Kahananui, and he omitted it because he thought it was of so little value that it was not worth while surveying the same.[31]
>
> If you wish to have a survey made of the land I will sell it to you at a private sale[32] at a nominal sum. This of course will involve the cost of another Patent."

About twelve days after this letter, on October 29, 1889, Grant 3437 in its final form (Ex. B) was issued.

---

[31] This again shows that the survey was not, and never purported to be, the "whole" of the lele of Kahanui as claimed by appellant.

[32] A private sale was lawful because this piece was valued at less than $300.00.

Replying to the Minister of the Interior's letter, on October 23, 1889 (Ex. I-2), Meyer again referred to the "additional piece of land" which had been the subject of the correspondence, and stated:

> "I must acknowledge the correctness that it would be illegal to add anything to a Royal Patent for a piece of land sold by survey, and never did expect anything of the kind—and I am perfectly willing therefore, to pay for the extra patent and also the nominal value which you see fit to put on in order to obtain the deed for this additional piece of land.
>
> "Regarding the survey of it, I presume and feel confident, that a sufficient description can be made out, from now existing surveys, without the necessity of making out an actual survey, and have a surveyor come up on purpose, which would probably prove to be very expensive.
>
> "Please accept my thanks for having the error in spelling, in the first patent corrected and in having a new and clean copy made out."

From further correspondence (Ex. I-1, P, and O) it appears that the ridge was not surveyed, except as to its length and some points. On June 25, 1890 Monsarrat wrote Meyer:

> ". . . you can make an application as I told you viz: All the land on the top of the ridge between Waihanau and Waialeia valleys and lying between the edge of pali on the East side of Waihanau and West side of Waialeia Valleys. I think this or something similar would do for a description.
>
> I enclose a rough tracing from my 1000 foot map[33] showing the ridge and the points located by me. From which you can get the length of the ridge and get some idea of the area. . . ." (Ex. O)

On May 5, 1891 the patent conveying the ridge was issued, being Grant No. 3539 (Ex. K). It contained a center

---

[33] This again shows the authorship of the maps.

line description and a map showing the intention to convey
land on top of the ridge between Waihanau and Waialeia
valleys and lying between the edge of pali on each side. J.
F. Brown of the Survey office wrote Meyer (Ex. L) that it
had been intended to include in this patent the words "that
tract of land lying on the top of the ridge between the Waihanau and Waialeia valleys, and bounded by the upper edge
of the palis of these valleys", but in view of the patent's map
being so clear to this effect the omission is not important.

The beginning point of Grant 3539 for the ridge piece,
"beginning at a point on the northern boundary of Grant
3437", is Point A, one of the points located from Monsarrat's
field notes as above stated (supra, p. 15), and marked on
Map II. There is no disagreement as to the location of Point
A nor as to the fact that "the beginning point of Grant 3539
calls for, in its description, this point A" (R. 88, 93, testimony of appellant's surveyor; and Ex. A being the map and
marking of points by appellant's surveyor), nor is there any
disagreement as to the fact that Grant 3539 touches Grant
3437 at only this one point, Point A (R. 88-89, 90, testimony
of appellant's surveyor).

In making the survey for appellant's application in the
Land Court, appellant's surveyor included the ridge in
Grant 3437, even though Meyer admitted it was not so included. Appellant's surveyor followed the p r o p o s e d
amended description of Grant 3437 that was not made, as
well as a great deal of other material extraneous to the grant
(infra, pp. 31-32):

4. **The Grant 3437 map is to be read with the description and is a
   part of the description.**

In each patent there is a map drawn on the second page,

intervening between the first and last pages. Thus, in Grant 3437, the first page (numbered 149 in the record book) bears the words of grant and the language of the description, the next page (numbered 150 in the record book) has drawn on it the sketch map made from Monsarrat's map, and the last page (numbered 151 in the record book) states the area, reserves mineral rights, and contains the habendum and testimonium clauses, followed by the signatures of the King and Minister of the Interior (Ex. B). The map thus is "a part of the patent on its face", as stated by the Supreme Court (R. 45).

Appellant assumes that the map is not a part of the description because not specifically referred to in the description (Br. 5, 27). Appellant cites no authorities; the authorities are to the contrary as would be supposed. Thus, in *Murray v. Klinzing*, 64 Conn. 78, 29 Atl. 244, 1894, the question was whether the court erred in treating the map on the deed as a part of the description of the land intended to be conveyed. The plaintiff argued that in the absence of an express reference to the map it was not a part of the description. The court held otherwise, saying:

> "Where a map or a diagram is drawn on a deed in such relation to, or connected with, the words of the deed, as to indicate to any reasonable person that the grantor intended it to be taken as a part of the description, then no reference is needed. It is entirely a question as to what the grantor intended to convey. If the map is on another paper, a reference might be necessary in order to identify it. When the map is on the deed itself, the court, of necessity, must examine it, and from it, taken together with the words of description, determine what the deed conveys."

In *Wailuku Sugar Co. v. Hawaiian Commercial and Sugar Co.*, 13 Haw. 583, 586, 1901, the instrument for construction was a land commission award. The question was whether the title ran to the center of the stream or only to its bank. The Court held the latter, although the language of the description ran "along" the stream. Applying the rule that a deed will be construed as excluding the bed of the stream if such intent "clearly appears from the language of the conveyance or from any map or plat made a part thereof" the Court held that the intention to exclude the bed of the stream was confirmed beyond doubt by a diagram contained in the Award, it being "over the signatures of the members of the Land Commission and may, therefore, be considered as a part of the Award itself."

The purpose of a reference to a map is to make it "as important a part of the description as if it had been actually copied in the deed."[34] This again shows that insertion of a copy of the map in the deed is the best method.

When a map is made a part of a deed or patent, everything that is shown on the map becomes a part of the description, and where the words of the description are general they are given certainty by the map, which is considered the more particular and controlling description.[35]

---

[34] *Werk v. Leland University*, 155 La. 971, 99 So. 716; *Slauson v. Goodrich Transportation Co.*, 99 Wis. 20, 74 N.W. 574; *McBryde Estate v. Gay and Robinson*, 15 Haw. 117, 121, 1903; 2 Devlin on Deeds, Third Ed., Sec. 1020; 2 Thompson on Real Property, Perm. Ed., Sec. 477; 8 Am. Jur. 750, Sec. 8.

[35] *McBryde Estate v. Gay and Robinson*, supra, 15 Haw. 117, 121-122; *Wailuku Sugar Co. v. Hawaiian Commercial and Sugar Co.*, supra, 13 Haw. 583, 586; *Lincoln v. Wilder*, 29 Maine (16 Shep.) 169, 180; *Vance v. Fore*, 24 Cal. 438, 1864; *McIver's Lessee v. Walker*, 9 Cranch (13 U.S.) 173, 1815, 3 L.Ed. 694; *Lotz v. Hurwitz*, 174 La. 638, 141 So. 83, 1932; *Dallum v. Breckenridge*, 6 Fed. Cases No. 3547, C.C.D. Tenn., 1812; *McCormick v. Huse*, 78 Ill. 363, 1875. *Kelekolio v. Onomea*, 29 Haw. 130, cited by appellant (Br. 34), was a case of an irreconcilable conflict between the head of the holua as shown by the map, and an auwai which was called for and was a definite and certain monument; the case is not in point.

We already have dealt with appellant's contention that the map in Grant 3437 is of doubtful origin (supra, pp. 14-15). The remaining argument made against the map is that it is not based on an actual survey along the disputed boundary (Br. 26, 29, 31, 41, 75). We will show in the next division of the argument that the map is sufficient for all practical purposes. That is all that is required.[36]

5. Upon application of the governing rules of law, the boundary is clear, certain and unambiguous, requiring a location that excludes the disputed area.

Grant 3437 commences at the Government Triangulation Station Puu Kaeo "on the edge of the Waikolu Valley." This is the southeast corner of the piece, as shown on the patent's map (See Map I). The boundary then runs west and south along the government land of Kamiloloa to a stone marked as indicated, then north and west along the land of Kaunakakai to a cross on a stone, then continues north and west along the land of Kalamaula to a cross on a stone, then again continues north and west along the land of Kalamaula "to a stone marked with a cross at the edge of Waihanau Valley." All of this boundary was located without dispute. The next call gives rise to the dispute. It reads:

> "Thence around the head of the [named] Valleys to the Govt. Survey Station Kaluahauoni. The direct bearing and distance being S. 79° 07′ E. (true) 8631 ft."

Of the valleys named the first, or western one, is the Waihanau Valley (at the edge of which is the stone marked with a cross to which the previous call carried), and the sec-

---

[36] *Arkansas v. Tennessee*, 269 U.S. 152, 156-157, 1925, 46 S.Ct. 31, 70 L.Ed. 206; *Hughes v. City of Carlsbad*, 53 N.M. 150, 203 P. 2d 995, 999, 1949.

ond valley or eastern one is the Waialeia Valley (See Map I).

The last call reads: "Thence along the edge of the Waikolu Valley to initial point." This again has been located without dispute, that is, from the Government Station Kaluahauoni along the edge of Waikolu Valley to the point of beginning.

Returning now to the call "around the head" of the Waihanau and Waialeia Valleys, it further appears by comparison of the map annexed to the appellant's application and the map annexed to the Territory's answer, and from the appellant's Exhibit A prepared by its surveyor, that the parties are in agreement as to the line from Point A to the Government Station Kaluahauoni. (Point A is one of the field note points marked for convenience of reference on Map II, it being undisputed that this point is located at the base of the ridge and also that this is the beginning point of the description of Grant 3539 and the only point at which this grant touches Grant 3437, supra, p. 20. Also, upon comparison of the maps annexed to the appellant's application and the Territory's answer, it appears that the parties have the same location for the line from the northwest tip of the land, that is, from the stone marked with a cross at the edge of the Waihanau Valley, as far as the place indicated by the red line on Map I, where appellant's line takes off north and east and the Territory's line continues south and east along the line shown on the patent map. Thus the call from the stone marked with a cross on the edge of the Waihanau Valley, thence around the head of the Waihanau and Waialeia Valleys to the Government Survey Station Kaluahauoni, which is the northern boundary of this piece, is located without dispute as to its extreme western portion and without dispute as to the eastern portion from the base of the ridge marked Point A on Map II to the Government Station Kaluahauoni. As correctly stated by the Supreme Court (R. 42) the issue was narrowed by the parties to the determination of the location of the middle western portion of the northern boundary. The parties stipulated that the issue was simply the boundary of the disputed area of approximately fifty acres delineated in green on the map annexed to the Territory's answer (R. 61) .[37]

From the words of the description it appears that the northern boundary meanders along the sinuosities of the edges of the valleys, and the Supreme Court so held (R. 49, 52). This appears from the fact that the line begins at the edge of the Waihanau Valley and proceeds "thence around * * *", ending at the edge of the Waikolu Valley at the Government Station Kaluahauoni. This calls for "the contour lines of continuous mountains meandering along the edges of the respective three adjoining valleys similar to that surrounding the ridge land of Royal Patent 3539" (R. 49) ; "a meander line commencing with 'a stone marked with a cross at the [western] edge of Waihanau Valley thence [curving along that edge in a southerly direction to the topmost part of the valley's upper end] around the head * * *' " (R. 52, bracket insertions by Supreme Court) ; "the valley's edge" (R. 52). Further, the call is not "around the head of the Waihanau Valley and around the head of the Waialeia Valley" but instead it is a call "around the head" of the two

---

[37] Appellant's brief reads as if the stipulation had divorced the issue from the rules of law governing the determination of such an issue (Br. 6, 15, 17, 58). The record speaks for itself.

valleys. From the direct bearing furnished it also appears that the direction of the line from its beginning at the edge of the Waihanau Valley to its end at the edge of the Waiholu Valley at the Government Station Kaluahauoni, is southeast.

The map further defines the intent as to the contour or thread the sinuosities of which are to be followed.[38] Calling the line a "meander line" does not affect the importance of the map. As stated in *Horne v. Smith*[39] in disposing of a contention that the boundary was the water line of the main body of a certain river, as opposed to the contention that the boundary was the water line of a bayou opening into the river:

> "* * * The basis of this contention is the familiar rule that a meander line is not a line of boundary, and that a patent for a tract of land bordering on a river conveys the land, not simply to the meander line, but to the water line, and hence, as claimed in this case, carries it to the water line of the main body of the river. * * *" (p. 42)
>
> "* * * It is * * * true that the meander line is not a line of boundary, but one designed to point out the sinuosities of the bank of the stream, and as a means of ascertaining the quantity of land in the fraction which is to be paid for by the purchaser. *Railroad Co. v. Schurmeir*, 7 Wall. 272; *Hardin v. Jordan*, 140 U.S. 371, 380. * * *" (p. 43)
>
> "But the question in this case is whether the boundary of these lots is the bayou or the main body of the river. That a water line runs along the course of the meander line cannot, of course, in the face of the plat and survey, be questioned, but that the meander line of the plat is the water line of the bayou rather than that of the main body of the river, is evident * * *.

[38] *Horne v. Smith*, 159 U.S. 40, 42-44, 15 S.Ct. 988, 40 L.Ed. 68; *Wailuku Sugar Co. v. Hawaiian Commercial and Sugar Co.*, supra, 13 Haw. 583, 586; *Lincoln v. Wilder*, supra, 29 Maine (16 Shep.) 169, 180; *Erskine v. Moulton*, 66 Maine 276, 280, 1877.

[39] Cited in the preceding note.

* * * the meander line, as shown on the plat, is, so far as these lots are concerned, wholly within the east half of sections 23 and 26, while the water line of the main body of the river is a mile or a mile and a quarter west thereof, in sections 22 and 27. * * *" (pp. 43-44)

Hence, appellant does not advance its case by stating that the northern boundary is a meander line and reiterating the rules applicable to meander lines (Br. 21-24, 26-31, 75). A meander line serves the purpose of locating the sinuosities which are to be followed, and that is its purpose in the patent's map.

Upon application of the correct rules we find from the patent as a whole, that is, from the general description by words and the particular description by the map, that the following is to be done in locating the northern boundary:

(1) It starts on the west side of Waihanau Valley at a point to be located by running the preceding boundary, and thus is defined as a stone marked with a cross on the edge of the valley.

(2) From this starting point the boundary meanders along the sinuosities of the edges of the valleys, as stated by the Supreme Court at R. 49, 52, reviewed supra.

(3) The starting point is the northernmost tip of the tract. From thence, the boundary runs in a sloping southeasterly direction to reach the head of the Waialeia Valley, and between this portion of the boundary and the western boundary that adjoins Kalamaula there is formed a thumb-shaped piece, as on the thumb of a right hand. Waihanau Valley is on the east side of this thumb with Waialeia Valley east of that.

(4) From the tip of this thumb (i.e. from the marked stone which is the starting point) to Kaluahauoni Govern-

ment Triangulation Station a direct bearing is given by the description, and if dotted in on the map it will be found that the northern boundary lies south of this direct bearing line, except for the extreme eastern tip of the boundary, not in dispute, where the line after passing along the head of the second valley, Waialeia, turns back along the edge of the third valley, Waikolu.

The conditions on the ground were shown both by the appellant and the Territory without disagreement as to any essential of this location when made under correct rules of law. Reference is made to the maps (appellant's Exs. A and M, the latter being a copy of the map attached to appellant's application), the contour and profile maps (Ct's Ex. 1 and appellant's Ex. N); the testimony of appellant's own surveyor McKeague, as noted infra; the testimony of the Territory's surveyor Newton, surveyor and engineer Towill, and engineers Howell and Jorgensen. Contrary to the statement made by appellant (Br. 4-5, 16-17, 42, 50, 78) these witnesses were on the ground.[40] But in any event there is no disagreement as to the ground conditions described in the delineation of the boundary location which follows. This delineation can be followed from Map II, which will be found to be the same in all essential particulars as the map and testimony of appellant's surveyor McKeague. Topic

---

[40] Newton made and mapped his survey at the time of the 1936 trial (R. 225, 228, Ex. 10); he retraced Monsarrat's survey on the ground and particularly located on the ground the portion of the boundary here in dispute (R. 227, 253-258). Towill made the aerial photographs and from them the mosaic contour map which is Territory's Exhibit 1 (R. 358) and also was on the ground (R. 376-378). Jorgensen was the engineer who in 1924 put in the water tunnel the intake of which is in the disputed area, and Howell was the engineer who made the further improvements of this water system in 1933; both of them, before doing the work, located the boundary on the ground at the point where the Territory places it (R. 382-384, 389-390; 392-394).

numbering of the below delineation follows that used above in outlining what is called for by the patent.

(1) The starting point of the northern boundary has been located by both parties. It is on the top edge of the Waihanau Valley, on the western side of the valley, at the stone marked with a cross. This is Point X according to Monsarrat's field notes and so designated on Map II.

(2) This top edge of valley can be and accordingly must be followed as it meanders southeast, past the point where appellant drops down 400 feet to the valley floor (R. 144-145; R. 366; Ct's Ex. 1) ; through the point identified as K in Monsarrat's field notes, and so designated on Map II, where this top edge of the valley is about 350 feet above the valley floor[41] (R. 144-146; Ct's Ex. 1) ; and to the point of overlapping spur ridges below described, at which point we are 280 feet above the valley floor (R. 366-367; Ct's Ex. 1) . All the way from the starting point at the marked stone, Point X, this contour has been distinct, as testified by appellant's surveyor McKeague.[42] At the point of overlapping spur ridges below described there is a sharp turn to the west to the point identified as Y in Monsarrat's field notes and so designated on Map II. However, the patent does not call for following a contour that runs west. It calls for a southeastern direction in order to reach the head of the Waialeia Valley. Nor does the patent call for running back to the

[41] The valley floor rises, as shown by appellant's Ex. N.

[42] Appellant's surveyor McKeague, referring to this contour as the top edge of the pali, said that it was distinct through and beyond Point K, and continues on around until it hits Point Y (R. 134, 149; for the points mentioned see Map II). This can be followed from the hachure marks on this surveyor's map, Exs. A and M.

As to the differentiation between the steepness of the pali in different portions, made by McKeague and touched on in appellant's brief, this is discussed, infra, pp. 33-34.

western or Kalamaula boundary of the tract as would be done if we followed the contour west to Point Y, for that would bite right through the thumb which on the contrary is depicted by the patent as attaining a gradually increasing thickness. Accordingly, looking for the contour intended to be followed in the southeastern direction toward the head of Waialeia Valley, we find that at this point there are overlapping spur ridges coming out from each side of the valley and causing an S bend in the stream at a pool called Waiau. Although appellant's surveyor McKeague, did not show on his own map the spur ridge coming down from the east side of the valley he admitted it was there and that there was a marked overlapping of these spur ridges (R. 148-149, 158-159, 162, 165), his testimony being:

"Q. A very marked overlapping. Correct?
A. That is right."

(R. 165)

These overlapping ridges at the S bend of the stream were held by the Supreme Court to mark the head of the valley (R. 51). They block off the view of the valley, and above this point the stream begins to branch out (R. 255-256, 364-366, 377-378, testimony of Newton and Towill; see Map II and appellant's Ex. A). Appellant argues that "the valley involved runs as a water shed several miles above * * *" (Br. 55). But this is not the material question. That the line of the overlapping spur ridges is the head of the valley intended by the patent is all that is material.

The turn around the valley's head cannot be north of this point, because the contour of the valley's edge has been clearly followed running south to this point. That the line has not been located still further south does not aggrieve the appellant.

Crossing over on the line of the overlapping spur ridges, therefore, we reach the point at the base of Grant 3539 which is Point A according to Monsarrat's field notes and so designated on Map II. From this point there juts out the ridge that divides the Waihanau Valley from the Waialeia Valley. The top of this ridge, between the palis that mark the east side of the Waihanau Valley and the west side of the Waialeia Valley, is Grant 3539 which touches Grant 3437 at this one point as above stated.

(3) The boundary as thus located runs in a sloping southeasterly direction to reach the head of the Waialeia Valley, and forms a thumb-shaped piece with Waihanau Valley on the east side of the thumb, all as indicated on the patent map.

(4) From the tip of this thumb to Kaluahauoni Government Triangulation Station the direct bearing, when dotted in as has been done in red on Map II, is the chord of a crescent that is formed by the slope of the thumb, and the boundary thus located lies south of this direct bearing line, except for the extreme eastern tip of the boundary, not disputed, where it turns back along Waikolu Valley. This all is as indicated by the patent's map.

The reason why the appellant's surveyor did not find this clearly located line is because he did not look for it. He rejected the patent's map (R. 117). He concluded that since Monsarrat wrote the description before Meyer made the application to purchase the land the description "was not intended to convey the land that was applied for by Mr. Meyer" (R. 84). It was the objective of appellant's surveyor to follow "the intent of where that boundary should be under the application made by Meyer for the land that was desired" (R. 83, also R. 71). To that end he examined the correspondence and made inquiries of members of the Meyer family, whom he called "kamaainas"[43] (R. 76-78). He also followed (R. 81) the wording of the proposed amended description (Ex. J) and included the ridge (R. 70-71), even though he knew and admitted that it was granted by Grant 3539 as a separate piece of land (R. 88-90); again his theory was that it was part of what Meyer applied for (R. 88). In short, his whole object was to survey what he thought would have been surveyed if a new survey had been made to conform to Meyer's application, instead of what was surveyed, sold at public auction, and actually patented. It needs no extended citation of authority to show that this was wrong.[44] Hence, the only materiality of his evidence lay in his depiction of conditions on the ground.

That appellant's location of the boundary does not follow the patent may be expected from the foregoing. It is reviewed below with topic numbering following that used above in outlining what is called for by the patent.

(1) Appellant correctly locates the starting point of the northern boundary, on the top edge of the Waihanau Valley on the western side of the valley.

(2) Appellant does not follow the top edge of the valley as it meanders southeast, but instead drops down 400 feet to

---

[43] The Territory consistently contended that these persons were not qualfied "kamaainas," but since the entire method by which the appellant located its line is wrong under the governing rules of law the point is not reached; it was not reached by the Supreme Court.

[44] 8 Am. Jur. 819, Sec. 102; *Sullivan v. New Orleans & N.E.R. Co.*, 9 La. App. 162, 119 So. 275, 276, 1928; *Edmonds v. Wery*, 27 Haw. 621, 1923. This particularly was wrong in the case of a public grant such as this one, the rule of construction in such a case being against the grantee. 6 Thompson on Real Property, Perm. Ed., Sec. 3365.

the valley floor (R. 144-145; R. 366; Ct's Ex. 1) just after completing the top of the thumb. From here appellant's line runs north and then crosses the floor of the valley to the ridge, interposing courses not called for, as the Supreme Court held (R. 54). This of course was improper.[45]

(3) By inclusion of the disputed area the thumb becomes a broad chimney with all of Waihanau Valley north of it, for the top of the chimney is supposed to be the head of the valley. Alongside this chimney piece is Waialeia Valley, not Waihanau Valley. But by the patent the Waihanau Valley was shown extending along the side of the thumb. This valley land, which by the patent was to be excluded, now is included in the chimney piece.

(4) When appellant's line is applied, the boundary is made to run north, across the direct bearing line, although (with the exception of the extreme eastern tip near Waikolu Valley where the boundary is not in dispute) it was to lie south of the direct bearing line. The surveyor could not have made a mistake about this. He stood at the northernmost tip of the land, at the marked stone, and took the direct bearing to the Government Triangulation Station Kaluahauoni. He intended the boundary line to meander along to the right, south of this line, and reproduced this intention in the patent, which governs.

Appellant's theory is that the top of a precipice is called for; it further is argued that appellant justifiably dropped down 400 feet to the valley floor because it crossed the valley floor at the top of a big waterfall (Br. 38). However, there is no call for the top of a precipice. This is a play on the Hawaiian word "pali" (Br. 37, 70) but that word is not men-

_____

[45] *Edmonds v. Wery*, supra, 27 Haw. 621, 624, 1923; *Re Waikapu Boundaries*, 31 Haw. 43, 51, 1929.

tioned in the grant either. (It was used at the trial as a convenient way to refer to the top edge of the valleys.) Nor would the word "pali" include a waterfall, which would be "wailele."[45a]

6. The 1891 purchase of the ridge as a separate piece in itself requires rejection of appellant's line.

There is a continuous ridge between Point A, which is the base of the ridge on the south, and the northern end of the ridge called Holae (R. 120-121, 129-130). Grant 3539 was for this ridge piece, described as jutting out from the northern boundary of Grant 3437 and touching it only at the base of the ridge, Point A (supra, p. 20). Meyer purchased the ridge piece in 1891, after agreeing that it was not included in Grant 3437; Meyer obtained the issuance of Grant 3539 to cover it (supra, pp. 17-19). Although Grant 3539 shows on its face that it is for a separate piece, as admitted by appellant's surveyor McKeague (R. 88), it was designated in the appellant's application as "on a portion of Grant 3437" (R. 15). The Territory's answer took issue with this (R. 21). The trial court stated the question ("the question for determination is whether or not Grant 3539 to R. W. Meyer, as a grant, was issued on a portion of Grant 3437 to R. W. Meyer, the same grantee, and in that connection raises the question in dispute as to the boundary of Grant 3437 * * *", R. 28) ; but the trial court failed to cope with the question so stated. The Supreme Court held (R. 40) that there were "two separate and distinct grants", and gave proper significance to this holding (R. 46-47).

Appellant has not solved, and cannot solve, the dilemma presented by the existence of the second grant. Because it

---

[45a] Andrews Hawaiian Dictionary. From "wai" meaning "water" and "lele" meaning "to jump."

could not be solved appellant's surveyor included the ridge in Grant 3437. His theory was (R. 70-71) that he could do this under the proposed amended description (Ex. j), which was not made. The theory of appellant's brief is not clear. Appellant does not state where its line is supposed to proceed after it is pushed across the valley floor at the Big Falls. If the line were then to run south along the ridge to Point A there would be presented a further dilemma. For although part of this area is a hog's back[46] the southern part is a grassy plateau (R. 120). Does the line pass east of this grassy plateau and include it in Grant 3437, on the theory that this part of the line is along the edge of Waialeia Valley? Or does it pass west of this plateau on the theory that this part of the line follows the edge of the Waihanau Valley? If the answer is the latter it is incompatible with the theory that the Waihanau Valley was left behind when the valley floor was crossed at the Big Falls, the supposed head of the Waihanau Valley. If the answer is the first one, then the south part of the ridge was included in Grant 3437; so why does Grant 3539 start at Point A? It is admitted that this is the starting point of Grant 3539 (R. 89, 93). Furthermore, why is Point A the only point at which Grant 3539 touches Grant 3437, if Grant 3539 ran along Grant 3437 (as it would have, had the disputed area been included in Grant 3437); it is admitted that Grant 3539 touched Grant 3437 only at the one point, Point A (R. 88-90). These questions

---

[46] The sketch map in Grant 3539 does not show this hog's back, as the ridge originally had not been intended to be patented and had not been surveyed, supra, pp. 18-19. (In contrast, the map of Grant 3437, which was surveyed, is remarkably accurate for so large a tract and in such terrain.) As to the map in Grant 3539, it served its purpose by showing the starting point, the relation of the two pieces, and that the second piece was the top of the ridge between the palis.

cannot be answered, and they present insurmountable obstacles to the acceptance of appellant's line. In order to reconcile with Grant 3539, the boundary of Grant 3437 necessarily must stay on the west side of the valley and not hit the ridge until Point A.

7. Parol evidence was not admissible to contradict the patent; this rule excludes from the case the evidence upon which appellant relies.

The well-settled rule[47] was stated by the Supreme Court as follows:

> "The crux of the case concerns the location of a portion of boundary, rather than a construction of the grant, and involves the admissibility of parol or extrinsic evidence. Upon the crucial point this court has authoritatively declared the settled law to be, where, as here, there is no ambiguity, that 'parol evidence is inadmissible to vary or contradict the terms of the grant.' (Ookala S. Co. v. Wilson, 13 Haw. 127, 131.) It further likewise declared that 'It is also settled that parol evidence is admissible when the question is one of location as distinguished from one of construction, that is such evidence is admissible to connect the land with the grant or to apply the grant to the land.' (Ookala S. Co., v. Wilson, supra.) These principles, simply stated, are decisive of the solution of the problem before this court, the objective being to give effect to nothing else but the grant's intention to convey land according to its surveyed description and map."

In another Hawaiian case[48] it was held that there was no ambiguity in the description of land demised, though the description included a statement, "being that portion of the said land suitable for the cultivation of sugar cane", and

---

[47] *Ookala Sugar Co. v. Wilson*, 13 Haw. 127, 131, 1900; *Territory v. Kapiolani Estate*, 18 Haw. 394, 396, 1907.

[48] *Notley v. Kukaiau Plantation Co.*, 11 Haw. 525, 529, 1898.

though there were eleven acres of land not suitable for the cultivation of sugar cane divided off from the rest by a high bluff stretching across the entire tract, the court stating the rule as follows:

> "* * * The principle of interpretation is that if there be a description of the property clear and definite, and sufficient to render certain what is intended to be demised, the addition of a wrong name, * * * will have no effect. That there was such a definite and certain description is clear, and it must prevail." (p. 529)

Hence, parol evidence should be taken to "connect the land with the grant", but not to create uncertainty where none exists. This is further developed in the cases, infra.

We have shown that the boundary is located with certainty by the patent itself, which contains its own determination of the Waihanau Valley's head. A surveyor can go out on the ground and locate it from the patent, without asking anyone: "Where is the head of the Waihanau Valley?" The starting point of the northern boundary is located from the preceding call, and if the surveyor stays where he belongs, which is on the top edge of the valley, the proper location unrolls like a carpet. How this is done is the *proper* purpose of the parol evidence. The *improper* purpose, which is appellant's, is to create uncertainty where none exists. It was and is appellant's object to show that the head of the Waihanau Valley is not where it was placed by the government surveyor.

The trial court held that the government survey constituted only an inconclusive opinion as to where the line should be (R. 29-31), and that the question for it to determine was where the head of the Waihanau Valley should be placed (R. 28-29). This the trial court proceeded to do without paying any attention to the context of the language in the description (which the Supreme Court held called for a line following the valley's edge). The trial court likewise paid no attention to the map (R. 31). Concluding from Meyer's application (without paying any attention to the laws governing public auctions) that the intention of the grantor was to convey "the whole of the lele of Kahanui" (R. 32), the Court decided that such was the governing factor, that the land "was purchased by name" (R. 32), that the ancient boundary of this land was at the big fall in Waihanau Valley, and that this big fall accordingly was the head of Waihanau Valley (R. 33-34). The evidence in this regard, held extraneous and inadmissible by the Supreme Court, is well summed up by it as follows:

"* * * That evidence consists of the testimony of various witnesses, the correspondence between the patentee and the Minister of the Interior, letters of Monsarrat and other documents. It deals generally with ancient boundaries and specifically with the big waterfalls. It tends to prove, assuming without deciding such probative tendency, that the top of those falls has been considered 'since ancient times' to be the head of the Waihanau Valley as a natural monument descriptive of an ancient boundary and was used and regarded by the patentee for the purpose of marking the middle western portion of the northern boundary of Royal Patent Number 3437." (R. 54-55.)

This is the same evidence now urged upon this court (Br. 3, 7-9, 11-14, 39-40, 46, 55-56, 69, 74, 76-77). As it is extraneous, there is no need to delve into its insubstantial character or into the appellant's numerous departures from the record in its brief.[49]

The Territory repeatedly objected to this extraneous evidence, pointing out that no uncertainty in the patent had been shown (e.g. R. 170, 173-174, 190). Error duly was assigned by the Territory to the trial court's overruling of such objections (R. 10-12, 44), and the evidence was excluded by the Supreme Court's decision (R. 48, 54-56). The error committed by the trial court in admitting it is very well epitomized in *Territory v. Kapiolani Estate*,[50] in which the court said:

> "* * * But as the only ground for admitting the evidence would be the uncertainty of the surveyed line it would be reversing the rule in such matters to regard the line as uncertain because of the evidence and to admit the evidence to explain the uncertainty produced by it. * * *" (p. 396)

That was a case of a land patent and a boundary description, both following the "Gay survey," which incorporated a map from which it appeared that the boundary, described as "returning on the Eastern Bank of the River," was set well back from, and not intended to follow, the water's edge, as held in an earlier case,[51] the rulings in which were adopted. In the later case (18 Haw. 394) the court held that by reason of this certainty "explanation by extraneous

---

[49] For example, Br. 56, where it is stated that "the kamaainas said [to Monsarrat] that the boundary was the head of Waihanau Valley." See also Br. 60. There is no such evidence. According to Monsarrat's letter of July 17, 1885, "the Kamaainas showed me a piece of Kahanui away mauka on the edge of the palis * * *." (Ex. 7-A)

[50] Supra, 18 Haw. 394, 396.

[51] *McBryde Estate v. Gay and Robinson*, supra, 15 Haw. 117, 122, 1903.

evidence" could not be permitted. The evidence thus excluded consisted of an explanation that the boundary was intended to include only the river within the banks and not the marshy fringes, because it was "always understood" by the "native residents" that this particular ili of Kuiloa only included the river and was merely a fishing right. The case is closely in point here.

In requiring that the land be "correctly surveyed" it of course was the purpose of the law to remove uncertainty and to not rely on evidence of ancient boundaries. The uncertainties of that type of evidence would increase year by year as the kamaainas died out, as was recognized. The map therefore was intended "as a final and conclusive reference for the location of the * * * line" and it was error to receive evidence as to the "true location," since this "introduced the uncertainty" which was sought to be avoided.[52]

As stated by the Supreme Court of the United States:[53]

> "The public had the option to declare the true mouth of the river, for the purposes of a survey and sale of the public land."

That was in a case in which there was a call for the mouth of the Chicago River in the field notes and plat of the survey. The Chicago River was the southern boundary. However, instead of following the river in its southerly bend to the natural mouth of the river, the plat showed a straight line, following an artificial channel cut through the sand bar formed by the bend in the river. The court held that the plat could not be contradicted; the only question in the case was whether the land sued for was within that platted, this

---

[52] *Wilson v. Chicago Lumber and Timber Co.*, 143 Fed. 705, 712-713 (C.A. 8th 1906).

[53] *Bates v. Illinois Central R. Co.*, 1 Black (66 U.S.) 204, 208, 17 L.Ed. 158, 1861.

question arising by reason of the land presently being under water in consequence of certain piers constructed after the plat was made.

In another case in the Supreme Court of the United States[54] the Court rejected the contention "that because the water mentioned on the plat is called Indian River the boundary must be taken as the water line of the river, and cannot be that of any intermediate bayou." The Court followed the case cited in the preceding note and said:

> "* * * obviously the surveyors surveyed only to this bayou, and called that the river. The plaintiff had no right to challenge the correctness of their action, or claim that the bayou was not Indian River or a proper water line upon which to bound the lots."[55]

8. The rule as to natural monuments does not govern this case.

It is claimed that the Big Falls marked the ancient boundary and was always understood in the Meyer family as being the head of the Waihanau Valley (Br. 11-14). But as already has been shown, the patent furnished its own interpretation of the head of the Waihanau Valley and is not subject to contradiction by the showing of a different one. The case is not one of a natural monument. There was no call for the Big Falls. As to the "head" of the Waihanau Valley, since it is sought to ascertain this by an ancient boundary or place name it is arguing in a circle to say that the case is one controlled by a natural monument. The argument really is that the case is controlled by the ancient boundary or place name. As stated by appellant's counsel in the trial court:

---

[54] *Horne v. Smith,* supra, 159 U.S. 40, 45-46.

[55] See also *Givens v. United States Trust Co.,* 260 Ky. 762, 86 S.W. 2d 986, 1935, reviewing several cases holding that the shape of the land as shown by the plat is controlling when it is evident where the surveyor placed objects or other boundary lines called for, even though he was mistaken in so placing them.

"The question of surveying does not enter into this deal at all and it is not proper cross-examination. How he would determine the head of a valley as described in a grant, when the valley is described by place name, is determined by where the place name ends, not where the physical contours of the land continue up several miles, several miles on up." (R. 136)

This argument permeates appellant's brief (Br. 11-14). In effect, it is an attempt to construe the patent as partly by survey and partly by name. Even the Land Commission, which had authority to make an award either by survey or by name, could not combine these methods.[56]

The correct rule as to natural monuments is that they prevail when more certain because there is less likelihood of a mistake being made as to them, "but where this reason fails the rule itself fails."[57] Thus, in an attempt to bring into the case a definite natural monument, appellant relies on the Big Falls. But there was no call for it, as the Supreme Court held (R. 55).

It is claimed that the Big Falls were the southern boundary of the land of Makanalua, but there is no call for the land of Makanalua. (That word appeared in the description as written on September 7, 1886 (Grant 3437 file, Exs. C-1 to C-3), and in the patent as issued a few days after the sale (Ex. J), as the designation of the second or easterly valley. This was corrected in the final form of the patent (Ex. B) to read "Waialeia.") Therefore, it is not necessary to consider whether a call for the land of Makanalua would have brought into the case the Pease survey, and if so whether the mention by Pease of "a certain mountain peak at the

---

[56] *Boundaries of Kewalo*, 3 Haw. 9, 16, 1886.
[57] *Ookala Sugar Co. v. Wilson*, supra, 13 Haw. 127, 132.

head of said gulch called 'Kaulahuki'" could be transformed by the appellant into a waterfall called Kaulahuki (see Br. 13-14, 39, 74). As shown by the patent on its face, and conceded by appellant (Br. 14), Kaulahuki was the name of a government triangulation station considerably south of the grant. The name was so used by Monsarrat in all his work in connection with this survey (R. 278).

Appellant further attempts to bring the Big Falls into the case by resort to Monsarrat's field notes, Exhibit 16 (Br. 3, 8, 11, 30, 42, 47-50, 56-57, 61-63, 73, 76-77). These were part of the public record, so held by the Supreme Court (R. 47), and resort could be had to them if necessary. However, the patent is clear without them. So far we merely have used four of these field note points (X, K, A, and Y) for convenience of reference to points on Map II.

Before taking up appellant's argument in detail, we wish to state that the field notes reconcile with the patent and with the government registered maps, and further confirm the Territory's location of the line. The field notes do *not* take the boundary through the Big Falls. On Exhibit 11 Monsarrat has marked in his own handwriting (R. 248) Points X, K, A, and Y, showing the boundary as running through X, K, and A. Appellant's surveyor McKeague plotted Point K (R. 99) as well as the other points (R. 68-69, 93); he placed them the same as on Monsarrat's map and all the surveyors are in agreement as to the location of these points (R. 258-259, 262-263). That the boundary runs from X to A *through Point K* (shown on Map II) again definitely requires the rejection of appellant's line and again confirms the Territory's line. The Supreme Court so held (R. 53).

Appellant's long and abstruse argument as to the field notes consists in an attempt to connect the word "waterfall" appearing on the sketch on page 112 of Field Book 2 (Ex. 16) with the Big Falls at which appellant wants the line to cross. Appellant admits that "the testimony would have been overwhelming for the appellee if these falls were Waiau" (Br. 49). But appellant argues that it should be deduced that the word "waterfall" on page 112 of the field book refers to the Big Falls because elsewhere in the field notes Monsarrat took two sights to the Big Falls, one from Kaohu Triangulation Station (Ex. 16, page 109, R. 346), and one from Point Z[58] (Ex. 16, p. 111, R. 346). Kaohu Triangulation Station and Point Z are points on the boundary of Kahanui 1, north of this tract. (Ex. A, map by appellant's surveyor McKeague.)

The word "waterfall" on page 112 is in the immediate vicinity of Point A, the base of the ridge, and therefore *not* the Big Falls but instead Waiau Falls,[59] as testified by Newton (R. 311). The straight lines on page 112 from Z to X, and from X to Kaluahauoni Triangulation Station, obviously are not a boundary line, because they cross the heads of the valleys, which are indicated on the field book page by rows of short parallel dashes, the same as used for that purpose on the work sheet map made by Monsarrat (Ex. 11). These straight lines Z to X and X to Kaluahauoni Triangulation Station merely indicate the taking of direct bearings between these points (R. 330), which in fact was done (p. 111 of the field book, Ex. 16).

---

[58] Mistakenly referred to by appellant (Br. 50) as Point Y.

[59] These are the falls at the S bend in the stream where the spur ridges overlap near Point A (marked in pencil on Ex. A and see Ex. N).

But even if appellant were given the latitude desired by it in the interpretation of the sketch on page 112 of the field book (Ex. 16) *the boundary could not run through the Big Falls.* When run through the Big Falls the boundary must come out on the ridge at Monsarrat's point "dry tree" as shown on appellant's Exhibit A, the map prepared by appellant's surveyor McKeague. The point "dry tree" plainly appears on the ridge on Monsarrat's sketch in the field book, and the straight line that appellant wants to convert into a boundary line goes nowhere near it.

The real importance of the field book sketch is that, by the rows of short parallel dashes, the sketch depicts the head of each valley with the ridge lying between them jutting out from Point A, and with "Waihanau Gulch" written in and shown as bordering the complete ridge, all the way.

Since the field notes reconcile with the patent and with the government registered maps, it is not necessary to determine which would prevail if the field notes did not reconcile. The trial court did not hold there was any conflict; instead it rejected the work of the government surveyor as only his opinion (R. 29-31).

9. Appellant's claims of "possession" play no part in the case.

Since there is in this case no issue of adverse possession, appellant's claims in this regard (Br. 10) need not be examined.[60] However, it is noteworthy that Albert Meyer, a member of the Meyer family, showed Jorgensen where the boundary went when Jorgensen went on the land to put in the water tunnel in 1924, and the place so pointed out was 1,000 to 1,500 feet above where the intake was put

---

[60] *In the Matter of the Boundaries of Pulehunui,* supra, 4 Haw. 239, 255, 1879.

(R. 382-383), hence did not include the disputed area. William Meyer, another member of the Meyer family, showed Carson and Samuel Wilder King the boundary when they went on the land to make an appraisal for the 1929 condemnation suit, the map of which followed the patent map (R. 411-413). This William Meyer showed them that the boundary crossed at a place called Waiau, where there was a pool, the place being marked by the witness Carson on Exhibit 21 (R. 354, 355, and see 379), and being the place where the government places the line.

The line always has been placed by the government where it is placed by it today and the government always has claimed the disputed area (supra, note 3). One has only to look at the government registered maps (Exs. 11-15) to see that this is so.[61] There is not one word of evidence that the Territory negotiated for the purchase of the disputed area, as implied by appellant (Br. 10). The 1929 condemnation suit (Br. 11) did not include the disputed area (R. 411-413).

When the government constructed and improved the water tunnel and intake in reliance on its title (both engineers having checked the boundary, Jorgensen with Albert Meyer's assistance in 1924, R. 382-383, and Howell in 1933, R. 392-394), there were no protests or claims of private ownership (R. 383-384, 390, 394).

---

[61] As to the lepers not being allowed to go beyond the Big Falls where appellant wants the line to cross, obviously the officials of the leper settlement had no authority to speak for the government as to where the line was and did not purport to do so when they decided how far up the valley the lepers might wander. (The leper settlement is situated on a peninsula far below the mountain area here involved, as shown on Ex. U.) The exhibit cited by appellant (Br. 9) was an affidavit admitted over objections (R. 86, 193-194) and clearly inadmissible.

10. The Supreme Court did not "retry the facts."

Appellant argues that the Supreme Court did not confine itself to issues of law and that it retried issues of fact. (Br. 5, 54-55, 58-59, 73). This is incorrect.

The rule applicable is the familiar one that the appellate court shall not reverse the trial court for any finding depending upon the credibility of witnesses or the weight of the evidence.[62] This of course leaves to the appellate court the materiality of the evidence in point of law. Appellant's case, and the trial court's decision upholding it, were based upon extraneous and inadmissible evidence, the Supreme Court held (R. 43-44, 48, 54-56).

The practice in the Land Court conforms to that in probate, and the proceeding is in the nature of a suit in equity.[63] The court is one of limited jurisdiction having power only to determine whether an applicant has sustained his claim of title.[64] Whether there is, in a Land Court proceeding, an issue of fact requiring trial as such is a question of law for the courts, whose prerogative it is to determine the probative tendency of the evidence and the conclusiveness of the record against the proponent of the issue.[65]

There is in this record no issue of fact that is not concluded by the Supreme Court's rulings of law. The Supreme

---

[62] Sec. 9564, c. 186, Revised Laws of Hawaii 1945. Appellant says (Br. 59) that writs of error to the land court are different from writs of error in other cases but this is not correct. Section 12635, which appears in chapter 307 relating to the land court, merely provides that a writ of error will lie, leaving it to chapter 186, relating to writs of error, to supply the provisions relating thereto. The applicability of chapter 186 to land court cases appears from the first section of the chapter and from *In re Kakaako*, 30 Haw. 494, 1928.

[63] Section 12600, Revised Laws of Hawaii 1945; *In re Atcherley*, 24 Haw. 507, 1918.

[64] *In re Rosenbledt*, 24 Haw. 298, 1918.

[65] *In re Kakaako*, supra, 30 Haw. 666, 671, 1928.

Court so held. This has been shown step by step in this brief. In summary:

(1) The land was sold at public auction by survey.

(2) The survey was made by M. D. Monsarrat, government surveyor, in 1885, who mapped the land in 1886 and wrote a description of it dated September 7, 1886. Monsarrat's field notes and maps are on file.

(3) The auction sale was held on October 4, 1888, and a few days afterward there was issued the patent afterward cancelled (Ex. j) containing the same sketch map appearing in the final patent.

(4) In November 1888, Meyer talked to Monsarrat and to Surveyor General Alexander about a change in the description. Meyer wanted the ridge piece included, but the Minister of the Interior decided it could not be included because the sale had been made at public auction. The Minister of the Interior offered to sell Meyer the ridge piece at private sale, it being deemed of a value below the amount at which a public auction would have been required. Meyer acknowledged that nothing could be added to the patent for the piece already sold, and stated his willingness to pay for the ridge piece. The patent for the piece already sold was issued and accepted after the making of minor corrections (mostly in spelling) ; and the same became Grant 3437, issued October 29, 1889.

(5) After further correspondence the ridge piece was sold to Meyer and patented as Grant 3539, issued May 5, 1891. It called for a piece jutting out from the northern boundary of Grant 3437 and touching it only at the base of the ridge, Point A. This point has been located by both parties without disagreement.

(6) In making the survey for appellant's application in the Land Court, appellant's surveyor included the ridge in Grant 3437, even though Meyer admitted it was not so included and purchased it as Grant 3539. The theory of appellant's application was and is that Grant 3539 was "on a portion of Grant 3437," whereas in point of law these were two separate and distinct

grants. Appellant cannot reconcile the two grants. Thus is presented an insurmountable obstacle to the establishment of the Grant 3437 northern boundary where appellant places it. Only by locating the boundary where the government places it can the two grants be reconciled.

(7) The line always has been placed by the government where it is placed by it today and the government always has claimed the disputed area.

(8) The correct rule of law is that the map in Grant 3437 is a part of the description. The map gives certainty to the words of the description, and is to be considered the more particular and controlling description.

(9) The patent itself locates the head of the Waihanau Valley with certainty, and the appellant had no right to adduce evidence that this was not the true location of the head of the valley. Such evidence introduced the very uncertainty which was sought to be avoided by the making of the sale by survey. The sale was not by name. "As the only ground for admitting the evidence would be the uncertainty of the surveyed line it would be reversing the rule in such matters to regard the line as uncertain because of the evidence and to admit the evidence to explain the uncertainty produced by it."

(10) The northern boundary, as fixed by the patent, is a boundary meandering along the edges of the valleys in a southeasterly direction. From the starting point of this boundary on the western side of the Waihanau Valley on its top edge, the line follows the same top edge south as far as it continues in the indicated direction and until it turns sharply west, then follows the line of overlapping spur ridges southeast to turn around the valley's head and connect with the head of the Waialeia Valley at Point A, the base of the ridge which divides the two valleys.

(11) The conditions on the ground were shown both by the appellant and the Territory without disagreement as to any essential of this location when made under correct rules of law.

(12) No other location conforms with the description and map in the patent.

(13) Appellant's surveyor did not find the correct line because he did not look for it. He did not retrace Monsarrat's survey. His objective was to follow "the intent of where that boundary should be under the application made by Meyer for the land that was desired," having in mind that Monsarrat wrote the description before Meyer made the application to purchase and the description "was not intended to convey the land that was applied for by Mr. Meyer."

(14) The rule as to natural monuments does not govern this case. The rule is attempted to be used to contradict the patent's location of the head of the Waihanau Valley and ascertain the line by an ancient boundary or place name, instead of by the surveyor's location of it expressed in the patent. In effect it is an attempt to construe the grant as one made by name, or partly by survey and partly by name.

(15) There was no call for the Big Falls or Kaulahuki. The "Kaulahuki" mentioned in the patent is a government triangulation station considerably south of the grant, as appellant concedes.

(16) The trial court did not find any conflict between the field notes and the patent. The Supreme Court's holding that they reconcile is the only conclusion that could be reached. Even if the appellant were given the latitude desired by it in the interpretation of the sketch on page 112 of the field book the boundary could not run through the Big Falls.

(17) The grant is clear, certain and unambiguous, requiring a location which excludes the disputed area.

The application was filed by appellant and was required to be sustained by it. Since the application was not sustained as to the disputed area, a severance of this area was in order.[66] The Supreme Court had power on reversal to direct modification of the decree[67] as was done (R. 57). "On

66 Section 12617, Revised Laws of Hawaii 1945.
67 Section 9564, Revised Laws of Hawaii 1945.

error * * * the entire record is brought up, and the judgment of the appellate court is such as the facts and law warrant as shown by the entire case."[68] The case comes within
the rule that when the record conclusively shows what judgment ought to have been given under the appellate court's
rulings on the law, the appellate court may direct such
judgment.[69]

---

[68] *Territory v. Cotton Bros.*, 17 Haw. 374, 378-379, 1906.

[69] *Santa Fe County v. Coler*, 215 U.S. 296, 306, 1909; *Irvine v. Angus*, 93 Fed. 629, 94 Fed. 959 (C.A. 9th 1899), cert. den. 175 U.S. 725 (on writ of error to a federal circuit court which held that plain-tiff was not a trustee for one Fair and therefore could not recover advances made for assessments on Fair's stock, Court of Appeals held that there was also involved a count for money paid for Fair's use and benefit, and that it itself would determine from the ad-mitted facts whether plaintiff was a mere volunteer in paying the assessments and also when there occurred such an implied promise by Fair to pay as would start the running of the statute of limita-tions—these issues having been resolved in favor of the plaintiff the Court of Appeals reversed the judgment for the defendant and directed that judgment be entered for the plaintiff); *Fellman v. Royal Insurance Co.*, 184 Fed. 577 (C.A. 5th 1911) (where "there was no substantial dispute about the actual facts" the Court held that its rulings on the law required judgment for the plaintiff in-stead of for the defendant and so directed); *Hazeltine Research, Inc. v. General Motors*, 170 F. 2d 6, 10 (C.A. 6th 1948); *Sbicca-Del Mac v. Milius Show Co.*, 145 F. 2d 389, 400 (C.A. 8th 1944); *Mc-Dade v. Caplis*, 154 La. 1019, 158 La. 489, 98 So. 625, 104 So. 218, 1923-1925 (suit alleging ownership of a lake of 100 acres, wherein trial court sustained the plaintiffs but appellate court held that 17.96 acres of land reclaimed from the lake had been transferred to one Smith—the 17.96 acres were ordered excluded and since there was no definite description of the area so excluded the trial court upon remand properly determined this upon a rule to show cause); *Bledsoe v. Doe*, 4 How. (Miss.) 13, 1839 (plaintiff in ejectment recovered, but on writ of error appellate court held that defendant's adverse possession required denial of the writ as to part of the land and ordered trial court to limit writ of possession to the remainder); *Dormer v. Dreith*, 145 Neb. 742, 18 N.W. 2d 94, 1945 (plaintiff sued to establish road easement by adverse user and prevailed, but appel-late court held evidence did not justify granting an easement over twenty feet in width and limited the decree to this width); *Gray v. Cosden*, 141 Okla. 183, 284 Pac. 288, 1930 (action for conversion in which trial court's judgment was reduced to the amount supported

(Note continued next page)

CONCLUSION

The appeal should be dismissed, or alternatively the judgment of the Supreme Court of Hawaii should be affirmed for failure of the appellant to show error therein (i.e., "manifest" error, "clear departure from ordinary legal principles.")

Dated at Honolulu, T. H., this 7th day of July, 1953.

Respectfully submitted,

RHODA V. LEWIS,
Deputy Attorney General,
Territory of Hawaii,

Attorney for Appellee.

---

[69] (Continued)

by competent evidence, after the appellate court had held certain evidence was incompetent) ; *Socony-Vacuum Oil Co. v. Lambert*, 180 S.W. 2d 456 (Tex. Civ. App.), 1944 (seaman's action for damages for personal injuries based on theory ship was sunk by a torpedo, and for care and maintenance—verdict and judgment for plaintiff held unsupported by any competent evidence as to the firing of the torpedo, on which the damages for personal injury depended, and judgment reduced to the amount for care and maintenance) ; *Colin v. De Coursey Cream Co.*, 162 Kan. 683, 178 P. 2d 690, 1947 (action for personal injuries in which the verdict included $1,760 for medical expenses but the appellate court found the evidence supported only $576 and reduced the judgment accordingly) ; *Hink v. Sherman*, 164 Mich. 352, 129 N.W. 732, 1911 (where jury found for plaintiff but there was "no substantive proof of any actual damages," judgment reduced to statutory minimum).

No. 13,545

IN THE

United States Court of Appeals
For the Ninth Circuit

R. W. MEYER, LIMITED,

$\quad\quad\quad\quad\quad\quad$ *Appellant,*

vs.

TERRITORY OF HAWAII,

$\quad\quad\quad\quad\quad\quad$ *Appellee.*

Appeal from the Supreme Court of the
Territory of Hawaii.

APPELLANT'S REPLY BRIEF.

PHIL CASS,
2186 City View, Eugene, Oregon,
SAMUEL SHAPIRO,
506 Stangenwald Building, Honolulu, T. H.,
Attorneys for Appellant.

FILED

AUG 6 1953

PAUL P. O'BRIEN
CLERK

Topical Index

No. 13,545

IN THE

United States Court of Appeals
For the Ninth Circuit

R. W. Meyer, Limited,

Appellant,

vs.

Territory of Hawaii,

Appellee.

Appeal from the Supreme Court of the
Territory of Hawaii.

APPELLANT'S REPLY BRIEF.

The Appellant respectfully submits:

The answering brief of the Appellee does not attempt to follow, in orderly sequence of reply, argument to the Appellant's opening brief, nor to answer in any fashion the material points of law and the cited evidence as they appear therein. Most of the matter set out in the answering brief is original matter alleging facts not found in the record or submitted to the Supreme Court of Hawaii, denying, without citation of record, the cited testimony of the witnesses, or urging, on appeal, that the findings of the lower Court are final and binding as to the law and the facts.

Replying to matters found in the answering brief as they are set out, Appellant shows (pages in Appellee's brief are shown as (AB   ):

JURISDICTIONAL STATEMENT. (AB 1.)

It is shown by the record and by the statement of Appellee in its brief that the value of the land involved or the damages sought is in excess of $5,000.00. While jurisdiction may not be conferred by agreement, facts constituting the jurisdictional qualification, may appear by record, affidavit, or by stipulation. The burden of sustaining the jurisdiction of this Court is met by reference to the record showspecifically the value claimed by the parties. The record shows on its face that the second cause of action is dependent on the decision of this appeal, since there can be no damage to occupancy, if there is no right of title.

STATEMENT OF THE CASE. (AB 4.)

ANSWERING "THE TRIAL COURT'S PRIMARY ERROR WAS IN HOLDING THAT THE GOVERNMENT SURVEY, EVEN THOUGH INCORPORATED IN THE PATENT, CONSTITUTED ONLY AN INCONCLUSIVE OPINION AS TO WHERE THE LINE SHOULD BE".

The trial Court did not so hold. The government survey in the patent is the description. The issue before the trial Court was the location of the described line on the ground. It has been the contention of Appellee throughout this case that the "map", so called, attached to the patent was the "survey", although on numerous occasions the Appellee differentiates between the "map" and "survey". There is no evidence that the "map" so attached represented any location work by any surveyor. It is positively shown that this sketch of the disputed boundary was "sketched in", was a "Meander line", was never intended to fix the boundary, but as Newton says, "It (the title) follows the monument". Further, the sketch was not on any government map at the time of the sale, but was added to those maps without survey afterwards. It is settled law that, in the absence of fraud, the description of a natural monument is superior to any plat or sketch unless it is shown affirmatively that the parties intended the sketch to control; that a meander line does not fix a boundary. The intention of the parties as shown by the correspondence, by the occupancy of the land to the falls by Meyer, and by the dispute over water rights by the leper settlement officials, shown in Mauritz' affidavit, was to convey the whole of the lele to the ancient boundary known to the parties as the "head of Waihanau valley" and shown in the surveyor's field book to be along the big falls.

––––––

APPELLEE'S STATEMENT THAT THE SKETCH WAS "INCORPORATED IN THE PATENT" IS WITHOUT JUSTIFICATION.

Numerous cases, cited in the opening brief, show that it was the practice in Hawaii, as in the federal land office, when land was purchased, to attach a sketch for the purpose, not of fixing boundaries, but to show the general location and shape of the land, and to determine the amount of acreage purchased. There is no showing in this case that there was any other purpose in attaching a sketch, without reference to it in the description, to this patent.

———

QUESTIONS INVOLVED. (AB 7.)

ANSWERING "DID THE SUPREME COURT OF HAWAII COMMIT REVERSIBLE ERROR BY HOLDING THAT THE GRANT IS CLEAR, CERTAIN AND UNAMBIGUOUS, REQUIRING A LOCATION WHICH EXCLUDES THE DISPUTED AREA"?

Here again, Appellee and the Supreme Court of Hawaii erroneously adopt the sketch as part of the description, and, having so adopted the sketch without supporting evidence of intent to control, or that the sketch represented a traversed, fixed boundary, and in spite of a definite ruling and proof to the contrary, hold that the sketch is all controlling, fixing the boundary contrary to the proven location of the described monument, and in total disregard of the undenied intent of the parties that the land held by Meyer, the whole of the lele, should be conveyed.

The Supreme Court is right in saying that the grant is clear, certain and unambiguous, as held by the trial Court. It is in error in rejecting the factual testimony, uncontradicted, as to the location of that line on the ground. It is further in error in adopting opinion testimony by persons unfamiliar with the natural boundary described, locating on the ground a boundary so described. The Supreme Court of Hawaii is also in error, in ruling that the Waihanau valley, the monument described, extends to a place above the boundary shown by witnesses, without any factual testimony to support its position.

The ruling by the Supreme Court in connection with the above finding, that the testimony of persons familiar with the ground, born and raised on the land, as to the location of Waihanau valley, below the big falls, and as to the boundaries of Waihanau valley as known from ancient times, is incompetent, is contrary to all known decisions requiring ground locations to be proved by such testimony. The decisions, all of them, hold that the grant must be tied to the land by such testimony and that surveyors may be used either to trace the footsteps of the original survey (in this case there were no such footsteps), or to identify the location of lost monuments which have been located mathematically or by technical means comprehensible to the profession. Their opinion otherwise as to facts of factual locations, the location of natural monuments, or artificial monuments not so identified or located, is immaterial.

THERE IS NO STATUTORY RULE OF EVIDENCE IN HAWAII DIFFERING FROM THE FEDERAL RULES OF PROOF OF BOUNDARIES. (AB 8.)

The Supreme Court of Hawaii, in its ruling, departed from the established law of Hawaii, fixed by the decisions of the Supreme Court of Hawaii before

annexation and cited in the opening brief adopting
the principles of the United States Supreme Court
and the decisions thereof to the effect that (a) in a
patent a natural monument takes precedence over
map and sketch locations; (b) that all boundary lines
must be tied to the grant by oral factual testimony;
(c) that the opinions of surveyors may not be taken
except for the technical determination of mathematically fixed locations; (d) that the existence in any
office of the government of a map is not proof of
a boundary; (e) that the field notes of a surveyor
are evidence, not only of what he did in connection
with a survey, but what he did not do; (f) that the
field notes of a surveyor are part of a map prepared
in accordance with the survey, and where the field
notes and the map differ the field notes control. In
this case, the definite location in the field book, on
page 112, of the big falls by triangulation, and the
location of the boundary line of Kahanui as passing
through those falls, above the location shown on the
sketch as being Waihanau valley, must control any
map or sketch, plat or diagram on which those landmarks do not appear in the ground location of the
described boundary.

ARGUMENT. (AB 9.)

APPELLEE ASSIGNS AS ERROR THE DECISION OF THE TRIAL
JUDGE THAT IT WAS THE INTENT OF THE PARTIES TO
CONVEY ACCORDING TO THE ANCIENT BOUNDARIES.
(AB 13.)

The intent of the parties became material only if
there was an ambiguity in the description. It also
was an obligation of the Courts to so construe the
grant, if possible, to effectuate the intent of the parties. We are concerned here with only the application
of that ruling to the present case in view of the testimony. The whole of the correspondence shows this
intent. The boundary is described as being the head
of Waihanau valley, which was the ancient boundary
by all of the testimony. In determining what was
the ground location of the described boundary, it was
important, first, to determine whether the boundary
was capable of ground location by parol testimony;
second, in case of a divergence in locations to determine whether the parties were familiar with that
location and whether their intent coincided with the
proven ground line. It cannot be understood why the
Supreme Court of Hawaii said that the testimony
of the witnesses, familiar with the ground, which
placed the boundary from landmark to landmark,
accurately following the line of the surveyor shown
on Appellant's map, but identifying the line on the
ground in absolute certainty, constitutes a variation
of the description because the patent does not contain
the step by step landmarks but describes the land
as following the meander of the head of the valley. It

was the "head of the valley" which the witnesses were pointing out, not the legal implications of the use of the name.

The only evidence or testimony as to the location of the "head of Waihanau valley" is in the statements of Appellant's witnesses. The opinions of Newton, Howell, Jorgensen and Carson were all, by their statements, opinions as to where the line of the sketch would lie if placed upon the ground. Not one of these witnesses had any factual knowledge of the "head of Waihanau valley" or pretended any knowledge of local land boundaries. None of their testimony, and there is no other, may be accepted to tie the grant to the land, or the land to the grant. Without that testimony there is not one iota of proof that the boundary claimed by the government and fixed by the Supreme Court of Hawaii exists other than in desire and imagination.

ANSWERING (AB 14) "IN NO PLACE DID THE WITNESS SAY THAT THE LAND WAS MAPPED AFTER THE GRANT OR THAT THE ORIGINAL MAP WAS CHANGED IN ANY MATERIAL RESPECT".

The witness Newton said the sketch of Kahanui was added to the government map after the grant (R. 321) the maps on record were all produced from the one survey by Monsarrat and are all copies of the original. with no record as to what was on the original at the time of the grant. The maps are progressive maps with matter added from time to time with no record as to who added, or on what authority the addition was made. The sketch boundary of the land of Kahanui shown on the government maps was certainly added sometime after the original was drawn. At the time of the grant Monsarrat had never been on the disputed boundary.

THE WHOLE CASE OF APPELLEE IS BASED ON NEWTON.

Newton was the government's prime witness. He was the custodian of the records produced at the trial, and it was his authentication of those records that made them admissible. It is his reproduction of the sketch line which is adopted by the government, although he knows little of that land, knew that he was not following Monsarrat's footsteps but was making a line of his own, and looked for no monuments because he knew there were none. The genuine character of the maps, sketches and records as being documents known to the parties to the grant and controlling the boundary line as it was known at the time of the patent is of the essence of the law of this case. If the maps produced cannot be shown to be original documents, but "progressive maps" of the type discussed in the various cases, Hawaiian and federal, cited in the opening brief, they certainly cannot be acceptable as proving the location of a line known to persons acting with mutual intent prior to their existence.

CONTOUR LINES DO NOT PROVE BOUNDARY LOCATIONS.

Much is made by the Appellee of the alleged contour of the upper valley as determining the boundary. Contour may be a criterion where there is a dispute as to a definite known boundary lost to the knowledge of the present generation. It has no bearing upon the location of a named boundary well known to numerous witnesses. Like intent, area, occupancy, and other vague indications of ownership which may be considered when other evidence directly to the point is unavailable. However, natural boundary lines of savage and primitive peoples such as the Hawaiians when these lands were bounded, tend to be those of impassable or defensible barriers. The line of the big falls is such that even today it bars the lepers from uncontaminated land. It is truly a line of the continual impassable palis surrounding the lower land. The terrain of the upper valley, on the contrary, is bounded only by a visual barrier, where the valley turns, and constitutes no such impediment to travel as to have been a barrier to the native mountaineers.

Box canyons are not unknown in the west. Wherever there are steep mountains there are gulches that end in cliffs. Most of these are known by name and bounded as box canyons by the cliff regardless of the extent of the watershed above or the height of the hills on either side. Such a box canyon is Waihanau, the name meaning "the water erupts" or the "birth of waters"; such would be the appearance of the big falls from below when the water was in flood.

CONCLUSION.

This is a boundary case. The origin of the dispute between the parties is plain. As Appellee explains, the government land office gave Jorgensen a map of the boundaries of the government land which had the meander line then indicated as a surveyed line, which was false. On the faith of this map, the government engineers laid out and constructed a waterworks at an expense of nearly a million dollars with its intake above the falls. At that time they were in negotiation with the Meyers to buy the land occupied by the Meyers and the Meyers were asked to and did remove their cattle from the land down to the big falls. After the tunnel was built, the claim was first made, in the condemnation suit of 1929, that the Meyers did not own the tunnel site, and offers to pay for the Meyer lands as excluding this portion were the cause of the breakdown of negotiations and the necessity for that condemnation action.

Since that time several actions have been started to collect rentals from the government for the use of the land, as recited by Appellee in the answering brief. These actions were thwarted by the jurisdictional rule that there can be no implied contract where the government claims to act by right, and it took an action by the legislature to authorize specifically the recovery of such claims in this cause in the second cause of action.

Actually, the issue before the Court narrows down to these questions: Where a clear, certain, unambiguous description is written into a description of land, naming a natural boundary, a monument known to all parties by name and location, and the land is sold at public auction according to the description given, can the fact that a sketch, without any of the indicia of a map, direction, distance, topography, scale, override the description and change the location of the boundary to a reproduction of the sketch line on the ground? Can the opinion testimony of surveyors without information as to the location or name of natural boundaries, be used to fix a line on the ground not determined by mathematics of technical traversed survey?

The judgment on appeal of the Supreme Court of Hawaii should be reversed and the decree of the trial Court ordered sustained.

Dated, Eugene, Oregon,
      August 5, 1953.

              Respectfully submitted,
                  PHIL CASS,
                  SAMUEL SHAPIRO,
                  By PHIL CASS,
                      Attorneys for Appellant.

No. 13552

IN THE

United States Court of Appeals

FOR THE NINTH CIRCUIT

RAFO IVANCEVIC, Consul General of the Federal Peoples'
Republic of Yugoslavia,

Appellant,

vs.

ANDRIJA ARTUKOVIC,

Appellee.

JAMES J. BOYLE, United States Marshal,

Appellant,

vs.

ANDRIJA ARTUKOVIC,

Appellee.

On Appeal From the United States District Court for the
Southern District of California, Central Division.

BRIEF FOR THE UNITED STATES AS AMICUS CURIAE AND APPENDIX.

WALTER S. BINNS,
United States Attorney.
CLYDE C. DOWNING,
Assistant United States Attorney,
Chief of Civil Division.
ARLINE MARTIN,
Assistant United States Attorney.
312 North Spring Street,
Los Angeles 12, California,
Attorneys for the United States.

Parker & Company, Law Printers, Los Angeles. Phone MA. 6-9171.

ridiculous

TOPICAL INDEX

TABLE OF AUTHORITIES CITED

iii.

INDEX TO APPENDIX.

No. 13552

IN THE

United States Court of Appeals

FOR THE NINTH CIRCUIT

———

RAFO IVANCEVIC, Consul General of the Federal Peoples'
Republic of Yugoslavia,

Appellant,

vs.

ANDRIJA ARTUKOVIC,

Appellee.

———

JAMES J. BOYLE, United States Marshal,

Appellant,

vs.

ANDRIJA ARTUKOVIC,

Appellee.

———

On Appeal From the United States District Court for the
Southern District of California, Central Division.

———

BRIEF FOR THE UNITED STATES AS AMICUS CURIAE.

———

Jurisdiction.

Jurisdiction of the District Court and of this court is as
set forth in the Brief of Appellants herein.

This Brief *Amicus Curiae* is filed pursuant to written
order of this court made and entered on October 3, 1952.

Statutes and Treaty Involved.

The pertinent provisions of the extradition laws of the United States (18 U. S. C. 3181 *et seq.*) and the Extradition Treaty concluded on October 25, 1901, between the United States and Serbia (32 Stats. 1890) are set forth in the footnotes to the opinion of the District Court [R. T. 65-71].

Statement of the Case.

In the proceedings which were instituted in the United States District Court for the Southern District of California, Central Division, the appellee sought, by a petition for writ of *habeas corpus,* to obtain his discharge from provisional arrest and detention with a view to extradition to Yugoslavia.

The facts are set forth in the opinion of the District Court [R. T. 35]. In essence, they are these:

The appellee, Andrija Artukovic, was provisionally arrested and detained with a view to extradition on August 29, 1951, at Los Angeles, California, pursuant to a warrant of arrest issued by Howard V. Calverly, United States Commissioner for the Southern District of California, Central Division, upon a complaint filed on that date by Mr. Rafo Ivancevic, Consul General of the Federal Peoples' Republic of Yugoslavia. The Yugoslav Ambassador in Washington, in a note dated August 30, 1951, addressed to the Secretary of State, formally requested the extradition of the appellee pursuant to the provisions of the Extradition Treaty of October 25, 1901, concluded between the United States and Serbia.

On September 12, 1951, the appellee filed in the United States District Court for the Southern District of California, Central Division, a petition for a writ of *habeas corpus*. The United States Marshal and the Yugoslav Government appeared, on September 17, 1951, by counsel, in opposition to the granting of the writ. An amended petition, filed on September 19, 1951, challenged the legality of the arrest and, of course, the extradition proceedings which were thereby initiated, on the grounds (1) that there had not been a compliance with applicable statutes; (2) that there was no extradition treaty in force between the United States and Yugoslavia; and (3) that the complaint on which the warrant of arrest had been issued showed on its face that the alleged crimes with which the appellee was charged were political offenses and hence did not warrant extradition either under the extradition statutes of the United States or under the extradition treaty depended upon by the Yugoslav Government in this case.

Counsel for the Yugoslav Government filed, on October 15, 1951, an amended complaint with the United States Commissioner and thereby remedied the defect in the original complaint which was made the basis for the first ground for challenging the legality of the arrest of the appellee.

The appellant and the Yugoslav Government concede that certain political and geographic changes involving

Serbia were effected between October 25, 1901, when the Extradition Treaty between the United States and Serbia was concluded and the present time. The appellant contended, however, that notwithstanding such changes as were effected, the treaty continued in full force and effect and that presently it is in effect between the United States and the Federal Peoples' Republic of Yugoslavia.

Inasmuch as the District Court did not give consideration to the question whether the crimes charged against the appellee are political offenses within the meaning of the treaty, the only question presented for determination by this court is whether the Extradition Treaty concluded on October 25, 1901, between the United States and Serbia is still in force and applicable between the United States and the Federal Peoples' Republic of Yugoslavia.

Interest of the United States.

The proceedings in this case involve the effect of a change in government or a change in the geographical limits, or both, of one party thereto upon the treaty relations of the United States with other governments and not alone its treaty relations with Yugoslavia. The Executive Branch of the Government has proceeded heretofore on the theory that, in the absence of the complete absorption of one of the high contracting parties to the treaty by a third country, a mere change in the form of government or the expansion or contraction of the geographical boundaries of that high contracting party did not affect the termination of the treaty relations with that party.

Consequently, unless the changed conditions were such as to suggest the desirability of new treaties, the prior treaties have been considered as remaining in full force and effect. This practice has been in conformity with the generally accepted principles of international practice and is believed to be sound. A departure from the established practice after this late date could cause great confusion since there is probably no country now existing with which the United States has concluded treaties that has not undergone some change, either with respect to the form of its government or with respect to its boundaries. Heretofore the Department of State has been looked to for a determination of the question whether a specific treaty is still in effect after such changes in government or boundaries. The decision of the District Court, if not reversed, will preclude such a determination.

As the decision, if not reversed, will affect the entire treaty structure, it is believed that the Government's interest in the case transcends in importance the interest of the parties to these proceedings whose sole interest is the matter of the possible extradition of the appellee. The Executive Branch of the Government is not presently concerned with this phase of the case and will not be concerned with it unless and until it shall have been certified to the Department of State by the extradition magistrate pursuant to the provisions of 18 U. S. C. 3184.

Summary of Argument.

I. The general rule of international law and practice sustains the continuance in force of the treaties of a state following a change in its territorial limits or in its form of government; it also sustains application of those treaties to newly annexed territory of a state.

II. Evidence indicates that the state formerly known as Serbia continued as an international juridical entity upon its enlargement into the Kingdom of the Serbs, Croats, and Slovenes in 1918, and consequently the treaty rights and obligations of that state continued in force and applied to the whole of its territory.

III. The United States and the Serb-Croat-Slovene State (later Yugoslavia), as well as other leading countries, have given open and continuous recognition to the continuance in force of the pre-war Serbian treaties and the application thereof to the whole territory of the Kingdom of the Serbs, Croats, and Slovenes, subsequently Yugoslavia.

IV. The United States and the Serb-Croat-Slovene State (later Yugoslavia) have openly and continuously acted, during the entire period since World War I, under and pursuant to the provisions of pre-war treaties concluded between the United States and Serbia.

V. Opinions of United States courts have recognized the force and effect of the treaties of commerce and consular relations concluded in 1881 between the United States and Serbia—treaties which rest their validity upon the same legal grounds as the validity of the 1901 extradition treaty, namely, consideration of Yugoslavia as a true successor State to the Kingdom of Serbia with respect to continuance of its treaty rights and obligations.

ARGUMENT.

I.

The General Rule of International Law and Practice.

The weight of authority among writers on international law, as well as customary international practice, supports the rule that territorial changes of a State, whether by addition or loss of territory, do not in general deprive that State of its rights or relieve it of its obligations under a treaty, unless the changes are such as to render execution of the treaty impossible. In the case of the enlargement of a State by addition of new territory, the weight of authority supports the principle that the territory annexed becomes impressed with the treaty obligations of the acquiring State.

1 Moore, *Digest of International Law* (1906), page 248, states:

> "Mere territorial changes, whether by increase or by diminution, do not, so long as the identity of the state is preserved, affect the continuity of its existence or the obligations of its treaties."

Crandall, *Treaties: Their Making and Enforcement* (2d ed., 1916), page 429, states the application of the rule to the territory annexed as follows:

> "It may be stated as a general principle that the territory of the annexed or incorporated state becomes impressed with the treaties of the acquiring state so far as locally applicable, to be determined in each instance by the character of the particular treaty and the nature of the union. The former Republic of Texas, upon its admission as a State into the Union on terms of equality with the other

States, undoubtedly became bound and privileged by all the treaties of the United States, of which it had become an integral part."

V Hackworth, *Digest of International Law* (1943), page 376, expresses the rule as follows:

"As a general rule territory of the annexed or incorporated state becomes impressed with the treaties of the acquiring state, so far as they are not locally inapplicable. This matter is usually the subject of an understanding between the annexing state and other treaty states at the time of the annexation, or of an affirmative declaration by the annexing state acquiesced in by other treaty countries."

McNair, *The Law of Treaties: British Practice and Opinions* (1938), page 436, states the view of the British Government as follows:

"In the view of the United Kingdom Government the general principle governing the operation of treaties, when the territorial extent of one of the parties has been increased, is that existing treaties automatically apply to the new territory acquired."

Proceeding to a discussion of British treaty relations with certain other countries, McNair states with respect to United States treaties:

"Since the Convention of Commerce of July 3, 1815, was made between Great Britain and the United States of America, much territory has been added to the latter contracting party, but there is no question that this and other treaties of the early nineteenth century apply to the whole enlarged territory of the United States of America."

In further support of the general rule with respect to continuance of treaty rights and obligations regardless of territorial changes is the Harvard *Research in International Law* published in the *American Journal of International Law,* Supplement, Part III, Law of Treaties, Volume 29 (1935), page 1066.* As a result of that research a draft convention on the Law of Treaties was formulated, containing as Article 26, "Effect of Territorial Changes," the following:

> "A change in the territorial domain of a State, whether by addition or loss of territory, does not, in general, deprive the State of rights or relieve it of obligations under a treaty, unless the execution of the treaty becomes impossible as a result of the change."

The rule as stated in that article is supported by reference to leading European as well as American authorities in international law including F. de Martens, 1 *Traité de Droit International* (Leo trans., 1883), page 370; Rivier 1 *Principes due Droit des Gens* (1896), pages 62-63; Fauchille, 1 *Traité de Droit International Public,* pt. 1 (1922), page 343; 2 Hoijer, *Les Traités Internationaux* (1928), page 474; Fiore, *International Law Codified* (Borchard trans., 1918), Article 151.

It is, furthermore, a universally accepted doctrine in international law that a change in the form of government of a contracting State does not serve to terminate its treaties. Authorities on this point are abundant and unani-

---

*Among the notable international law authorities who served as advisers on that research were Benjamin Akzin, Harvard and Radcliffe Bureau of International Research; Charles Cheney Hyde and Philip C. Jessup, Columbia University Law School; George W. Wickersham; George Grafton Wilson, Harvard University; Quincy Wright, University of Chicago; and Green H. Hackworth, formerly Legal Adviser of the Department of State and now a member of the International Court of Justice.

mous. For example, 1 Moore, *Digest of International Law,* page 249, states:

> ". . . though the government changes, the nation remains, with rights and obligations unimpaired. . . .
>
> "The principle of the continuity of states has important results. The state is bound by engagements entered into by governments that have ceased to exist; . . ."

2 Hyde, *International Law* (1945), page 1528, states:

> "It is accepted doctrine in which the United States has long acquiesced, that a change in the form of the government of a contracting State does not serve to terminate its treaties, or necessarily justify the attempt of any party to terminate them."

To the same effect, the Harvard Research into the Law of Treaties (A. J. I. L., Supp., pt. III, Vol. 29 (1935), p. 1044) states:

> "Forms of government and constitutional arrangements in these days are constantly being changed, and if the enjoyment of treaty rights and the duty of performance were dependent upon the continuance of the *status quo* in respect to the governmental organization or constitutional system of the parties, one State would never be able to count with certainty on rights which have been promised it by another. . . .
>
> "Turning now to the opinions of writers on international law, we find that they appear to be in complete agreement that, as a general principle, changes in the governmental organization or constitutional system of a country . . . have no effect on the treaty obligations of States which undergo such changes."

In support of that statement, the Harvard Research (pp. 1046-1055) cites numerous international law authorities from the seventeenth century (Grotius, *De Jure Belli ac Pacis*) to modern times, as well as the decisions of European and American courts and international tribunals. For example, it refers to the case of *Lepeschkin v. Gosweiler* (71 *Journal des Tribunaux et Revue Judiciaire,* 1923, p. 582) in which the Swiss Federal Tribunal stated:

> "It is a principle of international law, recognized and absolutely uncontested, that the modifications in the form of government and in the internal organization of a State have no effect on its rights and obligations under the general public law; in particular they do not abolish rights and obligations derived from treaties concluded with other States."

Customary international practice with respect to application of the treaties of a State to its newly annexed territory has been evidenced on numerous occasions. As can be seen in some of the preceding passages quoted, the United States itself presents an example of such application. There has been no question but that the treaties entered into by the United States during the early years of its history apply to territory annexed to the United States subsequent to that time, including the State of Texas, which was formerly a Republic.

The case of Italy presents a striking similarity to that of Yugoslavia. Between 1859 and 1861 Lombardy, Tuscany, Emilia, Parma, and the Kingdom of the two Sicilies united with Sardinia to form the Italian Kingdom. The Italian Government took the position that only Sardinia, of all those States, had maintained its juridical entity and that the treaties of Sardinia alone had survived the union.

These treaties were considered to have replaced those of the other uniting States and were extended to the whole territory included in the new union. The theory supporting this action was that the new Kingdom of Italy did not constitute a new State, but that instead an existing State, Sardinia, serving as a nucleus, had expanded into a larger State into which a number of other Italian States had been absorbed. It is true that there was considerable controversy among jurists as to the theory at the time; but the Harvard Research Comment cited above points out, on page 1073, the following:

"The controversy, however, has only an academic interest. The courts of both Italy and France held that the treaty of March 4, 1760, concluded between France and Sardinia, relative to the execution of judgments, survived the formation of the Kingdom of Italy and was applicable throughout the Kingdom of Italy and binding on both countries—this on the theory that the Italian Kingdom was merely an expansion or enlargement of the State of Sardinia. . . . For the French decisions, see, among others, the cases of *La Modération* c. *La Chambre d'Assurances* (Court of Paris, 1879), *Mantil* c. *Pompilis* (Tribunal Cor. of the Seine, 1883, 10 *Journal du Droit International Privé*, 1883, p. 500), and *Vincent* c. *Bardini, Dalloz,* 1901, 2.257 and the note thereon by Pic. See also the decision of the Court of Montpellier of July 10, 1872, in the case of *Iconomidis v. Coude* (6 *Journal du Droit International Privé,* 1879, p. 69), where it was emphasized that additions to the territory of a State have no effect upon the State's treaty obligations. . . . For the Italian jurisprudence, see, among others, the decision of the Italian Court of Cassation of December 3, 1927, in the case of *Gastaldi v. Lepage Héméry* (9 *Rivista di Diritto Internazionale,* 3d ser. 1930, p. 102), where the survival of the treaty of 1760 between France and Sardinia was affirmed, on the principle that the Italian State was merely an expansion of the Kingdom of Sardinia. See also the decisions of various Italian Courts cited or summarized in 5 *Journal du Droit International Privé* (1878), p. 244, and 6 *ibid.* (1879), p. 305 ff.

"It may be added that the Permanent Court of International Justice in the *Case of the Free Zones of Upper Savoy and the District of Gex,* recognized that the treaty of Turin of March 16, 1816, between Sardinia and Switzerland survived the transformations which resulted in the formation of the Italian Kingdom. *Publications of the P. C. I. J.,* Series A, No. 22, p. 18, and Series A, No. 24, p. 17.

"The conclusion deducible from the practice in the case of the formation of the Italian Kingdom is that when a State enlarges its territorial domain by the annexation of other States, its treaties continue to bind it."

Moreover, it has never been required under recognized international law or practice that in order for a treaty to be extended to newly annexed territory the treaty must have contained a specific provision for that purpose. The contention [T. R. 55] that the absence of such a provision in the extradition treaty with Serbia compels the conclusion that the treaty did not survive the series of events following the first World War so as to cover the territories which became part of the Serb-Croat-Slovene

State is not justifiable by legal authority or by precedent. No such provision was contained in the early bilateral treaties of the United States, which nevertheless were applied to this country's newly annexed territory. The comparison of the Serbian extradition treaty with the German extradition treaty under consideration in *Terlinden v. Ames,* 184 U. S. 270 (1902), with respect to the presence or absence of such a provision is not warranted in view of the widely different circumstances surrounding those States at the time the treaties were signed. The German Treaty was signed in 1852 on behalf of "Prussia and other States of the Germanic Confederation"; that confederation was then already in existence; a movement for a stronger union of German States was under way; and Prussia was surrounded by numerous autonomous German States which with considerable likelihood might wish to accede to the treaty. On the other hand, Serbia in 1901, when the extradition treaty was signed, was a single independent nation and there was no immediate likelihood that it would subsequently be joined by States then under the Austro-Hungarian Empire. As pointed out by the court [T. R. 56], "it is historically unlikely that such a provision would have been put in the treaty with Serbia. . . ." To require the presence of such a provision in order to apply a treaty at some later time to the newly annexed territory of a State does not accord with the logic of the situation or with accepted international practice.

II.

Evidence of Continuance of Serbia as an International Juridical Entity Upon Its Enlargement Into the Kingdom of the Serbs, Croats, and Slovenes.

Evidence that the State which had been known as Serbia continued as an international juridical entity upon its enlargement into the Kingdom of the Serbs, Croats, and Slovenes, and hence that it falls within the general rule cited above with respect to the continuance of its treaty rights and obligations and the extension thereof to its newly acquired territory, may be seen in the following:

The Serb-Croat-Slovene State from the outset of its formation in 1918 appears to have regarded itself as a successor State to Serbia, formed by the voluntary union with Serbia of certain other States. The Serbian Chargé d'Affaires submitted to the Department of State of the United States on January 6, 1919, a communication from his Government in which were set forth the facts of the union of the Serbian, Croatian, and Slovene provinces within the boundaries of the former Austro-Hungarian Monarchy "into one single State *with the Kingdom of Serbia* [italics supplied] under the dynasty of His Majesty King Peter [King of Serbia] and under the regency of the [Serbian] Crown Prince Alexander" followed by the decision of the National Assembly of Montenegro to unite with the newly formed Kingdom of the Serbs, Croats, and Slovenes. The communication further stated:

> ". . . His Royal Highness the Crown Prince has declared that he accepts with pleasure and thanks these decisions. A common Government for the King-

dom has been organized on the 21st of December. The Legations, Consulates and other Missions of the Kingdom of Serbia will be the Legations, Consulates and other Missions of the Kingdom of the Serbs, Croats and Slovenes." (*Foreign Relations of the United States,* 1919, Vol. II, p. 892.)

That Serbia was the nucleus about which the Kingdom of the Serbs, Croats, and Slovenes was formed seems clear from a study of the events which accompanied its formation. That Serbia consistently regarded itself as that nucleus and never at any time relinquished its claim to continuity as a State is made doubly clear by its action in accepting the union of other States *to it,* while at the same time declaring the continuance of the Serbian dynasty and the Serbian facilities for conducting international relations.

On pages 16-19 of its opinion the court quotes authorties who refer to the Serb-Croat-Slovene State or Yugoslavia as "a new state," "a new order," etc. The implication is that mere use of the word "new" implies a complete disavowal of and separation from the "old" State; *i. e.,* Serbia. The facts of the case, however, indicate otherwise. At the time of union of the other Serb, Croat, and Slovene provinces with Serbia in 1918, Serbia constituted more than one-third of the total area of the newly enlarged State and approximately one-third of the total population, far exceeding any other single State in the group. The other States turned to Serbia for their rulers, for their seat of government, for their constitutional guarantees. Belgrade, the capital of Serbia, remained the capital of the newly enlarged State. Serbian diplomatic representatives in other capitals of the world became the diplomatic representatives of the Serb-Croat-Slovene State. Serbian legations, consulates, and missions became the legations, consulates, and missions of the Serb-Croat-Slovene State. The Serbian ruling family remained in power, *accepting* sovereignty over the newly annexed provinces. The Serbian Constitution of 1903 continued in force until the adoption of a new Constitution in 1921. The Christmas Day (1918) proclamation of Prince Regent Alexander proclaimed the duty of the Government

> "to extend immediately to the whole territory of the Kingdom of the Serbs, Croats and Slovenes all the rights and liberties now enjoyed by the Serbs in accordance with the Serbian Constitution." (*Foreign Relations of the United States,* 1919, Vol. II, p. 897.)

It is noteworthy also that the United States Government from the outset regarded Serbia as a continuing State *to which* other States and provinces had joined themselves. In recognizing the new régime, this Government, in a note dated February 10, 1919, addressed to the Minister of the Kingdom of the Serbs, Croats, and Slovenes (*Foreign Relations of United States,* 1919, Vol. II, pp. 899-900) [T. R. 89-90], stated:

> ". . . the Government of the United States welcomes the union of the Serbian, Croatian and Slovene provinces within the boundaries of the former Austro-Hungarian Monarchy *to Serbia* and recognizes the Serbian Legation as the Legation of the Kingdom of the Serbs, Croatians and Slovenes." (Emphasis supplied.)

It was wholly within the constitutional power and prerogatives of the Executive Branch of the United States Government to accord such recognition to the State as a continuing entity.

1 Hyde, International Law (1945), 156;

Oetjen v. Central Leather Company, 246 U. S. 297-302;

United States v. Belmont, 301 U. S. 324, 330;

Guaranty Trust Company of New York v. United States, 304 U. S. 126, 137-139;

1 Hackworth, Digest of International Law, 161-166.

In the *Oetjen* case the court said:

"The conduct of the foreign relations of our Government is committed by the Constitution to the Executive and Legislative—'the political'—Departments of the Government and the propriety of what may be done in the exercise of this political power is not subject to judicial inquiry or decision."

Regarding the union of the Yugoslav peoples, the Secretary of State made public in Paris on February 7, 1919, the following statement, which like the note quoted above seems to regard the Serbian State as the continuing judicial entity in the newly formed union (Foreign Relations of United States, 1919, Vol. VII, p. 899) [T. R. 89]:

"On May 29, 1918, the Government of the United States expressed its sympathy for the nationalistic aspirations of the Jugo Slav race and on June 28 declared that all branches of the Slavish race should be completely freed from German and Austrian rule. After having achieved their freedom from foreign oppression the Jugo Slav[s] formerly under Austro-Hungarian rule on various occasions expressed the desire *to unite with the Kingdom of Servia.* The Servian Government on its part has publicly and officially *accepted* the union of the Serb, Croat and Slovene peoples. The Government of the United

States, therefore, welcomes the union while recognizing that the final settlement of territorial frontiers must be left to the Peace Conference for determination according to desires of the peoples concerned." (Emphasis supplied.) (1 Hackworth, *Digest of International Law* (1943), p. 221.)

A communication dated March 24, 1919, from the Minister for the Kingdom of the Serbs, Croats, and Slovenes to the Acting Secretary of State, a copy of which is attached marked Appendix "A-1," gives still another indication that both Governments from the outset regarded the Kingdom of the Serbs, Croats, and Slovenes as a continuation of the Serbian State under a new name. The use of the phrase "the change in the title" of the Government is noteworthy. That communication reads in part:

> "I have received your letter of March 21st, requesting that in view of the change in the title of my Government, I furnish the State Department with full powers running in the name of the new Kingdom of the Serbs, Croats and Slovenes . . .
>
> "I have not failed to communicate with my Government and have asked that in compliance with your request, His Excellency Mr. Dodge be furnished as soon as possible with a copy of the new full powers." (Dept. of State file No. 860 h. 5½.)

In a memorandum of May 31, 1921, copy of which is attached marked Appendix "A-2," the then Solicitor (Legal Adviser) of the Department of State, Fred K. Nielsen, reached the following conclusion in a case which was pending before him for official action:

> "The formation of the Kingdom of the Serbs, Croats and Slovenes apparently presents a situation

different from that arising out of the formation of the German Empire by the amalgamation of several independent states, which united to form a new entity, the German Empire. I believe it may properly be said that Serbia absorbed the territories which came to her as a result of the war and that these territories can properly, from the standpoint of our law, be regarded as covered by our treaties with Serbia . . ." (Dept. of State File No. 711.60h.)

In accordance with the accepted theory regarding continuity of States and their international obligations, the Serb-Croat-Slovene State, as hereinafter indicated, appears to have consistently regarded the Serbian treaties with other countries as continuing in force and applicable to the whole of its territory. That those treaties were likewise so regarded by the Principal Allied and Associated Powers, including the United States, Great Britain, France, Italy, and Japan, is clearly indicated in the preamble to the Treaty between the Principal Allied and Associated Powers and the Kingdom of the Serbs, Croats, and Slovenes for the Protection of Minorities, signed at St. Germain-en-Laye September 10, 1919 (III Treaties, etc., between United States and other Powers, Redmond, 3731 Senate Document 134, 75th Cong., 1 Hudson, *International Legislation,* 1931, p. 312). That preamble reads in part as follows:

"Whereas since the commencement of the year 1913 *extensive territories have been added to the Kingdom of Serbia,* and

"Whereas, the Serb, Croat and Slovene peoples of the former Austro-Hungarian Monarchy have of their own free will determined to unite with Serbia in a permanent union for the purpose of forming a single sovereign independent State under the title of the Kingdom of the Serbs, Croats and Slovenes, and

"Whereas the Prince Regent of Serbia and the Serbian Government have agreed to this union, and in consequence the Kingdom of the Serbs, Croats and Slovenes has been constituted and has assumed sovereignty over the territories inhabited by these peoples, . . .

"Whereas it is desired to free Serbia from certain obligations which she undertook by the Treaty of Berlin of 1878 to certain Powers and to substitute for them obligations to the League of Nations . . ." (Emphasis supplied.)

The treaty then declares in a clause preliminary to Article 1 that the Serb-Croat-Slovene State, in view of the obligations contracted under the "present" treaty, is discharged from the obligations of Article 35 of the Treaty of Berlin of July 13, 1878.

Further, Article 12 of the treaty provides:

"Pending the conclusion of new treaties or conventions, all treaties, conventions, agreements and obligations between Serbia on the one hand, and any of the Principal Allied and Associated Powers, on the other hand, which were in force on the 1st August, 1914, or which have since been entered into shall *ipso facto* be binding upon the Serb-Croat-Slovene State."

The wording of the preamble, the preliminary clause, and the article quoted above makes it amply clear that in view of the signers of that treaty the former Kingdom of Serbia had been *enlarged* into the Kingdom of Serbs, Croats, and Slovenes; that the latter kingdom at the time of the signing of the treaty was already bound by all the treaties of Serbia in force at the outbreak of World War I; that a specific treaty clause (that referring to the Treaty of Berlin) was necessary to relieve the Serb-Croat-Slovene State of any such treaty obligations; and that in the absence of such a clause the Serbian treaties continued to bind the Serb-Croat-Slovene State.

Accordingly, Article 12 is merely declaratory of the existing treaty obligations of the Serb-Croat-Slovene State; it does not create those obligations. It describes an existing condition to which it gives formal international recognition. The use of the words *"ipso facto"* in Article 12 is also meaningful. Webster defines that phrase thus: "By the fact or act itself; by the very nature of the case." In effect, then, the Article states not merely that the Serbian treaties shall bind the Serb-Croat-Slovene State but that *by the very fact* that they were in force between Serbia and the other powers on August 1, 1914, they shall bind the Serb-Croat-Slovene State.

Commenting on Article 12, Harvard Research on the Law of Treaties, cited above, has this to say on page 1075:

"This article appears to have been based on the view that the Yugoslav Kingdom was not a new State but an expansion of the Kingdom of Serbia. Serbia was admittedly the nucleus of the Yugoslav Kingdom, she had concluded treaties with foreign States which were in force at the time of the formation of the Yugoslav Kingdom, and it could hardly be maintained that her union with the other territories destroyed her capacity to perform the treaty obligations which she had assumed prior to the territorial and political transformations which she underwent."

The position of the United Kingdom Government with regard to the treaties of Serbia, already indicated in the above-mentioned Treaty of St. Germain-en-Laye, is clearly stated in McNair, *The Law of Treaties: British Practice and Opinions,* 1938, p. 443:

> "*Serb-Croat-Slovene State.* In the view of the United Kingdom Government this State has succeeded to the treaty obligations of Serbia, except in so far as it has been specifically released from them . . .
>
> "There seems to be no doubt that this case must be regarded as an enlargement of the territory of an existing State."

The Treaty between the Principal Allied and Associated Powers and the Serb-Croat-Slovene State for the Protection of Minorities, signed at St. Germain-en-Laye September 10, 1919, referred to above, like several other treaties which were bound in with the League of Nations, was never submitted to the United States Senate. This was natural, since ratification of such treaties obviously would have been incompatible with the Senate's refusal to approve United States participation in the League of Nations. Consequently, the United States did not ratify the Treaty with the Serb-Croat-Slovene State for the Protection of Minorities. It *was* ratified, however, by Great Britain, France, Italy, Japan, and the Serb-Croat-Slovene State and entered into force with respect to those governments along with the treaty of peace with Austria on July 16, 1929. (III Treaties, Conventions, etc., Redmond 3149.) The treaty thus became effective, and the provisions contained therein with respect to continuance of the pre-war Serbian treaties were formally confirmed as law among the ratifying States.

On page 20 of its opinion the court notes the fact that after World War I special provision was made in treaties with Germany, Austria, and Hungary regarding continuance in force of pre-war treaties. (III Treaties, Conventions, 3329, 3149, 3539.) From that fact the conclusion is drawn that "it was generally regarded at that time that previous treaties were abrogated unless specifically affirmed or provision made for their affirmation in a treaty ratified by the Senate." [T. R. 63.] It should be remembered, however, that Germany and Austria-Hungary had been at war with the United States and that the force of certain of their treaties with the United States may have been considered affected by that state of war. It is considered desirable, in bringing to an end a state of war, to have included specific treaty provisions regarding pre-war treaties for the following reasons: (1) that the victorious countries may determine which of their pre-war treaties with the vanquished States should be applied upon the return to peaceful relations; (2) that any doubts as to the status of particular treaties as a result of a war may be completely resolved; and (3) that a State which considers all treaties terminated *ipso facto* by a state of war may have a convenient procedure for reviving pre-war treaties. Serbia, however, was never at war with the United States and therefore the continuance in force of treaties between the two countries was never interrupted by reason of war. Consequently, the situation which existed between the United States and Serbia is not analogous to the situation which existed between the United States and Germany, Austria, or Hungary in regard to the purpose to be served by a specific treaty provision with respect to the application of pre-war treaties.

III.

Open and Continuous Recognition by the United States and Yugoslavia of the Continuance in Force of the Pre-war Serbian Treaties and of Their Enlarged Application.

The fact that the United States did not ratify the Treaty of St. Germain-en-Laye with the Serb-Croat-Slovene State makes the events that followed even more significant. On June 4, 1921, the Secretary of State addressed to the Minister of the Kingdom of the Serbs, Croats, and Slovenes in Washington a formal note, copy of which is attached marked Appendix "A-4." This inquired whether it was the view of the Government of the Kingdom of the Serbs, Croats, and Slovenes that the treaties which were in force between Serbia and the United States at the time of the formation of the Kingdom of the Serbs, Croats, and Slovenes were applicable to those parts of the new Kingdom not comprised within the territories of the former Kingdom of Serbia. It made particular reference to three treaties: the commercial convention of 1881, the consular convention of 1881, and the extradition treaty of 1901. (22 Stat. 963; 22 Stat. 968, and 32 Stat. 1890.) It is possibly worthy of note that the United States Government did not inquire the view of the Serb-Croat-Slovene Government with respect to *continuance in force* of the Serbian treaties; that appears to have been well settled. It inquired only with respect to the application of the treaties to territory not formerly comprised within the Kingdom of Serbia.

In reply, the Chargé d'Affaires by a note dated September 29, 1921, copy of which is attached marked Appendix "A-3," stated that the Government of the Kingdom of the Serbs, Croats, and Slovenes considered the treaties and conventions concluded between Serbia and the United States "as applicable to the whole territory of the Kingdom of the Serbs, Croats and Slovenes as constituted at present." (Note P. No. 429, Dept. of State file No. 711.60 H/3; V Hackworth, p. 375.)

Thus as early as 1921 the Serb-Croat-Slovene State in a formal diplomatic note to the United States Government had acknowledged not only the continuance in force of the pre-war Serbian treaties with the United States but the application of those treaties to the newly acquired territory.

In connection with this exchange of notes, 2 Hyde, *International Law* (1945), p. 1535, states:

> "It was logical and natural that the Government of the Kingdom of the Serbs, Croats and Slovenes, should have acknowledged to that of the United States in 1921, that it considered the treaties and conventions concluded between the Kingdom of Serbia and the United States as applicable to the whole territory of the Kingdom of the Serbs, Croats and Slovenes, as then constituted. The latter Kingdom embodied, in a territorial sense, the enlargement of the former Kingdom, and was the same State with a bigger body. It was also reasonable to contend, as did the United States in substance in 1921, that that Kingdom should regard those agreements as applicable to its territory which had formerly belonged to the Austro-Hungarian Empire."

From that time forward the Department of State, in reply to inquiries, particularly with respect to the commercial convention of 1881 the provisions of which were constantly being invoked in the carrying on of trade between the two countries, stated unequivocally that the treaties with Serbia were in force and applicable to the whole Kingdom, including territory not part of Serbia before the World War of 1914-1918. (V Hackworth, Digest of International Law, 375.)

The note of Secretary of State Hughes, dated June 4, 1921, to Defrees, Buckingham, and Eaton (cited in footnote 16 of the court's opinion and in V Hackworth p. 375) is of interest only as an indication that even prior to the receipt of the formal view of the Serb-Croat-Slovene State it was the considered opinion of the Department of State that the pre-war Serbian treaties applied to the newly acquired territory.

Thus far the continuance in force and enlarged application of the pre-war Serbian treaties appears to have been a decision taken and carried out by the Executive Branch of this Government. Based on accepted international practice and the acknowledged power of the President to conduct foreign relations, it was altogether proper that the Executive Branch should make the decision that the juridical entity which had been Serbia was continued in the enlarged Serb-Croat-Slovene State.

> 1 Hyde, International Law (1945), 156;
>
> *Oetjen v. Central Leather Company,* 246 U. S. 297-302;
>
> *United States v. Belmont,* 301 U. S. 324, 330;
>
> *Guaranty Trust Company of New York v. United States,* 304 U. S. 126, 137-139;
>
> 1 Hackworth, Digest of International Law, 161-166.

In 1928, however, the Congress of the United States in effect confirmed that Executive decision. By an Act approved March 30, 1928 (45 Stat. 399), it authorized the settlement of the indebtedness of the Kingdom of the Serbs, Croats, and Slovenes. In that settlement the debts of the Kingdom of Serbia to the United States were assumed by the Kingdom of the Serbs, Croats, and Slovenes and incorporated in the total amount of indebtedness on the same basis as the debts incurred by the latter Kingdom.

Reference here is to the fact that the "Principal of obligations acquired for cash advanced under Liberty Bond Act . . . $26,126,574.59," which is set forth in the Act of Congress was obviously calculated on the basis of the cash advanced to Serbia from August 1917 to November 1918, amounting to over 10 million dollars, plus advances of about 16 million in 1919, after the proclamation of the Serb-Croat-Slovene State. (See pp. 318-325, Combined Annual Reports of the World War Foreign Debt Commission.)

Congress thus endorsed the principle that the Serb-Croat-Slovene State was a continuation of the juridical entity that had been Serbia, to the extent that it would inherit Serbia's debts. Bynkershoek, *Questionum Juris Publici* (lib. II, ch. XXV, sec. 1, *Classics of International Law,* Frank trans., p. 276), as quoted in Harvard Research, page 1046, states:

> "The nation, however, is not changed with a change in the form of government. The same is certainly true of a state when it is governed now by this form, now by that. Otherwise one might suppose that a state in its present form is freed from the agreements and debts contracted under a different

form of government. Grotius agrees that this does not hold true in the case of debts; and the same argument that holds in the case of debts applies convincingly to agreements."

In 1945, following the establishment of the Federal Peoples' Republic of Yugoslavia, the Yugoslav Government confirmed its continued recognition of existing treaties and agreements with the United States. The United States Government, in a communication which specifically noted Yugoslavia's confirmation of the existing treaties and agreements, extended recognition to the Yugoslav Republic on April 16, 1946. This exchange of communications was noted by the court in its opinion [T. R. 42], and in footnote 5 thereof [T. R. 75]. This exchange is not the sole basis on which the Department of State relies in its assertion that the 1901 extradition treaty is in force with Yugoslavia. Contrary to that implication, it can be seen from the history of prior events as outlined herein that that exchange was but another step in the continuing chain of circumstances which proves the open and continuous recognition by the United States and Yugoslav Governments of the pre-war Serbian treaties.

The three United States-Serbian treaties which had been in force prior to World War I, including the extradition treaty, have been constantly carried on the records of the Department of State as treaties in force with the Serb-Croat-Slovene State and subsequently with Yugoslavia. In addition, from 1921 on, the Department has publicly and continuously declared the continuance in force of those treaties and their application to the Serb-Croat-Slovene State (Yugoslavia) as a whole.

Also evidencing the open and public recognition given by this Government of the continuance of the Serbian treaties are the Department's various treaty publications. For example, the compilation entitled *A List of Treaties and Other International Acts of the United States of America in Force December 31, 1932,* published by the Department in 1933, and a revision thereof published in 1941, carries as in force with Yugoslavia the 1901 treaty of extradition as well as the 1881 commercial and consular conventions. The loose-leaf treaty publication, *United States Treaty Developments,* started in 1947 has continuously carried in Appendix III(C) the following statement with regard to Yugoslavia:

"The treaties in force between the United States and Serbia at the time of the formation of the Kingdom of the Serbs, Croats and Slovenes (Dec. 1, 1918) were regarded by the Governments of the United States and the new Kingdom as applicable to the new Kingdom. State Department file 711.60h/1 and 3. The adoption of 'Yugoslavia' in place of 'the Kingdom of the Serbs, Croats and Slovenes' as the official title of the Kingdom on October 3, 1929, is understood not to have affected treaty relations.

"The establishment of the Federal People's Republic of Yugoslavia (November 1945) is understood not to have affected treaty relations between the United States and Yugoslavia. (Subsequent to the establishment of that Republic, the Yugoslav Government confirmed its continued recognition of existing treaties and agreements between the United States and Yugoslavia, and United States recognition of that Republic was extended on April 16, 1946.)"

Important evidence of the continuing force of the 1901 extradition treaty concluded with Serbia appears in connection with proposals in 1925 and 1927 for a new extradition treaty between the United States and the Kingdom

of the Serbs, Croats, and Slovenes. Two successive
Secretaries of State, Charles Evans Hughes on January
8, 1925, and Frank B. Kellogg on March 23, 1927, formally and officially, in instructions to the American
Minister in Belgrade took the position that the 1901
treaty was applicable to the whole Kingdom of the Serbs,
Croats and Slovenes. The instruction, copy of which is
attached marked Appendix "A-5," signed by Secretary
Hughes reads:

"On September 29, 1921, the Yugoslav Charge
d'Affaires ad interim informed the Department that
the Government of the Kingdom of the Serbs, Croats
and Slovenes considered the treaties and conventions
in force between the United States and the former
Kingdom of Serbia as applicable to the whole territory of the Kingdom of the Serbs, Croats and
Slovenes as at present constituted. In view of this
assurance and inasmuch as the extradition convention
concluded by the United States and Serbia on October 25, 1901, is, in the opinion of this Government,
a modern and comprehensive convention, the Department before considering the negotiation of a
new extradition convention would desire to be more
fully informed as to what useful purpose would thus
be served." (Inst. No. 543, to the American Minister,
Belgrade, dated January 8, 1925. Dept. file No.
760 h.00/12.)

The Yugoslav proposal for the negotiation of a new
extradition convention in 1924 carried with it no suggestion that the convention of 1901 was not still in force.
In a despatch dated February 14, 1925, copy of which is
attached marked Appendix "A-6," in reply to the instruction from which the above was quoted, Minister Dodge
said that the Director of the Treaties Section of the Yugo-

slav Foreign Office explained that it was desired "to make the new convention accord more completely" with the criminal legislation in the territories formerly belonging to Austria-Hungary and now forming part of Yugoslavia.

When this Government, on August 7, 1926, initiated steps to negotiate certain treaties with the Yugoslav Government "to supersede" early instruments on the same subjects, the Yugoslav Government again suggested the negotiation of a new extradition convention, among others. Thereupon Secretary Kellogg, in virtually the same words that Secretary Hughes had previously employed on this subject, instructed Minister Prince in Belgrade, on March 23, 1927, as follows:

'With regard to the negotiation of a new extradition convention you will recall that in instruction No. 543 of January 8, 1925, the Department pointed out that the extradition convention between the United States and Serbia, which is regarded both by this Government and the Government of the Serbs, Croats and Slovenes as being applicable to the whole territory of the Kingdom, is a modern and comprehensive convention. Pending the receipt of the more specific information concerning the proposal of the Government of the Serbs, Croats and Slovenes to supplant this convention which it is indicated on page 2 of despatch No. 2577 of February 14, 1925, would be furnished you, the Department is unwilling to consider the negotiation of a new treaty on this subject." (Inst. No. 64 to Belgrade, dated March 23, 1927. Dept. file No. 711.60 h 2/1. Printed in For. Rel., 1927, Vol. III, pp. 842-843.)

In 1934 the Yugoslav Government unequivocally stated, in a note verbale addressed to the American Legation in

Belgrade, that the 1901 extradition treaty was then in force. The American Legation had inquired of the Yugoslav Foreign Office whether the Yugoslav Government would agree to a supplemental extradition treaty with the United States adding to the list of extraditable crimes "crimes or offenses against the bankruptcy laws." The reply of the Yugoslav Government, copy of which is attached marked Appendix "B-1," reads in part as follows:

". . . the Royal Ministry for Foreign Affairs has the honor to inform the Legation that in the opinion of the Royal Ministry of Justice the extradition of criminals for offenses mentioned in the aforementioned note is already provided for under Article II, No. 7, of the above cited Convention [Convention of October 12/25, 1901] . . .

"As 'crimes or offenses against bankruptcy laws' are punishable by virtue of the provisions of the Penal Code of the Kingdom . . . it will be sufficient in each particular case, that the competent American authorities propound a legalized extract of the legislative provisions indicating that such crimes are also punished under the laws of the United States of America, and *the extradition requested will, in such case, be granted according to the Convention for extradition of criminals of 1901, which is now in force.*" (Emphasis supplied.) (Note p. No. 13524-IV of May 19, 1934; Dept. of State file No. 211.60H/10.)

As further public and formal evidence of the fact that both Governments regarded the United States-Serbian treaties as remaining in force, references to such treaties have been included in subsequent international agreements with Yugoslavia.

In an agreement between the United States and Yugoslavia effected by an exchange of notes at Washington signed May 4 and October 3, 1946, both the United States and Yugoslavia notes contain the following language:

". . . the most-favored-nation provisions of the Treaty for Facilitating and Developing Commercial Relations between the United States and Yugoslavia signed October 2/14, 1881 shall not be understood to require the extension to Yugoslavia of advantages accorded by the United States to the Philippines."

That agreement of 1946 was published in the Treaties and Other International Acts Series, as TIAS 1572, and in the *United States Statutes at Large,* Volume 61(3), page 2451.

An agreement between the United States and Yugoslavia, signed at Washington July 19, 1948, concerning settlement of pecuniary claims against Yugoslavia contained as Article 5 the following:

"The Government of Yugoslavia agrees to accord to nationals of the United States lawfully continuing to hold, or hereafter acquiring assets in Yugoslavia, the rights and privileges of using and administering such assets and the income therefrom within the framework of the controls and regulations of the Government of Yugoslavia, on conditions not less favorable than the rights and privileges accorded to nationals of Yugoslavia, or of any other country, *in accordance with the Convention of Commerce and Navigation between the United States of America and the Prince of Serbia, signed at Belgrade, October 2-14, 1881.*" (Emphasis supplied.)

This agreement was published in the Treaties and Other International Acts Series, as TIAS 1803, and was included in the *United States Statutes at Large,* Volume 62(3), page 2658.

Thus by formal international agreements between the United States and Yugoslavia, both governments have on two occasions officially recognized the United States-Serbian commercial convention of 1881 as continuing in force between the United States and Yugoslavia.

In the light of the numerous public declarations by this Government regarding continuance of the treaties and the inclusion of references to such existing treaties in other formal international agreements, it is difficult to perceive how it could properly be maintained either that Yugoslavia was not aware of the continuance in force of the extradition treaty or that the Senate of the United States had been deprived of the opportunity of extending its approval of application of the treaty with Serbia to the other States later forming part of the Kingdom of the Serbs, Croats and Slovenes. The Senate, in the light of the foregoing facts, must be presumed to have been aware of the application of the Serbian treaties to Yugoslavia and to have acquiesced in the power of the Executive branch of the Government to so consider their application. Yugoslavia, on its part, had given formal and official diplomatic assurance of the application of those treaties to all of its territories.

IV.

Open and Continuous Action by the Governments of the United States and Yugoslavia Under the Serbian Treaties.

It is noteworthy that an examination of the record reveals that both the United States Government and the Government of the Serb-Croat-Slovene State, and subsequently Yugoslavia, have acted openly and continuously under the provisions of the United States-Serbian treaties.

For example, the day-to-day consular relations between the United States and Yugoslavia are carried on under the terms of the consular convention of 1881 concluded between the United States and Serbia. Yugoslav consular officers are permitted to carry on their official work in various cities of the United States on a most-favored-nation basis, resting on the existence and validity of a consular convention assuring reciprocal treatment to American consular officers in Yugoslavia. That convention is, of course, the 1881 consular convention concluded with Serbia. (22 Stat. 968.)

In like manner commercial relations between nationals and companies of the United States and Yugoslavia in the territory of the other are carried on under the terms of the commercial convention of 1881 between the United States and Serbia. (22 Stat. 963.) Such rights as the right of entry, travel, and residence for business purposes, the right to acquire, possess, and dispose of property, the right to exemption from military service, the right of access to courts of justice, and numerous other rights have been consistently exercised, and are at this very moment being exercised, by nationals and companies of both countries under and in conformity with the terms of the 1881 treaty. To the knowledge of this Government, the validity of that treaty has not been questioned by the nationals or companies of either country acting under its provisions or bringing action under its provisions in a court of law.

The fact that action under the 1901 extradition treaty has not been taken with the same frequency and continuity arises, not from any difference in the force or effectiveness of the treaty, but in the very nature of the treaty itself. Extradition is not a subject of every-day application. It is altogether possible that neither party to an extradition treaty would request action under it for a period of many years at a time; it is possible even that action under an extradition treaty would never be requested. The force of the treaty is none the less real and the obligations of the parties to it none the less clear.

It is important to bear in mind in this respect that the extradition treaty rests for its validity on the same grounds as do the consular and commercial conventions of 1901; namely, that Yugoslavia is a true successor State to Serbia in so far as the continuance of treaty rights and obligations is concerned. If any one of those treaties can be considered in force, by the same token all must be considered in force.

V.

Opinions of United States Courts.

Courts in the United States on several occasions have considered cases in which reliance was placed upon the effectiveness as between the United States and Yugoslavia of the 1881 treaties of commerce and consular rights concluded between the United States and Serbia. By their decisions in those cases the courts have in effect recognized the continuance in force of the pre-war United States-Serbian treaties.

In *Lukich v. Department of Labor and Industries,* 176 Wash. 221, 22 P. 2d 388 (1934) the court made the following statement:

> ". . . December 27, 1882, a 'Convention of Commerce and Navigation' between the Kingdom of Serbia and the United States, which had theretofore been negotiated, was proclaimed. It is conceded that the present kingdom of Yugoslavia has replaced and absorbed the kingdom of Serbia, and that the convention above referred to is now in full force and effect between Yugoslavia and the United States . . ."

In *Urbus v. State Compensation Commissioner,* 113 W. Va. 563, 169 S. E. 164 (1933), the court held that the consular convention concluded with Serbia in 1881 must be given due significance as the law of the land in applying a state statute to a citizen of Yugoslavia. The opinion stated in part:

> "Yugoslavia, according to 23 Encyclopedia Britannica (14th ed.), page 916, is 'a convenient name for the Serb, Croat and Slovene State which originated at the end of 1918 by the union of parts of

the former Austro-Hungarian Empire with Serbia, and at a slightly later date with Montenegro.' The treaty between the United States and the other Principal Allied Powers on the one hand and The Serb-Croat-Slovene State on the other hand, signed at Saint Germain-en-Laye, on September 10, 1919, provided that all treaties between Serbia and any of the Principal Allied Powers which were in force on August 1, 1914, should be binding on the Serb-Croat-Slovene State. The treaty between the United States and Serbia in force in 1914, contained the following provisions: . . . [Here followed a quotation from the treaty].

"The Constitution of the United States, article 6, makes this treaty a portion of 'the Supreme Law of the Land,' and provides that 'the Judges of every State shall be bound thereby.' Consequently the treaty must be given due significance in applying a state statute . . ."

In another case, *Olijan v. Lublin,* 50 N. E. 2d 264 (1943), the court ruled inadmissible in evidence the affidavit of the Minister of Yugoslavia to the United States on the grounds that it failed to comply with the requirements regarding the taking of testimony of consular officers set out in the treaty of 1881 concluded between the United States and Serbia. In its opinion the court stated:

"It must be noticed in this case that the Consul General of the Kingdom of Yugoslavia has . . . invoked the jurisdiction of the court for the determination of the legal status of one of the subjects of the Kingdom of Yugoslavia. It would seem to follow that the evidence of its own ministers or consular officers should be presented in accord with its treaty provisions. The record in the case, insofar as the affidavit or certificate of the Minister of the Kingdom of Yugoslavia, fails to show that any of the requirements of the treaty were complied with before such testimony was taken."

The extradition treaty of 1901 is valid and effective between the United States and Yugoslavia on the same historical and legal grounds as are the 1881 treaties which were recognized by the courts in the above-cited cases. A holding that the extradition treaty is not in force is contrary to the decisions of the courts in those cases and a long record of continuous, open, and unchallenged action by both the United States and Yugoslavia under the pre-war United States-Serbian treaties.

In the case of *In re Thomas,* 12 Blatchf. 370, 23 Fed. Cas. 927, 930, which involved a request for extradition to Germany, the Circuit Court for the Southern District of New York said:

"It is further contended, on the part of Thomas, that the convention with Bavaria was abrogated by the absorption of Bavaria into the German Empire. . . . In the present case, the mandate issued by the government of the United States shows that the convention in question is regarded as in force both by the United States and by the German empire, represented by its envoy, and by Bavaria, represented by the same envoy. The application of the foreign government was made through the proper diplomatic representative of the German empire and of Bavaria, and the complaint before the commissioner was made by the proper consular authority representing the German empire and also representing Bavaria. It is also objected, that the complaint is insufficient. This objection is not tenable."

The opinion in the *Thomas* case was cited with approval in the case of *Terlinden v. Ames,* 184 U. S. 270, 287-288. The Supreme Court added:

"We concur in the view that the question whether power remains in a foreign State to carry out its treaty obligations is in its nature political and not judicial, and that the courts ought not to interfere with the conclusions of the political department in that regard."

The United States District Court for the Southern District of New York held, with respect to commercial treaties concluded between the United States, on the other hand, and Prussia and certain Hanseatic cities, that those treaties continued in force after the formation of the German Empire. *The Sophie Rickmers,* 45 F. 2d 413, 418.

The Supreme Court, in the case of *Disconto Gesellschaft v. Umbreit,* 208 U. S. 570, 581, said, with respect to the Commercial Treaty of May 1, 1828 between the United States and Prussia:

"This treaty is printed as one of the treaties in force in the compilation of 1904, p. 643, and has undoubtedly been recognized by the two governments as still in force since the formation of the German Empire. See *Terlinden v. Ames,* 184 U. S. 270; Foreign Relations of 1883, p. 369; Foreign Relations of 1885, pp. 404, 443, 444; Foreign Relations of 1887, p. 370; Foreign Relations of 1895, part one, 539.

"Assuming, then, that this treaty is still in force between the United States and the German Empire, and conceding the rule that treaties should be liberally interpreted with a view to protecting the citizens of the respective countries in rights thereby secured, is there anything in this article which required any different decision in the Supreme Court of Wisconsin that that given? . . ."

It may be observed in this relation that the Supreme Court cited the case of *Terlinden v. Ames.* It cited also the correspondence set forth in the volumes of the Foreign Relations for the years 1883, 1885, 1887 and 1895 wherein the Department of State had taken the position that the Treaty of May 1, 1828 was in force with respect to the German Empire. Unlike the Extradition Convention involved in the *Terlinden* case, the Commercial Convention of 1828 was not specifically revived or kept in force by a later treaty.

Conclusion.

For the foregoing reasons, it is respectfully submitted that the decision of the District Court granting the writ of *habeas corpus* should be reversed.

WALTER S. BINNS,
United States Attorney.

CLYDE C. DOWNING,
Assistant United States Attorney,
Chief of Civil Division.

ARLINE MARTIN,
Assistant United States Attorney.

Attorneys for the United States.

II to whom these presents shall come, Greeting:

I Certify That the annexed copy, or each of the specified number of
d copies, of each document listed below is a true copy of a document
official custody of the Archivist of the United States.

ecinal File, 1910-1929:
File Number 860h.51/2 dated March 24, 1919.
Memorandum from Fred K. Nielsen dated May 31, 1921.
File Number 711.60h/1 dated June 4, 1921.
File Number 711.60h/3 dated September 29, 1921.
File Number 760h.00/12 dated January 8, 1925.
File Number 760h.00/16 dated February 14, 1925.

ese documents are from the General Records of the
of State.

sstimony whereof, I, WAYNE C. GROVER, Archivist of the United States,
have hereunto caused the Seal of the National
Archives to be affixed and my name subscribed
by the Acting Chief Archivist, Diplomatic and
Judicial Branches   of the National Archives,
in the District of Columbia, this 3rd   day
of February   19. 53.

Wayne C. Grover
Archivist of the United States

By: [signature]

Appendix R-1 to Q - 6

My dear Mr. Polk:

I have received your letter of March 21 so requesting

that in view of the change in the title of my Government, if furnish

the State Department with full powers running in the name

new Kingdom of the Serbs/Croats and Slovenes,certifying what

action has been taken on my part with reference to loans by

United States to my Government and confirming my powers to

into agreements with the United States regarding loans,and to sign

obligations for advances thereunder to take such further action as

may be necessary or desirable in the premises as

I have not failed to communicate with my Government and

Hon. Mr. Polk,

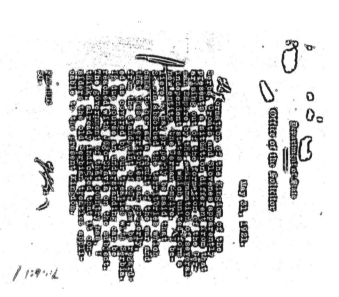

LEGATION OF THE KINGDOM
OF THE
SERBS, CROATS AND SLOVENES
WASHINGTON, D.C.

File No. 422.

DEPARTMENT OF STATE
DIVISION OF
NEAR EASTERN AFFAIRS
JUN 17 1921

SOLICITOR'S OFFICE
JUN 18 1921

The Chargé d'Affaires ad interim of the Kingdom of the Serbs, Croats and Slovenes presents his compliments to the Secretary of State, and referring to the latter's note verbale of June 4, 1921, so has the honor to advise him that the government of the Kingdom of the Serbs, Croats and Slovenes considers the treaties and conventions concluded between the Kingdom of Serbia and the United States as applicable to the whole territory of the Kingdom of the Serbs, Croats and Slovenes as constituted at the present.

m.60H/3

The Secretary of State presents his compliments
to the Minister of the Serbs, Croats, and Slovenes
and has the honor to inquire whether it is the view
of the Government of the Kingdom of the Serbs, Croats,
and Slovenes that the treaties and conventions which
were in force between the Kingdom of Serbia and the
United States at the time of the formation of the
Kingdom of the Serbs, Croats and Slovenes remain applicable to those parts of the new Kingdom which were
not comprised within the territories of the former
Kingdom of Serbia.

The inquiry is made in particular with reference
to the convention of former and navigation concluded
on October 14, 1881; the consular convention concluded
on October 14, 1881; and the extradition treaty concluded
on October 25, 1901.

The Honorable

H. Percival Dodge,

American Minister,

Belgrade.

Sir:

The Department has received your confidential despatch No. 244, of September 2, 1924, reporting that the Yugoslav Government is preparing drafts for a commercial treaty, consular and extradition conventions, and a convention for judicial assistance, which it intends to submit through the Legation for negotiation with the United States.

Note is made of the statement made to you by the Director of the Treaties section of the Foreign Office that the Yugoslav Government has made progress in the consideration of the naturalization convention proposed by this Government and that the delay in the matter has been due to a desire to await the passage of the new Yugoslav nationality law, which it was expected would be presented to the Parliament during the next session.

On September 23, 1924, the Yugoslav Chargé d'Affaires ad interim informed the Department that the Government of the Kingdom of the Serbs, Croats and Slovenes

Slovenes considered the treaties and conventions in force between the United States and the former ! Kingdom of Serbia as applicable to the whole territory of the Kingdom of the Serbs, Croats and Slovenes as at present constituted. In view of this assurance and in much as the extradition convention concluded by the United States and Serbia on October 25, 1901, is, in the opinion of this Government, a modern and comprehensive convention, the Department before considering the negotiation of a new extradition convention would desire to be more fully informed as to what useful purpose would thus be served.

The United States is not a party to any convention providing for mutual judicial assistance and the Department is not sufficiently informed as to the proposals which might be made by the Yugoslav Government in a draft of such a convention to be able to indicate whether it would be viewed favorably by this Government. As a help to the Department in reaching a decision on this matter, you are requested to transmit a copy of any such convention which the Yugoslav Government may already have concluded or to request of the Foreign Office a synopsis of the principal features of the draft which it is proposed to submit to the United States. You should make it understood, however, that this Government holds, for the

clusion of a convention providing for mutual judicial
assistance.

This Government will be glad in due course to
negotiate with the Yugoslav Government for the conclusion
of a treaty to replace the convention of commerce and
navigation and the consular convention concluded by the
United States and Serbia on October 14, 1881.

For reasons indicated below, however, the Department considers that it might be desirable if definite
action with respect to beginning such negotiations were
postponed for a time. A general treaty of commerce,
navigation and consular rights concluded by the United
States with Germany on December 8, 1923, is under consideration by the Senate. In the event that the
Senate gives its approval to the ratification of that
Convention, this Government probably would desire to
negotiate a treaty with Yugoslavia on the same general
lines with, of course, such alterations as particular
local conditions may make necessary. The treaty signed
by the United States and Germany contains provisions
for the regulation of the consular establishments of the
two countries which would render a separate convention
to cover consular matters unnecessary between the
United States and any country with which a similar
convention may be concluded. Pending action by the
Senate on the treaty between the United States and

Germany, the Department desires to defer the negotiation of commercial treaties and consular conventions with other countries.

It would be helpful, therefore, if, without disclosing the suggestion which has been put forward by the Yugoslav Government for the conclusion of a new commercial treaty and consular convention with the United States, you could discreetly bring it about that the submission of drafts to you be deferred for a short period. Should the matter not be raised further by the Yugoslav Government, you may consider it best not to make any mention of possible negotiations for a treaty of commerce of a consular convention until the Department instructs you further.

In case a situation develops which makes the negotiation of a general treaty of commerce, navigation and consular rights between the United States and Yugoslavia desirable, the Department would see no objection to the negotiations being conducted through the Legation at Belgrade, as the Yugoslav Government apparently desires.

I am, Sir,

Your obedient servant,

For the Secretary of State:

The Honorable
The Secretary of State,
Washington.

Sir:

I have the honor to acknowledge the receipt on the 29th ultimo of your instruction No. 543, File No. 860P.03/12 dated January 4th last, in reply to my despatch No. 341 of September 2nd, 1924, reporting that the Yugoslav Government was preparing drafts of a Commercial Treaty, Consular and Extradition Conventions and a Convention for Judicial Assistance which it intended to submit for negotiation with the United States.

In reply I beg to state that I have had a conversation with Dr. ...., the Director of the Treaties Section of the

as directed by your instruction, that the Government of the
United States holds, for the present, in reserve the decision
as to whether it will enter into negotiations for the conclusion of a Convention providing for mutual judicial assistance.
Regarding the negotiation of a Convention of Commerce
and Navigation and Consular Convention, I beg to state that
meeting Dr. Riza[?] a few days before the receipt of your
instruction, he informed me that he was drawing upon drafts
for these two Conventions. Upon the receipt of your [illegible]
tion, I accordingly thought it proper to tell to his [illegible]
tion the substance of that portion of it touching this [illegible]
Dr. Riza[?] replied that the Yugoslav-Italian treaty negotiations found in any case have referred him when submitting
his drafts to the legation the some time and that he would be
happy now to await the submission to his Government of a draft
for a general treaty of Commerce, navigation and consular
rights based upon the same general lines as those recently concluded between the United States and Germany.

I have the honor to be, Sir,

Your obedient servant,

[signature]

Joseph Dodge
[illegible] Minister

DEPARTMENT OF STATE

To whom these presents shall come, Greeting:

That the document hereunto annexed is a true and complete the translation of a note verbale dated May 19, 1934 from lav Ministry for Foreign Affairs to the American Legation de, which was transmitted to the Department of State osure to Despatch No. 127 of May 25, 1934 from the n Belgrade, the original of which is on file in the of State.

In testimony whereof, I, H. FREEMAN MATTHEWS, Acting Secretary of State, have hereunto caused the seal of the Department of State to be affixed and my name subscribed by the Authentication Officer of the said Department, at the city of Washington, in the District of Columbia, this ———————— third ———————— day of ———— February———— 1953.

H. Freeman Matthews
Acting Secretary of State.

By Barbara Hutchison
Authentication Officer, Department of State.

Ministry for Foreign Affairs.   from the Legation in Be -
                                  grade.

P.No. 13524 - IV.

Translation

Note verbale.

With reference to the American Legation's verbal note No. 59 of March 12, 1934, relating to a proposal made to conclude a supplemental agreement to the Convention for the Extradition of Criminals concluded between the Kingdom of Serbia and the United States on October 12/25, 1901, the Royal Ministry for Foreign Affairs has the honor to inform the Legation that in the opinion of the Royal Ministry of Justice the extradition of criminals for offenses mentioned in the aforementioned note is already provided for under Article II, No.7, of the above-cited Convention, which grants extradition for the following:

"Fraud or breach of trust committed by the manager, or a member or an official of a company, if such action is punishable under the laws of both countries, and if the amount of the sum, or the value of the property which was appropriated, amount to at least one thousand dinars or two hundred gold dollars."

According to this provision, it is not necessary that the act be punishable under the Penal Code,- it is sufficient that the punishment be prescribed by a special law.

As "crimes or offenses against bankruptcy laws" are punishable by virtue of the provisions of the Penal Code of the Kingdom (Article 344 and the following), it will be sufficient in each particular case, that the competent American authorities propound a legalized extract of the legislative provisions indicating that such crimes are also punished under the laws of the United States of America, and the extradition requested will, in such case, be granted according to the Convention for extradition of criminals of 1901, which is now in force.

Belgrade, May 19, 1934.

(Seal)

TOPICAL INDEX

TABLE OF AUTHORITIES CITED

MISCELLANEOUS

STATUTES

TEXTBOOKS

No. 13552

IN THE

United States Court of Appeals

FOR THE NINTH CIRCUIT

————

RAFO IVANCEVIC, Consul General of the Federal People's
Republic of Yugoslavia,

Appellant,

vs.

ANDRIJA ARTUKOVIC,

Appellee,

————

JAMES J. BOYLE, United States Marshal,

Appellant,

vs.

ANDRIJA ARTUKOVIC,

Appellee.

————

APPELLANTS' OPENING BRIEF.

————

Jurisdictional Statement.

This appeal is from an order of the United States District Court, Southern District of California granting a Writ of Habeas Corpus [R. p. 92] upon the petition of Appellee and for the release of Appellee upon bail pending appeal [R. p. 3]. Appellee was in the custody of the

United States Marshal, one of the Appellants herein, under a warrant of arrest issued by the United States Commissioner under a complaint in extradition filed by Rafo Ivancevic, as Consul-General of the Federal Peoples Republic of Yugoslavia, the other Appellant herein, seeking the return of Appellee to Yugoslavia for trial upon multiple murder charges.

Jurisdiction of the District Court is based upon Title 28, U. S. C. Sections 2241 *et seq.*

Jurisdiction of the Court of Appeals is based upon Title 28, U. S. C., Section 2253, as follows:

> "In a habeas corpus proceeding before a circuit or district judge, the final order shall be subject to review, on appeal, by the court of appeals for the circuit where the proceeding is had."

That the Consul-General may properly prosecute the appeal on behalf of his government as the real party in interest is based upon Rule 17(a), F. R. C. P., and on the case of *Ornelas v. Ruiz,* 161 U. S. 502 [see R. p. 104].

Extradition was sought under the terms of a treaty between the United States and Serbia for the mutual extradition of fugitives from justice signed at Belgrade October 25, 1901; ratification advised by the Senate January 27, 1902; ratified by the President March 7, 1902; ratified by Serbia, March 17, 1902; proclaimed May 17, 1902 (32 Stats., part 2, 1890). The text of said treaty is appended hereto as Appendix "A."

Statement of Case.

On August 29, 1951, a complaint in extradition was filed with the Honorable Howard V. Calverley, United States Commissioner for the Southern District of California by Appellant, Rafo Ivancevic, as Consul-General of the Federal Peoples' Republic of Yugoslavia. This complaint, which was subsequently amended, originally charged the Appellee Artukovic with twenty-three murders within the country of Yugoslavia and asked for his extradition under the terms of a treaty of extradition made between the United States of America and the Kingdom of Serbia in 1902 and alleged to be in full force and effect between the United States of America and the Federal People's Republic of Yugoslavia.

Appellee was arrested and a subsequent application for release on bail was denied by the Honorable United States Commissioner.

A petition for a writ of habeas corpus was filed with the United States District Court for the Southern District of California on September 12, 1951 [R. p. 3]. This petition originally sought nothing more than the release of petitioner upon bail pending the extradition hearing. However, at the suggestion of the District Court, an amended petition was filed in which the effectiveness of the extradition treaty was questioned as well as the sufficiency of the complaint in extradition.

At the commencement of the hearing upon the petition for a writ of habeas corpus, a formal appearance was filed upon behalf of Rafo Ivancevic, as Consul-General of the F. P. R. Y. [see R. p. 19] which was accepted by the Court [R. pp. 103-106].

A return to the Order to Show Cause on the petition for a writ was filed by the respondent, James J. Boyle, United States Marshal by the United States Attorney [R. p. 14].

During the course of hearings upon the petition and prior to the final decision of the Court, Appellee was released upon bail in the sum of $50,000 pending the final determination of the other issues presented [R. p. 289 *et seq.*].

Again, during the course of the hearings, an amended complaint in extradition was filed with the United States Commissioner, and a copy thereof presented to the District Court as Demanding Government's Exhibit H [R. p. 378]. Since this amended complaint charges Appellee with the murder of some 1277 persons (and in parallel counts with participation in such murders), repeating the list of names some three times in 24 similar counts and in a copy of the indictment or accusation filed in Yugoslavia and attached to the amended complaint, an order of this Honorable Court was obtained relieving Appellants from printing this material. The original exhibit is present in the Court's files.

During the course of the proceeding the position of the Consul-General of the Federal People's Republic of Yugoslavia was referred to by the Court and all parties as that of "the Demanding Government."

On behalf of the Demanding Government a certificate of the United States Secretary of State was filed as Exhibit DG.E [R. p. 362] stating that the provisions of the treaty of extradition in question which entered in force between the United States of America and the Kingdom of Serbia on June 12, 1902, continued in force and were applicable to the whole territory of the Kingdom of the Serbs, Croats and Slovenes, as constituted on December 1, 1938, and to the Kingdom of Yugoslavia, to which the name of the Kingdom was changed by a law of October 3, 1929; and further, that all of the provisions of said treaty continued in force and became applicable to the Federal People's Republic of Yugoslavia as proclaimed on November 29, 1945 and are presently in force between the United States of America and the Federal People's Republic of Yugoslavia.

A certificate of the Yugoslav Ambassador testifying to the present applicability of the treaty was also presented as Exhibit DG. F [R. p. 372].

During the course of argument and in memoranda filed with the District Court, counsel for all parties referred to various communications between diplomatic representatives of the United States of America and representatives of the Kingdom of the Serbs, Croats and Slovenes, the Kingdom of Yugoslavia, and the Federal People's Republic of Yugoslavia. All of these communications, official in nature, come within the rule of judicial notice. Several of them are set out as footnotes to the District Court's opinion [R. p. 35], and others will be referred to in the course of this argument.

It was contended by counsel for the Demanding Government that the treaty rights and obligations of the Kingdom of Serbia have continued uninterruptedly in force and effect and enure to, and are binding on the Federal People's Republic of Yugoslavia *for the reason*

*that a duly established treaty survives and continues to be
in force and effect notwithstanding any subsequent enlargement in the territory, or change in the form of the
government of either of the contracting powers and
enures to, and is binding on a successor state.*

It was further contended by counsel for the Demanding Government that the question whether a treaty survives changed conditions is political in its nature, and that
such a political decision as evidenced by the Exhibits
referred to above (and by other official correspondence)
when made by the Executive Branch of the Government
will not be overruled by the courts.

On July 14, 1952, the Court rendered its opinion [see
R. p. 35, *et seq*]. The opinion held that the Treaty of
Extradition with Serbia did not survive the formation
of the Kingdom of the Serbs, Croats and Slovenes in
1918.

On July 31, 1952, the Court entered its order granting
the petition for a Writ of Habeas Corpus, releasing the
Appellee and fixing bail in the amount of $5,000 pending
appeal [R. p. 92].

Notice of Appeal was filed by the Appellant Ivancevic,
as Consul-General on August 13, 1952 [R. p. 94]. On
September 29, 1952, Notice of Appeal on behalf of the
Respondent James J. Boyle, United States Marshal, was
filed by the United States Attorney [R. p. 99].

Thereafter, counsel for Appellant Ivancevic was substituted for the United States Attorney as attorney for
the United States Marshal [R. p. 399]. Both appeals
were perfected by the filing of designations of record and
statements of points on appeal, both in the District Court
and Court of Appeals.

Forword.

The matters presented by this appeal are of grave international importance. Not only is the entire treaty structure between the United States of America and the Federal Peoples' Republic of Yugoslavia affected, but the entire treaty structure of the United States with other nations is involved.

The question presented is that of the survival of treaty rights and obligations through a change in the form of government or territory of either of the Contracting Powers. Since almost every country with which the United States has treaty relations has been affected by changes in form of government and in boundaries since the conclusion of the treaties, the importance is readily seen.

Furthermore, since the succession of treaties through changes in the outward or inward form of International Persons is a matter recognized and accepted in International Law, a change in this rule, as contemplated by the decision of the District Court, might lead to unpredictable complications and consequences.

Questions on Appeal.

Actually the only question is whether Extradition Treaty which entered into force on June 12, 1902 between the United States of America and the Kingdom of Serbia is still in force between the United States of America and the Federal People's Republic of Yugoslavia. In its opinion, the District Court held that the creation of the Kingdom of the Serbs, Croats and Slovenes in 1918 terminated all treaty rights and obligations then existing between the Kingdom of Serbia and the United States.

Inherent in this question are two others, one purely of law, the second involving factual history relating to the *status* of Serbia through its transition into the Kingdom of the Serbs, Croats and Slovenes, the Kingdom of Yugoslavia, and the Federal People's Republic of Yugoslavia. These are as follows:

(a) Is the survival of treaty rights and obligations as affected by changes in the form of government or territory of the other contracting power, a political question to be decided by the Executive Branch of the United States Government, and is such a political decision of the Executive Branch controlling upon the courts?

(b) Did the Kingdom of Serbia retain its juridical entity in the formation in 1918 of the Kingdom of the Serbs, Croats and Slovenes, and/or did the Kingdom of the Serbs, Croats and Slovenes succeed the Kingdom of Serbia in such manner that treaties entered into by the Kingdom of Serbia survived and continued to be in force and effect with respect to the Kingdom of the Serbs, Croats and Slovenes?

SUMMARY OF ARGUMENT.

I.

The general rule of International Law is that treaty rights and obligations survive changes in territory and forms of government of either of the contracting powers.

(1) Territorial changes.

(2) Changes in form of government.

II.

The Kingdom of the Serbs, Croats and Slovenes was the successor to the Kingdom of Serbia, and as such the latter's treaty rights and obligations adhered to it.

(1) The formation of the Kingdom of the Serbs, Croats and Slovenes.

(2) Official interchange of correspondence between representatives of the Kingdom of Serbia, the United States of America and the Kingdom of the Serbs, Croats and Slovenes.

(3) Recapitulation of points indicating survival of juridical entity of Serbia.

III.

Questions of the survival in force and effect of treaties notwithstanding territorial and governmental changes, and the succession of states to treaty rights and obligations are political questions upon which the decision of the Executive Branch of the Government is controlling.

(1) The rule of Political Decision.

(2) Evidence of the Political Decision.

(3) Action taken pursuant to the Political Decision.

IV.

The question of Bail and Conclusion.

ARGUMENT.

I.

The General Rule of International Law Is That Treaty Rights and Obligations Survive Changes in Territory and Forms of Government of Either of the Contracting Powers.

The following authorities are cited in support of the contention by Appellants that treaty rights and obligations survive territorial changes of a state and changes in the form of government within a state.

1. Territorial changes:

"Mere territorial changes, whether by increase or by diminution, do not, so long as the identity of the state is preserved, affect the continuity of its existence or the obligations of its treaties."

> 1 *Moore, Digest of International Law* (1906), p. 248.

"It may be stated as a general principle that the territory of the annexed or incorporated state becomes impressed with the treaties of the acquiring state so far as locally applicable, to be determined in each instance by the character of the particular treaty and the nature of the union. The former Republic of Texas, upon its admission as a State into the Union on terms of equality with the other States, undoubtedly became bound and privileged by all the treaties of the United States of which it had become an integral part."

> *Crandall, Treaties: Their Making and Enforcement* (2d Ed., 1916).[1]

---

[1]Many other authorities on this point are set forth at length in the brief *amicus* filed on behalf of the United States Government. It would needlessly add to the work of the Court to repeat these citations here, but Appellants join in the views therein expressed and adopt such authorities as their own.

Indicative of the attitude taken toward an extension of territory by union are the views expressed concerning the formation of the Kingdom of Italy. This, we contend, is very similar to the situation presented by the union to Serbia of the other territories inhabited by Yugoslavs.

Lombardy, Tuscany, Emilia, Parma and the Kingdom of the two Sicilies united with Sardinia to form the Italian Kingdom between 1859 and 1861. The Italian Government took the position that only Sardinia, of all those states, had maintained its juridical entity and that the treaties of Sardinia alone survived the union, and were considered to have been extended to the whole territory. This was on the theory that the existing State of Sardinia, serving as a nucleus (*sic*—Serbia) had expanded into a larger State into which a number of others had been absorbed.

On this point, the Harvard Research into the Law of Treaties (A. J. I. L., Supp., Pt. III, Vol. 29 (1935), p. 1073) states:

> "The courts of both Italy and France held that the treaty of March 4, 1760, concluded between France and Sardinia, relative to the execution of judgments, survived the formation of the Kingdom of Italy and was applicable throughout the Kingdom of Italy and binding on both countries—this on the theory that the Italian Kingdom was merely an expansion or enlargement of the State of Sardinia. . . . For the French decisions, see, among others, the cases of *La Moderazione c. La Chambre d'Assurances* (Court of Paris, 1879), *Mantil c. Pompilis* Tribunal Cor. of the Seine, 1883, 10 *Journal du Droit International Prive*, 1883, p. 500), and *Vincent c. Bardini, Dalloz,* 1901, 2.2257 and the note

thereon by Pic. See also the decision of the Court of Montpellier of July 10, 1872, in the case of *Iconomidis v. Coude* (6 Journal du Droit International Prive, 1879, p. 69), where it was emphasized that additions to the territory of a State have no effect upon the State's treaty obligation. . . . For the Italian Jurisprudence, see, among others, the decision of the Italian Court of Cassation of December 3, 1927, in the case of *Gastaldi v. Lepage Hemery* (9 *Revista di Diritto Internazionals,* 3d. ser. 1930, p. 102), where the survival of the treaty of 1760 between France and Sardinia was affirmed, on the principle that the Italian State was merely an expansion of the Kingdom of Sardinia. See also the decisions of various Italian Courts cited or summarized in 5 *Journal du Droit International Privé* (1878), p. 244, and 6 *ibid.* (1879), p. 305 ff.

"It may be added that the Permanent Court of International Justice in the *Case of the Free Zones of Upper Savoy and the District of Gex,* recognized that the treaty of Turin of March 16, 1816, between Sardinia and Switzerland survived the transformations which resulted in the formation of the Italian Kingdom. Publications of the *P. C. I. J.,* Series A, No. 22, p. 18 and Series A, No. 24, p. 17.

"The conclusion deducible from the practice in the case of the formation of the Italian Kingdoms is that when a State enlarges its territorial domain by the annexation of other states, its treaties continue to bind it."

At the Paris Peace Conference in 1919, the Great Powers accorded to Serbia a position, juridically speaking, with respect to the Kingdom of the Serbs, Croats and Slovenes, parallel to that of Sardinia in the Kingdom of Italy. Thus, in the first instance, delegates bearing the credentials of the Kingdom of the Serbs, Croats and Slovenes were received only as representatives of Serbia. Later during the conference they were recognized as representing the Kingdom of the Serbs, Croats and Slovenes as the state to which the international rights and obligations of the former Kingdom of Serbia enured.[2]

Attention must be drawn at this point to a statement in the memorandum opinion of the District Court which seems rather specious. In his attempt to differentiate the rule of political decision in the case of *Terlinden v. Ames,* 184 U. S. 270, 22 S. Ct. 484, 46 L. Ed. 534, the court calls attention to the fact that the treaty *there* involved provided that it would be applied "to any other state of the Germanic Confederation, which may hereafter declare its accession thereto." The Trial Judge stated [R. p. 55]:

> "No provision is found in the treaty with Serbia of 1902 as that which existed in the treaties under consideration in *Terlinden v. Ames,* extending the terms to additional territory. And *it must be assumed that had the parties intended that the extradition treaty with Serbia of 1902 should apply to persons residing in territories which might subsequently come under the jurisdiction or sovereignty of Serbia, that the parties would have specifically stated that in the treaty.* The omission cannot be supplied by either Executive or Judicial construction." (Emphasis added.)

Since it is the generally accepted rule that an increase or decrease of territory does not affect the continued

---

[2]Temperley: A History of the Peace Conference of Paris, Vol. 5, p. 158.

existence of a treaty as long as the entity of the "international person" survives; or, juridical continuity is established between the personality of the old and new state, it would seem the more correct assumption that in the absence of a contrary provision, the parties intended that the accepted rule would apply and that the treaty would survive a change in territorial limits. The conclusion of the Trial Judge that the absence of a specific provision for continued validity prevents the survival of the treaty in the event of territorial or governmental change is not supported by any legal authority. On the contrary, it is a generally accepted rule that every juridical provision is to be interpreted in the sense of the general rule and not in that of an exception.

If the reasoning of the Trial Judge were accepted, then in the absence of a specific clause, no treaty right or obligation would survive the slightest change in the territorial boundaries of either of the contracting powers, and this would result in an absurdity, for treaties are made under the assumption of the state's stability and without regard to any possible changes in territory or form of government.

In any event, the reliance of the Court below on the provisions of the Prussian treaty referred to in *Terlinden v. Ames supra,* is misplaced. That was a treaty between the United States and one member of a group of sovereign and independent states joined together in a loose confederation. That such a treaty should specifically provide for the accession to it of other members of the confederation, does not support the contention that a treaty between two states loses its validity, in the absence of specific provision in the event of territorial or governmental changes resulting from union or otherwise.

Accordingly, Appellants urge that treaty rights and obligations survive territorial and governmental changes where the juridical personality of the Contracting Power continues or is succeeded to.

2. Changes in Form of Government.

It is also the accepted rule that treaties survive changes in the form of government of one of the contracting Powers.

The point is perhaps academic here, as the only change in the form of government in Yugoslavia was upon the formation of the present Federal People's Republic in 1945. The Court made no point of this in its decision which dealt only with the survival of the treaty in 1919 through the formation of the Kingdom of the Serbs, Croats and Slovenes. The point is well supported in the texts set out at length in the *amicus* brief filed on behalf of the United States Government, and in the interests of brevity will not be repeated here.

On this point, however, appellants wish to cite the case of *The Sapphire,* 78 U. S. 164. The case involved a collision between the French transport Euryale and the Sapphire. A libel was filed in the name of Emperor Napoleon III, then Emperor of France, as owner. During the proceedings Napoleon was deposed. One of the issues was the possible abatement of the action. The Court stated [p. 168]:

> "The reigning sovereign represents the national sovereignty and that sovereignty is continuous and perpetual, residing in the proper successors of the

sovereign for the time being. . . . On his (Napoleon's) deposition, the sovereignty does not change, but merely the person or persons in whom it resides. . . . *A deed to or treaty with a sovereign as such enures to his successors in the government of the country."*

Grotius, *The Rights of War and Peace* (Washington: M. Walter Dunn, 1901) pp. 120, 121 (Lib. II, cap. IX, Sec. VI), states:

"Nor does it make any difference in the argument, whatever the form of government may be, whether regal, aristocratical or democratical. The Roman people for instance was the same, whether under Kings, consuls or emperors. . . . It is evident that a state, which from a commonwealth has become a regal government, is answerable for the debts incurred before that change."

Also at pp. 184, 185 (Lib. II, cap. XVI, Sec. XVI):

"The nature of personal and real treaties . . . may properly be examined in this place. Indeed in all transactions with a free people, the engagements entered into with them are of a real nature; because the subject of them is a permanent thing. So permanent, that, although a republican be changed into a regal government, a treaty will remain in force. . . . But if a treaty be made with a King . . . it does not consequently follow that it is to be considered only as a personal and not a real treaty. For the name of a person may be inserted in a treaty . . . to point out the contracting parties. And this will be still more evident, if, as is usual in most treaties a clause is annexed declaring it to be perpetual, or made for the good of the Kingdom, or with the King himself and his successors, and it will also be considered a real treaty. . . .

"Other forms too besides those already named, and the subject itself, will frequently supply no improbable grounds for conjecture. But if the conjectures are equal on both sides, it will remain that favourable treaties are supposed to be real or permanent. . . . All treaties of peace or commerce are favourable."

It should be called to the attention of the Court that the treaty in question by its very terms [see Art. I, Appx. A] is binding on the government of Serbia (not merely on its King) and that it specifically provides [Art. XI] that it shall continue in force "for a period of six months after either of the contracting *governments* shall have given notice of a purpose to terminate it."

The Trial Judge apparently took the view [R. p. 57] that all treaty rights and obligations of Serbia terminated in 1919 unless the Kingdom of the Serbs, Croats and Slovenes was merely a "continuation" of the Kingdom of Serbia. Concluding that the Kingdom of the Serbs, Croats and Slovenes was not such a "continuation," but a "new" Kingdom, the Court below held that it neither acquired the rights nor became subject to the obligations of treaties previously entered into by Serbia. What the Trial Judge meant by "continuation" is not clear, but he apparently felt that if more than a change in name (*e.g.,* Persia to Iran, Siam to Thailand, Chosen to Korea) or relatively minor territorial and population accretions (*e.g.,* the transfer of certain Czech territory to Germany as the result of the Munich Agreement) was involved, a "new" state, free of treaty obligations and shorn of treaty rights was necessarily created.

This, appellants submit, is not the proper view. Treaties will survive, and continue in force and effect, under accepted principles of international law, where the contracting power retains its juridical entity, notwithstanding union with or absorption of extensive territories and populations, or where the resulting State is the successor to the contracting power.

II.

The Kingdom of the Serbs, Croats and Slovenes Has Juridical Continuity With the Former Kingdom of Serbia and Accordingly the Treaty Rights and Obligations of Serbia Were Transferred to the State of the SCS.

(1) The Formation of the Kingdom of Serbs, Croats and Slovenes.

As the Treaty here in issue was entered into in 1901 by the United States and Serbia and the demanding government herein is the Federal Peoples' Republic of Yugoslavia, it may be of assistance to the Court briefly to outline at this point the historical points marking the transition from Serbia to Yugoslavia.

Serbia (or Servia, which was then the common spelling) was in 1901 an independent, sovereign state. One of several contiguous areas populated by Yugo, or South, Slavs (Serbs, Croats, Slovenes, Macedonians, Montenegrins are South /or Yugo/ Slav nations), Serbia's absolute independence was recognized by the Treaty of Berlin in 1878 after centuries of Turkish rule and dependence. As a result of the Balkan Wars of 1912-13, Macedonia was also liberated from the Turks, and the larger part of that area was annexed to Serbia. In 1901, the only other Yugoslav people to have achieved independence were the Montenegrins, who had in fact maintained their independence through the centuries notwithstanding the efforts of the Turks to conquer them. However, Montenegro's independence was not actually recognized until the Treaty of Berlin in 1878. All other Yugoslav regions continued under foreign rule until 1918, as follows:

(1) Bosnia and Herzegovina were a Turkish province until 1908, although pursuant to the Treaty of Berlin, they had become an Austrian mandate in 1878 and were occupied and governed by that country. In 1908, Bosnia and Herzegovina were annexed by the Austro-Hungarian Monarchy, of which they became an integral part with limited autonomy in local matters. Klobuk, the village in which the Appellee was born in 1900 is in Herzegovina, not Croatia as the District Court [R. 49] states.

(2) Croatia and Slavonia, long under Hungarian domination, were reunited with Hungary under the so-called "Compromise" in 1868, after twenty years of separation, resulting from the Hungarian revolt against Austria in 1848. Integral parts of the Austro-Hungarian Monarchy, they were permitted only limited autonomy in local matters.

(3) Dalmatia and Carniola, and Carinthia, Styria and Istria (we are concerned only with parts of the latter three) were Austrian provinces and integral parts of the Austro-Hungarian Monarchy enjoying various degree of restricted autonomy in local matters.

(4) Vojvodina (Banat, Backa and Baranja), Medjumurje and Prekomurje were incorporated into Hungary and as such were integral parts of the Austro-Hungarian Monarchy.

The unification of the Yugoslavs was effected in 1918 (upon the disintegration of the Austro-Hungarian Monarchy resulting from World War I) by the voluntary *union with Serbia* of Montenegro and the regions of the former Austro-Hungarian Monarchy referred to above. The unified state of the Yugoslavs was first called the Kingdom of the Serbs, Croats and Slovenes, later the Kingdom of Yugoslavia, and since World War II, the Federal People's Republic of Yugoslavia.

Although the unification of the Yugoslavs into one nation with Serbia as its nucleus was achieved upon the defeat of the Austro-Hungarian Empire, it was in no sense a creation of the victors in their own interests. On the contrary, the Yugoslav unity realized in 1918 was the culmination of the centuries of persistent and continuous struggle which the South Slavs had waged against foreign conquerors, the Venetians, Turks, Austrians and Hungarians. In the course of their long struggle for liberty they had become conscious of their mutual interests and of the necessity for ultimate unity if they were to maintain the independence they were certain some day to win. This consciousness found expression in common cultural movements and political cooperation to the extent permitted by the circumstances. The partial independence won by Serbia in two uprisings (1804 and 1815) and the complete independence finally achieved by that country in 1878, gave the Yugoslav movement for liberty and union not only a great impetus, but a rallying point. A free Serbia provided the core around which Yugoslav independence and unity could be built. But the goal was to be achieved slowly, for not only were there the powerful conquerors to defeat, but the Balkans, on the cross-roads between East and West, were subject to other pressures and interests. However that may be, by the beginning of the twentieth century, the accomplishment of Yugoslav freedom and unity was considered an imminent task, and the successes of Servia and Montenegro in the Balkan Wars of 1912-13 brought both encouragement and a sense of reality to these twin ideals.

This course of development is reflected in the broad activity on the part of all Yugoslav peoples during World War I. Thus, the Serbian Government announced on December 7, 1914, that it considered the war as being "a struggle for the liberation and unification of all our unliberated brethren, Serbs, Croats and Slovenes" (F. Sisic, Documents on the Creation of the Kingdom of the Serbs, Croats and Slovenes (Zagreb, 1920) 10). The same aim was repeated on August 23, 1915 (*id.* 42). This view was also expressed by Yugoslav leaders who had fled Austria-Hungary and taken refuge in Allied countries. Thus, in refuting a statement of Count Tisza, Hungary's Premier, the Croatian Committee in Rome, forerunner of the Yugoslav Committee organized in London in 1915, announced through the press that Tisza's "efforts to separate the cause of the Croatian people from that of the Serbian people will remain futile" and that "the Croats have always declared that their ultimate goals were identical with the goals of their Serbian brethren" (*id.* 13). The Yugoslav Committee, organized in London by political and other refugees from Austria-Hungary and supported by Yugoslav immigrants everywhere, on May 6, 1915 addressed a Memoire to the governments of France, Great Britain and Russia in which it stated that "the struggle of Serbia and Montenegro is not a struggle of conquest to expand their borders; these two Serbian states are protagonists in the liberation of all Yugoslavs and their task is the task of all of us" (*id.* 25). More specifically, on December 18, 1916, upon the accession of Karl of Hapsburg to the thrones of Austria-Hungary, the Yugoslav Committee proclaimed that "all those territories inhabited by people of the same blood but bearing different names, the Serbs, Croats and Slovenes, should be taken from the Hapsburg dynasty and united with the Kingdom of Serbia" (*id.* 84).

In July, 1917, representatives of the Yugoslav Committee and of the Serbian Government met on the Island of Corfu and discussed "all questions pertaining to the future of a unified state of Serbs, Croats and Slovenes." Out of this meeting came the Corfu Declaration of July 20, 1917, which reaffirmed "the only and inalienable demand of our people * * * the basis of the principle of free self-determination of peoples, to be liberated from all foreign enslavement and united in one free, national and independent state." On July 29, 1917, the Montenegrin Committee for National Unification announced its acceptance in full of the Corfu Declaration and the union of Montenegro with a united Yugoslav nation (*id.* 100). Freedom and union in a Yugoslav state was the unalterable demand, and when on January 9, 1918, Lloyd George proposed to the British Parliament the federalization of Austria-Hungary as a possible solution of the problem, the Yugoslav Committee rejected his suggestion and confirmed its irrevocable position as set out in the Corfu Declaration (*id.* 112-3).

Meanwhile, Yugoslavs within Austria-Hungary were not quiescent. Thus, on January 31, 1918, the Yugoslav Club, which consisted of Yugoslav deputies in the Austrian Parliament, demanded the recognition of the right "of self-determination of peoples especially regarding the question of whether they desire a free state and the form in which they want it established" (*id.*, 120). The time of this demand is especially significant as it followed closely upon the capitulation of Russia to the Central Powers and peace negotiations at Brest-Litovsk. More specifically, on March 3, 1918, a conference of forty-three Croatian, Serbian and Slovenian political leaders in Austria-Hungary announced that "we demand our national independence and a state of Slovenes, Croats and Serbs founded on demoncratic principles" (*id.*, 126).

By the middle of 1918, the movement in Austria-Hungary toward Yugoslav unification began to take a more concrete form. On August 17, 1918, a National Committee was organized in Ljubljana in Slovenia, "as part of the general Yugoslav Committee." On October 6, 1918, the National Council of Slovenes, Croats and Serbs was established in Zagreb in Croatia as "the political body representing all Slovenes, Croats and Serbs" within the Austro-Hungarian Monarchy and its announced program was the "unification * * * into a national, free and independent state of Slovenes, Croats and Serbs, with a democratic form of government (*id.*, 174). The membership of the Council included representatives of all political parties of all the Yugoslav provinces or Austria-Hungary except Vojvodina.

On October 19, 1918, the National Council rejected Emperor Karl's proposal to reorganize the Austro-Hungarian Monarchy on federal lines and ten days later proclaimed the establishment of the "state of Slovenes, Croats and Serbs" (*id.*, 211). The same day the Croatian Sabor (Assembly) declared the independence of Croatia and Slavonia from Austria-Hungary and their adherence to the "common national sovereign state of Slovenes, Croats and Serbs on the entire ethnographic territory of those people" as the supreme authority of which the National Council was recognized (*id.*, 195, 196, 201). On November 8, 1918, the Serbian government, by an agreement reached at Geneva, recognized the National Council as "the lawful government of the Serbs, Croats and Slovenes dwelling in territory of the Austro-Hungarian Monarchy" (*id.*, 233). On November 24, 1918, the National Council resolved to "proclaim the unification of the State of the Slovenes, Croats and Serbs * * * with the Kingdom of Serbia and Montenegro into a unified State of Serbs, Croats and Slovenes" (*id.*, 255, 256). On November 26, 1918 the Great National Assembly of Montenegro submitted to the Serbian government its decision to unite with Serbia and to become a part of the State of Serbs, Croats and Slovenes. At the same time the Great National Council of Vojvodina, too, passed the same decision. On December 1, 1918 the unification of the Yugoslav people with Serbia was officially announced in Belgrade.

The subsequent forging of a unified Yugoslav state was not without its difficulties, for there naturally were differences of opinion with respect to the principles which should underlie the state and the organization of its government. However, there was no difference of opinion with respect to the basic principle—unification.

The foregoing survey shows clearly that during the course of World War I not only Serbia, which was one of the Allies, participated in the creation of the state of

Serbs, Croats and Slovenes, but also that representatives of Yugoslav peoples under Austro-Hungarian rule played a great role in, and made a major contribution to the unification of the South Slavs into one nation with Serbia. In this connection it will be noted that while at the outset the leadership was taken on behalf of the Yugoslav peoples in Austria-Hungary by exiles living elsewhere, in the last stages of the war they were joined by Yugoslavs who had remained in Austria-Hungary. The position of Serbia as a sovereign state enabled her to play in the unification of the Yugoslav peoples a role similar to that which Piemont (Sardinia) had played in the unification of the Italian nation.

In analyzing the historic development of the unification of Yugoslavia, the District Court made a number of inaccurate statements, which require rectification. We have already referred to the fact that Klobuk, where the Appellee was born in 1900, is in Herzegovina and not Croatia. At the time of the Appellee's birth, Herzegovina, as already indicated, was a Turkish province under Austrian-Hungarian mandate. Herzegovina is not, and was at no time a part of Croatia. In stating above that after the Balkan wars of 1912-13, the larger part of Macedonia was incorporated into Serbia, we have already indicated the error of the District Court in stating that Macedonia became part of Greece [R. p. 50].

The Court was also in error in stating that the National Council of Croats, Slovenes and Serbs, representing Yugoslavs within the boundaries of the Austro-Hungarian Monarchy also included representatives of Serbia. Serbia was never represented on this Council [R. p. 51].

The Court also was in error in stating that the United States in February, 1919, recognized the Serb-Croat-Slovene state as consisting of "all the Serbian, Croatian and Slovenian provinces within * * * the former Austro-Hungarian Monarchy and Montenegro" [R. p. 52]. Actually the United States welcomed the "union of the Serbian, Croatian and Slovenian provinces within the boundaries of the former Austro-Hungarian Monarchy *to Serbia*" and recognized "the Serbian legation as the legation of the Serbs, Croatians and Slovenes" (1 Hackworth, Digest of International Law, 221). Thus, the Court disregarded the juridically relevant fact that the creation of the state of the Serbs, Croats and Slovenes resulted from the union of the Yugoslav provinces of Austria-Hungary and Montenegro *with Serbia,* a sovereign, independent and internationally recognized state, which could juridically survive the unification. The Court avoids mentioning Serbia to which precisely the union was accomplished and the international juridical system of which survived becoming the international juridical system of the united Serb-Croat-Slovene State.[3]

---

[3]The foregoing material dealing with the formation of the Kingdom of the Serbs, Croats and Slovenes was prepared and submitted for inclusion in the brief by the Yugoslav Foreign Office. The reference from which the source material was taken, *F. Sisic, Documents on the Creation of the Kingdom of the Serbs, Croats and Slovenes* (Zagreb, 1920), apparently is available only in the Library of Congress. No. D651,Y 885 (Ferdinand Sisic: Dokumenti o postanku kraljevine Srba, Hrvata i Slovenaca, Zagreb, 1920).

(2) Official Interchange of Correspondence.

The Government of the United States was formally and officially advised by the Government of the Kingdom of Serbia of the development leading to the formation of the Serb-Croat-Slovene state by means of the following communications addressed to the Secretary of State by the Serbian Chargé d'Affaires in Washington:

(This and the succeeding communications appear as footnotes to the lower court's opinion beginning at page 83 of the Record. It appears in an official publication entitled Foreign Relations of the United States, 1919, Vol. II, Publication No. 661, Department of State, Government Printing Office, 1934.)

No. 176

Washington, November 11, 1918.

"Your Excellency: I have the honor to inform your excellency that the Serbian Government has recognized the National Council in Zagreb as the legitimate representative of the Serbians, Croatians and Slovenes who are residing within the boundaries of the former Austro-Hungarian Monarchy until the definite organization of one state which will comprise all Serbians, Croatians and Slovenes, when the Serbian Government and the National Council will create one common government who will protect the rights of the nation of all Serbians, Croatians and Slovenes.

"Until the organization of this Government Mr. Troumbitch, President of the Yugoslav Committee in London, has been entrusted with the mandate to represent the National Council in Zagreb with the Allied Governments.

"In bringing the above to the knowledge of Your Excellency I beg to present that the Serbian Government anticipates that the United States Government will recognize the National Council in Zagreb, the members of whom have been elected by the Parliament, as the legitimate government of the Yugoslavs (Serbians, Croatians and Slovenes) living within the boundaries of the former Austro-Hungarian Monarchy, and consider that government and its army as an ally.

"With renewed assurances, (etc.)

Y. Simitch."

Washington, undated

(Received January 6, 1919).

"Mr. Secretary: I am instructed by my Government to submit herewith the following communication:

"In accordance with the *decision* of the Central Committee *of the National Council of Zagreb which represents the State of all the Serbian, Croatian and Slovene provinces within the boundaries of the former Austro-Hungarian Monarchy,* a special Delegation has arrived at Belgrade on the 1st of December. This Delegation by one (a) solemn address, presented to his Highness the Crown Prince, has proclaimed the Union of all the Serbian, Croatian and Slovene provinces of the former Dualist Monarchy into one single State *with the Kingdom of Serbia* under the Dynasty of His Majesty King Peter and under the regency of the Crown Prince Alexander. In reply to this address His Royal Highness the Crown Prince has proclaimed the Union of Serbia with the above mentioned independent State

of Slovenes, Croats and Serbs into one single Kingdom: 'Kingdom of the Serbs, Croats and Slovenes',
His Highness has accepted the regency and will
form a common Government. On the 17th of December His Royal Highness the Crown Prince received
in audience a delegation from Montenegro. This
delegation has submitted to His Highness on the
26th of November the decisions of the Great National
Assembly of Montenegro. By virtue of these decisions His Majesty King Nikolas I, and his dynasty
have been declared destitute of all the rights upon
(to) the throne of Montenegro and the Kingdom of
Montenegro, united to Serbia under the dynasty of
Karageorgevich, is included in the Kingdom of the
Serbs, Croats and Slovenes. His Royal Highness
the Crown Prince has declared that He accepts with
pleasure and thanks these decisions. A common government for the new Kingdom has been organized
on the 21st of December. The Legations, Consulates and other Missions of the' Kingdom of Serbia
will be the Legations, Consulates and other Missions
of the Kingdom of the Serbs, Croats and Slovenes.

"Bringing the above to the knowledge of the United
States Government, *the Serbian Government* is
strongly convinced that their communication will be
met sympathetically: The Union of all the nations
of the Serbs, Croats and Slovenes in one single state,
which results from the imprescriptible right of the
people to dispose of their destiny.

"I take (etc.)

Y. Simitch."

Official cognizance was given by the United States
to these events by two significant diplomatic communications. The first [R. p. 89] was a telegram from the

Commission to Negotiate Peace to the Acting Secretary of State, from Paris, February 6, 1919, reading as follows:

"The Secretary of State will give out on February 7th the following statement in regard to the union of the Jugo Slav peoples, which you may give out to the press immediately:

" 'On May 29, 1918, the Government of the United States expressed its sympathy for the nationalistic aspirations of the Jugo Slav race and on June 28 declared that all branches of the Slavish race should be completely freed from German and Austrian rule. After having achieved their freedom from foreign oppression the Jugo Slav(s) formerly under Austria-Hungarian rule on various occasions expressed the *desire to unite with the Kingdom of Serbia. The Serbian Government on its part has publically and officially accepted the union* of the Serb, Croat and Slovene peoples. The Government of the United States, therefore, welcomes the union while recognizing that the final settlement of territorial frontiers must be left to the Peace Conference for determination according to desires of the peoples concerned.' "

The second of these communications, even more significant as it constituted the official recognition by the United States Government of the union with Serbia of the provinces within the former Austro-Hungarian Empire and Montenegro is the following communication, dated February 10, 1919, addressed by the Acting Secretary of State to the Serbian Legation [R. p. 89]:

"Sir: I have the honor to acknowledge the receipt of an undated Note from the Serbian Charge d'Affaires stating that in accordance with a decision of the Central Committee of the National Council of Zagreb, representing the State of all the Serbian, Croatian and Slovene provinces within the boundaries of the former Austro-Hungarian Monarchy, the Serbian Crown Prince has proclaimed the union of all the Serbian, Croatian and Slovene provinces of the former Dualist Monarchy with the Kingdom of Serbia in a single state all under the title of 'Kingdom of the Serbs, Croats and Slovenes' and under the regency of the Crown Prince Alexander.

"The Department further notes the statement contained in the Note that in accordance with the decision of a body proclaiming itself the Great National Assembly of the Kingdom of Montenegro, His Majesty King Nikolas I, and his dynasty, had been deposed from the throne of that country and had decreed the union of Montenegro with the Kingdom of the Serbs, Croats and Slovenes, and that this decision had been accepted by His Royal Highness the Crown Prince of Serbia.

"The Department further notes the statement that the Legation of Serbia in the United States will, hereafter, *be known as the Legation of the Kingdom of the Serbs, Croatians and Slovenes.*

"In reply I have the honor to inform you that the Government of the United States *welcomes the union of the Serbian, Croatian and Slovene provinces within the boundaries of the former Austro-Hungarian Monarchy to Serbia and recognizes the Serbian Legation as the Legation of the Kingdom of the Serbs, Croatians and Slovenes.*

"In taking this action, however, the United States Government recognizes that the final settlement of territorial frontiers must be left to the Peace Conference for determination according to the desires of the peoples concerned."

It is this communication to which the Court apparently refers [see R. p. 52] in its statement that "In February 1919 the United States recognized the Serb-Croat-Slovene State as consisting of 'all the Serbian, Croatian and Slovene provinces within the countries of the former Austro-Hungarian Monarchy and Montenegro.'" This is entirely incorrect as can be seen from the documents referred to above.

Quite to the contrary, the Kingdom of Serbs, Croats and Slovenes, or the Serb-Croat-Slovene State, as the Court called it, consisted of:

1. The Kingdom of Serbia, an independent Kingdom, an ally of the United States in World War I, and an existing international juridical entity to which the other elements were joined.

2. The former Kingdom of Montenegro.

3. The provinces formerly under the domination of Austria-Hungary, populated by Serbs, Croats and Slovenes (Yugoslavs) and for this reason referred to as Serbian, Croatian and Slovene provinces of Austria-Hungary.

Appellants submit that a very different conclusion might be justified had the Kingdom of the Serbs, Croats and Slovenes been merely an amalgamation of the Yugoslav provinces liberated from the subjugation of Austria-Hungary in World War I. Then there would have been no existing International Person or entity with which they had merged, attached or united. But the true and undisputed fact is that the Kingdom of Serbia was an existing International Person, a juridical entity. To this state as a nucleus, the other Yugoslav people cleaved. That they were welcomed and accepted upon a basis of equality does not weaken the continuity, juridically speaking, of the International Person in altered form.

On September 10, 1919, a treaty was signed by representatives of the Principal Allied and Associated Powers and Serb-Croat-Slovene State, known as the Treaty of St. Germaine-en-Laye (on the protection of minorities) [see R. p. 58, 3 Malloy (Redmond) 3731, Sen. Doc. No. 348, 67th Cong., 4th Sess.]. Probably because of the recent refusal of the United States Senate to ratify the Treaty of Versailles, and because of the inclusion in it of material treating with the League of Nations, this Treaty of St. Germaine-on-Laye was never presented for ratification by the Senate. Lodge, *The Senate and the League of Nations* (Scribner, 1925, p. 303). It was ratified and became effective between the British Empire, France, Italy, Japan and the Serb-Croat-Slovene State.

This treaty provides in part that all treaties, etc., of Serbia shall *ipso facto* be binding upon the Serb-Croat-Slovene State.

The Trial Court in its opinion [R. p. 62] states that if these treaties automatically became binding as we contend, it would have been unnecessary to have put in such a provision.

But the recitals in the treaty also state that it is desired to free Serbia from certain specific treaty obligations in the Treaty of Berlin. Conversely, if the treaty obligations of Serbia did not survive, it would have been unnecessary to have relieved the Kingdom of the Serbs,

Croats and Slovenes of these obligations by the treaty of St. Germaine-en-Laye.

Appellants set forth at some length excerpts from this Treaty of St. Germaine-en-Laye. It is not contended, of course, that this treaty became effective with the United States of America and thus recreated or revived a terminated obligation. It is cited simply to show an open international recognition of:

1. The continuation of the juridical entity of Serbia into the enlarged state of the Serbs, Croats and Slovenes.

2. The *ipso facto* succession of treaty rights with Serbia.

In support of these contentions, we call the Court's attention to the following provisions of the separate (fourth) Instrument annexed to the Treaty of St. Germain-en-Laye:

"Whereas since the commencement of the year 1913 extensive territories have been added to the Kingdom of Serbia, and

"Whereas the Serb, Croat and Slovene peoples of the former Austro-Hungarian Monarchy have of their own free will determined to unite with Serbia in a permanent union for the purpose of forming a single sovereign independent State under the title of the Kingdom of the Serbs, Croats and Slovenes, and

"Whereas, the Prince Regent of Serbia and the Serbian Government have agreed to this union, and in consequence the Kingdom of the Serbs, Croats and Slovenes has been constituted and has assumed sovereignty over the territories inhabited by these peoples, and

"Whereas, it is necessary to regulate certain matters of international concern arising out of the said additions of territory and of this union, and

"Whereas, *it is desired to free Serbia from certain obligations which she undertook by the Treaty of Berlin of 1878* to certain Powers and to substitute for them obligations to the League of Nations, and

"Whereas, the Serb-Croat-Slovene State of its own free will desires to give to the populations of all territories included within the State, of whatever race, language or religion they may be, full guarantees that they shall continue to be governed in accordance with the principles of liberty and justice . . . ."

Chapter II, Article 12 of this Instrument provides further:

"Pending the conclusion of new treaties or conventions, *all treaties,* conventions, agreements and obligations *between Serbia,* on the one hand, *and any of the Principal Allied and Associated Powers,* on the other hand, which were in force on the 1st August, 1914, or which have since been entered into, *shall ipso facto be binding upon the Serb-Croat-Slovene State.*" (Emphasis supplied.)

This Instrument to the Treaty of St. Germain-en-Laye does not create the treaty rights of Serbia, nor does it recreate or revive a right which has ceased to exist. It simply recognizes them as an existing condition.

Webster's New International Dictionary (2d Ed.) defines *"ipso facto"* as follows: "By the fact or act itself; as the result of the mere act or fact; *by the very nature of the case."*

Reduced to these words this Instrument to the Treaty of St. Germain states: All treaties between Serbia and any of the Allied and Associated Powers . . . shall *by the very nature of the case* be binding upon the Serb-Croat-Slovene State.

The recital of a fact as existing does not *create* the fact, contrary to the conclusion of the Trial Judge.

The Trial Court took cognizance [R. p. 91] of the opinion of Charles Evans Hughes, United States Secretary of State, who on June 4, 1921, in speaking of treaties with Serbia, wrote:

> "No formal understanding has been reached with the Government of the Kingdom of SCS as to the application of these agreements to the territory of that country which formerly belonged to the Austro-Hungarian Empire. It is the opinion of the Department that the treaties may properly be regarded as applicable to that territory." (V. Hackworth, Digest of International Law, 375.)

The Trial Court discounts the weight of this opinion because it was given in the form of private communication in a non-adversary proceeding. Yet it must be pointed out that the communication in question was not private communication, but an official one of the Secretary of State, as such, with respect to a matter peculiarly within his official charge. That it was directed to American citizens and not a foreign power does not make it "private." Moreover, that the question involved was one of law, and that the Secretary of State who wrote it was one of our greatest lawyers and later became Chief Justice of the United States, should cloak it with more than usual authority.

Moreover, the Trial Court wholly overlooked an official communication from the Yugoslav Charge d'Affaires to Secretary of State Hughes on September 29, 1921, when in response to an inquiry, it was stated:

> ". . . The Government of the Kingdom of the Serbs, Croats and Slovenes considers the treaties and conventions concluded between the Kingdom of Serbia and the United States as applicable to the whole territory of the Kingdom of the Serbs, Croats and Slovenes as constituted at the present." (V. Hackworth, Digest of International Law, 374, 375.)

(3) Recapitulation of Points Demonstrating the Survival of the Juridical Entity of Serbia.

For the convenience of the Court, it may be well to summarize at this time the various elements, factors, circumstances and points hereinbefore discussed which, Appellants submit, are, alone, sufficient to reverse the conclusion of the Trial Court that the treaty rights of Serbia did not survive to the Kingdom of the Serbs, Croats and Slovenes:

(1) The Kingdom of Montenegro declared its union with Serbia under the Dynasty of Karageorgevitch, the

Royal House of Serbia, and was included in the King-dom of Serbs, Croats and Slovenes.

(2) Vojvodina took the same decision.

(3) The Council of Slovenes, Croats and Serbs, pro-claimed the union of the Yugoslav provinces formerly within the Austro-Hungarian Monarchy with Serbia.

(4) The Serbian Legation officially informed the United States of the formation of the Kingdom of the Serbs, Croats and Slovenes.

(5) The United States of America welcomed the union of the "provinces within the boundaries of the former Austro-Hungarian Monarchy *to Serbia.*"

(6) The Karageorgevitch Dynasty was proclaimed to be and accepted as the dynasty of the Serb-Croat-Slovene State.

(7) Belgrade, the capital of Serbia, continued as the capital of the united state.

(8) Serbian diplomatic representatives (the legations, consulates and missions) became the representatives of the Serb-Croat-Slovene State.

(9) The Treaty of St. Germain-en-Laye recognized the *ipso facto* succession of treaty rights and obligations of Serbia.

(10) By direct communication the Government of the Serb-Croat-Slovene State stated that it considered the Serbian Treaties as applicable to the whole territory.

III.

The Question of Succession of States and Survival of Treaty Rights and Obligations Presents a Political Issue Upon Which the Decision of the Executive Branch of the Government Is Controlling.

Appellants contend that the material hereinbefore set out demonstrates the projection of the juridical entity of the Kingdom of Serbia into the Kingdom of the Serbs, Croats and Slovenes. Moreover a decision to this effect has already been made by the Executive Branch of the United States Government (viz.: The State Department) and we contend that this political decision is, under the prevailing rule, determinative of the matter and binding upon the courts. This discussion will fall into three sections:

(1) The Rule of Political Decision,

(2) Evidence of the Political Decision, and

(3) Action taken pursuant to the Political Decision.

The Constitution of the United States in enumerating the powers of the President, provides (Art. II, Sec. 2):

> "He shall have Power, by and with the Advice and Consent of the Senate, to make Treaties, provided two-thirds of the Senators present concur; . . ."

Appellants do not for a moment contend that the State Department by its own *"ipsi dixit"* [see R. p. 45 for the Trial Judge's views thereon] can *create* a treaty. Appellants do contend, however, and vigorously urge that the question whether a treaty, duly ratified by the Senate, is applicable, both as to rights and obligations thereunder, to a foreign country notwithstanding territorial and governmental changes is in its nature political and not judicial and that the courts should accept the conclusions of the Political Department in that regard.

Note here that we refer to power *remaining* in a foreign State to carry out its obligations.

It is *not* contended that the State Department could by its own *fiat transfer* treaty obligations from one International Person to another International Person. To draw an absurd illustration, the State Department could not determine that Serbian treaties applied to Norway or Venezuela. That would certainly violate the Constitutional limitation and usurp the treaty making prerogatives of the Senate.

Where, however, the determination to be made is whether or not the juridical entity of a nation extends into and continues in the form of a successor, that decision is peculiarly within the province of the Executive Branch of the government represented by the State Department which is familiar with the factual background. Particularly is this true where the treaty is executory in nature and requires positive action on the part of the Executive Branch.

The trial court seemed to indicate the view that the acceptance of the political decision indicated in *Terlinden v. Ames, infra,* would infringe on the treaty powers reserved to the Senate under Article II, Section 2 of the Constitution. But the decision is only that the other Contracting Party retains the power to meet treaty obligations. This in no way usurps any right of the legislative department, for *the legislative branch at all times has the power to declare a treaty abrogated.* (See *Chung Yim v.*

United States, 78 F. 2d 43, 46, citing: *Boudinet v. United States,* 11 Wall. 616, 20 L. Ed. 227; *Cheung Sum Shee v. Nagle,* 268 U. S. 336, 45 S. Ct. 539, 69 L. Ed. 985; and *Head Money Cases,* 112 U. S. 580, 5 S. Ct. 247, 28 L. Ed. 798.)

Let us proceed then to consideration of:

(1) The Rule of Political Decision.

Appellants respectfully contend that the views expressed by the United States Supreme Court in the leading case of *Terlinden v. Ames* (1902), 184 U. S. 270, 22 S. Ct. 484, 46 L. Ed. 534, are controlling on this phase. Since the case has been the subject of much study by counsel for all parties and by the trial court, it will be discussed herein at some length.

The case arose when the German Consul at Chicago filed an extradition complaint as the duly accredited agent of the German Empire and also the Kingdom of Prussia (forming a part of said German Empire) charging certain offenses by one Gerhard Terlinden. Ames was the United States Marshal who had custody of the accused.

In the Habeas Corpus proceedings two treaty questions were raised. The accused denied the existence of any treaty between the United States and the German Empire, and secondly, asserted that the extradition treaty with the Kingdom of Prussia of 1852 had terminated by the creation of the German Empire in 1871. This historical background as outlined by the Court is as follows: In 1852 the United States and the King of Prussia entered into an extradition treaty. At that time Prussia was a member of a loose grouping of German states styled the Germanic Confederation, and the treaty provided that it would be applicable not only to Prussia but also to certain specified members of the Germanic Confederation on whose behalf, as well as on its own, Prussia was acting, and to such other members of the Germanic Confederation as might later accede to it. In 1866 the Germanic Confederation became extinct and another loose grouping of German states, the North German Union or Confederation, was formed under the presidency of the King of Prussia. A treaty relative to naturalization entered into between the United States and Prussia in 1868 extended the applicability of extradition treaty of 1852 to all the States in the North German Union or Confederation. In 1871 the German Empire was founded by the union of the states belonging to the North German Union or Confederation and other German states, and a constitution was adopted whereby the King of Prussia became the German Emperor, imperial laws took precedence over those of the individual states, and jurisdiction over foreign affairs was placed in the imperial government.

The Court stated in part:

"It is contended that the words in the preamble translated 'an eternal alliance' should read 'eternal union,' but this is not material, for admitting that the Constitution created a composite State instead of a system of confederated States, and even that it was called a Confederated Empire rather to save the *amour propre* of some of its component parts than otherwise, *it does not necessarily follow that the Kingdom of Prussia lost its identity as such, or that the treaties theretofore entered into by it could not be performed either in the name of its King or that of the Emperor.* We do not find in this constitution any provision which in itself operated to abrogate existing treaties or to affect the Status of the Kingdom of Prussia in that regard. Nor is there anything in the record to indicate that outstanding treaty obligations have been disregarded since its adoption. So far from that being so, those obligations have been faithfully observed.

"And without considering whether extinguished treaties can be renewed by tacit consent under our Constitution, we think that on the question whether this treaty has ever been terminated, *governmental action in respect to it must be regarded as a controlling importance.* During the period from 1871 to the present day extradition from this country to Germany, and from Germany to this country has been frequently granted under the treaty which has thus been repeatedly recognized by both governments as in force." (*Terlinden v. Ames, supra.*)

It was to the last few words to this quotation to which the trial court referred [R. p. 46], implying that the action by which the government could recognize the existence of the treaty must be by extradition proceedings alone. Under a later heading appellants will show governmental action by *both* governments involved "repeatedly recognizing" the treaty obligations of Serbia as continuing in force.

After reciting an exchange of correspondence somewhat similar to the communication received from the Serb, Croat, Slovene State in September, 1921, recognizing the Serbian treaties as applicable to its entire territory, the Court in *Terlinden v. Ames* further states:

"Thus it appears that the German Government has officially recognized and continues to recognize the treaty of June 16, 1852 as still in force . . ."

And further:

> "*It is out of the question that a citizen of one of the German States, charged with being a fugitive from its justice, should be permitted to call on the courts of his country to adjudicate the correctness of the conclusions of the Empire as to its powers, and the powers of its members, and especially as the Executive Department of our Government has accepted these conclusions and proceeded accordingly.*" (Emphasis added.)

What wording could fit the instant case more perfectly?

In support of the reasons underlying this rule the Court in *Terlinden v. Ames,* the Supreme Court goes on to cite the case of *Doe v. Braden,* 16 How. 635, 656. In that case, Chief Justice Taney in declaring it to be the duty of the courts to interpret and administer a treaty according to its terms, said:

> "And it would be impossible for the Executive Department of the Government to conduct our foreign relations with any advantage to the country and fulfill the duties which the Constitution has imposed upon it, if every court in the country was authorized to inquire and decide whether the person who ratified the treaty on behalf of a foreign nation had the power by its constitution and laws, to make the engagements into which he entered."

Further quoting from *Terlinden v. Ames:*

> "We concur in the view that *the question whether power remains in a foreign state to carry out its treaty obligations is in its nature political and not judicial, and that the courts ought not to interfere with the conclusions of the political department in that regard.*" (Emphasis added.)

The Court goes on to show the distinction between a treaty to be considered or interpreted as a law where it operates itself without the aid of any legislative provision, and a situation where the treaty requires either party to perform a particular act (such as to deliver custody of the accused).

> "Treaties of extradition are executory in their character, and fall within the rule laid down by Chief Justice Marshall in *Foster v. Neilson*, 2 Pet. 314, 7 L. Ed. 435, thus: 'Our Constitution declares a treaty to be the law of the land. It is, consequently, to be regarded in courts of justice as equivalent to an act of the legislature, whenever it operates of itself without the aid of any legislative provision. But when the terms of the stipulation import a contract, *when either of the parties engages to perform a particular act, the treaty addresses itself to the political, not the judicial, department.*'
>
> ". . . *It cannot be successfully contended that the courts could properly intervene on the ground that the treaty under which both governments had proceeded had terminated by reason of the adoption of the German Empire, notwithstanding the judgment of both governments to the contrary.*" (Emphasis added.)

We interrupt the quotation from *Terlinden v. Ames, supra,* at this point to comment that the foregoing language is brought more clearly into focus if we consider the very nature of an extradition proceeding, and the manner and mode in which the fugitive is delivered to the demanding government.

Section 3184, Title 18, U. S. C. provides for the provisional arrest and detention of a fugitive upon a warrant issued by a Judge or Commissioner. A hearing is then held "to the end that evidence of criminality may be heard and considered." The section then provides:

> "If, on such hearing, he deems the evidence sufficient to sustain the charge under the provisions of the proper treaty or convention *he shall certify the same, together with a copy of all the testimony taken before him, to the Secretary of State, that a warrant may issue upon the requisition of the proper authorities of such foreign government, for the surrender of such person,* according to the stipulations of the treaty or convention; . . ." (Emphasis added.)

Section 3186 then provides:

> "*The Secretary of State may order the person committed* under sections 3184 or 3185 of this title *to be delivered* to any authorized agent of such foreign government, to be tried for the offense of which charged." (Emphasis added.)

The formal compliance with the requirements of the treaty is executed by the political department. The only recourse of the fugitive to the courts is by way of Habeas Corpus, not by appeal nor review. The "appeal," or ultimate determination of the case lies with the Department of State.

Nor is it unusual for the courts to accept the political determination of the Executive Branch in matters involving treaty rights and obligations of foreign governments. On the contrary, this is the usual practice, for the President "is the sole organ of the federal government in the field of International Relations." (*United States v. Pink,* 315 U. S. 203, 229; *Cf. In re Cooper,* 143 U. S. 472; *Taylor v. Morton,* 2 Curtis 454, 459, Fed. Cas. No.

13,799; *Union of Soviet Socialist Republics v. National City Bank,* 41 Fed. Supp. 353; *Chicago & S. Airlines v. Waterman,* 333 U. S. 103.)

(2) Evidence of the Political Decision.

We turn now to the matter of how the political decision has been indicated.

We have already adverted to the official opinion of the Secretary of State (later Chief Justice) Hughes in June, 1921, that the treaties theretofore concluded between the United States and Serbia were applicable to the Kingdom of the Serbs, Croats and Slovenes, and to the official confirmation of that view by the Yugoslav Charge d'Affaires in September, 1921. Their views related to all such treaties, there being three—the extradition treaty here in issue, the Convention of Commerce and Navigation of 1881 and the Consular Convention of the same year.

However, during the 1920's Yugoslavia expressed a desire to negotiate a new extradition treaty—one which would conform more closely to the legal concepts then prevailing than the existing treaty did. The United States declined to negotiate a new treaty, on *the express ground that the treaty here in issue was in force and effect and* was sufficiently comprehensive. Thus, on March 23, 1927, Secretary of State Kellogg instructed the American Minister to Yugoslavia as follows:

> "With regard to the negotiation of a new extradition convention you will recall that in instruction No. 543 of January 8, 1925, the Department pointed out that the extradition convention between the United States and Serbia, which is regarded both by this Government and the Government of the Serbs, Croats

and Slovenes as being applicable to the whole territory of the Kingdom, is a modern and comprehensive convention. Pending the receipt of the more specific information concerning the proposal of the Government of the Serbs, Croats and Slovenes to supplant this convention which it is indicated on page 2 of dispatch No. 2577 of February 14, 1925, would be furnished you, the Department is unwilling to consider the negotiation of a new treaty on this subject." (*Foreign Relations of the United States,* 1927, Col. III, pp. 842-843.)

In 1934, this time the United States Government raised the question of the conclusion of a supplemental extradition treaty, adding to the list of extraditable crimes "crimes or offenses against the bankruptcy laws." The mere reference to a "supplemental" treaty also clearly confirms that the United States Government has always considered the treaty of 1902 valid and in force. (Department of State file No. 211.60H/10; see also Appx. B-1 in *Amicus* Brief.)

Again, when the Yugoslav Minister requested the delivery of the appellee herein as a "war criminal" under the provisions of certain United Nations resolutions, Secretary of State Acheson [R. pp. 80-81] replied on May 14, 1951, that that result could only be achieved by resort to action *"pursuant to the provisions of the Extradition Treaty of October 25, 1901, in force between the United States and Yugoslavia."*

Again, on September 26, 1951, Secretary of State Acheson formally certified that the treaty here in issue was in full force and effect between the United States and The Federal People's Republic of Yugoslavia. Over the seal of the Department of State he said [Ex. DG-E, see R. p. 362]:

"That all of the provisions of the said treaty, which entered into force between the United States of America and the Kingdom of Serbia on June 12, 1902, continued in force and were applicable to the whole territory of the Kingdom of the Serbs, Croats and Slovenes, as constituted on December 1, 1918, and to the Kingdom of Yugoslavia, to which the name of the Kingdom was changed by a law of October 3, 1929;

"And that all the provisions of the said treaty continued in force and became applicable to the Federal People's Republic of Yugoslavia as proclaimed on November 29, 1945 and are presently in force between the United States of America and the Federal People's Republic of Yugoslavia.

"In testimony whereof, I, Dean Acheson, Secretary of State, have hereunto caused the seal of the Department of State to be affixed and my name subscribed by the Authentication Officer of said Department, at the city of Washington, in the District of Columbia, this twenty-sixth day of September, 1951."

And on September 28, 1951, the Yugoslav Ambassador duly accredited to the United States, certified to the same effect [Ex. DG-F, see R. p. 372], as follows:

"To Whom it May Concern:

I, Vladimir Popovic, Ambassador of the Federal People's Republic of Yugoslavia, officially state herewith that the Treaty between the United States and Serbia for the mutual extradition of fugitives from justice signed at Belgrade on October 25, 1901, and the ratifications of which were exchanged at Belgrade on May 13, 1902, has uninterruptedly been in force between the United States on one side and Serbia, and later Yugoslavia, on the other and that accordingly the provisions of that Treaty are applicable to matters of extradition of fugitives from justice between the United States and the Federal People's Republic of Yugoslavia.

"In testimony whereof, I have hereunto caused the seal of the Embassy of the Federal People's Republic of Yugoslavia to be affixed and signed this document at the city of Washington, D. C., U. S. A. this twenty-eighth day of September, 1951."

Further evidence of open and public recognition of the *decision* that the treaty rights and obligations survived is found in various State Department publications. A compilation entitled *"A List of Treaties and other International Acts of the United States of America in Force December 31, 1932,"* published in 1933, and revised and republished in 1941, lists the Extradition Treaty in 1901, as well as the Commercial and Consular Conventions of 1881 (all with Serbia) as being in force with Yugoslavia. The Treaty of Commerce and Navigation appears in 22 Stat. 964, *II Malloy* 1613. The Consular Treaty is in *II Malloy* 1618.

The loose leaf treaty publication, *"United States Treaty Developments,"* started in 1947 has carried the following statement with regard to Yugoslavia:

"App. III (C) . . . The treaties in force between the United States and Serbia at the time of the formation of the Kingdom of the Serbs, Croats and Slovenes (Dec. 1, 1918) were regarded by the Governments of the United States and the new Kingdom as applicable to the new Kingdom. State Department file 711.60h/1 and 3. The adoption of

'Yugoslavia' in place of 'the Kingdom of the Serbs, Croats and Slovenes' as the official title of the Kingdom on October 3, 1929 is understood not to have affected treaty relations."

Additional "evidence" by way of "action" is shown in an agreement signed at Washington July 19, 1948, concerning the settlement of pecuniary claims against Yugoslavia. This agreement appears in *Treaties and Other International Acts Series,* as TIAS 1803, and in *United States Statutes at Large,* Vol. 62(3), p. 2658.

"The Government of Yugoslavia agrees to accord to nationals of the United States lawfully continuing to hold or hereafter acquiring assets in Yugoslavia, the rights and privileges of using and administering such assets and the income therefrom within the framework of the controls and regulations of the Government of Yugoslavia, on conditions not less favorable than the rights and privileges accorded to nationals of Yugoslavia, or of any other country, *in accordance with the Convention of Commerce and Navigation between the United States of America and the Prince of Serbia,* signed at Belgrade, October 2-14, 1881." (Emphasis added.)

Although this agreement refers to the Convention of Commerce and Navigation, it is not the understanding of appellants that evidence of the decision be directed to the Extradition Treaty alone. The *decision* required for the survival of the Convention of Commerce and Navigation rests upon exactly the same factual foundation.

Thus, the *political* decision of the Executive Branch of the Government was made in 1921 and has been continuously adhered to up to the present day. It is that Yugoslavia (by whatever name its government is called) is bound by the obligations and entitled to the rights of Serbia under all treaties, including the extradition treaty here in issue, between Serbia and the United States.

The *decision,* then, was made in 1921 upon receipt of the assurance that the Serb, Croat, Slovene State considered the Serbian treaties applicable to the Kingdom of the Serbs, Croats and Slovenes. *Evidence* of the decision, open recognition and acceptance of the decision has appeared frequently, in fact in each successive decade to and including the present, as illustrated by the foregoing material.

(3) Action Taken Pursuant to the Political Decision.

This brings us to the consideration of the last subheading under this topic. The trial court, relying on the statement in *Terlinden v. Ames, supra,* that governmental action must be regarded as of controlling importance [See R. pp. 46-47], places considerable stress upon the failure to show that any extradition had been sought by either country since its effective date.

Treaty rights are not of such nature that they are affected by *laches.* Had it been shown that occasions had occurred when fugitives might have been extradited, but that either country failed to press for extradition because they considered the treaty terminated a different situation might be presented.

The mere fact that the criminals of the two countries were such home loving bodies that they did not wish to leave their native shores, or at least did not wish to sojourn in the other country, does not impress the writer as a very strong argument that treaty rights with Serbia did not survive the formation of the Kingdom of the Serbs, Croats and Slovenes.

But there has been government action in other respects than directed to this particular treaty, but *all based upon the identical political decision (concurred in by the Serb-Croat-Slovene State, the Kingdom of Yugoslavia, and the Federated People's Republic of Yugoslavia) that the treaty rights and obligations of Serbia survived into the Serb-Croat-Slovene State.*

The present extradition proceedings is one form of action.

The Convention of Commerce and Navigation, sometimes referred to as the Treaty for Facilitating and Developing Commercial Relations, signed in 1881, has twice been the subject of governmental recognition by action.

One instance was that referred to at the conclusion of the preceding subhead as "evidence." This was the settlement of pecuniary claims against Yugoslavia.

A very similar instance of action is indicated in an agreement between the United States and Yugoslavia appearing in *United States Statutes at Large,* Vol. 61(3), p. 2451, and published in the Treaties and Other International Acts Series, as TIAS 1572. This agreement was effected by an interchange of notes in 1946 and contains the following:

> ". . . the most-favored-nation provisions of the Treaty for Facilitating and Developing Commercial Relations between the United States and Yugoslavia signed October 2/14, 1881 shall not be understood to require the extension to Yugoslavia of advantages accorded by the United States to the Philippines."

Diplomatic and Commercial relations between the two countries have been carried on openly and continuously under the provisions of Serbian treaties.

Consular relations are carried on under the terms of the consular convention of 1881. Yugoslav consular officers carry on their official work on a most-favored-nation basis, bottomed on the existence of a consular convention assuring reciprocal treatment to American consular officers in Yugoslavia.

Likewise under the terms of the Commercial Convention of 1881 above referred to, there has been constant action between nationals of the two countries based upon the governmental decisions. Rights such as those of entry, travel, residence for business purposes, acquisition, possession and disposal of property, exemption from military service, access to courts of justice, inheritance and others have been consistently and continuingly exercised under this treaty.

"Action" has been reflected in proceedings before our courts. In *Lukich v. Department of Labor and Industries* (Wash., 1934), 29 P. 2d 388, the most favored nation clause of the Treaty of Commerce of 1881 (II Malloy 1613) was involved, and the Court said:

> "It is conceded that the present Kingdom of Yugoslavia has replaced and absorbed the Kingdom of Serbia, and that the convention above referred to is now in full force and effect between Yugoslavia and the United States."

In at least two cases the Consular Convention of 1881 between the United States and Serbia has been considered as applying to the Kingdom of Yugoslavia. These are the cases of *Urbus v. State Comp. Comm.*, 113 W.

Va. 563, 169 S. E. 164 (1993), and *Olijan v. Lublin,*
50 N. E. 2d 264 (1943). Since these cases are discussed
in the brief *amicus,* they will not be commented on here.
They are indicative only of a general acceptance of the
fact of survival and action thereunder.

Another example of governmental action was an Act
of Congress approved May 30, 1928 (45 Stat. 399),
which authorized settlement of the indebtedness of the
Kingdom of the Serbs, Croats and Slovenes and in which
the debts of the Kingdom of Serbia were incorporated
in the total amount.[4]

We would again point out that the 1881 treaties stand
on the same ground as the extradition treaties, and emphasize that if the extradition treaty is held not to be in
force and effect, *a fortiori,* the 1881 conventions must
be held to be nullities with the result that all the enumerated matters now governed by such treaties in accordance with the political decision long since made, would be
in jeopardy.

Very recently, on September 24, 1952, the California
District Court of Appeal in the case of *In re Arbulich's
Estate,* 113 A. C. A. 206, 248 P. 2d 179, accepted a certificate of the Secretary of State identical to Exhibit
FG-E [R. p. 362] as to the Treaty of Commerce of 1881
between the United States and Serbia. The case involves reciprocal rights of inheritance. It has not be-

---

[4]The analysis of this indebtedness is set out in the Government's
amicus brief and need not be repeated here.

come final at the time of this writing but is cited as another example of acceptance of the political decision and action thereunder.

Appellants suggest, however, that the *Arbulich* case points the way to the proper approach to all phases of this case. In that opinion, the Court states:

"The fact that the court disapproved of the form of the government of Yugoslavia was not relevant at all on the issue of reciprocity. Yugoslavia is a sovereign state and is recognized as such by the government of the United States. As long as some right of inheritance is recognized in that state, and the evidence here without conflict discloses that it is, the fact that such right differs from the right of inheritance in this country, or that as an individual a judge may disapprove of the form of government, are factors which are not relevant and should not be considered on the issue of reciprocity. This was clearly pointed out in the Estate of Kennedy, 106 Cal. App. 2nd 621, 235 P. 2nd 837, involving Romania, a country that is not only communistic, but within the sphere of influence of Russia, which Yugoslavia certainly is not. Some degree of socialization and nationalization has taken place in most European countries, a policy we as individuals may or may not approve, but as judges passing on the issue of reciprocity, the form of such governments is a false factor, and a matter for each sovereign country to determine for itself."

Conclusion.

(Reference to Bail.)

The issue to be determined is whether the treaty rights and obligations existing with Serbia prior to 1919 have survived and are now in force between the United States of America and the Federated People's Republic of Yugoslavia. Specifically, under the ruling of the trial court, the question is whether those treaty rights and obligations survived the transition of the Kingdom of Serbia into the Kingdom of the Serbs, Croats and Slovenes in 1919.

On this issue, Appellants respectfully submit:

1. That treaty rights and obligations by the generally accepted rules of International Law survive and continue to apply despite changes in forms of government or of territory. That such treaty rights and obligations succeed to so-called successor nations, if the juridical entity of the Contracting Power continues and is reflected in the successor. That such survival is not repugnant to the treaty-making limitations of our Constitution, as it deals only with termination, not creation of treaty obligations and rights.

2. That a juridical continuity exists between the Kingdom of Serbia, as an International Person and the Kingdom of the Serbs, Croats and Slovenes and that the former's treaty rights and obligations toward the United States remained in force and have been applicable to the entire area of the Serb-Croat-Slovene State or later, to the Federal People's Republic of Yugoslavia.

3. That the question whether a treaty, duly ratified by the Senate, is applicable, both as to rights and obligations thereunder, to a foreign country notwithstanding territorial and governmental changes, in its nature political and not judicial and that the courts should accept the conclusions of the Political Department in that regard.

4. That the Executive Branch of the United States Government, namely, the State Department, has by its decision determined that the treaty rights and obligations outlined in the Extradition Treaty with Serbia of 1902 remained in force also after her amalgamation, integration into the Kingdom of the Serbs, Croats and Slovenes in 1918; was in force and effect as to this Kingdom, and is presently in force and effect between the United States and the Federal People's Republic of Yugoslavia.

5. That such decision has been openly evidenced and recognized by the governments of both countries, and is properly in evidence in this instant case.

6. That the decision that the Kingdom of the Serbs, Croats and Slovenes was the juridical successor state to Serbia so that treaty obligations survive, applies to all treaty obligations, not alone to the Extradition Treaty, but to the Commerce and Consular Conventions of 1881, and that there have been numerous, repeated and continuing evidences of, and open recognition of such decision and of governmental and private action pursuant thereto.

Appellee is now released on $5,000.00 bail pending appeal [R. p. 92]. On September 19, 1951, bail was fixed at $50,000.00 [R. p. 289], which continued during the ten months during which the matter was before the District Court. Since the Commissioner has already held that he does not have jurisdiction to fix bail in a capital case, the reversal of the District Court and discharge of the writ could only lead to another application for bail by way of a new habeas corpus proceeding in the absence of some direction in the mandate. At the original hearing when bail was requested, counsel and the Court all agreed [R. p. 289] that the rule in *Wright v. Henkel,* 190 U. S. 40, 23 S. Ct. 781, 47 L. Ed. 948, was applicable, which, as the Trial Court paraphrased it, was "that ordinarily bail should not be granted in cases of foreign extradition, and that they (the courts) may do so, if at all only in cases where there are special circumstances."

Should the Court of Appeals hold that the Extradition Treaty in question is in force, there is no occasion for delay in proceeding before the Commissioner. We believe the other special circumstances outlined by the Trial Court to be inapplicable.

The attention of the Court is respectfully drawn to the following cases on the question of bail in extradition proceedings:

In re Klein, 46 F. 2d 85:

"... manifestly (in granting bail) they would *incur grave risk of frustrating the efforts of the executive branch of the government to fulfill treaty obligations.*"

United States v. McNamara, 46 F. 2d 84:

"If the bail, however, be drawn as to cause the money collected on forfeiture to flow to the demanding government, *the situation from an international viewpoint is ridiculous if not insulting.*"

Wright v. Henkel, 190 U. S. 40, 62:

> "The demanding government, when it has done all that the treaty and law requires it to do, is entitled to the delivery of the accused on the issue of the proper warrant, and the other government is under obligation to make the surrender; an obligation which it might be impossible to fulfill if release on bail were granted. The enforcement of the bond, if forfeited, would hardly meet the international demand; and the regaining of the custody of the accused would be surrounded with serious embarrassment."

The case of *Wright v. Henkel* did not actually hold that the Court had the power to grant bail in extradition: it merely refused to accede that it did not have the power.

If the matter be considered in the light of the argument under Point III(a) hereof and the language in *Terlinden v. Ames* to the effect that a treaty is executory in nature, a strong case could be made that since the obligation to deliver is that of the Political Department, the release of the prisoner should be only by its consent or under its (the Political Department's) jurisdiction.

Appellants respectfully urge, therefore, that the decision of the District Court should be reversed, the writ of habeas corpus discharged, and that Appellee be remanded to the custody of the United States Marshal to be held pending the conclusion of hearings before the United States Commissioner before whom the extradition complaint is pending.

Respectfully submitted,

RONALD WALKER,

Attorney for Appellants.

APPENDIX A.

1901 Extradition Treaty.

Concluded October 25, 1901; ratification advised by Senate January 27, 1902; ratified by President March 7, 1902; ratifications exchanged May 13, 1902; proclaimed May 17, 1902.

ARTICLES.

I Delivery of accused	VIII Prior offenses
II Extraditable crimes	IX Property seized with
III Procedure	fugitive
IV Provisional detention	X Persons claimed by
V Nondelivery of citizens	other countries
VI Political offenses	XI Expenses; duration; ratification
VII Limitations	

The United States of America and His Majesty the King of Servia, being desirous to confirm their friendly relations and to promote the cause of Justice, have resolved to conclude a treaty for the extradition of fugitives from justice between the United States of America and the Kingdom of Servia, and have appointed for that purpose the following Plenipotentiaries:

The President of the United States of America, Charles S. Francis, Envoy Extraordinary and Minister Plenipotentiary to His Majesty the King of Servia.

His Majesty the King of Servia, M. Michel V. Vouitch, President of His Council of Ministers, Ministers for Foreign Affairs, Senator, Grand Officer of the Order of Milosh the Great, Grand Cross of the Order of Takovo, Officer of the Order of the White Eagle etc. etc., who, after having communicated to each other their respective full powers, found in good and due form, have agreed upon and concluded the following articles:

Article I.

The Government of the United States and the Government of Servia mutually agree to deliver up persons who, having been charged with or convicted of any of the crimes and offenses specified in the following article, committed within the jurisdiction of one of the high contracting parties, shall seek an asylum or be found within the territories of the other: Provided, that this shall only be done upon such evidence of criminality as, according to the laws of the place where the fugitive or person so charged shall be found, would justify his or her apprehension and commitment for trial if the crime or offense had been committed there.

Article II.

Extradition shall be granted for the following crimes and offenses:

1. Murder, comprehending assassination, parricide, infanticide, and poisoning; attempt to commit murder; manslaughter, when voluntary.

.   .   .   .

Extradition is also to take place for participation in any of the crimes and offenses mentioned in this Treaty, provided such participation may be punished in the United States as felony and in Servia as crime or offense as before specified.

Article III.

Requisitions for the surrender of fugitives from justice shall be made by the Governments of the high contracting parties through their diplomatic agents, or in the absence of such through their respective superior consular officers.

If the person whose extradition is requested shall have been convicted of a crime or offense, a duly authenticated copy of the sentence of the Court in which he has been convicted, or if the fugitive is merely charged with crime, a duly authenticated copy of the warrant of arrest in the country where the crime has been committed, and of the depositions or other evidence upon which such warrant was issued, shall be produced.

The extradition of fugitives under the provisions of this Treaty shall be carried out in the United States and in Servia, respectively, in conformity with the laws regulating extradition for the time being in force in the State on which the demand for surrender is made.

Article IV.

Where the arrest and detention of a fugitive in the United States are desired on telegraphic or other information in advance of the presentation of formal proofs, complaint on oath, as provided by the statutes of the United States, shall be made by an agent of the Government of Servia before a judge or other magistrate authorized to issue warrants of arrest in extradition cases.

In the Kingdom of Servia the diplomatic or consular officer of the United States shall apply to the Foreign Office, which will immediately cause the necessary steps to be taken in order to secure the provisional arrest and detention of the fugitive.

The provisional detention of a fugitive shall cease and the prisoner be released if a formal requisition for his surrender, accompanied by the necessary evidence of criminality, has not been produced under the stipulations of this Treaty, within two months from the date of his provisional arrest and detention.

Article V.

Neither of the high contracting parties shall be bound to deliver up its own citizens or subjects under the stipulations of this Treaty.

Article VI.

A fugitive criminal shall not be surrendered if the offense in respect of which his surrender is demanded be of a political character, or if he proves that the requisition for his surrender has, in fact, been made with a view to try or punish him for an offense of a political character.

No person surrendered by either of the high contracting parties to the other shall be triable or tried, or be punished, for any political crime or offense, or for any act connected therewith, committed previously to his extradition.

If any question shall arise as to whether a case comes within the provisions of this article, the decision of the authorities of the Government on which the demand for surrender is made, or which may have granted the extradition, shall be final.

Article VII.

Extradition shall not be granted, in pursuance of the provisions of this Treaty, if legal proceedings or the enforcement of the penalty for the act committed by the person claimed has become barred by limitation, according to the laws of the country to which the requisition is addressed.

Article VIII.

No person surrendered by either of the high contracting parties to the other shall, without his consent, freely granted and publicly declared by him, be triable or tried or be punished for any crime or offense committed prior to his extradition, other than that for which he was delivered up, until he shall have had an opportunity of returning to the country from which he was surrendered.

Article IX.

All articles seized which are in the possession of the person to be surrendered at the time of his apprehension, whether being the proceeds of the crime or offense charged, or being material as evidence in making proof of the crime or offense, shall, so far as practicable and in conformity with the laws of the respective countries, be given up to the Country making the demand, when the extradition takes place. Nevertheless, the rights of third parties with regard to such articles shall be duly respected.

Article X.

If the individual claimed by one of the high contracting parties, in pursuance of the present Treaty, shall also be claimed by one or several other powers on account of crimes or offenses committed within their respective jurisdictions, his extradition shall be granted to the State whose demand is first received: Provided, that the Government from which extradition is sought is not bound by treaty to give preference otherwise.

Article XI.

The expenses incurred in the arrest, detention, examination, and delivery of fugitives under this Treaty shall be borne by the State in whose name the extradition is sought; Provided, that the demanding Government shall not be compelled to bear any expense for the services of such public officers of the Government from which extradition is sought as receive a fixed salary; and, provided, that the charge for the services of such public officers as receive only fees or perquisites shall not exceed their customary fees for the acts or services performed by them had such acts or services been performed in ordinary criminal proceedings under the laws of the country of which they are officers.

The present Treaty shall take effect on the thirtieth day after the date of the exchange of ratifications and shall not act retroactively.

The ratifications of the present Treaty shall be exchanged at Belgrade as soon as possible, and it shall remain in force for a period of six months after either of the contracting Governments shall have given notice of a purpose to terminate it.

In Witness Whereof, the respective Plenipotentiaries have signed this Treaty in duplicate and have hereunto affixed their seals.

Done at Belgrade this twenty-fifth (twelfth) day of October in the year of our Lord one thousand nine hundred and one.

CHARLES S. FRANCIS (Seal)
DR. MICHEL VOUITCH (Seal)

No. 13552

IN THE

United States Court of Appeals

FOR THE NINTH CIRCUIT

RAFEO IVANCEVIC, Consul General of the Federal People's
Republic of Yugoslavia,

Appellant,

vs.

ANDRIJA ARTUKOVIC,

Appellee,

JAMES J. BOYLE, United States Marshal,

Appellant,

vs.

ANDRIJA ARTUKOVIC,

Appellee.

APPELLEE'S BRIEF.

FILED

JUL 3 0 1953

**PAUL P. O'BRIEN
CLERK**

ROBERT T. REYNOLDS,
1000 National Press Building,
Washington, D. C.,

VINCENT G. ARNERICH,
639 South Spring Street,
Los Angeles 14, California,

EDWARD J. O'CONNOR,
530 West Sixth Street,
Los Angeles 14, California,
Attorneys for Appellee.

Parker & Company, Law Printers, Los Angeles. Phone MA. 6-9171.

TOPICAL INDEX

TABLE OF AUTHORITIES CITED

TREATISES

No. 13552

IN THE

United States Court of Appeals

FOR THE NINTH CIRCUIT

RAFEO IVANCEVIC, Consul General of the Federal People's Republic of Yugoslavia,

Appellant,

vs.

ANDRIJA ARTUKOVIC,

Appellee,

JAMES J. BOYLE, United States Marshal,

Appellant,

vs.

ANDRIJA ARTUKOVIC,

Appellee.

APPELLEE'S BRIEF.

Jurisdiction.

The jurisdiction of the Court of Appeals is based upon Title 28, U. S. C., Section 2253, as follows:

"In a *habeas corpus* proceeding before a circuit or district judge, the final order shall be subject to review, on appeal, by the court of appeals for the circuit where the proceeding is had."

Constitutional Provision, Treaty and Statute Involved.

Appellee has raised the question whether a treaty of extradition has been negotiated and ratified between the United States and Jugo-Slavia in accord with Article II, Section 2, United States Constitution.

Appellant and *Amicus Curiae* raised the question whether a treaty between the United States and Serbia concluded October 25, 1901 (32 Stats. 1890), is binding between the United States and Yugoslavia.

Summary of Argument.

I.

The applicable rule of international law is that bilateral treaties do not survive the extinction or disappearance of one of the high contracting parties thereto.

II.

Serbia was extinguished as a state, international person or "Juridical Entity" by its incorporation or amalgamation into the Serb-Croat-Slovene State in December, 1918.

    a. How the Serb-Croat-Slovene State was formed or created.

    b. Evidence as to the political acts of Serbia by which its international personality was extinguished.

    c. Physical evidence of the extinction of Serbia as an international state.

d. Recognition of the Serb-Croat-Slovene State as a new state by the several European states and the United States.

e. Recognition of the Kingdom of Serbs, Croats and Slovenes as a new state by the several European states.

f. Recognition of the Serb-Croat-Slovene State by the United States.

III.

A result of Serbia's extinction was the voidance of her treaties with the United States.

IV.
Rebuttal.

1. The creation of Italy compared with the creation of the Serb-Croat-Slovene State.

2. The Opinion of the Secretary of State, June 4, 1921, that the Serbian Treaties were applicable to the Serb-Croat-Slovene State was a misapprehension of prior political decision of the United States Government.

3. Distinguishing *Terlinden v. Ames,* 184 U. S. 270.

4. The debts of Serbia were normally assumed by Jugo-Slavia.

5. "Opinions of the United States Courts."

Statement of the Case.

Appellee accepts the statement of the case as set forth in appellant's brief, pages 3, 4, 5 and 6, and adds the following:

That the present extradition proceedings are based upon an alleged extradition treaty proclaimed May 17, 1902, between the Kingdom of Serbia and the United States of America; that Article VI of the said Treaty reads as follows:

> "A fugitive criminal shall not be surrendered if the offense in respect of which his surrender is demanded be of a political character, or if he proves that the requisition for his surrender has in fact been made with a view to try or punish him for an offense of a political character."

The periods referred to in this proceeding occurred during World War II and during the political strife between the Republic of Croatia and the communist forces of the Marshall Tito's Yugoslavian Government.

That Andrija Artukovic is a lawyer, a native of Croatia, and during the said period was Minister of Interior and Minister of Justice of the Croatian Republic [R. pp. 181-183, 189]; that the killings, if any occurred, were during the war and during the political strife and, as such, were of a political character and not subject to extradition under the terms of the said extradition treaty; that killings which occur during a war or during internal political strife are not extraditable. (*United States ex rel. Giletti v. Commissioner of Immigration*, 35 F. 2d 687; *In re Ezeta* (D. C. Cal.), 62 Fed. 972.)

That extradition hearings, as provided in the extradition statute, have not been held; that the defenses to the extradition proceeding have not been heard; that the only issue to be determined in this appeal is the United States District Court's decision concluding that there is no extradition treaty in existence between the Federal Peoples Republic of Yugoslavia and the United States of America.

Appellee's Position.

There is not in effect a treaty of extradition between the United States and Yugoslavia because there has not been negotiated and ratified between the two states an extradition treaty since the United States recognized the Kingdom of the Serbs, Croats and Slovenes, now known as Yugoslavia, as a new international state in 1919.

This premise is not disputed directly by appellant or *amicus curiae,* but it is urged by them that an extradition treaty negotiated and ratified between the United States and Serbia in 1901-1902, is valid and binding between the United States and Yugoslavia because the latter state is merely an enlarged or greater Serbia.

Per contra, appellee urges that the said Serbo-American extradition treaty is void because:

I. It is a recognized rule of International Law that bilateral treaties do not survive the extinction or disappearance of a contracting party thereto;

II. Serbia was extinguished as an international state or person or "juridical entity" upon its incorporation or amalgamation into the Serb-Croat-Slovene State in 1918; and

III. A result of Serbia's extinction as an international state was the voidance of her treaties with the United States.

ARGUMENT.

I.

The Applicable Rule of International Law Is That Bilateral Treaties Do Not Survive the Extinction or Disappearance of One of the Contracting Parties Thereto.

Appellee submits that appellant and *amicus curiae* have not applied the proper principle of International Law to the issue arising in this proceeding. It is not the intention of appellee, nor was it the purpose of the District Court, to challenge the correctness of the rule of International Law "that treaty rights and obligations survive changes in territory and forms of government of either of the contracting parties," whether or not "newly annexed territory," as seemingly misapprehended by appellant and *amicus curiae* in page after page of their briefs (see App. Br. pp. 9, 10-18, and *Amicus Curiae* Br., pp. 6, 7-15).

The District Court [R. pp. 57-62] and appellee are guided by the recognized principle of International Law that bilateral treaties do not survive the extinction or disappearance, as an international state, of one of the contracting parties thereto, and in support of said prinple of law the following authorities appear:

Hyde, International Law Chiefly as Interpreted and Applied by the United States, 1922, Volume II, page 83:

> "When a State relinquishes its life as such through incorporation into or absorption by another State, the treaties of the former are believed to be automatically terminated."

Oppenheim's International Law, Lauterpacht, Volume I, 5th Edition, 1937, page 745:

> "A treaty, although it has neither expired, nor been dissolved, may nevertheless lose its binding force by becoming void. And such voidance may have different grounds—namely, extinction of one of the two contracting parties, * * *."

Fenwick, International Law (Rev. Ed. 1934), page 122:

> "Whether coercive or voluntary, the extinction of the State as an International Person puts an end to its own international rights and obligations. * * *"

Research in International Law, Harvard, 29 A. J. I. L., Supp. Part III, 1935, pages 1165-1166:

> "Article 33(b). A treaty to which only two States are parties is terminated when one of the parties becomes extinct."

And our final authority is the United States Government, if we interpret correctly the following statement on page 4 of *Amicus Curiae* Brief, under subtitle "Interest of the United States":

> "* * * The Executive Branch of the Government has proceeded heretofore on the theory that, in the absence of *the complete absorption of one of the high contracting parties to the treaty by a third country,* a mere change in the form of government or the expansion or contraction of the geographical boundaries of that high contracting party did not affect the termination of treaty relations with that party." (Emphasis ours.)

The emphasized portion of the quotation is exactly the point upon which the District Court and appellee believe the instant case turns.

II.

Serbia Was Extinguished as a State, International Person or "Juridical Entity" by Its Incorporation or Amalgamation Into the Kingdom of the Serbs, Croats and Slovenes.

Upon this point a clear issue is raised between the District Court's decision and appellee's position, on the one hand, and the position of appellant and *amicus curiae*, on the other. *Amicus curiae* maintains as Point II of its argument that "Serbia continued as an international juridical entity upon its enlargement into the Kingdom of the Serbs, Croats and Slovenes" (Yugoslavia) (see Br. pp. 6, 15-24), in other words, Yugoslavia is an enlarged or greater Serbia. While appellants at first use the somewhat ambiguous terms, "successor to" and "has juridical continuity with," in alleging Yugoslavia's relationship to Serbia, finally, on page 34 of brief, appellants take the same position as *amicus curiae* and maintain the "continuation of the juridical entity of Serbia into the enlarged State of the Serbs, Croats and Slovenes."

The District Court [R. p. 61] and appellee support the view that Yugoslavia was a new state, not a greater or enlarged Serbia, but a state into which Serbia was incorporated or amalgamated, thereby causing the extinction or discontinuity of Serbia as an independent state or international person.

(a) How the Serb-Croat-Slovene State Was Formed or Created.

In determining whether Serbia was extinguished in the creation of Jugo-Slavia* *i. e.,* whether Jugo-Slavia was a new state or merely an enlargement or continuation of former Serbia, it is proper to consider the steps by which Jugo-Slavia was formed, and the elements which went into its making.

Naturally, it was not created on a moment's notice. The plan for its composition was formulated in July, 1917, at Corfu, by conferences between and among representatives of Serbia (its government-in-exile was situate there), and representatives of the putative State of the Slovenes, Croats and Serbs. There was issued a statement of their plans and purpose known as the Declaration of Corfu, a translation of which is attached as Appendix A. A copy of this declaration was forwarded to the United States State Department by its Special Agent (Dodge) at Corfu (see Foreign Relations U. S. 1918, Supp. 1, Vol. I, p. 829; also Appendix B).

Briefly, it provided for the voluntary union of Serbia, Montenegro and the then unformed State of the Slovenes, Croats and Serbs "to constitute a free, national and independent State," and that the said union was to have its own constitution, national assembly elected by universal suffrage, with equal, direct and secret ballot, flag, coat-of-arms, freedom of religion, equal use of Cyrillic and

---

*Appellee calls the Court's attention to the historical inaccuracy of referring to either the State of the Serbs, Croats and Slovenes or to the Kingdom of the Serbs, Croats and Slovenes as "Yugoslavia." The plain historical fact is that the term "Yugoslavia" had no official recognition prior to the proclamation of the dictatorship of King Alexander in 1929.

Latin alphabets, unification of the calendar, etc., under the dynasty of the Karageorgevic family, the ruling house of Serbia.

Thereafter, as admitted in Appellants' Brief, on October 29, 1918, the Southern Slavs, formerly of Austria-Hungary, proclaimed the establishment of the "State of the Slovenes, Croats and Serbs"; on November 8, 1918, the Serbian Government formally recognized the new state [see App. Br. pp. 23-24; also R. pp. 83-84]. On November 11, 1918, Serbia asked the United States to recognize the State of the Slovenes, Croats and Serbs and treat it as an ally [R. pp. 83-84].

Then on November 24, 1918, the government of the State of the Slovenes, Croats and Serbs took the first step toward the Union provided for in the Declaration of Corfu, and resolved to proclaim the unification of their state with Serbia and Montenegro "into a unified State of the Serbs, Croats and Slovenes" (App. Br. p. 24). On November 26, 1918, Montenegro took a similar decision (see App. Br. p. 24). It is clear that the declaration for unification made by the State of the Slovenes, Croats and Serbs was not one of annexation to Serbia; it was an open offer to unite with Serbia and Montenegro to constitute the new "free, national and independent State" described in the Declaration of Corfu. Before the union could be completed, Serbia had to declare, in turn, its union with the State of the Slovenes, Croats and Serbs.

And on December 1, 1918, Serbia received the resolution of unification proposed by the Slovene-Croat-Serb State, and in the clearest possible language *declared its union with that state to form a single kingdom* [see Note of Serbian Charge to Secretary of State, R. pp. 84-85].

The language of the Regent of the Serbian State declaring such union is so clear and unmistakable, and yet is so conveniently distorted by *amicus curiae* in lifting quotations out of the full text (Br. p. 15, 2nd par.) that appellee is impelled to quote here the pertinent language:

> "* * * The Delegation by one (a) solemn address, presented to his Highness the Crown Prince, has proclaimed the Union of all the Serbian, Croatian and Slovene provinces of the former Dualist Monarchy *into one single State* with the Kingdom of Serbia under the Dynasty of His Majesty King Peter and under the regency of the Crown Prince Alexander. *In reply to this address His Royal Highness the Crown Prince has proclaimed the Union of Serbia with the above mentioned independent State of Slovenes, Croats and Serbs into one single Kingdom:* 'Kingdom of the Serbs, Croats and Slovenes.' * * *."

It seems clear from the above quotation that the State of the Slovenes, Croats and Serbs proclaimed a union with— *not* an annexation to—Serbia into a single state—Jugo-Slavia. And it seems equally clear that before such a union can be completed, the other state of the intended union must be willing to accept the idea and join in the proclamation of the union. Therefore, appellee urges that the italicized sentence of the above quotation was an absolute necessity to the voluntary union by which Jugo-Slavia was formed, and that its meaning is so clear that it was necessary for appellants and *amicus curiae* to ignore it in arriving at the theory that Serbia continued as a "juridical entity" enlarged into Jugo-Slavia.

Thus in the formation of Jugo-Slavia there were joined three independent states—Serbia, Montenegro and the

State of the Slovenes, Croats and Serbs; *not* as appellants suggest (Br. p. 32) "an existing international juridical entity"—Serbia—to which the "other elements were joined." Serbia and Montenegro had long been recognized as International Persons, and the State of the Slovenes, Croats and Serbs was expressly recognized by Serbia, as admitted by appellants (Br. p. 24), and was belatedly recognized by the United States by its express recognition of the union forming Jugo-Slavia [Statement of Secretary of State, Feb. 7, 1919; R. p. 89].

(b) Evidence as to the Political Acts of Serbia by Which Its International Personality Was Extinguished.

If the foregoing is not enough to convince one that Serbia voluntarily ended its independent existence by a union with other states, we may also consider the acts of Serbia by which it ended its international existence. These acts were reported to the United States State Department and to the American Peace Mission at Paris by Special Agent Dodge on the scene at Belgrade in his notes to the American Secretary of State, December 24, 1918 (not published) and January 10, 1919 [R. pp. 85-88].

It is a matter of historical knowledge that Serbia in 1918, and for many years prior, was governed by a royal dynasty, a national parliament, elected to office, known as the Skuptschina, and an executive ministry or cabinet responsible to the Skuptschina, under a national constitution.

From Dodge's report we learn that after the union forming Jugo-Slavia, the Serbian Skuptschina held a "short session," elected delegates to the "National Council," and "adjourned presumably to meet no more." Thus the dissolution of the Serbian national parliament or legislature.

In the new state there was set up immediately a national provisional legislature known as a "National Council" composed of delegates from the Serbian Skuptschina, from the National Council of the former Slovene-Croat-Serb State, from Montenegro, from *Old Serbia, *Macedonia, Voivodina, Banat. In this provisional parliament were clearly represented all the peoples and minorities of the Kingdom, not only the Serbs.

Dodge informs us also that there was formed a Jugo-Slav ministry or cabinet of "representative character," "composed of men of all the political parties, regions, and creeds of the new State," from which it can only be understood the Serbian ministry was dissolved, and that the new ministry was also definitely Jugo-Slav in character, not Serbian. Thus the disappearance of another organ of the Serbian Government.

Dodge informs us further that immediate arrangements were made for election of a Constitutional Convention on the basis of "universal suffrage," something apparently not available in former Serbia, the said convention to frame a new constitution for the new state. Also that a "special ministry" had been appointed to draft electoral laws for the convention and plans for the constitution.

Summarizing, not only do we find the new Kingdom of the Serbs, Croats and Slovenes equipped or in process of being equipped with *new* national governmental organs, not transplanted Serbian organs of government, but we find that Serbia stripped itself of all governmental organs by which it might have independently engaged in formal relations with foreign States and thus have continued its

---

*Though annexed to Serbia in the wars of 1912-1913, not represented in the Serbian Skuptschina.

international existence. The only Serbian organ transferred to the new State was the royal dynasty, and it is important to note that this ruler no longer called himself the King (or Crown Prince) of Serbia, but referred to himself officially only as the King of the Serbs, Croats and Slovenes (Treaty of St. Germain, Sept. 10, 1919). The importance of these losses of identity by Serbia becomes the greater when it is remembered that the German States which formed the North German Union and the German Empire (the subject of inquiry by the Supreme Court in *Terlinden v. Ames,* 184 U. S. 270) retained their separate existence and governmental organs at least so far as to permit the individual German States to enter into diplomatic and treaty relations with foreign States, and further, that the Emperor of Germany continued to describe himself as the King of Prussia as well, and so described himself in a number of treaties and agreements with the United States executed after 1871 in behalf of the German Empire. (Malloy, Treaties, Conventions, etc., U. S., Vol. I, pp. 550, etc.) This comparison is more fully discussed later under the subhead, "Distinguishing Terlinden v. Ames."

Appellant (Br. p. 38) and *Amicus Curiae* (Br. p. 16) make much of the fact that the Legations, Consulate and other Missions of Serbia became the Legations, Consulates and other Missions of the Kingdom of the Serbs, Croats and Slovenes. Appellee urges that this has no importance as it would be only natural that the new Jugo-Slav State would use facilities of its components freely available to it.

Doubtless it used also buildings in Belgrade for its governmental offices which had formerly been so used by the Kingdom of Serbia. Additionally, the diplomatic service is merely an agent of an executive department of government, not an independent policy-maker, and as we have noted from Dodge, the Serbian ministry was dissolved and a new ministry representative of all Jugo-Slavia was formed. Appellee urges also that appellant and *amicus curiae* have strained the meaning of "Legations, Consulates and other Missions of Serbia" by interpreting them to mean "Serbian diplomatic representatives" (Br. pp. 38 and 16, respectively), and stating that they remained unchanged throughout the world. Without examining the rolls of each Serb-Croat-Slovene legation, consulate or mission to see what personnel changes occurred, appellee believes it sufficient to point out to this Court that the first Serb-Croat-Slovene Minister of Foreign Affairs (the chief of the diplomatic service) was not a "hold-over" from the dissolved cabinet of former Serbia, nor any other Serb, but was Ante Trumbitch, a Croat and spokesman for the State of the Slovenes, Croats and Serbs and a signer for those people of the Declaration of Corfu; and further that Trumbitch and Ivan Zolger, the latter a Slovene professor, were sent by the new State to Paris to join with delegates of former Serbia in representing the new State at the Peace Conference. In fact, Trumbitch (Trumbic) and Zolger were two of the three Serb-Croat-Slovene representatives who negotiated with the United States and others the Treaty of St. Germain, and Trumbitch is therein described as Minister of Foreign Affairs.

(c) Physical Evidence of the Extinction of Serbia as an International State.

While it is recognized that physical differences alone do not mark a new State or the end of an old State, yet together with the background of the formation of the Kingdom of the Serbs, Croats and Slovenes and the important political acts just detailed, the physical differences complete a picture that shows clearly a new State—one whose political and physical characteristics are entirely different than those of Serbia with whom the United States constitutionally entered into an extradition treaty in 1901-1902.

For instance, Serbia had a national flag and coat-of-arms. For the new State there was a new flag and new coat-of-arms, and the Serbian flag was used for internal domestic occasions or holidays just as, for example, the Lone Star flag of Texas. In former Serbia the official written language was in Cyrillic characters. In Jugo-Slavia, Cyrillic and Latin characters were officially used. Chronologically, old Serbia was on the Julian calendar; as agreed at Corfu, Jugo-Slavia was placed on the Gregorian calendar.

Appellant (Br. p. 38) has stressed the fact that Belgrade was the capital of both Serbia and Jugo-Slavia. Yet this was possibly the only mark of political geographic similarity between Serbia and Jugo-Slavia. Reference to any geographic authority will inform us that Serbia in 1914 was a state of approximately 37,000 square miles in size, approximately 4,000,000 population, entirely landlocked, and with an economy principally agricultural. But Jugo-Slavia in 1919 was a state approximately 96,000 square miles in size, slightly over 12,000,000 population, with a Croatian seacoast nearly 500 miles in length, and a diversified economy of agriculture, manufacturing, fishing, shipping and mining. Serbia, quite naturally, was populated principally by people of Serb descent whose religion was Greek Orthodox. Per contra, Jugo-Slavia was populated almost equally by Croats and Serbs, in lesser numbers by Slovenes, and with important minorities of Macedonians, Albanians, Germans and Hungarians. Slovenes are Roman Catholics, and Croats are Roman Catholics and Moslem.

(d) Recognition of the Kingdom of the Serbs, Croats and Slovenes as a New State by the Several European States and the United States.

While admitting, arguendo, the force of appellee's foregoing argument that Jugo-Slavia was a new State, yet it might be said, "True, there appears to have been a considerable change. But did the other States of the world, particularly the United States, take any political acts in relation to this changed situation, and if so what did their acts mean?"

Appellee submits that the established States of the world had a choice of attitudes toward the admittedly changed situation of the Kingdom of the Serbs, Croats and Slovenes of 1918-1919: they might regard the changes as merely an enlargement of Serbia despite their enormity, or they might regard the changes as creating a new State, an International Person with whom they had not previously had formal relations.

If the old States adopted the first attitude, *i. e.,* that the changes had merely enlarged Serbia, then it is submitted that no action—certainly not recognition—was required of them for all had long since recognized Serbia and had existing treaty relations with Serbia.

If, on the other hand, the old States adopted the second attitude, *i. e.,* that the changes had created a new state, then it is submitted that they might have taken several actions toward the new State, namely, recognition, treaty negotiations, etc.

Logically the next step is to examine history and determine what, if any, acts were taken by the old States in relation to the changed situation of the Kingdom of the Serbs, Croats and Slovenes. But, first, at the risk of putting the cart before the horse, the meaning, purpose and mode of recognition of new states are set forth according to recognized authoritative writers on International Law:

Moore, International Law Digest, Vol. I, 1906, page 72:

> "Recognition, says Rivier, is the assurance given to a *new* state that it will be permitted to hold its place and rank, in the character of an independent political organism, in the society of nations. The rights and attributes of sovereignty belong to it independently of all recognition, but it is only after it has been recognized that it is assured of exercising them. Regular political relations exist only between states that reciprocally recognize them. Recognition is therefore useful, *even necessary to the new state.* It is also the constant usage, when a state is formed, to demand it. * * *." (Emphasis added.)

Hackworth, Digest of International Law, Vol. I, 1940, page 161:

> "Recognition may be of new states, or new governments, or of belligerency. It is evidenced, in the case of a new state or government, by an act officially acknowledging the existence of such state or government and *indicating a readiness on the part of the*

recognizing state to enter into formal relations with it. * * *." (Emphasis added.)

"Whether and when recognition will be accorded is a matter within the discretion of the recognizing state. * * * In the United States recognition has in the past usually been accomplished by the President acting solely on his own responsibility, but, occasionally, in the case of new states, it has been accomplished by the President with the cooperation of Congress."

Oppenheim's International Law, Lauterpacht, Vol. I, 1937, pages 120-121:

"* * * Through recognition only and exclusively a State becomes an International Person and a subject of International Law; *and thereby acquires the capacity to enter into diplomatic relations and make treaties with the States which recognize it;* * * *." (Emphasis added.)

Further, on page 122:

"Sec. 72. *Recognition is the act through which it becomes apparent that an old State is ready to deal with a new State as an International Person and a member of the Family of Nations.* Recognition is given either expressly or impliedly. If a new State asks formally for recognition and receives it in a formal declaration of any kind, it receives express recognition. * * *." (Emphasis added.)

Further, on page 139:

"Sec. 75h. (c) As a rule States may acquire new territorial or other rights by unilateral acts, such as discover or annexation, or by treaty, without recognition on the part of third States being required for their validity."

Several points are brought out in the foregoing quotations which are pertinent to the issue herein, namely: (1) that recognition of States is given only to new States, *i. e.*, it is not required to be given to old States changing in name, size or form of government, or acquiring new territorial rights by annexation or treaty; (2) that such recognition necessarily precedes or accompanies diplomatic, treaty and other formal relations between the recognizing and recognized States, *i. e.*, that there do not exist between the recognizing and recognized States any diplomatic or treaty relations until recognition is given expressly or impliedly; and (3) recognition is granted at the discretion of the recognizing State.

(e) Recognition of the Kingdom of the Serbs, Croats and Slovenes as a New State by the Several European States.

Appellee submits that the acts of recognition of Jugo-Slavia detailed hereinafter should be considered not only by themselves but in comparison with acts of recognition extended by the same States during the same period to other new States, Czechoslovakia and Poland, and with the failure of these States to extend recognition to another State—Rumania—which was as greatly enlarged immediately after World War I as appellants and *Amicus Curiae* allege Serbia to have been.

Thus, Great Britain expressly recognized Jugo-Slavia on June 2, and France, on June 6, 1919; and recognition by Germany, Italy, Japan and other powers signatory to the Treaty of Versailles dates from execution of the Treaty on June 28, 1919. Authorities: (History of the Paris Peace Conference, Temperley, Vol. 5, page 157, Recognition of New States since 1919: also Foreign Relations of the United States, Paris Peace Conference, Vol. III, p. 603, and Vol. V, pp. 292-293, 312 and 338.)

In relation to each of these recognitions it should be remembered that these States had each recognized Serbia so long ago as, and continuously since, 1878. It cannot be assumed their acts of recognition were mere empty gestures, for each of them must be presumed to have been familiar with the rules of International Law; and, in fact, each of them has in its history extended many acts of recognition of new States.

Even more interesting are the express acts of recognition of Poland, Czechoslovakia and the Serb-Croat-Slovene State required of the defeated Central powers of World War I in the so-called "political clauses" of peace treaties negotiated with the latter states, and for ready comparison excerpts are set forth of several "political clauses" from the various treaties requiring recognition:

In the Treaty of Versailles with Germany, June 28, 1919:

"Part II—POLITICAL CLAUSES FOR EUROPE.

"Section VII. Czecho-Slovak State.

"Article 81. Germany, in conformity with the action already taken by the Allied and Associated Powers, recognizes the complete independence of the Czecho-Slovak State which will include the autonomous territory of the Ruthenians to the south of the Carpathians."

In the Treaty of St. Germaine-Laye with Austria, September 10, 1919:

"Part III—POLITICAL CLAUSES FOR EUROPE.

"Section II. Serb-Croat-Slovene State.

"Article 46. Austria, in conformity with the action already taken by the Allied and Associated

Powers, recognizes the complete independence of the Serb-Croat-Slovene State.

"Article 47. Austria renounces, so far as she is concerned, in favour of the Serb-Croat-Slovene State all rights and title over the territories of the former Austro-Hungarian Monarchy situated outside the fronts of Austria as laid down in Article 27, Part II (Frontiers of Austria) and recognized by the present Treaty, or by any Treaties concluded for the purpose of completing the present settlement, as forming part of the Serb-Croat-Slovene State."

Section III. Czecho-Slovak State.

"Article 53. Austria, in conformity with the action already taken by the Allied and Associated Powers, recognizes the complete independence of the Czecho-Slovak State, which will include the autonomous territory of the Ruthenians south of the Carpathians.

"Article 54. Austria renounces, so far as she is concerned in favour of the Czecho-Slovak State * * *."

In the Treaty of Trianon with Hungary, June 4, 1920, Articles 41, 42 and 48, 49 are identical to Articles 46, 47 and 53, 54, respectively, of the Austrian treaty quoted above.

So also were Bulgaria and Turkey required in identical clauses to recognize the Serb-Croat-Slovene State.

It should be noted that these "political clauses" are unequivocal recognitions of a *State,* not a government, and that the United States also was signatory to the treaties.

Also, in the above Treaties with Austria and Hungary, there were "political clauses" relating to Rumania— and quoted below is that from the Austrian treaty:

"Part III—POLITICAL CLAUSES FOR EUROPE.

"Section IV. Roumania.

"Article 59. Austria renounces so far as she is concerned in favour of Roumania all rights and title over such portion of the former duchy of Bukovina as lies within the frontiers of Roumania, which may ultimately be fixed by the principal Allied and Associated Powers."

See also Article 45 of the Treaty with Hungary.

In these treaties there are no "political clauses" of recognition of Rumania. Rumania was a greatly enlarged State as a result of World War I; having in 1914 an area of approximately 50,000 square miles and population of 7,000,000, and in 1919 an area of approximately 110,-000 square miles with population of 18,000,000. Thus, if Jugo-Slavia were merely an enlarged Serbia whose growth paralleled that of Rumania, then it may be concluded that only a "political clause" of renunciation to Jugo-Slavia would have been required of Austria and Hungary as given to Rumania.

In brief summary, there is a clear meaning to the fact that the several European States *and the United States* (signatory to each of these treaties) accorded the Serb-Croat-Slovene State a treatment identical to that accorded the admittedly new States of Czechoslovakia and Poland, and did not treat it in the manner accorded Rumania, admittedly an enlarged State. It is that the Serb-Croat-Slovene State was undoubtedly believed to be, and recognized as, a new State.

In fact, it seems that Jugo-Slavia also considered itself to be a new State, witness excerpt from note of May 12, 1921, from its Foreign Affairs Ministry to the German Embassy stating:

> "Therefore this legal office [of Foreign Affairs] stresses that, since it was not with the old Kingdom of Serbia that peace was made, but with the *new state* of the Serb-Croat-Slovene * * *." [R. p. 62.] (Emphasis added.)

Also in support of the theory that Jugo-Slavia was a new State are found the following European authorities on International Law:

Kaufman, Niemeyers zeitschrift fuer Internationales Recht, in Chap. XXXI, pp. 211-251, observes:

> "* * * The Serb-Croat-Slovene State is a new State. * * *."

Sack, Les Effets des Transfermations des Etate sur * * * leurs obligations * * * Paris, Sirey, 1927, I, p. 3: The Serb-Croat-Slovene State is shown as a new State.

Udina, L'estinizione dell' Impero Austro-Ungarico nel Diritto Internationale, 2d ed., pp. 288, 303, concludes that the Serb-Croat-Slovene State is a new State.

Guggenheim, Beitraege zur Voelkerrecht Lichen Lehre vom Staatenwechael (Staatenzukession), 1925, states:

> "The latest practice of states knows of one undoubted case of complete state discontinuity * * * where the old states disappeared and a new state

arose, *i. e.,* the disappearance of the Kingdom of Serbia (and Montenegro) which was followed by the new-established state of Yugoslavia. Serbia ceased to exist as a subject of international law. * * *."

Temperley, History of the Paris Peace Conference, Vol. 5, Recognition of New States since 1919, p. 157, shows Yugoslavia as a new State.

(f) Recognition of the Serb-Croat-Slovene State by the United States.

The most important guide to this Court in the instant proceeding must be the known acts and statements of the Government of the United States prior to, at and after the creation of the Serb-Croat-Slovene State and the disappearance of Serbia. Thus, appellee treats these at greater length than the acts of the European States.

There is little doubt as to the known international policy of the President, Woodrow Wilson, the Chief Executive of the United States Government, during and after World War I; openly, he advocated the self-determination of peoples as to their government and equally as strongly he opposed the annexation of alien territories and peoples by the victorious Allied and Associated Powers. The decision of the District Court [R. pp. 57-58, 91] took cognizance of such policy and attitude of the United States Government during and after World War I.

That the Chief Executive of the United States was interested in and aware of developments in the Balkans in 1918 leading to the formation of the Serb-Croat-Slovene State is evidenced by the series of public statements and diplomatic notes of the United States State Department and its representatives abroad concerning Serbia and the Serb-Croat-Slovene State in the period January-November 1918, published in Foreign Relations of the United States, 1918, Supp. 1, Vol. I, pages 790-870. Appellee believes that this background formed the basis for the acts of the United States Government detailed hereinafter.

That the American Chief Executive was interested in the proposed relation between Serbia and the then unborn State of the Slovenes, Croats and Serbs is reflected in the following brief despatch found in Foreign Relations U. S., 1918, page 823:

> "The Acting Secretary of State to the Special Agent at Corfu (Dodge)
>
> "Washington, August 7, 1918, 6 p.m.
>
> "Department desires from time to time confidential reports on Serbian Government's position as to character of relation to be established between Serbia and Yugo-Slav portion of Austria-Hungary if latter secure their liberty."

As we know from President Wilson's public statements that he opposed the domination of one people by another, it is a fair assumption from the above message that the President wished to satisfy himself that there was not being proposed or planned the substitution of a Serbian yoke for the Austro-Hungarian yoke then resting upon the Southern Slav people of the latter country; in other words, that the Serbian government had no intent to create a "greater Serbia" by the annexation or absorption of the Southern Slavs of Austria-Hungary if the latter should obtain their freedom.

Thus, the responses of Special Agent (Dodge) to the above request of August 7 are of considerable importance in analyzing the acts of the United States Government toward the Serb-Croat-Slovene State immediately following its formation in December, 1918. Dodge's responses of August 26 and September 13, 1918, reported in Foreign Relations U. S., 1918, pages 828 *et seq.* and 852 *et seq.* were in the record before the District Court, but as not designated in the record on appeal, these despatches are attached hereto for ready reference as Appendices B and C. Very briefly, it may be seen from these reports that according to official spokesmen of Serbia a new State was to be formed pursuant to the Corfu Declaration, that it was formed by a free and equal union, and that it was not to be a state of Serbian hegemony or superiority. The high offices held by the Serbian spokesmen lent credence to their statements and must have also impressed the U. S. State Department.

Thereafter, on October 14, 1918 (prior to the independence declaration of the State of the Slovenes, Croats and Serbs), the Serbian Government requested an American declaration that it favored the freedom of the Southern Slavs of Austria-Hungary and "their union with Serbia in a free and democratic State, such as was provided for in the Declaration of Corfu." Foreign Relations U. S., 1918, 1, I, p. 843.) To this request the United States responded on October 28, 1918, that the "United States has expressed itself freely in support of the right of the Jugo-Slavs to be entirely freed from Austrian domination and that it does not feel that it can go further in declaring a policy which manifestly depends upon the self-determination of the peoples involved." In short, the United

States was not going to favor or sponsor any cut and dried arrangement for a union proposed by one state in advance of self-determination by other states and peoples involved, which might smack of annexation or absorption by an existing State requesting such favor.

Then, as we have seen, followed the declaration of the independent State of the Slovenes, Croats and Serbs, October 29, 1918, Serbian recognition of such State, November 8, Serbian request that the United States recognize such State, November 11, and the declarations of three States, the State of the Slovenes, Croats and Serbs, November 24, Montenegro, November 26, and Serbia, December 1, for union into a single State, and the proclamation of the Kingdom of the Serbs, Croats and Slovenes.

The new State asked for recognition by the United States, and recognition was given by public statement of the Secretary of State (Lansing) at Paris, February 7, 1919. The telegram from the Commission to Negotiate Peace to Acting Secretary of State was as follows:

860h.01/26: Telegram

The Commission to Negotiate Peace to the Acting Secretary of State

Paris, February 6, 1919, 4 p.m.
[Received February 7, 1.32 a.m.]

622. The Secretary of State will give out on February 7th the following statement in regard to the union of the Jugo-Slav peoples, which you may give out to the press immediately:

"On May 29, 1918, the Government of the United States expressed its sympathy for the nationalistic aspirations of the Jugo Slav race and on June 28 declared that all branches of the Slavish race should be completely freed from German and Austrian rule. After having achieved their freedom from foreign oppression the Jugo-Slav[s] formerly under Austria-Hungarian rule on various occasions expressed the desire to unite with the Kingdom of Serbia. The Servian Government on its part has publicly and officially accepted the union of the Serb, Croat and Slovene peoples. The Government of the United States, therefore, welcome the union while recognizing that the final settlement of territorial frontiers must be left to the Peace Conference for determination according to desires of the peoples concerned."

All this statement has been transmitted Mr. Trumbitch [106] and telegraphed to Dodge at Belgrade.

Am[erican] Mission

[R. p. 89.]

Applying the rules of International Law set forth in this sub-heading, which it must be assumed that the United States Government knew, what did this act of recognition signify? First, that the United States recognized that the Kingdom of the Serbs, Croats and Slovenes was a new State. No other logical conclusion can be drawn from the act of recognition, for if the United States had believed the Serb-Croat-Slovene State to be an enlarged Serbia, no recognition would have been necessary as the United States had continuously recognized Serbia, at least since 1881. Second, that the United States was ready to enter into diplomatic, treaty and other relations with the new State, ergo, that it had no such relations then with the Serb-Croat-Slovene State.

But appellee is puzzled at the attempts of appellant and *amicus curiae* to ignore or minimize this act of recognition, which according to the foremost writers on International Law is a most important one. The treatment accorded United States' recognition of the Serb-Croat-Slovene State by appellants and *amicus curiae* suggests that perhaps they dispute the fact it was recognition of a new State; if so, appellee believes they will find no American authorities, including the United States Government itself, in support of their position. In support of its position appellee cites the following findings of American authorities:

Hackworth, Digest of International Law, Volume I, Chapter III, "Recognition" (broken down, among other categories, to "Recognition of New States," pp. 195-222, and to "Recognition of New. Governments," pp. 222-318), and the American recognition of the Serb-Croat-Slovene State in 1919 is placed squarely in the category "Recognition of New States," pages 219-222.

Also, Hyde, International Law Chiefly as Interpreted and Applied by the United States, Volume I, Second Revised Edition 1945, page 155:

> "The Department of State on April 7, 1924, found occasion to declare and its records disclosed the following information relative to the recognition by the Government of the United States of the following States:
>
> " 'The Kingdom of the Serbs, Croats and Slovenes (Yugoslavia): The Government of the United States recognized the Government of the Kingdom of the Serbs, Croats and Slovenes on February 7, 1919. Announcement was made of this recognition by the Secretary of State of the United States at

Paris on that date, while he was a member of the American Commission to Negotiate Peace; and subsequently in a note of February 10, 1919, addressed to the Minister of the Kingdom of Serbs, Croats and Slovenes at this capital, the Acting Secretary of State recognized the Legation of Serbia as the Legation of the Serbs, Croats and Slovenes.'

*   *   *   *   *   *   *   *

"*   *   * Communication to Mr. W. C. Hart, April 7, 1924."

Finally, Publication No. 661, Department of State, Foreign Relations of the United States, 1919, Volume II, pages 892-900, Recognition of Yugoslavia [see R. pp. 83-90]; compare also Recognition of Czechoslavkia, Foreign Relations U. S. *id.*, page 85, and of Poland, page 741.

Appellee cannot pass without taking opportunity here to correct the misunderstanding of appellants and *amicus curiae* as to the importance of the Acting Secretary of State's note of February 10, 1919, to the Jugo-Slav Minister (not the *Serbian* Legation as incorrectly stated by appellants in their brief, p. 30). Appellants (Br. p. 30) state incorrectly that said note of February 10, 1919, is "even more significant as it constituted the official recognition by the United States Government of the union with Serbia of the provinces within the former Austro-Hungarian Empire and Montenegro," for as the United States Government has said itself in the preceding quotation from Hyde, recognition of the Kingdom of the Serbs, Croats and Slovenes was made by the *Secretary of State February 7,* 1919, at Paris, and the note of the *Acting Secretary of State* on February 10, only recognized the

Serb-Croat-Slovene Legation. This fits squarely with the rules of International Law which state that recognition precedes diplomatic relations. Both *amicus curiae* and appellants have laid considerable stress on the language of the note of the Acting Secretary of State that union was "to Serbia," but neither the words nor the opinion of an underling, even if so intended, can modify those by the Secretary of State, the official spokesman in foreign affairs, which quite properly did not describe a union "to Serbia," and thus the February 10 note, other than recognizing the Legation of the Kingdom of the Serbs, Croats and Slovenes is of no legal consequence. As to the effect of American recognition of the Serb-Croat-Slovene Union upon the former Kingdom of Serbia, appellee might well be content to rest upon the words of Hyde, International Law etc., *id.,* pages 122-123:

"UNIONS OF STATES

"Sec. 31. Where International Personality of Members is Not Relinquished. States many and oftentimes do unite. In such event it becomes a matter of international concern whether any constituent member of the new State has retained its international personality by not relinquishing wholly its right to participate in foreign affairs. If such be the case, the union, however, described, is in a strict sense a group of states of international law each of which remains to be regarded as a distinct person in the family of nations. Unions of such a kind have appeared in various forms. * * * The German Empire under the constitution of April 16, 1871, is illustrative. While the several States comprising it retained rights to enable them technically to preserve their individual membership in the family of nations, to the outside world it was the German Empire—the Bundesstaat—which was of chief significance."

Pages 126-127:

"Sec. 32. Where International Personality of Members is Relinquished. *The terms of a union of States may mark the relinquishment by the members thereof of the privilege of dealing with the outside world, or of being held out to it as distinctive entities in whose behalf as such foreign relations are conducted* by an appropriate instrumentality. In such case the union becomes a person or State of international law of which the composition is a matter of unconcern to foreign powers. *They recognize the completeness of the merger,* and while it lasts, *necessarily regard as non-existent the former States which surrendered their international personalities.* * * *

"As a result of the World War the Serb, Croat and Slovene people of the former Austro-Hungarian Monarchy united of their own free will with Serbia in a permanent union *for the purpose of forming 'a single sovereign independent State under the title of the Kingdom of the Serbs, Croats and Slovenes.'*

"It suffices to observe that quite apart from the appropriateness of the accepted description of such types of unions, the family of nations is concerned solely with the result effected, namely, *the single political entity asserting an international personality which has supplanted for the purposes of statehood the several constiuents which were thus welded together.*"

Appellee urges that clearly implied in American recognition of the Kingdom of the Serbs, Croats and Slovenes as a new State is American recognition of the extinction, or non-existence, of Serbia and the other two states which united to form the Kingdom of the Serbs, Croats and Slovenes and this position is supported fully by the above-quoted language of Hyde, an American authority interpreting international law from the viewpoint of the United States.

III.

A Result of Serbia's Extinction Was the Voidance of Her Treaties With the United States.

Hence, upon Serbia's extinction and recognition thereof by the United States, and applying the rules of International Law as set forth in Point I hereof, the treaties between the United States and Serbia were void, and they could no more be made valid and binding between the United States and the Serb-Croat-Slovene State *by executive decree* than could treaties with the State of Slovenes, Croats and Serbs, also a component of the Kingdom of the Serbs, Croats and Slovenes had such treaties then existed.

Not only did the United States by its clear and un-equivocal recognition of the Serb-Croat-Slovene State recognize also the extinction of Serbia, but by other political acts closely following in time the United States recognized the non-existence of treaty relations with the new Serb-Croat-Slovene State.

The first of such acts was the negotiation with the new State of a treaty which, had it been ratified, would have brought into force between the United States and the Kingdom of the Serbs, Croats and Slovenes the treaties with former Serbia *in a constitutional manner.* This treaty is identified as the Treaty of St. Germain-en-laye, executed September 10, 1919 (III Malloy, Treaties, Conventions, International Acts, etc., between the United States and Other Powers, 1910-1923, pp. 3731 ff.).

Article 12 of such Treaty provided:

> "Pending the conclusion of new treaties or conventions, all treaties, conventions, agreements and obligations between Serbia, on the one hand, and any of the Principal Allied and Associated Powers, on the other hand, which were in force on the 1st August, 1914, or which have since been entered into, shall *ipso facto* be binding upon the Serb-Croat-Slovene State."

Here was a clear attempt to provide interim treaty relations for the new State until new treaties, taking into consideration the tremendous differences between the Kingdom of the Serbs, Croats and Slovenes and Serbia, could be negotiated. Appellant and *amicus curiae* would persuade the Court that the Serbian treaties were in effect between the Allied and Associated powers and the Kingdom of the Serbs, Croats and Slovenes regardless of the Treaty of St. Germain, and that the above article was merely declaratory of an existing fact and without legal significance —an unnecessary act. But such an interpretation assigns no purpose at all to the opening clause of the article, "Pending the conclusion of new treaties or conventions," nor does it recognize the future sense of the principal verb of the article, "shall be binding."

Had the Serbian treaties been effective without break by the extinction of Serbia, then quite naturally they would have continued effective until expiring of themselves or replaced by new treaties, thus the "Pending

* * *" clause would have been without purpose or unnecessary—a manner of doing things which appellant and *amicus curiae* have seemingly several times assigned to the States involved herein. It is urged that the opening clause was based on a then present and future situation recognized by the treaty negotiators, *i. e.,* that there were no treaty relations existing between the Allied and Associated powers and the Serb-Croat-Slovene State, and the contemplation that there would be early future treaty negotiations between such States, and a desire to bridge such gap in treaty relations. Thus, the principal verb, "shall be binding," with its sense *in futuro* from the time of effectiveness of the treaty, carries out perfectly the purpose and intent of the treaty negotiators in placing Article 12 in the Treaty of St. Germain.

Therefore, when the United States Senate did not ratify the Treaty of St. Germain (it not having been presented to the Senate), the treaty never became constitutionally effective between the United States and the Serb-Croat-Slovene State, and their treaty relations were left just as they were when the unratified treaty was negotiated—non-existent—a state of affairs which was recognized by the United States when the treaty was negotiated.

By a comparison of the St. Germain treaty with another treaty negotiated by the United States during the same period there is found a second act of the United States from which it may be inferred that the purpose of Article 12 was to bridge a gap in treaty relations with the Serb-Croat-Slovene State.

If any reason is assigned by appellant and *amicus curiae* for the incorporation of Article 12 into the Treaty of St. Germain, it is that Serbia had so greatly grown that it was felt necessary to affirm the existence of treaties with the state in its enlarged form. By the same reasoning we should find a similar clause in a similar treaty with Rumania—a State equally as enlarged by the same circumstances of World War I. We do find such a treaty—the Treaty of Paris, December 9, 1919, between the United States and other Allied powers, on the one hand, and Rumania, on the other, the text of which is set forth in III Malloy, Treaties, Conventions, International Acts, etc., pages 3724 ff. Comparing with the Treaty of St. Germain, it will be noted that the Articles of the two treaties are identical with two exceptions—one unimportant to this case, Article 7 of the Rumanian treaty protecting the Jews, which was not in the Serb-Croat-Slovene treaty—and one most important to this case, Article 12 of the Serb-Croat-Slovene treaty providing interim treaty relations, *which was completely omitted from the Rumanian treaty.* The simple reason is that Rumania was truly an enlarged State, and the treaty negotiators, being fully aware of the applicable principles of International Law, knew that it was not necessary to incorporate in the Rumanian treaty an article providing interim treaty relations because their treaty relations with Rumania had not been impaired by the enlargement of the Rumanian state.

In passing, it might be noted that the preamble of Rumanian treaty refers to "large accession of territory to the Kingdom of Rumania, just as appellant and *amicus curiae* would interpret the preamble of the Serb-Croat-Slovene Treaty of St. Germain, whereas the latter preamble in reality refers first to the enlargement of Serbia by annexations of territory resulting from the Balkan Wars of 1912-1913, and then refers to a "permanent union for the purpose of forming a single sovereign independent State" to which "the Prince Regent of Serbia and the Serbian Government have agreed," clearly distinguishing Rumania as an "enlarged State" and the Kingdom of the Serbs, Croats and Slovenes as a "new State."

Appellee asserts that herein are the acts or "political decisions" of the United States by which it recognized in 1919 the voidance of the Serbian treaties.

IV.
Rebuttal.

1. The Creation of Italy Compared With the Creation of the Serb-Croat-Slovene State.

Appellant (Br. pp. 11-12) and *amicus curiae* (Br. pp. 11-13) contend that the union of a number of Italian States with Sardinia to form the Kingdom of Italy presents a "striking similarity" to the present case, that it was the position of the Italian Government that only the Sardinian treaties were in effect between the United States and Italy, but appellant and *amicus curiae* are strangely silent as to the expressed position of the United States Government, naturally the first authority for the United States Courts, as to the effect of Italy's creation upon American treaties—particularly in view of source material so readily available to *amicus curiae*.

First, it is pointed out that the Italian Kingdom was not formed by the *voluntary* union of the several independent states, but was formed as the result of wars involving the several Italian states, culminated by Garibaldi's conquest of the Kingdom of the Two Sicilies in behalf of Sardinia. In contrast with the instant situation, Serbia was not at war with either Montenegro or the State of the Slovenes, Croats and Serbs. Further, it is clearly recognized in the concluding deduction of Harvard Research into the Law of Treaties, the authority for both appellant and *amicus curiae,* that "the case of the formation of the Italian Kingdom is that when a State enlarges its territorial domain *by the annexation of other states,* its treaties continue to bind.

But even then the United States apparently did not like the idea of annexation, a dislike publicly proclaimed by President Wilson. At the time of the formation of Italy in 1861, the United States had a treaty of commerce (since 1838) with the Kingdom of Sardinia (2 Malloy, Treaties, Conventions, etc., p. 1603) and a treaty of commerce with the Kingdom of the Two Sicilies (since 1855). The Italian Government maintained that only the Sardinian treaty was effective and binding upon new Italy. Let the following excerpt speak for the position of the United States:

Diplomatic Correspondence and Foreign Relations of the United States, 1864, Part 4, pages 327-328:

"Mr. Seward [Secretary of State] to Mr. Marsh [Minister to Italy]

"Department of State

"Washington, June 15, 1864

"No. 102

"* * *.

"Pursuant to the request made by you at the instance of the Secretary-General of the [Italian] Ministry of Foreign Affairs, the President instructs me to transmit the accompanying full power, authorizing

you to negotiate with His Majesty's Government a
new treaty of commerce to take the place of the
*existing treaties between the United States and the
kingdoms of Sardinia and the Two Sicilies.* * * *."
(Emphasis added.)

Thus, even in a clear case of annexation the United
States did not recognize the treaties of the annexing
State as binding upon the annexed State, and so, with-
out further words, the comparison of the formation of
Italy with that of Yugoslavia fails completely.

2. **The Opinion of the Secretary of State, June 4, 1921, That
the Serbian Treaties Were Applicable to Yugoslavia Was
a Misapprehension of Prior Political Decisions of the
United States Government.**

We come now to Appendix 2 of *Amicus Curiae* Brief,
the opinion of F. K. Nielsen, Solicitor, State Department, May 31, 1921, which was not before the District
Court. This memorandum apparently formed the basis
for the communication of the Secretary of State, June 4,
1921, to a private law firm in New York, expressing the
State Department's opinion that the Serbian treaties with
the United States were applicable to the territory of the
Serb-Croat-Slovene State acquired from Austria-Hungary.
This communication was considered by the District Court
[R. pp. 91-92].

It is urged that the basic premise of Solicitor Nielsen's
memorandum, *i. e.,* "it may be said that Serbia absorbed
the territories which came to her as a result of the war,"
is a misapprehension directly antithetical to and incompatible with the position and political decisions of the
United States taken in 1919, *i. e.,* recognition of and
treaty negotiation with the State of the Serbs, Croats

and Slovenes as discussed at length in Point III of Argument.

It has been pointed out repeatedly that had the United States Government in 1919 believed that the union forming the Kingdom of the Serbs, Croats and Slovenes was an act of Serbia absorbing or annexing territories, then, in accord with well-defined principles of International Law, the United States would *not* have recognized the Kingdom of the Serbs, Croats and Slovenes as a new state—an act which, however, the United States did take, and which was followed by all other allied and associated powers. Thus the Solicitor of the State Department in 1921— nearly two and a half years later—attempts by a departmental memorandum to disregard the political decisions of the United States publicly taken and widely recognized in 1919.

Further, the language of the public recognition of the Serb-Croat-Slovene State given by the United States Secretary of State, February 7, 1919, and the language to the preamble to the Treaty of St. Germain, September 10, 1919, between, among others, the United States and the Serb-Croat-Slovene State, do not support the basic premise of Solicitor Nielsen's memorandum of May 31, 1921, as may be seen from the following quotations:

From the public announcement of recognition of the Serb-Croat-Slovene State by the Secretary of State at Paris, February 7, 1919 [R. p. 89]:

"* * * *After having achieved their freedom from foreign oppression* the Jugo Slav[s] formerly under Autria-Hungarian rule on various occasions expressed the desire to unite with the Kingdom of Serbia. The

Serbian Government on its part has publicly and officially *accepted the union* of the Serb, Croat and Slovene peoples. * * *."

From the preamble to the Treaty of St. Germain with the Serb-Croat-Slovene State:

"Whereas the Serb, Croat and Slovene peoples of the former Austro-Hungarian Monarchy have of their own free will determined to unite with Serbia in a permanent union *for the purpose of forming a single sovereign independent State under the title of* the Kingdom of the Serbs, Croats and Slovenes, and

"Whereas *the Prince Regent of Serbia and the Serbian Government have agreed to this union, and in consequence the Kingdom of the Serbs, Croats and Slovenes has been constituted* * * *."

The United States specifically recognized that the Southern Slavs of Austria-Hungary had achieved their freedom from the domination of one people, and American policy in opposition to annexations or absorptions by victorious powers of World War I was well known. But the opinion of Solicitor Nielsen would hold that the United States sanctioned a change of dominations—from the Austro-Hungarian to the Serb—for the freed Southern Slavs, a position which the United States opposed and, upon basis of its searching inquiry as to the intentions of Serbia in the proposed union (see pp. 25-30 of this brief), a position which the United States did not take.

Then in the first paragraph of the preamble it is noted that the *express purpose* of the union was *to form a single sovereign independent state*. By this language alone, one realizes that it could not have been contemplated by the contracting parties that the union was an absorption or annexation by Serbia, *for Serbia had been for forty years a* "single sovereign independent State" and had she been absorbing or annexing territory it would have been unnecessary to form such a state as Serbia was already. Thus the express purpose of the union must have been to form *another* "single sovereign independent State"—not Serbia.

And to this proposition, both in the United States recognition of the Kingdom of the Serbs, Croats and Slovenes and in the treaty preamble, there is found the appropriate response for Serbia—Serbia "accepted" or "agreed to this Union," *i. e.,* to the formation of a new "single sovereign independent State"—an acceptance or agreement which would properly be given by a state in the process of extinguishing its own international personality. In contrast it would be unnecessary indeed that an absorbing or annexing state "accept" or "agree to" its own act of absorption or annexation. Thus by such quoted language the United States and other world states emphasized the fact that a new state—the Kingdom of the Serbs, Croats and Slovenes—was created and that Serbia had accepted this situation.

3. Distinguishing Terlinden v. Ames, 184 U. S. 270.

Throughout this proceeding the subject case has been held forth as a prohibition to judicial consideration of the issue arising herein. But appellee urges that there are the following fundamental differences between the creation of the North German Union and the German Empire (discussed at length by the Supreme Court) and the creation of the Serb-Croat-Slovene State and Yugoslavia, and thus between *Terlinden v. Ames, supra,* and the instant case.

In creating the North German Union and the German Empire it is clearly a fact that the German states did not give up their independent existences to the extent of stripping themselves of power to enter into relations with foreign states; "* * *, those [German] states are not hindered from independently regulating extradition by agreements with foreign states, * * *." (Moore, International Law, Vol. 5, p. 355; *Terlinden v. Ames, supra,* p. 286.) Nor did, for example, the State of Prussia lose its international identity as its King, who became the Emperor of Germany, officially titled himself as the King of Prussia in negotiating a number of treaties and conventions with the United States after 1871 (Malloy, Treaties, Conventions, International Acts, etc., Vol. I, p. 550).

This may be contrasted with Serbia's complete loss of identity and disappearance as set forth heretofore under Point II of Argument.

There is this second important distinction. Following the formation of the North German Union in 1866, that state and the United States concluded a treaty in 1868, a provision of which "extended to all the States of the North German Union" the extradition convention of 1852 between the United States and Prussia and other German States. This treaty was duly ratified in accord with our Constitution. Appellee submits that Article 12, Treaty of St. Germain between the United States and the Serb-Croat-Slovene State, hereinbefore discussed, was intended for a similar purpose, and that non-ratification of the latter treaty marks a second important distinction between *Terlinden v. Ames, supra,* and the instant case.

A third distinction brings us also to an important misquotation of *Terlinden v. Ames, supra,* pp. 290-291, by
appellant's counsel, a misquotation which he has now made
for the third time in these proceedings and to which error
his attention has been previously called. Not only is the
misquotation extremely pertinent to the issue arising here,
but it has been emphasized by italicization. It is found
in the second paragraph of the quotation appearing on
page 45 of Appellants' Brief, reading as misquoted:

> ". . . *It cannot be successfully contended that the
> courts could properly intervene on the ground that
> the treaty under which both governments had pro-
> ceeded had terminated by reason of the adoption of
> the German Empire, notwithstanding the judgment
> of both governments to the contrary.*"

It seems clear that appellant is attempting to draw a
parallel between the "adoption of the German Empire" in
Terlinden v. Ames, supra, and the proclamation of union
forming Jugo-Slavia in the instant case, and to persuade
this Court that the quoted language of the Supreme Court
in relation thereto should be controlling.

But let us see how the Supreme Court's language, correctly quoted, reads:

> ". . . it cannot be successfully contended that the
> courts could properly intervene on the ground that
> the treaty under which both governments had pro-
> ceeded had terminated by reason of the adoption OF
> THE CONSTITUTION of the German Empire, notwith-
> standing the judgment of both governments to the
> contrary." (Emphasis ours.)

Thus we find that the most important words of the
quotation have been left out, and the quotation becomes of

distinctive consequence in relation to the present issue for the simple reason that appellee has not raised the issue of the Constitution of the Serb-Croat-Slovene State terminating the validity of Serbian treaties, whereas the effect of the German Constitution was an important issue in *Terlinden v. Ames.*

This brings us naturally to appellants' quotation from *Terlinden v. Ames* (Br. p. 44), which he describes as fitting the instant case perfectly. But appellee has not called upon the courts of this country to "adjudicate the correctness of the conclusions" of Yugoslavia as to its powers under its Constitution or otherwise, but has called upon the courts of this country to determine whether a treaty of extradition has been lawfully concluded with Yugoslavia, provoking the further question whether by reason of recognized rules of international law the treaties with Serbia were voided and such voidance was recognized in political decisions taken by the United States in 1919.

4. The Debts of Serbia Were Normally Assumed by the Serb-Croat-Slovene State.

Amicus curiae has attempted to find in the action of the United States Congress in 1928 upon Serbian and Jugo-Slavia indebtedness an approval of its position, but the rule of International Law, expressed succinctly in the following quotation, suggests that such settlement of indebtedness was but a normal procedure:

I Hackworth, Digest of International Law, page 540:
"* * * Where the identity of the parent state is destroyed, the conquering or annexing power *or the new state* becomes heir to the debts of the destroyed country."

This parallels a rule of common business practice: If one takes over the assets of another (Jugo-Slavia took over the assets of Serbia), one must assume his liabilities (Jugo-Slavia assumed the debts of Serbia). Jugo-Slavia took over also the assets of Montenegro and the State of the Slovenes, Croats and Serbs, and assumed as well their debts (that of the latter being a portion of the Austro-Hungarian debt as prorated in the several peace treaties).

Thus the action of the United States Congress in settlement of the indebtedness of Jugo-Slavia has no significance in relation to treaties between the two states.

5. "Opinions of the United States Courts."

Amicus curiae (Br. p. 38 ff.) and appellant (Br. pp. 54-55) have quoted the decisions of several state courts in support of their position that the Serbian treaties are effective between the United States and Yugoslavia.

A cursory examination of the language quoted from the decision in *Lukich v. Department of Labor and Industries,* 176 Wash. 221, 22 P. 2d 388 (1934), reveals that it was *"conceded * * * that the [Serbian] convention above referred to is now in full force and effect between Yugoslavia and the United States,"* from which concession it may be seen that there was no determination upon the merits of the issue, and thus is of no value in determining the issue raised herein.

In language quoted from *Urbus v. State Compensation Commissioner,* 113 W. Va. 563, 169 S. E. 164 (1933), it is at once apparent that the Court labored under the misapprehension that either the Treaty of St. Germain was ratified and in force between the United States and the Serb-Croat-Slovene State or that the mere signing of the treaty bound the United States to Article 12 thereof which would have revived the Serbian treaties. This fundamental error of that Court destroys the comparative value of that case in relation to the present issue.

Another case quoted, *Olijan v. Lublin,* 50 N. E. 2d 264 (1943), does not pretend to determine the issue of validity of treaties.

The case of *In re Thomas,* 12 Blatchf. 370, 23 Fed. Cas. 927, involves a point similar to that in *Terlinden v. Ames, supra, i. e.,* that Bavaria continued its international existence as a state despite the formation of the North German Union and the German Empire. Indeed, after the formation in 1866 of the North German Union, the United States and Bavaria in 1868 negotiated and concluded a Treaty of Naturalization (1 Malloy, Treaties, Conventions, etc., p. 60), Article 3 of which expressly extended the life of an earlier extradition convention between these two states which was the subject of inquiry in *In re Thomas, supra.*

Conclusion.

It is respectfully submitted that the decision of the United States District Court granting the writ of *habeas corpus* be affirmed.

Respectfully submitted,

ROBERT T. REYNOLDS,
VINCENT G. ARNERICH,
EDWARD J. O'CONNOR,
Attorneys for Appellee.

APPENDIX "A."

Excerpted from

THE HISTORY OF THE PEACE CONFERENCE OF PARIS
Vol. 5.

by H. W. Temperley

pages 393-396, incl.

THE MANIFESTO (PACT) OF CORFU[1]

At the conference of the members of the late (Serbian) Coalition Cabinet and those of the present Cabinet, and also the representatives of the Jugo-Slav Committee in London, all of whom have hitherto been working on parallel lines, views have been exchanged in collaboration with the president of the Skupstina, on all questions concerning the life of the Serbs, Croats, and Slovenes in their joint future state.

We are happy in being able once more on this occasion to point to the completely unanimity of all parties concerned.

In the first place, the representatives of the Serbs, Croats, and Slovenes declare anew and most categorically that our people constitutes but one nation, and that it is one in blood, one by the spoken and written language, by the continuity and unity of the territory in which it lives, and finally in virtue of the common and vital interests of its national existence and the general development of its moral and material life.

The idea of its national unity has never suffered extinction, although all the intellectual forces of its enemy were directed aganist its unification, its liberty and its

---

[1]The Jugo-Slav Movement, by R. J. Koerner, pp. 100-5.

national existence. Divided between several states our nation is in Austria-Hungary alone split up into eleven provincial administrations, coming under thirteen legislative bodies. The feeling of national unity, together with the spirit of liberty and independence, have supported it in the never-ending struggles of centuries against the Turks in the East and against the Germans and the Magyars in the West.

Being numerically inferior to its enemies in the East and West, it was impossible for it to safeguard its unity as a nation and a State, its liberty and its independence against the brutal maxim of "might goes before right" militating against it both East and West.

But the moment has come when our people is no longer isolated. The war imposed by German militarism upon Russia, upon France and upon England for the defense of their honour as well as for the liberty and independence of small nations, has developed into a struggle for the liberty of the World and the Triumph of Right over Might. All nations which love liberty and independence have allied themselves together for their common defense, to save civilization and liberty at the cost of every sacrifice, to establish a new international order based upon justice and upon the right of every nation to dispose of itself and so organize its independent life; finally to establish a durable peace consecrated to the progress and development of humanity and to secure the world against a catastrophe similar to that which the conquering lust of German Imperialism has provoked.

To noble France, who has proclaimed the liberty of nations, and to England, the hearth of liberty, the Great American Republic and the new, free and democratic

Russia have joined themselves in proclaiming as their principal war aim the triumph of liberty and democracy and as a basis of the new international order the right of free self-determination for every nation.

Our nation of the three names, which has been the greatest sufferer under brute force and injustice and which has made the greatest sacrifices to preserve its right of self-determination, has with enthusiasm accepted this sublime principle put forward as the chief aim of this atrocious war, provoked by the violation of this very principle.

The authorized representatives of the Serbs, Croats, and Slovenes, in declaring that it is the desire of our people to free itself from every foreign yoke and to constitute itself a free, national and independent State, a desire based on the principle that every nation has the right to decide its own destiny, are agreed in judging that this State should be founded on the following modern and democratic principles:

(1) The State of the Serbs, Croats, and Slovenes, who are also known as the Southern Slavs or Jugo-Slavs, will be a free and independent kingdom, with indivisible territory and unity of allegiance. It will be a constitutional, democratic and parliamentary monarchy under the Karageorgevitch Dynasty, which has always shared the ideas and the feelings of the nation, placing liberty and the national will above all else.

(2) This State will be named "The Kingdom of the Serbs, Croats, and Slovenes." And the style of the Sovereign will be "King of the Serbs, Croats, and Slovenes."

(3) The State will have a single coat-of-arms, a single flag, and a single crown. These emblems will be composed

of the present existing emblems. The unity of the State will be symbolized by the coat-of-arms and the flag of the Kingdom.

(4) The special Serb, Croat, and Slovene flags rank equally and may be freely hoisted on all occasions. The special coat-of-arms may be used with equal freedom.

(5) The three national designations—Serbs, Croats, and Slovenes—are equal before the law throughout the territory of the Kingdom, and every one may use them freely upon all occasions of public life and in dealing with the authorities.

(6) The two alphabets, the Cyrillic and the Latin, also rank equally, and every one may use them free throughout the territory of the Kingdom. The royal authorities and the local self-governing authorities have both the right and the duty to employ both alphabets in accordance with the wishes of the citizens.

(7) All recognized religions may be freely and publicly exercised. The Orthodox, Roman Catholic and Mussulman faiths, which are those chiefly professed by our national, shall rank equally and enjoy equal rights with regard to the State.

In consideration of these principles the legislature will take special care to safeguard religious concord in conformity with the spirit and tradition of our whole nation.

(8) The calendar will be unified as soon as possible.

(9) The territory of the Kingdom of the Serbs, Croats and Slovenes will include all the territory inhabited com-

pactly and in territorial continuity by our nation of the three names. It cannot be mutilated without detriment to the vital interests of the community.

Our nation demands nothing that belongs to others. It demands only what is its own. It desired to free itself and to achieve its unity. Therefore it consciously and firmly refuses every partial solution of the problem of its national liberation and unification. It puts forward the proposition of its deliverance from Austro-Hungarian domination and its union with Serbia and Montenegro in a single State forming an indivisible whole.

In accordance with the right of self-determination of peoples, no part of this territorial totality may without infringement of justice be detached and incorporated with some other State without the consent of the nation itself.

(10) In the interests of freedom and of the equal right of all nations, the Adriatic shall be free and open to each and all.

(11) All citizens throughout the territory of the Kingdom shall be equal and enjoy the same rights with regard to the State and before the law.

(12) The election of the Deputies to the National representative body shall be by universal suffrage, with equal, direct and secret ballot. The same shall apply to the elections in the Communes and other administrative units. Elections will take place in each Commune.

(13) The Constitution, to be established after the conclusion of peace by a Constituent Assembly elected by

universal suffrage, with direct and secret ballot, will be the basis of the entire life of the State; it will be the source and the consummation of all authority and of all rights by which the entire life of the nation will be regulated.

The Constitution will provide the nation with the possibility of exercising its special energies in local autonomies delimited by natural, social and economic condition.

The Constitution must be passed in its entirety by a numerically defined majority in the Constituent Assembly.

The nation of the Serbs, Croats and Slovenes, thus unified, will form a state of about twelve million inhabitants. This State will be the guarantee for their independence and national development, and their national and intellectual progress in general, a mighty bulwark against the German thrust, an inseparable ally of all the civilized nations and states which have proclaimed the principle of right and liberty and that of international justice. It will be a worthy member of the new Community of Nations.

Drawn up at Corfu, July 7/20, 1917.

The Prime Minister of the Kingdom of Serbia and Minister for Foreign Affairs.

(Sgd.) Nikola P. Pashitch

The President of the Jugo-Slav Committee.

(Sgd.) Dr. Ante Trumbic

Advocate, Deputy and Leader of the Croatian National Party in the Dalmatian Diet, late Mayor of Split (Spalato), late Deputy for the District of Zadar (Zara) in the Austrian Parliament.

APPENDIX "B".

The Special Agent at Corfu (Dodge) to the Secretary of State.

No. 107   Corfu, August 26, 1918.

(Received October 8)

Sir: I have the honor to acknowledge the receipt, late on the 8th instant, of your telegram of the 7th instant, 6 p. m., informing me that confidential reports were desired by the Department from time to time regarding the position of the Serbian Government as to the character of the relation to be established between Servia and the Yugo-Slav provinces of Austria-Hungary in the event that the latter obtained their freedom.

Such reports will be furnished as desired. I may mention that during my residence here I have heard and seen in the Serbian and Yugo-Slav press little as to the details of this matter, the broad outlines of which are laid down in the so-called "Declaration of Corfu," the text and a translation of which were enclosed in my despatch No. 2 of July 27, 1917. The members of the Government and other Serbs with whom I have talked upon this subject always assume that the constitution of the desired Yugo-Slav state will be based upon the principles laid down in this declaration. Unfortunately at present several of the principal members of the Government, including Mr. Pashitch, are absent from Corfu and expecting to remain away for some time. I have, however, taken advantage of my recent trip to Salonica (to be reported in a later despatch) during which I was constantly with Mr. Hintchitch, Minister of Public Works, and Mr. Gavriolevitch, now in charge of the Foreign Office, to ascertain from them what I could as to this matter. In so doing I have of course made no mention of the Department's desire. The following is the substance of what I learned:

Mr. Nintchitch: The character of the relation to be established between Serbia and the Yugo-Slav populations of Austria-Hungary is determined in its outlines by the Act of Corfu which declares that the new state shall be a free democracy in which all the citizens shall be equal and having equal rights before the state and the law. It also prescribes that all elections whether national, departmental or communal shall be by universal, equal, direct and secret ballot. This act was signed by Mr. Pashitch, representing the Serbian Government, and by Dr. Ante Trumbitch, representing the other Yugo-Slav peoples. It was drafted at conferences at which there took part for Serbia, in addition to Mr. Pashitch, representatives of the principal other Serbian political parties and, in addition to Doctor Trumbitch, who is a Dalmatian, two other members of the Yugo-Slav Committee, one a Slovene and the other a Croatian. All the members of the conference unanimously approved of the act. Its text had immediately been published in Austria-Hungary and in Germany and became well-known to the Austro-Hungarian Yugo-Slav and, so far as could be ascertained, won the approval of a very large majority of them. Of course, owing to the strict censorship and the difficulty of direct communication with these Yugo-Slav as a whole, their sentiments could not be ascertained as exactly as they could in normal conditions. Nevertheless enough was known to make Mr. Nintchitch feel convinced that a very large majority of the Austro-Hungarian Yugo-Slav enthusiastically supported the act. Yugo-Slav abroad in Allied or neutral countries had also shown clearly their entire approval, including those in the United States.

The act only attempted to determine the broad outlines of the future government, as it had been considered unwise to go into details both because the members of the conference might not in that case be able to agree upon them unanimously and because such details might have caused differences of opinion outside the conference leading to discussion which in the present circumstances it was most important to avoid. Further the conference, which was not an elected body and was only in a sense representative, it being impossible to elect a truly representative body at the time, felt that it should not go beyond the outlines which all were practically certain to accept or attempt to bind the Yugo-Slav people as to details.

For the same reason and as freedom of expression was denied to the Yugo-Slavs in Austria-Hungary, it had been considered best to discourage any discussion of the details of the future government in the Serbian and Yugo-Slav press abroad. Very little such discussion had therefore appeared.

According to the Act of Corfu, the future state was not to be a federal one but a centralized state with local autonomies. So much was clear and was considered necessary, as the future state must be strong, as it would have enemies on or near its borders, Bulgaria and Germany: to the latter it must be a barrier to prevent German schemes of conquest in the Near East. Such a centralized state was understood to be desired by the Croatians and Slovenes. Regarding the organization of such a centralized state, Mr. Nintchitch declared that this would be left entirely to the decision of the freely-elected representatives of all the Yugo-Slav people. As soon as practicable after the Yugo-Slav of Austria-Hungary had obtained their freedom, a constitutional convention would be called and this convention would freely draft the constitution of the future state. According to the Act of Corfu, the members of the convention would be elected by equal, direct, secret and universal suffrage.

Mr. Nintchitch discussed a few further details as to the future form of government but was careful to mention that the ideas he expressed were merely his own personal ones. The capital of the new state he thought should be Belgrade but in that case the King would be obliged to be in residence during regular periods of the year at cities in Croatia, Slovenia, etc., and especially at Agram. He mentioned a strong argument, to his thinking, against the maintenance of the present boundaries of the Yugo-Slav portions of Austria-Hungary in the new state, for the Serbs in Croatia, Dalmatia, Bosnia and Hersegovina would in that case desire to be united with Serbia, and as they must have the right of self-disposition this would of itself produce a very material modification of the present boundaries. Moreover, the Croatians of Dalmatia, Bosnia and Herzegovina would also be desirous of being united to Croatia. There were, he thought, about three million Serbs left in the present Kingdom and as many more in the Banat (Bachka), Montenegro, Croatia, Dalmatia, Bosnia and Hersegovina. The new state would include from twelve to thirteen million inhabitants about one-half of whom would be Serbs.

In a general way Mr. Nintchitch thought that the political organization of the new state should be like that of the present Kingdom of Serbia although the departments into which it would be divided might well have more local autonomy. It would be a parliamentary form of government with the Parliament elected, as prescribed by the Act of Corfu, by equal, direct, secret and universal suffrage. Ministers would be responsible to Parliament. Each of the present Serbian departments has a local assembly elected by universal suffrage. Its legislative powers are determined by the various laws passed by the Skupshtina and are usually limited to small local matters such as primary schools, communal roads, minor sanitary and police matters, etc. The acts of these assemblies are, however, subject to the veto of the Minister of the Interior who is himself responsible to the Skupshtina. Under the new constitution the powers of the departmental assemblies might be considerably enlarged.

Mr. Nintchitch did not think that the various portions of the new Kingdom would be found to differ to any great extent in the degree of their culture and civilization nor that the undoubtedly different interests of different portions would present any difficulties to harmonious cooperation. The different interests would be given free expression through local autonomies and the freely elected central parliament. It was true, however, that Serbia would enter the new state in a far more exhausted condition than the other Yugo-Slavs. He admitted that the new constitution would naturally be a good deal of an experiment, but changes would subsequently be made as found necessary, and with the profound desire for union of all the component parts of the new state, an arrangement satisfactory to all would eventually be found.

The statements made to me by Mr. Gavrilovitch were, so far as they went, similar to those of Mr. Nintchitch. Mr. Gavrilovitch, however, appeared anxious to avoid entering into details or expressing any personal opinion, stating that all discussion of such matters should be left for after the war and for the constitutional convention. It was sufficient for the present to fight for the liberation of the Yugo-Slav portions of Austria-Hungary. After their liberation it would be time enough to discuss details of the future state which must be based upon the Act of Corfu.

I have (etc.)

H. Percival Dodge.

APPENDIX "C."

The Special Agent at Corfu (Dodge), temporarily at
Rome, to the Secretary of State.

No. 113   Rome, September 13, 1918

(Received October 21)

Sir: Referring to my despatch No. 107, of the 26th
ultimo, reporting, in accordance with your telegram of
August 7, 6 p.m., regarding the position of the Serbian
Government as to the character of the relation to be established between Serbia and the Yugo-Slav provinces of
Austria-Hungary in the event that the latter obtain their
freedom,—I have the honor to inform you that shortly
before leaving Corfu I had a conversation upon this subject with Mr. Stoyan Protitch, Acting President of the
Council and Minister for Foreign Affairs. Mr. Protitch
is generally considered to be closer to Mr. Pashitch than
any other of his colleagues and comes immediately after
Mr. Pashitch in importance in the Radical Party, which
is now in power.

    *   *   *   *   *   *   *   *   *

. . . I inquired of Mr. Protitch as to his view regarding the constitution of a future Yugo-Slav state. Mr.
Protitch replied that the foundations for such a state must
lie in the Declaration of Corfu, although this declaration
might be made even more democratic. All the present
Yugo-Slav portions of Austria-Hungary would enjoy absolute political equality with Serbia and there could be no
possibility of any Serbian hegemony or superiority of any

sort. Serbia moreover desired no such superiority. He saw no reason why sooner or later Bulgaria should not also join the Yugo-Slav state if she agreed to come in on the same footing as the others. Bulgarians spoke a tongue closely allied to Serbian and there was no very great racial difference between Bulgarians and Serbians, although the former had a considerable admixture of Turanian blood. This would be the logical solution and he greatly hoped it would some day be possible.

Regarding the details of the form of government, these must naturally be left to be decided by the constitutional convention which would be called and elected (as all elections were prescribed to be made by the Declaration of Corfu) by equal, direct, secret and universal ballot. His own idea was, however, that the future state must possess strength. The central Government must, therefore, control military, naval and foreign affairs, national finances and national economic and commercial matters. Also, the civil and criminal law must be uniform for the whole state. Outside of these matters, the rest and all local matters must be left to local assemblies. The administrative divisions of the state might remain as at present, each division having its local assembly, or the present divisions might be somewhat modified or possibly entirely new divisions might be made: All this depended upon the decisions of the constitutional convention. The central Government would be a ministry, responsible to Parliament as at present. Parliament itself might well be composed of two Chambers instead of one Chamber as at present.

Mr. Protitch emphasized the democratic character of the new state and the absolute equality of all its inhabitants and territories.

I have also recently had an interview with General Rachitch, Minister of War, in which I was able to turn the conversation to the same subject. General Rachitch stated that it was quite impossible to go into any details at present as all of these must be settled by the constitutional convention. Nevertheless, he might say that the new state must, of course, be built upon thoroughly democratic principles and upon the outlines so clearly laid down in the Declaration of Corfu. Complete equality would be guaranteed to all portions of the territories and their inhabitants. Serbia must enjoy no position in the new state in any way privileged or different from the other portions. If Serbia should become pre-eminent in the new state it would only be through the individual merits of her population.

Several of my colleagues with whom I have talked on this subject express the opinion that the present Serbia, in the possible future state, will tend to be over-shadowed by Croatia which is only slightly smaller in population and is far more advanced educationally, economically and financially. Croatia has also suffered far less than Serbia in the present and recent Balkan wars. In addition to enormous losses of productive capital, Serbia, it is generally assumed, has lost fully one-quarter of her population since the first Balkan War.

I have (etc.)

H. Percival Dodge

No. 13552

IN THE

United States Court of Appeals

FOR THE NINTH CIRCUIT

———

Rafo Ivancevic, Consul General of the Federal People's
Republic of Yugoslavia,

Appellant,

vs.

Andrija Artukovic,

Appellee.

———

James J. Boyle, United States Marshal,

Appellant,

vs.

Andrija Artukovic,

Appellee.

———

APPELLANTS' REPLY BRIEF.

———

Ronald Walker, Paul P. O'Br
1023 Rowan Building,
458 South Spring Street,
Los Angeles 13, California,
Attorney for Appellants.

Parker & Company, Law Printers, Los Angeles. Phone MA. 6-9171.

TOPICAL INDEX

TABLE OF AUTHORITIES CITED

No. 13552

IN THE

United States Court of Appeals

FOR THE NINTH CIRCUIT

———

RAFO IVANCEVIC, Consul General of the Federal People's
Republic of Yugoslavia,

Appellant,

vs.

ANDRIJA ARTUKOVIC,

Appellee.

———

JAMES J. BOYLE, United States Marshal,

Appellant,

vs.

ANDRIJA ARTUKOVIC,

Appellee.

———

APPELLANTS' REPLY BRIEF.

———

Introduction.

Before subjecting appellee's argument to the light of
analysis and the consequent exposure of its complete arti-
ficiality and lack of foundation in logic or law, appellants
believe that the attention of the Court should be directed
to the nature and scope of the issue which it is called upon
to decide. For what hangs in the balance on this appeal

is the continuing validity as between the United States and Yugoslavia of all of the treaties entered into between the United States and Serbia prior to the union with the latter of certain former Austro-Hungarian provinces and Montenegro. For, while technically only the Extradition Treaty of 1901 is involved in this case, actually the validity of the Convention of Commerce and Navigation of 1881 and of the Consular Convention of 1881 (2 Malloy 1613, 1618, 1621) is equally involved, as all three treaties stand upon the same footing. This, indeed, is recognized by appellee in his statement of Point III of his brief (p. 34).

As we have shown in our opening brief, both the Yugoslav* and United States Governments have considered these treaties to be in full force and effect, notwithstanding the union, and the relations between the two countries have been, and are now being conducted largely within their framework. Appellee's position is that both Governments are and have been wrong, and that the United States need not now respect any rights granted by it in such treaties to Serbia. But the coin has an obverse: the treaties grant rights not only to Serbia but to the United States, as well. Obviously, if Serbia's union with the

---

*For convenience sake, the words Yugoslav and Yugoslavia are used herein indiscriminately to refer to the Kingdom of the Serbs, Croats and Slovenes, the Kingdom of Yugoslavia and the Federal People's Republic of Yugoslavia. This is and has been the popular name for the country regardless of changes in its formal name which are irrelevant to the discussion herein.

other territories extinguished the rights so granted by the United States, by the same token the rights so granted to the United States have also been extinguished. That this is not an academic matter is witnessed by the importance which the United States Government attached to such rights, when, in 1946 as a condition of recognizing the republican government which had replaced the monarchy in Yugoslavia, the United States requested and received the new government's assurances that it recognized the continuing validity as between the United States and Yugoslavia of the latter's international obligations [R. pp. 75-78] which must, of necessity, have included those contained in the treaties concluded between the United States and Serbia which, as early as 1921, both countries had agreed had survived the organization of the Yugoslav union (V Hackworth, pp. 374, 375). Thus, the subtle appeal of appellee's argument that the organization of Yugoslavia relieved the United States of its obligations under its treaties with Serbia is at once dissipated when it is recognized that its inescapable consequence would be to deny to the United States rights which it claims and which Yugoslavia concedes.

In the light of the foregoing, let us consider the argument whereby the appellee would persuade this Court that treaty rights and obligations which both governments have recognized as obtaining, do not exist as a matter of law, and have not existed for some thirty-two years during which many of such rights and obligations have been claimed and fulfilled.

I.

The Union With Serbia of the Former Austro-Hungarian Provinces and Montenegro Did Not Result in the Extinguishment of Serbia's Treaties.

Appellee argues that as a matter of law, the voluntary union with Serbia of the former Austro-Hungarian provinces and Montenegro resulted *ipso facto* and *eo instante,* in the disappearance of Serbia and the consequent extinguishment of international treaties to which Serbia was a party. But, such a grotesque concept has no more validity under international law than it has in private law, and none of the authorities cited by appellee support it. They are all addressed to the situation created by the absorption of one state into the territory of another *existing* state which has its own already subsisting network of international rights and obligations. Serbia's acquiesence to the new union was not of this nature and did not result in the extinction of Serbia's treaty rights and obligations. This is accomplished when, as in the case of Japan's forceful annexation of Korea and as in the case of Hawaii's voluntary annexation to the United States for example, one sovereign power is absorbed into another existing sovereign power and the former's sovereignty is expressly extinguished. In this connection, it is significant that notwithstanding the extinction of Hawaii's sovereignty by the act of its annexation to the United States, the American Congress nevertheless thought it prudent specifically to abrogate treaties to which Hawaii had been a party, presumably because, even in such case, there was some apprehension that they would otherwise survive. (Joint Resolution, July 7, 1898, V Hackworth 361.)

Thus, it is merely an exercise in semantics to talk about the absorption of Serbia into Yugoslavia in the same context. Yugoslavia was nonexistent until the union with Serbia of the former Austro-Hungarian provinces and Montenegro. Until that moment, Yugoslavia was without form or substance and had neither sovereignty nor territory. It "absorbed" Serbia only by the *process of coming into being as its successor,* endowed with the rights and encumbered by the obligations of the sovereign which it had succeeded, and from which its own sovereignty was derived.

II.

Whether Yugoslavia Was or Was Not a "New" State Is Wholly Immaterial, Since if It Was a "New" State, It Was the Successor State to Serbia.

The remainder of appellee's argument in chief, consisting of a labored attempt to demonstrate that Yugoslavia was a "new" state, is as ineffective as it is irrelevant. That the royal dynasty of Serbia became the royal dynasty of Yugoslavia, that the Serbian parliament and cabinet was succeeded by a Yugoslav parliament and cabinet and that the Serbian legations and missions were transformed into Yugoslavia legations and missions (Appellee's Br. pp. 12-16), merely demonstrates, of course, that Serbia was succeeded by Yugoslavia. Very few of the European states have undergone no transformations and thus have not had new flags and coats-of-arms (see Appellee's Br. p. 16). Yet these circumstances have in no way affected the continuity of their international relationships, and the accretion in territory and population merely evidences the fact which is our starting point, to wit, that there was a voluntary union with Serbia of the former Austro-Hungarian provinces and Montenegro. The modernization of the calendar and other such trivia do not merit separate comment. It is only sterile and meaningless casuistry to split hairs as to whether Yugoslavia is a "new" state or merely an enlarged Serbia, for there is no inconsistency in considering Yugoslavia as a "new" state and at the same time as the successor to Serbia's international rights and obligations. Thus, while as appellee points out, Hackworth lists the recognition of Yugoslavia as that of a "new" state (Appellee's Br. p. 30), he also indexes the reference of Yugoslavia's recognition of, and Secretary Hughes' opinion with respect to the continuing validity of the Serbian treaties (V Hackworth 374, 375) under "Treaties—Sovereignty, change of" (VIII Hackworth 308). Furthermore, Hackworth's reference under "Treaties—State Succession" is *"See* Government, effect of change of, *supra;* Sovereignty, change of, *supra"* (VIII Hackworth 308). Thus, if Hackworth's method of indexing is relevant, it must be noted that in his indexing he recognized the consistency of a state being both a "new" state and a "successor" state, and in the continued existence of treaties where there has been a change in sovereignty by succession.

Indeed, a "new" state free of international treaty obligations and possessing no treaty rights comes into being only when such state is not the successor to any previous sovereignty. Recent examples are Israel and Tripolitania, neither of which is a successor to the sovereignty of the power previously having jurisdiction over its territories, each having been made, so to speak, "out of whole cloth." This was not the case with Yugoslavia which was formed by the voluntary union of former Austro-Hungarian provinces and Montenegro with the Kingdom of Serbia, an already existing sovereign state.

Thus, to say that Yugoslavia is a "new" state and therefore did not succeed to either the benefits or the obligations of Serbia, is to beg the question. On the basis of appellee's argument, Yugoslavia would have been the successor to Serbia if Serbia had conquered and absorbed Montenegro and the former Austro-Hungarian provinces, instead of having entered into voluntary union with them. The logical consequence of appellee's argument is that because Serbia did not annex and absorb the former Austro-Hungarian provinces and Montenegro, but entered into voluntary union with them, Serbia, for all international juridical purposes, must be deemed to have been annexed and absorbed by the former Austro-Hungarian provinces and Montenegro.

III.

"Recognition" Is Not Given Exclusively to "New" States Without Antecedents or Succession.

The even more extended discussion of "recognition" (Appellee's Br. pp. 17-31) is also completely devoid of both relevance and significance.

Appellee argues that "recognition" is extended only to "new" states, but United States recognized Yugoslavia, *ergo* Yugoslavia was a "new" state (see last paragraph page 17 and first paragraph page 20). Apart from the fallacy inherent in this argument that a "new" state may not also be the successor to the treaty rights and obligations of an "old" state, the Court will take judicial notice of the error in the premise. Thus, the United States "recognized" Russia shortly after achieving its own sovereignty, for it will be recalled that John Quincy Adams was appointed Minister to the Court of St. Petersburg in 1809 (Am. Dict. Biog.). Obviously, when the United States withdrew its "recognition" of Russia in 1917, or thereabouts, and again "recognized" Russia in 1933, following the Litvinov Agreement, the United States was withdrawing and extending its "recognition" not of Russia or the Russian state but of the regime or government then holding power in Russia. If "recognition" was applicable only to "new" states, as distinguished from regimes and governments, there would be no public issue today with respect to the "recognition" or "non-recognition" of China, and there would have been no occasion to rerecognize Yugoslavia in 1946 [R. pp. 75-78] upon the replacement of the monarchy by the republic. In these instances, as in the more frequent cases that arise as the result of coups d'etat and pronunciamientos in Latin American countries, the question of "recognition" or "non-recognition" pertains not to the state itself but to a regime newly come into power.

Of course, "recognition" may also involve a "new" state as in the case, for example, of Israel and Tripolitania. But the fact of "recognition" gives rise to no inference as to whether the recipient of such "recognition" is a new government in an "old" state or a "new" state, or, in the case of the latter, whether the "new" state is or is not a successor of some other state.

IV.

Appellee's Attempted Gloss on Article 12 of the Treaty of St. Germain Is Contrary to the Plain Meaning of That Provision.

Appellee argues (Br. p. 34) that the implication from the reference in the Treaty of St. Germain-en-Laye to Serbia's treaties constitutes a recognition that but for such reference the treaties between Serbia and the parties to such treaty (the United States Senate never ratified it) would have lapsed. But as appellants have already pointed out, in effect (Op. Br. p. 33) the reference that such treaties "shall *ipso facto* be binding on the Serb-Croat-Slovene State," must be taken to mean what it says, *i.e.,* that such treaties are "automatically" binding and not that they are not automatically binding but binding only because of the St. Germain-en-Laye treaty.

Appellee's distorted construction is impossible of application. The very words *"ipso facto"* make the inclusion of this paragraph in that treaty merely a recognition that such treaties *by the very nature* of the case were binding upon the new Kingdom. And surely the negotiation of new treaties would effectually dispose of old treaties. In no sense could the signing of this treaty by representatives of this government, be construed as a decision recognizing the termination of Serbian treaties. It was the exact reverse. It was a recognition that *ipso facto* they continued.

Counsel for appellants does not wish to belabor the point by repeating the arguments of his opening brief, but, since appellee places so much stress upon the point, takes the liberty of re-emphasizing the material appearing on pages 33-36 of his opening brief. Attention is directed, however, to the fact that where it was sought to *free* Serbia from a treaty obligation under the Treaty of Berlin of 1878, a specific paragraph was required, whereas all other treaties continued *ipso facto*.

V.

Appellee Has Wholly Failed to Weaken the Force and Effect of the Analogy of the Unification of Italy.

Appellee seeks to avoid the force of the arguments of appellants and *Amicus* as to the close analogy of the Italian union to the Yugoslav union by stressing the element of war and conquest in the former as distinguished from the peaceful and voluntary nature of the latter. We have already adverted to the absurdity of attaching a penalty to voluntary action, a penalty which would be contrary to the entire thrust of American foreign policy throughout its history. It should also be pointed out, however, that the very authority quoted by appellee at the conclusion of, and presumably as support for, this astounding proposition furnishes no such support since it does not even mention any such distinction. (See quotation from Harvard Research into the Law of Treaties, Appellee's Br. p. 39.)

In addition appellee ends up by completely cutting the ground from under his own feet. For in the remainder of his argument on this point he negates his own attempted distinction by arguing that in the case of Italy the annexation did not result in the carryover of the Sardinian Treaties to the annexed territories. While this argument appears to be strained and wholly incorrect it highlights the thorough confusion and inconsistency of appellee's approach. For the very argument he uses to reach this result, that the United States is opposed to forcible annexation and therefore did not recognize its effect, is squarely opposed to his earlier argument that it is the element of force and conquest which is essential for the transfer of sovereignty and of the international rights and obligations attached thereto.

The weakness of appellee's attempted distinction points up the fact that in all essential elements the formation of Yugoslavia corresponds to the formation of Italy, without the factor, recognized by appellee himself as negative, of the use of force. The unification of South Slav peoples was preceded by centuries of persistent common struggle against the oppressors—Turkey, Austro-Hungary, the Republic of Venice. In the course of this long-lasting struggle an awareness of the unity of their interests and of the necessity of unification as a guarantee of final success was developed. In the period of the awakening of national awareness, as well as of the strengthening of national movements and formation of national individuality, there appeared in various forms a deeper political and cultural cooperation as well as a completely formed national ideology on the unity of all South Slav peoples. Serbia, which through two uprisings (1804 and 1815) secured relative independence, and later full independence in the war against Turkey (1876-1878), became the center of the liberation struggle of the South Slav peoples as a potential nucleus around which unification could be completed.

Serbia, as an independent state and one which had greater political and material possibility, was able to develop the strongest activity for unification as the center of attraction for all South Slav peoples under the rule of Turkey and Austro-Hungary. This position of Serbia made it possible for her to play the role in the unification of the South Slav peoples which Piedmont played in the unification of the Italian peoples.

VI.

The Attempted Distinction of Terlinden v. Ames Serves Merely to Emphasize the Binding Force of That Decision.

The confusion in appellee's basic approach carries over to his labored attempt to distinguish *Terlinden v. Ames,* and thus to escape the binding force of that decision here. He purports to find the basis for that decision solely in the circumstance that the states composing the German Empire continued to exercise a certain power to enter into international arrangements with respect to extradition. But the abbreviated quotation at page 44 of appellee's brief fails to disclose what clearly appears from the remainder of the text quoted, that is that such power was by leave of the Imperial Government pending the exercise by it, in the field of extradition, of its plenary foreign affairs powers under the German Imperial Constitution. See *Terlinden v. Ames,* 185 U. S. at 285, 286, *id.,* 284, 285. Moreover, the Court, far from giving the circumstance relied on by appellee the weight he would give it, merely commented as follows after referring to it (185 U. S. at 286):

> "Thus it appears that the German Government has officially recognized, and continues to recognize, the treaty of June 16, 1852, as still in force, as well as similar treaties with other members of the Empire, so far as the latter has not taken specific action to the contrary or in lieu thereof."

It would hardly appear that appellee's point was the *ratio decidendi* of *Terlinden v. Ames.*

Furthermore, in none of the other cases following *Terlinden v. Ames,* and holding that treaties other than extradition treaties of the German States composing the Empire, survived the creation to the Empire, is any consideration given or reference made to any continuing power of any such state to enter into new international engagements in the fields covered by such treaties. See *The Disconto Gesselschaft v. Umbreit,* 208 U. S. 570; *The Sophie Rickmers,* 59 F. 2d 464; *Flensburger Dampfercompagnie v. United States,* 59 F. 2d 464. On appellee's thesis, in the absence of such a showing such treaties should have been deemed terminated as of the date of the organization of the German Empire, but in each case the continuing validity of the treaty was upheld.

Other attempts by appellee to distinguish *Terlinden v. Ames, supra,* are pure sophistry.* Appellee labors to show that a different set of historial facts were present in the formation of the German Empire than were present in the formation of the Kingdom of Serbs, Croats and Slovenes. Concedely, this is so. Appellee totally fails, however, to show that the legal principle delineated in

---

*In his attempt to avoid the effect of *Terlinden v. Ames, supra,* appellee strains at an unintentional omission (see Appellee's Br. p. 45) in one of Appellants' quotations from that case. Here Appellants used the words "adoption of the German Empire" instead of "adoption of the constitution of the German Empire". Counsel for appellants apologizes for the unintentional inaccuracy. but submits that it in no way changes nor distorts the clear meaning of the paragraph, nor the applicability of the rule announced to the formation of the Kingdom of the Serbs, Croates and Slovenes. Obviously what the court was referring to was the creation of the German Empire.

Terlinden v. Ames is not here applicable. This principle, restated, is that the question of whether a treaty survives political changes in the character of the other party to it, is in its nature essentially political and not judicial, and that the courts ought not to interfere with the conclusion of the Executive Branch in that regard.

In short, appellee's arguments cannot and do not avoid the rule of political decision. The continuing validity of the treaty here in question has been affirmed by both governments concerned, and under such circumstances, it "is out of the question," as the Court said in *Terlinden v. Ames,* 184 U. S. at 286, that a citizen of one of them, charged with being a fugitive, "should call on the courts of this country to adjudicate the correctness of the conclusions" of his own government and of our own.

Conclusion.

As presaged in the introductory comment herein, appellee's attempt to find a basis for overriding the positions of both the United States and Yugoslav governments and destroying a substantial portion of the basic fabric of the treaty relationships between the two countries has been shown to be wholly without support in either reason or authority. That the Union of the former Austro-Hungarian provinces and Montenegro with Serbia was voluntary and not imposed by force was and is a source of gratification. It is certainly not a basis for denying the Union's succession to Serbia in international relations, a succession recognized and acted upon over a period of

32 years by both Governments. If the judicial branch rather than the executive branch had had to make the decision, we believe the decision would undoubtedly have been the same for the reasons set forth in appellant's briefs and the *amicus* brief of the Government. Appellee's clear failure to distinguish *Terlinden v. Ames* emphasizes, however, that the decision was one for the executive branch and that its decision is controlling.

Respectfully submitted,

RONALD WALKER,
Attorney for Appellants.

No. 13602

United States
Court of Appeals
for the Ninth Circuit.

JAMES V. McCONNELL and MARGOT MURPHY McCONNELL,

Appellants,

vs.

PICKERING LUMBER CORPORATION,

Appellee.

Transcript of Record

Appeal from the United States District Court for the Northern District of California, Northern Division.

Phillips & Van Orden Co., 870 Brannan Street, San Francisco, Calif.—1-30-53

No. 13602

United States
Court of Appeals
for the Ninth Circuit.

JAMES V. McCONNELL and MARGOT
MURPHY McCONNELL,

Appellants,

vs.

PICKERING LUMBER CORPORATION,

Appellee.

Transcript of Record

**Appeal from the United States District Court for the
Northern District of California,
Northern Division.**

Phillips & Van Orden Co., 870 Brannan Street, San Francisco, Calif.—1-30-53

INDEX

[Clerk's Note: When deemed likely to be of an important nature. errors or doubtful matters appearing in the original certified record are printed literally in italic; and, likewise, cancelled matter appearing in the original certified record is printed and cancelled herein accordingly. When possible, an omission from the text is indicated by printing in italic the two words between which the omission seems to occur.]

NAMES OF ATTORNEYS OF RECORD

HERBERT BARTHOLOMEW,
  1240 Merchants Exchange Bldg.,
  San Francisco 4, California;

PEMBROKE GOCHNAUER,
  111 Sutter Street,
  San Francisco 4, California,

  Attorneys for Plaintiffs.

JOHN F. DOWNEY,

RALPH R. MARTIG,

DOWNEY, BRAND, SEYMOUR & ROHWER,
  500 Capital National Bank Building,
  Sacramento 14, California,

  Attorneys for Defendant Pickering Lum
  ber Company, a Corporation.

In the District Court of the United States for the Northern District of California, Northern Division

No. 6532

JAMES V. McCONNELL and MARGOT MUR-
· PHY McCONNELL,

Plaintiffs,

vs.

PICKERING LUMBER CORPORATION, a Corporation, DOE ONE, DOE TWO, and DOE
THREE,

Defendants.

COMPLAINT

Plaintiffs complain of defendants, and each of them, and for cause of action allege:

I.

The jurisdiction of this court is invoked under the provisions of Title 28 U.S.C.A., Section 1332. Plaintiffs are citizens of the State of New York. Pickering Lumber Corporation is a corporation incorporated under the laws of the State of Delaware. The matter in controversy exceeds, exclusive of interest and costs, the sum of Three Thousand Dollars ($3,000.00).

II.

Plaintiffs James V. McConnell and Margot Murphy McConnell, at all times hereinafter mentioned were, and they now are, husband and wife. On April 10, 1946, and all times mentioned herein prior thereto, plaintiff Margot Murphy McConnell was the owner of an undivided fractional interest in certain lands in Tuolumne County, California, commonly known as the McArthur and Ducey lands, together with the timber thereon.

III.

The true names and capacities, whether corporate, associate or otherwise, of defendants Doe One, Doe Two and Doe Three are unknown to plaintiffs and plaintiffs therefore designate them by such fictitious names and when their true names are discovered this complaint will be amended accordingly.

IV.

Pickering Lumber Corporation (hereinafter sometimes referred to as "defendant corporation") is a corporation organized and existing under and by virtue of the laws of the State of Delaware, with principal offices and place of business in Kansas City, Missouri. Said corporation at all times herein mentioned has been, and it now is, transacting business in California, and has designated D. H. Steinmetz, Standard, California, as its agent in California for the service of process. At all times mentioned herein defendant corporation has been, and it now is, engaged in the business of purchasing, cutting, milling, selling and distributing timber and lumber. In the contract attached hereto as Exhibit A, plaintiffs are designated as "Seller" or "Sellers" and defendant corporation is designated as "Purchaser."

V.

On the 10th day of April, 1946, defendant corporation made and entered into a written agreement with plaintiffs, in the above-entitled District and Division, concerning the acquisition by defendant corporation of plaintiffs' undivided fractional interest in said McArthur and Ducey lands and timber. A true copy of said agreement, with its attached Schedules A and B, is annexed hereto, marked "Exhibit A" and by this reference incorporated herein. Said lands consist of 154 parcels of 40 acres, or approximately 40 acres, each, and aggregate 6,172.60 acres, lying in the County of Tuolumne, State of California, and at the time of the negotiation of the aforesaid agreement said lands were held in undivided ownership as follows:

John F. Ducey, Detroit, Michigan—494.8/1360 undivided fractional interest, or the equivalent of approximately 2245.402 acres if divided.

Pickering Lumber Corporation (a defendant herein)—272/1360 undivided fractional interest, or the equivalent of approximately 1234.336 acres if divided.

Margot Murphy McConnell (a plaintiff herein), New York, New York—248.2/1360 undivided fractional interest, or the equivalent of approximately 1126.33 acres if divided.

Robert A. McArthur, Detroit, Michigan—130/1360 undivided fractional interest, or the equivalent of approximately 589.94 acres if divided.

Percy A. McArthur, Detroit, Michigan—117/1360

undivided fractional interest or the equivalent of approximately 530.946 acres if divided.

Ernest H. Fontaine, Jr., Trustee, Detroit, Michigan—85/1360 undivided fractional interest, or the equivalent of approximately 385.73 acres if divided.

Lawrence L. Brotherton, Detroit, Michigan—13/1360 undivided fractional interest, or the equivalent of approximately 58.994 acres if divided.

VI.

Section 10 of the agreement between plaintiffs and defendant corporation (Exhibit A) provides as follows:

"10-(A) Should Purchaser at any time prior to July 1, 1950, acquire the 494.8/1360 fractional interest of John F. Dusey in the property listed in Schedule A from him, his heirs or assigns or representatives, directly or indirectly, or at a partition sale of all the property described in Schedule A at a price higher than that provided herein for Sellers' interest, then Purchaser and Sellers hereby agree that the price provided in this contract for the Sellers' interest shall forthwith be adjusted upward by the amount necessary to make up the difference. Such additional amount shall be paid by Purchaser to Sellers as follows:

"(a) The additional amount due on all deeds taken up by Purchaser under this agreement prior to the date of purchase of such John F. Ducey interest shall be paid by Purchaser to Escrow Agent for the account of Sellers within 15 days;

"(b) The additional amount due on deed or deeds remaining in the possession of Escrow Agent at date Purchaser acquired the John F. Ducey interest shall be paid by Purchaser to Escrow Agent for the account of Sellers when Purchaser calls on Escrow Agent for delivery of any or all such remaining deeds.

"(B) The Purchaser further agrees with the Seller that, in the event it should purchase the said John F. Ducey interest at any time on or before July 1, 1950, that it will, within fifteen (15) days after making said purchase mail to the address of the Seller, notice of said purchase and the terms and conditions of same."

VII.

During the month of February, 1949, plaintiffs discovered that theretofore and on or about December 9, 1947, defendant corporation had acquired the 494.8/1360 fractional interest of John F. Ducey in and to certain parcels of said McArthur and Ducey lands (which parcels, plaintiffs have since learned, amounted to 40 parcels aggregating 1599.22 acres), at a price greatly in excess of the price of seventy-five dollars ($75.00) per acre heretofore paid to plaintiffs for their fractional interest therein. Plaintiffs have been unable to ascertain the exact price per acre paid by defendant corporation to said John F. Ducey, but believe said price to be approximately One Hundred Fifty Dollars ($150.00) per acre. Plaintiffs have done all things required to be done by them under the terms of

their said agreement with defendant corporation
(Exhibit A) and allege that defendant corporation,
in accordance with the provisions of said agreement,
owes plaintiffs an amount of money equal to the
difference between the price of Seventy-five Dollars ($75.00) per acre heretofore paid by defendant
corporation to plaintiffs and the higher price per
acre heretofore paid by defendant corporation in
acquiring said interest of said John F. Ducey, together with interest thereon from the time said
amount or amounts should have been paid to
Escrow Agent for the account of plaintiffs as required by said agreement (Exhibit A).

VIII.

Defendant corporation has never notified plaintiffs of its said purchase of said John F. Ducey's
interest as provided in subparagraph (B) of paragraph 10, quoted in Paragraph VI of this complaint, and has never paid any additional amount
or amounts to the Escrow Agent for the account of
plaintiffs, as provided in subparagraphs (a) and
(b) of said paragraph 10-(A).

IX.

Plaintiffs are informed and believe and therefore
allege defendant corporation rests its contention
that it does not owe plaintiffs any amount or
amounts of money under the terms of said paragraph 10, set forth in Paragraph VI of this complaint, upon the claim that the language of said
paragraph 10 relieves it from the obligation to pay
any additional amount to plaintiffs because it did

not acquire, prior to July 1, 1950, the 494.8/1360 fractional interest of said John F. Ducey in all 154 parcels of the said McArthur and Ducey lands, but only in 40 parcels thereof.

X.

Plaintiffs deny that the language of the said paragraph 10 of Exhibit A can be interpreted to excuse defendant corporation from paying to plaintiffs an amount equal to the difference between the price of Seventy-five Dollars ($75.00) per acre paid to plaintiffs and the higher price per acre paid by the defendant corporation to said John F. Ducey, and assert that the provisions, properly read, state that should defendant corporation, at any time prior to July 1, 1950, acquire the 494.8/1360 fractional interest of said John F. Ducey in all or in any parcels of the said lands at a higher price per acre than the price of Seventy-five Dollars ($75.00) per acre, then the said price of Seventy-five Dollars ($75.00) per acre should be forthwith adjusted upward by the amount necessary to make up the difference.

XI.

If the language of paragraph 10-(A) quoted in Paragraph VI of this complaint is susceptible of the interpretation now placed upon it and now relied upon by defendant corporation, then the said language, so interpreted, does not truly express the intention of the parties thereto at the time of the execution of said agreement.

In this regard plaintiffs allege:

1.   Prior to the execution of said agreement defendant corporation, acting by and through its then president, Ben Johnson, informed plaintiffs that defendant corporation wanted to purchase the fractional interest of said John F. Ducey in all of said lands and the fractional interest of each other co-owner in all of said lands, and that defendant corporation never would purchase, nor consider the purchase of, the fractional interest of said John F. Ducey, nor of any other of the co-owners, in any particular parcel or parcels of said lands nor any fractional interest in less than all of said lands. Plaintiffs believed said statements and at no time thereafter during the negotiations leading up to the execution of said agreement, which negotiations occurred over a period of several months, did the parties thereto consider nor discuss the purchase by defendant corporation of the fractional interest of said John F. Ducey, nor of any other co-owner, in only a part of said lands, nor the price to be paid plaintiffs in the event defendant corporation should thereafter acquire the fractional interest of said John F. Ducey in only a part of said lands. Defendant corporation prepared the written agreement (Exhibit A), including the language of paragraph 10-(A) thereof, and submitted the same to plaintiffs for their signature, and plaintiffs signed said agreement in the belief that it truly expressed the intentions of each party thereto. Plaintiffs therefore allege that Exhibit A was executed under a mutual mistake of each party thereto as to the

meaning and effect of paragraph 10 thereof in the event defendant corporation should acquire, on or before July 1, 1950, the fractional interest of said John F. Ducey in a part or parts of, but less than all of, said lands.

2. In the event said agreement was not executed under a mutual mistake of each party thereto as alleged in subparagraph 1. above, then and in that event, said agreement was executed under a mistake of plaintiffs as alleged in subparagraph 1. above, which defendant corporation at the time of execution thereof knew or suspected; at all times mentioned herein prior to the execution of said agreement defendant corporation knew or suspected that plaintiffs were unwilling to dispose of their fractional interest in said lands and to place in escrow deeds thereto for future delivery during the period from April 10, 1946, to July 1, 1950, at a price of Seventy-five Dollars ($75.00) per acre, unless they should receive as additional consideration therefor the difference in price between Seventy-five Dollars ($75.00) per acre and any higher price per acre provided in any agreement between defendant corporation and said John F. Ducey by which defendant corporation should acquire prior to July 1, 1950, the fractional interest of said John F. Ducey in all of or in any part or parts of said lands; and at the time of the execution of said agreement defendant corporation knew or suspected that plaintiffs would not execute said agreement if the language of paragraph 10-(A) thereof were susceptible of the inter-

pretation now placed upon it and now relied upon, by defendant corporation, namely, that paragraph 10 thereof should not apply in the event defendant corporation, at any time prior to July 1, 1950, should acquire the fractional interest of said John F. Ducey in a part of, but less than all of, said lands.

Wherefore, plaintiffs pray judgment against the defendant corporation as follows:

1. That the court declare that plaintiffs are entitled, under the terms of the agreement (Exhibit A) to receive from the defendant corporation such amount or amounts of money as may be found necessary to make up the difference between the price of Seventy-five Dollars ($75.00) per acre at which defendant corporation acquired plaintiffs' interest, and the higher price per acre at which defendant corporation acquired the interest of said John F. Ducey, in certain parcels of said lands, together with interest thereon from the time the same should have been paid in accordance with the terms set forth in subparagraphs (a) and (b) of paragraph 10-(A) of said agreement.

2. That if the language of the contract does not mean what plaintiffs claim it means, as stated in Paragraph X of this complaint, that by decree of this court the aforesaid agreement be reformed to conform with the actual agreement of the parties as alleged in Paragraph X of this complaint by the addition of the words "any of" after the word "in" and preceding the words "the property listed"

in the third line of paragraph 10-(A) of said agreement.

3. That the court decree that under the said agreement so reformed defendant corporation owes plaintiffs such amount or amounts of money as may be found necessary to make up the difference between the price of Seventy-five Dollars ($75.00) per acre at which defendant corporation acquired plaintiffs' interest, and the higher price per acre at which defendant corporation acquired the interest of said John F. Ducey, in a part of said lands, together with interest thereon from the time the same should have been paid in accordance with subparagraphs (a) and (b) of paragraph 10-(A) of said agreement.

4. For interest, costs of suit, and such and other and further relief as to the court may seem proper.

/s/ HERBERT BARTHOLOMEW,

/s/ PEMBROKE GOCHNAUER.

EXHIBIT A

An Agreement to Purchase and Sell entered into between Pickering Lumber Corporation, hereinafter referred to as Purchaser, and Margot Murphy McConnell and James V. McConnell, her husband, hereinafter referred to as Seller.

The date of this agreement is July 1, 1945.

The Sellers warrant that they own 248.2/1360 fractional interest in the McArthur and Ducey lands in Tuolumne County, California as set out in Schedule "A" attached and agree to sell all their rights, title and interest therein at the rate of $75.00 per acre, or a total consideration of $84,-474.87.

Terms:

(a) 20% ($16,894.97) is to be paid in cash to the Escrow Agent at the time of the closing of the transaction, delivery of the deeds and title insurance and signing of the Escrow Agreement.

(b) As to the balance, $67,579.90, payment is to be completed on or before July 1, 1950, and at not less than the rate of $13,515.98 on or before July 1, 1946-1947-1948-1949-1950. The Purchaser shall have the right to deposit with the said Escrow Agent at any time any sums that Purchaser may wish to deposit in addition to the minimum payments required as above set forth. In the event the Purchaser should deposit with said Escrow Agent any sum in excess of the minimum payments above set forth, such excess shall be credited toward the payment falling due for the next or succeeding years.

No interest is to be paid on the deferred deeds.

The Bank of America is to act as Escrow Agent under the transaction.

Twenty-five (25) deeds covering various parcels of the lands as selected by the Purchaser are to be deposited with the Escrow Agent and the full consideration for each deed shall be arrived at as stated above, less the 20% thereof paid in advance as specified above.

The Purchaser shall have the right to take up any deed it may select from the Escrow Agent and the Escrow Agent shall promptly deliver such deed to the Purchaser when there is a sufficient credit in Escrow Agent's hands to cover the payment specified for such deed.

Other Conditions:

1. The Purchaser will pay at its expense all taxes on the property involved for the fiscal year beginning July 1, 1945, and agrees to pay promptly the installments of future taxes when due.

2. The Sellers agree to warrant the title and furnish title policy at their expense, but the Purchaser agrees that the Escrow Agent may make the initial cash payment of 20% specified under "Terms (a)" in advance of the delivery of the title policy.

3. The grazing rights on all the lands embraced in this deal are granted to the Purchaser, beginning with the year 1946.

4. The contract will specify the valuation of and the balance due for taking up each deed.

5. No timber shall be cut off the lands described in any of the deeds covered by this contract until the Purchaser has received from the Escrow Agent the deed covering the land from which the timber is to be cut.

6. The Sellers will agree in the contract and/or in the Short Form of Agreement to convey rights-

of-way and easements to locate, construct, use and operate over, on, and across the land of the Seller described in the deferred deeds, such roads, railroads, skid roads, logging roads, camps and other facilities as may be reasonably necessary in connection with Purchaser's lumber and logging operations.

7.   Copy of this contract, together with the deeds referred to herein shall be escrowed with the Bank of America at the Sellers' expense.

8.   Appropriate Short Form of Agreement shall be executed covering the transactions.

9.   Revenue Stamps on each deed to be canceled at expense of Seller at the time such deed is delivered to Pickering Lumber Corporation.

10-(A).   Should Purchaser at any time prior to July 1, 1950, acquire the 494.8/1360 fractional interest of John F. Ducey in the property listed in Schedule A from him, his heirs or assigns or representatives, directly or indirectly, or at a partition sale of all the property described in Schedule A at a price higher than that provided herein for Sellers' interest, then Purchaser and Sellers hereby agree that the price provided in this contract for the Sellers' interest shall forthwith be adjusted upward by the amount necessary to make up the difference. Such additional amount shall be paid by Purchaser to Sellers as follows:

    (a)   The additional amount due on all deeds taken up by Purchaser under this agreement prior to the date of purchase of such John F. Ducey interest shall be paid by Purchaser to Escrow Agent for the account of Sellers within 15 days;

(b) The additional amount due on deed or deeds remaining in possession of Escrow Agent at date Purchaser acquired the John F. Ducey interest shall be paid by Purchaser to Escrow Agent for the account of Sellers when Purchaser calls on Escrow Agent for delivery of any or all such remaining deeds.

(B). The Purchaser further agrees with the Seller that, in the event it should purchase the said John F. Ducey interest at any time on or before July 1, 1950, that it will, within fifteen (15) days after making said purchase, mail to the address of the Seller, notice of said purchase and the terms and conditions of same.

Signed   6 April 1946.

/s/ MARGOT MURPHY
McCONNELL,

JAMES V. McCONNELL,

By /s/ JOHN L. McCORMICK,
Attorney.

Signed   10 April 1946.

PICKERING LUMBER
CORPORATION,

By BEN JOHNSON,
President.

"Schedule A"

Description of McArthur & Ducey Lands in
Tuolumne County, California

Description   Acreage

T. 5 N. R. 16 E.

Sec. 1—NW NE 37.45
        SW NE 40
        SE NE 40
        NE NW 37.35
        NW NW 37.25
        SW NW 40
        SE NW 40
        NE SW 40
        NW SW 40
        NE SE 40
        NW SE 40
        SE SE 40

Sec. 2—NE NW 37.14
        NW NW 37.11
        NE SE 40

Sec. 3—NE NE 36.96
        NW NE 36.69
        SW NE 40
        NE SW 40
        SW SW 40
        SE SW 40
        NW SE 40

Sec. 4—SW SE 40
        SE SE 40

Description   Acreage

Sec. 9—NE SW	40
SW SW	40
SE SW	40
NW SE	40
Sec. 10—SW NE	40
SE NE	40
NW NW	40
NE SW	40
SE SW	40
NE SE	40
NW SE	40
Sec. 11—NE NE	40
SW NE	40
SE NE	40
NE NW	40
SW NW	40
SE NW	40
NE SW	40
NW SW	40
NE SE	40
NW SE	40
SW SE	40
Sec. 12—NE SW	40
NW SW	40
SW SW	40
SE SW	40
NE SE	40
NW SE	40
SW SE	40

Description   Acreage

 Sec. 13—NE NE 40
    NW NE 40
    SW NE 40
    SE NE 40
    NE NW 40
    NW NW 40
    SW NW 40
    SE NW 40
    NE SE 40
    NW SE 40
    SW SE 40
    SE SE 40
 Sec. 14—NW NE 40
    SW NE 40
    NE NW 40
    SW NW 40
    SE NW 40
    NW NW 40
 Sec.15—SE NE 40
 Sec. 17—NE NE 40
    NW NE 40
    SE NE 40
    NE SE 40

T. 5 N. R. 17 E.
 Sec. 4—NE NW 40.05
    SW NW 40
    SE NW 40
 Sec. 5—SE NE 40
    NW NW 38.55
    SW SW 40

Description   Acreage

Sec. 6—NE NE 38.30
      NW NE 38.10
      SW NE 40
      SE NE 40
      NE NW 37.90
      NW NW 38.03
      · SW NW 40.84
      SE NW 40
      NE SW 40
      SE SW 40

Sec. 7—NE NE 40
      NW NE 40
      SW NE 40
      NE NW 40
      SE NW 40
      NE SW 40
      NW SW 42.10
      SE SW........................40
      NW SE 40
      SW SE 40

Sec. 8—NE NW 40
      NW NW 40
      SE SW 40
      SW SE 40

Sec. 17—NE NE 40
      NW NE 40

Sec. 19—NE NE 40

Description   Acreage

Sec. 20—NW NE 40
        NE NW 40
        NW NW 40

T. 6 N. R. 16 E.

Sec. 25—NE SE 40
        NW SE 40
        SW SE 40
        SE SE 40

Sec. 35—NE SW 40
        NW SW 40
        SW SW 40
        SE SW 40
        NE SE 40
        NW SE 40
        SW SE 40
        SE SE 40

T. 6 N. R. 17 E.

Sec. 30—SW NW 38.74
        SE NW 40
        NE SW 40
        NW SW 39.90

Sec. 31—SE SE 40

Sec. 32—SE NW 40
        NE SW 40
        SW SW 40
        SE SW 40
        NE SE 40
        NW SE 40
        SW SE 40

Description   Acreage

Sec. 33—SW NW 40
          SE NW 40
          NE SW 40
          NW SW 40

T. 4 N. R. 15 E.

Sec. 1—NE NW 39.22
          SE NW 40
          NE SW 40
          NW SW 40
          SW SW 40
          SE SW 40

T. 4 N. R. 15 E.

Sec. 12—SW NE 40
          NW NW 40
          SE NW 40
          NE SW 40
          SE SW 40

Sec. 13—NW NW 40
          SW NW 40

Sec. 14—NE NE 40
          SE NE 40
                                    ————
Total Acreage 6,171.68

SCHEDULE B

248.2/1360ths Interest
McArthur & Ducey Land and Timber

6,171.68 Acres

Recapitulation

Deed No.	Acres	Total Purchase Price	Less 20% Advance	Net Amount Due
1	240.	$ 3,285.00	$ 657.00	$ 2,628.00
2	280.	3,832.50	766.50	3,066.00
3	240.	3,285.00	657.00	2,628.00
4	360.	4,927.50	985.50	3,942.00
5	242.10	3,313.74	662.75	2,650.99
6	280.	3,832.50	766.50	3,066.00
7	276.90	3,790.07	758.01	3,032.06
8	238.10	3,258.99	651.80	2,607.19
9	160.	2,190.00	438.00	1,752.00
10	275.93	3,776.79	755.36	3,021.43
11	240.	3,285.00	657.00	2,628.00
12	200.	2,737.50	547.50	2,190.00
13	160.	2,190.00	438.00	1,752.00
14	200.	2,737.50	547.50	2,190.00
15	360.	4,927.50	985.50	3,942.00
16	200.	2,737.50	547.50	2,190.00
17	240.	3,285.00	657.00	2,628.00
18	200.84	2,749.00	549.80	2,199.20
19	312.05	4,271.18	854.23	3,416.95
20	227.90	3,119.38	623.87	2,495.51
21	320.	4,380.00	876.00	3,504.00
22	318.64	4,361.39	872.28	3,489.11
23	239.22	3,274.33	654.87	2,619.46
24	200.	2,737.50	547.50	2,190.00
25	160.	2,190.00	438.00	1,752.00
Total 6,171.68		$84,474.87	$16,894.97	$67,579.90

[Endorsed]: Filed August 23, 1951.

[Title of District Court and Cause]

NOTICE OF MOTION TO DISMISS

Defendant Pickering Lumber Corporation, a corporation, moves the Court to dismiss the action as to the defendant Pickering Lumber Corporation because the complaint fails to state a claim against said defendant upon which relief can be granted.

/s/ JOHN F. DOWNEY,

/s/ RALPH R. MARTIG,

DOWNEY, BRAND,

SEYMOUR & ROHWER,

Attorneys for Defendant Pickering Lumber Corporation, a Corporation.

To: Herbert Bartholomew, and Pembroke Gochnauer, Attorneys for Plaintiffs:

Please Take Notice, that defendant Pickering Lumber Corporation will bring the above motion on for hearing before this Court in the courtroom of said Court, in the Federal Building, 9th and I Streets, Sacramento, California, on the 29th day of October, 1951, at 10:00 o'clock in the forenoon of that day, or as soon thereafter as counsel can be heard.

/s/ JOHN F. DOWNEY,

/s/ RALPH R. MARTIG,

DOWNEY, BRAND,

SEYMOUR & ROHWER,

Attorneys for Defendant Pickering Lumber Corporation, a Corporation.

[Endorsed]: Filed October 9, 1951.

[Title of District Court and Cause]

ORDER

In their complaint plaintiffs seek to recover an additional sum from defendants based upon paragraph 10 of the contract between the parties hereto which provides for an increase of the price paid to plaintiffs for their undivided interest in several parcels of land equivalent to the amount greater than that received by them in the event that the interest of John F. Ducey in the parcels was sold. Plaintiffs contend Ducey sold his interest in a portion of the parcels for a higher price than received by the plaintiffs and plaintiffs interpret the contract to mean they should receive an equivalent increase on the theory that the agreement pertained to the sale of any number of parcels and not the entire unit. Defendants contend that the provision for an acceleration in the price would be effective only if Ducey's entire interest in all of the parcels was sold.

Plaintiffs pray—1, that the court declare that they are entitled to receive the higher price per acre because of the sale by Ducey of his interest in certain parcels; and 2, that if the language of the contract does not have the meaning plaintiffs attach to paragraph 10 that the agreement be reformed to conform with the actual agreement of the parties.

I do not find an ambiguity in the contract. It is therefore not subject to the interpretation which plaintiffs would place upon it. The allegations of the complaint do not set forth an agreement by the parties other than the writing herein to which it could be reformed. The averments are insufficient to permit reformation on the ground of mistake. It follows that the complaint should be dismissed.

Defendant's motion to dismiss is granted and the complaint herein is dismissed with leave to plaintiffs to file within fifteen days from the date hereof an amended complaint setting forth sufficient allegations to present the question of the propriety of reforming the agreement herein.

Dated: November 7th, 1951.

/s/ DAL M. LEMMON,
United States District Judge.

[Endorsed]: Filed November 7, 1951.

[Title of District Court and Cause]

NOTICE OF MOTION TO VACATE ORDER DISMISSING THE COMPLAINT DATED AND FILED NOVEMBER 7, 1951, AND FOR LEAVE TO FILE AMENDED COMPLAINT

Plaintiffs above-named move the Court to vacate the Order of this Honorable Court dated and filed November 7, 1951, because the same is contrary to law, and for leave to file plaintiffs' Amended Complaint, a copy of which is hereto attached and by this reference made a part of this Motion.

/s/ HERBERT BARTHOLOMEW,

/s/ PEMBROKE GOCHNAUER,
Attorneys for Plaintiffs.

To: John F. Downey, Ralph R. Martig, Downey, Brand, Seymour & Rohwer, Attorneys for Defendant Pickering Lumber Corporation, a corporation:

Please Take Notice that plaintiffs above named will bring the above Motion on for hearing before this Court in the courtroom of said Court, in the Federal Building, 9th and I Streets, Sacramento, California, on the 3rd day of December, 1951, at 10:00 o'clock in the forenoon of that day, or as soon thereafter as counsel can be heard.

/s/ HERBERT BARTHOLOMEW,

/s/ PEMBROKE GOCHNAUER,
Attorneys for Plaintiffs.

[Endorsed]: Filed November 23, 1951.

———

[Title of District Court and Cause]

MEMORANDUM

Plaintiffs' motion for leave to file their amended complaint is granted.

The submission of plaintiff's motion to vacate the order of this court dated November 7, 1951, is set aside. It will be resubmitted upon submission of any motion attacking the amended complaint.

Dated: January 3rd, 1952.

· /s/ DAL M. LEMMON,
United States District Judge.

[Endorsed]: Filed January 3, 1952.

———

[Title of District Court and Cause]

AMENDED COMPLAINT

Plaintiffs complain of defendants, and each of them, and for cause of action allege:

I.

The jurisdiction of this court is invoked under the provisions of Title 28 USCA, Section 1332. Plaintiffs are citizens of the State of New York. Pickering Lumber Corporation is a corporation incorporated under the laws of the State of Delaware. The matter in controversy exceeds, exclusive of interest and costs, the sum of Three Thousand Dollars ($3,000.00).

II.

Plaintiffs James V. McConnell and Margot Murphy McConnell, at all times hereinafter mentioned were, and they now are, husband and wife. On April 10, 1946, and at all times mentioned herein prior thereto, plaintiff Margot Murphy McConnell was the owner of an undivided fractional interest in certain lands in Tuolumne County, California, commonly known as the McArthur and Ducey lands, together with the timber thereon.

III.

The true names and capacities, whether corporate, associate or otherwise of defendants Doe One, Doe Two and Doe Three are unknown to plaintiffs and plaintiffs therefore designate them by such fictitious names and when their true names are discovered this complaint will be amended accordingly.

IV.

Pickering Lumber Corporation (hereinafter sometimes referred to as "defendant corporation") is a corporation organized and existing under and by virtue of the laws of the State of Delaware, with principal offices and place of business in Kansas City, Missouri. Said corporation at all times herein mentioned has been, and it now is, transacting business in California, and has designated D. H. Steinmetz, Standard, California, as its agent in California for the service of process. At all times mentioned ·herein defendant corporation has been, and it now is, engaged in the business of purchasing, cutting, milling, selling and distributing timber and lumber. In the contract attached hereto as Exhibit A, plaintiffs are designated as "Seller" or "Sellers" and defendant corporation is designated as "Purchaser."

V.

On the 10th day of April, 1946, defendant corporation made and entered into a written agreement with plaintiffs, in the above-entitled District and Division, concerning the acquisition by defendant corporation of plaintiffs' undivided fractional interest in said McArthur and Ducey lands and timber. A copy of said agreement, with its attached Schedules A and B, is annexed hereto, marked "Exhibit A" and by this reference incorporated herein. Said lands consist of 154 parcels of 40 acres, or approximately 40 acres, each, and aggregate 6,172.60 acres, lying in the County of Tuolumne, State of California, and at the time of the negotiation of the aforesaid agreement said lands were held in undivided ownership as follows:

John F. Ducey, Detroit, Michigan—494.8/1360 undivided fractional interest, or the equivalent of approximately 2245.402 acres if divided.

Pickering Lumber Corporation (a defendant herein)—272/1360 undivided fractional interest, or the equivalent of approximately 1234.336 acres if divided.

Margot Murphy McConnell (a plaintiff herein), New York, New York—248.2/1360 undivided fractional interest, or the equivalent of approximately 1126.33 acres if divided.

Robert A. McArthur, Detroit, Michigan—130/1360 undivided fractional interest, or the equivalent of approximately 589.94 acres if divided.

Percy A. McArthur, Detroit, Michigan—117/1360 undivided fractional interest, or the equivalent of approximately 530.946 acres if divided.

Ernest H. Fontaine, Jr., Trustee, Detroit, Michigan—85/1360 undivided fractional interest, or the equivalent of approximately 385.73 acres if divided.

Lawrence L. Brotherton, Detroit, Michigan—13/1360 undivided fractional interest, or the equivalent of approximately 58.994 acres if divided.

VI.

Section 10 of the agreement between plaintiffs and defendant corporation (Exhibit A) provides as follows:

"10-(A)   Should Purchaser at any time prior to July 1, 1950, acquire the 494.8/1360 fractional interest of John F. Ducey in the property listed in Schedule A from him, his heirs or assigns or representatives, directly or indirectly, or at a partition sale of all the property described in Schedule A at a price higher than that provided herein for Sellers' interest, then Purchaser and Sellers hereby agree that the price provided in this contract for the Sellers' interest shall forthwith be adjusted upward by the amount necessary to make up the difference. Such additional amount shall be paid by Purchaser to Sellers as follows:

"(a)   The additional amount due on all deeds taken up by Purchaser under this agreement prior to the date of purchase of such John F. Ducey interest shall be paid by Purchaser to Escrow Agent for the account of Sellers within 15 days;

"(b)   The additional amount due on deed or deeds remaining in possession of Escrow Agent at date Purchaser acquired the John F. Ducey interest shall be paid by Purchaser to Escrow Agent for the account of Sellers when

Purchaser calls on Escrow Agent for delivery of any or all such remaining deeds.

"(B) The Purchaser further agrees with the Seller that, in the event it should purchase the said John F. Ducey interest at any time on or before July 1, 1950, that it will, within fifteen (15) days after making said purchase, mail to the address of the Seller, notice of said purchase and the terms and conditions of same."

VII.

During the month of February, 1949, plaintiffs discovered that theretofore and on or about December 9, 1947, defendant corporation had acquired the 494.8/1360 fractional interest of John F. Ducey in and to certain parcels of said McArthur and Ducey lands (which parcels, plaintiffs have since learned, amounted to 40 parcels aggregating 1599.22 acres), at a price greatly in excess of the price of Seventy-five Dollars ($75.00) per acre heretofore paid to plaintiffs for their fractional interest therein. Plaintiffs have been unable to ascertain the exact price per acre paid by defendant corporation to said John F. Ducey, but believe said price to be approximately One Hundred Fifty Dollars ($150.00) per acre. Plaintiffs have done all things required to be done by them under the terms of their said agreement with defendant corporation (Exhibit A) and allege that defendant corporation, in accordance with the provisions of said agreement, owes plaintiffs an amount of money equal to the difference between the price of Seventy-five Dollars ($75.00) per acre heretofore paid by defendant corporation to plaintiffs and the higher price per acre heretofore paid by defendant corporation in acquiring said interest of said John F. Ducey, together with interest thereon from the time said amount or amounts should have been paid to Escrow Agent for the account of plaintiffs as required by said agreement (Exhibit A).

VIII.

Defendant corporation has never notified plaintiffs of its said purchase of said John F. Ducey's interest as provided in subparagraph (B) of paragraph 10, quoted in Paragraph VI of this complaint, and has never paid any additional amount or amounts to the Escrow Agent for the account of plaintiffs, as provided in subparagraphs (a) and (b) of said paragraph 10-(A).

IX.

Plaintiffs are informed and believe and therefore allege defendant corporation rests its contention that it does not owe plaintiffs any amount or amounts of money under the terms of said paragraph 10, set forth in Paragraph VI of this complaint, under the claim that the language of said paragraph 10 relieves it from the obligation to pay any additional amount to plaintiffs because it did not acquire, prior to July 1, 1950, the 494.8/1360 fractional interest of said John F. Ducey in all 154 parcels of the said McArthur and Ducey lands, but only in 40 parcels thereof.

X.

Plaintiffs deny that the language of the said paragraph 10 of Exhibit A can be interpreted to excuse defendant corporation from paying to plaintiffs an amount equal to the difference between the price of Seventy-five Dollars ($75.00) per acre paid to plaintiffs and the higher price per acre paid by the defendant corporation to said John F. Ducey, and assert that the provisions, properly read, state that should defendant corporation, at any time prior to July 1, 1950, acquire the 494.8/1360 fractional interest of said John F. Ducey in all or in any parcels of the said lands at a higher price per acre than the price of Seventy-five Dollars ($75.00) per acre, then the said price of Seventy-five Dollars ($75.00) per acre should be forthwith adjusted upward by the amount necessary to make up the difference.

XI.

If the language of paragraph 10-(A) quoted in Paragraph VI of this complaint is susceptible of the interpretation now placed upon it and now relied upon by defendant corporation, then the said language so interpreted does not truly express the intention of the parties thereto at the time of the execution of said agreement, and said agreement was executed by plaintiffs under a mistake on their part as to the meaning and effect thereof, which mistake was known or suspected by defendants at the time of the execution thereof. The circumstances constituting and giving rise to said mistake were as follows:

Plaintiffs executed said agreement under the understanding and belief that Section 10-(A) thereof meant plaintiffs should receive as the price of their interest in said McArthur-Ducey lands an amount equal to the difference between $75.00 per acre and any higher price per acre provided in any agreement between defendant corporation and said John F. Ducey made at any time prior to July 1, 1950, for the sale of said Ducey's interest in all of or any of said lands.

Soon after defendant corporation acquired in July, 1944, its said twenty per cent interest in said lands defendant corporation commenced negotiations with the owners of all other outstanding interests in said lands for the purchase of all outstanding interests. It was necessary for defendant corporation to acquire all outstanding interests in any parcel thereof before defendant corporation could cut any timber upon such parcel. The negotiations between defendant corporation and its co-owners were conducted in large part between defendant corporation and plaintiffs. All of said co-owners, except John F. Ducey, were then willing to sell their interests to defendant corporation if a fair price could be agreed upon. In March, 1945, plaintiff Margot McConnell met with all of her co-owners in Detroit, Michigan, and it was then agreed among them that all were willing to sell at that time at a price of $75.00 per acre. This fact was made known to defendant corporation. In June, 1945, defendant corporation prepared, signed and sent to its co-owners a proposed written agreement for the purchase of all of their interests at a price of $75.00 per acre. Said proposed agreement contained the same or substantially the same provisions as "Exhibit A" except that it omitted any pricing clause such as Paragraph 10 of "Exhibit A." Said proposed written agreement was not accepted by plaintiffs or any of the other co-owners because John F. Ducey refused or failed to sign it. Commencing approximately in November, 1945, defendant corporation began negotiations with plaintiffs for the purchase of plaintiffs' interest alone and informed plaintiffs that if defendant corporation could not acquire the interests of the other co-owners by agreement with them the acquisition of plaintiffs' interest would improve the position of defendant corporation in the event the institution of a partition suit should become necessary.

From the inception of defendant corporation's efforts to acquire plaintiffs' interest separate and apart from the interests of the other co-owners, plaintiffs refused to sell their interest in said lands at a price of $75.00 per acre and informed defendant corporation that plaintiffs were unwilling to **sell at** said price, and that plaintiffs must receive price protection against the acquisition by defendant corporation prior to July 1, 1950, of any other interest therein at a higher price per acre. During subsequent negotiations it was orally agreed between them that any such price protection clause which might be finally agreed upon would refer only to any higher price per acre to be paid to John F. Ducey in view of the size of his fractional interest and his past unwillingness to sell. During February, 1946, John F. Ducey, Robert A. McArthur, Percy A. McArthur and Ernest H. Fontaine, Jr., trustee, offered to sell their respective interests to defendant corporation at a price of $100.00 per acre and so informed plaintiffs. Thereafter, during February, 1946, Ben Johnson, then president of defendant corporation, came to New York and offered on behalf of defendant corporation to sign two agreements with plantiffs, one at a price of $75.00 per acre which could be shown to the other co-owners, and a second at a higher price per acre which would be a private agreement between plaintiffs and defendant corporation. Plaintiffs refused to consider this offer. It was thus apparent to plaintiffs that defendant corporation desired to acquire all outstanding interests in said property and plaintiffs believed that it would do so prior to July 1, 1950, at a price or prices in excess of $75.00 per acre.

On or about April 4, 1946, defendant corporation prepared and sent to plaintiffs for their signature the written agreement (Exhibit A) which was signed by both parties as alleged in Paragraph V of this amended complaint.

During July, 1951, plaintiffs learned from an inspection of the official records of Tuolumne County, California, that defendant corporation had agreed prior to July 1, 1950, with all of the co-owners of said lands other than John F. Ducey for the acquisition by defendant corporation of all of their respective interests in all of said lands and plaintiffs are informed and believe and on such information and belief allege that said interests were so acquired at a price or prices in excess of $75.00 per acre.

The contingency of the purchase by defendant corporation of the fractional interest of John F. Ducey in a part of but less than all of said lands was not discussed during the negotiations between plaintiffs and defendant corporation, but the plaintiffs at all times prior to, and at the time of executing said agreement understood and believed and defendant corporation at all said times knew or suspected that plaintiffs under the terms of said agreement understood and believed that plaintiffs would receive the difference between $75.00 per acre and any higher price per acre which might be agreed upon between defendant corporation and John F. Ducey at any time prior to July 1, 1950.

Wherefore, plaintiffs pray judgment against the defendant corporation as follows:

1. That the court declare that plaintiffs are entitled, under the terms of the agreement (Exhibit A) to receive from the defendant corporation such amount or amounts of money as may be found necessary to make up the difference between the price of Seventy-five Dollars ($75.00) per acre at which defendant corporation acquired plaintiffs' interest, and the higher price per acre at which defendant corporation acquired the interest of said John F. Ducey, in certain parcels of said lands, together with interest thereon from the time the same should have been paid, in accordance with the terms set

forth in subparagraphs (a) and (b) of paragraph 10-(A) of said agreement.

2.   That if the language of the contract does not mean what plaintiffs claim it means, as stated in Paragraph X of this complaint, that by decree of this court the aforesaid agreement be reformed to conform with the actual agreement of the parties as alleged in Paragraph X of this complaint by the addition of the words "any of" after the word "in" and preceding the words "the property listed" in the third line of paragraph 10-(A) of said agreement.

3.   That the court decree that under the said agreement so reformed defendant corporation owes plaintiffs such amount or amounts of money as may be found necessary to make up the difference between the price of Seventy-five Dollars ($75.00) per acre at which defendant corporation acquired plaintiffs' interest, and the higher price per acre at which defendant corporation acquired the interest of said John F. Ducey, in a part of said lands, together with interest thereon from the time the same should have been paid in accordance with subparagraphs (a) and (b) of paragraph 10-(A) of said agreement.

4.   For interest, costs of suit, and such other and further relief as to the court may seem proper.

........................,
Attorney for Plaintiffs.

Lodged November 23, 1951.
[Endorsed]:   Filed January 4, 1952.

[Title of District Court and Cause.]

MOTION TO DISMISS
AMENDED COMPLAINT

Defendant Pickering Lumber Corporation, a corporation, moves the Court to dismiss the action as to said defendant because the amended complaint fails to state a claim against said defendant upon which relief can be granted.

/s/ JOHN F. DOWNEY,

/s/ RALPH R. MARTIG,

DOWNEY, BRAND,
SEYMOUR & ROHWER,

Attorneys for Defendant Pickering Lumber Corporation, a Corporation.

[Endorsed]: Filed January 25, 1952.

[Title of District Court and Cause.]

ORDER

I believe that a ruling upon the motion to dismiss should be deferred until the trial. This is permissible under Rule 12 (d) of the Rules of Civil Procedure. c.f. Montgomery Ward & Co. vs. Schumacher, 3 F.R.D. 368; Bowles vs. Bissinger, 3 F.R.D. 494. It is so ordered.

March 26th, 1952.

/s/ DAL M. LEMMON,
United States District Judge.

[Endorsed]: Filed March 26, 1952.

[Title of District Court and Cause.]

ANSWER

Comes now defendant Pickering Lumber Corporation, a Delaware corporation, and for its answer to the Amended Complaint states:

First Defense

The Amended Complaint fails to state a claim against defendant upon which relief can be granted.

Second Defense

1. Defendant admits the allegations contained in Paragraph I of the Amended Complaint.

2. Defendant is without knowledge or information sufficient to form a belief as to the truth of the allegation of Paragraph II of the Amended Complaint that plaintiffs James V. McConnell and Margot Murphy McConnell, at all times therein mentioned, were husband and wife. Defendant denies each and every other allegation contained in Paragraph II of the Amended Complaint.

3. Defendant is without knowledge or information sufficient to form a belief as to the truth of the allegations contained in Paragraph III of the Amended Complaint.

4. Defendant denies that its principal offices and place of business are in Kansas City, Missouri, and denies that D. H. Steinmetz, Standard, California, is designated as its agent in California for the service of process, all as alleged in Paragraph IV of the Amended Complaint. Defendant admits all other allegations contained in Paragraph IV of the Amended Complaint.

5. Defendant admits that plaintiffs and defendant entered into a written agreement, in the above-entitled District and Division, on the 10th day of April, 1946, and that a copy of said agreement, with its attached Schedule "A," is annexed to the Amended Complaint, marked "Exhibit A" and by reference incorporated therein. Defendant denies each and every other allegation contained in Paragraph V of the Amended Complaint.

6. Defendant admits the allegation contained in Paragraph VI of the Amended Complaint.

7. Defendant admits that on December 9, 1947, it contracted with John F. Ducey for the purchase of his 494.8/1360 fractional interest in 1599.22 acres of timberland in Tuolumne County, California, comprising a part only of the 6171.68 acres described in Schedule "A" of the aforesaid agreement between defendant and plaintiffs. John F. Ducey's 494.8/1360 fractional interest in the remaining 4572.46 acres of the 6171.68 acres described in said Schedule "A" is now owned by said John F. Ducey and has never been acquired by defendant. Defendant is without knowledge or information sufficient to form a belief as to the truth of the averments that plaintiffs have been unable to ascertain the exact price per acre paid by defendant corporation to John F. Ducey, and that plaintiffs believe said price to be approximately $150.00 per acre. Defendant denies each and every other allegation contained in Paragraph VII of the Amended Complaint.

8. Defendant admits it has never given plain-

tiffs notice under the provisions of subparagraph (B) of paragraph 10 of the aforesaid agreement and admits it has never paid any additional amount or amounts to the Escrow Agent for the account of plaintiffs under the provisions of subparagraphs (a) and (b) of paragraph 10-(A) of said agreement. Defendant denies that it is or at any time was required under the provisions of subparagraph (B) of paragraph 10 of said agreement to give any type of notice whatsoever to plaintiffs; and defendant denies that it is or at any time was obligated under the provisions of subparagraphs (a) and (b) of paragraph 10-(A) of said agreement to pay any sums or amounts of money whatsoever to or for the account of plaintiffs. Defendant denies each and every other allegation contained in Paragraph VIII of the Amended Complaint.

9.   Defendant is not and never has been obligated under the terms of paragraph 10 of the said agreement with plaintiffs, or otherwise, to pay to or for the account of plaintiffs any additional amount or amounts of money whatsoever by reason of the purchase by defendant of John F. Ducey's 494.-8/1360 fractional interest in 1599.22 acres of the 6171.68 acres described in Schedule "A" of the aforesaid agreement. Defendant denies each and every other allegation contained in Paragraph IX of the Amended Complaint.

10.   Defendant denies each and every allegation contained in Paragraph X of the Amended Complaint.

11. Defendant admits that it negotiated for the purchase of the undivided interests in the land described in Schedule "A" attached to said agreement and admits that it negotiated with plaintiffs for the purchase of plaintiffs' undivided interest in said land. Defendant denies each and every other allegation contained in Paragraph XI of the Amended Complaint.

Third Defense

Any claim for relief stated in Paragraph XI of the Amended Complaint did not accrue within three (3) years next before the commencement of this action and is therefore barred by the limitations provisions of Section 338-4 of the California Code of Civil Procedure.

Wherefore, having fully answered, defendant prays that the Court deny the relief sought by plaintiffs; discharge defendant from all liability in the premises and award its costs; and that plaintiffs take naught by their action.

Dated: April 17, 1952.

/s/ JOHN F. DOWNEY,

/s/ RALPH R. MARTIG,

DOWNEY, BRAND,

SEYMOUR & ROHWER,

Attorneys for Defendant Pickering Lumber Corporation, a Corporation.

Receipt of copy acknowledged.

[Endorsed]: Filed April 19, 1952.

[Title of District Court and Cause.]

DEMAND FOR JURY TRIAL

To Defendant Pickering Lumber Corporation, a corporation, and to John F. Downey, Ralph R. Martig and Downey, Brand, Seymour & Rohwer, its attorneys:

You will please take notice that the plaintiffs in the above-entitled cause demand a jury, and that the claim for relief predicated upon the contract without reformation thereof be tried by a jury, and plaintiffs further demand that all issues of fact arising upon the claim for relief predicated upon reformation of said contract be tried by a jury.

/s/ HERBERT BARTHOLOMEW,

/s/ PEMBROKE GOCHNAUER,
Attorneys for Plaintiffs.

[Endorsed]: Filed April 25, 1952.

———

[Title of District Court and Cause.]

MOTION TO DISPENSE WITH JURY TRIAL ON REFORMATION ISSUES

Defendant Pickering Lumber Corporation, a corporation, moves the Court to dispense with a jury trial on the issues arising upon the claim for relief predicated upon reformation of contract as set forth in the complaint in the above action. This motion is made pursuant to Rule 39(a)(2) of the Federal Rules of Civil Procedure.

Dated: May 1, 1952.

/s/ JOHN F. DOWNEY,

/s/ RALPH R. MARTIG.

[Endorsed]: Filed May 1, 1952.

[Title of District Court and Cause.]

MEMORANDUM AND ORDER

This case affords a classical example of improvident plaintiffs struggling to enlist the aid of a court to extricate them from the web of their own imprudence.

The unsure nature of the plaintiffs' position is indicated by their varying and inconsistent contentions at various times:

(1) That the contract as drawn is clear and unambiguous, and should be construed in the plaintiffs' favor;

(2) If the contract isn't clear and unambiguous, it contains an "extrinsic" or "latent" "ambiguity," and parol evidence should be admitted to show what the parties meant by what they said;

(3) That if it isn't clear and unambiguous, it was entered into as the result of a mutual mistake, and should be reformed; and

(4) That the mistake, if any, wasn't mutual after all, but unilateral on the plaintiffs' own part—but even if so, the contract should be reformed in their favor, anyway!

1. The Original Complaint

On August 23, 1951, the plaintiffs, who are husband and wife, filed their original complaint. They alleged that they are citizens of the State of New York, and that the defendant is incorporated under the laws of Delaware. The complaint contained the following salient averments:

On April 10, 1946, the plaintiffs were the owners of an undivided fractional interest in lands in Tuolumne County, California, known as the McArthur and Ducey lands, together with the timber thereon.

The Pickering Lumber Corporation, the defendant, organized under the laws of Delaware, on April 10, 1946, entered into a written agreement with the plaintiffs concerning the acquisition by the defendant of the plaintiffs' above-mentioned undivided interest.

There are listed three "Doe" defendants, whose roles in this case have remained a mystery to the time of this writing. The Pickering Corporation will hereinafter be referred to as "the defendant."

The McArthur and Ducey lands consist of 154 parcels of about 40 acres each, and aggregate 6,172.60 acres. John F. Ducey, of Detroit, Michigan, at the time of the negotiation of the above agreement held an undivided interest of 494.8/1360 in that tract, or the equivalent of approximately 2,245.402 acres if divided. Margot Murphy McConnell, one of the plaintiffs, held an undivided interest of 248.2/1360, or approximately 1,126.33 acres if divided, in the same McArthur and Ducey lands. There were five other co-owners, each likewise holding an "undivided fractional interest." The defendant was one of the co-owners, with a share of 272/1360, or 20 per cent; or about 1,234.336 acres if divided.

Section 10 of the above agreement between the plaintiffs and the defendant reads as follows: ·

"10-(A) Should Purchaser (defendant) at any time prior to July 1, 1950, acquire the 494.8/1360 fractional interest of John F. Ducey in the property listed in Schedule A from him * * * or at a partition sale of all the property * * * at a price higher than that provided herein for Sellers' (plaintiffs') interest, then Purchaser and Sellers hereby agree that the price provided in this contract for the Sellers' interest shall forthwith be adjusted upward by the amount necessary to make up the difference * * *

"(B) The Purchaser further agrees with the Seller (sic) that, in the event it should purchase the said John F. Ducey interest at any time on or before July 1, 1950, that (sic) it will, within fifteen (15) days after making said purchase, mail to the address of the Seller (sic), notice of said purchase and the terms and conditions of same."

In February, 1949, the plaintiffs discovered that on or about December 9, 1947, the defendant had acquired Ducey's 494.8/1360 interest to certain parcels of the lands, which portions, the plaintiffs have since learned, amounted to 40 parcels aggregating 1,599.22 acres. The price was greatly in excess of $75 per acre, which had been theretofore paid to the plaintiffs for their fractional interest in the lands. The plaintiffs believe that the price paid by the defendant to Ducey was approximately $150 per acre.

The defendant has never notified the plaintiffs of its purchase of Ducey's interest, and has not paid any additional amount to the Escrow Agent named in the agreement, for the account of the plaintiffs.

The plaintiffs are informed that the defendant contends that it does not owe them any money under the agreement, on the ground that it did not acquire Ducey's fractional interest in all 154 parcels of the land in question, but only in 40 parcels thereof.

Such an interpretation of the contract is opposed by the plaintiffs, but they allege that if the agreement is indeed susceptible to such a construction, then the language of Paragraph 10-(A), supra, does not truly express the intention of the parties at the time of the execution of the contract. In this regard the plaintiffs allege:

Prior to the execution of the agreement, Ben Johnson, at that time president of the defendant, informed the plaintiffs that the defendant wanted to purchase Ducey's fractional interest in all the lands, and that the defendant would never consider the purchase of Ducey's fractional interest in less than all the land. At no time thereafter, during the negotiations leading up to the execution of the agreement, did the parties consider or discuss the purchase by the defendant of the fractional interest of Ducey or of any other co-owner in only a part of the lands, or the price to be paid to the plaintiffs in the event the defendant should thereafter acquire Ducey's interest in only a part of the tract.

The defendant prepared the written agreement, including paragraph 10-(A), and the plaintiffs signed it in the belief that it truly expressed the intention of the parties. The plaintiffs therefore allege that the contract was executed under a "mutual" mistake of each party as to the meaning of paragraph 10 in the event that the defendant should acquire, on or before July 1, 1950, Ducey's fractional interest in less than all of the lands in question.

In the event the agreement was not executed under a mutual mistake, then it was entered into under a mistake of the plaintiffs that the defendant at the time of the execution thereof knew or suspected. The plaintiffs were unwilling to dispose of their fractional interest and to place in escrow deeds thereto for future delivery from April 10, 1946, to July 1, 1950, at $75 per acre, unless they should receive as additional consideration therefor the difference in price between $75 and any higher price per acre provided for in any agreement between the defendant and Ducey by which the defendant should acquire Ducey's interest in all or any part of the lands. At the time of the execution of the agreement the defendant knew or suspected that the "plaintiffs would not execute said agreement if the language of paragraph 10-(A) thereof were susceptible of the interpretation now placed upon it and now relied upon, by defendant corporation, namely, that paragraph 10 thereof should not apply in the event defendant corporation, at any time prior to July 1, 1950, should acquire the fractional interest of said John F. Ducey in a part of, but less than all of, said lands."

The prayer is that the Court declare the plaintiffs are entitled, "under the terms of the agreement * * *, to receive from the defendant * * * such amount * * * of money as may be found necessary to make up the difference between * * * $75 per acre at which defendant corporation acquired plaintiffs' interest, and the higher price per acre at which defendant corporation acquired the interest of * * * Ducey in certain parcels of said lands," etc.

The plaintiffs also ask that if the contract "does not mean what plaintiffs claim it means," the contract be reformed by the Court to conform "with the actual agreement of the parties * * * by the addition of the words 'any of' after the word 'in' and preceding the words 'the property listed' in the third line of paragraph 10-(A) * * *"

Finally, the plaintiffs pray that under the agreement so reformed the Court decree that the defendant owes the plaintiffs the difference between the price of $75 per acre and the higher price per acre at which the defendant acquired Ducey's interest in a part of the lands, together with interest, etc.

2. The Original Complaint Is Dismissed

On October 9, 1951, the defendant corporation filed a motion to dismiss the action on the ground that the complaint failed to state a claim upon which relief could be granted.

On Novmber 7, 1951, the Court made an order reading in part as follows:

> "I do not find an ambiguity in the contract. It is therefore not subject to the interpretation which plaintiffs would place upon it. The allegations of the complaint do not set forth an agreement by the parties other than the writing herein to which it could be reformed. The averments are insufficient to permit reformation on the ground of mistake. It follows that the complaint should be dismissed.

> "Defendant's motion to dismiss is granted and the complaint herein is dismissed with leave to plaintiffs to file within fifteen days from the date hereof an amended complaint setting forth sufficient allegations to present the question of the propriety of reforming the agreement herein."

3. The Motion to Vacate the Order

On November 23, 1951, the plaintiffs moved the Court to vacate its order of November 7, 1951, as being contrary to law, and asked for leave to file an amended complaint.

On January 3, 1952, the Court granted the plaintiffs' motion for leave to file an amended complaint, and set aside the submission of the plaintiffs' motion to vacate the order of the Court of November

7, 1951. The motion was ordered to be resubmitted upon the submission of any motion attacking the amended complaint.

4. The Amended Complaint

On January 4, 1952, the plaintiffs filed an amended complaint. As they point out in their brief, the amended complaint differs from the original one in that it omits a claim for relief by way of reformation of the contract based upon the mutual mistake of the parties. Relief by way of reformation is sought, as an alternative to a claim for relief on the contract itself, bottomed upon the plaintiffs' mistake, which it is alleged was known or suspected by the defendant at the time the contract was executed. The plaintiffs' claim for relief on the contract as it stands has been left unchanged. The prayers of the two complaints are identical.

In their brief, the plaintiffs claim that the allegations of the original complaint regarding the plaintiffs' unilateral mistake "have been expanded and particularized." This is in professed accordance with Rule 9(b) of the Federal Rules of Civil Procedure. Summarized, the allegations of the amended complaint as to the plaintiffs' mistake are as follows:

The plaintiffs executed the agreement believing that Section 10-(A) meant that they should receive as the price of their interest an amount equal to the difference between $75 per acre and any higher price provided for in any agreement between the defendant and Ducey, for the sale of the latter's interest in all or any of the lands.

Soon after the defendant acquired, in July, 1944, its twenty per cent interest, it opened negotiations with the owners of all other outstanding interests in the lands, for the purchase of such interests. It was necessary for the defendant to acquire all outstanding interests in any parcel of the land before it could cut any timber thereon. The negotiations between the defendant and its co-owners were conducted in large part between the defendant and the plaintiffs. All of the said co-owners except Ducey were willing to sell if a fair price could be had.

In March, 1945, plaintiff Margot McConnell met with all her co-owners in Detroit. It was then agreed among them that all were willing to sell at that time at a price of $75 per acre. This was made known to the defendant, which, in June, 1945, prepared, signed, and sent to its co-owners a proposed agreement for the purchase of all their interests at that price. The proposal contained substantially the same provisions as the contract now being considered, except that it did not have any pricing clause, such as Paragraph 10, supra.

Because Ducey refused to sign it, that proposed agreement was not accepted by the plaintiffs or any of the other co-owners. Commencing about in November, 1945, the defendant began negotiations with the plaintiffs for the purchase of their interest alone, and informed them that if the defendant could not acquire the interests of the other co-owners, the acquisition of the plaintiffs' interest would improve the defendant's position in the event that a partition suit should become necessary.

From the inception of the defendant's efforts to acquire the plaintiff's interest separately from those of the other co-owners, the plaintiffs refused to sell at a price of $75 per acre. They informed the defendant of such unwillingness, and declared that they must receive "price protection" against the acquisition by the defendant, prior to July 1, 1950, of any other interest therein at a higher price. Later, it was orally agreed between them that any such price protection clause that might finally be agreed upon would refer only to any higher price to be paid to Ducey, in view of the size of his fractional interest and his past unwillingness to sell.

During February, 1946, Ducey and three other co-owners offered to sell their respective interests to the defendant for $100 per acre, and so informed the plaintiffs. Later that month, Ben Johnson, then president of the defendant, went to New York and offered, on behalf of the corporation, to sign two agreements with the plaintiffs, one at a price of $75 per acre, which could be shown to the other co-owners, and a second at a higher price, which would be a "private agreement" between the plaintiffs and the defendant. The plaintiffs refused to consider this offer.

It was thus apparent to the plaintiffs that the defendant desired to acquire all outstanding interests in the property, and they believed that it would do so before July 1, 1950, at a price in excess of $75 per acre.

On or about April 4, 1946, the defendant prepared and sent to the plaintiffs for their signature the agreement that constitutes Exhibit A, supra. This was signed by both parties.

During July, 1951, the plaintiffs learned from an inspection of the official records of Tuolumne County, that the defendant had agreed, prior to July 1, 1950, with all the co-owners other than Ducey for the defendant's acquisition of all of their respective interests in the lands. Such acquisition was effected at prices higher than $75 per acre, according to the plaintiffs' belief.

The contingency of the defendant's purchase of Ducey's fractional interest in less than all of the lands was not discussed during the negotiations between the plaintiffs and the defendant, but the plaintiffs at all times prior to and at the time of executing the agreement believed—and the defendant "knew or suspected" that the plaintiffs under the terms of the agreement so understood and believed—that they would receive the difference between $75 per acre and any higher price that might be agreed upon between the defendant and Ducey at any time prior to July 1, 1950.

5. The Motion to Dismiss the Amended Complaint

On January 25, 1952, the defendant filed a motion to dismiss the amended complaint for failure to state a claim upon which relief can be granted.

On March 26, 1952, the Court made the following order:

> "I believe that a ruling upon the motion to dismiss should be deferred until the trial. This is permissible under Rule 12(d) of the Rules

of Civil Procedure. Cf. Montgomery Ward &
Co. vs. Schumacher, 3 F.R.D. 368; Bowles vs.
Bissinger, 3 F.R.D. 494. It is so ordered.''

6. The Answer

The time to answer having been extended by
stipulation, on April 19, 1952, the defendant filed
its answer, consisting of three ''defenses.''

The first defense asserts that the amended complaint fails to state a claim against the defendant
upon which relief can be granted.

In its second defense, the Company denies that
its principal offices are in Kansas City, Missouri,
and that D. H. Steinmetz, of Standard, California,
is designated as its agent for the service of process.

While admitting the agreement of April 10, 1946,
the defendant denies all the allegations of the
amended complaint relating to the ownership of
the various undivided interests in the land in question—including its own share in the tract.

The answer admits that on December 9, 1947,
the defendant contracted with Ducey for the purchase of his 494.8/1360 fractional interest in
1599.22 acres of timber land in Tuolumne County.
It is alleged that Ducey's 494.8/1360 interest in the
remaining 4572.46 acres of the 6171.68 acres of the
tract is still owned by Ducey. The defendant denies
that it owes the plaintiffs the difference between
$75 per acre and the higher price alleged by the
plaintiffs to have been paid to Ducey by the
defendant.

It is admitted that the defendant has never given

the plaintiffs notice under the provisions of sub-paragraph B of paragraph 10 of the contract, supra, and that it has never paid any additional amounts to the Escrow Agent for the account of plaintiffs, under the provisions of the contract. The defendant denies that it has been obligated to do so under those provisions. It likewise denies that it is obligated to pay the plaintiffs any sum whatever by reason of its purchase of Ducey's fractional interest in 1599.22 acres. The answer challenges the plaintiffs' interpretation of Paragraph 10 of the contract, supra.

Regarding the plaintiffs' alternative claim for relief based upon their own alleged mistake, which has already been fully set forth herein, the defendant merely admits that it negotiated for the purchase of the undivided interests in the land described in the schedule attached to the agreement, including the plaintiffs' undivided interest therein. Every other allegation regarding the unilateral mistake is denied.

As its third defense, the Company asserts that any claim for relief due to the plaintiffs' alleged mistake did not accrue within three years before the commencement of this action, and is therefore barred by the limitations provisions of Section 338-4 of the California Code of Civil Procedure.

7. The Motions Relating to a Jury Trial

On April 25, 1952, the plaintiffs filed a demand for a jury trial, on the claim for relief predicated upon the contract either with or without reformation.

On May 1, 1952, the defendant filed a motion to dispense with a jury trial on the reformation issue. The motion was made pursuant to Rule 39(a)(2) of the Federal Rules of Civil Procedure.

8. The Planitiffs Are Not Entitled to Relief on the Contract as It Stands.

It is fundamental law that, when a copy of a contract is attached to a pleading, the contract itself, and not what the pleader alleges it to be, is determinative. This rule applies even on a motion to dismiss.

In Foshee vs. Daoust Construction Co., 7 Cir., 185 F. 2d 23, 25 (1950), the Court pointed out that "where the allegations of a pleading are inconsistent with the terms of a written contract attached as an exhibit, the terms of the latter, fairly construed, must prevail over the averments differing therefrom. (Cases cited)"[1]

We must turn, then, to the contract itself in order to ascertain the intention of the parties. A written contract "supersedes all the negotiations or stipulations concerning its matter which preceded or accompanied the execution of the instru-

---

[1]See also Pelelas vs. Caterpillar Tractor Co., 7 Cir., 113 F. 2d 629, 631 (1940), certiorari denied, 311 U.S. 700 (1940); Sinclair Refining Co. vs. Stevens, 8 Cir., 123 F. 2d 186, 189 (1941), certiorari denied, 315 U. S. 804 (1942); Zeligson vs. Hartman-Blair, Inc., 10 Cir., 126 F. 2d 595, 597 (1942); Eaves vs. Timm Aircraft Corp., 107 C.A. 2d 367, 370 (1951), petition for a hearing by the State Supreme Court denied (1952).

ment." Section 1625 of the California Civil Code.[2]

The plaintiffs contend, however, that the contract contains an "extrinsic ambiguity," within the ambit of Section 1856 of the California Code of Civil Procedure. That section reads as follows:

"An agreement reduced to writing deemed the whole. When the terms of an agreement have been reduced to writing by the parties, it is to be considered as containing all those terms, and therefore there can be between the parties and their representatives, or successors in interest, no evidence of the terms of the agreement other than the contents of the writing, except in the following cases:

"1. Where a mistake or imperfection of the writing is put in issue by the pleadings;

"2. Where the validity of the agreement is the fact in dispute.

"But this section does not exclude other evidence of the circumstances under which the agreement was made or to which it relates, as defined in section eighteen hundred and sixty, or to explain an extrinsic ambiguity, or to establish illegality or fraud. The term agreement includes deeds and wills, as well as contracts between parties." (Emphasis supplied.)

In the instant case, however, there is no ambiguity, either extrinsic or intrinsic, in the contract.

---

[2]See also United Iron Works vs. Outer Harbor Dock and Wharf Co., 168 Cal. 81, 84-85 (1914); Harding vs. Robinson, 175 Cal. 534, 537 (1917).

If there was any misconception or misapprehension regarding the agreement, it existed in the minds of the plaintiffs alone. The mistake, if any, was purely subjective with them, and, as we shall see presently, they are not in a posiiton to take advantage of it.

After quoting Section 1856, supra, the Supreme Court of California, in Barnhart Aircraft, Inc., vs. Preston, 212 Cal. 19, 21-22, 23-24 (1931), referred with approval to the following language used by Jones in his Commentaries on Evidence, volume 3, section 454:

" ' * * * Ambiguity in a written contract, calling for construction, may arise as well from words plain in themselves but uncertain when applied to the subject matter of the contract, as from words which are uncertain in their literal sense * * * Such an ambiguity never arises out of what was not written at all, but only out of what was written so blindly and imperfectly that its meaning is doubtful.

" 'It must be borne in mind that although declarations of the parties may in some cases be received to explain contracts or words of doubtful meaning, yet no other words can be added to or substituted for those of the writing. The courts are not at liberty to speculate as to the general intention of the parties, but are charged with the duty of ascertaining the meaning of the written language.' " (Emphasis supplied.)

Applying the foregoing language to the instant contract, there is absolutely no warrant for asserting that the words "fractional interest of John F. Ducey in the property" were "written blindly and imperfectly" or that their meaning is "doubtful"; and since "no other words can be added to or substituted for those of the writing," we cannot read "in the property" to mean "in any of the property."

Similarly, in Eastern-Columbia vs. System Auto Parks, Inc., 100 C.A. 2d 541, 545 (1950), it was said.

> "If the language of the instrument is clear and explicit the intention of the parties must be ascertained from the writing alone. Parol evidence is admissible only where the language used is doubtful, uncertain or ambiguous and only then in cases where the doubt appears upon the face of the contract. (Cases cited.)"[3]

Generally speaking, we may say that "the property," as used in the present contract, means "all the property." A closely similar question was presented to the Court in Russell vs. Stillwell, 106 Cal. App. 88, 92 (1930):

---

[3]See also Betts vs. Orton, 34 Cal. App. 397, 400 (1917); Courtright vs. Dimmick, 22 C.A. (2d) 68, 71 (1937), petition to have the cause heard in the California Supreme Court denied (1937); Miranda vs. Miranda, 81 C.A. 2d 61, 66-67 (1947), petition for a hearing by the California Supreme Court denied (1947).

"We can see but one construction that can be placed upon the words in the added clause 'the completion of the plans,' and that is all plans before mentioned in the contract—not merely preliminary plans. The words themselves require no explanation. If they did it could be found in the contract itself. In the absence of fraud, where the parties have reduced to writing what appears to be a complete and certain agreement, parol evidence will not be permitted for the purpose of varying the written contract."

Quoting a salutory admonition to be found in the California statutes themselves, our Court of Appeals, in Black vs. Richfield Oil Corporation, 146 F. 2d 801, 804 (1945), certiorari denied, 325 U.S. 867 (1945), said:

"The California law is admittedly controlling. A statute of that state (section 1858, Cal. Code Civ. Proc.) provides that, in the construction of an instrument, 'the office of the judge is simply to ascertain and declare what is in terms or in substance contained therein, not to insert what has been omitted, or to omit what has been inserted.' The local decisions, like those of the courts elsewhere, are in harmony with the elementary principle declared by the statute."

One of the authorities relied upon by the plaintiffs is Universal Sales Corporation, Ltd., vs. California Press Manufacturing Company, 20 C. (2d)

751, 776 (1942). The plaintiffs quote the following excerpt from what they term the "separate concurring opinion" of Mr. Justice Traynor:

"Words are used in an endless variety of contexts. Their meaning is not subsequently attached by the reader but is formulated by the writer and can only be found by interpretation in the light of all the circumstances that reveal the sense in which the writer used the words. The exclusion of parol evidence regarding such circumstances merely because the words do not appear ambiguous to the reader can easily lead to the attribution to a written instrument of a meaning that was never intended."

The plaintiffs have omitted the two opening sentences of Mr. Justice Traynor's opinion, immediately preceding the extract quoted supra. Those two sentences definitely establish that the justice dissented from the majority opinion in the very respect that is crucial here:

"I concur in the judgment. I do not agree with the premise implicit in the majority opinion that parol evidence as to the meaning of the contract was admissible only because the contract is ambiguous on its face."

This Court believes that the rule was correctly stated by Mr. Associate Justice Curtis, who gave the majority opinion:

"The fundamental canon of construction which is applicable to contracts generally is the ascertainment of the intention of the parties

(Civ. Code, sec. 1636), and in accordance with section 1638 of the Civil Code, the language of the agreement, if clear and explicit and not conducive to an absurd result, must govern its interpretation." (Page 760.)

To hold that the meaning of words "is not subsequently attached to them by the reader but is formulated by the writer" is too reminiscent of Humpty Dumpty's oft-quoted theory of semantics.[4]

9. The Plaintiffs Have Not Made a Showing That Entitles Them to a Reformation of the Contract.

Rule 9(b) of the Federal Rules of Civil Procedure reads in part as follows:

"In all averments of fraud or mistake, the circumstances constituting fraud or mistake shall be stated with particularity * * *"[5]

There has been given hereinabove a somewhat full summary of the plaintiffs' so-called "expanded and particularized" allegations purporting to deal with their unilateral mistake.

---

[4] " 'When I use a word,' Humpty Dumpty said in a rather scornful tone, 'it means just what I choose it to mean—neither more nor less.'
" 'The question is,' said Alice, 'whether you can make words mean so many different things.'
" 'The question is,' said Humpty Dumpty, 'which is to be master—that's all.' "
Lewis Carroll: "Through the Looking Glass and What Alice Found There," chapter vi, page 234 (M. A. Donohue & Co., Chicago and New York).

---

[5] See also Auerbach vs. Healy, 174 Cal. 60, 63 (1916).

Taking these allegations by their four corners, however, we find that while they are replete with details, the details are not pertinent to the question of the plaintiffs' asserted unilateral "mistake."

The most relevant statement in that connection is to be found in the very first paragraph of the plaintiffs' explanation. But the allegation in question, already quoted in full substance herein, is merely one of an ultimate fact; namely, that "Plaintiffs executed said agreement under the understanding and belief that Section 10-(A) thereof meant plaintiffs should receive as the price of their interest * * * an amount equal to the difference between $75 per acre and any higher price," etc.

There is absolutely nothing in the succeeding paragraphs that in the slightest degree bears upon the question of the execution of the agreement "by plaintiffs under a mistake on their part as to the meaning and effect thereof, which mistake was known or suspected by defendants at the time of the execution thereof."

On the contrary, the plaintiffs allege that "The contingency of the purchase of the fractional interest of John F. Ducey in a part of but less than all of said lands was not discussed during the negotiations between plaintiffs and defendant corporation."

Indeed, the very closing words of the plaintiffs' "expended and particularized allegations" regarding their alleged mistake fail to set forth that even they understood the contract to mean that if Ducey sold less than all his interest in the land to the defendant they would receive the differential be-

tween $75 per acre and the higher price paid to
Ducey:

> " * * * the plaintiffs at all times prior to,
> and at the time of executing said agreement
> understood and believed and defendant corpo-
> ration at all said times knew or suspected that
> plaintiffs under the terms of said agreement
> understood and believed that plaintiffs would
> receive the difference between $75.00 per acre
> and any higher price per acre which might be
> agreed upon between defendant corporation
> and John F. Ducey at any time prior to July
> 1, 1950.''

At that point in the plaintiffs' recital, bringing
to a culmination the lengthy narrative regarding
the negotiations, one would expect the plaintiffs to
make strong mention of their alleged understanding that the agreement covered Ducey's sale to the
defendant of his fractional interest in less than all
the lands. Yet as to that crucial feature of the
case, the plaintiffs' peroration contains no specific
word. "O most lame and impotent conclusion!"

From this eloquent lack of particularity on so
vital an issue, the Court is forced to the conviction
that there are no facts which the plaintiffs can
allege regarding even their own asserted subjective,
unilateral misunderstanding of the meaning of the
agreement. Their hindsight seems to be vastly
superior to their foresight.

Section 3399 of the California Civil Code lays
down the conditions under which a contract may be

revised by the courts on the ground of mistake:

> "When, through fraud or a mutual mistake
> of the parties, or a mistake of one party, which
> the other at the time knew or suspected, a writ-
> ten contract does not truly express the inten-
> tion of the parties, it may be revised, on the
> application of a party aggrieved, so as to ex-
> press that intention, so far as it can be done
> without prejudice to rights acquired by third
> persons, in good faith and for value."

In California, it is well settled that, before a
contract can be reformed on the ground of fraud
or mistake, the plaintiff must plead and prove a
definite agreement that pre-existed the instrument
sought to be corrected.

In Auerbach vs. Healy, supra, 174 Cal. at pages
62-63, the Supreme Court of California said:

> "The rules of pleading in actions for the
> reformation of contracts are well established,
> and should be familiar. The complaint should
> allege 'what the real agreement was, what the
> agreement reduced to writing was, and where
> the writing fails to embody the real agreement.'
> 34 Cyc. 972.) If the complaint seeks the correc-
> tion of a description of land, 'the pleading must
> describe the premises so as to render certain the
> location and boundaries.' (34 Cyc. 973.)"

Counsel for the plaintiffs contend, however, that
"as to a mistake of one party which the other at
the time knew or suspected" they "have been unable to find any California cases holding that it is
necessary to allege under these circumstances that

the parties did come to an agreement, and setting forth that agreement.''

There is, however, precisely such a case, decided recently by the Supreme Court of California and citing numerous authorities: Bailard vs. Marden, 36 C. 2d 703, 708-709 (1951). There the plaintiffs alleged both a mutual mistake and their own unilateral mistake, as is made clear on page 704 of the opinion.

With such a situation before it, the Court said:

"The purpose of reformation is to effectuate the common intention of both parties which was incorrectly reduced to writing. To obtain the benefit of this statute (Section 3399), it is necessary that the parties shall have had a complete mutual understanding of all the essential terms of their bargain; if no agreement was reached, there would be no standard to which the writing could be reformed.

"Otherwise stated, '(I)nasmuch as the relief sought in reforming a written instrument is to make it conform to the real agreement or intention of the parties, a definite intention or agreement on which the minds of the parties had met must have pre-existed the instrument in question.' (Authorities cited.) Our statute adopts the principle of law in terms of a single intention which is entertained by both of the parties. 'Courts of equity have no power to make new contracts for the parties, * * * (N) or can they reform an instrument according to the terms in which one of the parties understood it, unless it appears that the other party also had the same understanding. (22 Cal. Jur. section 2, p. 710). If this were not the rule, the purpose of reformation would be thwarted.''

Nowhere in the amended complaint now before this Court is there any suggestion of any "pre-existing agreement" to which the sought-for reformed instrument should conform. The verbose statement in the amended complaint contains no intimation that the plaintiffs envisaged any sale by Ducey to the defendant of his undivided fractional interest in only a part of the lands in question. On the contrary, the amended complaint specifically negatives such a suggestion, for, as we have seen, it alleges that the purchase by the defendant of Ducey's interest in "less than all" of the lands "was not discussed."

10. The Amended Complaint Shows on Its Face That the Action for Reformation Is Barred by the Statute of Limitations.

Under Rule 9(f) of the Federal Rules of Civil Procedure, "For the purpose of testing the sufficiency of a pleading, averments of time * * * are material * * *" Accordingly, where a complaint shows on its face that the action is barred by a statute of limitations, the defense can be raised by a motion to dismiss.

A recent case in point, decided by our Court of Appeals, is Suckow Borax Mines Consolidated, Inc., vs. Borax Consolidated, Ltd., 9 Cir., 185 F. 2d 196, 204 (1950), certiorari denied, 340 U.S. 943

(1951), rehearing denied, 341 U.S. 912 (1951). There the Court said:

> " * * * a complaint may properly be dismissed on motion for failure to state a claim when the allegations in the complaint affirmatively show that the complaint is barred by the applicable statute of limitations. This is because Rule 9(f) makes averments of time and place material for the purposes of testing the sufficiency of a complaint. (Many cases cited)"[6]

It is well settled that, where there is no applicable Federal statute of limitations, the statute of the State where the action is brought controls.[7]

Section 338 (4) of the California Code of Civil Procedure provides that "An action for relief on the ground of * * * mistake" must be brought within three years. The subsection further sets forth:

---

[6]See also Gossard vs. Gossard, 10 Cir., 149 F 2d 111, 113 (1945); Brictson vs. Woodrough, 8 Cir., 164 F 2d 107, 110-111 (1947), certiorari denied, 334 U.S. 849 (1948); 2 Moore's Federal Practice, 2d ed., Section 9.07, page 1920; 1 Barron and Holtzoff's Federal Practice and Procedure, Rules ed., Section 307, page 556.

---

[7]Johnson vs. Greene, DC Cal., 14 F Supp. 945, 947 (1936), affirmed, 9 Cir., 88 F 2d 683 (1937); Latta vs. Western Inv. Co., 9 Cir., 173 F 2d 99, 107 (1949), certiorari denied, 337 U.S. 940 (1949), petition for rehearing denied, 338 U.S. 840 (1949), motion for leave to file a second petition for rehearing denied, 338 U.S. 863 (1949), motion for leave to file petition for rehearing denied, 338 U.S. 889 (1949); Zellmer vs. Acme Brewing Co., 9 Cir., 184 F 2d 940, 942 (1950), 21 ALR 2d 253n. (1952).

"The cause of action in such case not to be deemed to have accrued until the discovery, by the aggrieved party, of the facts constituting the fraud or mistake."

The amended complaint states that the written agreement between the plaintiffs and the defendant was entered into on April 10, 1946. The original complaint, which, as we have seen, contained an alternative prayer for reformation of the contract, was filed on August 23, 1951, more than five years after the execution of the purchase agreement.

In an effort to escape the application of the statute of limitations, however, the plaintiffs allege in both the original and the amended complaint:

"During the month of February, 1949, plaintiffs discovered that * * * on or about December 9, 1947, defendant corporation had acquired the 494.8/1360 fractional interest of John F. Ducey," etc.

Although Section 338(4), supra, provides that the statute does not start to run until such time as the mistake or fraud is discovered, it is well established in California, as elsewhere, that the time will begin to run at such time as the plaintiffs could with reasonable diligence have ascertained the facts.[8]

The amended complaint should have contained allegations of facts showing why the alleged mistake, in the exercise of reasonable diligence, was not discovered until a time within the period of

---

[8]Shain vs. Sresovich, 104 Cal. 402, 405 (1894); Simpson vs. Dalziel, 135 Cal. 599, 603 (1902).

limitation. In other words, the party seeking to avoid the bar must plead facts excusing the failure to make an earlier discovery of the mistake.

In Bradbury vs. Higginson, 167 Cal. 553, 558 (1914), the Court said:

"It is true that the answer avers that the defendant did not discover the mistake until August, 1909, which was within three years of the filing of the answer. But a mere averment of ignorance of a fact which a party might with reasonable diligence have discovered is not enough to postpone the running of the statute. (Cases cited). It is necessary for the party seeking to avoid the bar to affirmatively plead facts excusing the failure to make an earlier discovery of the mistake or fraud relied upon."[9]

In California, an action for the reformation of a contract may be barred even though the time for bringing a suit on the contract itself has not yet run. In Bradbury vs. Higginson, supra, 167 Cal. at page 559, the Court, referring to Gardner vs. California Guar., etc., Co., 137 Cal. 71, used the following language:

"The opinion in the Gardner case contains, further, an expression to the effect that an action for the reformation of a contract is not barred so long as an action on the contract

---

[9]See also Montgomery vs. Peterson, 27 Cal. App. 671, 675-676 (1915); Johnson vs. Ware, 58 C.A. 2d 204, 207 (1943); Prentiss vs. McWhirter, 9 Cir., 63 F 2d 712, 713 (1933), 172 ALR 290 (1948).

itself might be brought. If this be the correct rule, we do not consider it applicable to a case like the one before us, where the reformation is not merely incidental to the main relief sought, but is an essential prerequisite to the asking of any relief." (Emphasis supplied.)

The plaintiffs seek to avoid the incidence of the statute of limitations by relying upon the provisions of Paragraph 10-(B), to the effect that the defendant agreed with the plaintiffs that, in the event that it should purchase the Ducey interest it would, within 15 days, notify the plaintiffs to that effect. It is conceded that the defendant did not give the plaintiffs such notice.

The short answer to this contention, of course, is that the defendant did not purchase the Ducey interest in all of the property, but in only a part of it. This feature of the case has already been fully discussed herein, and need not be labored here.

Since the defendant did not purchase the Ducey interest in all of the lands, it was not required to give the plaintiffs the notice specified in Section 10-(B).

A statute of limitations is not a technical device by means of which meritorious claims may be defeated. It is a statute of repose, and is looked upon favorably in Anglo-American jurisprudence. In Wood vs. Carpenter, 101 U.S. 135, 139 (1879), the Court said:

> "Statutes of limitation are vital to the welfare of society and are favored in the law.

They are found and approved in all systems of enlightened jurisprudence. They promote repose by giving security and stability to human affairs. An important public policy lies at their foundation. They stimulate to activity and punish negligence. While time is constantly destroying the evidence of rights, they supply its place by a presumption which renders proof unnecessary. Mere delay, extending to the limit prescribed, is itself a conclusive bar. The bane and antidote go together."[10]

11. Conclusion

Insofar as the claim for relief on the contract as it stands is concerned, it is admitted that the plaintiffs have left their pleadings unchanged. Accordingly, the Court adheres to its ruling of November 7, 1951, to the effect that there is no ambiguity in the contract in its present form.

In their Amended Complaint, the plaintiffs have failed (a) to set out any pre-existing agreement according to which the contract should be reformed, and (b) to give a cogent and persuasive explanation as to how they came to make their alleged "unilateral mistake."

Finally, the Amended Complaint is barred by the three-year statute of limitations, insofar as it relates to the reformation of the contract.

Accordingly, the Amended Complaint is dis-

---

[10]See also Shain vs. Sresovich, supra, 104 Cal. at page 406.

missed, and judgment is rendered in favor of the defendant.

Dated: September 3d, 1952.

/s/ DAL M. LEMMON,
United States District Judge.

[Endorsed]: Filed September 3, 1952.

United States District Court for the Northern District of California, Northern Division

Civil Action File No. 6532

JAMES V. McCONNELL and MARGOT MURPHY McCONNELL,

Plaintiffs,

vs.

PICKERING LUMBER CORPORATION, a Corporation, DOE ONE, DOE TWO and DOE THREE,

Defendants.

JUDGMENT OF DISMISSAL

Defendant Pickering Lumber Corporation having filed herein its motion to dismiss plaintiffs' amended complaint on the ground that it fails to state a claim upon which relief can be granted, and having further filed its answer herein whereby as its first defense it asserts that plaintiffs' amended complaint fails to state a claim against the defendant on which relief can be granted; and the Court having heard arguments and considered briefs on defendant's motion to dismiss, and being fully advised in the premises and having heretofore filed its memorandum and order thereon, now therefore pursuant to said memorandum and order:

It Is Hereby Ordered, Adjudged and Decreed that defendant's motion to dismiss plaintiffs' amended complaint be and the same is hereby granted and plaintiffs' amended complaint is hereby dismissed with prejudice; and judgment is hereby rendered in favor of the defendant and against the plaintiffs, and defendant is awarded its costs of suit herein in the sum of One Hundred Seventy Dollars ($170);

It Is Further Ordered, Adjudged and Decreed that plaintiffs' motion to vacate the order of this Court of November 7, 1951, dismissing plaintiffs' original complaint, as being contrary to the law, be and the same is hereby denied.

Dated: September 16, 1952.

/s/ DAL M. LEMMON,
Judge of the United States
District Court.

[Endorsed]: Filed September 16, 1952.

Affidavit of mailing attached.

Entered September 16, 1952.

[Title of District Court and Cause.]

NOTICE OF APPEAL FROM JUDGMENT OF DISMISSAL

To Pickering Lumber Corporation, a Corporation, and to John F. Downey, Ralph R. Martig, and Downey, Brand, Seymour & Rohwer, Its Attorneys:

You and Each of You will please take notice that James V. McConnell and Margot Murphy McConnell, plaintiffs above named, hereby appeal to the Court of Appeals for the Ninth Circuit from the final Judgment of Dismissal entered in this action on the 16th day of September, 1952.

Dated this 9th day of October, 1952.

/s/ HERBERT BARTHOLOMEW,

/s/ PEMBROKE GOCHNAUER,
Attorneys for Appellants.

[Endorsed]: Filed October 15, 1952.

[Title of District Court and Cause.]

STATEMENT OF POINTS UPON WHICH APPELLANTS INTEND TO RELY

The points upon which the appellants intend to rely upon this appeal are as follows:

1. The District Court erred in dismissing plaintiffs' amended complaint sua sponte after an answer

had been filed, the issues were joined, depositions of the parties had been taken and filed and the case had been regularly set for trial.

2. The District Court erred in vacating, sua sponte, its own Order of March 26, 1952, deferring until the time of trial a ruling on defendant's motion to dismiss the amended complaint.

3. The District Court erred in vacating, sua sponte, its Order of January 3, 1952, resubmitting plaintiffs' motion to vacate its Order of November 7, 1951, dismissing plaintiffs' original complaint.

4. The District Court erred in dismissing plaintiffs' amended complaint upon the asserted ground that said amended complaint failed to state a claim for relief upon a written contract.

5. The District Court erred in dismissing plaintiffs' amended complaint upon the asserted ground that said amended complaint failed to state a claim for relief for reformation of a written contract based upon a mistake by plaintiffs as to the meaning and effect thereof which mistake was known or suspected by defendant at the time of the execution thereof.

6. The District Court erred in dismissing the plaintiffs' amended complaint upon the asserted ground that said amended complaint shows on its face that the action for reformation is barred by the Statute of Limitations.

7. The District Court erred in dismissing plaintiffs' amended complaint on the basis of allegations

contained in the plaintiffs' original unverified complaint and in defendant's unverified answer.

8. The District Court erred in dismissing plaintiffs' amended complaint without leave to amend and without resort to pre-trial conference or to a consideration of the depositions of the plaintiffs and of the officers of defendant corporation, which depositions were then on file with the court; and in accepting, as indicated in its opinion, statements of counsel in unverified pleadings as a substitute for valid evidence of the ultimate facts.

Dated this 21st day of October, 1952.

/s/ HERBERT BARTHOLOMEW,

/s/ PEMBROKE GOCHNAUER,
Attorneys for Appellants.

A copy of the within Statement of Points Upon Which Appellants Intend to Rely was served upon defendant Pickering Lumber Corporation and its attorneys of record herein by depositing a copy thereof in the United States mail at San Francisco, California, addressed to: John F. Downey, Ralph R. Martig, of Downey, Brand, Seymour & Rohwer, 500 Capital National Bank Building, Sacramento 14, California, on October 21, 1952.

/s/ HERBERT BARTHOLOMEW.

[Endorsed]: Filed October 22, 1952.

[Title of District Court and Cause.]

CERTIFICATE OF CLERK TO RECORD ON APPEAL

I, C. W. Calbreath, Clerk of the District Court of the United States for the Northern District of California, do hereby certify that the foregoing and accompanying documents listed below, are the originals, or certified copies of originals filed in this Court in the above-entitled case, and that they constitute the record on appeal as designated herein by the parties.

Complaint.

Notice of motion to dismiss.

Order, dated Nov. 7, 1951.

Notice of motion to vacate order dismissing the complaint dated and filed Nov. 7, 1951, and for leave to file amended complaint.

Memorandum, dated Jan. 3, 1952.

Amended complaint.

Motion to dismiss amended complaint.

Order dated March 26, 1952.

Answer of defendant Pickering Lumber Co.

Demand for jury trial.

Motion to dispense with jury trial on reformation issues.

Memorandum and order, dated Sept. 3, 1952.

Judgment of dismissal.

Notice of appeal.

Supersedeas bond on appeal.

Statement of points upon which appellants intend to rely.

Designation of contents of record on appeal.

In Witness Whereof, I have hereunto set my hand and the seal of said Court this 30th day of October, 1952.

[Seal]   C. W. CALBREATH,
                        Clerk.

By /s/ C. C. EVENSEN,
            Deputy Clerk.

———

[Endorsed]: No. 13602. United States Court of Appeals for the Ninth Circuit. James V. McConnell and Margot Murphy McConnell, Appellants, vs. Pickering Lumber Corporation, Appellee. Transcript of Record. Appeal from the United States District Court for the Northern District of California, Northern Division.

Filed October 31, 1952.

/s/ PAUL P. O'BRIEN,
Clerk of the United States Court of Appeals for the Ninth Circuit.

In the United States Court of Appeals
for the Ninth Circuit
No. 13602

JAMES V. McCONNELL and M A R G O T
MURPHY McCONNELL,

Appellants,

vs.

PICKERING LUMBER CORPORATION, a Corporation,

Appellee.

STATEMENT BY APPELLANTS OF POINTS
ON WHICH THEY INTEND TO RELY ON
APPEAL

Appellants, James V. McConnell and Margot
Murphy McConnell, refer to the Statement of
Points upon which Appellants Intend to Rely, filed
in the office of the Clerk of the United States District Court for the Northern District of California,
Northern Division, on October 15, 1952, and incorporate said statement of points as fully as though
said points were specifically set forth herein.

In addition to the foregoing, appellants hereby
designate the following additional point upon which
they intend to rely on appeal:

The District Court erred in entering judgment
for defendant Pickering Lumber Corporation and
against the plaintiffs.

Dated: November 19th, 1952.

/s/ HERBERT BARTHOLOMEW,

/s/ PEMBROKE GOCHNAUER,
Attorneys for Appellants.

[Endorsed]: Filed November 19, 1952.

No. 13,602

United States Court of Appeals
For the Ninth Circuit

JAMES V. McCONNELL and
MARGOT MURPHY McCONNELL,

Appellants,

vs.

PICKERING LUMBER CORPORATION,

Appellee.

APPELLANTS' OPENING BRIEF.

HERBERT BARTHOLOMEW,
1240 Merchants Exchange Building, San Francisco 4, California,
PEMBROKE GOCHNAUER,
111 Sutter Street, San Francisco 4, California,
Attorneys for Appellants.

PERNAU-WALSH PRINTING CO., SAN FRANCISCO

Subject Index

Table of Authorities Cited

Cases   Pages

Codes

Rules

Texts

No. 13,602

United States Court of Appeals
For the Ninth Circuit

JAMES V. McCONNELL and
MARGOT MURPHY McCONNELL,
                                            Appellants,
   vs.

PICKERING LUMBER CORPORATION,
                                            Appellee.

APPELLANTS' OPENING BRIEF.

STATEMENT OF JURISDICTION.

1. Jurisdiction of District Court.

The complaint and amended complaint alleged that appellants are citizens of New York; appellee is a Delaware corporation; and the matter in controversy exceeds, exclusive of interest and costs, the sum of $3,000.00. (Tr. pp. 3, 29.) The answer to the amended complaint admitted said facts. (Tr. p. 42.)

The District Court had original jurisdiction based on diversity of citizenship. 28 U.S.C. section 1332.

2. Jurisdiction of Court of Appeals.

This appeal is taken from a judgment of dismissal entered September 16, 1952 (Tr. pp. 77-78), wherein appellee's motion to dismiss the amended complaint on the ground that it failed to state a claim was granted with prejudice and a judgment for costs was rendered in favor of appellee. The notice of appeal was filed October 15, 1952 (Tr. p. 79), within the time limited by 28 U.S.C. section 2107.

The judgment of dismissal constituted an adjudication upon the merits. Federal Rules of Civil Procedure, Rule 41 (c). It was a final decision by the District Court and jurisdiction of this appeal is conferred upon this court by 28 U.S.C. sections 1291 and 1294 (1).

PROCEEDINGS IN THE DISTRICT COURT.

Appellee moved to dismiss the original complaint under Rule 12 (b) (6) for failure to state a claim on which relief can be granted. (Tr. p. 25.) On November 7, 1951 the District Court granted the motion and dismissed the complaint on contract because "I do not find an ambiguity in the contract." The Court held the averments insufficient to permit reformation but granted leave to file an amended complaint for reformation. (Tr. pp. 26, 27.)

Appellants moved to vacate the order of November 7, 1951, and lodged with the Court their proposed amended complaint, *which was identical with the original complaint except as to the allegations in paragraph XI thereof concerning reformation.* (Tr. pp. 27-40.)

On January 3, 1952, the District Court granted leave to file the amended complaint and set aside the submission of the motion to vacate its order of November 7, 1951, to be resubmitted with any motion attacking the amended complaint. (Tr. pp. 28, 29.)

On January 25, 1952, appellee moved to dismiss the amended complaint under Rule 12 (b) (6). (Tr. p. 41.)

On March 26, 1952, the District Court entered an order stating, "I believe that a ruling upon the motion to dismiss should be deferred until the trial * * * It is so ordered." (Tr. p. 41.)

Appellee filed its answer to the amended complaint on April 19, 1952. (Tr. pp. 42-45.)

On April 25, 1952, appellants filed a demand for a jury trial on their claim upon the contract without reformation and also as to "all issues of fact" on their claim for reformation. (Tr. p. 46.)

On May 1, 1952, appellee filed a motion to dispense with jury trial on reformation issues. (Tr. p. 46.)

On September 3, 1952, the district judge filed a "memorandum and order" directing a dismissal of the amended complaint and a judgment for appellee (Tr. pp. 47-77), and pursuant thereto, on September 16, 1952, entered a "judgment of dismissal" (Tr. pp. 77, 78) whereby he granted appellee's motion to dismiss the amended complaint (of January 25, 1952); dismissed the amended complaint with prejudice; rendered judgment for appellee and awarded it costs in the sum of $170.00; and denied appellant's motion to vacate the order of November 7, 1951, dismissing the original complaint.

This appeal is taken from said "judgment of dismissal."

STATEMENT OF THE CASE.

The claim against appellee is to recover the unpaid balance of the purchase price of certain timber lands in Tuolumne County, California, under a written contract. (Tr. pp. 3-24.) The issue involves the meaning and application of a price escalator clause, section 10 of the contract. The amended complaint (Tr. pp. 29-40) sets forth the contract and the opposing interpretations placed upon it by appellants and appellee and asks relief under the contract as written. In the alternative, if the contract is construed as appellee interprets it, appellants allege the contract was executed by them under a mistake on their part as to its meaning and effect which was known or suspected by appellee, and ask reformation for "mistake of one party, which was known or suspected by the other," in accordance with section 3399 of the *Civil Code of California*. The charging allegation of the original and amended complaints in this respect is in the very language of said code section. (Tr. pp. 11, 35, 39.)

The original complaint alleged both mutual mistake and unilateral mistake as a basis for reformation. (Tr. p. 10.) The amended complaint alleged unilateral mistake only. These alternative claims are criticized in the "Memorandum and Order" of the District Court as "varying and inconsistent contentions" although the pleading of alternative claims is permitted by Rule 18 (a) of the Federal Rules of Civil Procedure.

The amended complaint and attached contract reveal the following situation:

Appellee corporation was engaged in the lumber business in California. (Tr. p. 30.) Appellee corporation, appellant Margot Murphy McConnell, who resides in New York, and five individuals, all residing in Michigan, held in undivided ownership 154 parcels of timber lands in Tuolumne County, California, aggregating 6172.60 acres. In terms of percentages John F. Ducey owned 36.38 per cent, appellee corporation 20 per cent, appellant Margot McConnell 18.25 per cent and the other four people the remaining 25.37 per cent among them—in other words, three of the seven co-owners held approximately 75 per cent of the property. (Tr. pp. 30-32.) Appellee desired to buy the interests of its co-owners. Appellee prepared the written agreement covering purchase of appellant's interest at an initial price of $75.00 an acre. (Tr. p. 38.) This agreement is dated July 1, 1945, but was signed by appellants April 6, 1946, and by appellee April 10, 1946. It contains the following pricing clause:

> "10-(A)—Should Purchaser at any time prior to July 1, 1950 acquire the 494.8/1360 fractional interest of John F. Ducey in the property listed in Schedule A from him, his heirs or assigns or representatives, directly or indirectly, or at a parti-

tion sale of all the property described in Schedule A at a price higher than that provided herein for Sellers' interest, then Purchaser and Sellers hereby agree that the price provided in this contract for the Sellers' interest shall forthwith be adjusted upward by the amount necessary to make up the difference." (Tr. p. 32.)

In February, 1949, appellants discovered that appellee had purchased, in December, 1947, the entire 494.8/1360 fractional interest of John F. Ducey in 40 of the 154 parcels "listed in Schedule A" at a price greatly in excess of $75.00 per acre and believed to be approximately $150.00 per acre. Appellee has made no payment to appellants under the price escalator clause (Tr. p. 33) nor has it notified appellants of its purchase from Ducey as required by paragraph (B) of section 10 of the agreement. (Tr. p. 34.)

Appellants are suing here for the difference between $75.00 per acre paid to them and the higher price per acre paid by appellee to John F. Ducey together with interest thereon from the time such payment should have been made as provided in section 10 of the agreement. Appellee's failure to pay is believed to be based on its contention that section 10 of the agreement is completely inoperative because appellee did not acquire, prior to July 1, 1950, the fractional interest of John F. Ducey in all 154 parcels of the property but only in 40 parcels thereof. (Tr. p. 34.)

It is then alleged, in substance, that if the contract is construed to mean that appellee corporation must buy the interest of John F. Ducey in "all" of the property listed in Schedule A, then it was executed by appellants under a mistake on their part as to the meaning and effect of the language "the property listed in Schedule A," which mistake was known or suspected by appellee at the time of the execution of the contract. At the time appellants executed said contract it was their understanding that Section 10-(A) meant that they would receive for their interest in the McArthur-Ducey lands an amount equal to the difference between $75.00 per acre and any higher price per acre provided in any agreement between appellee corporation and John F. Ducey, and made prior to July 1, 1950, for the sale of Ducey's interest *in all or any* of said lands. (Tr. p. 35.)

Appellants were induced into this mistake by the following circumstances: After appellee corporation acquired its twenty per cent interest in said lands in July, 1944, and in order for it to cut timber on any of said lands, it began negotiations to buy out the interests of all the other owners. These negotiations were largely carried on between appellants and appellee corporation, and all co-owners, except John F. Ducey, were willing to sell if a fair price could be obtained. In March, 1945, appellant went to Detroit, met with all of her co-owners, and they agreed to sell their interests at a price of $75.00 per acre, which fact was made known to appellee corporation, for in June of that year appellee corporation prepared and submitted a proposed contract at this price (Tr. p. 36) which contained substantially all the provisions of the contract here in issue, except it omitted the pricing clause, paragraph 10. John F. Ducey refused to sign this contract. Thereupon appellee corporation entered into negotiations with appellants for the purchase of their interest and informed appellants that the acquisition of their interest would improve the corporation's position in the event of a partition suit.

Appellants refused to sell their interest at $75.00 per acre unless protected against the acquisition by appellee corporation of any of the other interests at a higher price per acre. This demand was subsequently narrowed to include only the interest of John F. Ducey because he owned the largest outstanding interest, and because of his past unwillingness to sell. (Tr. p. 37.) In February, 1946, all the other co-owners offered to sell their interests to appellee corporation for $100.00 per acre, which fact was made known to appellants. The same month Ben Johnson, the then president of appellee corporation, proposed to appellants in New York that they enter into two contracts, one at $75.00 per acre which would be shown to the other co-owners, and another at a higher price per acre, which would be a private agreement between them. Appellants refused to consider this. By reason of these negotiations it became apparent to appellants that appellee corporation desired to purchase all outstanding interests in said property and appellants believed it would do so prior to July 1, 1950.

In April, 1946, the parties entered into the contract here in controversy, which contract was prepared and submitted by the appellee corporation.

In July, 1951, appellants discovered that appellee corporation had, prior to July 1, 1950, agreed with all of the other co-owners, except John F. Ducey, to buy all of their interests in all of said lands and that appellants are informed and believed that the prices received by them exceed the sum of $75.00 per acre. (Tr. p. 38.) In paragraph VII it is alleged that in February, 1949, appellants learned that appellee corporation had purchased all of John F. Ducey's interest in 40 of the 154 parcels at a price greatly in excess of $75.00 per acre. It is then alleged that although the contingency of the purchase by appellee corporation of the fractional interest of John F. Ducey in a part of but less than all of said lands was not discussed between appellee corporation and appellants, that appellants, under the terms of the agreement, understood and believed that appellants would receive the difference between $75.00 per acre and any higher price which might be agreed upon between appellee corporation and John F. Ducey at any time prior to July 1, 1950.

The foregoing factual allegations of the circumstances giving rise to appellants' mistake, known or suspected at the time by appellee, were all made pursuant to Rule 9 (b) of the Federal Rules of Civil Procedure. The amended complaint was expanded to include these allegations after the District Court had on November 7, 1951, granted appellee's motion to dismiss the original complaint, with leave only to amend as to the reformation issue. (Tr. pp. 26-27.)

SPECIFICATION OF ERRORS RELIED UPON.

Appellants' statement of the points on which they intend to rely on this appeal are set forth at pages 79, 80, 81 and 84 of the record. They are nine in number but may be summarized as follows:

1. The District Court held that the amended complaint does not state a claim upon which relief can be granted either for breach of the written contract which is incorporated therein, nor, in the alternative, for the reformation of said contract under California Civil Code, section 3399 for a mistake of one party which the other at the time of its execution knew or suspected.

This holding, we contend, was error.

2. The District Court held that the amended complaint shows on its face that the action for reformation is barred by the statute of limitations.

This holding, we contend, was error.

3. In March, 1952, the District Court ordered that a ruling upon appellee's motion to dismiss the amended complaint "be deferred until the trial." Thereafter appellee answered, depositions of the parties were taken and filed and the case was set for trial. In September, 1952, the District Court on its own initiative, without notice, hearing, pretrial conference, or motion for judgment on the pleadings, dismissed the amended complaint with prejudice and entered judgment for appellee.

The dismissal of the amended complaint, we contend, was error.

SUMMARY OF ARGUMENT.

We will show:

1. The amended complaint states a claim for relief upon the contract as written.

2. The amended complaint states a claim on which relief can be granted by way of reformation.

3. The claim for relief by way of reformation was not barred by the statute of limitations.

ARGUMENT.

I. THE AMENDED COMPLAINT STATES A CLAIM FOR RELIEF UPON THE CONTRACT AS WRITTEN.

The claim on the contract turns upon the meaning and application of the words in the price escalator clause—"in the property listed in Schedule A". Said Schedule A lists 154 parcels of land. Appellee subsequently acquired 40 of these parcels at a higher price. Can the clause be construed to mean *"in all or any of the property"* as appellants allege or must it be construed as meaning *"in all the property"* as the District Court held?

The "Memorandum and Order" of the Court below sets forth the basis of its ruling. Citing the parol evidence (integration) rule and its exceptions (interpretation rules) in the case of ambiguity, either patent or latent, the learned judge says:

> "In the instant case, however, there is no ambiguity either extrinsic or intrinsic, in the contract." (Tr. p. 61.)

and further (Tr. p. 63):

> " * * * we cannot read 'in the property' to mean 'in any of the property' * * * Generally speaking, we may say that 'the property,' as used in the present contract, means *all* the property.' " (emphasis supplied.)

In so holding, and denying appellants the right at a trial to prove what the parties meant by what they said, the District Court erred in the following respects:

1. The so-called "integration" rule—that all prior and contemporaneous negotiations are merged into and expressed by the written agreement—is not involved, although the District Court apparently believed it was involved.

2. In holding "the property," as used in the present contract, means "all the property" and under no circumstances could it mean "any of the property" or "all or any of the property," when the word "the" and the term "the property" have been judicially construed to mean either "all" or "any" depending upon the context and the circumstances under which they were used.

3. The decision ignores or overlooks the fact that the parties place conflicting and opposite meanings on the language; that the language was prepared by appellee and must be construed against it, and that other terms of the contract itself lend support to the appellant's construction of it.

4. Finally, the decision holding "the property" means "all the property" proves the ambiguity, for it

is clearly established that an ambiguity exists whenever it is necessary to add words to a writing to make its meaning clear.

RULES OF CONSTRUCTION WHICH SHOULD HAVE BEEN APPLIED ON MOTION TO DISMISS.

The denial to appellants of a day in Court was not in harmony with the spirit and purpose of the Federal Rules of Civil Procedure. Speaking to the California Bar in 1947, Judge Goodman said (7 F.R.D. 449):

> "In the pleading stage of civil litigation in Federal Courts is found the most beneficial impact of what we may well call the new spirit in Federal Civil Procedure * * *
>
> "The adroit procedural maneuvering of the earlier days in the pleading stage, often invoked to deprive a litigant of his day in court, is now relegated to the archives. Motions to dismiss, motions to strike, motions to make more certain, motions for bills of particulars, while still permissive under the new rules, are, in fact, no longer available as a means of frustration or to delay the final reckoning of trial. The pleading state of litigation should be, and is made simple. Our philosophy now is that only that need be stated that gives a fair notice to the opponent of the general nature of the cause or defense."

See also,

> *Securities & Exchange Comm. v. Time Trust, Inc.,* (D.C. Cal. 1939), 28 F. Supp. 34, 41;
>
> *Van Dyke v. Broadhurst,* (D.C. Pa. 1939), 28 Fed. Supp. 737, 740;

In re Stroh (D.C. Pa. 1943), 52 F. Supp. 958,
961;

Porter v. Shoemaker, (D.C. Pa. 1947), 6 F.R.D.
438, 440;

2 *Moore's Federal Practice,* (2d Ed.) 1605.

In *Topping v. Fry,* (C.C.A. 7, 1945) 147 F. 2d 715,
a judgment of dismissal was reversed although "The
complaint is so poorly drafted that it is difficult to determine upon what theory the action is based." The
Court says at page 719:

"Under the liberalized procedure provided for
by the new rules, we think it is error to dismiss
a complaint with prejudice if it appears that any
relief could be granted on the facts stated."

A complaint should not be dismissed under Rule
12(b)(6) for "failure to state a claim upon which relief can be granted" unless——

"It appears to a certainty that the plaintiff
would be entitled to no relief under any state of
facts which could be proved in support of the
claim asserted to him."

Cool v. International Shoe Co., (1944 C.C.A.
8th), 142 F. 2d 318, at 320;

Pennsylvania R. Co. v. Musante-Phillips, Inc.,
(D.C. Cal. 1941), 42 F. Supp. 340, 341;

2 *Moore's Federal Practice,* (2d Ed.), p. 2245.

In *Continental Collieries v. Shober,* (1942, C.C.A.
3d), 130 F. 2d 631, the Court after stating the above
rule said at page 635:

"No matter how likely it may seem that the
pleader will be unable to prove his case, he is en-

titled, upon averring a claim, to an opportunity
to try to prove it."

On motion to dismiss, the facts alleged are taken
as true.

> *Clark v. Nebersee Finanz-Korp.,* (1947), 322
> U.S. 480, 68 S. Ct. 174, 92 L. Ed. 88.

Here appellants' claim on contract is clearly stated.
The contract is set forth in full (Tr. pp. 13-24); the
opposing constructions of it are spelled out (Tr. pp.
34, 35); and relief is asked in accordance with the
contract terms. (Tr. pp. 39, 40.) All issues had been
framed by appellee's answer. (Tr. pp. 42-45.) Depositions of the parties had been taken and filed and the
case had been set for trial. (Tr. pp. 80, 81.) Nearly
thirteen months had elapsed between the filing of the
original complaint on August 23, 1951 (Tr. p. 24) and
the judgment of dismissal on September 16, 1952. (Tr.
p. 78.) As to the contract claim the amended complaint
is identical with the original complaint. (Tr. p. 54.)
The District Court granted a motion to dismiss in November (Tr. p. 27), resubmitted his ruling in January
(Tr. p. 29) in March deferred further rulings until
trial (Tr. p. 41), and finally decided the case in September (Tr. p. 78) *sua sponte,* without trial or pretrial conference. Apparently, appellee was satisfied
to proceed to trial for it could have filed a further
"speaking motion" for summary judgment under
Rule 56 if it had believed the evidence developed in
the depositions of the parties did not support appellants' claim. Finally, the District Court could have

resorted to a pretrial conference. The net result of the unusual procedure adopted was to deny to appellants not only a trial but any opportunity to present to the Court extrinsic evidence to support their claim as to the meaning of the contract language.

THE DISTRICT COURT'S CONSTRUCTION OF THE CONTRACT CARRIES NO WEIGHT IN THIS COURT.

In the absence of extrinsic evidence in aid of the construction of a written instrument, an appellate Court is not bound by the trial Court's interpretation and will independently ascertain the meaning of the instrument's provisions from the language thereof as a matter of law.

> *Transport Oil Co. v. Exeter Oil Co.*, (1948), 84 Cal. App. (2d) 616, 620;
>
> *Moore v. Wood*, (1945), 26 Cal. (2d) 621;
>
> *Estate of Platt*, (1942), 21 Cal. (2d) 343.

In *Trubowitch v. Riverbank Canning Co.*, (1947), 30 Cal. (2d) 335, the rule is stated, at page 339:

> "It is settled in this state that an appellate court is not bound by a trial court's construction of a contract or other written instrument based solely upon the terms of the instrument" (citing cases).

This honorable Court is called upon to examine the allegations of the amended complaint and all provisions of the written contract incorporated therein, and unless this Court is convinced from its own independent consideration thereof that appellants "would be entitled to no relief under any state of facts which could be proved in support of the claim'', it must reverse the judgment herein.

> *Cool v. International Shoe Co.*, supra;
>
> *Pennsylvania R. Co. v. Musante-Phillips, Inc.*, supra;
>
> 2 *Moore's Federal Practice*, (2d Ed.), p. 2245.

RULES OF INERPRETATION WHICH SUPPORT APPELLANTS' CONSTRUCTION OF THE CONTRACT.

1. **A contract must be construed against the party who prepared it.**

The amended complaint alleged that appellee prepared the contract. (Tr. p. 38.) Appellee is also the promisor. Also alleged are the opposite interpretations which the parties have placed upon it. (Tr. pp. 34, 35.) Our codes provide the following rules of interpretation:

> *Civil Code*, Sec. 1654. *Words to be taken most strongly against whom.* In cases of uncertainty not removed by the preceding rules, the language of a contract should be interpreted most strongly against the party who caused the uncertainty to exist. The promisor is presumed to be such party; except in a contract between a public officer or body, as such, and a private party, in which it is presumed that all uncertainty was caused by the private party.
>
> *Civil Code*, Sec. 1649. *Interpretation in sense in which promisor believed promisee to rely.* If the terms of a promise are in any respect ambiguous or uncertain, it must be interpreted in the sense in which the promisor believed, at the time of making it, that the promisee understood it.

Code of Civil Procedure, Sec. 1864. *Of two constructions, which preferred.* When the terms of an agreement have been intended in a different sense by the different parties to it, that sense is to prevail against either party in which he supposed the other understood it, and when different constructions of a provision are otherwise equally proper, that is to be taken which is most favorable to the party in whose favor the provision was made.

2. **A contract must be construed to avoid an absurdity.**

"The property listed in Schedule A" consists of 154 parcels, each of 40 acres or thereabouts, aggregating 6,171.68 acres. (Tr. pp. 18-24.) If "the property" can only mean "all the property" as the District Court held (Tr. p. 63); and if "there is no ambiguity, either extrinsic or intrinsic," as it further held (Tr. p. 61), then it must follow that the price escalator clause, as the District Court construes it, could never operate unless appellee elected to purchase "all" 154 parcels. Operation of the pricing clause depended, in any case, upon a future voluntary act by appellee. Appellee could always escape its own promise by omitting from its future purchase a single parcel, or even a fraction of one parcel!

The result of such a construction is to render the clause meaningless and absurd.

Even had the operation of the clause hinged upon the future act of a third party rather than the promissor, its meaning could not be clear and unambiguous.

Rule 8 (f) requires that "all pleadings shall be so construed as to do substantial justice."

Section 1638 of the *Civil Code* provides:

> *§ 1638 Intention to be ascertained from language.* The language of a contract is to govern its interpretation, if the language is clear and explicit, and does not involve an absurdity.

Hence, under the above code provision even if we were to concede, as the District Court contends, that the clause is "clear and explicit" we would still reject the construction given by the District Court because it involves an absurdity.

3. A contract must be construed as a whole.

Section 1641 of the *Civil Code* provides:

> *§ 1641. Effect to be given to every part of contract.* The whole of a contract is to be taken together, so as to give effect to every part, if reasonably practicable, each clause helping to interpret the other.

There are other provisions of the contract which support appellants' construction of it.

a. The property listed in Schedule A is not a single parcel or tract of land. If it were one parcel only, the ruling that "the" was intended to mean "all the" would be more plausible. Instead Schedule A lists separately 154 parcels spread over 3 townships and 3 ranges. Although Schedule A as prepared by appellee does not include a map as is usually the case, anyone familiar with section maps can see from the descriptions that the 154 parcels are not contiguous. (Tr. pp. 18-23.) It becomes relevant and important, therefore, to inquire whether appellee would be apt to purchase the Ducey interest in all 154 parcels or only in those parcels which it needed to cut during the term of the contract.

b. Section 10-(A) first covers the contingency of a direct purchase of the Ducey interest "in the property listed in Schedule A." Later in the same sentence it covers the contingency of a partition sale of "*all* the property described in Schedule A." (emphasis supplied.) The use of all in one instance and its omission in the other certainly does not support the District Court's holding that the parties clearly meant "all" in both instances. To the contrary it must be assumed the parties intentionally omitted "all" in the first instance, and therefore "the property" was not intended to mean *all* the property.

Expressio unius est exclusio alterius.

> *Jones v. Robertson,* (1947), 79 Cal. App. (2d) 813.

c. Reading the contract as a whole it is apparent that the pricing clause was the real consideration moving to seller (appellants), since the purchase price was payable over a term of years, the price escalator clause was intended to fix the real price at the value of sellers' interest to buyer, *as fixed by the buyer,* within such term.

As construed by the District Court, the contract means that the parties intended that during the same term appellee could pay one price to appellants and a higher price to Ducey for their fractional interests in the same timber. Stated differently, the District Court has read the contract to mean the parties intended that appellee was free to pay one price to appellants and a higher price to Ducey, unless appellee should elect to buy Ducey's interest in every tree on every parcel. This interpretation is unreasonable and it renders the clause ineffective for any practical purpose.

On the other hand, the interpretation which appellants allege, and have been denied an opportunity to prove, gives the pricing clause vitality and meaning.

EVIDENCE IS ADMISSIBLE TO EXPLAIN A PATENT OR LATENT AMBIGUITY.

The District Court erred in denying appellants the right to prove the intended meaning of the contract by evidence of the circumstances prior to and contemporaneous with its execution. The right to prove the contract means what appellants allege it means is clearly conferred by the California Codes.

Civil Code, Sec. 1647. *Contracts explained by circumstances.* A contract may be explained by reference to the circumstances under which it was made, and the matter to which it relates.

Code of Civil Procedure, Sec. 1860. *The circumstances to be considered.* For the proper construction of an instrument, the circumstances under which it was made, including the situation of the subject of the instrument, and of the parties to it, may also be shown, so that the judge be placed in the position of those whose language he is to interpret.

The duty of the Court to ascertain the intention of the parties before construing the contract is equally clear.

> *Civil Code,* Sec. 1636. *Contracts, how to be interpreted.* A contract must be so interpreted as to give effect to the mutual intention of the parties as it existed at the time of contracting, so far as the same is ascertainable and lawful.

Also, Section 1859 of the *Code of Civil Procedure* provides "* * * and in the construction of the instrument the intention of the parties, is to be pursued, if possible * * *."

See also,

> *Restatement of the Law of Contracts,* Secs. 230, 235;
>
> *Wachs v. Wachs* (1938) 11 Cal. (2d) 322.

The District Court's judgment is based upon the so-called "integration" rule (*Civil Code,* Section 1625; *Code of Civil Procedure,* Section 1856), by which a written agreement supersedes all prior and contemporaneous negotiations or stipulations (Tr. pp. 60, 61) and its corollary, that if the language is clear and explicit, the intention of the parties must be ascertained from the writing alone (Tr. p. 63). The Court below refers to the so-called "interpretation" rules (Tr. p. 61) permitting extrinsic evidence to explain patent or latent ambiguity, but the Court says that neither exists. (Tr. p. 61.)

Patent ambiguity is dismissed with the statement "There is absolutely no warrant for asserting that the words 'fractional interest of John F. Ducey in the property' were 'written blindly or imperfectly' or that their meaning is 'doubtful'." (Tr. p. 63.)

It seems unnecessary and inappropriate to restate at this point the reasons which bear out appellants' opposing interpretation, nor to cite to this Court many cases in which the Courts have liberally applied the interpretation rule as to patent ambiguity to the writings before them. This Court had a similar situation in *Hanney v. Franklin Fire Ins. Co. of Philadelphia* (1944 C.C.A. 9th) 142 F. (2d) 864, an action upon an insurance policy, and for reformation of it. Each party claimed the policy was clear but they disagreed as to its meaning. The trial Court dismissed under Rule 12 (b) and this Court reversed.

Latent, or extrinsic ambiguity is dismissed by the District Court with the statement that none exists. (Tr. p. 61.) To the contrary, we maintain that even if no ambiguity existed on the face of the contract as the District Court contends, appellants are certainly entitled to prove that an extrinsic or latent ambiguity arose after the contract was signed by appellee's purchase of the Ducey interest in part of the property, and to explain its meaning in the light of this subsequent event.

Parol evidence is admissible to show that a latent ambiguity exists, and to explain it.

Pacific Ind. Co. v. California Elec. Works (1938) 29 Cal. App. (2d) 260, 272;

Estate of Donellen (1912) 164 Cal. 14;

Estate of Domencini (1907) 151 Cal. 181.

Language which is clear when written may become ambiguous in the light of future events.

F. P. Cutting Co. v. Peterson (1912) 164 Cal. 44;

Barham v. Barham (1949) 33 Cal. (2d) 416.

The *Barham* case, supra, involved the interpretation and effect to be given to a property settlement agreement in the light of a remarriage and divorce. There was no ambiguity in the agreement.

In *Millet v. Taylor* (1914) 26 Cal. App. 161, parol evidence was held admissible to prove that "one equal half part of all the proceeds," as used in a lease, meant one half the *net* proceeds. The Court said this was "a latent ambiguity."

Under the District Court's ruling here one may wonder how an extrinsic ambiguity could be shown to exist in any case when the Court felt the language of the writing to be clear!

ADDING "ALL" TO THE CONTRACT IN ORDER TO CLARIFY ITS MEANING IS PROOF OF THE AMBIGUITY.

In support of its construction of the contract the District Court says (Tr. p. 63):

> "Generally speaking, we may say that 'the property,' as used in the present contract, means 'all the property'."

Not only was the learned judge in error in deciding that *"the"* must mean, or that it generally does mean, *"all the,"* but he erred also in deciding that "In the instant case, however, there is no ambiguity," (Tr. p. 61) when he found it necessary to read "the" to mean "all the."

> "Once something has to be read into a contract to make it clear, it can hardly be said to be susceptible of only one interpretation."
>
> *Union Oil Co. v. Union Sugar Co.* (1948) 31 Cal. (2d) 300, at p. 306. (Reversing trial Court's construction of written contract, though based on conflicting evidence of intent.)

And the comment in the above case at page 306 is particularly applicable:

> "It would have been error for the trial court to read something into the contract by straining 'to find a clear meaning in an ambiguous document, and having done so exclude the extrinsic evidence on the ground that so construed no ambiguity exists'."
>
> *Body-Steffner Co. v. Flotill Products* (1944) 63 Cal. App. (2d) 555, 562.

The *Body-Steffner* case, supra, is notable not only as indicating how carefully the California Appellate Courts reexamine the trial Courts' construction of an instrument, but in addition, the latitude permitted in the use of extrinsic evidence to aid the Court in deciding its intended meaning. In reversing, for refusing to receive extrinsic evidence that contract language had an opposite meaning by custom and usage, the Court says, at page 562:

"Our conclusion that these contracts are ambiguous on their face makes it unnecessary for us to determine in this case whether parol evidence should not be admitted in every case to show the sense in which the parties used the language embodied in their contracts, even though the language used would normally have a clear and settled meaning. There is a considerable body of opinion among students of the subject whose conclusions are entitled to the greatest respect that parol evidence should always be admissible to show the sense in which the contracting parties used and understood the language of their written contracts (cf. concurring opinion of Traynor, J., in *Universal Sales Corp. v. California, etc. Mfg. Co.*, (1942) 20 Cal. (2d) 751, 776."

"THE PROPERTY" HAS NO PRECISE MEANING.

Cases defining the word "the" well illustrate that "the" has no exact meaning, and that the word must be interpreted in light of the context in which it is used. In the case of

Anundsen v. Standard Printing Co. (Iowa, 1905) 105 N.W. 424,

the Court held that the words "the property," as used in an Iowa statute giving preference to labor claims "when the property of any company * * * shall be seized * * *," did not mean "all of the property." After observing that the word "the" has sometimes been construed to mean "all of the" and sometimes not, the Court said at page 426:

"But at most, it is nothing more than a definitive adjective, as opposed to an indefinite article.

* * * And there seem to be no settled rules for its construction. Much must of necessity be left to the context, and to the objects and purposes of the statute in which it is found."

In

Howell v. State (Ga. 1927) 138 S.E. 206, 210, the Court held that the words "the warden" as used in a statute providing who should serve as executioner, meant "any warden," so that although the state penitentiary had three wardens, any one of them could serve. While agreeing that grammatical niceties should not be resorted to without necessity, the Court observed that in the construction of statutes the Courts should apply common sense and not the logical refinement of the schoolman.

The California Courts have had occasion to define "the" to mean "any" in at least two instances. In the case of

Craig v. Boyes (1932) 123 C.A. 592, 596, it was held that the words "the proximate cause," as used in the California Guest Law, means "a" proximate cause of injury. The Court referred to numerous authorities including *Noyes v. Children's Aid Society*, 70 N.Y. 481, 484, and the *Anundsen* case, *supra;* it quoted the above quoted passage from the *Anundsen* case with approval and then said that the quoted rule was applicable to the case before it.

And in

City of Oakland v. Hogan (1940) 41 C.A. (2d) 333,

it was held that the Port Commission of Oakland was the legislative body of the City of Oakland within the language of C.C.P. Section 811: "the legislative body of any municipal corporation," although it is primarily an administrative body and not the principal legislative body of that city. In so holding, the Court reversed a judgment for defendants based on an order sustaining their demurrers to the amended complaint. The effect of the decision is a holding that "the legislative body" means "a legislative body." With respect to the meaning of the word "the" the Court cited the *Noyes* and *Craig* cases, supra, and said, at page 343:

> "* * * An examination of the citations *pro* and *con* leads to the conclusion that its context and the apparent intent of the party or parties responsible for the use of the italicized word control in its interpretation and construction rather than the strict grammatical definition of the word."

The cases cited above demonstrate the error of the District Court in its holding that "the property" means "all the property," and that extrinsic evidence is inadmissible to prove that it was intended to mean "any of the property."

II. THE AMENDED COMPLAINT STATES A CLAIM ON WHICH RELIEF CAN BE GRANTED BY WAY OF REFORMATION.

As the Court below has noted (Tr. p. 34) the only difference between the original and the amended complaints is contained in the allegations of paragraph XI of each with respect to a claim for reformation. The original alleged both a mutual mistake and a unilateral mistake. (Tr. pp. 9-12.) The allegations were held defective for failure to allege an agreement other than the writing to which it could be reformed. (Tr. p. 27.) There is no point, of course, in arguing as to error in the Court's ruling on the original complaint. We concede that *as a matter of proof as distinguished from a matter of pleading,* it is necessary in the case of *mutual* mistake to show an antecedent agreement to which the writing can be reformed.

The amended complaint omits any claim of mutual mistake. (Tr. pp. 35-39.) It states a claim under *Civil Code* Section 3399 for a mistake of appellants which was known or suspected by appellee when the contract was signed. It states that appellants executed the agreement under the understanding and belief that it meant "Ducey's interest in all of or any of said lands." Circumstances leading up to the contract which support appellants' understanding of it are set forth. The final allegation is that appellants "at all times prior to, and at the time of executing said agreement understood and believed and defendant corporation at all times knew or suspected that plaintiffs under the terms of said agreement understood and believed that plaintiffs would receive the difference between $75.00 per acre and any higher price per acre which might be agreed upon between defendant corporation and John F. Ducey at any time prior to July 1, 1950." (Tr. p. 39.)

The District Court has dismissed these allegations without leave to amend. The relative portion of the Court's opinion is preceded by a heading averring that appellants "have not made a showing that entitles them to a reformation." (Tr. p. 66.) The opinion says the allegations are "replete with details"; that the opening statement "is merely one of an ultimate fact"; and that the final allegation is "most lame and impotent" because it did not repeat the opening averment that they understood the agreement covered Ducey's sale of his fractional interest "in less than all of the lands." (Tr. pp. 67, 68.)

Appellants' claim is, first, that the contract prepared by appellee means they should receive the benefit of any better deal which appellee might make with Ducey and secondly, if it cannot be so construed, it should be reformed because appellants so understood its meaning and appellee knew or suspected they so understood its meaning. This claim is abundantly clear from the pleading. The pleading is drawn in the language of Section 3399 of the *Civil Code*.

The *real basis* of the District Court's ruling however, rests not upon the language of the amended complaint, but upon the erroneous premise that appellants "must plead and prove a definite agreement that pre-existed the instrument sought to be corrected." (Tr. p. 69.) Thus the Court returned to its ruling of November 7, 1951, dismissing the original complaint which alleged both mutual mistake and unilateral mistake. (Tr. p. 27.) The Court below could see no difference between stating a claim for mutual mistake and a claim for unilateral mistake. In either case plaintiffs must *plead* a definite pre-existing agreement.

The District Court erred:

1. In failing to distinguish between mutual mistake and "a mistake of one party, which the other at the time, knew or suspected."

2. In applying what the Court believed to be the California rule as to pleading and proof to a motion for failure to state a claim under Rule 12 (b).

3. In dismissing the amended complaint with prejudice.

Civil Code, Section 3399 confers separate, distinct and alternative rights of action for mutual mistake and "a mistake of one party, which the other at the time knew or suspected." The difference is noted by the courts.

> Auerback v. Healy (1916) 174 Cal. 60, 63;
> *F. P. Cutting v. Peterson* (1912) 164 Cal. 44, 50;
> *Burton v. Curtis* (1928) 91 Cal. App. 11, 13;
> *Bank of America v. Granger* (1931) 115 Cal. App. 210, 220;
> *Eagle Indemnity Co. v. Industrial Acc. Comm.* (1949) 92 Cal. App. (2d) 222, 229.

Here, after protracted negotiations, appellee prepared a written proposal and sent it to appellants who signed it. (Tr. p. 38.) The District Court held in effect that such a writing can never be reformed for a mistake of one party which was known to the other because "the plaintiff must plead and prove a definite agreement that preexisted the instrument." The District Court is clearly in error. It is not necessary to plead and prove two agreements.

The rule applicable is clearly stated in the *Eagle Indemnity* case, supra, which upheld reformation of an insurance policy for mistake of one party known to the other. The Court says at page 229:

"Petitioner argues that the commission by ordering reformation of the policy created a new contract for the parties. Of course, reformation cannot be ordered so as to create a new and different contract for the parties (22 Cal. Jur. 710) but where, as here, the case falls within the language of Civil Code, section 3399, 'when through * * * a mistake of one party, which the other * * * knew or suspected, a written contract does not truly express the intention of the parties * * *' *the contract which was intended by the party acting under unilateral mistake known or suspected by the other, is, as a matter of law, the contract of the parties.* (Bank of America v. Granger, 115 Cal. App. 210, 220.)" (Emphasis supplied.)

In the *Granger* case, supra, suit was based upon a written guaranty in favor of an extinct corporation and for reformation of it for mutual mistake. A judgment for defendant was reversed on appeal. In distinguishing mutual mistake from unilateral mistake, the Court said at page 220:

"The defendant Thomas contends that the defendants knew whom they were guaranteeing in that they intended to guarantee only the United Bank and Trust Company of California. We do not think that is the record. However, for the purposes of this decision, assuming such to be the record, then the only effect is to rest the case on a harsher clause contained in our statute.

There is certainly no evidence that the plaintiff or its predecessors in interest actually intended to obtain guaranties running in favor of a corporation extinct. Addressing itself to a similar contention in the case of *F. P. Cutting Co. v. Peterson,* supra, on page 50 of 164 Cal. (127 Pac. 163, 165), the court said: 'If they had declared that they did not then expect that the price list would be printed and that they approved the wording with that idea, it would be a virtual confession that they believed that the guaranty would be nugatory and intended to perpetrate a fraud upon the defendant if a lower price was fixed by the association without printing the price list. The mistake would then come within the class of mistakes described in section 3399 as "a mistake of one party, which the other at the time knew or suspected".' The point is without merit."

See also, 22 Cal. Jur. 721;
　　　Burton v. Curtis, supra;
　　　Starr v. Davis (1930) 105 Cal. App. 632;
　　　Stevens v. Holman (1896) 112 Cal. 345.

The opinion of the Court below cites only two cases, *Auerback v. Healy* (1916) 174 Cal. 60, and

Bailard v. Marden (1951) 36 Cal. (2d) 703, in support of the proposition that appellants must "plead" "a definite agreement that preexisted the instrument." Each of them was discussed by *both* parties in the briefs below and neither supports the proposition.

Both the *Auerback* and *Bailard* cases came before the appellate Court after a trial on the merits, not at the pleading stage.

The *Auerback* case did not involve a mistake of one party known to the other, but a mutual mistake because a draftsman failed to insert a block number in a deed. That the portion of the opinion quoted by the District Court (Tr. p. 69) refers to pleading *mutual* mistake is clear from what immediately follows at page 63 of 174 Cal.:

> "It is necessary to aver facts showing how the mistake was made, whose mistake it was, and what brought it about, *so that the mutuality may appear.*" (emphasis supplied.) "* * * In this state mutuality is not always necessary. It is sufficient if there was 'a mistake of one party, which the other at the time knew or suspected.' (Civ. Code, sec. 3399.) But the *facts* showing a mistake of that character, *in such a case,* must likewise be alleged." (Emphasis ours.)

Thus it is clear the *Auerback* case does not support the theory of the District Court. Even the above dicta as to unilateral mistake says only that under rules of pleading in the state Court the *"facts"* must be alleged—not "a definite agreement that preexisted the instrument," or two agreements.

In the *Bailard* case the plaintiffs did plead both mutual and unilateral mistake but the portion of the opinion quoted (Tr. pp. 70, 71) clearly refers to reformation based on *mutual* mistake, and to the proof rather than the pleading. The opinion deals with the evidence and the findings rather than sufficiency of the pleading. The Court apparently agreed with the defendant's contention that the evidence did "not support the conclusion that the transaction was based upon a mutual mistake," and that there was no evidence "of any knowledge or suspicion by them" (the defendants) of any mistaken belief by plaintiffs. The opinion in the *Bailard* case does not cite any of the cases which we have cited and quoted above, and the language of the opinion cannot be taken to overrule them.

In effect, the District Court held that reformation can never be obtained where, as in the case at bar, one party prepares a written agreement and submits it to the other who signs it, because the claimant "must plead and prove a definite agreement that pre-existed the instrument sought to be corrected." (Tr. p. 69.)

The District Court's opinion quotes correctly a statement in one of our briefs below. (Tr. p. 69.) We reiterate, we have been unable to find any California case holding that in pleading a cause of action for a mistake of one party which the other at the time knew or suspected, it is necessary to allege an agreement preexisting the written instrument. And, of course, we have found no authority to support the theory that such an allegation is necessary to state a claim under the Federal Rules of Civil Procedure.

III. THE CLAIM FOR RELIEF BY WAY OF REFORMATION IS NOT BARRED BY THE STATUTE OF LIMITATIONS.

The District Court ruled that the amended complaint shows on its face that the action for reformation of the contract is barred by the three year statute of limitations, *California Code of Civil Procedure,* Section 338. (Tr. pp. 71-76.) It is submitted that this ruling is clearly erroneous.

The amended complaint reveals on its face the following facts relevant to this point:

Appellants are residents of the State of New York. Appellee is a Delaware Corporation with its principal office and place of business at Kansas City, Missouri. It transacts business in California. The timber lands in question are in California. John F. Ducey is a resident of Detroit, Michigan. (Tr. pp. 29-31.) The purchase by appellee of the Ducey fractional interest occurred December 9, 1947, which fact was discovered by appellants in February, 1949. (Tr. p. 33.) The contract between the parties required appellee to notify appellants of its purchase of the Ducey interest, which notification provision reads as follows:

"(B) The purchaser further agrees with the Seller that, in the event it should purchase the said John F. Ducey interest at any time on or before July 1, 1950, that it will, within fifteen (15) days after making said purchase, mail to the address of the Seller, notice of said purchase and the terms and conditions of same." (Tr. p. 17.)

Appellee never gave notice as required by this provision.

Section 338 of the *Code of Civil Procedure* provides, in part, as follows:

"338· Within three years:

*　　　*　　　*　　　*　　　*　　　*　　　*

4. An action for relief on the ground of fraud or mistake. The cause of action in such case shall not be deemed to have accrued until the discovery, by the aggrieved party, of the facts constituting the mistake."

The discovery was made well within three years of the filing of the original complaint. The District Court casts some confusion on this by pointing out that the original complaint was filed more than five years after the execution of the purchase agreement. (Tr. p. 73.) This fact has no relevancy to the point here in issue. It is further to be observed that the Court made no mention of the limitations question in its orders dated November 7, 1951 (Tr. pp. 26-27), January 3, 1952 (Tr. pp. 28-29), and March 26, 1952. (Tr. p. 41.) The point was first made in the memorandum preceding the judgment herein appealed from.

The District Court stated that the amended complaint should have contained facts showing why the alleged mistake, in the exercise of reasonable diligence, was not discovered until a time within the limitations period. It is submitted that sufficient facts, as reviewed above, have been alleged to relieve appellants of the bar. *The notice provision could have only one purpose,* i.e., to require appellee to notify appellants in New York of a California transaction with Ducey, a Michigan resident. It it were necessary under the Federal Rules to add a further statement that appellants relied on said notice provision, then the Court should have afforded appellants an opportunity to amend their complaint to include such allegation. The defect, if it is a defect, was equally apparent in the original complaint but the Court ignored it.

With respect to the failure of appellee to give the notice required of it, and appellee's defense of the statutory bar (Tr. p. 45), the rule is settled that the doctrine of equitable estoppel will prevent a defendant from relying on the statute of limitations where the defendant previously, by deception or any violation of duty toward plaintiff has caused plaintiff to permit the statutory period to elapse. In such cases it is held that the defendant has wrongfully obtained an advantage which the Court will not allow him to hold. Estoppel to plead limitations may arise from agreement of the parties, from defendant's conduct, or from his silence when under an affirmative duty to speak.

56 *Corpus Juris Secundum* pp. 962-964;

Verdugo Cañon Water Co. v. Verdugo (1908) 152 Cal. 655, 681-684;

Miles v. Bank of America N.T. & S.A. (1936)
17 Cal. App. (2d) 389, 397-398.

In the *Verdugo* case, supra, the Court, after noting that active fraud or deceit is not essential to invoking estoppel, quoted with approval the following from *Thompson v. Simpson,* 128 N.Y. 289, 28 N.E. 632:

> " 'An estoppel may arise also from silence as well as words. But this is only where there is a duty to speak, and the party upon whom the duty rests has an opportunity to speak, and knowing the circumstances require him to speak, keeps silent.' And upon the subject of duty it is further said: 'It is not necessary that the duty to speak should arise out of any agreement, or rest upon any legal obligation in the ordinary sense. Courts of equity apply to the case the principles of natural justice, and whenever these require disclosure they raise the duty and bind the conscience and base upon the omission an equitable forfeiture to the extent necessary to the protection of the innocent party.' "

The District Court took note of appellants' reliance upon the notice provision of the contract and commented as follows:

> "The short answer to this contention, of course, is that the defendant did not purchase the Ducey interest *in all of the* property, but only in a part of it. * * * Since the defendant did not purchase the Ducey interest *in all of the lands,* it was not required to give the plaintiffs the notice specified in Section 10-(B)." (Tr. p. 75.) (Emphasis supplied.)

Again the District Court "read something into the contract," a practice condemned in the *Body-Steff-ner* case, supra. In this instance it has added to the notice provision (section 10-(B)) the words "in all of the property" in order to construe it against appellants. In the first instance the Court held appellants have no claim under the contract because "in the property" means "in all the property." In this second instance the Court held appellants' claim to reform the contract is barred by limitations because, in the clause requiring notice for their protection, the words "the said John F. Ducey interest" means the said John F. Ducey interest "in all of the property."

It seems unnecessary to restate here the reasons contained in foregoing portions of this brief which demonstrate the Court's error. In construing sections 10-(A) and 10-(B) the Court read something into the contract to make its meaning clear, and having done so, has excluded all evidence on the ground that so construed no ambiguity exists.

See

Union Oil Co. v. Union Sugar Co., supra;

Body-Steffner Co. v. Flotill Products, supra.

In each instance appellants have been ushered out of Court at the pleading stage and denied an opportunity to prove their claim.

IV. THE DISTRICT COURT ERRED IN DECIDING THIS CASE
ON ITS MERITS AT THE PLEADING STAGE.

The decision of the District Court was most unusual. The Court has in effect decided the case on its merits at the pleading stage without permitting appellants to have their day in Court.

After the case was at issue the Court could have resorted to a pretrial conference. If the appellee had so desired it could have filed a motion under Rule 56 —a so-called "speaking motion"—whereby the Court would have been properly informed as to the positions of the respective parties, the evidence which they or it considered material or decisive, and the testimony to be adduced could have been explored in the light of the depositions of the plaintiffs and the officers of defendant corporation which were on file with the Court.

Instead of resorting to such regular and normal procedure the District Court, on its own initiative, reversed its prior ruling on the motion to dismiss and rendered judgment for appellee corporation. The memorandum and order preceding the judgment reveals that the Court was persuaded to take this action by consideration of other pleadings in the case, whereas a motion to dismiss under Rule 12 (b) (6) —like the old general demurrer—is addressed only to the pleading attacked, which in this case, was the amended complaint.

CONCLUSION.

It is respectfully submitted that the judgment should be reversed with directions to the District Court to set the case for trial on the claims for recovery upon the contract and, in the alternative, for reformation of the contract.

Dated, San Francisco,
    March 16, 1953.

        Respectfully submitted,

           HERBERT BARTHOLOMEW,
           PEMBROKE GOCHNAUER,
              Attorneys for Appellants.

In the

United States Court of Appeals

For the Ninth Circuit.

No. 13,602.

JAMES V. McCONNELL AND
MARGOT MURPHY McCONNELL, *Appellants.*

vs.

PICKERING LUMBER CORPORATION, *Appellee.*

BRIEF FOR APPELLEE.

CHARLES E. WHITTAKER,
1500 Dierks Building,
Kansas City, Missouri,
JOHN F. DOWNEY,
RALPH R. MARTIG,
Anglo Bank Building,
Sacramento, California,
Attorneys for Appellee.

WATSON, ESS, WHITTAKER, MARSHALL
& ENGGAS,
15th Floor Dierks Building,
Kansas City, Missouri,

DOWNEY, BRAND, SEYMOUR & ROHWER,
Anglo Bank Building,
Sacramento, California,
Of Counsel.

FILE

APR 16 1

PAUL P. O'B

INDEX.

Table of Cases.

Statutes.

Federal Rules of Civil Procedure.

In the

United States Court of Appeals

For the Ninth Circuit.

No. 13,602.

JAMES V. McCONNELL AND
MARGOT MURPHY McCONNELL, *Appellants.*

vs.

PICKERING LUMBER CORPORATION, *Appellee.*

BRIEF FOR APPELLEE.

Basis of Jurisdiction.

The recitals of fact appearing on pages 1 and 2 of appellants' brief, under the heading of "Statement of Jurisdiction," are correct and, therefore, are not here repeated.

Proceedings in the District Court.

Likewise, the recitals of fact appearing on pages 2, 3 and 4 of appellants' brief, under the heading of "Proceedings in the District Court," are substantially correct.

STATEMENT OF THE CASE.

Appellants' "Statement of the Case" is not, in all respects, accurate or complete and is argumentative, and, therefore, unsatisfactory, and we will endeavor to make a plain and concise statement, presenting the questions involved and the manner in which they arise.

This action was commenced by appellants on August 23, 1951 (R. 24[1]). The original complaint sought recovery upon a written contract (attached to and made a part of the complaint as "Exhibit A"—R. 13-24) which was signed by the parties under date of April 10, 1946, or, in the alternative, to reform it upon the ground of "mutual mistake" but if not shown, then on the ground of "mistake of plaintiffs known or suspected by defendants" (R. 3-24).

Appellee moved to dismiss for failure of the complaint to state a claim upon which relief could be granted (R. 25). The court, on November 7, 1951, sustained that motion and dismissed the complaint (R. 26) because, said the court (R. 26-27), *"I do not find an ambiguity in the contract.* It is therefore not subject to the interpretation which plaintiffs would place upon it. The allegations of the complaint *do not set forth an agreement by the parties other than the writing herein to which it could be reformed.* The averments are insufficient to permit reformation on the ground of mistake * * *." But leave was granted (R. 27) "to file * * * an amended complaint setting forth sufficient allegations to present the question of the propriety of reforming the agreement herein."

---

[1]References to the Transcript of Record will be preceded by the letter "R" and, unless otherwise noted, references to appellants' brief will be preceded by "p" or "pp," and, unless otherwise noted, local citations are to the official reports, and emphasis in all quotations has been supplied by us.

On November 23, 1952, appellants filed a motion to vacate the order of November 7, 1951, sustaining appellee's motion to dismiss, upon the ground that "the same is contrary to law," and for leave to file an attached "amended complaint" (R. 27). On January 3, 1952, the court filed a memorandum granting appellants leave to file the amended complaint, and saying that appellants' motion to vacate the order of November 7, 1951, sustaining appellee's motion to dismiss the original complaint, would be considered upon submission of any motion attacking the amended complaint (R. 28, 29). Thereafter, on January 4, 1952, the "amended complaint" was filed (R. 29-40). The original complaint, being now an "abandoned pleading," will not be further noticed here.

The amended complaint (R. 29-40), omitting caption and jurisdictional averments, alleged, in substance, the following:

The appellants are husband and wife; that, on April 10, 1946, appellant Margot Murphy McConnell owned an undivided 248.2/1360ths interest (1126.33 acres if divided), appellee owned an undivided 272/1360ths interest (1234.336 acres if divided), John F. Ducey owned an undivided 494.8/1360ths interest (2245.402 acres if divided) and four others owned, collectively, an undivided 345/1360ths interest (1565.610 acres if divided), in 6172.60 acres of timbered lands in Tuolumne County, California, commonly known as the "McArthur and Ducey lands" (R. 29-31).

That on April 10, 1946, appellants and appellee made and entered into a written agreement concerning the acquisition by appellee of appellants' undivided fractional interest in those lands, which "Agreement, with its attached schedules A and B, is annexed hereto, marked 'Exhibit A' and by this reference incorporated herein" (R. 31). The agreement appears at pages 13 to 24 of the record.

That numbered paragraph 10-(A) of the Agreement reads as follows:

"10-(A). Should Purchaser at any time prior to July 1, 1950, *acquire the 494.8/1360 fractional interest of John F. Ducey in the property listed in Schedule A* from him, his heirs or assigns or representatives, directly or indirectly, or at a partition sale of all the property described in Schedule A at a price higher than that provided herein for Sellers' interest, then Purchaser and Sellers hereby agree that the price provided in this contract for the Sellers' interest shall forthwith be adjusted upward by the amount necessary to make up the difference. Such additional amount shall be paid by Purchaser to Sellers as follows:

"(a). The additional amount due on all deeds taken up by Purchaser under this Agreement prior to the date of *purchase of such John F. Ducey interest* shall be paid by Purchaser to Escrow Agent for the account of Sellers within 15 days;

"(b). The additional amount due on deed or deeds remaining in possession of Escrow Agent at date Purchaser *acquired the John F. Ducey interest* shall be paid by Purchaser to Escrow Agent for the account of Sellers when Purchaser calls on Escrow Agent for delivery of any or all such remaining deeds.

"(B) The Purchaser further agrees with the Seller that, *in the event it should purchase the said John F. Ducey interest* at any time on or before July 1, 1950, that it will, within fifteen (15) days after making said purchase, mail to the address of the Seller, notice of said purchase and the terms and conditions of same."

That in February, 1949, appellants discovered that appellee had acquired, on or about December 9, 1947, the

494.8/1360 fractional interest of John F. Ducey *in 1599.22 acres of said lands,* at a price in excess of the rate of $75 per acre paid to appellants for their fractional interest in the McArthur and Ducey lands, and that they believe the price paid to Ducey was at the rate of approximately $150 per acre.

That appellee has never notified appellants of its purchase "of said John F. Ducey's interest as provided in subparagraph (B) of paragraph 10," of the Agreement, and has not paid any additional amount to the escrow agent for account of appellants.

That appellants have done all things required of them under the terms of the Agreement and that appellee, "in accordance with the provisions of said Agreement, owes plaintiffs an amount of money equal to the difference between the price of Seventy-five ($75) Dollars per acre heretofore paid by defendant corporation to plaintiffs and the higher price per acre heretofore paid by defendant corporation in acquiring said interest of said John F. Ducey," with interest.

That appellants are informed and believe that appellee rests its contention of nonliability "under the claim that the language of said paragraph 10 relieves it from the obligation to pay any additional amount to plaintiffs because it did not acquire, prior to July 1, 1950, the 494.8/1360 fractional interest of said John F. Ducey in all 154 parcels of said McArthur and Ducey lands, but only in 40 parcels thereof"; that appellants deny that the language of paragraph 10 of the Agreement "can be interpreted to excuse defendant corporation from paying to plaintiff an amount equal to the difference between the price of Seventy-five ($75) Dollars per acre paid to plaintiffs and the higher price per acre paid by the defendant corporation to said John F. Ducey," and allege that the provisions of said paragraph 10 when "properly read, state that should defendant corporation, at any time prior to July 1, 1950, acquire the 494.8/1360 fractional interest of said John F. Ducey *in all or in any parcels of the said lands* at a higher price" than was paid to appellants, then the price per acre paid to appellants "should be forthwith adjusted upward by the amount necessary to make up the difference."

The amended complaint is exactly the same as the original complaint to this point.

Then, going to the reformation matter, the amended complaint alleged that if the language of paragraph 10-(A) of the Agreement is susceptible of the interpretation placed upon it by appellee it does not truly express the intention of the parties thereto at the time made "and said Agreement *was executed by plaintiffs under a mistake on their part as to the meaning and effect thereof, which mistake was known or suspected by defendants,*" and that the circumstances giving rise to said mistake were as follows:

That appellants executed the Agreement "under the understanding and belief that Section 10-(A) meant plaintiffs should receive" an increased price if, prior to July 1, 1950, appellee purchased "said Ducey's interest *in all of or any of* said lands."

That soon after appellee acquired its undivided fractional interest in the McArthur-Ducey lands (alleged to be a 20% interest), in July, 1944, it commenced negotiations for the purchase of all outstanding interests therein; that it was necessary for appellee to acquire all outstanding interests in these lands before it could cut any timber thereon; that the negotiations were largely conducted between appellee and appellants; that all the co-owners, except John F. Ducey, were willing to sell if a fair price could be agreed upon; that in March, 1945, appellant Margot McConnell met with all co-owners in Detroit, Michigan, where it was agreed that all would sell at a price of $75 per acre, which was made known to appellee, and, in June, 1945, appellee prepared, signed and sent to the co-owners a written agreement for the purchase of their interests at that price; the proposed agreement was substantially in the same terms as the contract in suit, except it did not contain any provision similar to paragraph 10 of the contract in suit; that said proposed agreement was not executed because Mr. Ducey refused to sign it; that commencing in November, 1945, appellee began negotiations with appellants for the purchase of their interest alone and informed them that, if it could not acquire the interests of all the co-owners by agreement, acquisition of appellants' interest would improve its position in the event of a partition suit.

That from inception of appellee's efforts to acquire appellants' interest separately from those of the other co-owners, appellants refused to sell at a price of $75 per acre; that they informed appellee of such unwillingness and declared that they must receive "price protection" against the acquisition by appellee, prior to July 1, 1950, of any of the other interests at a higher price; that it was later orally agreed that any such price protection clause which might finally be agreed upon would refer only to any higher price paid to John F. Ducey, in view of the size of his fractional interest and his past unwillingness to sell.

That during February, 1946, John F. Ducey and three other co-owners offered to sell their respective interests to appellee for $100 per acre, and so informed appellants; that later that month the president of appellee went to New York and there offered, on behalf of appellee, to sign two agreements with appellants, one at $75 per acre, which could be shown to the other co-owners, and the other at a higher price which would be a "private agreement" between the parties; that appellants refused to consider that offer.

That *"it was thus apparent to plaintiffs that defendant corporation desired to acquire all outstanding interests in said property and plaintiffs believed that it would do so prior to July 1, 1950, at a price or prices in excess of $75 per acre."*

That on or about April 4, 1946, appellee prepared and sent to appellants for signature the Agreement in suit which was signed by both parties.

That during July, 1951, appellants learned from an inspection of official records of Tuolumne County, California, that appellee had agreed, prior to July 1, 1950, with all co-owners, other than John F. Ducey, for acquisition of all of their interests in these lands at a price which appellants believe was in excess of $75 per acre.

That *"The contingency of the purchase by defendant corporation of the fractional interest of John F. Ducey in a part of but less than all of said lands was not discussed during the negotiations between plaintiffs and defendant corporation,"* but that appellants "understood and believed" and appellee "knew or suspected" that appellants understood and believed that appellants would receive the difference between $75 per acre and any higher price per acre which might be agreed upon between appellee and John F. Ducey at any time prior to July 1, 1950.

The amended complaint they prayed:

1. That the court declare appellants to be entitled, under the terms of the Agreement, to receive such amount as may be found necessary to make up the difference between the price of $75 per acre paid to appellants and

any higher price per acre paid to John F. Ducey for his interest "in certain parcels of said land," with interest.

2. That if the language of the contract "does not mean what plaintiffs claim it means" that the Agreement be reformed *"by the addition of the words 'any of' after the word 'in' and preceding the words 'the property listed' in the third line of paragraph 10-(A) of said Agreement."*

3. That the court decree that under the Agreement, *"so reformed,"* appellee owes appellant such amount as may be found to be the difference between $75 per acre at which appellee acquired appellants' interest in these lands, and any higher price per acre at which appellant acquired the interest of said John F. Ducey "in a part of said lands" together with interest.

Thereafter on January 25, 1952, appellee served and filed its motion to dismiss the amended complaint upon the ground that it fails to state a claim upon which relief can be granted (R. 41). That motion to dismiss was briefed and argued before the court (R. 78) but the court, by order of March 26, 1952, decided to defer ruling thereon until the trial (R. 41). Appellee then filed its answer setting up, as its first defense, that "The amended complaint fails to state a claim against defendant upon which relief can be granted" (R. 42-45).

On September 3, 1952, the District Judge filed an elaborate "Memorandum and Order" (R. 47-77) sustaining appellee's motion to dismiss the amended complaint, pointing out, in great detail, the reasons and authorities that compelled his action, and he concluded (R. 76):

> 1. "Insofar as the claim for relief on the contract as it stands is concerned, it is admitted that the plaintiffs have left their pleadings unchanged. Accordingly, the court adheres to its ruling of November 7, 1951, to the effect that there is no ambiguity in the contract in its present form.

2. "In their Amended Complaint, the plaintiffs have failed (a) to set out any pre-existing agreement according to which the contract should be reformed, and (b) to give a cogent and persuasive explanation as to how they came to make their alleged 'unilateral mistake.'

3. "Finally, the Amended Complaint is barred by the three-year statute of limitations, insofar as it relates to the reformation of the contract.

4. "Accordingly, the Amended Complaint is dismissed, and judgment is rendered in favor of the defendant."

On September 16, 1952, the court entered judgment (R. 77), adjudging that appellee's motion to dismiss appellants' amended complaint "be and the same is hereby granted and plaintiffs' amended complaint is hereby dismissed with prejudice; and judgment is hereby rendered in favor of the defendant and against the plaintiffs, and * * * plaintiffs' motion to vacate the order of this Court of November 7, 1951, dismissing plaintiffs' original complaint, as being contrary to the law, be and the same is hereby denied."

From that judgment appellants have appealed to this Court (R. 79) contending, in substance, in their "Specification of Errors Relied Upon" (p. 10), that the District Court erred in holding: (1) that the amended complaint does not state a claim upon which relief can be granted upon the contract as written, (2) that the amended complaint does not state a claim upon which relief can be granted to reform the contract, (3) that the amended complaint shows on its face that the action for reformation of the contract is barred by the Statute of Limitations, and (4) that the court, after deciding on March 26, 1952, to defer ruling on appellee's motion to dismiss the amended complaint until the trial, and after answer was filed and depositions taken and the case set for trial, erred in dismissing the amended complaint with prejudice and entering judgment for appellee, without further notice, hearing, pre-trial conference or any motion for judgment on the pleadings.

Summary of the Argument.

1. There is no uncertainty or ambiguity in the contract as written. The questioned clause of paragraph 10-(A) of the contract says (R. 16), "Should Purchaser at any time prior to July 1, 1950, acquire the 494.8/1360 fractional interest of John F. Ducey *in the property listed in Schedule 'A,'*" at a higher price than paid to appellants for their fractional interest in said lands, a price adjustment would be due appellants. Inasmuch as the amended complaint alleges that appellee acquired Ducey's fractional interest in only 1599.22 acres (R. 33), or in only about 25 per cent of the 6,171.68 acres "listed in Schedule 'A'" (R. 24 and 31), it follows that the amended complaint did not state a claim upon which relief could be granted upon the contract as written.

2. Appellants ask "reformation" of the contract as written by adding to the questioned clause of paragraph 10-(A) the words "any of" after the word "in" and preceding the words "the property listed" (R. 40), so that "as reformed" the clause would read: "Should Purchaser at any time prior to July 1, 1950, acquire the 494.8/1360 fractional interest of John F. Ducey in *any of* the property listed in Schedule 'A.'"

Appellants do not allege that the parties ever agreed to those terms, but in very truth the amended complaint alleges exactly the contrary, by saying (R. 39), "The contingency of the purchase by defendant corporation of the fractional interest of John F. Ducey *in a part of but less* *than all of said lands was not discussed during the negotiations between plaintiffs and defendant corporation, * * *."*

Thus appellants do not allege that the contract failed to record the *real agreement* of the parties. They do not allege that the parties had agreed that the questioned clause of paragraph 10-(A) of the contract was to say "in *any of* the property listed in Schedule 'A,' " rather than to say, as it does say, "in the property listed in Schedule 'A,' " which was 6,171.68 acres. In fact, they say the exact contrary by alleging (R. 39), as above quoted, that such matter "was not discussed."

Therefore appellants do not allege an agreement of the parties, other or different than the one written and signed, to which the written contract should or could be reformed. The effect is that appellants seek to remake the contract to suit themselves—not to reform it to make it accord with the *real agreement* of the parties, which, from all that appears in the amended complaint, it already does.

Therefore the amended complaint fails to state a claim upon which reformation could be granted.

3. The written contract in suit was signed April 10, 1946 (R. 17). This action to reform that contract was filed August 23, 1951 (R. 24), more than five years after execution of the contract. Appellants allege (R. 35) that they executed the agreement "under a mistake on their part as to the meaning and effect thereof," without in any way explaining why their alleged mistake could not, with reasonable diligence, have been discovered within three years from the making of the contract, and, therefore, the complaint for reformation is barred by the California three-year Statute of Limitations (Section 338(4) of the California Code of Civil Procedure).

4. The action of the District Court in ruling on appellee's motion to dismiss the amended complaint after answer was filed and depositions were taken and the case **set for trial, without** further hearing, pre-trial conference or any motion for judgment on the pleadings, was neither irregular nor in any way prejudicial to appellants.

ARGUMENT.

Appellants are not entitled to relief on the contract as written and signed.

The written contract is attached to and made a part of appellants' amended complaint. It is clear, certain and unambiguous.

Appellants' whole case, upon the contract as written, is based upon their palpably erroneous contention that the last seven words of the clause in paragraph 10-(A) of the contract reading, "Should Purchaser at any time prior to July 1, 1950, acquire the 494.8/1360 fractional interest of John F. Ducey *in the property listed in Schedule 'A'*" (R. 16), mean "in all or in any parcels of the said lands" (R. 35).

Appellants make this contention even though they admit such was never agreed to, by alleging, in their Amended Complaint (R. 39), that "the contingency of the purchase by defendant corporation of the fractional interest of John F. Ducey *in a part of but less than all of said lands was not discussed during the negotiations.*"

The language "in the property listed in Schedule 'A'" certainly does not mean "in all or in any parcels of the said lands," as appellants contend.

It is fundamental law that, when an unambiguous contract is attached to and made a part of the complaint, the terms of the contract, and not what the pleader alleges, is determinative. In *Foshee* v. *Daoust Construction Co.,* 7 Cir., 185 F. 2d 23, 25 (1950), the court pointed out that "where the allegations of a pleading are inconsistent with the terms of a written contract attached as an exhibit, the terms of the latter, fairly construed, must prevail over the averments differing therefrom. (Cases cited.)"[2] This rule applies with equal force on a motion to dismiss. In *Zeligson* v. *Hartman-Blair, Inc.*, 10 Cir., 126 F. 2d 595, 597 (1942) the court declared, "The motion to dismiss admitted all facts well pleaded, but it did not admit the legal effect ascribed by the pleader to the writing. The writing was attached to the first amended complaint as an exhibit and its legal effect is to be determined by its terms rather than by the allegations of the pleader."[3]

The familiar rule that parol evidence is not admissible to alter, vary or contradict the terms of a written contract is so ingrained in the law of California as to be codified in a statute. Section 1625 of the California Civil Code provides:

> "The execution of a contract in writing, whether the law requires it to be written or not, supersedes all the negotiations or stipulations concerning its matter which preceded or accompanied the execution of the instrument."

We must turn, then, to the contract itself to determine the intention of the parties.

The questioned clause in the contract is clear, definite, certain and of single meaning, and it means what, and only what, it plainly says, namely, "Should Purchaser at any time prior to July 1, 1950, acquire the 494.8/1360 fractional interest of John F. Ducey in the property listed in Schedule 'A' " at a price higher than paid to appel-

---

[2]See also *Pelelas* v. *Caterpillar Tractor Co.*, 7 Cir., 113 F. 2d 629, 631 (1940), certiorari denied, 311 U. S. 700 (1940); *Sinclair Refining Co.* v. *Stevens*, 8 Cir., 123 F. 2d 186, 189 (1941), certiorari denied, 315 U. S. 804 (1942); *Zeligson* v. *Hartman-Blair, Inc.*, 10 Cir., 126 F. 2d 595, 597 (1942); *Eaves* v. *Timm Aircraft Corp.*, 107 C. A. 2d 367, 370 (1951).

[3]To the same effect are *St. Louis K. & S. E. R. R. Co.* v. *United States*, 267 U. S. 346; *Equitable Life Assurance Society* v. *Brown*, 213 U. S. 25; *Flanigan* v. *Security-First National Bank of Los Angeles*, D. C. S. D. Cal., 41 F. Sup. 77, 79 (1941); *DeLoach* v. *Crowley's, Inc.*, 5 Cir., 128 F. 2d 378, 380 (1942).

lants for their fractional interest in said lands, then a price adjustment would be due appellants. It is, we believe, impossible to comprehend how that clause could be more definite or certain. It is, also, we believe, inconceivable that the clause could have more than one significance to reasonable men, or could possibly mean "any of the property listed in Schedule 'A,' " as appellants argue.

Appellants argue (p. 13) that, in view of the liberality in pleading allowed by Federal Rules of Civil Procedure that "only that need be stated that gives a fair notice to the opponent of the general nature of the cause of action," and they cite cases (pp. 13, 14) holding that "it is error to dismiss a complaint with prejudice if it appears that any relief could be granted on the facts stated."

We agree that it is error to dismiss a complaint with prejudice if it appears that relief could be granted on the facts stated. Here, however, the questioned phrase reading "in the property listed in Schedule 'A' " as a matter of law does not mean, as appellants claim for their basis of recovery, "in all or in any parcels of said lands," and, therefore, no "relief could be granted on the facts stated."

Appellants say (p. 16) that the District Court's construction of the contract "carries no weight in this court" and they there cite cases holding that "an appellate court is not bound by a trial court's construction of a contract or other written instrument based solely upon the terms of the instrument." While we agree that this Court is not bound by the District Court's construction of the terms of the contract—for that is a question of law—we do believe that it is both incorrect and unseemly to say that the District Court's construction of the contract "carries no weight in this Court."

Appellants argue (p. 17) that inasmuch as appellee prepared the contract it must be construed against it, and they there cite and quote in full Section 1654 of the Civil Code of California (which deals only with "cases of uncertainty" in contracts), and Section 1649 of the Civil Code of California (which deals only with contracts "in any respect ambiguous or uncertain"), and Section 1864 of the Code of Civil Procedure of California (which deals only with contracts subject to "two constructions"). Obviously none of those sections has any application here because the questioned clause of the contract is not uncertain, ambiguous or subject to two constructions, and there is no room for construction.

Appellants say (p. 17), "Also alleged are the opposite interpretations which the parties have placed upon it." They thus appear to take the position that their bare allegations of their own mistaken understanding of the terms of the contract render it uncertain or create an ambiguity. Of course that is not the law. That position is directly met in *Eaves* v. *Timm Aircraft Corp.*, 107 C. A. 2d 367, 237 Pac. 2d 287 (1951), where the court said (p. 290):

> "Plaintiff seeks to recover not upon the contract as written but as enlarged in material respects by defendant's representations as to its meaning wholly at variance with its unambiguous expressions. Such recovery under the guise of interpretation may not be allowed where the terms used are unambiguous and have no local or technical meaning."

Appellants argue (p. 18) that if the contract be enforced as written it would result in an absurdity in that "appellee could always escape its own promise by omitting from its future purchase a single parcel, or even a fraction of one parcel." That argument is wholly without merit. Any such evasive subterfuge would be squarely met by the rules of "diminimus" and of "substantial performance."

But if appellants were allowed to rewrite the phrase "in the property listed in Schedule 'A' " to say, as they would like, "in all or in any parcels of the said lands" then they would thereby inject real uncertainty into the contract—uncertainty as to whether the price advance was to apply only to that portion of the property listed in Schedule A in which Ducey's interest has been purchased, or to all the property listed in Schedule A, and thus the present clear terms of the contract really would be rendered ambiguous.

Appellants say, and cite cases holding (pp. 19-21), that the contract should be construed as a whole. Surely so. That is exactly what was done. Not only is the questioned clause in paragraph 10-(A) of the contract clear in itself but, moreover, consistently therewith and inconsistent with appellants' claims, paragraph 10-(A)(a) (R. 17) refers "to the date of purchase of such John F. Ducey interest" and paragraph 10-(A)(b) (R. 17) employs the phrase "at date Purchaser acquired the John F. Ducey interest," and paragraph 10-(B) (R. 17) uses the phrase "in the event it should purchase the said John F. Ducey interest." Everything in the contract is consistent with the fact that the clause in paragraph 10-(A) of the contract reading "in the property listed in Schedule A" means in the 6,171.68 acres "listed in Schedule A," and is inconsistent with plaintiffs' claim that it means "in all or in any parcels of said land."

Appellants are virtually forced to concede that the phrase "in the property listed in Schedule 'A,'" as used in the contract, could only have referred to the 6,171.68 acres "listed in Schedule A," for they allege (R. 39), "The contingency of the purchase by defendant corporation of the fractional interest of John F. Ducey *in a part of but less than all of said lands was not discussed during the negotiations between plaintiffs and defendant corporation.*"

But the crux of appellants' contention is (p. 23) that there is a "latent" or "extrinsic" ambiguity in the questioned phrase *not appearing "on the face of the contract" and that they are entitled to offer parol evidence "to prove that an extrinsic or latent ambiguity arose after the contract was signed, by appellee's purchase of the Ducey interest in part of the property, and to explain its meaning in the light of this subsequent event."* But they do not allege any facts constituting a latent or extrinsic ambiguity.

In claimed support of their position they cite *Pacific Ind. Co. v. California Electric Works,* 29 Cal. App. 2d 260, 272, 84 Pac. 2d 313 (1938); *Estate of Donnellan,* 164 Cal. 14, 127 Pac. 166 (1912); *Estate of Dominici,* 151 Cal. 181, 90 Pac. 448 (1907); *F. P. Cutting Co. v. Peterson,* 164 Cal. 44 (1912); *Barham v. Barham,* 33 Cal. 2d 416, 202 Pac. 2d 789 (1949), and *Millett v. Taylor,* 26 Cal. App. 161, 146 Pac. 42 (1914). Each and every one of those cases involved an ambiguity or uncertainty in a contract or in a will and not one of them supports appellants or has any application to an action on a clear and unambiguous contract such as this. They in fact hold that, even in a suit on an ambiguous contract, extrinsic parol evidence is not admissible to show a different intent from that disclosed by the language of the instrument.[4]

---

[4]The *Pacific Indemnity Co.* case involved an ambiguity as to who were the obligees in a contract of indemnity. The court held that parol evidence was admissible to solve the ambiguity, and said: "The rule, therefore, is that if there is any reasonable room for doubt as to what the contract means or as to what the exact words thereof apply to, then parol evidence is properly admitted."

In Re Donnellan's Estate involved an ambiguity in decedent's will as to the identity of a legatee. It gave a legacy "to my niece, Mary, a resident of New York, said Mary being the daughter of my deceased sister, Mary." Decedent's deceased sister, Mary, had two daughters. One named Mary, who lived in Ireland and had never been in New York, another named Annie, who long had lived in New York, and the question was which was intended to have the legacy—the one whose name was stated in the will or the one who lived in New York. The court held that parol evidence was admissible to determine this extrinsic ambiguity and said, "Again, it is fundamental that in all cases where extrinsic evidence is admissible to aid in expounding the will the evidence is limited to this single purpose. It is considered for the purpose of explaining and interpreting the language of the wll, *and is never permitted to show a different intent or a different object from that disclosed though, perhaps obscurely, by the language of the will itself.*"

In Re Dominici's Estate involved almost the same situation and exactly the same ruling as *In Re Donnellan's Estate.*

The *Cutting Comany* case involved a contract for the sale and future delivery of canned tomatoes. The price to be reduced if the "opening *printed* prices for the season" of a trade association were less than stated in the contract. The association did not *print* an opening price list for the season but announced prices less than the contract prices. Defendant, when sued for the contract prices, sought reformation on the ground of "mutual mistake" *in that both parties contracted in view of the opening prices to be announced by the association and expected them to be printed.* The trial court denied reformation, but on appeal his action was reversed on the ground that mutual mistake was shown and the court said, "If they (plaintiffs) had declared that they did not then (when the contract was signed) expect that the price list would be printed, and that they approved the wording with that idea, it would be a virtual confession that they believed that the guaranty would be nugatory and intended to perpetrate *a fraud* upon the defendant if a lower price was fixed by the association without printing the price list. The mistake would then come within the class of mistakes described in Section 3399 as 'a mistake of one party, which the other at the time knew or suspected.' "

The *Barham* case involved an antenuptial agreement made between a husband and wife who were later divorced and who subsequently remarried. The contract was ambiguous (as to whether it controlled marital rights acquired by the second marriage) and was susceptible to two constructions. The court held that, in such a case, extrinsic evidence was admissible, saying, "When the language used is fairly susceptible to one of two constructions, extrinsic evidence may be considered, not to vary or modify the terms of the agreement but to aid the court in ascertaining the true intent of the parties * * *, not to show that the parties meant something other than what they said but to show what they meant by what they said."

In this case, however, as said by the District Court (R. 61), "There is no ambiguity, either extrinsic or intrinsic, in the contract. If there was any misconception or misapprehension regarding the agreement, it existed in the minds of the plaintiffs alone. The mistake, if any, was purely subjective with them * * *."

Appellants' contention is squarely met by the applicable California cases. In *Barnhart Aircraft, Inc.*, v. *Preston*, 212 Cal. 19, 21-22, 23-24, 297 Pac. 20 (1931), the Supreme Court of California, after quoting Section 1856 of the California Code of Civil Procedure (set forth in full in the District Court's opinion at R. 61) referred approvingly to the following language by Jones in his Commentaries on Evidence, Vol. 3, Section 454:

" '* * * ambiguity in a written contract, calling for construction, may arise as well from words plain in themselves but uncertain when applied to the subject matter of the contract, as from words which are uncertain in their literal sense * * *. *Such an ambiguity never arises out of what was not written at all, but only out of what was written so blindly and imperfectly that its meaning is doubtful.*

" 'It must be borne in mind that although declarations of the parties may in some cases be received to explain contracts or words of doubtful meaning, *yet no other words can be added to or substituted for those of the writing.* The courts are not at liberty to speculate as to the general intention of the parties, but are charged with the duty of ascertaining the meaning of the written language.' "

The *Millett* case involved a lease saying that lessees would give the lessors "one equal half part of all the proceeds and crops produced on said farm." The court held that this language was so indefinite as to whether gross or net proceeds were meant that extrinsic parol evidence was admissible to explain the ambiguity.

In *Eastern-Columbia* v. *System Auto Parks, Inc.*, 100
C. A. 2d 541, 545, 224 Pac. 2d 37 (1950), the court said
on this point:

> "If the language of the instrument is clear and
> explicit the intention of the parties must be ascer-
> tained from the writing alone. Parol evidence is ad-
> missible only where the language used is doubtful,
> uncertain or ambiguous and only then in cases where
> the doubt appears upon the face of the contract."

In *United Iron Works* v. *Outer Harbor Dock & Wharf
Co.*, 168 Cal. 81, 141 Pac. 917 (1914), the court said:

> "Appellants undertook by parol evidence of the
> 'surrounding circumstances' to show that there was
> such a warranty given even if it were not expressly
> embodied in the written contract. The objections to
> the admission of this evidence were sustained, and
> this is the first one of the asserted errors; the conten-
> tion being that under Section 1647 of the Civil Code
> and Section 1860 of the Code of Civil Procedure such
> evidence was clearly admissible. In this, however,
> appellant errs. These sections but enact the common-
> law rule. It was never within their contemplation
> that a contract reduced to writing and executed by
> the parties shall have anything added to it or taken
> away from it by such evidence of 'surrounding cir-
> cumstances.'
>
> "This rule of evidence is invoked and employed
> only in cases where upon the face of the contract
> itself there is doubt and the evidence is used to
> dispel that doubt, not by showing that the parties
> meant something other than what they said, but by
> showing what they meant by what they said."

In *Russell* v. *Stilwell*, 106 Cal. App. 88, 92, 288 Pac. 785
(1930), the court, on a very similar question, said:

> "We can see but one construction that can be
> placed upon the words in the added clause 'the com-

pletion of the plans,' and that is all plans before-
mentioned in the contract—not merely preliminary
plans. The words themselves require no explanation.
If they did it could be found in the contract itself.
In the absence of fraud, where the parties have reduced to writing what appears to be a complete and
certain agreement, parol evidence will not be permitted for the purpose of varying the written contract.''

This Court in the case of *Black* v. *Richfield Oil Corp.*,
9 Cir., 146 F. 2d 801, 804 (1945), had the following to say
on this point:

"The California law is admittedly controlling. A
statute of that state (Section 1858, Cal. Cod. Civ.
Proc.) provides that in the construction of an instrument, 'the office of the judge is simply to ascertain
and declare what is in terms or in substance contained therein, not to insert what has been omitted,
or to omit what has been inserted.' The local decisions, like those of the courts elsewhere, are in harmony with the elementary principles declared by the
statute.''

Appellants argue (pp. 24-25) that the District Court in
saying in his opinion (R. 63) that, "Generally speaking,
we may say that 'the property,' as used in the present
contract, means 'all the property,' '' added the word
"all" to the questioned clause and that this addition of a
word proves that the questioned clause is ambiguous. It is
too obvious for debate that the appellants' premise is
erroneous. The District Court did not add the word "all,"
or any words, to the questioned clause of the contract. He
merely defined what it means in other words. Certainly
in defining a word or phrase in a contract it is necessary
to use other words, else you do not define; but by so defin-

ing you do not add the words of the definition to the instrument.

The questioned clause of the contract says, "Should Purchaser at any time prior to July 1, 1950, acquire the 494.8/1360 fractional interest of John F. Ducey *in the property listed in Schedule 'A,'*" at a higher price than paid appellants, then a price adjustment would be due appellants (R. 35). Appellees are alleged to have purchased, in that time, Ducey's interest in only 1599.22 acres, or about 25 per cent, of the 6,172.60 acres "listed in Schedule 'A'" (R. 24, 31), and appellants allege that "the contingency of the purchase by defendant corporation of the fractional interest of John F. Ducey in a part of but less than all of said lands was not discussed during the negotiations between plaintiffs and defendant corporation," and, therefore, appellants' amended complaint clearly failed to state a claim upon which relief could be granted upon the contract as written, and it follows that the court's action in sustaining appellee's motion to dismiss the complaint, as to the claim on the contract as written, was clearly right.

The amended complaint shows on its face that appellants are not entitled to a reformation of the contract.

Appellants seek "reformation" of the contract as written by adding to the questioned clause of paragraph 10-(A) the words "any of" after the word "in" and preceding the words "the property listed" (R. 40), so that "as reformed" the clause would read: "Should Purchaser at any time prior to July 1, 1950, acquire the 494.8/1360 fractional interest of John F. Ducey in *any of* the property listed in Schedule 'A,'" at a higher price than paid appellants, then a price adjustment would be due appellants.

Appellants do not allege that the parties ever agreed to those terms, but in very truth the amended complaint alleges exactly the contrary, by saying (R. 39), ''The contingency of the purchase by defendant corporation of the fractional interest of John F. Ducey *in a part of but less than all of said lands was not discussed during the negotiations between plaintiffs and defendant corporation,* * * *.''

Thus appellants do not allege that the contract in suit failed to record the *real agreement* of the parties. They do not allege that the parties had agreed that the questioned clause of paragraph 10-(A) of the contract was to say ''in *any of* the property listed in Schedule 'A,' '' rather than to say, as it does say, ''in the property listed in Schedule 'A,' '' which was 6171.68 acres. In fact, they say the exact contrary by alleging (R. 39), as above quoted, that this matter ''was not discussed.''

Therefore appellants do not allege an agreement of the parties, other or different than the one written and signed, to which the written contract should or could be reformed.

But appellants say that inasmuch as they alleged in the amended complaint (R. 36) that they ''executed said agreement under the understanding and belief that Section 10-(A) thereof meant plaintiffs should receive as the price of their interest in said McArthur-Ducey lands an amount equal to the difference between $75 per acre and any higher price per acre provided in any agreement between defendant corporation and said John F. Ducey made at any time prior to July 1, 1950, for the sale of said Ducey's interest in all of or any of said lands'' and that (R. 35) ''said agreement was executed by plaintiffs under a mistake on their part as to the meaning and effect thereof, which mistake was known or suspected by defendants at the time of the execution thereof'' it is unnecessary for appellants to allege that the parties made a definite agreement covering the subject prior to the written contract and that the written contract does not conform to the real agreement of the parties and should be reformed to do so, arguing (p. 32) that "it is not necessary to plead and prove two agreements."

Certainly it is not necessary, or even possible, in a reformation case, "to plead and prove two agreements," but it is necessary to plead that the parties made a definite agreement, covering the subject, prior to the writing and that the writing, through mistake or fraud, fails to correctly set forth the *real agreement* of the parties to which the writing should be reformed.

Plaintiffs cite cases[5] which they claim support their contention but examination of them discloses that in every instance a definite agreement pre-existed the instrument sought to be reformed and asked reformation of the writing to accord with the real agreement of the parties.

This is just plain common sense for it is obvious that you cannot "reform" a written contract to make it say something never agreed to by the parties. That would be to remake, not reform, a contract. You cannot "reform" to something that never existed. You cannot "reform" something to nothing. That would be to chase a negative through a vacuum.

The law is well settled in California that before a contract can be reformed on the ground of fraud, or mistake of any kind, including unilateral mistake or mistake of one party, the plaintiff must plead and prove a definite

---

[5]*Auerback* v. *Healy,* 174 Cal. 60, 63, 161 Pac. 1157 (1916); *F. P. Cutting Co.* v. *Peterson,* 164 Cal. 44, 50, 127 Pac. 163 (1912); *Burton* v. *Curtis,* 91 Cal. App. 11, 13, 266 Pac. 1029 (1928); *Bank of America* v. *Granger,* 115 Cal. App. 210, 220, 1 Pac. 2d 479 (1931); *Eagle Indemnity Co.* v. *Ind. Acc. Comm.,* 92 Cal. App. 2d, 222, 229, 206 Pac. 2d 877.

agreement that pre-existed the instrument sought to be reformed.

The very first case cited on this point by appellants of *Auerback* v. *Healy,* 174 Cal. 60, 63, 161 Pac. 1157 (1916), is a leading case against them. There the Supreme Court of California said on the point (pp. 62-63):

> "The rules of pleading in actions for the reformation of contracts are well established, and should be familiar. The complaint should allege 'what the real agreement was, what the agreement reduced to writing was, and where the writing fails to embody the real agreement.' (34 Cyc. 972.)"

The recent California case of *Bailard* v. *Marden,* 36 C. 2d 703, 708-709, 227 Pac. 2d 10, settles this question, in California, beyond all controversy. There the plaintiffs alleged both a mutual mistake and their own unilateral mistake. The court said:

> "The purpose of reformation is to effectuate the common intention of both parties which was incorrectly reduced to writing. To obtain the benefit of this statute (Section 3399), *it is necessary that the parties shall have had a complete mutual understanding of all the essential terms of their bargain; if no agreement was reached, there would be no standard to which the writing could be reformed.*
>
> "Otherwise stated, *'(I)nasmuch as the relief sought in reforming a written instrument is to make it conform to the real agreement or intention of the parties, a definite intention or agreement on which the minds of the parties had met must have pre-existed the instrument in question.'* (Authorities cited.) *Our statute adopts the principle of law in terms of a single intention which is entertained by both of the parties.*
>
> "Courts of equity have no power to make new contracts for the parties, * * * *(N) or can they reform an*

*instrument according to the terms in which one of
the parties understood it, unless it appears that the
other party also had the same understanding.* (22 Cal.
Jur. Section 2, p. 710). If this were not the rule, the
purpose of reformation would be thwarted."

Inasmuch as the amended complaint does not allege a
definite agreement, or any agreement, between the parties, pre-existing the written contract in suit there is no
standard to which the contract in suit could be reformed,
and inasmuch as the amended complaint says (R. 39) "The
contingency of the purchase by defendant corporation of
the fractional interest of John F. Ducey in a part of but
less than all of said lands was not discussed during the
negotiations between plaintiffs and defendant corporation" there is no basis whatever for "reforming" (actually
rewriting) the questioned clause of the contract by adding,
as appellants ask (R. 40), the words "any of" after the
word "in" and preceding the words "the property listed"
so as to make said clause read "in *any of* the property
listed in Schedule 'A'."

It follows that the amended complaint failed to state a
claim upon which relief could be granted by way of reformation of the contract and the action of the court in sustaining appellee's motion to dismiss was undoubtedly correct.

**The amended complaint shows on its face that the action
for reformation is barred by limitations.**

The written contract in suit was signed April 10, 1946
(R. 17). This action to reform that contract was filed August 23, 1951 (R. 24), more than five years after execution of the contract.

Appellants allege (R. 35) that they executed the agreement "under a mistake on their part as to the meaning

and effect thereof." They do not in any way explain why their alleged mistake could not, with reasonable diligence, have been discovered within three years from the making of the contract.

Rule 9(f) of Federal Rules of Civil Procedure, provides: "For the purpose of testing the sufficiency of a pleading; averments of time * * * are material * * *."

This Court in the case of *Suckow Borax Mines, Consolidated, Inc.* v. *Borax Consolidated, Ltd.,* 9 Cir. 185 F. 2d 196 (1950), said that:

> "* * * a complaint may properly be dismissed on motion for failure to state a claim when the allegations in the complaint affirmatively show that the complaint is barred by the applicable statute of limitations. This is because Rule 9(f) makes averments of time and place material for the purposes of testing the sufficiency of a complaint (many cases cited)."

Where there is no applicable Federal statute of limitations, the statute of the state in which the action is brought controls.[6]

Section 338(4) of the California Code of Civil Procedure provides that "An action for relief on the ground of * * * mistake" must be brought within three years, but "The cause of action in such case not to be deemed to have accrued until the discovery, by the aggrieved party, of the facts constituting the fraud or mistake."

In an effort to escape the effect of the statute of limitations, appellants alleged in the amended complaint (R. 33) that:

> "During the month of February, 1949, plaintiffs discovered that theretofore and on or about Decem-

---

[6]*Johnson* v. *Greene*, D. C. Cal., 14 F. Sup. 945, 947 (1936), affirmed, 9 Cir., 88 F. 2d 683 (1937); *Latta* v. *Western Inv. Co.*, 9 Cir., 173 F. 2d 99, 107 (1949).

ber 9, 1947, defendant corporation had acquired the 494.8/1360 fractional interest of John F. Ducey in and to certain parcels of said McArthur and Ducey lands," etc.

Although, under the terms of Section 338(4), the statute does not start to run until such time as the mistake or fraud is discovered, the cases are unanimous in holding that the statute begins to run at the time when plaintiff, with reasonable diligence, could have ascertained the facts.[7]

The party seeking to avoid the bar of the statute must plead facts excusing failure to make earlier discovery of the mistake, and, failing to do so, as appellants have here, the statute is not tolled.

In *Bradbury* v. *Higginson,* 167 Cal. 553, 558, 140 Pac. 254 (1914), the Supreme Court of California said (p. 255, 256):

> "It is true that the answer avers that the defendant did not discover the mistake until August, 1909, which was within three years of the filing of the answer. But a mere averment of ignorance of a fact which a party might with reasonable diligence have discovered is not enough to postpone the running of the statute (cases cited). It is necessary for the party seeking to avoid the bar to affirmatively plead facts excusing the failure to make an earlier discovery of the mistake or fraud relied upon."[8]

The California law is clearly to the effect that an action for reformation of a contract may be barred by limi-

---

[7]*Simpson* v. *Dalziel*, 135 Cal. 599, 67 Pac. 1080 (1902); *Montgomery* v. *Peterson*, 27 Cal. App. 671, 151 Pac. 23 (1915); *Shain* v. *Sresovich*, 104 Cal. 402, 38 Pac. 51 (1894).

[8]See also *Johnson* v. *Ware*, 58 C. A. 2d 204, 207, 136 Pac. 2d 101, (1943); *Prentiss* v. *McWhirter*, 9 Cir., 63 F. 2d 712 (1933).

tations even though the time for bringing a suit on the contract itself has not yet run. This question was squarely decided in the case of *Bradbury* v. *Higginson, supra*, 167 Cal. at page 559 where the court, referring to *Gardner* v. *California Guarantee Co.*, 137 Cal. 71, 69 Pac. 844, said as follows:

> "The opinion in the Gardner case contains, further, an expression to the effect that an action for the reformation of a contract is not barred so long as an action on the contract itself might be brought. If this be the correct rule, we do not consider it applicable to a case like the one before us, *where the reformation is not merely incidental to the main relief sought, but is an essential prerequisite to the asking of any relief.*"

Appellants seek to avoid the effect of the statute by relying upon the provisions of paragraph 10-(B) of the contract (R. 17), providing "In the event it (appellee) should purchase the said John F. Ducey interest at any time on or before July 1, 1950, that it will, within fifteen (15) days after making said purchase, mail to the address of the Seller, notice of said purchase and the terms and conditions of same," and upon the fact that appellee did not advise them of its purchase of Ducey's interest in a part of the lands.

The complete answer is that appellee did not "purchase the said John F. Ducey's interest" in the 6171.68 acres of land "listed in Schedule A" attached to the contract, but in only 1599.22 acres, or about twenty-five per cent, of the 6172.60 acres "listed in Schedule A," and since appellee did not "purchase the said John F. Ducey's interest" "in the property listed in Schedule 'A'" appellee was not required to give appellants the notice specified in Section 10-(B) of the contract.

Inasmuch as the contract in suit was signed April 10, 1946, and this action to reform it was not filed until August 23, 1951, more than five years after execution of the contract, and inasmuch as appellants do not allege facts showing that they could not have discovered their claimed mistake within three years from the making of the contract, it follows that the amended complaint shows upon its face that the action for reformation of the contract is barred by limitations.

The action of the District Court in ruling on appellees' motion to dismiss the amended complaint after answer was filed and depositions were taken and the case set for trial, without further hearing, pretrial conference or a motion for judgement on the pleadings, was neither irregular nor in any way prejudicial to appellants.

Appellants argue (p. 41) that the court erred in deciding "the case on its merits at the pleading stage without permitting appellants to have their day in court." Appellee's motion to dismiss the amended complaint followed the method prescribed by Federal Rule of Civil Procedure 12(b), (6), for challenging the legal sufficiency of the complaint to state any cause of action against appellee. The court was bound to pass upon that motion. How could it be error for the court to pass upon that motion "at the pleading stage"? And it seems to us to be ridiculous to argue that the sustaining of the motion denied appellants "their day in court" for, certainly, it would be idle for a court to, and he never should, waste the time and incur the expense involved in going through a trial and hearing witnesses to establish the facts which the pleadings admit. Surely, to allow a litigant his day in court, the judge is not deprived of the right, nor relieved from the duty, of passing upon a pending motion to dismiss the complaint, and the litigant has "his day in court" equally whether the facts are established on evidence or are admitted by the pleadings. One cannot profitably elaborate a truth so simple.

Appellants further argue that the court should have resorted to a pretrial conference. Why? There were no issues of fact to be settled. The question before the court was one of law on facts contained in the amended complaint and admitted by the motion to dismiss. Pretrial conference could not have changed the facts or the law and would have been idle.

Appellants also argue that appellee could have filed a "speaking motion" under Rule 56 "whereby the court would have been properly informed as to the positions of the respective parties." Appellee did not so move. Its position was, and is, that the amended complaint "fails to state a claim upon which relief can be granted," and, to present that question, it followed the prescribed procedure of Rule 12(b) and filed a motion to dismiss upon that ground, and that issue had to be decided by the court. A motion for summary judgment, under Rule 56 (called by appellants a "speaking motion") was not called for, because appellee was not contending that "depositions, and admissions on file, together with the affidavits, if any, show that there is no genuine issue as to any material fact," but was contending simply that the amended complaint failed to state any cause of action against appellee and, hence, of course, the appropriate means of raising that question was a motion to dismiss.

We emphasize that here the court was very liberal with appellants. After sustaining appellee's motion to dismiss the original complaint and telling appellee that he did so, as to the action on the contract as written, because (R. 26) "I do not find an ambiguity in the contract," and that he did so, as to the action for reformation, because (R. 27) "the allegations of the complaint do not set forth an agreement by the parties other than the writing herein to which it could be reformed," he granted leave to appellants (R. 27) "to file * * * an amended complaint setting forth sufficient allegations to present the question of the propriety of reforming the agreement herein." Yet appellants' amended complaint left the averments of the action on the contract unchanged, and did not, on the reformation issue, "set forth an agreement by the parties other than the writing herein to which it could be reformed."

The court having thus pointed out to appellants precisely the deficiencies in their complaint, and having thus given them two opportunities to meet those deficiencies, and appellants having shown in their amended complaint that there was no agreement between the parties antedating the writing, there was nothing left for the court to do but pronounce the judgment of the law on the facts alleged by the amended complaint and admitted by the motion to dismiss, which required the entry of judgment for appellee.

Conclusion.

Before concluding we want to take this opportunity to say that the opinion of the District Court is as temperate, thorough, well reasoned and sound as any we have been privileged to see in a long time, and it is doubtful that any judge could improve upon it.

In conclusion we submit that it is clear beyond debate that appellants' amended complaint failed to state a claim upon which relief could be granted and the action of the court in sustaining appellee's motion to dismiss and in entering judgment for appellee was clearly right.

Respectfully submitted,

CHARLES E. WHITTAKER,
1500 Dierks Building,
Kansas City, Missouri,
JOHN F. DOWNEY,
RALPH R. MARTIG,
Anglo Bank Building,
Sacramento, California,
Attorneys for Appellee.

WATSON, ESS, WHITTAKER, MARSHALL
& ENGGAS,
15th Floor Dierks Building,
Kansas City, Missouri,

DOWNEY, BRAND, SEYMOUR & ROHWER,
Anglo Bank Building,
Sacramento, California,
Of Counsel.

No. 13,602

United States Court of Appeals
For the Ninth Circuit

———

JAMES V. McCONNELL and
MARGOT MURPHY McCONNELL,
Appellants,

vs.

PICKERING LUMBER CORPORATION,
Appellee.

APPELLANTS' CLOSING BRIEF.

———

HERBERT BARTHOLOMEW,
1240 Merchants Exchange Building, San Francisco 4, California,
PEMBROKE GOCHNAUER,
111 Sutter Street, San Francisco 4, California,
Attorneys for Appellants.

MAY 4 1953

PAUL P. O'BRIEN

Subject Index

Table of Authorities Cited

Codes

Rules

Texts

No. 13,602

United States Court of Appeals
For the Ninth Circuit

JAMES V. McCONNELL and
MARGOT MURPHY McCONNELL,
                                    Appellants,

VS.

PICKERING LUMBER CORPORATION,
                                    Appellee.

APPELLANTS' CLOSING BRIEF.

INTRODUCTION.

Appellee concedes (p. 1) that statements in our opening brief with respect to the jurisdiction of this Court and of the District Court are correct. Likewise no exception is taken to our recital of the proceedings in the District Court.

However, appellee asserts that our statement of the case (pp. 4-9 of our opening brief) "is not, in all respects, accurate or complete and is argumentative" (p. 2). No inaccuracy, omission nor argument is cited to support the general assertion. Nor have we found any. We believe the statement of the facts in our opening brief is fair and accurate.

Appellee, of course, may make his own summary of facts and he has done so. We find no specific conflict between ours and his. Aside from the differences in language, appellee seems to have given his version of the facts in order to quote selected parts of the contract, the amended complaint, and the District Court's "Memorandum and Order" and to emphasize, by italics, some of the words in those selections. At best, this treatment of the facts is a form of argument. Emphasis placed on language taken out of its entire context means very little.

Turning to appellee's direct argument, which is summarized at pages 11-13 of his brief, we find he argues four points, viz.: (1) "there is no uncertainty or ambiguity in the contract as written"; (2) the contract cannot be reformed because appellants do not allege an agreement preceding the writing to which the writing "should or could be reformed"; (3) the complaint for reformation is barred by the three-year statute of limitations because suit was not filed within three years from the "execution of the contract" and, they say, appellants do not explain why they could not, with reasonable diligence, have discovered their mistake within three years "from the making of the contract"; and (4) the action of the District Court "was neither irregular nor in any way prejudicial to appellants." Each of these points, except (4) above, was contained in the "Memorandum and Order" of the District Court and all four are answered in our opening brief. We will examine briefly appellee's reply to our opening brief.

ARGUMENT.

THE AMENDED COMPLAINT STATES A CLAIM FOR RELIEF UPON THE CONTRACT AS WRITTEN.

The argument contained on pages 11 to 28 of our opening brief as to the error of the District Court in holding appellants have failed to state a claim based on the contract as written is treated at pages 14 to 24 of appellee's brief.

At pages 13 to 16 of our opening brief we stated, with supporting authorities, the rules of construction applicable to appellants' claim on contract. Appellee (at p. 16) answers, without citing any authority, only by asserting that the language of the contract "as a matter of law" does not support appellants' claim as to its meaning. If, by this assertion, appellee is saying that the phrase "in the property listed in Schedule A" means, *"as a matter of law"* "in all the property listed in Schedule A" and cannot mean "in all or in any of the property listed in Schedule A", he is clearly in error. At pages 26 to 28 of appellants' opening brief it is shown that the words "the" and "the property" have no exact meaning, citing:

> *Anundsen v. Standard Printing Co.* (Iowa, 1905) 105 N. W. 424;
>
> *Howell v. State* (Ga., 1927) 138 S. E. 206, 210;
>
> *Craig v. Boyes* (1932) 123 C. A. 592, 596;
>
> *Noyes v. Children's Aid Society,* 70 N.Y. 481, 484;
>
> *City of Oakland v. Hogan* (1940) 41 C. A. 2d 333.

Appellee has made no attempt to answer this part of our brief.

The above cited cases clearly demonstrate that "in the property" has no precise or exact meaning "as a matter of law", or otherwise, and that the court below was wrong in construing the phrase to mean in all the property and in denying appellants an opportunity to prove their claim as to its meaning in this contract.

Appellee concedes (p. 16) that this Court is not bound by the District Court's construction of the contract. Apparently he also concedes, by silent acquiescence, appellants' contention:

"This Honorable Court is called upon to examine the allegations of the amended complaint and all provisions of the written contract incorporated therein, and unless this Court is convinced from its own independent consideration thereof that appellants 'would be entitled to no relief under any state of facts which could be proved in support of the claim', it must reverse the judgment herein" (opening brief pp. 16, 17).

To the codified rules that the contract must be construed against appellee who prepared it and is the promisor, appellee answers (pp. 16, 17) only that "there is no room for construction" "because the questioned clause of the contract is not uncertain, ambiguous or subject to two constructions". Appellee hopes to convince this Court that the contract is "clear, certain and unambiguous" by constant repetition of the statement that such is the fact. Constant repetition of a statement is a technique employed in advertising and propaganda as a means of convincing the reader that the statement is true. It is not a legal argument.

Appellee next notes (p. 17) appellants' assertion that the amended complaint alleges that the parties here have placed opposite interpretations upon the contract. He assumes quite correctly that appellants contend that the fact the parties have construed the language differently is a circumstance which a court will consider in reaching its own interpretation. But he says (p. 17), "Of course that is not the law", citing *Eaves v. Timm Aircraft Corp.* (1951) 107 C. A. 2d 367. We submit that appellee is mistaken as to the law and the *Eaves* case, supra, does not support his theory.

In the recent case of *MacIntyre v. Angel* (1952, hearing by Supreme Court denied April 24, 1952) 109 C. A. 2d 425, an agreement jointly signed and purporting, by the terms "we agree" and "we will make every effort", etc., to assume joint undertakings, was not intended as a joint and several undertaking but as separate and severable undertakings. The court says at page 429:

> "Thus it appears that the parties are in disagreement as to the meaning of the writing which they signed, as was the case in *Wachs v. Wachs,* 11 Cal. 2d 322, 325 (70 P. 2d 1085), *Woodbine v. Van Horn,* 29 Cal. 2d 95, 104 (173 P. 2d 17), and *Union Oil Co. v. Union Sugar Co.,* 31 Cal. 2d 300, 305 (188 P. 2d 470). As in each of those cases, the writing seems susceptible to either of the in-

terpretations respectively urged by the parties. We cannot to a certainty and with sureness, by a mere reading of the document, determine which is the correct interpretation.''

In *Hanney v. Franklin Fire Ins. Co.* (1944, C.C.A. 9) 142 F. 2d 864, this Court took note of the opposite interpretations of the parties.

Indeed it seems fair to say that a court looks in the first instance to the construction placed upon the contract by the parties themselves. See *Woodbine v. Van Horn,* supra.

The *Eaves* case, supra, arose from a written contract whereby defendant agreed to pay for plaintiff's services in obtaining an "affiliation" between defendant and another corporation. No affiliation occurred, but defendant subsequently leased one of its plants. The court observed (p. 370) that, the cause of action "asserts the claim that while the writing said one thing it was represented by defendant to mean something quite different." The case holds that affiliation did not, and could not be interpreted to cover a lease.

Obviously, a contract covering Blackacre cannot be interpreted to cover Whiteacre, but a contract covering "the property" may be found to cover either or both, and the fact that the parties have interpreted it differently is a part of the evidence which a court will consider before deciding "what the parties meant by what they said".

As his answer to our point that operation of the price escalator clause, as appellee wrote it, depended upon a future voluntary act by appellee and the construction of the District Court rendered it absurd because appellee is thereby given the option to escape its own promise, appellee says (pp. 17, 18) "any such evasive subterfuge would be squarely met by the rules of 'diminimus' (sic) and of 'substantial performance'". This answer begs the question. We stated fundamental rules of interpretation "* * * does not involve an absurdity", *Civil Code,* section 1638; "interpretation must be reasonable," *Civil Code,* section 3541. Another important rule of interpretation favors a construction of a contract as bilateral, affording protection to both parties, rather than unilateral. *Woodbine v. Van Horn,* supra.

Appellee says, in effect, these rules are not pertinent here because, if the contingency occurred, appellants could recover on the contract because the rules of *de mininis* and substantial performance come into play. At what point would they come into play? And why should general rules of interpretation not be applied because some other rule of law may be invoked?

At page 19 of our opening brief we pointed out that even if the words "in the property" were "clear and explicit", as the District Court contends, this Court's construction of them must be rejected because it involves an absurdity, citing section 1638 of the *Civil Code of California.* Appellee has ignored this rule. But in *MacIntyre v. Angel,* supra, the court applied the rule and at p. 429 of 109 C. A. 2d, stated it as follows:

" 'But this (referring to section 1638, *Civil Code*) *does not mean that a portion only of a written instrument, although it is clear and explicit, may be selected as furnishing conclusive evidence of the intention of the parties.* Section 1641 of the Civil Code embraces the true rule in providing that the whole of a contract is to be taken together, so as to give effect to every part, if reasonably practical, each clause helping to interpret the other.' (*Universal Sales Corp. v. California Etc. Mfg. Co.,* 20 Cal. 2d 751, 760, [128 P. 2d 665]." (Emphasis ours).

Appellee says next (p. 18) "But if appellants were allowed to rewrite the phrase 'in the property listed in schedule A' " "then they would thereby inject real uncertainty into the contract" as to how much appellee owes! The suit on contract is not an attempt to "rewrite" it, only to construe it. And we are injecting no new uncertainty into the contract. But even if a proper construction of one phrase in the contract raises an issue as to the meaning of another, that is not a valid excuse for denying it proper construction. The appellee cannot escape liability because the litigants may disagree as to how much he owes.

Appellee concedes (p. 18) of course that the contract must be construed as a whole. He then cites three references in section 10 of the contract to "the John F. Ducey interest" arguing that such references are consistent with his interpretation of the contract and inconsistent with appellants' interpretation of it. These references obviously are to "the 498.8/1360 fractional interest of John F. Ducey". Appellee does not explain and we fail to see how they clarify or help the Court to determine whether "in the property" means "in *all* the property" or "in *any* of the property".

On the other hand, appellants cited, at pages 19 to 21 of their opening brief, other provisions of the contract which support their interpretation of it. Appellee has made no attempt to answer. In other words, while contending the contract is clear appellee ignores, and must be deemed unable or unwilling to answer, other cited provisions of the contract which are inconsistent with his claim as to its meaning.

Appellee refers (pp. 11, 12, 19, 24, 25) to a part of an allegation in paragraph XI of the complaint (R. 39) that "The contingency of the purchase by defendant corporation of the fractional interest of John F. Ducey in a part but less than all of said lands was not discussed during the negotiations between plaintiffs and defendant corporation, * * *", omitting in each instance the gist of the allegation contained in the same sentence. He argues in effect that the above quoted part is "contrary to" and "virtually" a concession that "in the property" means in *all* the property.

We see no contradiction or inconsistency between a lack of discussion during negotiations and appellants' understanding of the contract which appellee subsequently prepared and submitted, but even if it were wholly inconsistent, appellee's argument is unsound. Paragraph XI states appellants' claim for reformation, not their claim upon the contract, and Rule 8(c)

of the *Federal Rules of Civil Procedure* expressly
authorizes a party to state "in one count", "as many
separate claims or defenses as he has regardless of
consistency and whether based on legal or on equitable
grounds or on both."

Appellee can take no possible comfort from what
he thinks is an inconsistency between our claim on
contract and part of an allegation in our alternative
claim for reformation of the contract.

At page 19 appellee lists some of the cases we have
cited dealing with patent and latent ambiguity, and
dismisses them with the observation that "each and
every one of those cases involved an ambiguity or uncertainty," whereas the contract here is "clear and
unambiguous". He follows up (pp. 21-23) by restating
quotations and authorities cited by the court below
(Tr. pp. 62-64). There is little to be gained by listing
cases which admitted extrinsic evidence because the
writing was ambiguous and those which held the
writing to be clear on its face. The issue is presented
in many cases. As noted in *Body-Steffner Co. v. Flotill Products* (1944) 63 C. A. 2d 555, 562, there is
considerable opinion that parol evidence should always be admissible, regardless of ambiguity, to show
"the sense in which the contracting parties used and
understood the language of their written contracts".
What is significant is the fact that wherever there is
possible doubt as to meaning the California courts
avoid the harsh rule of exclusion which was invoked
here by declaring the writing is not clear and thereby
admitting extrinsic evidence as to its meaning.

See:

> *MacIntyre v. Angel,* supra;
> *Body-Steffner Co. v. Flotill Products,* supra;
> *Wachs v. Wachs,* supra;
> *Universal Sales Corp. v. Cal. etc. Mfg. Co.,*
>   supra;
> *Woodbine v. Van Horn,* supra;
> *Union Oil Co. v. Union Sugar Co.,* supra.

Appellee says (p. 23) that "it is too obvious for debate that the appellants' premise is erroneous"; the District Court did not *add* the word "all" to the clause; "he merely defined what it means in other words". Well, let us look at the record. He dismissed the complaint on the ground "that there is no ambiguity in the contract" (Tr. p. 76); from all that appears he believed the contract was clear on the basis of the clause "in the property listed in schedule A"; and what he said was,

> "Generally speaking, we may say that 'the property', as used in the present contract, means 'all the property' ". (Tr. p. 63.)

Thus the District Court "read something into a contract to make it clear"—the word *"all"*—thereby demonstrating its ambiguity (*Union Oil Co. v. Union Sugar Co.* (1948) 31 C. 2d 300, 306) and having done so excluded "extrinsic evidence on the ground that so construed no ambiguity exists"—a practice which is condemned as error in the *Union Oil Co., Body-Steffner Co.* and *MacIntyre* cases, supra.

THE AMENDED COMPLAINT STATES A CLAIM FOR RELIEF BY WAY OF REFORMATION.

It is unnecessary and not the function of this brief to restate the argument nor recite the authorities contained in our opening brief. The basic issue which is argued there, with cited authority, is the error of the District Court in failing to note the difference between "a mutual mistake of the parties" and "a mistake of one party, which the other at the time knew or suspected," and therefore holding that in pleading a claim of mistake of the latter type it is necessary to allege "a definite agreement that preexisted the instrument sought to be corrected" (Tr. p. 69).

Appellee, in his brief, does not come to grips with this issue. His argument follows that of the Court below that it is "well settled" in California that before a contract can be reformed on the ground of fraud or mistake the plaintiff must plead and prove "a definite agreement that preexisted the instrument." Appellee has added the assertion, without any supporting authority, that this suggested rule applies to "mistake of any kind, including unilateral mistake or mistake of one party" (p. 26). The only authorities cited by either appellee or the District Court are the cases of *Auerback v. Healy* (1916) 174 C. 60, and *Bailard v. Marden* (1951) 36 C. 2d 703, both of which are cited and distinguished at pages 33-35 of our opening brief.

In brief, the case here is this: appellee, in California prepared a purchase agreement and sent it to appellants in New York who signed and returned it. Appellee then signed. Appellants at the time understood and believed, and appellee knew they so understood and believed, that the price escalator clause meant that in the event appellee should acquire Ducey's interest in all or any of the property (within the fixed period) at a higher price than $75 per acre, appellants would receive the same price per acre as Ducey.

There was no "definite agreement that preexisted the instrument". Appellee contends, and the court below held, that the writing cannot be reformed. Our code (C. C. Sec. 3399) does not say so. Neither does any case we have been able to find.

Appellee argues (p. 26) that you cannot reform a written contract to make it say something the parties never agreed to, for that would be to remake, not reform, a contract. Such was the contention in *Eagle Indemnity Co. v. Industrial Acc. Comm.* (1949) 92 C. A. 2d 222, and the court answered that reformation for "a mistake of one party, which the other * * * knew or suspected" did not "create a new or different contract" because "the contract which was intended by the party acting under unilateral mistake known or suspected by the other, is, as a matter of law, the contract of the parties." (See quotation at p. 32 of our opening brief.)

The above interpretation by the California Court of section 3399 of the California Civil Code is "admittedly controlling" in this Court. *Black v. Richfield Oil Corp.* (C.A. 9, 1945) 146 F. 2d 801, 804. Applied here, it means appellants have stated a claim which, if true, "is, as a matter of law, the contract of the parties." This shows the error of the District Court in dismissing the claim for the stated reason: "Nowhere in the amended complaint now before this Court is there any suggestion of any 'preexisting agreement' to which the sought-for reformed instrument should conform." (Tr. p. 71.) If the rule quoted by the District Court from the *Auerback* and *Bailard* cases, supra, that a "preexisting agreement" or "complete mutual understanding" could be applied to a claim for a mistake of one party which the other at the time knew or suspected"—and no California case has said that it does—then, even so, *Eagle Indemnity,* supra, says the claim stated in our amended complaint "is, as a matter of law, the contract of the parties". Thus an agreement is stated "to which the sought-for reformed instrument should conform."

THE ACTION FOR REFORMATION IS NOT BARRED BY LIMITATIONS.

Appellee has adopted (pp. 28-32) the reasoning contained in the opinion of the District Court (Tr. pp. 71-76) that the claim for relief by way of reformation is barred by the three year statute of limitations, *California Code of Civil Procedure,* Section 338 (4), as assertedly revealed on the face of the amended complaint. The gist of this argument is that the amended complaint does not allege facts excusing appellants' failure to discover the purchase by appellee of the

John F. Ducey interest (which occurred December 9, 1947) before February, 1949 (Tr. pp. 73, 74; Appellee's Brief, pp. 29-31) and that appellee's failure to give appellants' notice of said purchase, in accordance with the requirements of the notice provision contained in paragraph 10 (B) of the contract is no excuse because appellee was only required to give notice in the event it purchased the Ducey interest "in all of the property" (Tr. p. 75; Appellee's Brief, p. 31).

The notice provision of the contract was obviously inserted for the protection of appellants, who lived in New York and who had no ready facility whereby to inform themselves of a transaction involving the purchase and sale of subject California timberland between John F. Ducey, a resident of Michigan, and appellee, a Delaware corporation having offices in Missouri and California, in the absence of written notice thereof. As noted, supra, and in our opening brief (p. 40), the District Court construed the notice provision against appellants by reading into paragraph 10A the word "all", the reading of which into the contract is a practice condemned as error in the *Body-Steffner, Union Oil* and *MacIntyre* cases, supra.

Even if we admitted, for purposes of argument, that any such strained reasoning as advocated by appellee was valid in law, we submit it is not valid in equity,— and the action for reformation is an equitable action— because of the operation of the equitable doctrine of estoppel. This doctrine prevents a defendant from raising the defense of the statute of limitations where he has previously, by deception or any violation of duty toward plaintiff, caused plaintiff to permit the statutory period to lapse. The reason for the rule is that in such cases the defendant has wrongfully obtained an advantage which the court will not allow him to hold.

56 *Corpus Juris Secundum,* pp. 962-964;

Verdugo Canon Water Co. v. Verdugo (1908) 152 Cal. 655, 681-684;

Miles v. Bank of America N.T. & S.A. (1936) 17 Cal. App. 2d 389, 397-398.

We discussed this point in our opening brief (pp. 38-39). Appellee has not answered it. We believe it is unanswerable.

———

THE DISTRICT COURT ERRED IN DENYING APPELLANTS AN OPPORTUNITY TO PROVE THEIR CLAIMS.

Appellee argues (p. 32) that the action of the District Court "was neither irregular nor in any way prejudicial to appellants." The contention seems to be that the amended complaint shows that appellants have no claim either on the contract or for reformation of contract, and therefore the dismissal of the action after it was at issue and before trial was not prejudicial to appellants. We see no need to answer further an argument which is based on an erroneous premise. We feel we have demonstrated that appellants do have a claim on contract, and in the alternative, a claim for reformation. A denial of the opportunity to prove their claims is certainly prejudicial to them.

Appellee contends (p. 33) that there was no occasion for pretrial conference, and that a motion for summary judgment was not called for because appellee was not contending that the depositions show there was no definite issue as to any material fact, but was contending simply that the amended complaint failed to state a claim.

Well, the motion to dismiss was filed in January. In March the court deferred a ruling on it "until the trial". In April appellee filed its answer. Thereafter depositions of the parties were taken and the case was set for trial. In September, the court, *sua sponte,* filed a "memorandum and order" dismissing the amended complaint and rendering judgment for appellee. No ruling on the merits was called for at the time of judgment; neither party was "contending" in the sense that a ruling was then in order; and the depositions, while on file, had not been put before the Court. No doubt appellee was as surprised as the appellants were by the unexpected ruling (and far more pleased!). The point is that appellants assumed that the court would not rule further on the motion to dismiss "until the trial" when the evidence and depositions would be before it, and they had every right to so assume in the absence of any pretrial conference or motion under Rule 56.

CONCLUSION.

We feel that the foregoing, together with our opening brief, demonstrates to a certainty that the judgment herein must be reversed and the appellants permitted to have their day in court.

Dated, San Francisco, California,
    May 1, 1953.

        Respectfully submitted,
            HERBERT BARTHOLOMEW,
            PEMBROKE GOCHNAUER,
                Attorneys for Appellants.

No. 13,602

IN THE

United States Court of Appeals
For the Ninth Circuit

James V. McConnell and
Margot Murphy McConnell,

Appellants,

vs.

Pickering Lumber Corporation,

Appellee.

APPELLANTS' PETITION FOR A REHEARING,

After Decision by the United States Court of Appeals
for the Ninth Circuit, on November 18, 1954.

Herbert Bartholomew,
1240 Merchants Exchange Building, San Francisco 4, California,

Pembroke Gochnauer,
111 Sutter Street, San Francisco 4, California,

*Attorneys for Appellants
and Petitioners.*

FILED

DEC 1 0 1954

PAUL P. O'BRIEN,
CLERK

Pernau-Walsh Printing Co., San Francisco

Subject Index

Table of Authorities Cited

No. 13,602

United States Court of Appeals
For the Ninth Circuit

JAMES V. McCONNELL and
MARGOT MURPHY McCONNELL,

$\qquad$ *Appellants,*

VS.

PICKERING LUMBER CORPORATION,

$\qquad$ *Appellee.*

APPELLANTS' PETITION FOR A REHEARING,

**After Decision by the United States Court of Appeals
for the Ninth Circuit, on November 18, 1954.**

*To the Honorable William Denman, Chief Judge, and
to the Honorables William Healy and Walter L.
Pope, Circuit Judges of the United States Court
of Appeals for the Ninth Circuit:*

This Honorable Court, by its opinion filed herein
November 18, 1954, has held that in pleading a case
for reformation of a contract under Section 3399 of
the Civil Code of California, and particularly that
portion thereof authorizing reformation when, through
the mistake of one party, which the other at the time
knew or suspected, a written contract does not ex-

press the intention of the parties, it is necessary to plead an antecedent agreement or understanding between the parties to which the agreement can be reformed. It is respectfully submitted that in so holding the Court has departed from firmly established California law and from the general authority in such cases provided. It is to this point alone to which this petition for rehearing is most respectfully addressed.

ARGUMENT.

I.

IN AN ACTION FOR REVISION OF A CONTRACT ON THE GROUND OF THE MISTAKE OF ONE PARTY, KNOWN OR SUSPECTED BY THE OTHER, THE PLAINTIFF NEED NOT PLEAD ANY PRIOR MUTUAL AGREEMENT.

The decision of this Court proceeds upon the theory that in all actions for reformation under Section 3399 of the Civil Code of California there must have been a prior mutual agreement between the parties. *If this were so then it is submitted that relief by way of reformation could be granted under Section 3399 only in cases of mutual mistake.* And this despite the fact that Section 3399 is written in the disjunctive—"fraud *or* a mutual mistake * * * *or* a mistake of one party, which the other knew or suspected." Clearly, this section provides the remedy of revision under three types of circumstance, of which mutual mistake is only one.

By way of example let us suppose that A and B contracted to buy and sell the ship Peerless, and that at the time the contract was signed A thought he was buying the large ship Peerless anchored in San Francisco Bay and well known in the Bay Area, and B knew this, but B was thinking of another ship Peerless anchored somewhere off the coast of Mexico. Further assume there had been no discussion or "antecedent agreement" of what ship Peerless was the object of sale. Would the court deny relief because A could not in good faith plead any "antecedent agreement?" The express provisions of Section 3399 are clearly calculated to afford the equitable remedy of reformation under such circumstances.

Closely analogous is *Wilson v. Moriarty* (1891) 88 Cal. 207 wherein the trial court ordered the reformation of a lease. The trial court made the following finding of fact, pages 208-209:

> "That when plaintiff executed said lease, she did not understand said lease to be a lease for ten years, with the privilege of ten years more, but she understood said lease to be for a single term of five years. And the defendant then and there, at the time of the execution of said lease by plaintiff, well knew that the plaintiff did not understand the same to be for ten years, with the privilege of renewal, and well knew that she understood the same to be for a single term of five years, and the defendant fraudulently induced the plaintiff to misunderstand said instrument and to execute the same under such misunderstanding."

In affirming the judgment below the Supreme Court said of this finding, page 209:

"These facts, if justified by the evidence, undoubtedly support the judgment. Section 3399 of the Civil Code provides that 'when, through * * * a mistake of one party, which the other, at the time, knew or suspected, a written contract does not truly express the intention of the parties, it may be revised on the application of a party aggrieved, so as to express that intention, so far as it can be done without prejudice to rights acquired by third persons in good faith, and for value.' "

The *Wilson* case has never been overruled. It is good law today.

Another case in point is *Stevens v. Holman* (1896) 112 Cal. 345, an action to reform a mortgage. The parties here were substituting a new note and mortgage, cancelling the old. The respondent mortgagee had supposed he was getting a mortgage covering more land than was the case. At page 349 the Supreme Court stated the facts as follows:

"Respondent supposed that the description did include all such land, and accepted the mortgage under the mistaken notion that he was thereby getting a lien upon all the land which appellants had promised to mortgage. Appellants knew that the description did not embrace all said land; but they, and each of them, 'knew that plaintiff believed that the mortgage, as executed by them to him, did include all the land they, and each of them, had agreed to mortgage as aforesaid, and that plaintiff was deceived in so believing, and took and accepted said mortgage with the mistaken belief that the same did embrace all the land said defendants had agreed to mortgage to him.' "

In affirming the judgment of the trial court authorizing reformation, the court said, at page 352:

"Most of the adjudged cases upon the subject deal with mutual mistakes; but the code provides expressly for the kind of mistake involved in this action. By section 3399 of the Civil Code it is enacted as follows: 'When, through fraud or a mutual mistake of the parties, or a mistake of one party, *which the other at the time knew or suspected,* a written instrument does not truly express the intention of the parties, it may be revised on the application of a party aggrieved, so as to express that intention, so far as it may be done without prejudice to rights acquired by third parties in good faith.' " (Emphasis supplied by the court).

Attention is also invited to *Carpenter v. Froloff* (1939) 30 C.A. (2d) 400, wherein a judgment of nonsuit in favor of defendant was entered by the trial court, which judgment was reversed and the cause remanded on rehearing by the District Court of Appeal. At page 408 the court said:

"Although a reversal of the judgment is required, we have for the guidance of the trial court on a retrial, given consideration to appellants' contention that the remedy of reformation of a contract is to be granted only for the purpose of making the contract conform to the mutual agreement and intention of the parties thereto; *but in this state mutuality is not always necessary.* It is sufficient if there was, as is alleged in the pleadings here, 'a mistake of one party, which the other at the time knew or suspected' (Civ. Code, sec. 3399); and the pleadings herein set forth the facts showing a mistake of that character. (*Auerbach v. Healy,* 174 Cal. 60 (161 Pac. 1157).)'' (Emphasis supplied.)

The foregoing is cited as a correct statement of California law. The facts of the case reveal some prior understanding between the parties of what was intended to be conveyed. This circumstance of prior understanding exists in some, but not all of the cases. The existence of such circumstances does not detract from the force of the legal statement, and does not justify this Honorable Court in casting aside the correct statement of the legal principle, which is precisely what this Court has done in respect of the following cases:

> *Eagle Indemnity Co. v. Industrial Accident Commission* (1949) 92 C.A. (2d) 222, 229;
> *F. P. Cutting Co. v. Peterson* (1912) 164 Cal. 44, 50;
> *Burton v. Curtis* (1928) 91 C.A. 11, 13;
> *Bank of America v. Granger* (1931) 115 C.A. 210, 220;
> *Auerbach v. Healy* (1916) 174 Cal. 60, 63.

In the latter case the Supreme Court of this State said:

> "It is necessary to aver facts showing how the mistake was made, whose mistake it was, and what brought it about, so that the mutuality may appear."

Here is the rule of pleading as to mutual mistake. The Court then immediately goes on to cite the rule of pleading required in the type of case before this Court, as follows:

> "*In this state mutuality is not always necessary. It is sufficient if there was 'a mistake of one party, which the other at the time knew or suspected.'* (Civ. Code, sec. 3399.) *But the facts showing a mistake of that character, in such a case, must likewise be alleged.*" (Emphasis supplied.)

We agree that *in cases of mutual mistake* one must plead the prior understanding, because the prior understanding furnishes the standard to which the mistakenly executed agreement must be reformed. But if there is no prior *mutual* agreement this is no reason to deny relief under the other circumstances provided for in Section 3399. And certainly it cannot be said that these other circumstances are to lose their vitality because there was no prior mutual agreement—a circumstance not contemplated, or always possible in cases of fraud or the mistake of one known or suspected by the other.

In this latter case—the mistake of one, which the other at the time knew or suspected—the court is not without a standard to which the contract can be reformed. The standard here is that stated in *Eagle Indemnity Co. v. Industrial Accident Commission* (1949) 92 C.A. (2d) 222, 229, to-wit:

> "The contract which was intended by the party acting under unilateral mistake known or sus-

pected by the other, is as a matter of law, the contract of the parties.''

It is respectfully submitted that this is not only good California law, it is also recognized by leading text authorities. To illustrate we refer to 3 *Corbin on Contracts* page 445 where in discussing this very question it is said:

"In some cases one who knows of another's mistake and says nothing will find himself bound by a contract that he did not intend to make. Suppose one party assents to a writing, being mistaken as to the terms that it contains or as to the ordinary meaning of the terms that it contains; and the other, with knowledge of this mistake, likewise assents. *The language of an agreement will be interpreted according to the meaning given to it by one party if the other had actual knowledge that such was the meaning so given.* It is certain that such a bad actor will not be permitted to enforce the agreement according to its words in their usual meaning. The mistaken party is certainly entitled to rescission; but he may, instead, get reformation and enforcement as reformed." (Emphasis supplied.)

At pages 468-469 of the same work Mr. Corbin says this:

"Reformation may be a proper remedy *even though the mistake is not mutual.* If one of the parties mistakenly believes that the writing is a correct integration of that to which he had expressed his assent and the other party knows that it is not reformation may be decreed. The conduct of the other party in permitting the first to execute the erroneous writing and later attempting to enforce it may be regarded as fraudulent; *but it is enough to justify reformation that he knows the terms proposed by the first party and the meaning thereof and leads that party reasonably to believe that he too assents to those terms. This makes a contract; and the writing may be reformed to accord with it.* The fact that the first party was negligent in failing to observe that the writing does not express what he has assented to does not deprive him of this remedy." (Emphasis supplied.)

The rule is stated somewhat less precisely in 45 *Am. Jur.* p. 621 wherein *Stevens v. Holman,* 112 Cal. 345, is cited among supporting authority.

Section 505 of the *Restatement of the Law of Contracts* states the proposition laid down in the *Eagle Indemnity* case, supra, this way:

"If one party at the time of the execution of a written instrument knows not only that the writing does not accurately express the intention of the other party as to the terms to be embodied therein, *but knows what that intention is,* the latter can have the writing reformed *so that it will express that intention.*"

"*Comment:*

a. Under the rule stated in §71 (c) knowledge by one party that the other is under a mistake as to the meaning of his words or acts prevents them from operating as an offer or acceptance. In cases covered by the rule stated in the present

Section, there may be therefore not even a voidable contract; but knowledge of one party not only that the other party's intention is something different from what the writing expresses, but also what that intention is, *is sufficient ground for reforming the writing to conform to the unexpressed intention.* * * *

b. The rule stated in this Section is applicable whether the mistake was caused by misrepresentation by the other party or not.

Illustration:

1. A and B enter into a written contract for the transfer by A to B of certain land. B believes the conveyance contracted for will transfer ownership of underlying minerals, whereas it will not. A knows B's belief when the contract is executed. It will be reformed *to conform to B's understanding."* (Emphasis supplied.)

The California Annotations specifically state that this section is in accord with California Law. The early California cases, *supra,* bear this out, as does the *Eagle Indemnity* case.

In short, the concepts of offer and acceptance, of the meeting of minds, of mutuality, are not conditions precedent to the reformation of a contract executed under a mistake by one party which the other at the time knew or suspected. In this type of mistake the contract intended by the party acting under mistake is, as a matter of law, the contract of the parties. The agreement intended by the mistaken party becomes the real agreement of the parties.

II.

THIS IS A CASE BORDERING ON FRAUD—
EQUITY IS REQUESTED.

A perplexing aspect of this case is that appellants, in filing their amended complaint, abandoned their claim based upon mutual mistake because they could not honestly plead any "antecedent agreement," and rested their claim for reformation on their mistake, known or suspected by the respondent. This claim *is pleaded in the very language of the statute* (C.C. Sec. 3399)—not once, but twice (Transcript of Record, pp. 35 and 39). And still appellants are held required to plead a case of *mutual mistake*. We do not claim mutual mistake, but a mistake of appellants which respondent at the time knew or suspected. What did respondent know or suspect? The fact the written contract did not express the intention of appellants.

In concluding its opinion this Honorable Court observes we make no claim to the existence of other facts to bolster the amended complaint. We make no claim to the existence of other facts to support any theory of mutual mistake.

We did develop facts in the depositions of the several parties to this litigation which most assuredly bolster the case under that portion of Section 3399 of the Civil Code upon which we rely.

Appellants case, very briefly, is that Mrs. McConnell wanted price protection in the event respondent bought her uncle John Ducey's interest, or any part of his interest for a higher price than that paid to her. Respondent knew this. We now know from the depositions that respondent drafted the language of Section 10 A of the contract under the full realization it would undoubtedly be forced to buy a portion of John Ducey's interest before the year 1950. Respondent intentionally then set about drawing the language of the contract so clearly as to exclude any increase in price to Mrs. McConnell unless they bought *all* of John Ducey's interest. Despite all this, an officer of respondent thereafter negotiated in New York City with Mrs. McConnell, her husband and her lawyer and carried on the representation respondent would never buy less than all of John Ducey's interest. And so the contract was executed, and eventually respondent purchased a part of John Ducey's interest, just as it knew it would when respondent drafted the contract language.

By its opinion this Honorable Court seems to criticise appellants for not seeking to further amend their amended complaint between the time of the order of dismissal and the entry of judgment of dismissal. We respectfully submit this would have been a useless act in view of the conclusion by the trial court that appellants had to plead a prior agreement. Furthermore, the judgment of dismissal was an appealable order.

The mistake of one party, at the time known or suspected to the other, frequently involves situations bordering upon fraud, if not actual fraud. Our code section 3399 covers both fraud and the mistake of one, so that neither eventuality will be denied equitable relief. Mr. Williston recognizes these distinctions and overlaps in quoting from Thayer, Unilateral Mistake As a Ground for the Avoidance of Legal Transactions, Harvard Legal Essays (1934) 467, 468, as follows:*

> "The situation in which the mistake is truly unilateral is where one person is aware of the other's error. This is treated in Roman and Continental law under the heading of fraud and is more and more coming to be so considered with us."

We sincerely believe that this case is one demanding the relief of equity; that the denial thereof would result in a manifest injustice and a deviation from the objects and purposes of Section 3399 of the Civil Code.

Upon the foregoing grounds we earnestly submit that this petition for rehearing should be granted by this Honorable Court.

Dated, San Francisco, California,
December 8, 1954.

Respectfully submitted,
HERBERT BARTHOLOMEW,
PEMBROKE GOCHNAUER,
*Attorneys for Appellants
and Petitioners.*

---

*5 Williston on Contracts (Rev. Ed.), pp. 4387-4388.

CERTIFICATE OF COUNSEL.

I hereby certify that I am of counsel for appellants and petitioners in the above entitled cause and that in my judgment the foregoing petition for a rehearing is well founded in point of law as well as in fact and that said petition for a rehearing is not interposed for delay.

Dated, San Francisco, California,
December 8, 1954.

HERBERT BARTHOLOMEW,
Of Counsel for Appellants
and Petitioners.